The Second World War

A Global History

TEDDY J. ULDRICKS
University of Nevada, Las Vegas

ROWMAN & LITTLEFIELD
Lanham • Boulder • New York • London

Dedicated to Aaron, Evangeline, Seth, and Wyatt
In the hope that they never experience the horrors of war

Executive Acquisitions Editor: Ashley Dodge
Assistant Acquisitions Editor: Laney Ackley
Sales and Marketing Inquiries: textbooks@rowman.com

Credits and acknowledgments for material borrowed from other sources, and reproduced with permission, appear on the appropriate pages within the text.

Published by Rowman & Littlefield
An imprint of The Rowman & Littlefield Publishing Group, Inc.
4501 Forbes Boulevard, Suite 200, Lanham, Maryland 20706
www.rowman.com

86-90 Paul Street, London EC2A 4NE

British Library Cataloguing in Publication Information Available

Library of Congress Cataloging-in-Publication Data

Names: Uldricks, Teddy J., 1943- author.
Title: The Second World War : a global history / Teddy J. Uldricks.
Description: Lanham : Rowman & Littlefield, 2024. | Includes bibliographical references and index.
Identifiers: LCCN 2023013661 (print) | LCCN 2023013662 (ebook) | ISBN 9781538172230 (hardcover) | ISBN 9781538172247 (paperback) | ISBN 9781538172254 (epub)
Subjects: LCSH: World War, 1939-1945.
Classification: LCC D743 .U39 2024 (print) | LCC D743 (ebook) | DDC 940.53—dc23/eng/20230414
LC record available at https://lccn.loc.gov/2023013661
LC ebook record available at https://lccn.loc.gov/2023013662

∞™ The paper used in this publication meets the minimum requirements of American National Standard for Information Sciences—Permanence of Paper for Printed Library Materials, ANSI/NISO Z39.48-1992.

Contents

PART V: A WORLD MADE BY WAR

Preface

Dear Reader,

In writing this book, I seek to provide a clear, balanced, one-volume introduction to the Second World War for general readers and students. I place the war in a broader context from the Meiji Restoration in Japan and the unification of Germany through the traumas of the First World War, the Russian Revolution, the Great Depression, the gradual erosion of the British and French Empires, the emergence of national liberation movements among colonial peoples, the anarchy of twentieth-century China, and the halting emergence of American power. While examining the long- and short-term causes of the war, I emphasize the ideological, economic, and geopolitical objectives of its participants. I investigate the degree to which World War II was a race war and also a war against racism. I also introduce the reader to the best in recent scholarship on the war and explore the controversies that still rage over certain aspects of that conflict. This book highlights some novel approaches to studying the Second World War, including the role of food in the conflict, sex in war, and the ecological impact of the war.

Supplementing the narrative of political decision-making and military operations, I highlight the experience of ordinary people at war—soldiers in combat, workers in factories, prisoners of war, persecuted minorities, etc. I examine the critical importance of home fronts; World War II was a total war that required the total mobilization of societies. I examine the role of women, both on home fronts and in the armed forces. In addition, I explore the civil wars that erupted within the broader global conflict in many places. I emphasize the global nature of the conflict in which the European and Pacific theaters of operation were interconnected in political, military, and ideological ways. I also devote much more attention to the ferocious Russo-German conflict on the eastern front and to the agonies of China at war than is typical for English-language histories of the war. Finally, I survey the transformed world that emerged when the war ended as well as the collective memory and national myths that give meaning to that horrendous conflict in various national cultures. Inevitably, in a book of global scope, I have relied on the work of other historians for topics beyond my area of expertise. This book is based mainly on secondary and published documentary sources. The sections dealing with American, Soviet, and German developments are partial exceptions.

Thanks to Readers and Others Who Have Helped

Knowledgeable readers will immediately see the intellectual debt I owe to Gabriel Goro-detsky, whose pathbreaking work as well as friendship and counsel have been important to me all along the way. I owe a similar debt of gratitude to Gerhard Weinberg, whose writings, presentations, and hours of conversation have helped to shape my view of the Second World War. Special thanks go to Keith Schoppa, who reviewed the Asian sections of the manuscript in painstaking detail. Special thanks also go to Samuel Oppenheim and Harold Goldberg, who read the entire manuscript and made a host of useful suggestions. I also thank Larry Holmes, Grant Hardy, Austin Dean, Irwin Wall, Tracey Rizzo, Yana Pitner, William Spell-man, Michael Green, Ben Tipton, Bruce Menning, James Shenton, Michelle Tusan, and John Carlton for their comments on portions of earlier drafts of this work. Of course, any remaining inaccuracies are entirely my responsibility. Thanks also to Ashley Dodge, Laney Ackley, and Janice Braunstein at Rowman & Littlefield, who have been extremely helpful in seeing my manuscript into print.

Note on Chinese, Japanese, and Russian Names

Chinese and Japanese names are given in traditional fashion, family name first, except in the bibliography whenever a book's title page uses the Western order of given name preceding family name. Transliteration of Chinese names presents a special problem because a few personal and place names are so familiar in an older spelling that their modern pinyin version seems strange. Therefore, most Chinese names are rendered in pinyin, with Wade-Giles transliteration given in parenthesis at first mention, with exceptions for the most commonly known names (e.g., Chiang Kai-shek instead of Jiang Jieshi, Canton instead of Guangzhou), which are given in the most familiar spelling followed by the pinyin version in parentheses. I have used the Library of Congress transliteration system for Russian names and terms (thus, Trotskii, not Trotsky), except in quotations and bibliographical entries where the original transliteration has been kept. I have also kept commonly used spellings of some names where the LC transliteration might be confusing (thus Yalta, not Ialta).

Teddy J. Uldricks
Las Vegas, Nevada

Acronyms, Titles, and Terms

ABDA	American, British, Dutch, Australian naval task force
Afrika Korps	German and German-led Italian forces in North Africa
Axis	alliance of Nazi Germany, Fascist Italy, Imperial Japan, and other states
Barbarossa	code name for German attack on the USSR, June 22, 1941
Blitzkrieg	"lightning war," rapid combined-arms assaults
CCP	Chinese Communist Party
Chetniks	Serbian resistance forces loyal to the king
comfort stations	Japanese brothels with sex slavery
Cominform	Communist Information Bureau, established 1947
Comintern	Communist International, Third International
Duce	leader (Italian)
EAM	National Liberation Front (Greece)
EDES	National Republican Greek League
ELAS	Greek Peoples Liberation Army
Emperor Showa	reign title of Japanese emperor Hirohito
FDR	US president Franklin D. Roosevelt
Freikorps	paramilitary unit (German)
Führer	leader (German)
Gestapo	Secret State Police (German)
GI	"government issue," US soldier
GKO	State Defense Committee (Soviet)
Grand Alliance	alliance of Great Britain, the USSR, America, and many other states
GRU	Soviet military intelligence
gulag	Soviet prison camp system
Guomindang (GMD)	Chinese Nationalist Party
Herrenvolk	master race
Issei	first-generation Japanese Americans, noncitizens
Kaiser	emperor (German)
Kempeitai	Japanese military and civilian political police
Kremlin	seat of the Soviet government
Kriegsmarine	German navy
Kokutai	national polity, national essence (Japanese)
KPD	German Communist Party
Kapo	concentration camp prisoner serving as a guard or assistant

Kristallnacht	"night of broken glass," nationwide anti-Jewish pogrom in Germany, November 9–10, 1938
Kwantung Army	Japanese forces stationed in the Liaodong Peninsula, China, AKA Kanto Army
Lager	POW and concentration camps (German)
Landser	German soldier
Lebensraum	living space
Luftwaffe	Air Force (German)
Magic	US system for decrypting Japanese coded messages
Maquis	French rural resistance bands
marshal	Highest rank in some armies (above general)
Milice	Vichy French paramilitary police
NATO	North Atlantic Treaty Organization
NCO	noncommissioned officer
Nisei	second-generation Japanese Americans, US citizens
NKVD	Peoples Commissariat of Internal Affairs (Soviet secret police)
NSB	National Socialist Movement (Dutch)
NSDAP	National Socialist German Workers' Party (Nazi)
OKH	high command of the (Nazi) German army
OKW	high command of the (Nazi) German armed forces
OSS	Office of Strategic Services (US)
Ostheer	German army in the East
OUN	Organization of Ukrainian Nationalists
Overlord	code name for Allied landings in Normandy, France, June 6, 1944
panzer	tank (German)
PCF	French Communist Party
PLA	People's Liberation Army (Chinese Communist)
POW	prisoner of war
Quai d'Orsay	French Ministry of Foreign Affairs
RAF	Royal Air Force (British)
Red Army	army of the Soviet Union
Reich	Empire (German)
Reichswehr	armed forces of the Weimar Republic (Germany)
SA (*Sturmabteilung*)	Nazi paramilitary storm troopers, "Brownshirts"
SD (*Sicherheitsdienst*)	Nazi security and intelligence service
SHAEF	Supreme Headquarters Allied Expeditionary Force
Shoah	the Holocaust, the genocide of European Jews
SOE	Special Operations Executive (British)
SPD	Socialist Party of Germany
squadristi	Italian Fascist paramilitary units
SS (*Schutzstaffel*)	Nazi Party paramilitary forces
Stavka	high command of Soviet armed forces
Third Reich	Nazi Germany
Third Republic	government of France, 1870–1940
Tommy	British soldier
Ultra	British system for decrypting German coded messages
UNO	United Nations Organization
Untermenschen	subhumans (Nazi term)

USSR	Union of Soviet Socialist Republics (Russia)
Ustasha	Croatian ultranationalist regime and forces
Vichy	seat of collaborationist French government in unoccupied southern France
Volk	people (German)
Volksdeutsche	ethnic Germans outside the Reich
Waffen SS	SS divisions with full military armament
WACS	Women's Army Corps (US)
WAVES	Women Accepted for Volunteer Emergency Service (US Navy)
Wehrmacht	armed forces of the Third Reich

Part I

THE ORIGINS OF WAR

CHAPTER 1

From War to Peace

The guns fell silent on the western front on November 11, 1918. The First World War had ended. Eighteen million people had died, and still more were gravely wounded. Hundreds of thousands of civilians had been abused in occupied lands and thousands of women raped. Millions of widows and orphans grieved for their lost men while millions more were driven from their homelands in the aftermath of the fighting. The deep-seated problems that caused the war had scarcely been resolved. Worse yet, the unparalleled destructiveness of the "Great War" created new sets of issues to bedevil the peace of Europe and the world. Historian Robert Gerwarth suggests that the ethnic and class hatreds unleashed by World War I generated a "genocidal logic" that spawned the horrors of the Second World War.[1] The supposed "war to end all wars" was followed not by an era of harmony and tranquility but by a twenty-year crisis, an armed truce that exploded into the still more murderous global conflict of 1937–1945. This crisis of the Western mind and spirit was not limited to international affairs; it permeated domestic political, economic, social, and intellectual realms.[2] Modern physics (relativity and indeterminacy), Freudian psychology, the boom-and-bust economic cycle, corruption in parliamentary politics, and the most deadly war in European history sapped whatever residual Enlightenment confidence in progress and harmony was left by the early twentieth century. The war demonstrated that science, technology, and industrialization were not only engines of progress but also instruments of destruction.

Authoritarian alternatives tempted many who had lost faith in liberal democracy. The weakening hold of Christianity in Europe combined with the apparent eclipse of liberalism to open the door to new faiths on the far right and the far left. Radical and self-confident ideologies—Marxism-Leninism and fascism—arose to challenge liberal-democratic capitalism. A perceived "crisis of modernization" caused some to view the postwar order as hopelessly unworkable.

Not everyone was pessimistic about the future, however. For American president Woodrow Wilson, British prime minister David Lloyd George, and French premier Georges Clemenceau, the Entente victory in the Great War seemed to be a triumph for liberal democracy as well. Yet that victory would prove short-lived, challenged not only by ultranationalism, fascism, and communism but also by the stirrings of civil war and anticolonial struggle in many places. This is not to suggest that the Second World War was somehow inevitable. Neither the European crisis that provoked the war in 1914 nor the new conflicts generated during the struggle predetermined the recurrence of hostilities twenty years later. Nevertheless, the postwar heritage of unfulfilled national and imperial aspirations, combined with the disrupted balance of power in both Europe and Asia, made a renewal of the conflict possible, even probable.

World War II is usually said to have begun on September 1, 1939, when German armies swept into Poland, and to have ended on September 2, 1945, when Japanese emissaries signed the surrender document on board the battleship *Missouri* in Tokyo harbor. Yet, viewed in a broader perspective, the Second World War was clearly only a part—though a crucially important part—of a much longer historical process that involved the realignment of power both among the great states of Europe and also between the Continent and the rest of the world. The unification of Germany in 1871 had fundamentally upset the European balance of power, all the more so because of the militaristic and imperialistic nature of the new Reich. The First and Second World Wars were in large part bloody exercises in redefining the role of Germany in Europe. The concurrent decline of other traditional great powers magnified the instability caused by the advent of Germany. Neither the Ottoman (Turkish) Empire nor the Austrian Empire survived the Great War. Although it was not clear in 1918, even Britain and France had passed the zenith of their strength, though they had not yet been eclipsed by the two emergent superpowers, the Soviet Union and the United States. The rise of militant and mutually hostile nationalisms in eastern Europe further complicated this chaotic European scene.

Similarly in Asia, the readjustment of power relationships and the growth of national liberation movements in the colonial lands virtually ensured military conflict. In 1900, the Western powers appeared supreme. During the preceding century, they had overrun Asia and Africa, dividing the colonial spoils among themselves. In direct challenge to this European hegemony, Japan emerged as the first non-Western country to industrialize and thus acquire the basis for modern military power. Its surprising victory in the Russo-Japanese War of 1904–1905 established Japan as a great power. Japan, which like Germany had entered the imperial scramble late, wanted a share of the colonial plunder. Japan's struggle to displace Western imperialism with its own Greater East Asia Co-Prosperity Sphere is the central theme of the Pacific war. In contrast, China, traditionally the strongest power in East Asia, suffered precipitous decline. The Qing (Ch'ing) dynasty of the Manchu emperors had collapsed in 1911, and its demise inaugurated an era of fragmentation and civil war. Chinese weakness virtually invited Japanese aggression. Beyond the rivalry of Western and Japanese imperialism, the Pacific war also involved the forceful assertion of national independence by India, Vietnam, and almost every other subject population.

The Consequences of War

When the European states went to war in August 1914, none of them anticipated the momentous changes their action would precipitate. Each belligerent looked forward to a short, victorious campaign, and each justified its declaration of war in the noblest terms. After a Serbian terrorist assassinated Archduke Franz Ferdinand, heir to the Habsburg throne, the Austrian Empire proclaimed itself forced to war by this intolerable provocation. Germany justified its participation as an obligation to its Austrian alliance partner. Furthermore, propagandists for the Central powers argued that they were fighting to preserve Western civilization from Slavic barbarism as well as to gain imperial equality with France and Great Britain. Among the Allies, the Russians stressed their desire to defend their Slavic "little brother," Serbia. France was attacked by Germany and was also obliged to assist its Russian ally. England entered the fray in response to the German assault on Belgium and France.

The American president, Woodrow Wilson, characterized the war as a moral crusade for democracy and national self-determination, and against militarism and authoritarianism, when the United States entered the war in 1917.

Beneath these high-sounding public war aims, the powers fought covertly for more tangible gains. The British sought to acquire Berlin's African colonies and, most importantly, to destroy the German fleet that threatened the Royal Navy's command of the seas. The French intended to recover the provinces of Alsace and Lorraine, crush the German military threat, and perhaps even repartition the Reich. Britain and France also agreed to divide the Middle East between them after defeating Germany's Turkish ally. The Russians planned to annex the German and Austrian portions of Poland, crush their old Turkish rival, and take possession of Constantinople and the Straits. Austria intended to shore up its power in the Balkans and to prevent internal disintegration of the empire through a vigorous show of force abroad. Berlin developed the most ambitious goals. The Germans intended to destroy what they regarded as the menacing encirclement of the Triple Entente. According to the September Program drawn up soon after the outbreak of war, French military power was to be broken, and the Reich would make modest territorial gains at the expense of Belgium, Holland, and France. England would be forced to abandon its continental alliances and support an expanded German presence in Africa and the Pacific. The Russian Empire was to be shattered. Besides considerable land to be incorporated directly into the Reich, the rest of Eastern Europe was to be reorganized as German satellite states, including the former tsarist territories of Finland, the Baltic, Belorussia, and Ukraine.

The achievement of these various grandiose aims depended on a quick and decisive victory, which each belligerent anticipated. These expectations were soon disappointed. The initial massive offensives, on which each side wagered, were defeated by newly developed defensive strategies using intricate systems of trenches, barbed wire, machine guns, and massed artillery. The conflict on the western front degenerated into a stalemated war of attrition. Frontal assaults bought a few hundred yards of enemy territory at the cost of tens of thousands of casualties. This system of immobile trench warfare did not dominate the eastern front as completely as in the West. The Russian lines were never broken, although the Germans pushed them back some three hundred miles. Before 1918, Germany was unable to win a decisive victory in the East.

The Russian Revolutions

Tsarist Russia was the most vulnerable member of the Triple Entente. This autocratically ruled, only partially industrialized, and largely peasant land could not meet the demands of modern war. By the opening of 1917, poorly led and ill-equipped Russian soldiers were deserting by the thousands. Cold and hunger gripped the cities. In March (February by the Russian calendar), a bread riot in the capital escalated to revolutionary proportions, toppling the regime of Tsar Nicholas II. Initially the Western Allies welcomed this revolution, for it brought to power a liberal-democratic Provisional Government that pledged to prosecute the war more effectively than its predecessor had. But the unwillingness of the new regime to end the war or to enact sweeping land reforms and its inability to improve the country's sorry economic plight soon undermined its authority. Promising "bread, land, and peace," the Bolsheviks overthrew the Provisional Government in November (October in the Russian calendar) and proclaimed a Soviet Republic.

At first the Allies, hoping to preserve the eastern front, were cautious in their approach to the communist government, although they deplored its radicalism. The Soviet leaders, however, had neither the resources nor the desire to continue the war. In March 1918, the Bolsheviks signed a separate peace with the Central powers. The war in the East was over. This Peace of Brest-Litovsk stripped Russia of its populous, rich western borderlands, from the Baltic down to Ukraine. Furthermore, the Germans imposed a huge indemnity on their prostrate enemy. Brest-Litovsk exposed the full rapacity of Berlin's war aims.

These developments convinced the Allies that the Bolsheviks were German agents. Before coming to power, the Bolshevik party had received money from the German army command, which had also arranged for Vladimir Lenin's return to Russia through Germany from his exile in Switzerland. Brest-Litovsk, which the Western powers believed betrayed both the alliance and Russia, appeared to prove that the Bolsheviks were in the kaiser's pay. The Allies feared that the elimination of the eastern front would permit the Germans to transfer great numbers of troops to the West and thus achieve a breakthrough there before the arrival of fresh American forces could give the Entente predominance. The Western powers were also angered by the revolutionary, antiwar propaganda promulgated by Moscow all over Europe and by the Soviet regime's repudiation of foreign debts. Vladimir Lenin condemned the First World War as a bloody crisis of capitalism, fought for the redistribution of colonial spoils among the great powers. His government published the Allies' secret treaties and issued a Decree on Peace denouncing the imperialist nature of the war and appealing to the working classes of the belligerent states for "a just and democratic . . . immediate peace without annexation . . . and without indemnities." Under these circumstances, the Allies were quick to give aid to the anticommunist ("White") movement when the Russian civil war broke out in the summer of 1918.

Beyond providing supplies, equipment, and training for the White forces, Allied troops intervened directly to seize the northern ports of Murmansk and Archangel, various points on the Caspian and Black Sea coasts, and Vladivostok on the Pacific. The Allies initially justified these landings as necessary to keep stockpiles of war matériel from falling into German hands. The anti-Bolshevik thrust of the intervention became clear as the operation continued long after the German surrender. Lacking great military prowess, the Soviet government responded with the only weapon at its command, revolutionary propaganda. Lenin hoped to overthrow the Western powers by stimulating revolutionary movements among their working classes. Ultimately, both the Allies and the Russian communists failed in their objectives. The limited Western military forces in Russia could not compensate for the divisiveness and political ineptitude among the White armies. By 1921, after a dramatic but inconclusive war with Poland, the Bolsheviks consolidated their hold on Russia. Yet their hopes for broader revolution were disappointed. Neither shrill propaganda nor the expenditure of a few million rubles sufficed to bring down the Allied governments. Although both sides were forced to recognize each other's continued existence and eventually establish normal diplomatic relations, this early conflict between Soviet Russia and the Western democracies had far-reaching consequences. Many in the West came to view the USSR as fundamentally unreliable, immoral, and, above all else, dedicated to the destruction of existing society. Hitler, Mussolini, and the Japanese militarists would later manipulate these fears to their advantage. Similarly, the Soviet leaders developed an image of their country as encircled by menacing imperialist forces waiting for another opportunity to crush the socialist experiment. These attitudes, too, were later to play an unfortunate part in preventing the Western states and the USSR from cooperating against Nazi aggression.

The Peace of Versailles

While the Russian civil war still raged in 1919, the victorious Allied leaders met in Paris to draft a peace and reconstruct a war-torn continent. President Wilson projected a vision of humankind's future sharply different from that of Lenin. He delivered his famous Fourteen Points speech before Congress on January 8, 1918, both to counter Bolshevik propaganda and to publicize American war aims (as differentiated from those of the Allies). The American president called for a just and lasting peace based on open diplomacy, free trade, arms reductions, a fair adjustment of colonial claims with some consideration for the wishes of the populations involved, the freeing of all conquered territory, freedom for the Poles, autonomy for the peoples of the Habsburg and Ottoman Empires, and the creation of a League of Nations. It was to be a peace without forcible annexations or indemnities for the victor, a peace based on the principle of national self-determination, a durable peace made possible by the democratization of international affairs. This liberal peace program, put forward unilaterally by Wilson, was not binding on the Allies. They endorsed the president's speech as a basis for peace, but with many reservations. Nonetheless, when the German authorities sought to end hostilities, they addressed themselves directly to Wilson and asked for an armistice based on their unrealistic interpretation of the Fourteen Points.

The ensuing Paris Peace Conference met in an atmosphere of impossible expectations. The Germans hoped for leniency from the victors, despite Berlin's aggression against Russia, France, and Belgium; its introduction of poison gas and unrestricted submarine warfare; and its imposition of a brutal peace on defeated Russia. A host of long-suppressed peoples clamored for Allied recognition of their national independence. Liberal internationalists of the Wilsonian viewpoint anticipated a new era of peaceful and democratic relations among free peoples. The task of settling the key issues fell to the big three: President Wilson, British prime minister David Lloyd George, and French premier Georges (the Tiger) Clemenceau. Neither the Germans nor the Soviet regime were allowed to participate in the negotiations. Wilson came to Paris as the living symbol of hope for a just and moderate settlement. However, even the president was convinced of Germany's responsibility for the war and therefore its obligation to compensate the victims of its aggression. Moreover, Wilson was unable to impose his views on his colleagues. He was frequently forced to compromise as the negotiations progressed. His efforts also suffered from inadequate support at home. The American public had already grown weary of Europe's problems. Worse yet, the Congress, dominated by hostile Republicans whom Wilson had largely ignored, did not share the president's vision of an expanded global role for the United States.

The French premier challenged Wilson's views. Clemenceau sought, above all else, to protect France from the awful specter of a resurgent Germany. France had lost a higher proportion of its population during the war than any other belligerent, and combat had ravaged a significant part of the country, while German factories and fields were untouched. Moreover, during its retreat in 1918, the German army had deliberately laid waste to the entire northeast section of France. The greater industrial capacity and population of Germany constituted an ongoing threat to France. To offset these dangers, the French intended to disarm Germany, make Berlin pay for the damage it had done in France, detach the Rhineland from the Reich, and perhaps even reverse the unification of 1871. Beyond that, Clemenceau wanted to maintain the alliance with Britain and the United States and even expand it as a vehicle for broad economic cooperation. Lloyd George frequently occupied the middle ground between Clemenceau and Wilson. The British intended to acquire several colonial possessions from Germany and Turkey, but they also hoped to revive Germany as a trading partner as soon as possible. Moreover, London had no wish to foster French hegemony on the Continent. Great Britain had always sought to preserve a balance of power in Europe.

The peace terms that resulted from this clash of personalities and divergent national interests inevitably reflected painful compromise. France had to give way on several points. Germany was not divided into a series of separate states, and it did not lose the Rhineland. France recovered Alsace-Lorraine and was awarded coal mines in the Saar region in compensation for French mines destroyed by the Germans. The Saarlanders, however, voted to return to Germany in a 1935 plebiscite. The Reich lost its overseas colonies. To forestall further aggression, the German army was limited to one hundred thousand long-term volunteers (to prevent the buildup of a large reserve force) and forbidden to have tanks, heavy artillery, military aircraft, or poison gas. The navy was similarly scaled down in size and deprived of all submarines. As a further guarantee of demilitarization, the Germans were prohibited from stationing any troops in the Rhineland. The Allies were to garrison this area for fifteen years.

Article 231—the war guilt clause—proved to be the most controversial provision of the peace settlement: the Germans were forced to admit, however insincerely, their guilt for launching an aggressive war. This admission became the basis for insisting that Germany pay reparations to the victims of its aggression. The Reich was ordered not only to pay for the damage caused by its invading armies in France, Belgium, and elsewhere but also to reimburse such Allied expenses as pensions for veterans and widows. The Allies were unable to agree, however, on the exact amount to charge Germany, so the decision was left to a Reparations Commission that did not complete its work until 1921. In the meantime, the German government was to begin preliminary payments of one billion gold marks per year, plus some coal deliveries for France. All the Allies, except the United States, had gone deeply into debt to finance their war efforts, and they were unwilling to impose that debt on their own populations. In their view, the Reich, as the aggressor, should be made to pay. The Germans were aghast at this apparent violation of the Fourteen Points, even though they had imposed reparations on France after the Franco-Prussian War and had forced Russia to pay a staggering indemnity at Brest-Litovsk.

In Eastern Europe, the Allies recognized, rather than created, a series of new nation-states from the Baltic to the Black Sea. Finland, Estonia, Latvia, and Lithuania seceded from the defunct Russian Empire and formed independent countries. Poland reappeared on the map of Europe as a sovereign state for the first time since the late eighteenth century, with land taken from the former Russian, German, and Austro-Hungarian Empires. The case of Poland well illustrates the impossibility of constructing a just and mutually satisfactory settlement in Eastern Europe, where competing national, economic, and historical claims abounded. The various ethnic groups were so interspersed throughout the region that the "clearly recognizable lines of nationality" of which President Wilson spoke simply did not exist. The Allies were reluctant to force mass population transfers (as would happen after World War II). Therefore, they separated the German province of East Prussia from the rest of the Reich by the creation of a Polish Corridor to the Baltic Sea. The corridor was an economic necessity for Warsaw, and most of its inhabitants were Poles; but at its head stood the largely German port of Danzig that became a free city under the auspices of the League of Nations. The former German province of Upper Silesia, an ethnically diverse zone, was eventually divided between Germany and Poland, though not before considerable fighting by local nationalist forces. To the south, another area of mixed population, Teschen, wit-

Europe after World War I

Europe after World War I

nessed fighting between Poles and Czechs before its division. The outcome of the Russo-Polish War in 1920 determined the eastern borders of Poland. Although Warsaw's bid to extend its sway deep into the territory of the former tsarist empire was rebuffed by the Red Army, the resulting frontier incorporated many Ukrainians and Belorussians into Poland.

The Habsburg, or Austro-Hungarian, Empire completely disappeared, replaced by a small, ethnically German Austria, forbidden to merge with the Reich, and by a truncated Hungary, deprived of two-thirds of its former territory. Czech national aspirations were satisfied by the creation of Czechoslovakia, although this new state contained a substantial German minority within its western border (the Sudetenland), a region of Hungarian settlement inside its southern boundary, and a Ruthenian population (related to the Ukrainians of the USSR) in the east, as well as part of the disputed Teschen region mentioned above. Romania expanded enormously by seizing Bessarabia from Russia along with Transylvania,

Bukovina, and part of the Banat from Hungary. Serbia grew into the great, multinational South Slav state of Yugoslavia. France supported the growth of Poland, Czechoslovakia, Romania, and Yugoslavia in the hope of building a counterweight to Germany in the East, as well as a rampart against the further westward spread of communism. Elsewhere, Germany lost small patches of land to Belgium and Denmark, while Italy received Alpine areas up to the Brenner Pass and some territory at the head of the Adriatic Sea as its reward for having joined the Allies in 1915.

President Wilson and his liberal-internationalist admirers saw the creation of the League of Nations as the capstone of the peace settlement. Its initial membership included forty-one Allied and neutral states, all of whom were represented in the General Assembly. Significantly, neither Germany nor Soviet Russia was a League member at first. The smaller League Council initially included Britain, France, Italy, and Japan, as well as four additional members elected from the General Assembly. League states pledged themselves to respect each other's territorial integrity and not to go to war without first pursuing diplomatic or judicial solutions to their disputes. The League Covenant provided for sanctions, such as economic blockades or even military action, against aggressor nations, but such strictures could be invoked only by unanimous vote of the council. The League also took nominal charge of the Central powers' overseas possessions, parceling them out to various Allied countries as "mandates." Although the creation of the League of Nations was almost universally praised, views of its nature and purpose differed widely. Wilsonians looked upon the League as a vehicle for the democratization of international affairs, the only real guarantee of peace. In sharp contrast, the French saw the League more as a tool for enforcing the peace settlement on the defeated enemy states and for maintaining Allied unity.

After months of intricate negotiations, the treaty, comprised of 440 clauses and running to over two hundred pages of text, was presented to the German delegation at the Palace of Versailles on May 7, 1919. The Germans were bitterly hostile to its provisions, but there was little they could do. The German army had already given up most of its heavy weapons and had retreated to indefensible positions under the terms of the armistice. The Allies threatened to recommence hostilities if their terms were not accepted. The German representatives were thus forced to sign the Treaty of Versailles on June 28, 1919. Similar peace settlements were signed with the other Central powers over the next several months—the Treaty of Saint Germain with Austria, the Treaty of Trianon with Hungary, the Treaty of Neuilly with Bulgaria, and the Treaty of Sèvres with the Ottoman Empire.

Sèvres shattered the Ottoman Empire. Its non-Turkish territories were divided among Britain, France, Italy, and Greece. The harshness of these terms provoked a nationalist explosion among Turks, leading to the Turkish War of Independence. Allied occupation forces were driven from Anatolia. The most savage fighting occurred between Turkish and Greek forces, involving large-scale massacres of Armenians, Greeks, and Turks as well as forced population transfers. Turkey emerged as an independent republic, while the much less punitive Treaty of Lausanne (1923) replaced Sèvres. Nonetheless, the outcome of the First World War enhanced the dominance of Britain and France in the Middle East. Egypt had been a British protectorate since 1882. Even before the war, England effectively controlled the Persian Gulf, while French influence permeated Lebanon and Syria. The 1916 Sykes-Picot Agreement and subsequent decisions at the Paris Peace Conference left Britain in control of Palestine and France dominant in Syria. The Middle East had long been an area of great power rivalry, but the early twentieth-century discovery of vast oil reserves there dramatically increased its economic and strategic value. Moreover, in 1917, British foreign secretary Arthur Balfour publicly declared his government's support for a national home for the Jewish people in Palestine. Far from establishing peace and stability in the region, the postwar settlements were plagued by unrest and violence.

The widespread sense of hopeful expectation, which at first pervaded the Paris Peace Conference, dissolved into severe disappointment as the terms of the settlement became known. Not surprisingly, the Versailles Treaty outraged many Germans. The war guilt clause, reparations, unilateral disarmament, and territorial losses all seemed to violate the Wilsonian principles upon which the Germans had appealed for peace. For them, Versailles was *Der Diktat*, a punitive, rapacious settlement unfairly imposed by the victors. In contrast, many Frenchmen regretted that the treaty had not gone nearly far enough in eroding the aggressive potential of Germany or bolstering French security. Italians bemoaned their insufficient share of the spoils. They grumbled about their "mutilated victory," their "lost peace." Optimists who had hoped that the peace conference would inaugurate an era of justice in world affairs were also disheartened. One of their number, the British diplomat Harold Nicolson, later complained of the "rapid deterioration in moral awareness" at the conference and deplored the "ghastly hypocrisy of the Paris Treaties."[3] Subsequently, many historians have also been critical of the peace treaties. American diplomat and historian George F. Kennan lamented that "this was a peace which had the tragedies of the future written into it as by the devil's own hand."[4] They have pointed out the many obvious violations of the principles of open diplomacy, national self-determination, and a peace with no annexations or indemnities. Historian Sally Marks argues that "throughout the interwar period there was no firm foundation for permanent peace since three of the four strongest continental powers [i.e., Germany, Italy, and the USSR] were intensely dissatisfied with the *status quo*."[5]

In Eastern Europe there was scarcely a state that did not harbor some territorial aspirations against its neighbors and that did not include several minority nationalities. Poland, for example, fought six wars against its various neighboring states in its first three years of existence! All of eastern Europe, from Finland to Greece, saw savage ethnic violence. Poles fought Russians, Ukrainians, Lithuanians, Germans, and Czechs. The Czechs also fought Hungarians, who in turn fought Romanians. Serbs battled Italians, while Greeks and Turks slaughtered each other. The terrible ethnic cleansing during and following the Second World War was prefigured in 1918–1923. Beyond that, several of these new countries were economically marginal as well, fragments torn from the larger economies of the former empires.

In retrospect, it seems that the peacemakers of 1919 have been judged unfairly. In the view of historian Margaret MacMillan, "when war came in 1939, it was the result of twenty years of decisions taken or not taken, not of arrangements made in 1919."[6] Considering Germany's aggressive war aims and the exceptionally punitive terms it imposed on defeated Russia, it is difficult to argue that the Allied statesmen treated the Reich too harshly. Given the passionate hatreds aroused by the war and the fearful toll of casualties, it is amazing that Germany was not thoroughly partitioned. For that matter, many of the treaty restrictions (reparations, disarmament, etc.) were never fully enforced. Even a peace along strictly Wilsonian lines (involving, for example, the loss of provinces with Polish majorities) would still have been unacceptable in Germany. In the ethnic mélange of Eastern Europe, conflicting claims of historical precedent, economic necessity, and nationalism were beyond harmonizing. The infamous corridor that bisected Germany was vital to Poland for economic reasons, just as the Sudetenland (also populated by Germans) was strategically crucial to Czechoslovakia's defense. Nor were the Allied leaders solely responsible for the settlement in Eastern Europe. Without an army on the scene to impose their will, the Allies often had to acquiesce in the decision of arms reached by clashing nationalist forces. Despite the inevitable creation of national minorities within the new nation-states, never before had the political boundaries of Europe so closely approximated patterns of ethnic settlement. In the view of historian Adam Tooze, "Versailles lived up to its claim to have married diplomacy with expert decision-making in a new and enlightened fashion."[7]

Most importantly, the stability of the peace arrangements was undermined from the very beginning when one of the fundamental assumptions on which they were based—the continued active participation of the United States in European affairs—proved false. President Wilson had misjudged the changing mood of the American people, who were fast losing their enthusiasm for foreign involvement, just as he underestimated the strength of his opposition in Congress. Ultimately, the US Senate rejected the Versailles Treaty, membership in the League of Nations, and the special security guarantee for France that the president had promised. The peace of Europe was not doomed by this American retreat from responsibility, but its foundations were certainly dramatically weakened.

Postwar Germany

The pressures of war and of defeat brought about revolutionary upheaval in Germany. On September 29, 1918, General Erich Ludendorff advised Kaiser Wilhelm II that the German army could no longer fend off the Allied onslaught. An armistice was unavoidable. The general further suggested that the government in Berlin be reorganized on broader, more democratic, and civilian lines. This might curry favor with Wilson and, even if the negotiations with the Allies eventually fell through, it would give the army time to organize a last-ditch resistance inside the Reich. It might also calm the wave of revolution in Germany. Ludendorff hoped that this reassertion of civilian authority would allow him to shift the blame for Germany's defeat from the army to the reformist politicians of the new administration. The army command strenuously fostered the *Dolchstoss* legend (the "stab in the back" myth), according to which the army was supposedly winning the war in the trenches until its efforts were undercut by defeatism and treason on the home front. The myth shifted the blame to liberals, Jews, socialists, and even to the entire working class.

Events soon burgeoned beyond Ludendorff's control. Sailors of the German High Seas Fleet mutinied at Kiel in October when their officers ordered a suicidal attack on the British fleet. Such an engagement could well have undermined the armistice negotiations. The rebellious sailors formed a council, modeled after the Russian soldiers' and workers' soviets of 1917, and the movement quickly spread to military units and factories elsewhere. A revolution expelled the king of Bavaria and created a socialist regime in Munich. Massive peace demonstrations swept Berlin. On the advice of his senior commanders, the kaiser abdicated and fled to Holland. It suddenly seemed that Germany might follow the course of Russia from authoritarian monarchy to communist revolution. That Germany did not experience a radical social revolution and become a proletarian dictatorship was in large part due to the efforts of the German Socialist Party (SPD). Radical in rhetoric but reformist in practice, the SPD had no desire to play the role of Bolsheviks by plunging their country into chaos, civil war, and dictatorship. Its leaders, Philipp Scheidemann and Friedrich Ebert, therefore established a parliamentary republic on November 9, 1918. The more militant Independent Socialists and the proto-communists hoped to foment a much more sweeping socialist revolution. But SPD leaders, supported by the majority of workers, were intent upon securing a democratic government for Germany first, and only then pursuing their social and economic aims through parliamentary means. Under their sponsorship, a constitutional convention met at Weimar in January 1919 to found a democratic republic. The delegates established a two-chamber legislature with a cabinet and chancellor responsible to it. The constitution also provided for a president with strong powers who was independent of the parliament. The traditional German states retained much of their authority in a federal structure. Universal adult suffrage crowned this sweeping political reform.

Tragically, large sections of the German public never accepted the Weimar Republic as anything more than a temporary expedient. Various right-wing elements merely tolerated democracy as a means to appease President Wilson and as a buffer against communism. The military officer corps gave the republic, at best, a grudging and conditional loyalty. For them, as well as for civilian nationalists, Weimar was a regime of weakness and defeat that could never restore Germany's greatness. Far too many officers felt that they, rather than the duly elected government, were the true embodiment of the national will. The peace treaty, which mandated a small army with long terms of enlistment, had the unanticipated effect of isolating the rank-and-file soldiers from society and making them more susceptible to their commanders' antirepublican sentiments. The *Freikorps* (army units that had refused to demobilize, paramilitary groups, and private armies) rejected the republic even more emphatically. These counterrevolutionary volunteers and battle-hardened thugs regarded the SPD-led government as hardly better than the communists whom they pledged to destroy. Violence was their creed. "People told us that the war was over," one of them commented. "That made us laugh. We ourselves are the War. Its flame burns strongly in us. It envelops our whole being and fascinates us with the enticing urge to destroy."[8] German industrialists also withheld their support, fearing that the current moderate socialist regime was only a stepping stone to Bolshevism. Broad elements of the middle classes shared these fears. In their view, its association with socialism forever tainted the republic. Finally, anti-Semites condemned the democratic experiment as a Jewish plot. What made this situation especially menacing was the failure of Ebert and Scheidemann to purge these unreliable elements from the army, the civil service, and dominant positions in the economy. Fearing civil war and chaos, the moderate socialist leaders felt compelled to reach an accommodation with the officer corps and bureaucracy.

In its first years, the Weimar Republic faced mortal danger from the extremes of left and right. Early in January 1919, the Revolutionary Shop Stewards movement sparked an uprising aimed at pushing the German revolution much further to the left. The leaders of the newly formed German Communist Party (KPD), Rosa Luxemburg and Karl Liebknecht, quickly stepped in to assume leadership of the insurrection. The socialist government ministers were compelled to call upon the army and right-wing *Freikorps* units to put down this challenge from the far left. They suppressed the revolution brutally, murdering Luxemburg and Liebknecht after taking them prisoner. A few months later, the army and *Freikorps* once again meted out savage repression against the rebels who proclaimed a Bavarian Soviet Republic in Munich. The officers and their paramilitary allies were happy to slaughter leftists in the guise of defending the regime, but their true attitude toward the republic was made clear during the Kapp Putsch in March 1920. The Erhardt Brigade, one of the *Freikorps* units, seized Berlin in an attempted counterrevolution. This time the army refused the government's order to crush the rebellion. General von Seeckt bluntly told the minister of defense that his troops would not fight against their fellow veterans who made up the rebel force. The republic was saved, however, because the trade unions paralyzed the country with a nationwide general strike and the civil service refused to cooperate in the coup. The putsch collapsed after four days. Democracy in Germany was off to an uncertain beginning. In elections held later that same year, the coalition of parties that supported the republic (the SPD, the Democratic Party, and the Catholic Center Party) won only 44 percent of the seats in the Reichstag.

After mid-1920, a series of coalition cabinets dominated by bourgeois moderates and right-of-center republicans replaced the socialist-led administration. Neither the socialists nor their moderate and conservative successors were able to solve Germany's severe economic problems. The chief difficulty was the lack of agreement among the political parties on how to pay the costs of the war, which had been fought largely on credit. In lieu of a policy, matters were allowed to drift, and the war debt was absorbed through inflation. The rate of inflation, which had grown steadily since the early years of the war, reached disastrous proportions by 1923. Early in 1920, ten marks were needed to buy what one mark could have purchased in 1914. By the middle of 1922, the same transaction required a hundred marks, and by 1923, 2,500 marks. Shoppers now carried their nearly worthless currency in wheelbarrows rather than wallets. Some factories even paid their workers twice each day so that the wages could be spent before the next round of price hikes. Inflation severely affected working people. Although wages rose sharply, they could never keep pace with the rise in prices. The workers' standard of living declined, and their most potent political weapon, the industrial strike, lost its effectiveness during these hard times. The lower middle class was hit even harder than blue-collar workers were. Many people who lived on fixed incomes, such as pensions, savings, and small investments, or on the profits from small businesses were bankrupted. Retirement funds, painstakingly accumulated over the years, became worthless almost overnight. While it would have been logical to denounce the former imperial government, which had caused the problem, devastated bondholders and marginal businessmen tended to blame the republic.

The cabinet of Gustav Stresemann, which took office in August 1923, managed to stem the crisis only by drastic deflationary measures. His government issued new currency, issuing one new mark for each trillion marks of the old paper currency, while massive American loans stabilized the economy. The Weimar Republic thus survived a series of early crises and, after 1923, entered a period of relative stability and prosperity. These were years of economic boom in which all the major industrial sectors for the first time surpassed their prewar levels of production and profit, while the standard of living improved markedly. The economic surge helped to produce a parallel improvement in the political climate. The coup attempts, assassinations, and paramilitary street clashes that had marred the republic's early years declined sharply. The election of Field Marshal Paul von Hindenburg, a living symbol of the nation's past glories, as president in 1925 helped many conservative and nationalistic Germans reconcile themselves to the republican regime. Under Stresemann's chancellorship, the Reich also entered into a process of détente with the Allied powers. Germany was gradually shedding its image as the defeated pariah and was becoming an accepted member of the European community. If these favorable trends had continued for a longer period, the republic might well have engendered loyalty and a sense of legitimacy among wider sections of the population. Unfortunately, after 1929, the Great Depression and the rise of Nazi violence aborted these promising developments.

The Rise of Italian Fascism

While Germany experienced an incomplete revolution in the wake of the First World War, a thorough counterrevolution traumatized Italy. Italy emerged from the war burdened with staggering debts, suffering uncontrollable inflation, seemingly cheated of the fruits of victory, and awash in violence. A wave of bloody strikes and plant seizures swept the cities. In the countryside, hordes of impoverished peasants began to take over the fields and drive off their landlords. The parliamentary system, with its three leading parties—the socialists, the liberals, and the Catholics—had neither the confidence nor the courage to deal with these crises. Powerful segments of Italian society became dissatisfied with the government. Big business and wealthy estate owners wanted a regime that would protect their property. Many war veterans, coming home to social chaos and unemployment, were deeply alienated. Ultranationalists, who felt that the peace settlements had deprived Italy of its just rewards, were similarly discontented. These various disaffected elements found a common leader in Benito Mussolini. The appeals of fascism were not solely or even primarily economic. A serious cultural and spiritual crisis gripped Europe in the 1920s and 1930s. The secularizing tendencies of the late nineteenth century combined with the horrors of the First World War to call traditional values, beliefs, and institutions into question. Mussolini's Fascism promised a total political, economic, social, and spiritual rebirth of Italy, recapturing the greatness of ancient Rome.

Mussolini was a former socialist newspaper editor who had forsaken Marxism for chauvinism and imperialism during the war. He had never been an orthodox Marxist, but early in his political life he had been a militant opponent of the Catholic Church and an advocate for social justice. Mussolini was a political chameleon who shed old beliefs and adopted new ideas as needed. He was also a skilled opportunist. Above all, the future dictator was a man of supreme ego. After the conclusion of peace, he emerged as a spokesman for renewed military glory and territorial expansion. He organized his first *Fascio di combattimento* (combat group) in Milan in March 1919. The Fascist movement spread rapidly, but in the early days neither its hierarchy nor its ideology were yet firmly defined. Regional party chieftains (local strongmen who, unlike Mussolini, generally came from right-wing backgrounds) often resisted their leader's authority. It was also under their influence that the vestigial hostility to aristocrats and capitalists, which Mussolini still harbored from his socialist days, was pruned from the Fascist creed, to be replaced by a fervent anti-Marxism. These local party chiefs even hired out their *squadristi* (goon squads) to suppress striking workers or rebellious peasants. The Fascists thus posed as champions of property and of law and order against the alleged communist menace. Respectable middle-class politicians and newspaper editors condoned this mounting reign of terror, so long as it was directed against the left and the lower classes.

The Socialist Party unintentionally gave Mussolini his opportunity by launching a general strike in August 1922. The strike was poorly executed and unpopular with the public. The Fascists used the strike as an excuse to destroy Italian socialism. They sacked socialist and trade union headquarters and smashed leftist newspaper offices. In numerous towns where socialists or communists had been elected to office, the *squadristi* deposed the municipal governments and took power by force. Acts of public humiliation frequently accompanied these events. Deposed officeholders were forced to drink castor oil and soil themselves in front of crowds. The national government, with no workable majority in the hopelessly divided parliament, did nothing. The Fascists were clearly preparing a coup, but that proved unnecessary. With the support of clerical and military groups, King Victor Emmanuel III agreed to appoint Mussolini as prime minister. He assumed power on October 30, 1922, just in time to welcome the now anticlimactic March on Rome by his followers.

Having acquired power by pseudo-legal means, Mussolini moved slowly to consolidate his hold on the country. During the next two years, socialist and liberal leaders were gradually purged from the government by a combination of political maneuvering and violence. The Fascists revised election laws to give themselves an artificial majority in parliament. Many establishment politicians supported this legalized coup because they imagined that drawing Mussolini and his Fascists into the parliamentary system would somehow tame or limit them. Historian Martin Clark puts it colorfully: "The turkeys, thinking they were being invited to the feast, voted for Christmas."[9] A critical turning point came in June 1924 when Fascist terrorists murdered socialist leader Giacomo Matteotti. This atrocity outraged many Italians and galvanized opposition to Fascism. Although caught off guard at first—he apparently had not ordered Matteotti's assassination—*Il Duce* (the leader) soon recovered his composure, instituted a police crackdown on oppositionists, and assumed personal, dictatorial rule. All political parties other than the Fascists were disbanded, while freedom of speech and the press disappeared. Yet, despite his claims, Mussolini never gained truly totalitarian sway over his country. His regime was repressive but never a fully totalitarian police state. Moreover, the monarchy, the army, the church, the industrialists, and the big landowners remained independent centers of power.

After coming to power, Mussolini disbanded the *squadristi*, transforming them into a government-controlled militia, and merged the Fascist Party with the conservative and monarchist Nationalist Association—and thereby defanged Fascism. That was a precondition of his accommodation with Italy's elites. They were his allies rather than compliant subordinates. He neutralized one potential source of opposition, the papacy, by the Lateran Treaties of 1929, which healed the long-standing breach between the Vatican and the Italian state. The Duce continued to talk about the need for a second revolution—in part sincerely and in part as a lever against his conservative allies—but, in Clark's view, "Fascism became boring."[10]

The Fascists loudly proclaimed their intention to renovate Italian society, to sweep away the selfish individualism and class conflict of the liberal system and replace it with corporatism. This scheme envisioned the harmonious cooperation of all elements of society for the greater national good. The labor unions were dissolved, and both workers' strikes and employers' lockouts were prohibited. New labor-management syndicates were supposed to guarantee peaceful and equitable relations among the classes. In practice, however, corporatism was a front for the triumphant alliance of party officials, industrialists, and landowners who exploited the workers and peasants. Despite his boasts in public, the Duce understood that he only shared power with conservative elites and that the Italian people were not the fanatical warriors of his dreams. He longed to complete his fascist revolution. Only war, he imagined, could do that. A successful campaign to spread Italian hegemony throughout the Mediterranean world would allow him to subordinate the monarchy, the army, and the rich to his will. The crucible of combat would supposedly transform the independent-minded and pleasure-loving Italian people into Roman warriors. As early as 1927, Mussolini had told his military chieftains that war was inevitable.[11] In the winter of 1932–1933, he tried to persuade the army and the crown to attack Yugoslavia, but without success.

Mussolini was among the first to realize that, in the age of mass society and mass media, politics is theater. The Fascist regime mobilized huge political spectacles as well as art and architecture to bolster the image of the regime. The Fascists also attempted to implement policies through mass mobilization campaigns—the Battle for the Lira (to prop up the sagging currency), the Battle against the Mafia (a lost cause!), the Battle for Wheat (to achieve national self-sufficiency in food), the Battle for Births (to expand the Italian population). His real goal, however, was much more ambitious. He wanted to transform the Italian people. Historian Roger Griffin emphasizes the transformative goals of Fascism, terming its ideology a "palingenetic form of populist ultra-nationalism."[12] Relying on shared myth and appealing to emotion rather than reason, Mussolini's Fascism sought a national rebirth that would change not only the government, economy, and society, but also the hearts of Italians as well. Along with public art and spectacle, the party, state-sponsored mass organizations, and the education system promoted fascist values. The ideas propagated included "fascism as continuing revolution, social justice, the glories of ancient Rome, the cleansing function of war and violence, the religious spirit of the new political creed, the omniscience of the leader."[13] The ultimate goal was to create the New Fascist Man—a fervent patriot, a true believer in Mussolini, and a fearless warrior. The project was never more than superficially successful. The family, the rural community, and the Catholic Church all provided alternative foci of loyalty. Similarly, among industrial workers, sympathy for socialism and communism remained strong, even if temporarily muted. Moreover, the regime's failure to achieve prosperity, social justice, and international respect eventually undermined its hold on most of its people.

Fascism worked no economic miracles for Italy, though Mussolini boasted that he made the trains run on time. Italy remained one of the poorer countries in Europe. The new regime managed to end the chronic violence in the streets, if only by making its perpetrators the lawful authorities. The conservative elites, who backed Mussolini, were well satisfied. The regime eliminated the threat of communism and smashed the unions. The controlled press created an image of a supremely powerful, infallible Duce—an object of faith and adoration for the masses. Most of all, Mussolini sought to sustain his popularity by promising to restore the greatness of Rome. However, Italy lacked the resources needed to make dramatic conquests. It was not nearly so far down the path toward national unity and industrial modernization as its prospective ally, Germany, or its future enemies, France, Britain, and the United States. Mussolini wanted to pursue a bold foreign policy designed to raise Italy to equality with the great powers; but this goal proved to be far beyond the country's limited economic and military means, and the unsuccessful attempt would lead to tragic consequences not only for the Fascist regime, but also for the entire nation.

For all its crudeness and violence, Mussolini and his Fascist regime had their foreign admirers. For instance, after visiting Italy and enjoying a personal meeting with the Duce, Winston Churchill told reporters, "I could not help being charmed, like so many other people have been, by Signor Mussolini's gentle and simple bearing and his calm detached poise in spite of so many burdens and dangers. Secondly anyone could see that he thought of nothing but the lasting good, as he understands it, of the Italian people. . . . If I had been an Italian I am sure that I should have been wholeheartedly with you [Mussolini] from the start to finish in your triumphant struggle against the bestial appetites and passions of Leninism."

The Allies and the Peace

Fear largely conditioned French policy in the immediate postwar years. The Great War had left France bereft of a generation of young men and economically drained. Moreover, most

Frenchmen realized that Germany, despite its recent defeat, had the population and industrial resources to make a quick recovery. Yet, for the moment, with Germany and Russia prostrate, France enjoyed a position of hegemony in Europe. Its army was the largest and best on the Continent. However, the cornerstone of the French security system crumbled when the US reneged on its promise of a continuing alliance and the British government, now having second thoughts of its own, seized on the American repudiation of their joint obligation as an excuse to withdraw its offer as well.

The French, abandoned by their allies, were determined to use their current position of strength to ensure their future security. In place of an alliance with Washington and London that never materialized, French diplomacy created a system of alliances in eastern Europe involving Poland, Czechoslovakia, Romania, and Yugoslavia. The newly reestablished Polish state fielded a large army. As long as the Reich remained essentially disarmed, these Polish forces provided a credible threat on Germany's eastern frontier. The other three states in the French system, the so-called Little Entente, were fervid defenders of the peace settlement because each of them had gained substantially by it. This assortment of small powers in the East was hardly a satisfactory replacement, however, for France's pre-1917 ally, Imperial Russia. The tie with Poland was in many ways a liability, since both Germany and the USSR, once they regained their strength, were likely to advance serious territorial claims against the Warsaw regime. Only one of the Little Entente states, Czechoslovakia, bordered on Germany, so the mutual efforts of that group were directed mainly at the threat of Hungarian revisionism. In the West, the Franco-Belgian Military Agreement of 1920 served to bolster France's western frontier.

In addition to concluding alliances with these small powers, the French sought to enhance their security by unilaterally enforcing the peace terms on Germany. The French hoped that this would facilitate their economic recovery while retarding the reestablishment of German military and economic power. The reparations issue was especially critical. Paris needed the German payments not only to finance reconstruction and to maintain the value of the franc, but also to repay large American loans, which the fiscally conservative Republican administrations of the 1920s refused to cancel. In April 1921, the Reparations Commission finally agreed on a total figure for Germany's obligation—132 billion gold marks, approximately $33 million—payable in installments of two and a half billion marks each year (though between 1918 and 1931 German payments would average only one and a half billion marks per year[14]). Even this apparently large sum, calculated to appease public opinion, was less burdensome than it appears because the Allies never expected the Germans to pay more than 38 percent of the total. German economists knew that these payments were manageable, but they never admitted that in public.[15]

French insistence on full compliance with the Versailles terms was matched by German determination to avoid fulfilling these obligations. Most Germans rejected the war guilt clause, which was the moral justification for the burdens imposed on the Weimar Republic. There soon developed what can only be described as a nationwide conspiracy to violate the treaty. Allied representatives charged with overseeing reparations transfers or supervising disarmament found their missions constantly hindered by the local citizenry as well as by Weimar officials. The German state governments organized militias to circumvent the limitation on the national army. Berlin also attempted to strengthen its position by negotiating a series of agreements with the other great power fundamentally hostile to the European status quo, the USSR. At the Genoa Conference in 1922, called to deal with continental economic problems, the Soviet delegation played skillfully on German fears of Allied intentions. The resulting Rapallo Treaty gave each signatory considerable leverage. Both Moscow and Berlin had now broken out of diplomatic isolation. Even before Rapallo, the Red Army and the Reichswehr had begun a fruitful, but highly secret, collaboration. On Soviet territory, German officers could train with all those essentials of war forbidden them at Versailles—large troop formations, heavy artillery, air power, tanks, and poison gas. In return, Red Army officers, few of whom had professional training, were schooled in German military science.

This clash of French determination and German resistance culminated in 1923. Exasperated by the dozens of strategies the Germans had devised to avoid their obligations, Prime Minister Raymond Poincaré sent a technical control commission, and a small Franco-Belgian military force to protect it, to the coal syndicate headquarters in Essen. The French did not anticipate strong opposition from Berlin over this incursion because any turmoil might spark a communist revolution. Contrary to these expectations, German industry and the Weimar regime responded with a campaign of widespread passive resistance. Poincaré had to dispatch several divisions of French troops plus thousands of engineers and railway workers to extract the required coal deliveries. The Ruhr invasion ultimately proved a disaster for all concerned. The Germans learned that their flagrant violations of the peace terms could provoke further military occupation of their country, which the tiny Reichswehr was powerless to prevent. The passive resistance campaign had nearly bankrupted the government and driven the already soaring inflation rate to astronomical heights. The crisis had also precipitated sharp social conflict throughout Germany. The communists made significant gains in the Ruhr, Saxony, and Thuringia, while in Munich a previously little-known band of right-wing extremists, the Nazis, staged a coup. The results were scarcely better for the French. What they were able to extract from the Ruhr did not cover the costs of the military operation, which produced the same destabilizing effects on the French economy as it had in Germany. The occupation also split France politically, with most of the left in opposition. Ultimately, the French had to admit that, despite their military superiority, they simply could not force Germany to honor the treaty.

The French policy of enforcing the peace produced such poor results, in part, because Great Britain failed to support it. English sentiment for punishing Germany declined rapidly after the war. In Britain, as in the United States, growing numbers of historians, journalists, and political leaders began to think that the disaster of August 1914 was not solely the result of ruthless German aggression. Some historians argued that St. Petersburg had been more culpable than Berlin; others suggested that an overly rigid structure of hostile alliances had led to an automatic war, beyond the power of any statesman to prevent. A few Britons, and many more Americans, had come to believe that their country's participation in the war had been a mistake. The punitive aspects of the Versailles settlement were based on the premise of German guilt. If serious doubts arose about that guilt, then the treaty itself was hardly defensible. In this light, French insistence on strict enforcement seemed unreasonable.

The British government also had practical reasons for declining to support French efforts. Balance of power had long been a cardinal principle of British foreign policy. For centuries, English diplomacy had sought to block any state from establishing hegemony on the Continent. Only a balance among the European states could ensure the island kingdom's independence. Moral and ideological considerations aside, many Britons could justify their decision for war in 1914 as essential to prevent German domination of Europe. After 1918, however, with the power of Germany and Russia crippled, France appeared to dominate the Continent. Rigorous enforcement of the treaty could only worsen that imbalance. Even British leaders who did not suspect France of hegemonic ambitions begrudged the money and troops required to keep Germany in permanent subjection. With troubles in Ireland, India, and elsewhere in its global empire, Great Britain had to husband its limited resources carefully. Every soldier stationed on the Rhine meant one fewer available in Palestine or Singapore. Anticommunism also played a role in London's foreign policy. Many conservatives feared that enforcing a harsh peace would only throw Germany into complete chaos and thereby facilitate the spread of Bolshevism.

The argument that did most to undermine British support for the Versailles Treaty was neither moral, nor strategic, nor ideological, but economic. Soon after the peace conference in December 1919, the English economist John Maynard Keynes published *The Economic Consequences of the Peace*. Keynes accused Allied statesmen of imposing a Carthaginian peace designed to cripple Germany's industry, strip the country of its natural resources, and starve its population. Not only was the treaty unjust, according to Keynes, but it was also economically impossible to fulfill. He claimed that Germany was financially incapable of paying such huge indemnities and that even if the payments could be made, they would do more harm than good to the Allied economies. For better or worse, Germany was tied to the rest of Europe. If the German economy remained a shambles, the rest of the continent would stagnate too. Keynes's thesis created an immediate sensation. It convinced many Britons that a moderate policy calculated to reintegrate Germany politically and economically into the European state system was the only sound course.

French critics exposed several fallacies in Keynes's arguments, but to no avail. Keynes was wrong in contending that it was physically impossible for Germany to meet its reparations payments, yet in a broader sense he may have been correct that it was not *psychologically* possible for the Germans to make such sacrifices for the benefit of their Allied enemies. A sufficiently ruthless conquering army can take all the movable wealth from a defeated country and even enslave its population, but the Versailles terms were to be carried out over an extended period and without an army of occupation. The treaty required German cooperation. Without that cooperation, no amount of stiffened Allied will could make the treaty work. Keynes's book gave ammunition to Germans who did not want to execute the peace terms, and to Britons who did not wish to make them do so.

This British change of heart caused considerable tension between Paris and London. The French viewed even a defeated and disarmed Germany as a grave menace to their security, whereas British foreign secretary Austen Chamberlain predicted that Germany could not again pose any military threat before 1960 or 1970! The British frequently pressed their cross-Channel ally to make concessions to Germany, although, Frenchmen noticed, such concessions never dealt with Germany's former fleet and colonies or similar issues that impinged on England's interests. This growing Anglo-French rift over whether to enforce the treaty provisions broke open in the Ruhr invasion. The British government openly voiced its disapproval of that operation.

The disastrous Ruhr occupation caused each of the powers to reevaluate its policies. The Stresemann cabinet quickly abandoned passive resistance in the Ruhr and initiated overtures for an understanding with Paris. Premier Édouard Herriot, who had replaced the belligerent Poincaré in May 1924, was equally anxious to reach some accommodation with Berlin. The new Labour government in Britain, led by Ramsay MacDonald, was willing to take a more active part in continental security arrangements in order to facilitate the budding détente. This emerging conciliatory mood first bore fruit in the form of the Dawes Plan. An international commission, chaired by the American banker Charles G. Dawes, met in London during the summer of 1924 to reorganize the reparations system. The commission recommended an eight-hundred-million-mark loan for Germany, a temporary moratorium on payments, and thereafter greatly reduced payments during the ensuing four years, until in 1929 when the full two-and-a-half-billion-mark annual payment would resume. Tax reform, some international supervision of the German economy, and substantial loans from America facilitated the funding of reparations payments. Any decision about revising the total amount of German reparations was postponed until 1929. One of the most difficult issues in Franco-German relations seemed well on its way to resolution. MacDonald boasted that the agreement finally ended an era of hostility and the threat of renewed war. Many Frenchmen disagreed.

The Locarno Accords, an even more sweeping exercise in accommodation, supplemented the Dawes Plan in 1925. Stresemann, anxious to prevent any repetition of the Ruhr invasion and hoping to get the Allied troops out of the Rhineland before their scheduled withdrawal in 1935, proposed a Franco-German guarantee of their common frontier. A general West European security agreement emerged from negotiations among Stresemann, Austen Chamberlain, and French foreign minister Aristide Briand. Germany, France, and Belgium acknowledged the sanctity of their mutual frontiers and pledged not to resort to war in settling disagreements among themselves. Britain and Italy signed the pact as guarantors. They would intervene if any of the parties violated the borders. The Allies agreed to early evacuation of their occupation forces in the Rhineland, while the Germans promised not to garrison the region. Germany was to join the League of Nations, which would supervise execution of the pact. Stresemann was unwilling, however, to recognize the permanence of Germany's eastern frontiers. Nevertheless, he did sign arbitration treaties with Czechoslovakia and Poland. France, therefore, reaffirmed its support for its eastern allies by strengthening its mutual assistance treaties with them.

Beyond the specific provisions of the accords, the negotiations produced a great burst of optimism—the Locarno spirit. The old, hostile intransigence gave way to the hopeful diplomacy of compromise. The *New York Times'* headlines proclaimed, "France and Germany Ban War Forever." Briand, Stresemann, and Chamberlain received the 1926 Nobel Peace Prize for their efforts. Hopes for peace reached new, but clearly unrealistic, heights in 1928 when Briand and American secretary of state Frank Kellogg cosponsored a multilateral agreement to abolish war. In signing the Kellogg-Briand Pact, the United States, Japan, and the European powers pledged to "renounce war as an instrument of national policy." Unfortunately, the treaty contained no mechanism to compel its signatories to honor their promise.

Great Britain, and even France, had abandoned coercion in favor of conciliation in dealing with Germany. Briand and Chamberlain hoped that reasonable concessions would inspire a "moral disarmament" in Berlin. They believed that if Germany no longer felt threatened or persecuted by the Allied powers but were accepted as an equal partner in cooperative European development, the Germans would learn to live in peace with their neighbors. The British and French also hoped that making concessions to "good Germans" like Stresemann would undermine the influence of militaristic, vengeful elements in Germany. This was a policy of appeasement, though, unlike the much-criticized appeasement of the 1930s, it was a program based on moral and practical political considerations and carried out from a position of strength. On the German side, Stresemann followed a policy of "fulfillment." He intended to demonstrate Germany's reliability to the Allies by voluntarily, if selectively, honoring the treaty. The fulfillment strategy was designed to disarm the Allies' suspicions and thereby persuade them that the most punitive features of the peace treaty were no longer necessary. Stresemann made no secret of his desire to redraw the eastern boundaries of the

Reich. He wanted to reestablish the borders of 1914 and, in a few instances, expand even beyond them into areas of German settlement then under foreign control. Although Stresemann did not forswear the use of force in principle, the goal of his foreign policy was the peaceful restoration of Germany's prewar position of strength.

In the following years, the Locarno spirit flagged but did not die. An international committee under the chairmanship of American banker Owen D. Young revised the reparations provisions once more in 1929. The Young Plan reduced Berlin's yearly payment by an additional 20 percent and abolished the system of foreign supervision over the German economy. Despite the continual revision of the reparations obligation in Germany's favor, the German Nationalist and Nazi parties bitterly denounced the Young Plan. When the ensuing Great Depression convulsed the German economy, reparations were eliminated altogether at the Lausanne Conference in 1932. The Reich had paid only a tiny fraction of its original liability. Likewise, the irritant of Allied occupation disappeared in June 1930 when the last French troops marched home from the Rhineland.

The disarmament issue, however, proved impossible to resolve. The disarming of Germany in 1919 was intended as merely the first step, as Article 8 of the treaty specified, toward "the reduction of national armaments to the lowest level consistent with national safety" for all the powers. Whatever chance for genuine arms limitation there may have been in the wake of Locarno was lost. The World Disarmament Conference did not convene until February 1932, and by then conditions were far less favorable for success. The French feared that any decrease in their military superiority over Germany would only facilitate German aggression. Berlin clamored for equality of armaments, which really meant not disarmament but permission for the Reichswehr to rearm up to the level of its potential adversaries. Hopes for arms control foundered on mutual suspicion and a general unwillingness to give up any of the prerogatives of sovereignty. The Germans withdrew from the conference after the fall of the Weimar Republic. Hitler recalled his delegate in October 1934, fearing that continued participation would expose his rapidly increasing but still covert rearmament program.

Was the hopeful spirit of Locarno an illusion? Perhaps it was not entirely without promise. Although even the "good Germans" wanted substantial treaty revision, it was not men like Stresemann and the parliamentary system he represented that led Germany to war in 1939. Locarno was at the very least the first step toward a mutual reconciliation of interests, a détente. Tragically, these promising developments were cut short by the death of Stresemann, the effects of the Great Depression, and the rise of Adolf Hitler.

From Weimar Republic to Third Reich

The Wall Street crash of October 1929, which plunged the United States into the Great Depression, soon precipitated an economic crisis in Germany as well. A massive flow of American dollars had sustained Weimar prosperity in the years 1924 to 1929. These loans not only covered reparations payments but also financed the expansion of German industry. The Great Crash cut off that supply of money and prompted the recall of these short-term loans. Furthermore, the crash deprived Germany of key export markets. The Depression caused unemployment to mount sharply. By late 1929 there were already 1,368,000 Germans out of work; by 1932 that figure had risen to 6,014,000.

The political effects of the Depression were even more traumatic than its economic impact. The hordes of unemployed men clogging the city streets were now much more susceptible to radical Nazi and communist propaganda. Middle-class fears of financial and social disaster, dormant since 1924, revived once more. Widespread unemployment also undermined the effectiveness of labor strikes, the most powerful weapon of the democratically inclined trade unions. Industrialists, desperate to save their fortunes, condoned more radical political measures than these otherwise conservative men normally would have accepted. The army was also deeply disturbed by the prospect of decreasing military budgets just at the point when covert expansion was to have accelerated. These events were interconnected and mutually reinforcing. The Depression weakened liberal democracy while the political crisis made governments less able to deal with the Depression. In Germany, the Depression undermined the confidence of the Weimar regime's supporters and caused them to squabble among themselves. At both political extremes, the allegedly superior authoritarian systems of Fascist Italy and Stalinist Russia challenged German liberal democracy. Economic crisis in itself did not cause the victory of National Socialism. The United States endured even more severe fiscal strains and yet emerged with its democratic tradition strengthened in the form of the New Deal. The social and political response to economic disaster differed greatly between Germans and Americans. In Germany the crisis created a climate of desperation and violence where the previously unthinkable—a Nazi takeover—became a possibility.

The pro-republican coalition of moderate socialist through moderately conservative parties broke apart under the weight of the Depression. The last truly democratic government of the Weimar era resigned in the spring of 1930. Heinrich Brüning, a conservative from the Catholic Center Party, served as chancellor from March 1930 to June 1932, but he was never able to build a viable parliamentary majority. In the Reichstag elections of September 1930, all the parties that supported Weimar democracy received a combined total of only 47 percent of the vote, while the conservative, authoritarian, and monarchist parties of the traditional right garnered almost 21 percent. Ominously, the Nazis captured 18.5 percent of the ballots, and the communists accounted for over 13 percent. New elections in July 1932 did not improve the situation in parliament. This time the pro-republican parties received just under 39 percent of the vote, and the parties of the old right got only 8.5 percent; the communists raised their share to over 17 percent of the ballots cast, and the Nazi total exploded to nearly 39 percent, making the Nazis the most popular party in the country. Thus, at the low point of the Depression, scarcely a third of the electorate voted in support of the democratic regime. Conversely, nearly two-thirds of the voters chose parties that sought to bring down the republic. Although the SPD managed to retain its urban working-class constituency, the middle-class moderate parties virtually ceased to exist. The Nazis, meanwhile, made dramatic electoral gains at the expense of the old-line conservative parties. Many Germans became so disillusioned with the political process that they no longer saw any point in participating. Parliamentary democracy simply could not operate under such circumstances.

Lacking a parliamentary majority, Chancellor Brüning was forced to rule through the executive power of President von Hindenburg. Article 48 of the Weimar constitution provided for temporary government by presidential decree during times of national emergency. Brüning employed this temporary expedient for over two years. Following the economic orthodoxy of his day, Brüning tried to combat the depression with a policy of deflation, which entailed reduced government spending, wage reductions, and attempted price controls. At the same time, the government had to provide some unemployment benefits, even if at a reduced level, and it sponsored a program of land resettlement for poor peasants. The chancellor used his emergency powers to restore order on the streets by banning the Nazi storm troopers.

Brüning hoped to win a popular mandate for his administration, despite its painful deflationary measures, by achieving great diplomatic success. He attempted to create a customs union with Austria, a measure forbidden by the Versailles Treaty, and to secure the right to armaments equality with the Western powers. Brüning failed in all these endeavors. The French blocked his foreign policy initiatives. Industrialists deeply resented the costs of welfare payments, while landowners were equally displeased at the prospect of land reforms. The deflationary strategy for dealing with the Depression only worsened the crisis. Workers, unions, and the SPD reacted sharply against decreased welfare payments. Moreover, the chancellor's resort to the ballot box in 1932 failed to produce a workable parliamentary majority.

By July 1932, President von Hindenburg had lost faith in his chancellor's ability to deal with the multiple crises facing the Reich. Two short-lived administrations, the first under aristocratic Franz von Papen and the second under General Kurt von Schleicher, failed to win parliamentary majorities or to deal with the nation's growing problems. General Schleicher's cabinet was soon brought down by the intrigues of his old rival, von Papen. Baron von Papen proposed to tap Nazi electoral strength by forming a new administration in which Hitler would participate. Inclusion of the Nazis would, he hoped, finally make a parliamentary majority possible, but von Papen and his conservative allies had no intention of really sharing power with the upstart Austrian demagogue. Von Papen, Alfred Hugenberg of the Nationalist Party, and other representatives of industry, the army, and the bureaucracy intended to retain power. Hitler would serve only as a figurehead. For his part, Hitler was more eager than before to consider entering a coalition government. He sensed that he might acquire power by legal, or rather, pseudo-legal, means. He also realized that this might be his last opportunity. The Depression seemed to have passed its peak in late 1932, and Nazi returns in the second Reichstag election of that year had begun to drop. Furthermore, the frequent electoral campaigns had nearly drained the party treasury. Restive party factions also threatened to challenge Hitler's leadership. For all these reasons, he was anxious to seize the opportunity. On January 30, 1933, Adolf Hitler became chancellor of a right-wing coalition cabinet.

The Rise of Adolf Hitler

The future dictator of Germany, Adolf Hitler, was born on April 20, 1889, in the small Austrian town of Braunau. He was the son of a Habsburg customs official. Contrary to the picture of poverty and family strife Hitler would later create in his memoirs, his childhood was apparently a happy one, and he was a good student in the lower grades. He did not do as well when his father sent him to a more demanding secondary school to prepare him for a civil service career. The quality of his schoolwork declined steadily and, after his father died in 1903, Adolf dropped out of school at the age of fourteen. The next ten years were a decade of isolation, alienation, and frustration for Hitler. For a while he lived in Linz, Austria, without an occupation or apparent goal in life. In 1907, he moved to Vienna to study art, only to be rejected by the Imperial Academy of Fine Arts for lack of talent. Hitler stayed on in the Habsburg capital, living on his orphan's pension and a substantial inheritance from an aunt. The fact that he sometimes frequented Viennese flophouses does not reflect poverty, as he later claimed, but his attempt to elude the Austro-Hungarian authorities who sought him for draft evasion. These years in Vienna were crucial to Hitler's ideological development.

Vienna at that time was the scene of brilliant cultural and scientific advance, but Hitler was caught up in the slimy underside of Viennese intellectual life. He learned much from the virulent anti-Semitism and demagogic techniques of Mayor Karl Lueger. He absorbed the crude social Darwinism and racism then prevalent in central Europe. He also encountered the Pan-German chauvinism of Baron von Schönerer. Much of the Nazi creed can be traced back to the beer hall philosophers and the ultra-right-wing polemics of prewar Vienna.

The outbreak of World War I came as a deliverance for Hitler. He had already migrated to Munich, conveniently out of reach of the Austrian conscription officials. He reacted to the news of war with relief and thanksgiving. His years of aimless wandering were over. Now at age twenty-five, Hitler finally had a cause that gave meaning to his life. He immediately joined a Bavarian regiment of the German army. Hitler saw combat, serving as a dispatch carrier on the western front. He was decorated several times for bravery, receiving the Iron Cross (First Class), an unusual distinction for an enlisted man. Hitler seems to have enjoyed the war, probably because in it he found a sense of self-worth. Shortly before the end of the war, Hitler was temporarily blinded during a gas attack. He received the stunning news of Germany's surrender while he was recuperating. Hitler was devastated. Historian John Lukacs argues that Hitler's immediate postwar experiences in Munich were critical to the crystallization of his beliefs and hatreds. The twin traumas of Germany's defeat and living under the Bavarian Soviet Republic moved anti-Semitism to the core of Hitler's consciousness.[16]

Hitler remained in the army after the armistice as an information officer. He was ordered to penetrate and report on a small radical-rightist, anti-Semitic group in Munich known as the German Workers' Party (DAP). Its doctrines were similar to those that attracted Hitler in Vienna. Soon he quit the army, joined this party, and even became a member of its executive committee. The party leadership found Hitler a valuable contributor to their cause because of his skills as a fiery street-corner agitator. Railing against the supposed unfairness of the Versailles Treaty and the alleged treason of the socialists and Jews who betrayed Germany, he managed to attract a mass audience, something that the party had never before enjoyed. He also helped procure financial support from conservative groups and from the army, which in turn enabled the party to acquire its own newspaper, the *Völkischer Beobachter* (the People's Observer). Within a year Hitler had become the dominant figure in the DAP. The force of his personality and his infectious fanaticism enabled him to eclipse the party's original leaders. By the end of 1921, Hitler became the Führer (supreme leader) of the now renamed National Socialist German Workers' Party (the NSDAP or Nazi Party).

The Nazis were only one of dozens of rabidly nationalistic, anti-Semitic, anti-Marxist, revisionist, and vengeful political groups infesting postwar Germany. All of them played on the pervasive fears and hatreds unleashed in these troubled times. Many of them advocated a national rebirth to lift Germany out of defeat, degradation, and despair. These groups appealed especially to veterans humiliated by Germany's defeat and unable to readjust to civilian life, and to lower-middle-class elements—artisans, shopkeepers, small businessmen—who feared being crushed between the socialist labor movement and the giant corporations. The Nazis proclaimed themselves champions of the "little man." At this early stage, National Socialist ideology contained an anticapitalist current as strong as its anticommunist thrust. The party promised to deliver the independent store or the family business from the ruthless competition of the big chain stores and multinational corporations. Restless, violence-prone veterans were drawn into the party's paramilitary force, the *Sturmabteilung* (abbreviated SA, but also known as the storm troopers or Brownshirts). The party used these direct-action squads to disrupt the political activities of rival groups and to intimidate opponents. The SA specialized in street fighting—with fists, clubs, knives, and pistols. The Nazis appealed to the romantic nationalism and the cult of militarism so widespread in Germany. Using uniforms, insignia, banners, and torchlit parades, the Nazis tried to identify themselves with the German tradition of strength and power, in contrast to the Weimar image of weakness and humiliation.

Having won control of the tiny German Workers' Party, Hitler was determined to seize power in all of Germany. His first attempt in 1923 was an ill-fated coup d'état known as the Beer Hall Putsch. Hitler was confident that the inflation crisis, the French occupation of the Ruhr, and communist resurgence in Saxony and Thuringia provided a good opportunity to topple the despised republic. The local military authorities had already usurped power from the legitimate Bavarian state government. Hitler intended to take control of Munich by force, compel the regional army command to join him, and then march on Berlin. It was to be a repetition of Mussolini's successful March on Rome the previous year. Hitler had gained the support of General Ludendorff, whose participation in the coup was supposed to paralyze any resistance from the army or conservative forces. On November 8, Nazi forces overwhelmed a right-wing political meeting in the Bürgerbräukeller, arrested the state governor as well as leading police and army officials, and forced them all to proclaim their support for the coup. Other detachments of storm troopers, under Captain Ernst Röhm, took over the Bavarian War Ministry. The following day Hitler, with Ludendorff at his side, led a column of supporters to seize the rest of the state government apparatus. He had miscalculated, however. Most Reichswehr units in the area did not rally to the putsch. Under this circumstance, it was relatively easy for a cordon of Bavarian State Police to break up the Nazi march with a few volleys of rifle fire.

Hitler was slightly injured in escaping the disaster, and he was arrested soon thereafter. Along with a group of fellow conspirators, he was tried for high treason in 1924. Sympathetic Bavarian judges allowed Hitler to turn his trial into an indictment of the Weimar Republic. "I alone bear the responsibility," he proclaimed, "but I am not a criminal because of that. If today I stand here as a revolutionary, it is as a revolutionary against the revolution. There is no such thing as high treason against the traitors of 1918." Hitler was sentenced to a mere five-year prison term, the statutory minimum, for his attempt to destroy Weimar democracy. He served only a few months of his term in comfortable conditions at Landsberg prison before he was paroled. The state police wanted to deport Hitler to Austria, but his homeland refused to take him back. The conservative Bavarian state bureaucrats obviously did not regard treason to the republic as a serious crime. Hitler was free by Christmas of 1924 to resume his political crusade.

Hitler used his stay at Landsberg prison to write the first volume of *Mein Kampf* (My Struggle)—part political credo, part fictionalized autobiography. Above all, he wanted to produce a work that would make people take him seriously as a political thinker. He did not succeed. Verbose, turgid, and irrational, *Mein Kampf* mirrored the mind of its creator. Yet the book expressed, however opaquely, the principal elements of Hitler's ideology. He outlined his racist theory that the various nationalities were inherently unequal. The Aryans, which meant the Germans, were the master race (*Herrenvolk*), while the other peoples of the world were ranked in a descending order of racial quality with Asians and Africans at the bottom. Hitler tied this assertion of ethnic inequality to a social Darwinist notion of racial evolution. The various nationalities and races, he claimed, were locked in a desperate struggle for survival. Either the Aryans would assert their superiority by dominating the inferior races, or they would be swamped by mongrelized and debased hordes of Slavs, Asians, and Africans. The very process of struggle would purify and toughen the Germanic *Volk*.

The German people supposedly needed living space (*Lebensraum*) for their develop-ment. This desire for additional space sprang, in Hitler's mind, not from there being too many Germans but *too few*. When he came to power, mothers who bore large numbers of children received medals as well as more tangible rewards. The future of war and conquest that he envisioned would require much larger armies and many more resources than those available within Germany's postwar borders. The space Hitler had in mind was Eastern Europe. Ultimately, he thought, the German people would have to dominate this region, en-slaving or exterminating its Slavic population. What menaced the *Volk* at the moment, how-ever, was the supposed Jewish world conspiracy. Hitler claimed that "the Jews" employed capitalism, liberalism, Marxism, pacifism, homosexuality, and other diabolical weapons to divide and subdue the German nation. Behind virtually every development that he opposed, Hitler saw the sinister hand of the Jew. His depiction of Jews was highly inconsistent. He saw them as both the racial scum of humanity and as a supremely wily opponent. Thus, in Hitler's mind, "the Jews" were the chief enemy, who mobilized and led all other enemies to destroy the German people. These ideas were not unique to Hitler, but what was new about his anti-Semitism was his belief that this struggle would redeem the nation and allow Germans to achieve their full potential. Historian Saul Friedländer calls this "redemptive anti-Semitism," a "synthesis of a murderous rage and an 'idealistic' goal."[17]

Hitler also implored his compatriots to abandon rationalistic, atomistic liberalism for a life of mystical unity with the nation, violent action, and unquestioning obedience to him—Führer and *Volk* united in destiny. *Mein Kampf* did little to popularize the Nazi cause. It was not widely read until after the NSDAP had become a serious contender for power. It sold over six million copies by 1940, but few readers, including high-ranking Nazis, had the persistence to slog through the dense volume. Yet the book cannot be dismissed as unim-portant. Although the cautious policy followed during the first years of Hitler's reign seemed to belie the radicalism of *Mein Kampf*, once Germany had fully rearmed, Hitler's racist and imperialist ravings reemerged in genocide and global war.

Hitler had relatively little to say about the United States in these early years. Not well informed about the nature of American society, initially he had seen the United States as a racist and imperialist model for Germany—a nation that ruthlessly exterminated the red man and enslaved the black man. His view changed from admiration to disgust and fear as he learned more about America. On one hand, he came to see the United States as a mon-grelized nation, led in the 1930s by a cripple (FDR), who was surrounded by Jewish advi-sors. On the other hand, he understood the tremendous economic strength of the United States and its potential to achieve not only economic but also military hegemony throughout the world. Hitler expressed these fears in his untitled, unpublished second book written in 1928.[18] Germany needed *Lebensraum*, he believed, to acquire the human, industrial, and natural resources that would enable it to challenge America for world domination.

While Hitler was in prison, the party atrophied under the weak leadership of Alfred Rosenberg. Upon his parole at the end of 1924, Hitler set about rebuilding his belea-guered, factionalized party. Reflecting on the collapse of the Beer Hall Putsch, he reached an important conclusion. Power could not be seized against the opposition of the Reichs-wehr and other centers of conservative strength. This realization led Hitler to proclaim a "legality policy." The party would protect itself by creating at least a facade of legality. It would participate in electoral politics. It was a sensible strategy, since not only Hitler but, in effect, the Nazi Party as well was on probation. Pseudo-legality was never more than a temporary stratagem for the Führer. He never accepted the constitutional limitations of the parliamentary system, and he never abandoned his reliance on paramilitary violence in the streets. By employing semilegal means to build his political and parliamentary strength, he hoped to make his movement acceptable to the officer corps, the higher bureaucracy, and the industrialists. He then intended, by raising the level of anarchistic street violence, to create a situation in which those conservative groups would hand over emergency power to the Nazis to preserve order.

If Hitler were to appease Germany's conservative elites, he first had to eliminate two aspects of his movement that they found objectionable—the independent power of the SA and the strain of anticapitalism in the Nazi creed. The army of the Weimar Republic was more thoroughly professional and aristocratic than it had been even under Kaiser Wilhelm II. Although they valued the right-wing paramilitary formations as potential auxiliaries, the officers feared that Ernst Röhm and his SA intended to replace, or at least dominate, the Reichswehr. Röhm aspired to lead the Nazi Party as well. He also disagreed fundamentally with the legality tactic. Hitler temporarily checked this threat to his position by forcing Röhm to resign in 1925. At the end of the decade, Hitler also began to construct a counter-weight to the SA in the form of the SS (*Schutzstaffel*). Over the next several years, Heinrich Himmler built up what began as a two-hundred-man unit of bodyguards into a mighty political and military force.

Hitler also had to purge the anticapitalist wing of the Nazi Party. That segment of the NSDAP, led by Gregor and Otto Strasser, took the anticapitalist plank of the party platform as seriously as the nationalistic and anti-Semitic planks. Appealing to working-class and lower-middle-class hostility to banks, landlords, chain stores, and big business in general, these Nazi radicals had established party organizations in previously hostile areas, especially northern Germany and the Rhineland. However, their talk of nationalizing heavy industry and large estates frightened precisely those industrialists and conservative agrarians whom Hitler was trying to reassure. Moreover, as with the SA, the growth of a radical Strasserite faction in the party threatened Hitler's control over the movement. Once again, Hitler outmaneuvered his opponents. The party abandoned their radical program early in 1926 at a conference packed with south German Nazi district leaders loyal to the Führer. A hostile critique of bourgeois capitalism remained formally part of Nazi ideology, but it ceased to have any operative significance. An ever-increasing emphasis on anti-Semitism replaced the anticapitalist appeal. Hatred of Jews had always been an important ingredient of Nazism, but now it emerged as the main thrust of the NSDAP. Shifting the focus of hatred from the capitalist system to the Jews pleased most industrialists and military officers, who were anti-Semitic themselves. Anti-Semitism also provided an effective diversion for the mass following that Hitler sought to beguile. The Nazis had a deceptively simple answer to all the seemingly intractable problems facing Germany—they were the Jews' fault. Hitler's wily political shifts did not mean that he had abandoned his hostility to big business. For the moment, however, it suited him to downplay Nazi anticapitalism just as it was politically necessary to suppress Nazi hostility to Christianity. There would be time to deal with those enemies after he had gathered all power in his hands.

Hitler and his followers set about rebuilding their shattered party with considerable energy and ingenuity. They used the radio and air travel as never before. In many respects, the Nazis introduced the techniques of modern political campaigning into Germany. They preached their message at an emotional and intellectual level that no German could fail to grasp. They oversimplified every issue, appealing to the lowest prejudices and hatreds. All would be well, they shouted, if Germans cast off the shackles of Versailles, overthrew the bastard republic, expropriated rapacious Jewish businessmen, and established a truly Germanic, Nazi-led regime. Many Germans found Hitler's oratory spellbinding. The energy and passion of his voice touched a responsive chord in them.

The Nazis attempted to reach a broad spectrum of the German nation. The NSDAP met with only modest success among the proletariat, however. The socialists and communists divided most of the urban working class between them. The Nazis fared somewhat better among peasants in Protestant areas. A long-term agricultural recession had radicalized the farmers, but socialism had not taken hold in the countryside. The anti-Marxism and the simple solutions proffered by the Nazis attracted significant numbers of lower-middle-class people traumatized by economic disaster. Salesmen, tradesmen, and small shopkeepers were the backbone of the party. Nationalists, militarists, and *Freikorps* thugs responded enthusiastically to Hitler's denunciations of Versailles and Weimar. Anti-Jewish bigots, of course, found a ready welcome in the National Socialist camp. The Nazis also promised to bridge the deep social and economic divisions that set one German against another by fostering a sense of national community (*Volksgemeinschaft*). This doctrine had considerable appeal for a nation torn by violent party and class conflicts. Hitler concealed many of his plans from his audiences, most importantly that he intended war—unlimited war, war at any cost and any risk.

Through skillful organizational work, brilliant propaganda, and verbal pyrotechnics, Hitler was able to resuscitate the NSDAP. The party boasted a hundred thousand members and twelve Reichstag deputies in 1928. For all his successes, however, Hitler still presided over a minor fringe party with sharply limited influence in Germany. What stood in Hitler's way for the moment was the prosperity of the later 1920s and the relatively successful foreign policy of Stresemann. The Weimar Republic seemed to be working all too well. Few Germans saw any need for the desperate political remedies Hitler offered. The Great Depression soon changed their minds.

Hitler began to acquire a nationwide following even before the Depression struck. In 1929, the Nazis allied with Alfred Hugenberg's German National People's Party (the DNVP) and other right-wing groups to crusade against the Young Plan. This new reparations arrangement, which required German payments through the year 1988, outraged all nationalists. Although the campaign failed to block the Young Plan, Hugenberg's press empire brought Hitler's name and ideas to the attention of millions of Germans. Then with the onset of the Depression, Nazi fortunes soared. The legality strategy was beginning to pay off. For much of the middle class, the psychological effects of the crisis proved even more devastating than its economic impact. Besides worrying about their potential loss of income or status, many Germans manifested a fear of communist revolution disproportionate to the danger. They looked to the Nazis for protection against the specter of Bolshevism. In the election of 1930, large numbers of respectable burghers deserted centrist or conservative parties and, for the first time, cast National Socialist ballots. The result increased Nazi representation in the Reichstag from 12 to 107 deputies. The worse the economy became, the greater the Nazi successes. After the mid-1932 elections, the NSDAP had 230 seats in the parliament, making it the largest single party in the country. Nearly 40 percent of voters backed the Nazis in 1932. Fear, anger, and misperceptions of their own economic interests drove some of them, but many found Nazi ideas of assertive nationalism and racial community appealing. Hitler was both a fanatical true believer and an extraordinarily cynical politician. The masses were like sheep to him; he told them what they wanted to hear and then led them in the direction he required them to go.

The decline of Germany's centrist and nationalist parties was already well underway before the Great Depression. For many voters, those parties seemed both ineffective and too invested in protecting the rich and the powerful while ignoring the plight of ordinary Germans. The decade-long depression in agricultural prices hurt farmers (29 percent of the population) and those townsmen who depended on their trade. Splinter parties and interest groups, however, could not produce meaningful reforms for their constituents. The National Socialists benefited immensely from the deterioration of moderate and conservative parties. More and more Germans found the Nazi promise of a true people's community irresistible. Even some of the working class was seduced by the Nazis' powerful slogan, "Work and bread!" At the height of the Depression, as much as a third of the Nazis' electoral support came from working-class voters. Surprisingly, very large numbers of more affluent Germans voted for the NSDAP too. Even the relatively well-to-do shared a pervasive sense that the Weimar Republic was a hopeless morass and that the nation required a dramatic rebirth.[19] None of this means that most Germans had signed on for the Holocaust, global war, and the privations that the latter inevitably entailed. Even though a careful examination of Hitler's speeches and writings, as well as those of other Nazi leaders, gave evidence of future ethnic cleansing and aggressive warfare, that is not what most of the Führer's sympathizers chose to see.

It was this electoral strength, combined with SA muscle in the streets, that tempted the conservative elites to make common cause with National Socialism. They intended to co-opt Hitler into a right-wing coalition cabinet that they would control and that, with Nazi support, would command a Reichstag majority. The elites intended to use this majority in the legislature to destroy both Marxism and parliamentary democracy in Germany and to deal with the Depression. After that, they planned to throw Hitler and his thugs back into the gutter from which they crawled. They had made a fatal mistake.

Gleichschaltung: The Revolution after Power

Adolf Hitler became chancellor of the Reich on January 30, 1933, not by armed revolt or by majority vote but through the intrigues of an aristocratic cabal. Under these circumstances, Hitler had to proceed with caution. The Nazis received only three positions in the new government: the chancellorship for Hitler, the Ministry of Interior for Wilhelm Frick, and a ministerial chair without portfolio for Hermann Göring, who also assumed the key post of minister of interior for the Prussian state. Frick and Göring now possessed considerable power over the police and judicial system in much of the country. The Nazis hoped to increase their share of power still more in the Reichstag elections of April 1933, but they were disappointed. Even using their position in the government to control the mass media and employing the SA to intimidate all opponents, the NSDAP still received only 44 percent of the vote. National Socialism had failed to win over Catholic Center, Social Democratic, and Communist Party voters. The coalition cabinet had a precarious Reichstag majority only when the deputies of the Nationalist Party, which had received 8 percent of the vote, supported the Nazis. If Hitler had continued to play the parliamentary game, he would have been dependent on his conservative allies, just as they had intended.

An unexpected stroke of fortune rescued Hitler from this political dilemma. On February 27, 1933, a deranged Dutch communist, Marinus van der Lubbe, set fire to the Reichstag building. Although this was the isolated act of a crazed individual, Hitler proclaimed the threat of an incipient communist revolution. With this excuse, he unleashed a full-scale campaign of SA terror across Germany and began to dismantle the institutions of Weimar democracy. To meet this supposed Bolshevik menace, President von Hindenburg signed an emergency decree, "for the protection of the people and the state," temporarily suspending the protections of the Weimar constitution and giving Hitler broad executive authority. The SA immediately began to eliminate the German Communist Party. With Weimar civil rights nullified and the Nazi-controlled police looking the other way, the storm troopers were free to perpetrate every outrage on anyone who opposed the destruction of democracy.

Temporary emergency powers were insufficient for Hitler's purposes. The Führer therefore demanded Reichstag passage of an Enabling Act, granting the chancellor the authority to make new laws without recourse to the parliament or the president. It gave him dictatorial powers. Securing a majority for this legislation required ruthlessness and supreme political skill, since it involved asking the Reichstag to vote itself out of existence. Communist Party opposition presented no problem; all its deputies were in prison or had fled the country. The Catholic Center delegates were won over with the promise that the new regime would negotiate an agreement with the Vatican protecting religious freedom in Germany. Right-wing delegates were stampeded by the anticommunist hysteria and intimidated by threats of violence. On March 23, 1933, the measure carried by a vote of 441 to 92. Only the Social Democrats had the courage to vote against it. Although the Enabling Act explicitly limited the chancellor's emergency powers to four years, in practice it established a Nazi dictatorship in perpetuity. The Weimar Republic was dead. Germany soon would be transformed into the Third Reich.

Hitler bolstered his position with two agreements negotiated with segments of the traditional elite—the industrialists and the officer corps. He assured Hjalmar Schacht, representing the business community, that there would be no second revolution, no expropriation of big corporations for the benefit of the "little man." In return, the industrialists agreed to support the party and refrain from using their enormous economic strength to block the Nazi destruction of the Weimar political system. Just the opposite, such big companies as IG Farben, Deutsche Bank, and AEG bankrolled the Nazi Party and underwrote Hitler's personal expenses. The new regime curtailed democracy and destroyed the labor movement—just what the big corporations wanted. The Führer worked out a similar arrangement with General Werner von Blomberg of the army high command. The generals pledged not to interfere in domestic politics, that is, not to interpose the only force in Germany capable of suppressing Nazi violence. Besides accelerating the rearmament program, Hitler promised not to undermine the position of the professional military officers in the army command structure. There was also a tacit understanding between Hitler and the civil service. Nazi propaganda had promised to purge the elitist and supposedly corrupt state bureaucracy, but once in command of the state, the party leadership needed the cooperation of experienced civil servants. In exchange for formal professions of allegiance to National Socialism, government workers, except Jews and known leftists, kept their jobs.

The SA was the main obstacle to fulfilling these promises to Germany's conservative elites. Once again under Ernst Röhm's leadership, the storm troopers were anxious to take command of the army, displace the bureaucrats, and humble big business. Hitler's response to this challenge was murderously effective. On the "Night of the Long Knives," June 30, 1934, SS squads swooped down upon the SA leadership. They summarily executed Röhm and his henchmen. General von Schleicher and Gregor Strasser, leader of the Nazi Party's radical wing, were also killed. Baron von Papen was arrested. Although Hitler's thugs violently crushed their opponents, most people seem to have accepted the Nazi takeover willingly. They applauded the destruction of the Communist Party, the abolition of the fractious political parties and parliament, and the promise of a united, resurgent Germany.

As soon as the Enabling Act subverted the Weimar constitution, Hitler launched the *Gleichschaltung* (meaning "coordination," or figuratively, Nazification) of all German society. The NSDAP formalized its monopoly of political power by outlawing the Socialist and Communist Parties and by pressuring the other parties into disbanding themselves. There was little protest against these measures since many Germans had already rejected the parties and the parliamentary process as divisive and corrupt. Similarly, socialist and Catholic labor unions were abolished, and all nongovernmental workers were brought under the Nazi Labor Front. The federal structure of Germany, which reserved considerable authority for the states, was undermined as well. Locally elected officials were replaced by Nazi governors appointed by Berlin.

All social and professional organizations were either brought under party guidance or dissolved. The Nazis were eliminating the organizational basis for any potential opposition to their reign. Not even the churches were exempt. The various publicly supported Lutheran and Reformed Churches were united in the state-controlled German Evangelical Church. The Catholic Church was protected from such a complete Nazi takeover by the terms of a concordat signed with the government preserving its churches and schools but silencing its voice in politics. Joseph Goebbels's Propaganda Ministry took control of all the mass media—radio, the press, and motion pictures. In schools and universities, the faculty were purged and curricula revised to conform to the party line. The Nazis sought to control the flow of information and the associational life of the German people because they needed to transform the national mentality. "The ultimate goal, once the people had been won for Nazi ideals," historian Ian Kershaw argues, "was already envisioned: the psychological preparation of the German people for the inevitable war to establish supremacy."[20]

Terror now became an official policy of the state. All ideas contrary to the tenets of National Socialism were suppressed. A campaign against "cultural Bolshevism" culminated in widespread book burnings on May 10, 1933. Works by Bertolt Brecht, Albert Einstein, Sigmund Freud, Franz Kafka, Karl Marx, Erich Maria Remarque, Helen Keller, and many others were consigned to the flames. Socialists and other dissenters were subjected to constant harassment, physical harm, and even murder. The infamous concentration camp system had its beginnings in the first year of Nazi rule with the internment of thousands of communists, trade union officials, liberals, and uncooperative churchmen. Jews were savagely persecuted. In 1933, all non-Aryans were excluded from government posts, and two years later the Nuremberg Laws deprived Jews of German citizenship and prohibited their marriage to Aryans. In addition, a campaign of extralegal violence forced many Jews to flee the Reich. Reflecting on a boycott of Jewish businesses, enforced by intimidating storm troopers, Arnon Tamir, a Jewish teenager, concluded that "you could do with the Jews whatever you liked, that nobody stood up for them, that a Jew was an outlaw."[21]

The Nazi Party expanded greatly after Hitler's rise to power, though it still included only a small fraction of the German population. However, over time, with its control of the mass media and the schools, the Nazis managed to convince most Germans that the Führer's view of the world was correct. Most came to believe that Germany had been betrayed by traitors in 1918, that the Allies had treated Germany unfairly, that the Weimar Republic had failed the German people, that stern measures were required to purge Germany of internal enemies, and that, under Hitler, German was now experiencing real freedom. By imposing the pseudo–law and order of the SA-man's truncheon, the Nazis ended the anarchy of the streets that had marred the republic's last years. For many frightened people in the middle classes, the loss of democracy appeared a small price to pay for the elimination of the dreaded communist bogey. The constantly reiterated Nazi themes of anti-Semitism, anticommunism, and hostility to the Versailles system took people's minds off their daily problems. Their anger was conveniently redirected toward scapegoats and outside enemies. Nazi propagandists could plausibly claim that the Führer and his policies were popular with most Germans.

With power now firmly in his hands, Hitler proceeded to "solve" Germany's problems. A massive rearmament program combined with extensive public works projects created full employment for workers and large profits for industrialists. The expansion of the armed forces and the growth of concentration camps absorbed excess labor. The country seemed to recover very rapidly from the Depression. It was not an entirely rosy picture, however. The taxing demands of rapid rearmament required continuing sacrifices by the German people. The new regime severely constricted civilian consumption. Living standards remained significantly below those of France, Britain, and the United States.[22]

Hitler's apparent success in overcoming the difficulties that had plagued the Weimar Republic was largely illusory. None of his measures really solved anything. They only masked real problems and created new ones. Full employment, for example, was based on economically unproductive armaments expenditures. Worse yet, after an initial burst of expansion, the rearmament program would have to level off or find a new justification for its continued acceleration—namely, war. Even though unemployment was virtually eliminated, living standards dropped. Both food and consumer goods were in short supply. Nonetheless, Hitler's popularity was undeniable. In the view of Adam Tooze, "for many millions, the reconstruction of the Wehrmacht was clearly the most successful aspect of the regime's domestic policy and the collective mass-consumption of weaponry was a more than sufficient substitute for private affluence."[23] Nor did National Socialism heal the deep social divisions that rent the country. Nazi propaganda proclaimed a new Germany of open opportunity for peasants and workers, the lower middle class, and young people. In reality, the traditional elites—landowners, big business, bureaucrats, and the officer corps—retained their near monopoly of wealth and prestige. Even the rank and file of the NSDAP did not benefit much from their Führer's conquest of power. Only the Nazi hierarchy reaped the social and financial rewards of victory. The founding of the Third Reich did not create a tightly organized, disciplined, totalitarian society. While the Führer held the power of life and death over every German, in practice most administrative responsibility was delegated to subordinates. Hitler was uninterested in anything besides his two favorite subjects, art and war. He secured his own position by deliberately creating a jumble of conflicting authority and personal rivalry below him. One historian has described the situation as "the division of domination into thousands of little empires of ambitious men, domains that were largely unchecked by law, that had been replaced by Hitler's will, which was largely a mirage."[24]

The economic recovery that Germany experienced in the 1930s was predicated on the necessity of war, although Hitler did not tell that to his adoring audiences. The Four Year Plan, introduced in 1936, aimed at the establishment of short-term economic self-sufficiency as a prelude to armed aggression. Experts, both at the time and subsequently, criticized the seeming irrationality and imbalance of Nazi economic plans, but such criticism ignores the fact that the mobilization of resources within Germany's 1919 boundaries was intended merely to provide the basis for greater expansion. Hitler was convinced that the Reich could not achieve real prosperity without the conquest of additional resources and living space abroad. A prolonged period of peace would have been disastrous for Hitler. His economic policy would have collapsed and he would soon have lost any justification for continued re-armament and for the constant demands on the German people for obedience and sacrifice. Despite the consumer sacrifices that his policies entailed, the Führer's continuing popularity rested largely on a widespread sense of renewed national strength and on the series of brilliant diplomatic victories that he won during his first seven years in power. By the spring of 1939, the resistance of the Western Allies had stiffened. The era of easy victories was past. For Hitler, war had become inevitable.

Notes

1. Robert Gerwarth, *The Vanquished: Why the First World War Failed to End* (New York: Farrar, Straus & Giroux, 2016), 13.

2. Richard Overy, *The Interwar Crisis*, 3rd ed. (London: Routledge, 2017), 3–10.

3. Harold Nicolson, *Peacemaking 1919* (New York: Grosset & Dunlap, 1965), 189–90.

4. George F. Kennan, *American Diplomacy, 1900–1950* (New York: Mentor, 1952), 60.

5. Sally Marks, *The Illusion of Peace: International Relations in Europe, 1918–1933* (New York: Palgrave, 2003), 156.

6. Margaret MacMillan, *Paris 1919: Six Months That Changed the World* (New York: Random House, 2003), 493–94.

7. Adam Tooze, *The Deluge: The Great War, America and the Remaking of the Global Order, 1916–1931* (New York: Viking, 2014), 282–83.

8. Klaus Theweleit, *Male Fantasies*, vol. 1, *Women, Floods, Bodies, History* (Minneapolis: University of Minnesota Press, 1987), 16.

9. Martin Clark, *Mussolini* (Harlow: Pearson, 2005), 76.

10. Clark, *Mussolini*, 108.

11. MacGregor Knox, *Hitler's Italian Allies: Royal Armed Forces, Fascist Regime, and the War of 1940–1943* (Cambridge: Cambridge University Press, 2000), 9.

12. Roger Griffin, ed., *Fascism* (Oxford: Oxford University Press, 1995), 4.

13. Tracy H. Koon, *Believe, Obey, Fight: Political Socialization of Youth in Fascist Italy, 1922–1943* (Chapel Hill: University of North Carolina Press, 1985), xvii.

14. Tooze, *The Deluge*, 369.

15. Gerwarth, *The Vanquished*, 202.

16. John Lukacs, *The Hitler of History* (New York: Vintage, 1997), 57–75.

17. Saul Friedländer, *Nazi Germany and the Jews*, vol. 1, *The Years of Persecution, 1933–1939* (New York: Harper Perennial, 1998), 3, 73–112.

18. Gerhard Weinberg, ed., *Hitler's Second Book: The Unpublished Sequel to Mein Kampf* (New York: Enigma Books, 2006).

19. William F. Hamilton, *Who Voted for Hitler?* (Princeton, NJ: Princeton University Press, 1982); Thomas Childers, *The Nazi Voter: Social Foundations of Fascism in Germany, 1919–1933* (Chapel Hill: University of North Carolina Press, 1983).

20. Ian Kershaw, *Hitler, 1889–1936: Hubris* (New York: Norton, 1999), 96.

21. Quoted in Laurence Rees, *The Holocaust: A New History* (New York: PublicAffairs, 2017), 61.

22. Adam Tooze, *The Wages of Destruction: The Making and Breaking of the Nazi Economy* (New York: Penguin, 2006), 94, 97.

23. Tooze, *The Wages of Destruction*, 659.

24. Edward N. Peterson, *The Limits of Hitler's Power* (Princeton, NJ: Princeton University Press, 1969), 446.

.R 2

ǝ Origins of War in Asia

While Hitler prepared to plunge Europe into war, hostilities had already commenced in Asia. The issues and events immediately preceding the outbreak of war in East Asia in 1937 were different from the circumstances precipitating conflict in Europe two years later, but the underlying causes of fighting on both continents were remarkably similar. Everywhere, nationalism and imperialism provided the impetus for aggression. In Asia, these themes manifested themselves in the rise of Japanese power and the parallel decline of China's fortunes. The gradual erosion of Britain's imperial position, coupled with the increase of American strength in the Pacific region, and the spread of national liberation movements among the colonial peoples further complicated the situation.

The Rise of Japan

Japan had been a "closed country" since the early seventeenth century—isolated by the shogun (the chief military commander) to prevent both Western penetration and the strengthening of maverick regional lords through foreign contact. Nonetheless, when American commodore Matthew C. Perry sailed into Tokyo harbor in July 1853, inaugurating the so-called opening of Japan, he found a society that had already begun the process of modernization. A long period of peace under the Tokugawa Shogunate (1603–1868) had fostered significant changes in traditional Japanese society. The rise of commercially oriented urban centers and the partial conversion of the samurai from feudal warriors to educated, salaried bureaucrats evidenced the beginnings of a national transformation. The intrusion of the Western powers greatly accelerated the pace of change. Under Perry's guns, the shogunate agreed to end its long-standing policy of national isolation and establish trade relations with the United States and subsequently with other Western states. Japanese leaders realized that the economic opportunities resulting from contact with the West also entailed the risk of Western imperial domination. They were keenly aware of the growing European encroachments on Chinese sovereignty in the aftermath of the Opium Wars. Rebels overthrew the Tokugawa Shogunate in 1868 in large part because it had been unable to deal with this foreign threat.

This successful rebellion, called the Meiji Restoration, ushered in a period of extremely rapid change in almost every aspect of Japanese life. The country soon lost its decentralized feudal character, while its rigidly hierarchical class structure gave way to increasing social mobility. Ultimately Japan became the first non-Western country to experience an industrial revolution. The oligarchic rulers of Meiji Japan understood that only by developing Western-style economic and military power could they protect their homeland from colonial subjugation. The government actively fostered industrial growth, always with an eye toward

34

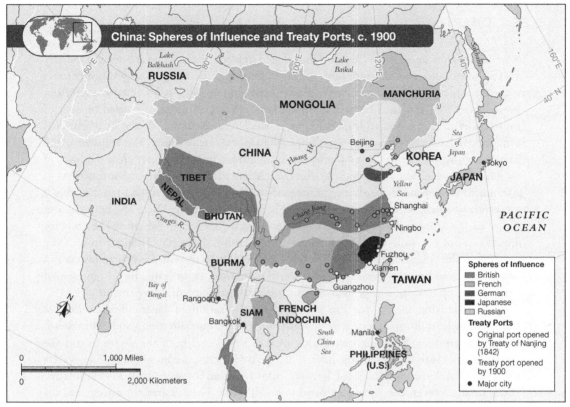

By 1900 various powers had taken control of parts of China, though the country did not formally lose its independence.

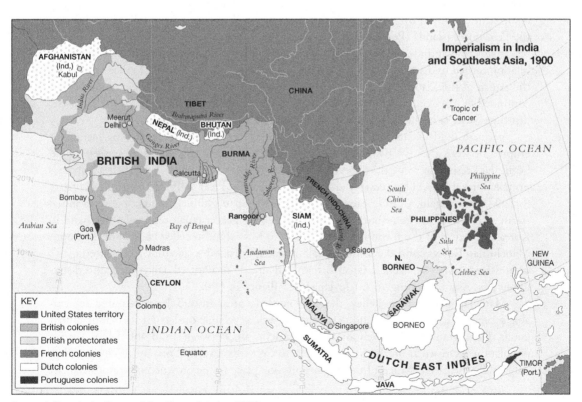

Imperialism in India and Southeast Asia, 1900

its strategic significance. In 1873, Japan introduced universal education for boys and military conscription in order to renovate both the labor force and the army. The government also required restructuring. Japan received its first constitution in 1889, proclaimed as a gift from the emperor, who was thus beyond its limitations. The constitution, modeled on that of Imperial Germany, created an Imperial Diet in which a lower house, elected by a restricted suffrage, was balanced by an appointed upper chamber. Furthermore, the emperor could dismiss the lower house in favor of new elections, and his imperial decrees had the force of law until they were later acted upon by the Diet. Many of the most important functions of government lay beyond the authority of the parliament. The emperor appointed the cabinet or executive branch, which was not immediately responsible to the Diet. The emperor also controlled the army and navy, whose chiefs reported directly to the throne. The emperor himself did not normally take an active part in governing, however. Thought to be a descendant of the sun goddess, his majesty was above quotidian politics. His ministers ran the country, wielding real power. This system was far from democratic, but it represented Japan's first step toward European-style constitutional, participatory government.

The underlying motive for this sweeping reorganization of Japan—the creation of a Western-style military force, state-sponsored rapid industrialization, and widespread, government-encouraged cultural emulation of the West—had been the desire to end the unequal treaties with the imperialist powers. By the mid-1890s, the humiliating foreign control of tariffs and visiting foreigners' freedom from Japanese law were gradually eliminated. By this time, however, the Japanese aspired to much more. They desired the esteem and the tangible benefits of great power status. They could not reach that goal peacefully.

The Japanese first tested their newly developed strength against China. War broke out between Tokyo and Beijing (Peking) in 1894. They fought over control of China's vassal state, Korea. Western observers expected a Chinese victory, but the modern tactics and equipment employed by Japan led to a stunning triumph. China had to relinquish Taiwan, the Pescadores Islands (Penghu), the Liaodong Peninsula in southern Manchuria, and Korea. It also paid an indemnity to Tokyo. Japan had at last become an imperial power. Its jubilation turned to dismay the following year when Russia, Germany, and France insisted on the return of the Liaodong Peninsula. Japanese resentment mounted as these same powers continued to carve out profitable concessions in China. Even more galling for the Japanese, just three years later the Russians took control of the Liaodong Peninsula.

Japanese and Russian imperial ambitions collided frequently in the following years. War erupted between the two rivals in 1904. The Japanese began this war, just as they would begin the Pacific war some thirty-seven years later, with a surprise attack on their adversary's principal naval base. They destroyed the Russian Pacific Fleet at Port Arthur on February 8, 1904. Once again, outside observers underrated Japan's ability, predicting an eventual tsarist victory, but St. Petersburg was forced to sue for peace. Japan received a free hand in Korea and return of the Liaodong Peninsula. The Russians also ceded control of the South Manchurian Railway and the southern half of Sakhalin Island to Japan. Even before Japan's impressive victory over Russia, Great Britain had already recognized Tokyo's enhanced stature in East Asia by signing an Anglo-Japanese Alliance in 1902.

Many Japanese came to believe that they needed a great empire. Japan required dependable sources of coal, iron ore, and petroleum as well as reliable outlets for its manufactured goods. Demographic trends reinforced this conclusion. Between 1873 and 1913, Japan's population increased from thirty-five million to over fifty-two million, and it continued to rise rapidly thereafter. Much of this expansion took place in the crowded new industrial cities of Tokyo, Yokohama, Nagoya, and Kobe. Some Japanese intellectuals began to perceive the need for what Hitler would later call *Lebensraum*. An expanded empire on the mainland of Asia and in the Pacific island chains seemed to be the solution.

The Japanese victory over the tsarist empire and the simultaneous Russian Revolution in 1905 sent shock waves throughout Asia. For the first time, the apparently inexorable advance of Western imperialism had been rebuffed. A "colored" people had defeated the supposedly invincible white man. Beyond that, in St. Petersburg and Moscow working-class rebels had come close to toppling the autocratic Romanov dynasty. This combination of events electrified native nationalist forces all over Asia. Many Japanese saw themselves as the natural leaders of a Pan-Asian liberation movement. They believed that politically, economically, and, above all, morally Japan provided the example that all the peoples of East Asia should follow. Japan would lead them from Western domination to harmony and prosperity under its own paternal guidance. Many anti-imperialist Asian students and intellectuals looked to Japan as a model and a potential leader in the struggle against colonialism. Tokyo became a haven for Indian nationalists and Chinese rebels, including the future leader of republican China, Sun Yat-sen. At this early stage, however, it was not clear whether Japan would realize its imperial aspirations in harmony with or in conflict against the Western powers, nor whether the other peoples of East Asia would be Japan's partners or its victims.

The outbreak of the First World War offered Japan an irresistible opportunity to extend its empire in cooperation with Britain and France. Tokyo declared war on Germany in August 1914 and quickly overran the Shandong (Shantung) Peninsula, Germany's principal concession in China, as well as its Pacific island holdings—the Marshalls, Marianas, Carolines, Palau, and Yap. In exchange for sending a flotilla for Mediterranean convoy duty in 1917, Japan received Allied sanction, by secret treaty, for its acquisition of German colonial possessions. Participation in the war greatly increased the government's popularity and stimulated an economic boom.

Japanese leaders also viewed the war as a chance to improve their position in China. At the beginning of 1915, they presented Twenty-One Demands to the recently established republican regime in Beijing. Most of the demands, grouped in five parts, extended or elaborated existing Japanese prerogatives in China. The fifth group of demands, however, contained the requirement that Japanese advisors serve throughout the Chinese government and a further provision for Japanese penetration of Chinese military and police forces. The Chinese leaders regarded these demands as a grave threat to their national existence. Lacking any significant military strength with which to defy Japan, they relied on skillful diplomacy and infinite procrastination. The clumsiness and brutality of the Japanese initiative also aroused opposition abroad. The United States was determined not to let China slip completely under the domination of any foreign state. President Wilson bluntly refused to recognize the legitimacy of Japan's demands. The Chinese ultimately bowed to the partial implementation of demands in groups one through four, but Tokyo was forced to drop those in group five. Subsequently, the United States also renounced the Lansing-Ishii Agreement that had recognized Tokyo's special interests in China.

While China's current weakness served Japanese interests, the Bolshevik Revolution in Russia created a perplexing combination of danger and opportunity. Military men and politicians in Tokyo feared the attraction of communism to their own proletariat. In addition, the anti-imperialist thrust of Leninism challenged Japan's envisioned role as liberator of Asia. Yet the travail of revolution and civil war in Russia held advantages for Japan as well. A series of mutually antagonistic, weak regimes replaced the tsarist autocracy, Tokyo's great rival in East Asia. The situation in Siberia was especially chaotic. Bolshevik detachments, anti-Bolshevik forces, and various local movements competed for power there. Japan not only joined the Western intervention at Vladivostok on the Russian Pacific coast; it sent more troops there than all the other Allies combined. The Imperial Army fought the Bolsheviks and sponsored a number of right-wing, pro-Japanese governments in the region. Japanese army commanders hoped to establish a puppet regime in eastern Siberia. This transparent ambition provoked strenuous protest from the Allies. Prime Minister Hara Kei (Hara Takashi) had to restrain the army. The eventual consolidation of Soviet power, continuing pressure from the Allies, and the increasing costs of the operation persuaded the Japanese to abandon Siberia in 1922, two years after the other powers had withdrawn.

While intervention in Russia had proved unfruitful, the Paris Peace Conference rewarded Japan for its participation in the world war. The Western powers confirmed Japanese possession of the Shandong Peninsula and Germany's former colonies and gave Japan a permanent seat on the Council of the League of Nations. However, the Japanese could not overcome Western resistance to their desire for a declaration of racial equality in the League Covenant. British and French colonial considerations and American domestic politics prohibited any such admission. Some Japanese suspected that the moralistic platitudes of Wilsonianism as well as American "Open Door" pronouncements on China only masked a cynical, racist policy. US immigration laws that excluded Asians and outrages committed against Japanese and Chinese immigrants in California strengthened these suspicions.

Japan's experience in dealing with the Western powers since 1853 had fostered two contrasting foreign policy orientations. Some Japanese, especially in the diplomatic corps and the business community, emphasized the common interests of Japan and the Western states. They looked to cooperation with the West and multilateral diplomacy as the best means for achieving their country's aims. They saw Japan as part of the great power imperialist system. Prosperity, economic development, and peaceful expansion were their goals. Many who held this view also supported the evolution of a liberal parliamentary system in Japan. Other Japanese strongly opposed these ideas, most conspicuously military men and nationalist intellectuals, who believed that the interests of Japan were fundamentally different from those of the Occidental empires. They stressed Japan's unique national character and supposed mission in Asia. They had little faith in Western cooperation. They believed that only Japan's own strength, above all its military forces, could guarantee national progress. They wanted to make Japan dominant in East Asia, with the Western states excluded or at least subordinated. Advocates of this viewpoint tended to reject Western political and social institutions, except military technology, as unsuitable for Japan. Although the clash of these conflicting approaches had emerged soon after the "opening" of the country, Japanese foreign policy in the latter half of the nineteenth century had been relatively coherent because it was dominated by the small group of senior statesmen who had led the Meiji Restoration. By the twentieth century, most of these oligarchs were dead or in retirement. Tokyo's foreign policy had lost its former unity of purpose and had begun to oscillate between multilateral cooperation and unilateral belligerence. In World War I, Japan's participation in the Entente displayed the former orientation, while the Twenty-One Demands evidenced the latter tendency.

During the 1920s, however, the overall thrust in Japan's relations with the West was cooperative. The Japanese political system appeared to be evolving along democratic lines, while in foreign affairs Tokyo's efforts were oriented toward harmony with Europe and America. The Western victory in World War I seemed for many Japanese to prove the superiority of democracy. Conversely, Germany's defeat and the fiasco of intervention in Siberia

diminished the appeal of militarism. The postwar years saw the establishment of
system and the apparent beginning of cabinet responsibility to parliament. Fro
1932, it became the common practice, though not a legal requirement, for the le
strongest party in the Diet to become prime minister. Passage of a universal mar
frage law in 1925 increased the electorate from three million to over twenty-five million. The
civil bureaucracy became more thoroughly professional and ceased to be the exclusive do-
main of the samurai. Labor unions were legalized, and workers were protected by a new set
of health insurance and industrial safety laws. Spending on public works projects increased,
while the military budget shrank 50 percent between 1919 and 1926. Although the army
and navy ministers had to be military men, the revised law of 1913 permitted the premier to
select service ministers from the retired list, thus giving these ministries some independence
from the armed services they were supposed to control.

In the realm of foreign affairs, Japan pursued a moderate policy emphasizing economic
expansion and the peaceful penetration of Chinese and Western markets. Japan's foreign
trade grew significantly, while Japanese investors cooperated with their Western counterparts
in developing the Chinese economy. Japan participated in the Washington Conference of
1921–1922, which reaffirmed China's territorial integrity and the principle of equal trade
opportunity there. The Japanese relinquished control over the Shandong Peninsula and
waived several privileges gained through the Twenty-One Demands. The powers agreed
to limit their battleship tonnage according to a ratio of 5:5:3:1.7:1.7 for the United States,
Britain, Japan, Italy, and France, respectively. Furthermore, the United States and England
pledged not to build fortifications west of Hawaii or east of Singapore. A relative balance of
naval power was thus established in the Pacific. These arrangements were supplemented at
the London Naval Conference of 1930, which fixed a 10:6:6 ratio for cruisers among Great
Britain, America, and Japan and sanctioned parity in submarines. Premier Tanaka Giichi,
who came to power in 1927, proclaimed a more aggressive "positive policy" toward China,
but even under General Tanaka, Japanese diplomacy continued to focus on safeguarding
Tokyo's economic position in cooperation with the Anglo-American powers and the League
of Nations. The Tanaka government also signed the Kellogg-Briand Pact outlawing war.

These progressive trends in domestic politics and foreign policy did not survive far
into the 1930s, for Japan's course toward democracy and international cooperation was not
popular with all segments of society. While these trends were supported by diplomats, businessmen, liberals, party officials, and a portion of the intelligentsia, they were vigorously opposed by conservatives, military men, and ultranationalists. The democratic and egalitarian
tendencies developing in Japanese society appalled traditionalists. They were morally outraged by the sight of Western-clad, cigarette-smoking couples walking hand in hand down
the Ginza. The "Moga" (modern girl) phenomenon—financially, emotionally, and sexually
independent young women who were dismissive of traditional values—seemed particularly
offensive to conservatives. For many Japanese, the political party system, with its close ties
to big business, appeared inherently corrupt. It is unlikely that Japanese politicians were any
worse than their American or West European counterparts, but to the still prevalent Confucian morality, the institutionalized clash of private interests and personal ambitions seemed
improper. Despite the introduction of universal manhood suffrage, a deep commitment to
democratic values had not yet developed among broad sectors of society. In many areas, local
notables, veterans' organizations, or other groups controlled large blocks of votes.

The Imperial Army was remarkably successful in its pervasive penetration of both the
education system and rural society (i.e., that part of the nation least affected by industri-

alization and modernization). Its leaders used various civic organizations and the military training curriculum required of boys "to ensure military popularity, spread a nationalistic ideology, and build the army a solid basis of support."[1] They sought to identify the emperor and the army as the legitimate sources of authority (not the constitution, legal code, prime minister, cabinet, or any concept of popular sovereignty) in order to gain support from the rural majority of the nation for militarism, authoritarian politics, and an aggressive foreign policy. General Ugaki Kazushige, the minister of war, wrote in his diary in 1925:

> Party politics is like a three-cornered battle and interrupts the flow of events. Only one party can hold power at any time. Thus, the work of leading our seventy million fellow citizens under the throne as a truly unified and cooperating nation in both war and peace, however you think about it, has been assigned to the army. . . . Only the army, which touches 200,000 active soldiers, 3,000,000 reserve association members, 500,000 to 600,000 middle school students, and 800,000 youths has the qualifications to accomplish this task.[2]

By the 1930s, Japanese public opinion began to turn away from the incompletely developed liberal parliamentary system, with its acceptance of diversity and conflicting interests, in favor of a more disciplined society of uniformity and national unity. Even though the parties really represented the interests of rural landowners and urban industrialists, conservatives feared that the moderate liberalism of the 1920s might be only a stepping stone to radical revolution. The growth of the labor movement and the founding of the Japanese Communist Party seemed especially menacing. In response to such fears, the Diet passed the Peace Preservation Law of 1925, which prohibited groups from advocating either the abolition of private property or any change in the "national polity" or "national essence" (*kokutai*). A Special Higher Police Force was established to repress "dangerous thought."

Japan's experiment with liberalism and internationalism also suffered from the poor performance of the economy during the 1920s. The wartime prosperity ended abruptly with the advent of peace. World demand for Japanese products declined suddenly, while competing goods from the Allied states returned to the export markets. The nation also endured severe bouts of inflation and deflation. In addition, a series of strikes by factory workers and demonstrations by rural tenant farmers rocked the country. To make matters worse, the biggest cities, Tokyo and Yokohama, experienced a series of earthquakes, tidal waves, fires, and epidemics. Violent race riots exploded in the capital after the 1923 earthquake. Some police and army units used the excuse of civil unrest to kidnap and murder political radicals. Moreover, the country's agriculture was devastated by fluctuations of the economy. The prices farmers received for rice and silk cocoons fell dramatically. Some desperately poor farm families sold their daughters into child prostitution to avoid starvation. The government only exacerbated the situation by returning to the gold standard in 1929—a disastrously ill-timed decision coming just before the Great Depression. This priced many Japanese goods out of the market.

Japan's success in establishing itself as an important part of the world economy opened the country to the worst effects of the global depression. Wages dropped sharply and unemployment soared to over three million. With the American and European markets for luxury goods evaporating, the price of Japanese silk fell by two-thirds in less than a year. Public opinion tended to blame the party system for the depression. In this view, the parties were tainted by their presumed corruption and their supposedly unethical ties to big business and great landowners. Although the government went off the gold standard late in 1931, producing an immediate increase in exports, it was too late to save parliamentary government in Japan. Dramatic increases in government spending on armaments stimulated a domestic economic revival, except for the agricultural sector, which remained depressed until 1936. Japan was the first nation to recover from the Great Depression. Yet despite a reviving economy, many Japanese believed that their country was still in the grip of a monstrous crisis that required desperate measures. This misconception made otherwise cautious and peace-loving citizens ready to accept radical changes in both domestic and international affairs.

Military and civilian nationalist circles attacked the conciliatory foreign policy of the party cabinets as weak and unworthy of a great nation. In their view, the government's emphasis on peaceful economic expansion in cooperation with China and the Western powers had failed to protect the country's national interests. Japan, they argued, must pursue a more aggressive foreign policy that did not subordinate its vital needs to Anglo-American desires and that did not forswear the use of force. The global depression also seemed to undercut the premises of the multilateral approach. As foreign trade plummeted and other countries erected protective tariff barriers, advocates of a more militant policy asserted that Japan must seek prosperity and security through unilateral action. Furthermore, military officers feared that the growth of civilian authority in the 1920s threatened the traditional independence of the armed services. Cabinets dominated by political parties and the business community had cut the military's share of the net domestic product from 7.7 to 3 percent during these years. Reliance on peaceful, diplomatic means afforded military officers little opportunity for promotion and glory.

A consensus was gradually emerging among military men, traditionalists, and nationalist intellectuals that if Japan were to remain a unique, great, and free nation, its foreign and domestic policies required a radical reorientation. The country would have to abandon what they perceived as its slavish imitation of Western social and political models. Instead, it must reassert those values and customs that were held to be quintessentially Japanese. Similarly, the government must end what they saw as its subservience to British and American leadership and adopt a bold policy of independence, even confrontation. Several overseas developments reinforced these beliefs. The apparent success of authoritarian, autarkic regimes in Italy, Russia, and Germany seemed to suggest that liberal internationalism was no longer the best alternative for Japan. Moreover, the reemergence of Russia as a great power under Stalin's ruthless hand raised a new threat to Tokyo. In its new Soviet guise as the bearer of international communism, a powerful Russia now seemed more dangerous than ever.

Most of all, however, it was events in China that engendered a sense of crisis in Tokyo. Japan had supplied arms and money to the rebels who overthrew the Manchu ruler of China in 1912. At first, Tokyo had not considered the emergence of Chinese nationalism as a threat to Japanese interests. With the increasing success of the Guomindang (Kuomintang) under Chiang Kai-shek (Jiang Jieshi) in the later 1920s, it suddenly seemed that feeble and fragmented China might be transformed into a united, industrialized, and modernized power. In that case, not only would Japan's position in China be undermined, but Japan might be eclipsed, even subjugated, by an expanding Chinese empire.

China: From Empire to Republic

The Japanese responded to the nineteenth-century onslaught of Western imperialism by copying European economic and military institutions in order to maintain their independence.

China, in contrast, was too large, too disorganized, too ill led, and, above all, too confident of its own superiority to attempt such a radical transformation. In consequence, the first test of strength between the Middle Kingdom and European powers, the First Opium War of 1839–1842, ended in disaster for Beijing. A series of humiliating, unequal treaties followed this defeat. Although China was not formally partitioned like Africa, the various powers progressively extended their domination over "concessions" along the China coast and up the Yangzi (Yangtze) River valley. They took control of China's tariff system and forced the Chinese to grant them extraterritoriality. That is, foreigners in China were not subject to the country's laws but were governed and judged by their own officials. The enfeebled Qing (Ch'ing) dynasty was powerless to break the Western grip on China through either reform or rebellion.

By the beginning of the twentieth century, ardent Chinese nationalists, who longed to see their country liberated from foreign domination, concluded that the ineffectual Manchus had to be overthrown. Developments in Japan greatly impressed these young rebels. They hoped that a similar process of industrialization and modernization would give China the strength to reassert its independence. Sun Yat-sen was one such rebel, a Cantonese from a well-to-do peasant family who had obtained a Western-style education at mission schools. In 1894, Sun founded a secret revolutionary society dedicated to overthrowing the dynasty and establishing a republic. The authorities soon discovered the group, and Sun had to flee abroad. In exile, Sun elaborated an ideology centering on his Three Principles of the People: nationalism, democracy, and the people's welfare.

Meanwhile in China, Sun's group and other nationalistic secret societies attempted several insurrections, but each one ended in failure. Finally, on October 10, 1911, a successful rebellion flared at Wuchang. The Qing dynasty disintegrated rapidly. The army, police, and Mandarin bureaucracy had lost faith in the Manchus. The only effective military force at the government's disposal were European-style regiments commanded by General Yuan Shikai (Yüan Shih-k'ai), but Yuan, recognizing that dynastic collapse was inevitable, entered negotiations with the rebels. Sun Yat-sen rushed home from exile in time to be elected provisional president of the first Chinese Republic in 1912. Sun's group, the Guomindang or GMD (Kuomintang or KMT), or National People's Party, had neither an army of its own nor a widespread political organization in China. The rebels therefore had to compromise with Yuan Shikai, even though they distrusted him. Sun resigned the presidency in favor of Yuan. Yuan, as the Guomindang suspected, was not committed to constitutional rule. During 1913, the ambitious general employed a combination of political manipulation and naked violence to oust his Nationalist partners from government. Surviving Guomindang members fled to Guangzhou (Canton) far to the south, out of the reach of Yuan's troops. Yuan now reigned as a military strongman. In 1915, he proclaimed himself president for life. Shortly before his death the following year, he founded a new dynasty with himself as its first emperor.

Under Yuan Shikai, China was a united republic in name only. With command of a modernized army and the support of the central government bureaucracy, Yuan firmly controlled Beijing and its surrounding provinces in north China. His hold over the provinces of central China was considerably less secure, and he had no real authority in the south or in the remote interior regions. Power in China had fragmented. The country was in the grip of warlords. These were men whose rule depended solely on their military power. They seldom had much political skill or any social base of support. Some of them had been provincial military commanders, others simply bandit chieftains. They led mercenary armies that fought only to augment their personal power and fortune. Though he bore the title of president, Yuan Shikai was only the most powerful of the warlords. After his death in 1916, the capital at Beijing became the prize in a bloody contest among rival warlord factions. It was a period of rampant lawlessness and near anarchy in China. The situation invited further foreign penetration and exploitation.

Chinese humiliation and outrage boiled over in the form of the May Fourth Movement in 1919. The announcement that the Paris Peace Conference had awarded Germany's former rights on the Shandong Peninsula to Japan precipitated this crisis. On May 4, several thousand college students converged on Tiananmen Square in protest. They were especially angry that the warlord regime in Beijing had already recognized Japan's gains in Shandong. The demonstrators assaulted one pro-Japanese official and set fire to the house of a cabinet minister. They also organized a countrywide boycott of Japanese goods. The rampaging students were reacting against more than just one provision of the Versailles Treaty. They were attacking a whole tradition of backwardness, weakness, and subjection. The movement marked the first stirrings of national consciousness in China, if only among the most educated and modernized segments of society.

This was precisely what the floundering Guomindang needed. At this juncture, Sun's Nationalist Party also got some help from an unexpected source—the Soviet Union. Lenin had decreed that, in the underdeveloped nations of Asia, so-called bourgeois national liberation movements like Sun's were progressive and thus suitable allies for the proletariat. In addition, the Kremlin saw Chinese nationalism as a counterweight to the menace of Japanese imperialism. The Russians therefore offered Sun an alliance. If he would accept the newly formed and tiny Chinese Communist Party into the Guomindang, the USSR would supply him with money, weapons, and advisors. The deal proved advantageous for all parties. The Soviet political advisors and the Chinese communists introduced Bolshevik organizational discipline into the Guomindang. The GMD began to emerge as a mass party. Red Army advisors helped to build an army for the Guomindang as well. Chiang Kai-shek received special training in Moscow and then took command of the Nationalists' Whampoa Military Academy. As the GMD enlarged the area in south China under its control, the Communist Party was able to come into the open and build its strength too. From a tiny nucleus of intellectuals at its founding in 1921, the CCP grew within a few years to a respectable membership of fifty thousand, including many factory workers.

Despite its usefulness, the marriage of convenience between the Nationalists and the Communists could not last. The alliance began to unravel after the death of Sun Yat-sen in 1925. The right wing of the GMD feared the growth of Communist power. Conservatives found their champion and a successor to Sun Yat-sen in Chiang Kai-shek. For the moment, though, Chiang still needed Soviet support. In July 1926, he launched the Northern Expedition, with the assistance of Russian advisors and equipment. Although the Guomindang armies faced great hordes of warlord troops, the GMD fought with determination and ideological conviction. Sometimes the warlord mercenaries fought hard. On other occasions they fled from battle or joined the Nationalists. Chiang's forces soon reached the Yangzi River in central China. As his military success increased, Chiang's need for his Communist allies decreased correspondingly. In April 1927, he established a new capital at Nanjing (Nanking), purged Communist cadres from the GMD leadership, and launched a massacre in the Communist stronghold of Shanghai. The CCP responded with a belated series of urban uprisings that were brutally crushed. The Communist leaders had to go underground in the cities or seek safety in the remote countryside. A second Northern Expedition extended the Guomindang's control all the way to Beijing. Many warlords chose to join the movement rather than fight against it. Chiang appeared to have won a complete victory. He seemed to have smashed Communist power and united China once again, except for a few outlying provinces.

However, Chiang's victory was far from complete in several respects. He had not overcome the heritage of national disunity. The Republic of China lacked some of the core characteristics of a modern nation-state. The relationship between some of the more distant provinces and the central government in Nanjing was quasi-feudal. Chiang Kai-shek had accepted many of the warlords into the Guomindang, which meant confirming them in power as GMD generals or provincial governors of their strongholds. Such newly converted "Nationalists" continued to regard the areas under their control as personal fiefs. They carried out national policies in their regions only when it was expedient for them to do so. For example, Zhang Xueliang's acceptance of Manchurian unification with China was more like an alliance than a submission to central authority. In the decade between 1927 and 1937, Chiang had to fight one major war and several lesser campaigns against his rebellious warlord allies, as well as a Muslim revolt. These conflicts almost bankrupted the Nanjing government. In 1937, when the Japanese attacked, Chiang controlled only twelve of the country's eighteen provinces. Historian Hans van de Ven suggests that "as the leader of the Nationalists he was more the convener of a fractious alliance than the chief of a disciplined and structured organisation working towards a single purpose."[3] China's flawed unification proved a critical weakness when war came. The Japanese takeover of Manchuria in 1931 stimulated more cooperation among the Chinese than ever before, but Chiang still faced a serious problem of political fragmentation in China.

The Guomindang never became a truly national party either. The nationalist and reformist orientation of the GMD made it attractive in China's big cities. The party appealed mainly to people in the relatively small modernized sector of the economy, concentrated along the seacoast and along the lower Yangzi valley. Elsewhere, and especially among China's peasant masses, the GMD never generated much support—a fatal weakness in this largely peasant land. In part, the Guomindang failed to win mass allegiance because it was never able or willing to translate Sun Yat-sen's Three Principles of the People into national policy. The GMD had made a beginning at implementing the nationalism principle, which entailed national unification, to be followed by the elimination of foreign control and the restoration of China to great power status. However, Chiang's regime only paid lip service to the other principles—democracy and the people's welfare. The GMD developed into a right-wing, authoritarian dictatorship, ironically patterned after the Soviet Communist Party. The Guomindang also did little to improve the lot of peasants and urban workers. Given Chiang's reliance on financiers, merchants, big landowners, and warlords for support, no sweeping socioeconomic reforms could be expected of him. China did make some progress under Chiang's leadership, especially in industrialization, public works, and economic stabilization. The agricultural sector, however, languished—the countryside left to the tender mercies of the landlords.

Most importantly, the Guomindang did not develop an adequate ideological base. After its partial success in unifying the country, the GMD ceased to be a cause that inspired great numbers of Chinese. It was merely a geographically distant regime whose polices were even more remote from the daily concerns of China's peasants. To combat the problems of Chinese inertia and disunity and the challenge of communism, Chiang Kai-shek launched the New Life Movement in 1934. It was a mass mobilization campaign to promote cultural reform and neo-Confucian morality while fighting corruption and nepotism as well as Marxism and Western liberalism. Its most dynamic element, the violence-prone Blue Shirt Society (modeled on Mussolini's *squadristi*), alienated most Chinese. Ultimately, the movement failed to produce the significant increase in national unity and discipline that Chiang sought.

Chiang also had not laid the Communist specter to rest. After his coup against the Communists in 1927, a remnant of the party leadership escaped to the Jinggang (Chingkang) Mountains on the border between Jiangxi (Kiangsi) and Hunan Provinces. By appealing to peasant hatred against the landlords, Zhu De (Chu Te) and Mao Zedong were able to establish a Communist base area, proclaiming a Chinese Soviet Republic in November 1931. In response, Chiang determined to finish the task he had left incomplete in 1927–1928. Beginning in 1930, he launched a series of "extermination campaigns" against the Communists. He employed the best of his German-trained, well-equipped troops in these operations, even though China faced a grave new military threat from Japan. The last of these extermination campaigns threatened to extinguish the CCP. In desperation, over a hundred thousand Communists broke out of the Nationalist encirclement and began the Long March—a circuitous, 5,600-mile trek on which they fought Nationalist, warlord, and minority ethnic forces almost daily.

For the most part, the Western powers responded positively to China's nominal unification. They slowly began to dismantle the apparatus of foreign domination. Japan's reaction to the rise of the Nationalist government was quite different. In a sense, the advance of Guomindang authority served Japanese interests by restoring law and order on the mainland and erecting a barrier to communist revolution. However, many in Tokyo feared that a resurgence of Chinese nationalism would ultimately weaken Japan's position in China. There had already been incidents of violence against Japanese businessmen in China and boycotts of Japanese goods. As Nationalist forces overran Shandong, the Tanaka government sent troops to protect Japanese residents. A bloody clash occurred at Jinan (Tsinan). In May 1928, Japanese officers, believing that they had been fired upon from a Foreign Ministry liaison office in the city, arrested the Chinese official in charge of the office, cut off his tongue, gouged his eyes out, and shot him. Tokyo threw twenty-one thousand soldiers into this volatile situation. Clearly overmatched, Chiang Kai-shek withdrew most of his troops from the region. Japanese forces attacked the two remaining Nationalist regiments, killing many Chinese soldiers and civilians. The Japanese belief that control of their interests in China, and especially in Manchuria, was threatened caused a reorientation of the political system in Tokyo and led to the pursuit of a much more aggressive foreign policy. Moreover, as historian Rana Mitter suggests, "for the Japanese militarists the Jinan incident seemed to prove that China could be treated shamelessly without fear of consequence."[4]

The Manchurian Incident

If there were a Japanese equivalent to Mussolini's March on Rome and Hitler's seizure of power, which set Italy and Germany on the course to authoritarianism and war, it was the Manchurian Incident of 1931. Japan had long viewed Manchuria as crucially important to its security and prosperity. Tokyo regarded it as a buffer against Russian aggression as well as a prime source of vital raw materials. The Japanese presence was already extensive in the Liaodong Peninsula and along the South Manchurian Railway. Previously, Tokyo had been content to exploit Manchuria peacefully and to control events there from behind the scenes through its patronage of the provincial warlord Marshal Zhang Zuolin

(Chang Tso-lin). When even this former bandit leader proved insufficiently compliant with Japanese wishes, staff officers of Japan's Kwantung occupation army, acting on their own authority, assassinated Zhang in 1928. The Old Marshal's successor, his son Zhang Xueliang (Chang Hsüeh-liang), was even less amenable to Japanese control. The Young Marshal declared his allegiance to the Chinese Nationalist government, which in turn appointed him its commander in Manchuria. The Guomindang then began to push for the abolition of Japan's special rights in the province.

Militant young Japanese army officers of the Kwantung occupation force feared that the civilian government in Tokyo was sacrificing Japan's position on the mainland and bowing before the dictates of the Western powers. In 1929, Tokyo formally recognized the Guomindang regime as the legitimate government of China. The following year, Prime Minister Hamaguchi Yuko forced through ratification of the London Naval Agreement against bitter opposition from the armed services. The officers believed that weak civilian leaders were betraying national security in the face of mortal threats from Chinese nationalism and Soviet communism. While Japanese officers demanded the strictest discipline and unquestioning adherence to orders from their troops, those officers seldom manifested the same discipline and obedience. Many of them believed that they were more patriotic and possessed a keener sense of the national interest than the government or even their own high command.

A crisis mentality gripped military and ultranationalist circles. The navy fumed over the limitations imposed by the 1930 London Naval Conference on future warship construction. The army feared that it, too, might be constrained by the impending League of Nations disarmament conference. A consensus was building for dramatic, violent action. An ultranationalist assassinated Prime Minister Hamaguchi in October 1930. This murder was followed by the killing of several other civilian leaders who favored cooperation with the Western powers and a less aggressive policy in China. Civilian government and party officials bowed to the pressure, accepting "national unity" cabinets that greatly strengthened the military. The emperor opposed both this political violence and the military's insistence on a more aggressive foreign policy, but his opposition was weak and ineffective.

Japan's Kwantung Army, stationed in China's Guandong (Kwantung) Peninsula, took matters into its own hands. A group of its staff officers led by Colonels Itagaki Seishiro and Ishiwara Kanji planned direct military action in Manchuria. Their scheme was supported by some high-ranking members of the General Staff in Tokyo, but when word of the affair leaked out, the emperor and the cabinet insisted that army headquarters suppress the plot. The high command dispatched General Tatekawa Yoshitsugu to restrain the conspirators. Tatekawa, however, sympathized with the plan and deliberately delayed carrying out his orders until it was too late. During the night of September 18, 1931, Japanese soldiers exploded a charge near the South Manchurian Railway line. Itagaki and his coconspirators then proclaimed that this incident was the work of Chinese saboteurs. In "retaliation," the next morning their forces attacked and quickly overran the Manchurian army base at Mukden (Shenyang). This clumsy charade fooled no one.

The conspirators had taken an enormous gamble. They had not only evaded their orders but had also precipitated combat in a region where enemy forces outnumbered their own by twenty to one. They counted on the likelihood that, once battle was joined, it would inevitably escalate, and their superiors could not let a small contingent of Japanese troops be annihilated or otherwise back down without an unacceptable loss of face. These calculations were correct. Despite the Tokyo government's desire to limit hostilities, Japanese troops poured into central Manchuria from Guandong and Korea. As historian Sarah Paine put it, "the Kantō Army had hijacked foreign policy."[5] Commanders on the scene continued to escalate their operations, using such phrases as "strategic necessity" and "defensive measure" to justify their actions. Cabinet officials and the emperor were furious over the Kwantung Army's insubordinate behavior, but they did nothing to curb it.

Japan had now taken the first step on the path to all-out war with China (and ultimately with the Western powers as well), even though the emperor and the cabinet opposed this course. This bizarre development was made possible by the weakness of the Showa emperor and of liberal, constitutional government in Tokyo, as well as by what Japanese historian and political activist Ienaga Saburo has termed "diffuse complicity." "The Manchurian Incident," he writes, "actually was a broad criminal conspiracy between a local unit and Tokyo army leaders. . . . Thereafter, one by one agencies of the Japanese state, some enthusiastically, others passively, joined the cabal and kept the war going for fifteen years."[6] The cabinet of Wataksuki Reijiro resigned, but authorities in Tokyo could not give up territories won with the sacrifice of Japanese blood. The emperor's courtiers even feared for their own and his majesty's safety if he were to openly denounce the conduct of his disobedient officers. The threat of a military coup was never far from their minds.[7]

The Tokyo government refused the army's plan to annex Manchuria formally, fearing a possible hostile Soviet reaction. Instead, the army set up the nominally independent puppet state of Manchukuo (meaning "Land of the Manchus"), which it controlled. The army installed the former Qing emperor, Puyi (P'u-i), as its figurehead sovereign, though the commander of the Kwantung Army was the real governor of Manchukuo. Japanese officers hoped that this tactic would allay domestic and foreign criticism of their coup and make the result less painful for the Chinese government to accept. The Japanese kept Manchurian foreign and military affairs as well as transportation and communications under their own control. Manchurian local civil and military authorities were persuaded or coerced to declare their independence from China and serve the new regime. Initially, the occupiers succeeded in fostering broad cooperation from local elites throughout Manchuria. For officeholders and the wealthy, collaboration with the Japanese secured their positions and property.

Japanese atrocities against the civil population, which would become all too common in the following years, began during the initial fighting in Manchuria. At the village of Pingdingshan, Japanese troops machine-gunned and bayoneted some three thousand men, women, and children. The army justified these outrages as a necessary part of the struggle against guerrilla fighters and Chinese soldiers in civilian dress. A Japanese veteran later explained, "Even though we are told not to kill civilians, you just cannot tell them apart."[8]

Japanese aggression posed a dilemma for Chiang Kai-shek, Marshal Zhang Xueliang, and the peoples of Manchuria. Neither leader wanted to lose one of China's most valuable provinces, but neither wanted a war with a great power. Mitter suggests that Japanese occupation "presented China with a crisis different from previous instances of foreign intervention, as it demanded for the first time a clear choice between acquiescence and resistance to full-scale occupation."[9] Initially, under orders from Chiang, the Young Marshal's forces did not offer strong opposition to the aggressors. Chiang feared that any fighting between Japanese and Nationalist troops might not be contained in Manchuria but might spill over into north China. He also had some hope for foreign assistance through the League of Nations. Marshal Zhang ordered his troops to lay down their arms, but some Chinese and Manchurian units fought nonetheless. There were fierce engagements in some areas, but this resistance was neither coordinated nor effective. After four weeks of sometimes hard fighting, the better-equipped Japanese forces were in possession of south Manchuria.

Chiang's hesitancy to confront the Japanese at this point sprang from weakness. His troops were able to defeat the warlords' mercenaries, but they were no match for the tanks, heavy artillery, and modern aircraft of the Japanese army. Although the total forces available to Chiang exceeded two million troops, approximately three-fifths of that total consisted of provincial soldiers whose discipline, equipment, training, and political loyalties left much to be desired. Chiang did not want a military confrontation with Japan before he had the opportunity to train and equip much more powerful forces. Moreover, he was also intent on eliminating his Communist rivals and consolidating control over quasi-independent regions of the country before dealing with the foreign enemy. His slogan in those trying days was "First unity, then resistance [to the Japanese]." His famous remark that the Japanese were a disease of the skin while the Chinese Communists were a disease of the heart suggests that Chiang both miscalculated the menace of Japanese imperialism and failed to understand that a weak Guomindang response to Japanese aggression would discredit the GMD in its domestic struggle with the Communists.[10] However, in Mitter's judgment, given Chiang's military weakness relative to Tokyo, as well as his continuing problems with the Communists, warlords, and opponents within his own party, "to fight the Japanese as well would have been suicidal."[11]

The Western powers undertook no effective action to block Japanese expansion. China appealed to the League of Nations for assistance, citing Japan's violation of the League Covenant and of the 1922 Nine Power Treaty that guaranteed Chinese territorial integrity. The League appointed a commission of inquiry, chaired by Lord Lytton, that traveled to East Asia to investigate the situation. The resulting Lytton Report exposed the falseness of Japanese claims to be acting in self-defense and in cooperation with legitimate Manchurian separatist forces. The League condemned Japan's aggression. Japanese ambassador Matsuoka Yosuke responded by denouncing the League and pulling Japan out of the organization. For Japanese nationalists, condemnation by the League was just another hypocritical example of the Western imperial powers' desire to deprive Japan of equal status. The League could not go beyond moral censure unless the Western powers were ready to impose effective sanctions on Tokyo.

Hopes for collective security against aggression foundered on this point. France was too preoccupied with European affairs. Great Britain was unwilling to risk war in a region where Japan's military and naval forces were far stronger than its own, especially since London could not count on American support. President Herbert Hoover and Secretary of State Henry L. Stimson were deeply concerned over this violation of numerous international agreements, but they discouraged London and Paris from taking action against Japan. The United States simply declared its nonrecognition of any abridgment of American rights or Chinese sovereignty in Manchuria. The Soviet Union, its rearmament program not yet completed and its forces locked in a bloody struggle to collectivize the peasantry, chose to acquiesce in the Japanese absorption of Manchuria. The League had failed the first test of collective security. That failure not only reinforced Japanese expansionism but also heartened Benito Mussolini and Adolf Hitler, who would soon launch their own wars of conquest. If anything, the barrage of Western denunciations followed by no effective action tended to stifle criticism of the Manchurian affair within Japan and unite the nation in support of a more aggressive policy.

The Manchurian Incident marked a turning point for Japan in both its internal and external affairs.[12] It seemed to prove the superiority of bold, forceful action to cautious diplomacy and compromise. The achievements of diplomats and civilian politicians paled beside the glorious exploits of Japan's warriors. Such views emanated most strongly from the ultranationalist civilian and military secret societies that proliferated in the late 1920s and early 1930s. Whether in or out of uniform, men in these groups castigated the supposed corruption of party politics and the selfishness of the capitalist system, as well as the alleged weakness of current Japanese foreign policy. They demanded the complete renovation of society, a return to the national essence (*kokutai*). In practice that meant glorification of the emperor, emphasis on martial spirit, and a cult of unity and sacrifice, all channeled in support of an expansionist foreign policy.

The secret societies never developed into mass parties. Instead, their impact was felt through terrorism and insurrection. The assassinations of several political leaders, discussed above, drew the sympathy of the minister of war, General Araki Sadao—not for the victims but for their murderers. The assassins, he believed, had not acted for "fame or personal gain, nor are they traitorous. Their acts were performed in the sincere belief that they were for the benefit of Japan."[13] Although the Seiyukai Party had won an overwhelming victory in the last parliamentary elections, the new cabinet after Prime Minister Inukai Tsuyoshi's murder was a nonpartisan, so-called national unity government headed by retired admiral Saito Makoto. This marked the end of cabinets dominated by democratically elected leaders. Moreover, extremist groups did not limit themselves to isolated assassinations. On several occasions they also attempted to overthrow the government, twice in 1931 alone.

Not even the armed services escaped the strife and violence. The army officer corps was polarized between the Imperial Way faction (Kodoha) of General Araki and the rival Control faction (Toseiha). Beyond careerism, regional rivalries, and personal hostilities, the two groups disagreed on strategic issues. The Kodoha faction believed the army must prepare for an inevitable war with the USSR, while the Control officers looked to China and the Pacific as the more likely field of expansion. The Imperial Way group stressed the paramount factor of "spirit" in battle, whereas the Toseiha emphasized the importance of modern weaponry, tactics, and total national mobilization. When Araki was forced to step down in 1934 and the Control faction began to purge its opponents from the high command, outraged Kodoha officers stormed into the office of the leading Toseiha general, Nagata Tetsuzan, and hacked him to death with a sword. The orgy of violence reached a climax with the attempted military coup of February 26, 1936. Rebel troops seized downtown Tokyo, occupied the major government buildings, and executed a number of high-ranking government and military officers. The insurrection collapsed after three days, however, because the emperor denounced it and the navy brought warships into Tokyo harbor with their guns leveled at rebel positions. The insurgent officers were promptly executed. Just because the coup was suppressed, however, does not mean it failed entirely. Even in defeat, the coup served further to intimidate supporters of democracy and international cooperation.

Unlike Germany and Italy, in Japan the ultranationalist radicals never came to power. The secret societies and terrorist groups declined rapidly after 1936. Japan did not experience a successful fascist revolution. The evolution of Japanese politics was considerably subtler. "Rather, what happened," writes historian Albert M. Craig, "was a small shift in the balance between elites, the advantage passing from the parties to the military. This small shift produced an enormous change in political climate and policy, setting Japan upon the course that led to disaster in World War II."[14] Now, "national unity" cabinets brought together military officers, bureaucrats, various experts, and a few token party ministers. The next two prime ministers were both retired admirals. Political parties were not abolished in the 1930s; there was no need for such a measure. Each of the two major parties contained a strong faction that welcomed a much more aggressive foreign policy and that did not object to the growth of military influence in government.[15] During the 1920s, the government had faced vociferous criticism of its foreign policy in parliament, but during the following decade, few in the Diet complained of Japan's ever more reckless course in international affairs.

It is ironic that the military command emerged significantly strengthened from the 1936 insurrection. The incident might have been used to tame the army, but instead the civilian leadership chose to allow the Control faction more latitude than ever so that it could purge the ultraradical officers associated with the Kodoha. The armed service chiefs gained two important levers of power at this time. In 1936, the requirement that the army and navy ministers be officers on active duty was restored. The armed forces thus gained veto power over the government. If a new prime minister or his proposed cabinet was unacceptable to them, the service chiefs could block the formation of the new government by preventing any of their officers from taking the service ministries. The army or navy could also bring down an existing cabinet whose policies they disliked by withdrawing the service ministers and refusing to appoint new ones.

The military further bolstered its influence in the government by an even more insidious device—intimidation. Whenever senior commanders objected to a policy or politician, or when they wished to impose their own view on the government, they would sorrowfully inform the civil authorities that unless the course they recommended was followed, they might not be able to restrain the impetuous, violence-prone younger officers. The attempt of Ugaki Kazushige, a man unacceptable to many of his fellow officers, to form a government in 1937 prompted the army chiefs to employ both techniques to block Ugaki. They refused to provide an army minister for the new cabinet. General Nakajima of the military police warned Ugaki bluntly: "The younger officers are very upset and the situation is delicate. Therefore, the army minister has asked me to tell you that he wishes you would decline the premiership."[16]

The Widening War in China

The army used its growing influence over the government to foster Japanese expansion in China. Contrary to widespread Western opinion, there never was a well-thought-out, step-by-step plan of aggression that carried Japan inexorably from Mukden to the Marco Polo Bridge (Lugouqiao) and on to Pearl Harbor. The so-called Tanaka Memorial, which has been cited as evidence of such a master plan, is a spurious document.[17] There was, however, a consensus among the military and much of the civilian leadership that Japan needed to adopt more forceful measures to protect its interests on the increasingly turbulent international scene of the 1930s. There was general agreement that Japan had to prevent both the expansion of Soviet power in East Asia and the spread of communism in China, that Tokyo must consolidate its control over Manchuria, and that China ought to remain fragmented and weak. There was spirited disagreement, however, as to which specific military and diplomatic policies were best suited to achieve these commonly accepted goals.

A few rabid expansionists, like Ishiwara Kanji, clearly envisioned a future of war and conquest. "It should be our basic national defense policy," Ishiwara wrote in 1933, "first to establish control over China quickly and skillfully, then to create a self-sufficient economic bloc encompassing Japan, China, and Manchukuo, and finally to use force against the Soviet army and the American and British navies to protect our East Asian union."[18] Most Japanese, though, were not anxious to plunge into war with three of the greatest powers on earth, even if Japan could fight them one at a time. Foreign Minister Matsuoka believed that the strongest nations would establish regional hegemony in their areas of the globe. He looked forward to the emergence of four great power blocs: the Americas under US leadership, central Eurasia under Soviet Russia, Euro-Africa controlled by Germany and Italy, and East Asia dominated by Japan. Peace would result, Matsuoka hoped, because each of the dominant powers would respect the others' spheres of influence.

While debates over Japan's course raged in Tokyo, the Japanese army proceeded to extend its sway over more and more of China. Under pressure from their own government, as well as from the Western powers, not to precipitate open war in China, Japanese commanders adopted the tactic of piecemeal subversion. They targeted the five provinces of north China adjacent to Manchuria. Guomindang control was weak in these areas. Warlords and local officials in this region had converted to the Nationalist cause in 1928 out of political expediency rather than any real dedication to the GMD. By exerting pressure on north China, the Kwantung officers hoped to detach these provinces from the Nanjing regime and make them Japanese satellites. Japan's field commanders pursued their own foreign policies, often in conflict with each other, while ignoring instructions from Tokyo.

As a preliminary step, Japanese troops seized the Shanhaiguan (Shanhaikwan) gateway in January 1933 and then overran Rehe (Jehol) Province under the pretext that Zhang Xueliang was marshaling forces there to reconquer Manchuria. Rehe was thereupon incorporated into Manchukuo. Kwantung Army forces also moved against Hebei (Hopeh) Province, launching two attacks south of the Great Wall of China. Then in May 1933, the Japanese commanders negotiated the Tanggu (Tangku) Truce with local north Chinese officials, which set up a twenty-one-district demilitarized zone. Japanese security officers brought the Chinese police force in this area under their control. The army authorities much preferred to deal with the weak provincial and district officials of north China, whom they could easily overawe, than with Chiang Kai-shek's government. In 1935, they forced the governor of Hebei to sign the He-Umezu Agreement and the governor of Chahar Province to sign the Qin-Doihara (Ch'in-Doihara) Agreement that banned the Nationalist Party and GMD troops from those provinces while opening them to further Japanese penetration.

In order to foster a complete break between the northern provinces and the Guomindang regime at Nanjing, the Japanese Kwantung Army supported a North China Autonomy Movement. Doihara Kenji, a military intelligence officer, called a "state founding conference" for north China, but none of the area's warlords attended. Chinese officials in the north, like Song Zheyuan (Sung Che-yüan) who headed the Hebei-Chahar Political Council, were pulled in three directions by Japanese pressure, orders from the Nationalist government, and their own desires for personal power. Meanwhile, the Japanese used the cooperation of Mongol prince De Wang (Teh Wang) and the forces of warlord Li Shouxin (Li Shou-hsin) to extend their control over much of Inner Mongolia. The Kwantung Army also used its growing presence in north China to wage economic warfare against Nanjing. Under army protection, smuggling operations grew to such a large scale that the customs revenues of the Nationalist government plummeted.

Chiang Kai-shek did not respond forcefully to these Japanese inroads in northern China, just as he had not defended Manchuria. He feared Japan's military superiority, and he still intended to eliminate Chinese communism before any attempt to expel the foreign invaders. Chiang even proposed a Sino-Japanese treaty of friendship in 1935. However, since Nanjing refused to renounce its sovereignty over north China and become little more than a Japanese client state, no diplomatic settlement was possible. Some patriotic Chinese sharply criticized Chiang's policies. They feared that once again their country was falling into disunity and foreign control. Nonetheless, Chiang insisted on launching yet another extermination campaign against the Communists in 1936. The Manchurian troops of Zhang Xueliang who spearheaded this drive were reluctant to fight fellow Chinese, whatever their politics, while the Japanese enslaved their homeland.

A remnant of the Chinese Communist Party, now under the leadership of Mao Zedong, had survived the Long March and established a new base area at Yan'an in Shaanxi (Shensi) Province in northwestern China. There the Communists organized new political cadres and a guerrilla army of nearly eighty-five thousand men. Mao's success in reviving the CCP was due in part to his skill in harnessing the force of Chinese anger against the invaders. In Shaanxi, the Communists played down the more revolutionary aspects of their program and emphasized the need for national defense against the Japanese aggressors. Anxious about the twin threats of fascism in Europe and Japanese expansionism in Asia, the USSR, operating through the Moscow-dominated Communist International, appealed for a "united front" of all communists and noncommunist patriots against fascism and Japanese militarism. Comintern chief Georgi Dimitrov specifically enjoined the CCP to join with all forces who opposed the Japanese, including the Nationalists.[19] Within the CCP, Wang Ming enthusiastically endorsed the united front cause, while Mao Zedong was lukewarm in his support for the idea. Outside the party, this call struck a responsive chord among many non-Communist Chinese, including Zhang Xueliang, who implored the Guomindang government to take a more resolute stand against Tokyo's incursions.

Continuing Japanese aggression began to change the priorities of many Chinese leaders, but existing hatreds were hard to displace. Even Chiang Kai-shek now considered the Japanese the most dangerous long-term enemy of his country. He secretly sent representatives to discuss the possibility of cooperation with the CCP, but at the same time the generalissimo told several of his associates that he was in the "last five minutes" of his campaign to exterminate the Chinese Communists.[20] Zhang Xueliang was also in covert negotiations with the Chinese Communists to replace Chiang as leader of China and create a broad anti-Japanese alliance.[21] At this point, Mao favored a broad coalition of anti-Japanese forces, but one excluding Chiang Kai-shek. He sought to advance the cause of revolution *within* the struggle against the invader.

It is in this context that the bizarre Xi'an (Sian) Incident took place. Chiang Kai-shek flew to Xi'an in December 1936 to urge Zhang to more vigorous action against the Communists. Instead of complying, Zhang arrested his commander. Mao Zedong pressed Zhang to kill the GMD leader, but Stalin vetoed the project. Now all the crestfallen Zhang could do was force his boss to negotiate with Communist representatives and refuse to release him until he agreed to a united front, including the CCP. Although Nationalist and Communist forces seldom cooperated, despite various promises of unity, the incident greatly increased the pressure on Chiang Kai-shek to take a more determined stand against Japanese encroachments. For his efforts, Zhang Xueliang was arrested and remained in Guomindang custody until 1988. Although the Nationalists, Communists, and regional military leaders were increasingly drawn together by their shared fear of and hatred for the Japanese, each side in this united front maneuvered to use resistance to the invader to strengthen its own forces while weakening those of its rivals. The civil war would continue within the context of the national liberation struggle.

Moscow supported Chiang Kai-shek and his Nationalist regime because Stalin believed that only Chiang could unite China in successful resistance to Japanese aggression. That was important to the Soviet leader because, while the Japanese were fighting a major war in China, they would be much less likely to attack the USSR. Stalin feared that the recently signed Anti-Comintern Pact between Germany and Japan presaged a joint attack on Russia. For that reason, the Soviet-controlled Comintern instructed the Chinese Communists to moderate their radicalism and join forces with the Guomindang in defending the country. General Vasilii Chuikov (of later Stalingrad fame), who served as Chiang's chief military advisor in 1940, recorded Stalin's remarks during a briefing:

> It would seem that the Chinese communists are closer to us than Chiang Kai-shek and that our aid should be given mostly to them. But such aid would make it look as if we were exporting revolution to a country with which we have diplomatic relations. The CCP and the working class are still too weak to lead the struggle against the aggressor. . . . Apart from that, the imperialist powers will scarcely allow Chiang Kai-shek to be replaced by the Communist Party.[22]

The Japanese continually worried about the possibility of Soviet intervention as they expanded into China. Although the USSR had appeased Japan by selling its interest in the Chinese Eastern Railway to Tokyo in 1934, Russia began to provide modest amounts of equipment for the Nationalist army. Some Japanese officers were alarmed by the rapid increase in Soviet military capabilities. They believed that by 1936 Stalin's industrialization and rearmament programs had once again made Russia a serious threat to Japanese security.

Tokyo also hoped to compensate for its deteriorating relations with London and Washington by drawing closer to Nazi Germany and Fascist Italy. The persistent agitation of Japan's pro-German military attaché in Berlin, Oshima Hiroshi, finally bore fruit in the form of the Anti-Comintern Pact of November 25, 1936. In this pact Germany and Japan (with the addition of Italy in 1937) pledged to "exchange information on the activities of the Communist International" and to "take no measures which would tend to ease the situation of the USSR" if any of the signatories went to war with the Soviet Union. The pact fell short of an alliance, but Tokyo hoped it would make the Russians more cautious.

As military men and diplomats in Tokyo worried about a nonexistent Soviet threat, hostilities in China escalated into a major war that neither the Japanese government nor Chiang Kai-shek wanted. While the cabinet and even the high command in Tokyo sought some accommodation with Nanjing, Japanese commanders on the scene pursued virtually unlimited objectives. Japanese leaders pressed Nanjing for a comprehensive agreement, including an anticommunist military alliance, lower tariffs on Japanese goods, and the embedding of Japanese military advisors throughout the Nationalist army. Chiang's government balked at these terms, which would have compromised Chinese sovereignty. The drift toward war was now unstoppable. Ever since the antiforeign Boxer Rebellion in 1900, the great powers had maintained garrisons in the Tianjin-Beijing (Tientsin-Peking) area to protect their citizens. Great Britain kept just over a thousand and France fewer than two thousand soldiers in the region, but the Japanese garrison at Tianjin numbered ten thousand heavily armed troops. The commanders of that garrison planned, on their own initiative, to seize the Marco Polo (or Lugouqiao [Lukouchiao]) Bridge (ten miles west of Beijing) and an adjacent railway station. Possession of these objectives would allow them to control the vital railway link between Beijing and central China. The Japanese officers at Tianjin hoped thereby to gain more leverage in dealing with the regional Chinese administrative authorities, the Hebei-Chahar Political Council. They did not mean to provoke all-out war; they merely intended one more small encroachment on the sovereignty of China.

The Japanese did not expect to encounter serious resistance, but on the night of July 7, 1937, while supposedly on maneuvers near the Marco Polo Bridge, Japanese soldiers exchanged fire with Chinese troops of the nearby Wanping garrison. Both sides brought up reinforcements, and a menacing situation developed. The Japanese were greatly outnumbered by the Chinese 29th Army under General Song Zheyuan (Sung Che-yüan). Despite the numerical superiority of Chinese forces on the scene, General Song was anxious to avoid further conflict. He and the Japanese commander were on the verge of working out a local settlement of the crisis when Tokyo and Nanjing undermined their efforts. The Japanese high command, still deeply concerned over the possibility of a clash with the USSR, did not want to be mired in full-scale war on the mainland, but neither the generals nor the government of Prince Konoe Fumimaro were willing to see the Japanese army humiliated. A negotiated settlement and a withdrawal of its forces at Lugouqiao in the face of Chinese military superiority would involve an intolerable blow to the army's prestige. Therefore, Tokyo rushed five divisions plus air cover to the scene to bolster Japan's weak position. Konoe and the army still hoped for a peaceful resolution of the incident, but they would only accept a settlement in which the Chinese backed down.

The Nanjing regime was even less inclined than Tokyo to seek a test of strength at this juncture, but Chiang Kai-shek was under heavy domestic pressure to offer firm resistance to any further Japanese advance. Chiang nominally commanded approximately two million troops, but they were of mixed quality and loyalty. About nine hundred thousand were reasonably well trained and armed and were directly under his command or were provincial troops loyal to him. The remainder were less well-equipped warlord or Communist troops whose loyalty to Chiang Kai-shek was marginal. Nonetheless, Chiang's German military advisor, General Alexander von Falkenhausen, assured him that his German-trained Central Army was now ready to confront the Japanese enemy.

The generalissimo concluded: "If we do not accomplish this [standing up to Japan], after taking an inch they will reach for another foot with no end to it."[23] Chiang therefore began to move more divisions northward, and he ordered General Song to reject Japanese demands. Japan had finally reached the point where its belligerent actions inevitably led—the only alternative to an unbearable loss of face was all-out war. Japanese forces attacked the Chinese 29th Army on July 27, 1937. After two days of fighting, General Song abandoned Beijing. Some Nationalist divisions fought fiercely, but the commanders of other units accepted bribes to retreat without fighting. On August 8, Japanese troops entered the undefended northern capital. In retaliation, the Nationalist air force bombed the Japanese residential section and naval installations at Shanghai on August 14. The Tokyo government proclaimed that "the Chinese, overconfident of their national strength, contemptuous of our own power, and also in league with the communists, have assumed toward Japan an increasingly arrogant and insulting attitude," and that Japan was "now forced to resort to resolute action to bring sense to the Nanking government by punishing the atrocious Chinese army."[24]

Japan asserted its air and naval strength from the first days of the war. In addition to pounding GMD troop concentrations, the Imperial Air Force bombed Nanjing and other Nationalist cities, while the navy established a blockade along the China coast. Although outnumbered by the Chinese at every engagement, the Imperial Army held several advantages beyond naval and air support—heavy weaponry (mainly artillery and tanks), intelligence, and combat effectiveness. The Japanese usually knew the location and movement of major enemy formations because they had broken the Nationalist army's codes. Moreover, an American military observer estimated that a Chinese division had only one-third to one-twelfth the combat punch (calculated as the number of troops multiplied by their firepower) of a Japanese division.[25]

In mid-August, Chiang initiated major fighting in the Shanghai area. He thought that he could draw pressure away from his hard-pressed troops in the north by bombing Imperial Navy ships at Shanghai and attacking the much smaller Japanese garrison there. Chiang understood that Japanese mobility and firepower gave the enemy a natural advantage on the plains of north China that they would lose in urban warfare. This gamble ultimately backfired. The people of Shanghai paid a terrible price for that mistake. On August 14, Chinese bombers attacked the Japanese cruiser *Izumo* anchored on the Huangpu River near the city center. Some of the bombs fell wide of their target, killing more than a thousand civilians. Subsequent air raids by the Japanese killed a great many more. Chiang committed his best German-trained and equipped divisions to this campaign, reinforced by two hundred thousand warlord troops. Initially, Nationalist forces enjoyed an overwhelming advantage over the Japanese garrison. Both sides fought ferociously. Chiang's troops pushed the enemy back steadily in bloody street fighting. However, the Japanese quickly brought in a two-hundred-thousand-man strike force in an attempt to defeat the Guomindang on its home ground.

The tide of battle soon turned. Imperial troops were supported by devastating naval gunfire from ships patrolling Shanghai's rivers, while the Chinese lacked adequate artillery and antitank weapons. By the last week of October, the Guomindang defenders had been pushed back to Suzhou Creek west of the city. Japanese infantry forced a crossing of the "creek" (too deep to wade across and in some places one hundred to three hundred feet wide) against devastating Chinese fire. Chiang told his troops, "Even if we have only one soldier and one bullet left, we must fight to the end."[26] Their fate was sealed when the Japanese staged an amphibious landing to the southwest of Shanghai at Hangzhou Bay with 120,000 additional troops. Chiang confided to his diary that his failure to defend that landing zone was "our biggest strategic mistake."

The fighting was costly for both sides. Some Japanese units experienced casualty rates as high as 80 percent, and the Imperial Army lost over forty thousand men in this engagement. The Chinese, raked by superior enemy firepower, suffered some 187,000 casualties before beginning their retreat from Shanghai toward Nanjing on November 9. These losses included 60 percent of the elite Central Army forces Chiang had committed to the campaign, weakening the generalissimo not only against the Japanese but also in relation to his own warlord generals. Nationalist forces, anticipating that they might be pushed out of Shanghai, had prepared a stout defensive line of concrete blockhouses in the vicinity of Wuxi, about fifty miles west of Shanghai, but their retreat disintegrated into a panicked rout. Too few of them regrouped behind the Wuxi line to hold the onrushing enemy. Unreliable regional troops fled their posts, letting the Japanese through. Although the Chinese suffered a crushing defeat at Shanghai, Chiang's commitment of his best troops demonstrated his intention to resist the invader and thereby helped him weld together a coalition of Nationalist, regional, and Communist forces.

Chiang Kai-shek also hoped to elicit foreign support by escalating the fighting at Shanghai because that city was the focal point of Western interests in the country. He failed completely in this objective, however. At that point the Western powers were preoccupied with the looming menace of Hitler in Europe and were intimidated by Japan's military superiority in East Asia. Neither the League of Nations nor the Nine Power Treaty Conference did anything more than talk about the problem. President Roosevelt fully expected war with Japan at some point in the future, but isolationist sentiment in the United States and the growing menace in Europe kept him from acting decisively. America's military weakness also limited the president's options.[27] Verbal condemnation and moral support were as far as any of the Western powers would go. The United States did not even respond strongly when Japanese planes sank the US gunboat *Panay* on the Yangzi River near Nanjing, nor did the British government when the HMS *Ladybird* was bombed. The wounding of Britain's ambassador by a strafing Japanese plane produced only protests. Facing the Depression, the rising threat of Germany in Europe, and widespread antiwar sentiment in the democracies, neither London nor Washington dared push the Japanese too hard.

Hitler terminated all support for China in January 1938, shifting to a pro-Japanese foreign policy. Now only the Soviet Union provided some help for China—signing a nonaggression pact with that country in August and subsequently providing 897 combat planes, 872 tanks, 1,150 trucks, 5,700 machine guns, 50,000 rifles, quantities of ammunition, and a 100-million-yuan loan. Though more assistance was to follow, even the Russians flirted with the possibility of ending aid to the Nationalists in exchange for Tokyo's promise not to exterminate the Chinese Communist Party.[28] Nevertheless, by 1941 the Soviets had sent 5,000 military advisors and pilots, 1,235 planes, and 1,600 artillery pieces to the Nationalist army. After the German invasion of the USSR in June 1941, Stalin would have little to spare for the Chinese.

A War against the People

The Japanese committed widespread atrocities against Chinese soldiers and civilians from the beginning. The Imperial Army had made no provision for housing and feeding large numbers of prisoners of war. The Japanese executed thousands of surrendering Nationalist troops during and after the battle for Shanghai as the most expedient way of dealing with the problem. Officers sometimes engaged in competitions with each other to "cut down a hundred" with their swords. Japan's press reported these exploits in the context of heroic attacks on enemy pillboxes and camps, but in reality most of the body count represented the killing of defenseless prisoners. Imperial forces took out their wrath on the civil population, too. There was an orgy of murder, torture, rape, theft, vandalism, and arson, not just during the battle but also in the weeks that followed. Chinese civilians were shot or bayoneted without cause, women of all ages were raped, valuables were stolen, and whole villages were burned to the ground.

One survivor of this carnage, Zhang Bingnan, recounted the following brutal scene near Wuxi:

> There were two young women in the group, one seventeen and unmarried, and the other pregnant. Both were taken off to separate houses and raped by one "devil" after another. . . . Having raped the two women, the soldiers turned to arson and mass murder. Some soldiers dragged the two women back to the garden, while others took on the job of setting fire to all the houses. . . . The soldiers rammed a

broom into the vagina of the younger woman and then stabbed her with a bayonet. They cut open the belly of the pregnant women and gouged out the fetus.[29]

Such actions caused the Chinese to dub the invaders "Eastern Devils" and "animal soldiers." Racist disdain for the local population partly explains why Imperial troops behaved so
badly. Schools in Japan had taught their pupils that the Chinese were inferior to them. Popular culture reinforced this image. Uno Shintaro, an army officer, admitted candidly, "On
the battlefield, we never really considered the Chinese humans. When you're winning, the
losers look really miserable. We concluded that the Yamato [Japanese] race was superior."[30]

Atrocities happen in every army in every war and are usually the product of either
soldiers who snap under the extreme stress of combat or men with a preexisting criminal
disposition. In either case, an individual or small group of soldiers is responsible for the
mayhem. In China, however, the very structure and culture of the Japanese armed forces
sparked these atrocities. Japanese political scientist Masao Maruyama argues that the Imperial Army was a rigidly hierarchical, oppressive, and often brutal system that fostered
the "transfer of oppression," and therefore Japanese soldiers, harassed and abused by
their superiors, took out their pent-up rage on the prisoners of war and enemy civilians
who came under their control.[31] Moreover, most Japanese soldiers were young peasants
recruited from rural districts. While attitudes about sex and gender roles were changing to
some degree in Japan's major cities, these young soldiers still tended to see all women as
inferior and as merely servants of their needs.

This escalating cycle of violence exploded after the Imperial Army took Nanjing.
Japanese investigative journalist Honda Kasuichi suggests a typical chain of events: "It often
happened that one or two Japanese soldiers ventured into a village to hunt down women or
to do a little looting, and there they fell into the hands of either guerrillas or villagers exacting revenge for the invasion. Japanese troops would then pile into the area looking for the
missing soldiers. As vengeance, they would burn the village and kill all the inhabitants."[32]

In the case of these atrocities in China, however, explanations that focus on the devi-
ance of individuals or small groups (though that certainly did play a role) are inadequate.
The outrages were far too widespread and continued for much too long to have escaped
the attention of senior commanders. Historian Sabine Frühstük argues that "the systematic
nature of both types of sexual violence [i.e., rapes and violent assaults] makes clear that most
instances were not the crimes of a handful of men acting outside the control of the Japanese
state and military administration."[33] Beyond just condoning these crimes, Japanese officers
saw the carnage as a means to intimidate the Chinese into surrendering (though in fact it
had the opposite effect). Although after the war the victors never found any written order
for mass murder and indiscriminate terror, the savagery was so pervasive and prolonged that
it could not have been perpetrated solely at the initiative of individuals and small groups of
renegade soldiers. Based on extensive interviews with victims and perpetrators, Honda concludes, "The massacres that unfolded everywhere were systematic acts based on policies of
the upper echelons of the Japanese military."[34] Japanese atrocities were motivated by a lethal
mixture of racist and sexist attitudes, combat-induced hysteria, lust to avenge the deaths of
comrades, and deliberate (even if unwritten) policy decisions.

Having defeated the Nationalist forces at Shanghai, the Imperial Army General Staff did
not intend to expand the war in central China at this point. However, the Japanese commanders on the scene, Generals Matsui Iwane and Yanagawa Heisuke, wanted to pursue

the retreating Chinese and attack Nanjing. They believed that capturing the Guomindang capital would force Chiang Kai-shek to sue for peace. They therefore ignored their orders and chased the fleeing Chinese ferociously. Chiang understood that Nanjing could not be defended successfully with the battered forces now available to him. Yet he determined to fight for the capital anyway, because the enraged patriotism of his countrymen demanded it, and also to demonstrate to world opinion China's determination to defy the aggressor. The Japanese generals planned to batter Nanjing day and night from the air while two spearheads encircled the city. The Chinese patched together a one-hundred-thousand-man force to defend the GMD capital, but many of them were shell-shocked veterans from Shanghai or raw recruits just learning to use their rifles.

By December 10, the Japanese had overrun the outer rings of Nanjing's defenses, and they began an assault on the walled city itself. The fighting was savage and extremely costly to both sides. The Japanese used concentrated artillery fire and explosive charges to breach some of the gates and enter the city in fierce, sometimes hand-to-hand fighting. The Nationalist defense began to collapse at this point. General Tang Shengzhi ordered his troops to withdraw from Nanjing. Unfortunately, many of his units never received the order or they were unable to fight their way through the encircling enemy. Soon hordes of panicked civilians and demoralized soldiers clogged the streets and waterways, desperately fleeing the onrushing adversary. After the debacle, Chiang Kai-shek told his people, "The outcome of this war will not be decided at Nanking or in any other big city; it will be decided in the countryside of our vast country and by the inflexible will of our people. . . . In the end we will wear the enemy down. In time the enemy's military might will count for nothing. I can assure you that the final victory will be ours."[35] He confided to his diary, "We can use our capacities of endurance to achieve our goal in a protracted battle."[36]

The Japanese had hoped that the capture of Nanjing would force the Guomindang to capitulate. The Nationalist regime did not surrender; rather, the Japanese army's own barbarous actions provoked an explosion of anger and resistance by the Chinese nation. There in the capital took place an atrocity that shocked the world—the rape of Nanjing. General Matsui Iwane had promised, "Though harsh and relentless to those who resist, the Japanese troops are kind and generous to noncombatants and to Chinese troops who entertain no enmity to Japan."[37] However, during the citywide search for Chinese soldiers in hiding, his troops loosed an orgy of murder, rape, and pillage. Even Nazi observers were shocked. These atrocities were triggered in part by Japanese soldiers who, angered by the fierce Chinese resistance that had claimed the lives of so many of their comrades, wreaked a bloody revenge. Beyond that, however, the Japanese once again used indiscriminate terror to cow the Chinese into submission. The massacre was not merely a spontaneous outburst by troops driven half mad by the horrors of combat. The Japanese army maintained its order and discipline while it carried out the virtually systematic plunder of the city.

Conflicting visions of anti-imperialist ideology also fueled the rampage. "Even if there was no meticulous plan for the massacre in Nanjing," Rana Mitter argues, "the wider ideological clash between Japan and China was a central cause of the tragedy. . . . The notion that China might have developed its own vision of nationalism, in which Japan was as much an aggressor as the West, did not fit into the worldview of the invaders."[38] Over twenty thousand women were raped. A third of the city burned to the ground. More than two hundred thousand (some Chinese sources say three hundred thousand) Chinese military prisoners and hapless civilian victims were slaughtered in and around Nanjing. Some were machine-gunned in big batches; others were used for bayonet practice.[39] Tang Junshan, a fifteen-year-old resident of the capital, witnessed a brutal example of this terror. Japanese soldiers took a large group of Chinese military and civilian captives to a big pit, already partly filled with dead bodies. The prisoners

> were divided into four groups of equal size and made to stand on four sides of the pit. . . . Then the head cutting began. . . . The four teams were having a head cutting contest. As each head was cut off, blood spurted up and the body fell over. The heads were lined up in back. . . . The seventh and last person in the first row was a pregnant woman. The soldier thought he might as well rape her before killing her. . . . As he was trying to rape her, the woman resisted fiercely. . . . The soldier abruptly stabbed her in the belly with a bayonet. She gave a final scream as her intestines spilled out. Then the soldier stabbed the fetus, with its umbilical cord clearly visible, and tossed it aside.[40]

A Japanese soldier, Azume Shiro, later reminisced, "At home I was a good father, a good brother, a good husband; however, after a month on the battlefield, I killed without remorse. I'm often at a loss as to why this happened."[41] Many Imperial soldiers apparently had no qualms about their bloody mission; they even sent photographs back home of themselves beheading Chinese men and holding naked Chinese women.

Foreign journalists in China reported the atrocious behavior of Japanese forces globally. American moviegoers, for example, saw the gruesome aftermath of the rape of Nanjing on newsreel footage in theaters. The Japanese press reported none of the atrocities. They published stories about Imperial troops treating prisoners with care, passing out candy to children, and helping to rebuild the local economy. The Japanese press depicted the struggle with China as a moral crusade. Prime Minister Konoe proclaimed that Japan was fighting for a "New Order in East Asia." Under Tokyo's benign guidance, Asia would be liberated from the white man's thrall and led to a new era of prosperity and harmony. From this viewpoint, the Guomindang was nothing more than a tool of Western imperialism. Discussions in the Japanese press often spoke of the Chinese as if they were spoiled, rebellious children who did not know what was good for them and who needed to be disciplined. That view found wide support among the Japanese public.

The Japanese never admitted to the outside world, or even to themselves, that they were actually at war with China. They always referred to the conflict as the "China Incident." They deluded themselves that one more battle, one more big victory, and the fighting would end. Tokyo had stumbled into a major war, which it had not intended, did not understand, and could not win. However, none of that was apparent at the end of 1937. Early the following year, when Chiang failed to accede to Japanese demands, Konoe withdrew recognition of the Guomindang government and publicly declared that a negotiated settlement was no longer possible. The Japanese were now committed to the conquest of China.

By the opening of 1938, Japan had increased its combat forces in China to sixteen divisions, plus numerous support units and air groups, which represented over half of the Imperial Army's strength. Nevertheless, the Japanese faced vastly larger Chinese armies on every battlefield and had to rely on superior discipline, training, tactics, and equipment to win victories. Chiang Kai-shek's Central Army was well armed and trained, but much of it had been decimated in the fighting at Shanghai. Elsewhere, Chinese provincial commanders led large infantry armies that were no match for Japanese mobility and firepower. The Chinese lacked almost everything required by modern armies—sufficient aircraft, artillery, transport, communications, and standardized weaponry—everything but flesh and blood.

Leadership was a problem, too. Their experiences in China's civil wars scarcely prepared Chiang's commanders to face Japan's well-equipped and well-led armies. Too often, Chinese military operations lacked the thorough planning, flexibility, and responsiveness required in modern combat.

The incomplete nature of Guomindang "unification" of China in the 1920s continued to hinder the Nationalists' war effort a decade later. The reliability of provincial commanders was sometimes a problem. Han Fuju, a former warlord and now the GMD governor of Shandong Province, attempted to negotiate his own settlement with the Japanese in order to preserve his personal power base. When that failed and the enemy attacked in December 1937, Chiang Kai-shek ordered Han to fight to the last man, but instead he and his troops abandoned the provincial capital, Jinan, to the enemy. Han fled the province, deserting his army. He was subsequently executed for dereliction of duty. Chiang was sending a strong message to other independent-minded generals who might put their own interests above the defense of the nation. Some Chinese commanders finally saw the need for a well-coordinated strategy under a unified central command.[42] Beyond some awakened patriotism, many of the warlord generals came to understand that unless they banned together, the enemy would destroy them one by one. The generalissimo also used the national defense effort to weaken warlord power, sending their armies to fight the Japanese whenever he could while holding forces loyal to him in reserve.

The major focus of combat in 1938 shifted to the central section of the Yangzi River valley. The Japanese planned to bring large forces from the north and from Nanjing to converge on the railway junction of Xuzhou. From there they would launch a two-pronged campaign along the valley with the ultimate objective of taking the Wuhan industrial complex, comprising the cities of Wuchang, Hanyang, and Hankou (Hankow). The Chinese took a stand at Xuzhou. Chiang needed to convince both the Chinese people and potential Western allies that his regime had the determination and the ability to defend the country. The two sides fought each other to a bloody standstill north of Xuzhou. Chinese defenses in this area depended on a mixture of troops loyal to the central government and those of a quasi-independent provincial commander, Li Zongren (Li Tsung-jen), who had previously tried to oust Chiang Kai-shek by force. The Japanese conquest of Manchuria convinced Li to rally to the Nationalist cause, though he and Chiang continued to treat each other with suspicion. The Chinese temporarily checked the enemy advance at Taierzhuang (Tai-erh-chuang) northwest of Xuzhou, where a force of 133,000 men led by General Tang Enbo defeated two enemy columns. Combat within the cramped old city involved brutal house-to-house fighting. The Imperial Army lost eight thousand troops in this engagement.

Chiang pressed for a renewed offensive, but it soon ground to a halt. The Chinese were forced to retreat when the Japanese marshaled ten divisions and renewed the attack. Instead of the easy victory the Japanese had anticipated, the capture of Xuzhou took five months of bitter, bloody fighting—though once accomplished it allowed them to connect their operations in northern and central China. The Japanese took thirty thousand prisoners at Xuzhou, but two hundred thousand Chinese soldiers escaped to fight another day. The victory at Taierzhuang and the heroic defense of Xuzhou served as a much-needed morale boost for the Nationalist army and the people of China.

The Guomindang lost more of its best units in May and June in savage fighting around the critical railroad junction of Lan-feng. Poor coordination of forces turned a promising victory into bitter defeat. Nationalist troops attempted to slow Japanese progress in June by opening dikes on the Yellow River in Henan Province and flooding the countryside, a desperate measure that harmed the peasants immeasurably but halted the enemy only temporarily. More than eight hundred thousand people in Henan, Anhui, and Jiangsu Provinces died, either drowned in the flooding or subsequently succumbing to hunger and disease. Four million were made homeless. The floods destroyed the annual harvest and reduced agricultural production in the region for several years.[43] Historian Diana Lary argues that the breaching of the Yellow River dikes reflected "upper-level panic" on the part of the GMD regime.[44] The breaching of the dikes was not an isolated disaster. Retreating Nationalist armies implemented a scorched-earth policy to deny resources to the Japanese enemy. War hysteria frequently led to irrational decisions—blowing up bridges and blocking harbors—that harmed the Chinese people more than they impeded the enemy. The Guomindang regime paid a heavy political price for these actions, which alienated many Chinese.

The campaign for Wuhan began in earnest in June 1938. The Japanese assembled four hundred thousand troops commanded by General Hata Shunroku. The Chinese amassed twice that number under General Chen Cheng. The Nationalist government had transferred its capital to Hankou (one of the Wuhan tri-cities) just before the fall of Nanjing. Japanese authorities were sure that Chiang Kai-shek would give up once they took his new capital. After all, how many disastrous defeats could the Chinese absorb? The Japanese planned this campaign for the fall so that their forces could feed themselves by seizing the recently harvested rice crop and take advantage of high river levels for transportation. Though outnumbered more than two to one, Japanese forces relied once again on control of the air, superior firepower, and, in this operation, poison gas (euphemistically called "special smoke") to overcome the Chinese defenders. By the beginning of October, the two prongs of the Japanese offensive were closing in on the Wuhan complex. Naval units striking up the Yangzi supplemented the overland attack on Hankou. Soviet "volunteer" pilots inflicted serious losses on the Imperial Air Force but could not prevent Japanese troops from entering the city. GMD soldiers hastily abandoned the town in October. The bloody campaign cost the Japanese 100,000 men, while the Chinese lost 250,000.

The Nationalists had lost a rich source of customs revenue and the only major industrial center remaining under their control. Chiang Kai-shek had already begun moving his government a month earlier, determined not to make an essentially suicidal last stand as he had done at Nanjing. The GMD also managed to evacuate some of Wuhan's industry westward. Soon thereafter, Guangzhou (Canton), the last big city still in Nationalist hands, fell to seaborne assault. With the bulk of Nationalist forces engaged around Wuhan, the six Chinese divisions defending Guangzhou were quickly overwhelmed by three Imperial divisions with strong naval and air support. Finally, after the fall of Wuhan, there seemed no way to defend the important Hunan Province capital of Changsha one hundred miles to the south. Acting on faulty intelligence and in a panic, Chiang ordered the city burned to deny it to the Japanese. It was a tragedy for the civilian population and a terrible mistake since the enemy did not assault the area for over a year. The year 1938 thus ended in defeat, but the Guomindang leadership was neither desperate nor depressed. Chiang adopted a new strategy of strategic retreat and protracted war. A long war of attrition would wear down the enemy and perhaps crack its will to continue.

The Japanese finally assaulted Changsha with a one-hundred-thousand-man force in September 1939, but General Xue Yue (Hsüeh Yüeh) brilliantly combined traditional and guerrilla tactics to repulse them. That autumn the Nationalists employed eighty divisions to launch their own broad offensive of coordinated attacks from north-central China to the southwest. The campaign soon faltered, however. One of the regional commanders, Yan

Xishan, withdrew his troops from the operation after cutting a deal with the enemy to preserve his Shanxi power base. In the southwest, the Japanese launched an invasion of Guangxi Province. They captured its capital, Nanning, in November. Nationalist forces finally halted this enemy advance after two months of fierce combat, but their own offensive was derailed by the need to defend south China. Elsewhere, in May 1940, the Japanese overran a key transit point in Chongqing's supply route, the city of Yichang in Hubei (Hupeh) Province.

The defeat at Wuhan had been a terrible loss, but it was also another important step in mobilizing the Chinese people to defend their country. Tens of thousands of students and intellectuals rallied to the cause, many of them joining the Communist Party in the process. Stephen MacKinnon argues that "the Wuhan experience had changed China's collective consciousness—reshaped politics, society and culture."[45] This may overestimate the militancy of the Chinese peasants, but certainly many Chinese students saw themselves locked in a global antifascist movement; for them, the defense of Wuhan was part of the same struggle as the defense of Madrid from Franco's forces. Guomindang propaganda picked up that theme, depicting the Chinese war effort as part of the global antifascist struggle.

To the northwest, the Japanese attempted smaller operations to secure Chahar Province. There, Nationalist and Communist troops planned operations to block this move, but preemptive strikes by the enemy against GMD forces seemed at first to guarantee Japanese success. However, Communist troops of the Eighth Route Army, commanded by Lin Biao, staged a highly successful ambush of a seventy-wagon, eighty-truck enemy supply column at the Ping-hsing Pass. Reinforcements from the Kwantung Army finally reached the besieged remnant and reclaimed the area, but it was a costly victory for the Japanese, who suffered high casualties and suppressed neither the Nationalist nor the Communist forces in the region.

The "Soviet Threat"

The Japanese high command's initial disinclination to see the Marco Polo Bridge Incident and the subsequent outbreak of fighting in Shanghai as an expansion into all-out war did not spring from any lessening of their desire to dominate and exploit China, but rather from their growing concern about Soviet power. After the suppression of the 1936 military mutiny in Tokyo and of the Kodoha faction in the officer corps, reformist officers pushed to expand and modernize the Imperial Army to meet this perceived Soviet threat. Some officers even began talking about securing Chinese cooperation in a campaign against the Soviet Union. Other officers, looking at the same supposed Russian menace, reached the opposite conclusion—that they must smash China's independence before confronting Stalin's legions. General Tojo Hideki, chief of staff to the Kwantung Army, expressed this view, remarking "that preparing for war against the Soviet Union without crushing the Nanjing government 'to remove the menace to our rear' was 'asking for trouble.'"[46]

While Japanese armies in China marched from victory to victory, a new crisis threatened in Manchuria. The Kwantung Army, which guarded Manchuria's northern frontiers against the USSR, had been weakened by the transfer of many troops to China. By late 1937, only six Japanese divisions and five air groups faced, by Tokyo estimates, twenty Soviet infantry divisions, four or five cavalry divisions, 1,500 tanks, and a slightly higher number of aircraft. An increasing number of minor border incidents beginning in 1935 further heightened the tension, finally leading to serious military clashes in 1938 and 1939. The first of these, called the Zhanggufeng (Changkufeng) Incident by the Japanese and the Lake Khasan Incident by the Russians, took place where the borders of the USSR, Manchuria, and Korea met. Boundaries in this area, which included Zhanggufeng hill, were imprecise and disputed. On July 11, 1938, Japanese troops stationed on the Korean side of the border noticed some forty Soviet soldiers apparently digging defensive positions on the hill. When informed of this development, the high command and the government in Tokyo advised extreme caution. They did not want any further outbreak of hostilities to jeopardize preparations for the Hankou offensive; but commanders on the scene were eager for action. Japanese forces attacked Zhanggufeng hill early on the morning of July 31 and secured its crest after three hours of heavy fighting. The Soviets counterattacked two nights later with two divisions and heavy tank, artillery, and air support. Fearing escalation, Moscow and Tokyo settled the incident diplomatically, with both sides withdrawing to their original lines.

An even more serious clash took place the following year along the disputed Halha River boundary between Manchuria and Soviet-dominated Outer Mongolia. The Nomonhan (or Khalkhin-gol) Incident began on May 11, 1939, when a band of seventy or eighty Mongolian troopers crossed the river and exchanged fire with soldiers of the Manchukuo army. Two days later the Japanese dispatched a cavalry regiment to the scene. The Outer Mongolian troops at first fell back, but on May 28, Soviet forces, using tanks and artillery, surrounded and destroyed the Japanese regiment. The Kwantung Army retaliated with a successful air strike against the Tamsagbulag air base in Outer Mongolia and with a division-strength offensive across the Halha River on July 1. On the following evening, several hundred Soviet tanks attacked the Japanese. The Japanese were forced back across the river the next night. They discovered that their thinly armored tanks and small-caliber antitank guns were inadequate in combat against Soviet forces. The Japanese brought up heavy artillery hoping to overwhelm the Russian positions with a massive bombardment. Soviet gunners responded with an even more powerful fusillade. The Japanese learned, to their chagrin, that the opposing Soviet forces were four or five times larger than their own and included numerous tank and air units. In the ensuing fighting, which one officer referred to as the struggle of flesh against iron, the Japanese suffered staggering casualties—seventeen thousand men killed, wounded, or missing in action. Soviet troops drove the Japanese back to the boundary line that Moscow claimed and then began building fortifications there.

The Kwantung Army planned to amass virtually all its strength in Manchuria for a counterattack to avenge this humiliating defeat. The army's commanders assumed that their operation would expand into a general war with the USSR. With victory in China still beyond their grasp and war breaking out in Europe, the Japanese government and high command could not permit any escalation of hostilities with the Russians. Japanese authorities were shocked by both the poor performance of the Kwantung Army and by the Nazi-Soviet Pact, signed in August. Tokyo now feared that the Russians, freed from the threat of a two-front war, might launch an offensive into Manchuria. They called off the Kwantung Army offensive and settled the incident diplomatically, to Soviet advantage. The peaceful resolution of these border battles was disturbing news for the Chinese, who had hoped that a Soviet-Japanese war might break out. Feeling less threatened in its relations with Berlin and Tokyo, Moscow began to curtail its aid to the Nationalist cause.

The disastrous results of the Zhanggufeng and Nomonhan Incidents had a profound effect on future Japanese policy. One major faction in the Imperial Army and many civilian leaders too had advocated eventual war against the Soviet Union. For them, southern China, Southeast Asia, and the Pacific were of secondary importance. These two manifestations of Soviet might, however, demonstrated that an anti-Soviet crusade would be much more difficult than anyone had envisioned. Many Japanese who had anticipated war with the USSR now warmed to the idea of diplomatic accommodation with Moscow. That view was strengthened in August when Germany signed the Nazi-Soviet Pact, without any prior notice to Tokyo. While these two "incidents" led to a reevaluation of Japan's overseas goals, they did not have much impact on Japanese military doctrine. The army continued to stress the importance of "spirit" and hand-to-hand combat, despite the bitter lessons administered by superior Soviet firepower. Similarly, although the Japanese had come to respect Soviet military strength, they missed the broader implication of their defeats—that they were ill prepared for all-out war with any major Western power whose population and industrial resources far exceeded their own.

Meanwhile in China, the Japanese had won an impressive series of tactical victories, but they could not win the war. They had expected Chiang Kai-shek to give up after the fall of Hankou. Instead, the generalissimo moved the seat of his government far up the Yangzi River to Chongqing (Chungking) in Sichuan (Szechwan) Province. In the big early battles along the relatively flat coastal lowlands, superior mobility and firepower gave Japan decisive advantages. Then, as the focus of action shifted into the vast rugged interior, those advantages dissipated. Japanese armies were in danger of being swallowed up by the seemingly limitless land and people of China.

The war in China did not end with Japan's capture of the cities on or near the coast, but its nature changed. It ceased to be a war of large-scale, decisive engagements; it became a test of endurance. Chiang Kai-shek's best divisions had been smashed in 1937–1938, and the Nationalist army was increasingly short of equipment. It could no longer afford to face

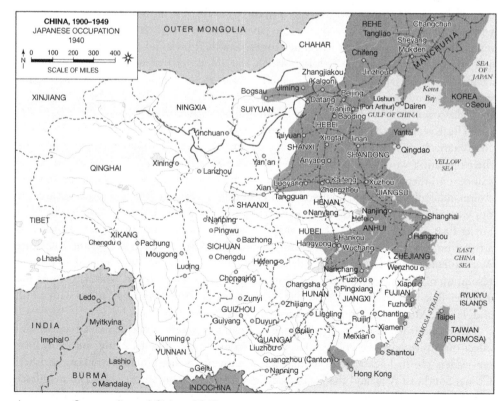

Japanese Occupation of China, 1940

the Japanese in great frontal engagements. The Chinese now had to attack from the flanks and from the rear. They had to take advantage of mountain passes and river gorges to set ambushes. The Japanese continued to push back the Guomindang's areas of control, though more slowly and not without losses. During May 1939, General Li Zongren repulsed and inflicted heavy casualties on a Japanese invasion force at Zaoyang (Tsaoyang) in Hubei Province. The Japanese were also repelled three times at Changsha by troops of General Xue Yue. Chiang Kai-shek and his generals have been accused of having no coherent strategy to defeat Japanese aggression.[47] The Nationalist military command had long anticipated that the enemy would be able to conquer coastal China because of Japan's superior naval and air power. The Chinese leader now intended to fight a prolonged war of attrition that would wear down the enemy.

The new Nationalist strategy involved drawing the enemy deeper and deeper into the hinterland until his lines of supply and communication snapped and his weakened forces could be counterattacked successfully. Chiang Kai-shek's troops also employed guerrilla tactics—infiltrating behind enemy lines in civilian clothes, staging ambushes, assassinating commanders, disrupting communications, and spreading chaos. Battered as it was, the Nationalist army still had enough strength to launch a nationwide series of offensives employing eighty divisions in the winter of 1939–1940. Most of these attacks soon ground to a halt, however, because the troops lacked air cover, armor, enough artillery, and adequate supplies. Moreover, with things seeming to go badly for the Nationalist cause, some regional commanders began to hedge their bets by negotiating secret agreements with the enemy. The "united front" between the GMD and the Communists also continued to fray, as Communist forces attacked some government units.

On the Japanese side, blockade of the hinterland now replaced battles of annihilation as Tokyo's strategy for victory. By controlling the coast, the Japanese cut off the major supply routes to Nationalist forces in the interior. Japanese bombers punished Guomindang cities. The small Nationalist air force, even augmented by squadrons of Soviet "volunteers," was unable to stop them. Japanese forces were not entirely quiet in this period. They launched an offensive in the summer of 1940 that, after very heavy fighting, secured the agriculturally rich north Hubei region. They paid a heavy price for this victory, losing between thirty thousand and forty thousand men.

According to conventional concepts of warfare, the Japanese should have won the war at this point. They had destroyed the enemy's best armies, captured its largest cities, controlled its transport system, and dominated the economically richest parts of its country. Yet that enemy—in Chongqing and in Yan'an—refused to give up. The Japanese did not know it yet, but they were locked in a life-and-death struggle in the first phase of the Second World War. The extension of that war around the globe in Europe was not long in coming. In Berlin, Adolf Hitler had conceived a plan of aggression more coherent and even more megalomaniacal and murderous than those of the Japanese militarists.

Notes

1. Richard J. Smethurst, *A Social Basis for Prewar Japanese Militarism: The Army and the Rural Community* (Berkeley: University of California Press, 1974), xiv.

2. Smethurst, *A Social Basis for Prewar Japanese Militarism*, viii.

3. Hans van de Ven, *China at War: Triumph and Tragedy in the Emergence of the New China* (Cambridge, MA: Harvard University Press, 2018), 4.

4. Rana Mitter, *Forgotten Ally: China's World War II* (Boston: Houghton Mifflin Harcourt, 2013), 82.

5. S. C. M. Paine, *The Wars for Asia, 1911–1949* (Cambridge: Cambridge University Press, 2012), 46.

6. Saburo Ienaga, *The Pacific War: World War II and the Japanese, 1931–1945* (New York: Pantheon, 1978), 63.

7. Noriko Kawamura, *Emperor Hirohito and the Pacific War* (Seattle: University of Washington Press, 2015), 39–48.

8. Louise Young, "Ideologies of Difference and the Turn to Atrocity: Japan's War on China," in *A World at Total War: Global Conflict and the Politics of Destruction, 1937–1945*, ed. Roger Chickering, Stig Förster, and Bernd Greiner (Cambridge: Cambridge University Press, 2005), 342.

9. Rana Mitter, *The Manchurian Myth: Nationalism, Resistance, and Collaboration in Modern China* (Berkeley: University of California Press, 2000), 2.

10. Lloyd E. Eastman, *The Abortive Revolution: China under Nationalist Rule* (Cambridge, MA: Harvard University Press, 1974), 246. Cf. Jay Taylor, *The Generalissimo: Chiang Kai-shek and the Struggle for Modern China* (Cambridge, MA: Harvard University Press, 2011), 83, who argues that the fighting at "Jinan had confirmed Chiang's rather new belief that Japan was China's greatest enemy, a more serious threat for the indefinite future than the European powers, the Communists, or the rebellious warlords."

11. Mitter, *Forgotten Ally*, 63.

12. Cf. Sandra Wilson, who argues that, "Nevertheless, neither the war with China nor the Pacific War was inevitable or predestined, and the 1930s do not represent a steady escalation towards war." Wilson does recognize, however, that the "incident" did strengthen nationalism and militarism while weakening the parliamentary system. *The Manchurian Crisis and Japanese Society, 1931–33* (New York: Routledge, 2002), 4–5.

13. Quoted in Marius Jansen, *Japan and China: From War to Peace* (Chicago: Rand McNally, 1975), 387.

14. John K. Fairbank, Edwin O. Reischauer, and Albert M. Craig, *East Asia: Tradition and Transformation* (Boston: Houghton Mifflin, 1978), 703.

15. John Dower argues that the difference between civilian "moderates" and the militarists was "slow" or "soft" imperial expansion versus "go fast" imperialism. *Empire and Aftermath: Yoshida Shigeru and the Japanese Experience, 1878–1954* (Cambridge, MA: Harvard University Press, 1979), 85.

16. Quoted in Ienaga, *The Pacific War*, 40–41.

17. John J. Stephan, "The Tanaka Memorial (1927): Authentic or Spurious?," *Modern Asian Studies* 7, no. 4 (1973): 733–45.

18. Quoted in Akira Iriye, "The Failure of Military Expansionism," in *Dilemmas of Growth in Prewar Japan*, ed. James William Morley (Princeton, NJ: Princeton University Press, 1971), 112.

19. *The Communist International, 1919–1943: Documents*, vol. 3, *1929–1943*, ed. Jane Degras (London: Oxford University Press, 1956), 356.

20. Taylor, *The Generalissimo*, 123–27.

21. Hans van de Ven depicts Zhang Xueliang as supportive of Chiang Kai-shek's continued leadership, as long as the generalissimo agreed to unite all factions against the Japanese. Failing that, Zhang proposed an alliance with the Communists and other regional military commanders, excluding Chiang. *War and Nationalism in China* (London: RoutledgeCurzon, 2003), 177–88.

22. Vasilii I. Chuikov, *Mission to China: Memoirs of a Soviet Military Adviser to Chiang Kaishek* (Norwalk, CT: EastBridge, 2004), 16.

23. Quoted in Paine, *The Wars for Asia*, 128.

24. Quoted in Jansen, *Japan and China*, 394–95.

25. Frank Dorn, *History of the Sino-Japanese War* (New York: Macmillan, 1974), 6–10.

26. Quoted in Yang Tianshi, "Chiang Kai-shek and the Battles of Shanghai and Nanjing," in *The Battle for China: Essays on the Military History of the Sino-Japanese War of 1937–1945*, ed. Mark Peattie, Edward Drea, and Hans van de Ven (Stanford, Stanford University Press, 2011), 152.

27. David Kaiser, *No End Save Victory: How FDR Led the Nation to War* (New York: Basic Books, 2014), 120.

28. Paine, *The Wars for Asia*, 178. According to historian Bruce A. Elleman, in October 1940 the Russians and Japanese concluded a secret agreement whereby Moscow was to stop supplying arms to the Nationalist army and restrain the Chinese Communist Party from attacking the Japanese, and in exchange

Japan would allow the CCP to survive unmolested in Shensi, Kansu, and Ninghsa. "The 1940 Soviet-Japanese Secret Agreement and Its Impact on the Soviet-Iranian Supply Route" (Working Papers in International Studies, Hoover Institution, Stanford University, I-95-5, May, 1995), 1. Elleman reproduces the text of this agreement from the Japanese foreign policy archives and adduces evidence of Soviet compliance with its terms.

29. Honda Katsuichi, *The Nanjing Massacre* (Armonk, NY: M. E. Sharpe, 1999), 63–64.

30. Haruko Taya Cook and Theodore F. Cook, eds., *Japan at War: An Oral History* (New York: New Press, 1992), 150.

31. Masao Maruyama, *Thought and Behavior in Modern Japanese Politics* (London: Oxford University Press, 1963), 18.

32. Honda, *The Nanjing Massacre*, 278.

33. Sabine Frühstük, "Sexuality and Sexual Violence," in *The Cambridge History of the Second World War*, vol. 3, *Total War: Economy, Society and Culture*, ed. Michael Geyer and Adam Tooze (Cambridge: Cambridge University Press, 2015), 433.

34. Honda, *The Nanjing Massacre*, 194.

35. Quoted in Keiji Furuya, *Chiang Kai-shek: His Life and Times* (New York: St. John's University Press, 1981), 557.

36. Quoted in Yang, "Chiang Kai-shek and the Battles," 150.

37. Quoted in Janet Chen, Pei-kai Cheng, and Michael Lestz, eds., with Jonathan D. Spence, *The Search for Modern China: A Documentary Collection*, 3rd ed. (New York: Norton, 2014), 327.

38. Mitter, *Forgotten Ally*, 143.

39. Jonathan Spence gives much lower victim numbers: twenty thousand women raped, thirty thousand Chinese POWs, and twelve thousand civilians murdered, but he notes that other estimates "were as much as ten times higher, and it is difficult to establish exact figures." Jonathan D. Spence, *The Search for Modern China*, 3rd ed. (New York: Norton, 2013), 401.

40. Honda, *The Nanjing Massacre*, 162–64.

41. Mark Eykholt, "Aggression, Victimization and Chinese Historiography of the Nanjing Massacre," in *The Nanjing Massacre in History and Historiography*, ed. Joshua A. Fogel (Berkeley: University of California Press, 2000), 16.

42. Stephen MacKinnon, "The Defense of the Central Yangtze," in Peattie et al., *The Battle for China*, 182.

43. Micah S. Muscolino, *The Ecology of War in North China: Henan Province, the Yellow River, and Beyond, 1938–1950* (Cambridge: Cambridge University Press, 2015).

44. Diana Lary, *The Chinese People at War* (New York: Cambridge University Press, 2010), 61. In contrast, Hans van de Ven argues that "some strategic justification existed for the decision." *War and Nationalism in China*, 226. He contends that the flooding prevented a rapid exploitation of their victory at Xuzhou. Cf. Chinese historian Ma Zhonglian, who demonstrates that "Japanese forces stopped their westward advance of their own volition. There is no evidence to show that breaking the dikes at Huayuankou caused them to halt their advance." Quoted in van de Ven, *China at War*, 107.

45. Stephen R. MacKinnon, *Wuhan, 1938: War, Refugees, and the Making of Modern China* (Berkeley: University of California Press, 2008), 96.

46. Edward J. Drea, "The Japanese Army on the Eve of the War," in Peattie et al., *The Battle for China*, 107.

47. Edward Dreyer, *China at War, 1941–1949* (London: Longman, 1995); Frank Dorn, *Sino-Japanese War, 1937–1941* (New York: Macmillan, 1974); Dick Wilson, *When Tigers Fight: The Story of the Sino-Japanese War, 1937–1945* (New York: Penguin, 1983).

CHAPTER 3

Hitler's Drive to War

The conscious policy of aggression pursued by Adolf Hitler was the principal cause of the Second World War.[1] Hitler believed he was destined to lead the German people to European supremacy and ultimately to global hegemony. He wanted what traditional Weimar German nationalists had sought: the elimination of Versailles Treaty constraints on German power, the absorption of Austria into the Reich, the destruction of Poland, and the incorporation of Germans in Czechoslovakia and elsewhere into a greater Germany. But he wanted much more than this. Rudolf Hess, who later became deputy Führer to Hitler, reflected his master's thinking in a 1927 letter: "World peace is certainly an ideal worth striving for; in Hitler's opinion it will be realizable only when one power, the racially best one, has attained complete and uncontested supremacy."[2]

Hitler's theory of racial conflict led him to conclude that both the geographical and population base of Germany required great expansion. Otherwise, the *Volk* would be swamped by hordes of inferior races. This necessary *Lebensraum* could be conquered only at the expense of Poland and Soviet Russia. Thus, war with those two countries was inevitable. To the west stood another ancient enemy, France. French use of African colonial troops in Europe during and after the Great War convinced Hitler that France posed a grave threat to Germany—the contamination of the master race by African blood. Hitler was sure that the French would never willingly permit the German conquest of Eastern Europe, so he planned to strike against France before dealing with the USSR. Early in 1934 the Führer told leading military and party officials that "brief, decisive blows first against the West and then against the East will be necessary." This speech was not publicized, but he had written as much openly in *Mein Kampf*. That bizarre manifesto, written ten years before the National Social-ist seizure of power, could not serve as a precise blueprint for Nazi foreign policy, but Hitler adhered to the general goals he laid down there with remarkable consistency. Although dur-ing his first years as chancellor he exhibited extraordinary diplomatic and tactical flexibility, his conceptions of race war and *Lebensraum* remained unalterable foundations of his policy.

Where Hitler deviated from the line projected in *Mein Kampf*, it was to pursue an even more aggressive course. For example, he had criticized Kaiser Wilhelm II for blundering into a two-front war in 1914 against powerful enemies on each flank. Hitler also criticized Imperial Germany's colonial and naval expansion policies, which he believed had needlessly provoked Great Britain into joining the campaign against the Reich. The Führer intended not to repeat those mistakes. He planned to fight a series of short, decisive wars, knocking out one opponent at a time. He also hoped to keep England from allying with his prospec-tive victims by (temporarily) forswearing overseas colonial acquisitions or any fleet-building program that would challenge the Royal Navy. In addition, he hoped to convince London that it needed German assistance to counter an alleged Soviet threat to Britain's position in

India and the Middle East, and the supposed American challenge to British naval power. Yet, when Great Britain refused to acquiesce in Germany's bid for continental hegemony, Hitler revised his plan and readily accepted the risk of war with England. By 1937, his thinking about the colonial question had also changed. The Nazi Party opened a Colonial Policy Office, and Hitler began to plan the conquest of an empire in Africa that would include possessions taken from France, Belgium, and England as well as the reclamation of Imperial Germany's former African colonies.

Similarly, Hitler ignored his own dictum about avoiding a two-front war when he attacked the Soviet Union in 1941 at a time when the war in the West was still far from won. Moreover, he repeated the worst mistake of Imperial Germany's warlords when he gratuitously declared war on the United States soon after the outbreak of Japanese-American hostilities at Pearl Harbor. Hitler's initial image of America was relatively favorable. He was impressed by the pervasive climate of racism in the United States and especially by its restrictive immigration laws that barred Asians and severely limited the entry of southern and eastern Europeans. The white settlers' ruthless suppression of the Native Americans and enslavement of Africans was, in Hitler's view, a valuable model for the German people. America's tribulations in the Great Depression, however, drastically lowered the Führer's opinion of the United States. He came to see America as a weak and effeminate nation whose Nordic vitality had been sapped by race mixing. As the Roosevelt administration assumed an increasingly hostile position against German aggression, Hitler accepted the logic of his admirals who had long sought a naval war with the United States. After annihilating the USSR and either conquering Britain or making an ally of it, Hitler intended to launch yet another major war, this time against America.

Besides the hoped-for alliance with England, Hitler wooed two other collaborators for his New Order, Italy and Japan. Italian ambitions for a re-creation of the Roman Empire in the Mediterranean region did not conflict with the Führer's plans, at least in their earlier formulation. He planned to weaken any western front that might materialize against German expansion by detaching Italy from it. To this end, he willingly sacrificed the interests of Germans living under Italian governance in the South Tyrol. Hitler was also attracted to Mussolini, whose Fascist movement had served as a prototype for National Socialism. It was an attachment that would have fatal consequences for the Duce and the Italian people. Hitler also saw the Japanese as prospective allies. He looked down on Asians as inferior beings, but he was impressed by the bold, ruthless action of the Japanese to secure their aims in Manchuria and China. Additionally, an alliance with Japan would tie down much of Britain's and America's military strength in the Pacific, thus facilitating the German conquest of Europe. It is unlikely, however, that his allies in Rome and Tokyo would have fared well if Hitler had been fully successful in carrying out his aggressive designs. Hitler did not want a mere redivision of the world among Germany and its allies; he sought *Weltherrschaft*— absolute global dominion. He kept the extent of his lust for conquest from the public, but his closest associates knew his intentions.[3]

When Hitler became chancellor in early 1933, he could not implement his grandiose plans of aggression immediately. He was partially constrained by his political alliance with Germany's conservative elites, who supported extensive border revisions but did not share the Führer's obsessive megalomania. Moreover, Hitler did not command the military power necessary to force radical changes in the map of Europe. Despite numerous violations of the Versailles disarmament provisions, the Reichswehr was still no match for the powerful French army, and even the outcome of a test of arms with Poland would have been in doubt. Hitler had to proceed cautiously and disingenuously at first. Throughout much of Europe and North America, the Nazis had a deservedly terrible reputation. Hitler had to conceal his true intentions to prevent the formation of a coalition of powers to block any German advance and to forestall the even more chilling prospect of direct foreign intervention to depose the Nazi regime. He had to hide his plans from the German people as well. Although most Germans favored the abrogation of the Versailles Treaty and the absorption of German-speaking populations contiguous to the Reich border, they even more strongly desired peace. Therefore, between 1933 and 1939, the Führer emphasized his desire for a peaceful resolution of Germany's grievances.

Yet Hitler was convinced that he could not afford to wait too long before launching his great campaign for world domination. The economic policies that brought Germany out of the Depression assumed war at an early date, which, after victory, would make it possible to save the economy from collapse by exacting tribute from the vanquished. Also, rapid rearmament in the mid-1930s gave Germany significant advantages over its potential opponents, but those advantages were only temporary. When the other European powers and America began expanding their own military capabilities in response to the German buildup, Hitler faced the prospect of losing whatever margin of superiority Germany possessed, unless he unleashed war quickly. Finally, Hitler's conception of his own role in world history reinforced the decision for war. Believing in his unique destiny to lead Germany to greatness, he was grimly aware of his advancing age. Hitler was fifty years old in 1939. He could not wait much longer before launching his bid for world power, lest his health or his energy fail him.

Although Hitler must bear primary responsibility for the outbreak of hostilities in Europe, other factors facilitated his drive for war. The inequities of the Versailles settlement are a case in point. Hitler was able to use the real and imagined injustices of the treaty, first to mobilize support for National Socialism among the German people and then to outmaneuver Western statesmen. He was never deeply concerned about these matters in themselves, whether it was the demand for a return to the 1914 borders or the alleged indignities inflicted on ethnic Germans in Czechoslovakia and Poland. These were merely issues he exploited for his own purposes. Paradoxically, an overwhelming desire for peace on the part of Western statesmen and electorates paved the way for Nazi aggression. British, French, and American political leaders desperately sought to avoid a repetition of the carnage of 1914–1918. The economic havoc wrought by the Great Depression strengthened their determination to maintain the peace. In their anxiety to prevent the recurrence of war, they permitted Hitler to wreck the Versailles system, rearm Germany, and launch his plan of conquest without any forceful opposition. A great majority of voters in the Western democracies supported the policy of appeasement. Neither the men at the top nor the man on the street was anxious to face the unpleasant alternatives of capitulation or war that Hitler offered them. Before 1939, the most common political insult was not "appeaser" but "warmonger."

Not everyone remembered the Great War in the same way. Frenchmen focused on the enormous costs and awful sacrifices of the war. Englishmen thought about the frightful costs too, but unlike the French, many of them came to see the conflict as a needless waste, to be avoided at all cost in the future. Many young Germans, in contrast, agonized over their defeat in 1918, the revolutionary wave that followed it, and the supposed injustices of the Versailles Treaty system. For too many of them, the experience of 1914–1918 had not discredited militarism and war. It had radicalized them and awakened a thirst for revenge.

The cold war atmosphere that poisoned relations between the Western powers and the Soviet Union throughout the interwar period also contributed to Hitler's initial series of easy victories. The Western states repeatedly declined to cooperate with the USSR against German aggression. London and Paris seemed paralyzed by the specter of communism, while authoritarian and fascist movements subverted legitimate, pro-Western governments from Spain to Romania. On the Soviet side, the political ruthlessness and apparent instability that characterized Stalin's Russia made the USSR a much less attractive ally for the Western camp.

Hitler's Cautious First Steps

Bent on global conquest, Hitler tailored both his domestic and foreign policies to preparing the nation for war. Since he believed that German forces were on the verge of victory in the First World War when a collapsing home front betrayed them, Hitler immediately set about the "moral" rearmament of the German people. The Nazis quickly subverted Weimar parliamentary institutions and began the repression of Jews, liberals, socialists, and communists. Beyond that, National Socialist propaganda in the press and in the schools attempted to replace democratic and humanitarian values with ruthlessness, a lust for combat, and the willingness to sacrifice everything to follow the Führer's path of conquest. Hitler's conservative political and military allies supported all these measures. The expansion and reequipping of the army could not, however, be accomplished with such speed and openness. While Germany remained weak and France strong, Hitler had to conceal the rearmament program as well as his aggressive long-term intentions. As he told a group of high officials soon after taking office, "the most dangerous time will come during the creation of the military forces. Then we will discover whether France has statesmen. If they do, they will not grant us the necessary time, but will fall upon us at once."

With Hitler as chancellor, the pace of covert rearmament, which had already begun during the Weimar period, accelerated greatly. However, the progress of the World Disarmament Conference endangered this hidden growth of German arms. The prospect that the powers finally might agree on an arms reduction program, including careful inspections, threatened to expose the secret German buildup. Hitler abruptly withdrew Germany's representative from the conference in October 1933 to prevent such a disclosure. To mask the real reason for abandoning the conference, the Germans successfully shifted the focus of attention to the issue of national equality. In Berlin's view, such equality required France to dismantle much of its military strength while Germany continued to expand its own. When the French refused, Hitler blamed Paris for the failure of the conference. The Führer used a similar strategy to pull Germany out of the League of Nations the same month. Fearing that membership in any such multilateral body would limit his foreign policy options, Hitler denounced the League as a tool of French hegemony and recalled the German delegate from Geneva while proclaiming his peaceful intentions toward France.

Hitler masked his real ambitions in several other ways. For the first few years after coming to power, he left the conservative, non-Nazi, veteran diplomats in place at the German Foreign Ministry. The presence of such old-line officials as Foreign Minister Konstantin von Neurath was intended to reassure the world that, despite the violence of Nazi rhetoric, Germany would continue to pursue a peaceful foreign policy. Foreigners, who were taken in by Neurath's assurances that the responsibilities of power would tame the Nazis, did not realize how far-reaching were the ambitions of even these respectable non-Nazi diplomats. Neither could they have foreseen how ruthlessly Hitler would jettison his conservative allies once they had served their purpose. Hitler improved his image outside of Germany by posing as an anticommunist champion. He portrayed himself as the man who had saved Germany from Bolshevism. What Europe most needed, he claimed, was a strengthened, rearmed Germany to serve as a rampart against the spread of communism. Such pronouncements appealed to Western conservatives who feared that the ravages of the Depression and the machinations of the Communist International might well undermine the social order.

Hitler's most effective ploy in masking his aggressive intent was rapprochement with Poland. That country and all it entailed—Silesia, the corridor, Danzig—were anathema to Nazis and to traditional German nationalists alike. Since 1919, German diplomats and military officers had viewed the destruction of Poland as the first step toward restoring the greatness of the Reich. Given what the Nazis had previously said about dismantling the Versailles settlement and acquiring *Lebensraum* in the East, Hitler's rise to power caused considerable alarm in Warsaw. In the spring of 1933, rumors spread that Poland, perhaps joined by France, might launch a preemptive strike against the new Nazi regime. It is still uncertain whether the Polish leader, Marshal Jozef Pilsudski, ever seriously contemplated such action or merely spawned the rumors for diplomatic effect in Berlin. Whatever the truth, the result was the German-Polish nonaggression pact in 1934. Anti-Polish German generals and diplomats were aghast at this collusion with the enemy, but Hitler had achieved a great diplomatic triumph. The pact partially undermined both the French and the Soviet security systems. It also seemed to demonstrate that the Nazis were not wild-eyed radicals bent on destroying the Versailles system.

Amid these early successes, Hitler suffered one significant foreign policy setback—the failure of his first attempt to incorporate Austria into the Reich. The fragmentation of the Habsburg Empire in 1918, combined with the Allied prohibition against an Austro-German union, left a rump Austria with poor economic prospects and with an electorate evenly divided between mutually antagonistic Social Democrats and conservative Catholics. During the 1920s, many Austrians had favored merging with Germany, but after the Nazi seizure of power, neither the socialists nor the Catholics were anxious to join the Third Reich. Hitler hoped, however, that the impact of the Depression and the example of his own success in Germany would soon bring the Austrian Nazis to power through the ballot box. Thereafter, presumably, the two Nazi regimes would merge. Engelbert Dollfuss, the right-wing Austrian chancellor, frustrated these plans by suspending parliamentary government, banning all political parties including the Nazis and the socialists, and instituting an authoritarian regime. Hitler responded with strong economic and political pressure against Vienna, but Dollfuss stood firm supported by Italy and Hungary. The Führer thereupon permitted the Austrian Nazis to stage a coup against the Dollfuss regime. In July 1934, the conspirators seized several government buildings in Vienna and murdered the chancellor. They had badly underestimated the obstacles in their path. Mussolini, anxious to keep a reviving Germany away from Italy's northern frontier, mobilized a hundred thousand troops on the Brenner Pass in support of the Austrian government. Meanwhile, loyalist paramilitary units suppressed the Nazi insurrection and installed a clerical, authoritarian regime under Kurt Schuschnigg. Hitler had no alternative but to bow to superior force and disavow any connection with the attempted putsch in Vienna. He realized now that before he could incorporate Austria, he would have to come to terms with Mussolini.

Mussolini's show of strength had reduced Hitler and his Austrian Nazi minions to impotence. The German dictator had no effective response to a hundred thousand Italian troops. Force, or even the threat of force, was not yet part of the Führer's arsenal because the Reich still lacked the military power to make such threats credible. Behind the scenes, however, Hitler and his generals worked feverishly to correct that disagreeable reality. In 1934, the army organized cadres for twenty-four divisions and began to supply its troops with the various types of heavy weapons, including tanks, forbidden by the Versailles Treaty. Hitler forced them to increase their expansion plans repeatedly. While he left the details of rebuilding the army to the generals, Hitler put one of his own associates, Hermann Göring, in charge of creating a new air force. Göring launched an intensive effort to produce four thousand warplanes by the fall of 1935. The staggering cost of such massive rearmament programs and their long-term effects on the economy did not worry Hitler. He anticipated the spoils of war to pay those expenses. He fired Hans Luther, the fiscally conservative president of the Reichsbank, and replaced him with Hjalmar Schacht, who provided the armed forces with virtually unlimited credit.

This rapid, large-scale buildup of German military strength could not be kept secret for long—nor was it even desirable to do so. Hitler's incessant complaining about the Versailles settlement would work for only so long. At some point he would have to threaten or perhaps even use force to achieve his objectives. In publicly unveiling German rearmament, Hitler once again demonstrated his skill at shifting the blame to others. When the British authorized some modest budget increases for the Royal Air Force (RAF) and the French lengthened the army conscription period from twelve to sixteen months, the Führer seized the opportunity to renounce treaty limitations on German armed forces. On March 9, 1935, Göring openly proclaimed the existence of his Luftwaffe, and a week later Berlin announced the reintroduction of military conscription with the aim of building a 550,000-man army. As usual, a propaganda campaign that stressed Germany's peaceful intentions accompanied these disclosures. From this point on, however, there were no more attempts to conceal rearmament. Instead, the Nazis deliberately exaggerated the growing power of the armed forces to lend maximum force to Hitler's saber-rattling. The Luftwaffe, for example, used international air shows, the 1936 Olympics, and visits by such prominent foreign fliers as Charles Lindbergh to create an illusion of awesome strategic power far beyond the actual strength of the German air force.

The Western powers vigorously denounced German rearmament, but they took no effective measures to stop it. In Geneva, the Council of the League of Nations protested Hitler's unilateral action and set up a committee to consider sanctions against Germany in the event of any further violations of treaty provisions. British, French, and Italian leaders met at Stresa in April to condemn Germany and to affirm their determination to preserve the status quo in Austria and elsewhere. This proclamation, which sounded like a bold, united challenge to Hitler's designs, was in fact merely the hollow rhetoric of statesmen whose policies were rapidly diverging.

Great Britain helped to undermine Western unity by signing an Anglo-German Naval Agreement on June 18, 1935. The British feared the renewal of a naval arms race with Germany, as had happened prior to World War I, so they readily accepted Berlin's offer to limit the German fleet rebuilding program to one-third the size of the Royal Navy. The agreement may have given Englishmen a temporary sense of security, but it did so at the price of legitimizing the German arms buildup. Worse yet, they negotiated the treaty without consulting France or Italy. Hitler also immediately violated the treaty's limitations by authorizing two new super battleships, the *Bismarck* and the *Tirpitz*.

Mussolini Switches Sides

Four months later, Mussolini took a step that ended any possibility that the World War I Allies would reunite to prevent Hitler from destroying the Versailles settlement. He invaded Ethiopia (Abyssinia). By the mid-1930s, the Fascist regime in Rome had lost nearly all its vitality and much of its glamour. To make matters worse, the Fascists now faced stiff competition as the champions of Europe's radical right from the more dynamic Nazi regime. The Duce saw expansion abroad as just the tonic his flagging movement needed. He had weakened the most radical and dynamic elements of the Fascist movement by compromising with the traditional elites, but he still longed for that "second revolution." Ethiopia, lying between the two existing colonies of Italian Somaliland and Eritrea, offered a tempting target, though more because of its vulnerability than for its economic value. First, Mussolini needed a pretext for aggression. Italian penetration well beyond the ill-defined border between Ethiopia and Italian Somaliland finally provoked a military incident at the desert oasis of Walwal. With this feeble excuse, in October 1935 Mussolini launched an invasion that he had been preparing for months. The Italians committed 650,000 men against Emperor Haile Selassie's ill-equipped militia. The Abyssinian warriors were blasted by long-range artillery, raked by machine-gun fire, and sprayed with poison gas. The forces of Marshal Pietro Badoglio occupied the Ethiopian capital, Addis Ababa, by May 1936. Defeating the Abyssinian army in open combat was relatively easy, but pacifying the country, even with methods of unstinting brutality, proved beyond the power of the occupying forces. Even though victorious, the war failed in its intended political purpose in Italy. It was not popular with the people and led to serious inflation.[4]

The international repercussions of the Italian assault on Ethiopia led to a fundamental shift in Mussolini's foreign policy away from cooperation with the Western democracies and toward alliance with Hitler. For some time, Britain and France had recognized the primacy of Italian interest in Ethiopia, but they could not support the Duce's blatant aggression in Africa. The League of Nations denounced the invasion of Abyssinia and imposed limited economic sanctions on Italy. The British and French governments were anxious, however, not to alienate Mussolini. They needed Italy as an ally against a resurgent Germany. The resulting policy of half measures aroused the Duce's ire without hindering his conquest of Ethiopia. Crucially, the embargoes leveled against Italy were not extended to oil, the one commodity that was vital to the Italian offensive. Moreover, the French and British worked out an agreement that might have ended the fighting by giving Italy almost two-thirds of Ethiopia, had not the terms been leaked in the press and then withdrawn under a barrage of public outrage.

The Italo-Ethiopian war further undermined the League of Nations. The League was chartered to deter aggression through a series of escalating sanctions, and even joint military action, by its members against an aggressor state. However, the system failed decisively in the 1930s. Neither moral nor limited economic sanctions had saved Manchuria from the Japanese onslaught in 1931. Now similar measures failed once more to halt Italy's invasion of Abyssinia. Far from being deterred, the conquerors showed their disdain by quitting the League. Japan and Germany had already done so. In 1937, Mussolini withdrew his representative from Geneva.

Hitler took advantage of the crisis to violate yet another provision of the Versailles settlement. On March 7, 1936, he sent ten thousand troops into the demilitarized Rhineland. The army high command warned Hitler that this brazen violation of German treaty obligations might prove suicidal, since the French army could easily overwhelm the token forces moving beyond to the Rhine. Events proved the Führer's political foresight superior to that of his generals. Apart from some protests, the Allies did nothing. Once again, Hitler initiated a propaganda campaign to throw the Western leaders off balance. He blamed a recently signed Franco-Soviet defensive treaty as provocation for remilitarizing the Rhineland. He claimed that he was only exercising the sovereign rights of any free state. He even offered to negotiate far-reaching agreements with France and Belgium demilitarizing both sides of their borders with Germany—an offer he knew they would refuse since it meant dismantling the extensive system of French border fortifications.

Moving ten thousand troops to the Rhine did not immediately threaten France, but the long-term strategic impact of this act was immense. Since 1919, an unprotected Rhineland had served as a hostage for German good behavior. In theory at least, French forces could occupy the area unopposed at any time to force German compliance with its obligations. With no German defensive works to breach, the French army could also provide rapid assistance to any of its East European allies, particularly Poland or Czechoslovakia, that Germany might attack. Now that leverage was gone.

In planning his Rhineland coup, Hitler had been assured by Mussolini that Italy would not cooperate with Britain and France to oppose any German violation of the Versailles or Locarno provisions. Mild as it was, Anglo-French opposition to the Abyssinian invasion had turned Mussolini against his former partners in containing German expansion. In January 1936, Mussolini informed Hitler that he would no longer oppose Austria becoming a German satellite. The alliance of First World War victors to contain Germany was decisively shattered as Rome moved more and more into the orbit of Berlin. Mussolini aspired to dominate the Mediterranean region and to build a great empire in Africa as well—goals that would bring him into conflict with Britain and France. He convinced himself, contrary to the facts, that those two nations had become weak through moral decay, while Italy, under Fascist leadership, had become the greatest power on the Continent. More than anything else, the Duce's policy was based on massive self-deception. The Nazis played skillfully to his vanity, using the one weapon Mussolini could never resist—flattery. Mussolini sent his foreign minister, his son-in-law Galeazzo Ciano, to Berlin in the fall of 1936. There Hitler told the young man that Mussolini was "the first statesman in the world, to whom no one else could even remotely be compared." By November, the flattered Duce was speaking openly of a Rome-Berlin axis. Hitler further smoothed the path toward Italo-German cooperation by ignoring (temporarily) the complaints of the German population in the South Tyrol region of Italy.

Events in Spain also drew Germany and Italy closer together. In July 1936, the Spanish army and a coalition of other right-wing elements led by General Francisco Franco rebelled against the leftist republican government of Spain. Both Hitler and Mussolini threw their support behind Franco. The two dictators provided air and sea transport to bring Franco and his Spanish Foreign Legion from North Africa to Spain. Besides giving money and equipment to the Spanish rebels, Mussolini eventually poured sixty thousand Italian "volunteers" into the conflict. Hitler sent the Kondor Legion, an eleven-squadron air unit detached from the Luftwaffe. The Germans used the Spanish civil war as a testing ground for new weapons and tactics. Both the Führer and the Duce fought to crush what they saw as the seeds of Bolshevism in Spain and to set up a compatible fascist regime there. France at first promised to aid the republic, but soon an Anglo-French Non-Intervention Agreement all but choked off outside assistance for the Loyalist cause. Germany and Italy also signed the agreement but did not let that technicality hinder their operations in Spain. Nazi and Fascist aid was crucial to the ultimate success of Franco's insurrection. The Spanish civil war reinforced international trends that grew out of the invasion of Ethiopia. Hitler and Mussolini were drawn into a closer relationship, and they both grew to feel more strongly than ever that Britain and France were weak and timid. It was in this context that Italy joined the Anti-Comintern Pact in 1937, which Germany and Japan had concluded the previous year. Although this pact, nominally against communism, was far from a binding military alliance, it clearly prefigured the Berlin-Rome-Tokyo axis of World War II.

Hitler Takes the Offensive

With German rearmament now well underway, with Italy converted from an enemy to an ally, and with the British and French backing away from every challenge, Hitler could now assert himself boldly. He summoned his senior foreign policy and military advisors for a special conference at the Reich chancellery on November 5, 1937. Hitler told them that territorial expansion was imperative in the near future to preserve and enlarge the German race. France and Britain would most certainly oppose any expansion of the Reich, so "Germany's problem could only be solved by means of force." It was essential to act quickly. Germany would have to make its bid for power by the period 1943–1945 at the latest. Otherwise its relative strength would decline as its opponents completed their rearmament programs. Favorable international developments, such as the outbreak of civil war in France or an Italo-French conflict, might make it possible to absorb Austria and overthrow Czechoslovakia even sooner. The army ought to be prepared to move as early as 1938. Neither the foreign minister, Baron von Neurath, nor the military chiefs, Generals von Blomberg, von Fritsch, and Göring and Admiral Raeder, voiced any criticism of Hitler's intent to wage aggressive wars of conquest. They merely brought up short-range objections on matters of timing and preparation. Only General Ludwig Beck, the chief of the General Staff, who was not present at this meeting, seriously questioned Hitler's long-term plans for Germany.

Despite the overall willingness of the professional diplomats and military officers to follow him on a course to war, Hitler was not pleased with them. His confidence in his own judgment—and destiny—grew with every crisis, with each time the potentially devastating Western reaction, about which his diplomats and generals had warned, failed to materialize, and each time his determination and boldness paid off with a bloodless victory. As the time for war drew near, Hitler wanted to bolster his control of German diplomacy and military power and rid himself of these timid, slow-moving, old-line professionals. A purge of the army high command and a drastic reshuffling in the foreign service quickly followed. The marriage of General Blomberg, the minister of war, early in 1938 to a former prostitute with a police record scandalized the officer corps. Blomberg was forced to resign, whereupon Hitler abolished the office of minister of war and assumed personal command of the armed forces. He then created a separate high command structure, the Oberkommando der Wehrmacht (OKW), to serve as his personal military staff, with the pliant General Wilhelm Keitel as its senior officer. The Nazis hatched a plot to bring down the commander-in-chief of the army, General Fritsch. They concocted charges of homosexuality against Fritsch, and Hitler dismissed him on that basis. His replacement, General Walther von Brauchitsch, was an officer who supported the Führer without question. In addition, sixteen other senior commanders were dismissed and forty-four others abruptly transferred.

The army offered no serious resistance to this purge. The expansion program that brought the army from a mere hundred thousand men to well over half a million had destroyed the former homogeneity and inner cohesion of the officer corps. Hitler was widely popular among the younger officers, and he could always find men to do his bidding, both in the influx of new recruits and in some careerist elements among the veteran commanders. The military leaders were also aware that his series of foreign policy successes had made the Führer more popular than ever among the German people. Opposing his will would have been highly difficult at best. Moreover, despite his early promise to allow the Reichswehr a monopoly of military power, Hitler was already creating a counterweight to the army in the form of Himmler's heavily armed SS detachments, some of which would soon develop into full-scale military units, the infamous Waffen SS divisions. Although some sections of the military, especially the intelligence office (the Abwehr), continued to harbor anti-Nazi sentiment, Hitler had largely broken the independence of the armed services.

A thorough shake-up at the Foreign Office paralleled these events in the army command. Hitler replaced Foreign Minister von Neurath with a Nazi, Joachim von Ribbentrop, who had impressed the Führer by negotiating the Anglo-German Naval Agreement of 1935. High-ranking non-Nazi career diplomats were recalled from their posts in Tokyo, Rome, and Vienna. In tightening his grip on Germany's diplomatic and armed services, Hitler was freeing himself from the last vestiges of control by those conservative allies who had arranged his appointment as chancellor in 1933, and he was preparing to dismantle the Versailles system completely.

As Hitler's power grew, he eased out old-line conservatives from controlling positions in the economy. Hjalmar Schacht lost his post as minister of economic affairs to a loyal Nazi, Walther Funk. Two other committed Nazis, Richard Darré and Herbert Backe, controlled agriculture. Göring's Four Year Plan operations and his Reichswerke Hermann Göring (the world's largest industrial conglomerate) gave Hitler's corpulent minion enormous power over the German economy. The Führer had no patience with professional economists who advised a slowdown in the rearmament drive and the reintegration of Germany into the global economy. Industrial leaders who worried that the breakneck pace of rearmament might ultimately be bad for business were simply steamrolled by the Führer's directives. No important decision on economic matters (like the allocation of scarce steel supplies) could be taken without Hitler's approval.

Subverting Austria

Austria was Hitler's first victim. He had written in *Mein Kampf*, "German-Austria must return to the great German motherland. . . . One blood demands one Reich." In 1934, the threat of Italian intervention had undermined the Nazi coup in Vienna; now the Duce had given Hitler a free hand in Austria. Support for union with Germany began to grow among some Austrians. After losing Mussolini's patronage, Austrian chancellor Kurt Schuschnigg still hoped to preserve his country's independence by rallying a broad coalition of support while suppressing the most radical of the Austro-Nazis. He was unwilling, however, to lift restrictive measures against labor unions and the socialists. His tactics failed. In the vain hope of dividing the Austrian Nazis among themselves, the chancellor appointed one of their apparently more moderate spokesmen, Artur Seyss-Inquart, to his cabinet. Hitler then pressured Schuschnigg to make a series of concessions to Seyss-Inquart on coordinating

German Expansion without War, 1933–1939

Vienna's policy with that of Berlin. These concessions gravely compromised Austria's sovereignty. Even worse treatment awaited Schuschnigg when he visited Hitler in January 1938 at Berchtesgaden, where the Führer gave the unfortunate Austrian leader a three-hour berating and forced him to agree to even more sweeping concessions, including the appointment of Seyss-Inquart as minister of the interior, a position that controlled the Austrian police.

Schuschnigg made one last desperate attempt to fend off the subversion of Austria. On March 9, he announced a nationwide plebiscite on the question of Austria's future, to be held in four days. The framing of the ballot proposal and the staffing of election boards virtually guaranteed a favorable vote for Schuschnigg. He hoped that a resounding rejection of an *Anschluss* at the polls would make it too embarrassing politically for Hitler to take Austria by force. The Führer responded by ordering the army to prepare an invasion and by unleashing the Austrian Nazis to do their worst. This time Mussolini made no objection.

The intense pressure forced Schuschnigg to cancel the plebiscite. Hitler next demanded Schuschnigg's replacement as chancellor by Seyss-Inquart, but even that capitulation did not satisfy the Führer. Göring thereupon drafted a telegram for Seyss-Inquart to send requesting the German army to restore order in Austria. German troops crossed the border on the morning of March 12, 1938. Later that day, Hitler drove across the frontier to his former hometown of Linz, where he received a tumultuous reception. Austria was formally incorporated into the Reich the following day. A great many Austrians found it expedient to become enthusiastic supporters of their new Führer's agenda. Hitler had destroyed yet another part of the Versailles system and at the same time had taken a further step in his plan for racial expansion. Germany grew overnight by the addition of another six and a half million subjects to a nation of eighty million people. Beyond its demographic significance, the incorporation of Austria also had great strategic impact. Suddenly German power was brought to bear directly on the borders of Hungary and Yugoslavia, while the western defenses of Czechoslovakia were outflanked to the south.

Destroying Czechoslovakia

Hitler next turned against Czechoslovakia. Like so many Austro-Germans, he had nurtured a deep-seated prejudice against Czechs from childhood. The Czechoslovak state, in existence only since 1918, was doubly damned in Hitler's view. It was a despised liberal-democratic regime, and it was the bulwark of the French alliance system in Eastern Europe. The Führer needed to destroy the Czech state as a prerequisite to conquering *Lebensraum* at the expense of Poland and the USSR. To undermine Czechoslovakia, Hitler skillfully exploited ethnic frictions within that multinational state. The country included over seven million Czechs, five million Slovaks (some of whom chafed under Czech leadership), 750,000 Magyars (Hungarians), 500,000 Ruthenians, 90,000 Poles, and over three million Germans who lived along the western border of the state in the Sudetenland.

The Czech and Slovak majority had not treated the German minority badly. Yet the Depression was particularly severe among the Sudeten Germans, and they complained that the Czech-dominated civil service discriminated against them. Such grievances, real and imagined, stimulated the growth of a Sudeten Nazi party (or Sudeten German Party) under the leadership of Konrad Henlein. Hitler was not genuinely concerned for the welfare of the Sudeten Germans. For him they were merely an instrument that he could manipulate to destroy the Czech state. Henlein and his fellow Nazis did nothing to improve the situation of the Sudeten Germans. Rather, they strove to inflame relations between the German minority and their Czech compatriots. The last thing Hitler wanted was a resolution of these ethnic conflicts. The Führer and Henlein agreed that in dealing with the Czech authorities, "we must always demand so much that we can never be satisfied." The object was to create a crisis so severe that it would require intervention by Germany.

Henlein hurled a set of audacious demands, known as the Karlsbad Program, at the Prague government in April 1938. The list included a pro-German foreign policy, local autonomy for German-speaking areas, compensation for German victims of alleged Czech discrimination, and full freedom for Nazi propaganda and activity in Czechoslovakia. Although the Czech government was willing to meet the German minority more than halfway, no compromise could satisfy the Sudeten Nazis or their master in Berlin. Fear of war swept Europe as German pressure mounted against Czechoslovakia in a campaign so like the recent one leading to Austria's downfall. In late May, the Czechs partially mobilized their forces while the British, French, and Soviet governments warned that they would not stand idle in the face of German aggression. Hitler's ambition was temporarily thwarted, but on May 30 he informed his military commanders that "it is my unalterable decision to smash Czechoslovakia by military action in the near future." While Czech president Edvard Beneš emerged from the May crisis even more determined to oppose Hitler's designs, the Western powers had been severely frightened by their own show of resistance. The British resolved not to risk war again for the sake of Czechoslovakia. French prime minister Edouard Daladier warned his British allies that more was at stake than just the security of a medium-size ally—that Hitler sought "the domination of the Continent in comparison with which the ambitions of Napoleon were feeble." London would not listen. Prime Minister Neville Chamberlain was willing to accept virtually any solution to the Sudetenland question, provided the Germans did not impose it on Czechoslovakia by force.

The situation threatened to explode again in September when serious rioting erupted in the Sudetenland. Czech authorities responded by imposing martial law on the region, whereupon Henlein fled to Germany to instigate border raids by Sudeten Nazi paramilitary forces. At this perilous moment, Chamberlain decided to intervene personally, employing face-to-face diplomacy with Hitler to avert war. He flew to Germany three times in September 1938, in frantic attempts to give the Sudetenland to the Führer lest he take it by force. The British prime minister and the French premier determined to impose any required territorial concessions on Czech president Beneš so that the Western powers could avoid the prospect of war in Eastern Europe.

The negotiations with Hitler were especially difficult because he did not want to acquire the Sudetenland peacefully. The supposed tribulations of the German minority there had never been more than a pretext for the Führer. He wanted war—not a second world war, but a short, localized conflict that would gain another victory for him and result in the complete destruction of the Czech state. Hitler constantly raised his demands, repeatedly telling the exasperated prime minister that what he and Henlein had previously insisted upon was no longer enough. For a while even Chamberlain despaired of maintaining the peace. Air-raid procedures were instituted in London, and French troops began to man their border fortifications. Fearing a German attack, authorities distributed gas masks to the people of London, while a third of Parisians fled their capital. At the last moment, however, pressure from the Western leaders as well as Mussolini persuaded Hitler to agree to a four-power conference on the Czech crisis.

Hitler, Mussolini, Chamberlain, and Daladier met in Munich on September 29 to decide the fate of Czechoslovakia. Neither the Czechs nor the Russians, who also had a great stake in the security of Eastern Europe, were allowed to attend the conference. Their participation would have only upset the four-power consensus to partition Czechoslovakia.

British prime minister Neville Chamberlain, French premier Edouard Daladier, Hitler, Mussolini, and Italian foreign minister Galeazzo Ciano at the Munich Conference, September 30, 1938.
Source: Wikimedia Commons

Chamberlain exhibited his lack of concern for Czech rights when he told the House of Commons one day prior to the meeting, "How horrible, fantastic, incredible it is that we should be digging trenches and trying on gas masks here because of a quarrel in a far-away country between people of whom we know nothing."

At Munich, the four leaders agreed to transfer the Sudetenland from Czechoslovakia to the Reich and to guarantee the independence of the remainder of Czechoslovakia. Some portions of the Sudetenland, where ethnic Germans were not a majority, were supposed to have plebiscites, but they were never held, as German troops quickly occupied the entire province. In the name of national self-determination and peace, some 2,825,000 Germans and 800,000 Czechs were brought under Hitler's control. Far from expressing his delight, the Führer complained in private that Chamberlain had stolen his war and spoiled his chance for a triumphal entry into Prague. Oddly, it was the British prime minister who left Munich in an exultant mood. He had persuaded Hitler to sign an Anglo-German agreement on September 30 pledging that both powers would use diplomatic rather than military means to settle any further disputes. Chamberlain landed in England amid cheering crowds, to whom he waved the agreement and announced, "I believe it is peace for our time."

Though he was petulant over losing the opportunity to crush Czechoslovakia in combat, Hitler had won still another easy victory. Once again, his intuition that the Western leaders would do almost anything to avoid war had proven correct. Once more, the fears of his generals, that the undeniably stronger Anglo-French forces would call Hitler's bluff and crush Germany, proved baseless. In the wake of Munich, the strategic situation shifted further in Germany's favor. Before 1937, a German attack on Czechoslovakia could only have come through the well-prepared Czech defense system in the Bohemian mountains. After the incorporation of Austria into the Reich, German troops could attack south-central Czechoslovakia, thus partially outflanking the Czech defenses. Nonetheless, German generals still could not be certain of victory in battle against the Czechs' thirty-five well-equipped divisions. Any substantial aid rendered by Prague's allies, France and Russia, would have made the situation hopeless for Germany. All that changed after Munich. The defensive bulwark of the Sudetenland was now lost. Czechoslovakia's alliances were exposed as just so many scraps of worthless paper. The Czechs retained a powerful army, but its morale, along with that of the civil government, plummeted.

Hitler was anxious to exploit this weakness to eliminate what was left of Czechoslovakia. Within only a few days after the Munich Conference, he was already making plans for military action against the Czechs. These preparations were unnecessary, however, for Czechoslovakia soon collapsed under the pressure of the political campaign that Germany waged against it. Hitler encouraged the separatist movement within the Slovak population. Prodded by the Nazis, Slovak leader, Father Josef Tiso, proclaimed Slovakian independence. Czechoslovakia seemed about to self-destruct. During this new crisis, Göring told Czech president Emil Hácha, who had replaced Beneš, that if he did not formally request a German protectorate over Bohemia and Moravia, the heartland of Czechoslovakia, the Luftwaffe would obliterate Prague from the air. Deserted by its allies and with civil war brewing, the Czech regime could resist no longer. German troops marched into Prague unopposed on March 15, 1939. The following day Bohemia and Moravia became Reich protectorates under the control of Konstantin von Neurath. Slovakia became a German satellite.

Hitler also encouraged Poland and Hungary to act on their long-standing grievances against Czechoslovakia. The Poles moved into the disputed Teschen region while Hungarian forces seized the Carpatho-Ukraine. Czechoslovakia disappeared from the map. German authorities arrested many Czech political leaders, intellectuals, and academics, and they closed the universities. The Czechs did not experience the worst repression that was soon to befall the Poles and Russians, however, because the Reich needed to keep Czech industry humming in its service. Hitler had bested the Western leaders, improved his geostrategic position for further conquests, acquired the valuable Skoda arms complex, and, in disarming the Czech army, secured enough weaponry for ten additional Wehrmacht divisions.

The German occupation of Prague finally shook the Western leaders from their lethargy. Hitler had brazenly violated his pledge to respect what remained of Czechoslovakia, and in absorbing areas where the population was preponderantly Czech, he was clearly not motivated by any legitimate desire to protect fellow Germans. It was now hard to avoid the conclusion that Hitler sought not only some justifiable rectifications in the Versailles system but actual domination of the Continent. Britain had already reversed its interwar policy of avoiding military commitments in Europe in February 1939 when it promised France "immediate co-operation in the event of a threat to her vital interests from whatever quarter." Then, after the Germans moved into Prague, Britain and France issued guarantees of support to several potential East European victims of Nazi aggression—Poland, Greece, Romania, and Turkey. The British and French knew that they could not successfully defend these remote countries against German attack, but they hoped that the threat of a two-front war, which their guarantees implied, would be sufficient to deter Hitler from continued aggression. They completely misunderstood Hitler, believing that no *rational* person would want to start another world war.

Nothing could have been further from the truth. The Führer was convinced that when he manufactured the next crisis, neither of the Western powers would actually fight. The fate of Prague, he thought, had demonstrated the value of their guarantees. He intended to fight France and Great Britain, but at times of his own choosing, after he had destroyed the French alliance system in Eastern Europe. A few days after occupying Prague, the Germans pressured Lithuania to cede the long-disputed Memel area to them. Then Mussolini took the offensive again. On March 24, 1939, the Duce's troops landed in Albania. That impoverished Adriatic country had been a virtual satellite of Italy for some time, but Mussolini believed that Italy must continue to expand abroad or be eclipsed by the growth of Nazi Germany. Albania would provide a springboard for the projected invasion of Greece and a confrontation with British power in the Mediterranean. This comic-opera invasion was so badly bungled that, despite the absence of any real opposition, one Italian diplomat lamented, "If only the Albanians had possessed a well-armed fire brigade, they could have driven us back into the Adriatic."[5] The state-controlled Italian press suppressed the embarrassing details of this "glorious victory."

The pathetic Italian victory over Albania could not alter the fact that Rome was progressively losing its independence in foreign affairs and falling under the domination of Berlin. Reichsbank president Hjalmar Schacht had largely succeeded in subordinating the Italian economy to serve German needs. Mussolini unwittingly furthered this process by concluding a formal alliance with Hitler, the Pact of Steel, on May 22, 1939. Without receiving any substantial benefit for Italy, Mussolini promised to aid Hitler with all his forces if Germany were involved in war. The treaty contained no escape clauses limiting its duration or making an exception for aggressive warfare. The Duce had bound his fate and that of his nation to the destiny of a megalomaniac whose lust for conquest knew no limits. Mussolini seems to have accepted this tragic alliance merely to save face. The Germans had no illusions about Italian military power, but they hoped that the specter of an apparently powerful Rome-

Berlin alliance would be enough to intimidate England and France into dishonoring their East European commitments. For the same reason, Hitler also tried to negotiate a similar alliance with Japan, already his partner in the Anti-Comintern Pact. Berlin and Tokyo could not come to terms, however, because the Japanese wanted a military pact aimed against the Soviet Union, which carried no hint of hostility toward Great Britain, while the Germans desired precisely the reverse. Yet even without a German-Japanese alliance, Hitler was convinced that the British were too timid to take any effective action against him.

Smashing Poland

In carrying out his quest for *Lebensraum*, Hitler's next victim was Poland. He told his military commanders on May 23, 1939, "Further successes cannot be achieved without bloodshed. . . . It is a matter of expanding our living space in the east. . . . There is therefore no question of sparing Poland, and the decision remains to attack Poland at the first suitable opportunity. . . . There will be war."[6] To undermine Poland, Hitler seized on the issues of Danzig, a free German city run under League of Nations auspices, and the Polish Corridor that separated East Prussia from the rest of Germany. Once again, he treated the world to a barrage of anguished complaints about Polish mistreatment of its German minority and the tragedy of their separation from their fatherland. Hitler demanded Danzig and an extraterritorial roadway to East Prussia across the corridor. The real purpose of these claims, however, was to destabilize Poland in preparation for its destruction. Unlike the Czechs, though, the Polish regime of Colonel Josef Beck was determined not to give in to Hitler.

The Poles relied on the strength of their own large army and on the Anglo-French guarantee. (It is a grim irony of interwar diplomacy that the Allies callously sacrificed Czechoslovakia, the only democratic government in eastern Europe, to Nazi aggression and then issued a guarantee of support to an authoritarian Polish regime that had joined in destroying the Czech state.) If the Poles would not capitulate, war was the only alternative for the Führer. At the beginning of April, he ordered the army to prepare for an invasion of Poland by September 1, 1939. To heighten the pressure on Warsaw and on London, he renounced the nonaggression pact of 1934 with Poland and the 1935 Anglo-German naval convention. Europe was about to descend into a second great conflagration that would dwarf even the monumental destructiveness of the First World War.

Why Appeasement?

British and French statesmen had acquiesced to Hitler's demands on almost every occasion. Between 1933 and 1939, they had permitted the transformation of Germany from a virtually disarmed state to a mighty nation possessing, to outside appearances at least, one of the most powerful armed forces in the world. This policy of appeasement has been widely criticized since the outbreak of World War II. Writing in 1948, Winston Churchill lamented, "How easily the tragedy of the Second World War could have been prevented; how the malice of the wicked was reinforced by the weakness of the virtuous. . . . It was a simple policy to keep Germany disarmed and the victors adequately armed for thirty years, and in the meanwhile, even if a reconciliation could not be made with Germany, to build ever more strongly a true League of Nations capable of making sure that treaties were kept or changed only by discussion and agreement."[7] This view does not do justice to the British, French, and American political leaders of the 1930s. Appeasement may well have been a mistaken policy, especially after 1937, but the alternatives were not as simple, easy, and obvious as Churchill made them seem in retrospect.

For the British (less so for the French), appeasement was, first, a moral policy, pursued not out of fear but because it seemed the right thing to do. Wilsonian liberal and nationalist principles had been violated in the Versailles settlement. The German residents of Austria, the Sudetenland, Memel, Danzig, and Silesia obviously had not been accorded the right of self-determination. Germany was virtually defenseless, while France was heavily armed. The Reich was split in two by an alien corridor. The British policy of appeasement began in the 1920s to meet these presumably justified German grievances.

Beyond morality, there was also an argument for appeasement on practical grounds. As the largest and most industrious population in central Europe, the Germans could not be held in subjection indefinitely. Many were convinced, Prime Minister Chamberlain among them, that Germany would inevitably reassume its position of dominance (conceived primarily in economic terms) in central and eastern Europe. Acquiescing in these developments, rather than vainly opposing them, seemed the more prudent course in London. Moreover, preserving the artificial postwar dominance of France on the Continent, at Germany's expense, was not in the best interests of England either. The achievement of a continental balance, which implied the strengthening of Germany and perhaps even the weakening of France, seemed the most sensible policy for Great Britain.

Sympathy for Nazism was never a serious basis for appeasement in the Western states. Even though fascist-style movements, like Oswald Mosley's English Blackshirts, sprang up in all the democracies, they remained isolated fringe groups with no impact on national policy. However, the repulsiveness of the Nazi regime did not curtail British efforts to seek an accommodation with Germany. Doubtless, many in England regretted that they had not freely given to democratic Weimar leaders in the 1920s those concessions that Hitler now extorted from them. Yet the British hoped that by meeting Germany's seemingly legitimate grievances, Hitler would be tamed or perhaps even replaced by more moderate political leaders. The Führer certainly knew how to play to such sentiments in London. He masked every aggressive thrust with diatribes against the inconsistencies and inequities of the Versailles settlement. Each time Hitler leveled a new ultimatum, he assured the Western powers that it was his last demand. Many Britons and Americans did not understand until it was too late that Hitler was never interested in a just accommodation of German grievances. They were only issues to exploit in his drive to dominate Europe.

Even though the crudely violent Nazi regime appalled many in the West, conservatives could justify the repression on anticommunist grounds. Appeasement took place during the Great Depression, a time when millions of people were out of work in the democracies. A widespread fear of revolution gripped the propertied classes. Hitler's methods may have been brutal, but they achieved dramatic results. He had physically liquidated the KPD, the largest communist party outside of the Soviet Union. As late as 1938, such British dignitaries as Lord Halifax and Sir Horace Wilson could openly praise the Führer for defending Western civilization from Bolshevism. Such thinking strongly influenced Britain's response to the Spanish civil war.

In parallel with the clash between the legitimate government in Madrid and the military rebels under Franco, a second struggle was taking place—an anarchist revolution. Thousands of landless peasants were taking over the vast estates of Spain and dividing them into anarchist communes. Just as bad in the eyes of Western conservatives, the republic was receiving outside aid from the USSR. Soviet military advisors and political commissars infested Loyalist-held areas. Support for the republic, even though it was a legitimate, democratic government under attack by Nazi- and Fascist-backed rebels, was, according to this line of reasoning, simply playing into Stalin's hands. Harold Nicolson, a respected British diplomat, described the Republican regime as "a mere Kerensky government at the mercy of an armed proletariat."[8] The Spanish civil war was, in one sense, a surrogate war between fascism and democracy, which the Western powers lost by default—in no small part because of their fear of communism.

Nazi outrages against German Jews did not unite people in the democracies against Berlin either. Outside of Jewish communities abroad, persecution of German Jews did not arouse enough public indignation in the West to alter foreign policy in London, Paris, or Washington. Part of the explanation for this lack of response was the broad current of anti-Semitism that pervaded not just the Third Reich but Western society as a whole. British ambassador Sir Horace Rumbold once remarked how much he was "appalled by the number of Jews" in Berlin. In the United States at this time, violence, including lynchings, against blacks, Jews, and other minority groups occurred frequently. The Nazi regime was not discredited abroad by a tidal wave of moral revulsion as it should have been because its racist ideas were at least partly shared in the democracies. Beyond that, the worst atrocity stories coming out of Germany were often dismissed as Jewish propaganda.

The democratic states also experienced a severe crisis of self-doubt in the 1930s, which further inhibited them from taking a resolute stand against Nazi aggression. The Great Depression triggered the crisis. Twelve million men were unemployed in the United States, while one in every four Britons was on welfare. American industrial production fell by 47 percent; French production declined by 24 percent. The Depression injured more than just the Western economies; it wounded the very spirit of the democracies. Everywhere, dazed, despondent men stood in long breadlines or huddled in soup kitchens. Executives who had managed large corporations only a year before now found themselves selling five-cent apples on the street corner. Something seemed to have gone wrong with the capitalist, liberal, democratic system. In contrast, the state-controlled presses in Germany, Italy, and Soviet Russia proclaimed that the Führer, the Duce, and the Vozhd had solved all economic problems and there was no depression there. In the West, a few people hoped, while many more feared, that liberal democracy would not survive—that totalitarianism of the left or the right was the wave of the future. The bright confidence and easy self-assurance of the victorious Allies of 1919 had dissipated. Nagging doubts about the prospects of their economies and the viability of their form of government hindered the Western societies as they faced the brutal challenges of the fascist dictators.

Ultimately it was the fear of war, more than anticommunism or racism or self-doubt, that provided the most powerful incentive for appeasement in the West. The painful memory of the staggering sacrifices of lives and treasure exacted during the Great War hung like a pall over the statesmen and the people alike. Some revisionist historians were arguing that it had all been a mistake, an error of judgment, a waste. Beyond historical questions, it also appeared that the recent development of weapons of mass destruction (long-range bombers, improved poison gases, etc.) had made war no longer acceptable as a means of settling international disputes. Perhaps most Englishmen would not have gone as far as the Oxford Union Society debaters who voted in 1933 that they would not, under any circumstances, take up arms for king or country, but certainly most Britons, Frenchmen, and Americans would have supported almost any policy likely to keep them out of another major war. Western statesmen therefore made every effort to satisfy the belligerent dictators and, in a crisis, even sacrificed small, faraway countries—an Abyssinia or a Czechoslovakia—because the alternative was too horrible to contemplate. The experience in the First World War had been at least as traumatic for the Germans as for their Western opponents. Yet that experience seemed to produce different attitudes in Berlin than those harbored in Paris and London. Most Germans did not want another world war, but many of them longed to reverse their 1918 defeat. Militarism and mass violence had not been discredited in Germany as it had been in France.[9]

By the time of Munich, it was becoming clear to many Britons that Hitler wanted considerably more than simple justice for Germany. Now, however, Britain and France were no longer dealing with a weak Weimar Germany but instead with an apparently well-armed and powerful Nazi regime. The Nazis created the illusion of overwhelming strength by claiming to have more troops and weapons than they actually possessed. The Western countries obligingly fell into the trap by consistently overestimating German power. For example, during the Rhineland crisis of 1936, French general Maurice Gamelin claimed that the German army had 120 divisions when in fact it had only 30.[10] This vast overestimation of German strength provided Western leaders with an excuse to bow before threats of violence and acquiesce to naked aggression. In 1938 and 1939, appeasement had become a policy of retreating before apparently superior force in order to avoid war and gain time for rearmament.

Great Britain's military position was complicated immensely by the difficulties of protecting its worldwide empire. Beyond the British Isles themselves, royal forces had to defend such widely scattered holdings as Gibraltar, Malta, and Suez in the Mediterranean, much of Africa, India, the Malay Peninsula, and even parts of the south China coast. It had been fairly easy to conquer a vast empire in the eighteenth and nineteenth centuries against relatively light native opposition. Defending it was quite another matter, especially given the weakened condition in which England had emerged from the First World War.

Any aggressive move by Germany, Italy, or Japan threatened some British outpost directly or menaced its line of communications and supply. No wonder the chiefs of staff stood solidly behind appeasement in December 1937 when they informed the cabinet, "We cannot . . . exaggerate the importance, from the point of view of Imperial defense, of any political or international action that can be taken to reduce the number of our potential enemies or to gain the support of potential allies." The Dominion governments favored appeasement, too. The Canadians, Australians, New Zealanders, and South Africans were reluctant to send their young men back to the European killing grounds for a second time within twenty years.

Despite England's Versailles and Locarno obligations and its extensive colonial commitments, its military forces, especially the army, had not been adequately maintained. British military planning and spending in the 1920s was governed by the assumption, laid down by the cabinet in 1919, that there would be no major war in Europe for the next ten years. The government reconfirmed this ten-year rule on an indefinitely continuing basis in 1928. It was not rescinded until 1932 in response to Japanese aggression in Manchuria. During this period, defense expenditures were concentrated on the Royal Navy. The British strove to maintain a main fleet as strong as any other navy in the world—a fleet that could be dispatched anywhere and still leave enough ships in home waters to defend against the next strongest European fleet (always assuming that the powerful US Navy would not be an opponent). Building and maintaining such a mighty fleet left few funds for the rest of the armed forces. Between 1923 and 1933, the army received less than 10 percent of the annual arms budgets. Even if Chamberlain had wanted to use force to block German annexation of Austria or Czechoslovakia, which he did not, he could not have found sufficient British troops to defend their frontiers.

Great Britain began a rearmament program in the early 1930s, but its progress was hindered by the Depression and by British forecasts of the sort of war England might have to fight in the near future. Though aware of the growing menace in Europe and the Far East, Treasury officials feared that excessive levels of military spending would jeopardize the nation's precarious recovery from the Depression. In consequence, as late as 1938 the British were still spending only 8 percent of their gross national product on arms, whereas the figures for Germany and Japan were 22 and 17.4 percent, respectively. British planners also assumed that a new conflict with Germany would involve a long struggle of attrition like the Great War. In that case, England's economic strength would be its greatest weapon, and it would have been foolish to upset that economic stability with overly ambitious military expenditures. The Nazis, who carried through just such a crash rearmament program, operated under a very different set of assumptions. They planned for a short war, or series of wars, in which aggregate strength at the outset, rather than economic staying power, would be decisive. Hitler did not worry about the long-term impact of his massive arms buildup on the German economy since he always intended to exploit the conquered nations to support his home front. By 1938, the progress of German rearmament and the belligerence of Hitler's foreign policy forced the British to abandon their more cautious approach and launch a full-scale arms procurement program. The time lag involved in designing new weapons, retooling factories, and training critically needed skilled labor meant that British statesmen were still constrained to play for time even though they were rapidly shedding their illusions about Nazi aims.

Widely believed but ill-founded claims about the potential of strategic bombing also fostered appeasement in Great Britain. The airplane had played a relatively unimportant, if highly romanticized, role in the First World War. Subsequently, however, some military theorists, most notably Giulio Douhet in Italy, Hugh Trenchard in England, and Billy Mitchell in America, came to regard strategic bombing as the decisive weapon in a future war. These men believed that no effective defense was possible against the long-range heavy bomber and that strategic bombing could both cripple the industrial capacity of an enemy nation as well as break the will to resist of its civilian population. The specter of massive bombing raids obliterating London and Paris obsessed Western statesmen. Advocates of strategic bombing pointed to the apparent lessons of the Spanish civil war, especially the devastating bombing of Guernica by planes of the German Kondor Legion, as well as to the terrifying Japanese bombing of Chinese cities. "The fear of ferociously destructive air raids," historian Peter Fritzsche asserts, "sat as deeply in the bones of Europeans in the 1930s as the fear of nuclear attack would during the Cold War a generation later."[11]

Hitler took full advantage of the widespread fear of this new and terrible form of warfare. He and Göring deliberately created the impression that the Luftwaffe could destroy the cities of Europe at will, even though German air power was developed as a tactical support force for the army and had little real strategic capability. By 1938, British military thinking had evolved away from the fatalism implicit in the strategic bombing doctrine. Some RAF commanders had begun to suspect that the bomber could indeed be stopped. In that year, the Treasury authorized funds for a thousand of the new Hurricane interceptors. Work also began on constructing a radar network and developing an integrated air defense command. But it would take time to complete these defensive measures. Meanwhile, all of England seemed open to destruction from the skies—a powerful argument for buying time through continued appeasement.

The French, too, drifted toward a policy of appeasement, although they did not have the barrier of the English Channel protecting them from the Reich, and though most French political and military leaders had fewer illusions than their British counterparts about the long-term prospects for peace with Germany. When the Nazis came to power in Berlin, it seemed for a while that the French response would be vigorous indeed. Foreign Minister Louis Barthou and veteran diplomat Alexis Léger worked to strengthen France's Eastern European alliance system and forge new links with Italy and Soviet Russia, a combination that would have encircled the Reich. After the assassination of Barthou in October 1934, however, French foreign policy faltered in dealing with Hitler.

The reasons for French paralysis in the face of a growing Nazi menace are complex. The political structure of the Third Republic was partly at fault. Under the pressure of constant foreign policy and economic crises, government cabinets rose and fell with alarming frequency. Some lasted less than a month. The combination of a fragmented electorate and a multiparty system meant that only fragile coalition governments were possible. Moreover, electoral disarray reflected profound ideological divisions within the nation. On the right, quasi-fascist groups and ultranationalist organizations openly repudiated the republic. Serious antirepublican rioting, which erupted in Paris on February 6, 1934, led many Frenchmen on the left to fear an imminent right-wing coup. At the opposite political extreme, the French Communist Party denounced liberal democracy and even national defense as bourgeois snares to entrap the working class. Nationwide strikes in May and June of 1936 that led to the occupation of numerous factories by their workers convinced many conservatives that the real danger facing France was not Hitler but social revolution. France lacked national unity when confronted by the challenge of German expansionism.

France was clearly the strongest country in Europe when Hitler became chancellor of the Reich, but a national crisis of confidence paralyzed French will to use that power until it was too late. Memories of the Great War haunted France in the 1930s. Historian Eugen Weber argues that for France, "the 1930s begin in August 1914. For fifty-one months thereafter, 1,000 Frenchmen were killed day after day, nearly 1 of every 5 men mobilized, 10.5 percent of the country's active male population."[12] The years 1935 to 1939 have been called the "hollow years," when the annual draft class of young men was only half its usual size because of the carnage twenty years before. The French were only too well aware of how narrowly they had avoided defeat in 1918 and how crucial Allied assistance had been in the process. Nor could they ignore the statistical reality of Germany's significantly larger population and industrial base. Many Frenchmen believed that another war with Germany was inevitable; few had any confidence that it could be won without considerable outside help.

French military plans reflected this pessimism. The generals expected the next war to begin with a German assault. They anticipated that French forces would remain on the defensive for two years while France and its allies built up an overwhelming superiority of men and equipment before launching their own offensive against Germany. The centerpiece of this defensive strategy was the Maginot Line, a massive system of powerful concrete and steel fortifications protecting the Franco-German border, from Switzerland in the south to Luxembourg in the north. Heavy artillery in the line was shielded in bombproof casements and manned by troops living deep in underground bunkers. The German onslaught, it was hoped, would be broken on the impregnable Maginot Line while France mobilized its army, built up matériel, and awaited help from its allies. The French also belatedly began to strengthen their armed forces, raising the term of service for draftees from one to two years in 1935. Military spending increased from 12.8 billion francs in 1935 to 93.7 billion in 1939.

Allies were as important as fortifications in French military planning. Paris negotiated pacts with Poland, Czechoslovakia, Romania, and Yugoslavia to threaten the Germans with the possibility of a two-front war if they attacked France. The French also hoped that Italy would play a significant role in the anti-Hitler coalition, but Mussolini's venture in Ethiopia undercut that prospect. Great Britain held the central position in the projected French alliance system. England and its empire could supply the additional manpower and resources needed to defeat Germany. For that reason, France had sought a binding mutual security pact with London ever since 1919. The British, however, had been reluctant to make that commitment until the German annexation of Czechoslovakia finally persuaded them to do so at the beginning of 1939. Even then the strategic position of France was weak compared to what it had been in 1914. Then, Italy and Imperial Russia had been allies of France—and subsequently the United States had joined the French war effort. Now, Mussolini's Italy was bound to the Third Reich, and in August 1939 the USSR became a quasi-ally of Nazi Germany as well. France had only a fickle British partner and nothing more than verbal support from America.

Reliance on static defensive fortifications and on foreign allies betrayed the underlying French lack of confidence in their own ability to deal with the growing Nazi threat. French leaders anticipated German rearmament, remilitarization of the Rhineland, and the *Anschluss*—and they determined in advance not to oppose any of these measures by force. It was easy to rationalize their inaction. They believed that they could not move against Hitler without British support, which of course was not forthcoming. French and British appeasement policies reinforced each other. Each side used the other's reluctance to rationalize its own inaction. French generals also supported appeasement by constantly overestimating German military strength. During the Rhineland crisis, the army told the cabinet that they might face as many as three hundred thousand German troops on the Rhine, giving Germany a two-to-one advantage. In reality, only a token force marched into the Rhineland, one that the French army could have easily overwhelmed.

Hitler's challenges to France's East European partners exposed the hollowness of the French alliance system. The French had always assumed that Germany would attack them first. The treaties with Poland, Romania, Czechoslovakia, and Yugoslavia were to draw them into war in support of France. But the Führer chose to strike eastward first. Paris never intended to fight in support of its client states in eastern Europe. The French army had neither the plans nor the immediate tactical capability to send troops to Eastern Europe. It was not even prepared to launch a major assault into the Rhineland to relieve pressure on the eastern front should the Germans attack Czechoslovakia or Poland. The whole point of the alliance system was to create the appearance of a mighty political-military combination that would deter German violations of the Versailles settlement and thereby prevent war. In Hitler, however, the French faced a German leader who not only did not fear war but actively sought it. Under this circumstance, the alliances with Eastern European states were liabilities rather than assets.

It seemed for a while in 1936–1937 that France might take a more determined stand against Nazi Germany. The Popular Front government of Premier Leon Blum, a coalition of liberals and moderate socialists with communist support, came to power on an avowedly antifascist platform. A peculiar reversal had occurred in French politics. The right wing, normally the champion of military prowess and a strong foreign policy, had accepted appeasement of Italy and Germany. They feared that war against the fascist dictatorships would create the conditions for widespread European revolution, just as had happened in 1917–1920. In contrast, the left, which was normally pacifist and antimilitarist, now supported rearmament and an antifascist policy both at home and abroad. The Blum government took office having pledged to strengthen French defenses, to create a more powerful alliance—including the USSR—for containing German aggression, to revitalize the economy, and to improve the lot of the workingman through moderate reform. Premier Blum hoped to establish a French New Deal, but he possessed neither the electoral mandate nor the broad constitutional powers enjoyed by President Roosevelt. The socialist premier was constrained on one side by anxious conservatives and moderates who feared that the Popular Front presaged a full-scale revolution and on the other side by the radical wing of his own Socialist Party who expected their victory at the polls to result in sweeping socioeconomic changes. Blum himself worried about the prospect of civil war in France.

The Spanish civil war was the most explosive foreign policy issue facing the Popular Front. Blum intended to support the loyalist republican forces. Opposition from Britain, his Radical Party coalition partners, and the professional diplomats of the Quai d'Orsay soon eroded the premier's resolve to help the besieged Madrid government. Blum bowed to this pressure and reluctantly accepted the policy of nonintervention. Even he feared that too deep an involvement in Spain might well draw France into war with Germany. So France, governed by an antifascist Popular Front government, watched helplessly while Mussolini and Hitler provided the critical margin of assistance needed to assure the triumph of a right-wing, fascist-supported dictatorship in Spain.

Beyond the Spanish issue, the Popular Front regime was not successful in its attempts to build a strong containment ring around the Third Reich. Blum was not able to secure firmer commitments for French security from Great Britain, nor was he able to translate a previously signed Franco-Soviet pact into an effective military alliance. In addition, Belgium defected from the French security system in March 1936, opting for neutrality. They feared that, with Europe increasingly aligned into two rival blocs, their small state would be crushed in the impending clash of the great powers. The defense of northern France now became even more problematic. Ultimately the Popular Front fell victim to the morass of foreign and domestic problems besetting it, as well as to its own internal contradictions. The electoral combination of the Radical, Socialist, and Communist Parties had never been harmonious. Each new crisis intensified their mutual distrust. In April 1938, the Popular Front government gave way to a politically middle-of-the-road cabinet under Edouard Daladier. Just five months later, Daladier would travel to Germany to sign the Munich Agreement.

Appeasement was also practiced by the United States, but across the Atlantic, it was better known as isolationism. Isolationism is something of a misnomer as it is commonly used to characterize American foreign policy in the 1920s and 1930s. The term conjures up an image of a totally isolated United States, neither knowing nor caring about events in the rest of the world. That picture is quite misleading. During these years, the US intervened militarily in Nicaragua and Haiti, was active in international disarmament negotiations, and played a significant part in European affairs (in the Dawes and Young Plans, for example). There was, however, a widespread disenchantment with American participation in the First World War and with the peace treaty that ended it. Many Americans came to believe that their country had been drawn under false pretenses into a European conflict that was none of their business. The unsavory picture of the victors at Paris squabbling over the spoils combined with Bolshevik revelations of secret Allied treaties to undermine the image of the war as a moral crusade for democracy and national self-determination. In 1934–1935, a Senate investigating committee claimed to have unearthed evidence showing that the United States had been propelled into the Great War by greedy bankers and arms manufacturers. Americans were revolted by the carnage of war and by the apparent duplicity of their recent allies. The public lost interest in foreign affairs, reverting to an attitude of smug and disdainful superiority toward the outside world. Above all, the majority of Americans were determined not to let the nation be lured into the quagmire of European war again. In government, the isolationist impulse expressed itself as a firm refusal to enter into alliances and most types of binding commitments, whether it be a guarantee of French security or membership in the League of Nations. Ultimately, isolationism entailed a refusal to assume those responsibilities in world affairs that America's wealth and power thrust upon it—responsibilities that Britain and France, severely weakened by the First World War, could no longer fully shoulder.

Menacing developments in the early 1930s—the Japanese invasion of Manchuria, the rise of Hitler to power in Germany, and Mussolini's invasion of Ethiopia—convinced Americans that another major war might soon break out in Europe or Asia. The Congress was especially anxious to avoid repeating the sort of violations of American neutral rights that had led to the US declaration of war in 1917. For that reason, Congress passed a series of Neutrality Acts between 1935 and 1937 that banned the sale of arms and ammunition or the granting of loans to belligerent powers, prohibited US ships from sailing into war zones, warned Americans that they could travel on the vessels of warring states only at their own risk, and required any nation at war to pay cash for American goods and transport those purchases in their own ships. The neutrality legislation applied uniformly to all parties at war, aggressors and victims alike. The intent of these laws was merely to keep the United States out of war, but they sometimes worked to the advantage of already well-armed predator nations by cutting off American supplies and equipment from any country that had been attacked.

President Roosevelt was considerably more realistic in his assessment of Hitler than was Prime Minister Chamberlain. As early as 1935, FDR told some of his cabinet officers privately that the Führer was an international gangster, a bandit who would someday have to be stopped. The president was similarly outraged by Japanese and Italian aggression, but he was constrained from taking firm action against the aggressors by the pervasive anti-interventionist sentiment among the public and in Congress. Roosevelt had hoped, for example, that the neutrality statutes would be framed to give the president discretionary power to apply them against aggressor states but not against countries legitimately defending themselves. Congress refused. Roosevelt invoked the arms embargo in good conscience during the Italo-Ethiopian war because only the Italians had any possibility of buying significant amounts of American armaments. The situation was different in Asia. There, China desperately needed American war matériel to defend itself from the Japanese attack. Fortunately, the legislation did grant the president authority to determine where and when a state of war existed. FDR took advantage of the technicality that the "China Incident" was an undeclared war to avoid invoking the Neutrality Acts and thus cutting off aid to China.

The efforts of President Roosevelt to oppose aggression were severely hampered by isolationist sentiment, by the multifaceted threat of war in both Europe and Asia, and by American military weakness. The land forces had been allowed to atrophy after 1918. The interwar US Army numbered only about 110,000 men (no bigger than the army of the quasi-disarmed Weimar Republic!), and it was so poorly equipped that some recruits had to drill with wooden rifles. The navy, on the other hand, remained a powerful force. FDR favored it with the lion's share of the defense budget. Saddled with these handicaps, the president initially had no effective means of blocking the aggressors. His caution (in some cases, timidity) has led some historians to conclude mistakenly that Roosevelt was an isolationist.

Politics, it is said, is the art of the possible, and FDR was a consummate political artist. He realized that he had neither the public support nor the military power to halt Nazi or Japanese expansionism. Given the strength of US isolationism, to move too boldly would have diminished his own political popularity and undermined support for his programs to end the Depression. Roosevelt was too smart a politician to take on a fight that could not be won. For the time being, all he could do was strengthen America's defenses and begin the painfully slow process of remolding public opinion—alerting it to the serious danger Nazi Germany posed for American security. In 1935, the president requested the nation's first peacetime billion-dollar defense budget, though a sum that large was not appropriated before 1938. Roosevelt justified expansion of the armed forces as a deterrent to would-be aggressors. "The American nation," he told Congress, "is committed to peace, and the principal reason for the existence of our armed forces is to guarantee our peace." The administration also mutually reinforced its foreign and domestic policies by using Public Works Administration money to build the aircraft carriers *Enterprise* and *Yorktown*, four cruisers, more than a hundred planes for the army, and some fifty military airfields.

Persuading the American public to support a more vigorous stance against aggressors proved to be no easy task. Congressional isolationists and such public pressure groups as the America First Committee and the No Foreign War Committee rose in a storm of protest any time US policy veered too closely parallel to that of the League of Nations or of Britain and France. In support of League sanctions against Mussolini, in 1935 Roosevelt proclaimed a "moral embargo" to persuade Americans voluntarily not to supply the Italian war machine. The effort failed as American oil companies scrambled for lucrative Italian oil contracts. Similarly, after the Marco Polo Bridge Incident in China, American firms continued to provide the petroleum products and scrap metal on which the Japanese war effort depended. FDR willingly followed the Anglo-French policy of nonintervention in the Spanish civil war in the vain hope of preventing a wider European conflict. The US government did nothing to help the Spanish republic defend itself from the Nazi- and Fascist-backed rebellion, although a force of American volunteers, the Abraham Lincoln Brigade, fought on the Loyalist side.

The president made his boldest attempt yet to sway public opinion and influence foreign governments in his "quarantine" speech in Chicago on October 5, 1937. He warned his countrymen, "The epidemic of world lawlessness is spreading. When an epidemic of physical disease starts to spread, the community approves and joins in a quarantine of the patients in order to protect the health of the community against the spread of disease. . . . War is a contagion. . . . It can engulf states and peoples remote from the original scene of hostilities. We are determined to keep out of war, yet we cannot ensure ourselves against the disastrous effects of war and the dangers of involvement." Roosevelt's words remained an empty gesture, however, because he could not back them with firm action. They did not deter the aggressors.

Hitler despised the American president as the ineffectual, Jew-ridden head of a mongrelized nation. Nor did FDR's verbal encouragement stiffen the resistance of Britain and France to Nazi encroachments. Chamberlain commented at the end of 1937, "The power that had the greatest strength was the United States of America, but he would be a rash man who based his considerations on help from that quarter."[13] Japanese atrocities in China, Hitler's belligerence, and the anti-Jewish horrors of *Kristallnacht* deepened American hostility to the aggressors and bolstered support for increased defense spending but did not alter the nation's resolve to avoid US participation in foreign wars. Moreover, in 1937, the economy deteriorated once more, and the president's political opponents massed for an attack on his domestic programs. Under these circumstances, he could do little to hinder Hitler's plans. During the Munich crisis, FDR could only make personal pleas to the dictators for a negotiated settlement. Historian Robert Dallek suggests that "Hitler and Mussolini probably viewed Roosevelt's appeals as gestures by a powerless man."[14]

The president was able to take firmer action against the menace of Nazi subversion in the Western Hemisphere. Under US prodding, the Pan-American Conference issued the Declaration of Lima in December 1938 pledging the American republics to take concerted action against the fascist threat to hemisphere security. Roosevelt also overcame considerable opposition to providing the French air force with new Douglas DB-7 bombers. However, even the German absorption of Czechoslovakia in March 1939, which convinced a majority of Americans that the United States ought to provide arms for the Western democracies, did not enable FDR to push a revision of the Neutrality Acts through Congress. His congressional opponents accused him of seeking foreign adventures to buoy up the embattled New Deal at home. Once more, the president was thrown back on rhetoric in lieu of more substantive responses to aggression. In April, he asked Hitler and Mussolini to promise publicly that they would not attack thirty-one specified nations for at least ten years. Predictably, the dictators treated this gambit with contempt. Roosevelt took this and similar purely verbal initiatives primarily for their domestic effect in order, as he phrased it, to "put the bee on Germany."

All three of the great Western democracies practiced appeasement of the aggressors, each in its own way and for its own differing motives. Could it have been different? Critics of appeasement suggest so. Churchill claimed that, "if the French government had mobilised [during the 1936 Rhineland crisis], there is no doubt that Hitler would have been compelled by his own General Staff to withdraw, and a check would have been given to his pretensions which might well have proved fatal to his rule."[15] This interpretation is highly dubious. The French army easily could have pushed one Wehrmacht division out of the Rhineland, but that action would have united almost all Germans behind the Führer as never before. As long as Hitler could conceal each forward thrust behind supposedly legitimate German grievances, he was on solid ground. Preventive war in 1933 or Western military intervention in Germany in 1935 or 1936 would have cast the Allies as aggressors and Hitler as a martyr. Even aiding the Austrian Republic in 1937 would have been problematic.

The situation changed qualitatively at Munich, however. Although Hitler once again appeared as the champion of an allegedly persecuted German minority, it was not on that basis that London and Paris betrayed Prague. Chamberlain, in fact, maintained a well-cultivated ignorance of the real situation in the Sudetenland. This time, to avoid the risk of war, the Western powers surrendered millions of innocent Czechs to Nazi oppression. Most importantly, Britain and France missed the first politically and strategically suitable opportunity to disrupt the pattern of German aggression. The Czechs possessed a powerful army (thirty-five well-armed divisions to the Germans' forty), readily defensible terrain, and an excellent arms industry. On the western border of the Reich, only ten understrength divisions manned the fragile Siegfried Line against the sixty divisions that the French could have thrown against them—if they had the will. Determined Anglo-French resistance to Hitler in 1938 would have received no more than verbal encouragement from Washington, but it might have secured decisive assistance from Moscow.

The USSR and Collective Security

The Soviet Union was not initially hostile toward the Nazi regime when it first came to power in Germany. The Moscow-dominated Communist International and its German affiliate, the KPD, deluded themselves that the Nazi phenomenon embodied a last desperate stage of German capitalism, a prelude to its imminent demise. National Socialism would undermine bourgeois democracy and thereby prepare the ground for revolution. The Kremlin leaders also hoped that, despite Hitler's radical anticommunist rhetoric and talk of *Lebensraum*, Germany would continue the Rapallo tradition of friendship with the USSR. On that assumption, the Russians renewed their 1926 commercial treaty with Germany just four months after Hitler became chancellor of the Reich. Ideologically, dealing with a fascist regime was no more repugnant than dealing with the liberal-democratic states. Moreover, the Soviets still regarded England as their chief enemy. They needed Germany, just as they had during the 1920s, as a counterweight to this presumed British threat.

Hitler soon demonstrated, however, that he had no interest in continuing the Rapallo relationship with the USSR. The Nazis butchered the KPD, Germany negotiated a nonaggression pact with Poland (the traditional enemy of both Moscow and Berlin), and the Führer refused to sign a mutual guarantee of frontiers with the Soviet Union. Stalin had to face the grim possibility that the responsibilities of power might not tame the Nazis, as so many Western statesmen expected, and that the bloodcurdling rantings of *Mein Kampf* might indeed be the foreign policy of the Third Reich. Soviet policy in Europe, therefore, altered dramatically in 1934 by espousing collective security. The Soviets attempted to build a solid front of antifascist nations encircling Germany, the combined strength of which, they hoped, would deter Hitler from aggression or decisively defeat the Reich if war could not be avoided. To this end, Russia threw its weight behind the League of Nations, Soviet diplomats sought treaties of mutual assistance with the Western powers, and the Comintern tried to construct a united front against fascism of all the "progressive" political forces in Europe.

The Soviet Union had always been hostile to the League, regarding it as an imperialist, counterrevolutionary tool. Yet, in 1934, the USSR joined the League, and Soviet commissar of foreign affairs Maksim Litvinov emerged as the strongest advocate at Geneva for collective security against aggression. "Germany," Litvinov warned, "is striving not only for the restoration of the rights trampled underfoot by the Versailles Treaty, not only for the restoration of its prewar boundaries, but is building its foreign policy on unlimited aggression, even going so far as to talk of subjecting to the so-called German race all other races and peoples." The Soviet commissar had discerned the essence of Nazi intentions. Denouncing appeasement as a suicidal policy, Litvinov warned the League delegates at Geneva that appeasing the aggressors only made them stronger. The peace-loving countries must stand up to the aggressor states before the balance of power tipped in their favor. Despite setbacks to the League's ability to thwart aggression in Manchuria and Abyssinia, the Russians still hoped to revitalize the international organization as an effective instrument of collective security. Supplementing multilateral diplomacy in Geneva, the USSR attempted to negotiate mutual defense treaties with its neighbors in Eastern Europe and, more importantly, with Britain and France. In 1935 the Soviet Union signed mutual defense pacts with France and Czechoslovakia, though in the latter case the Russians were not obligated to come to Prague's aid unless France did so first.

The Popular Front line, adopted by the Third International in 1935, embodied another aspect of the Soviet collective security drive. After years of vilifying the noncommunist left as the workingman's worst enemy, the Comintern executed a complete reversal, now urging communists everywhere to join with socialists, trade unionists, and even liberals in antifascist electoral coalitions. The twofold objective was to prevent the seizure of power by fascist movements in any other countries and to elect governments that would pursue an anti-German, pro-Soviet foreign policy. Supporting rearmament and a strong defense of their homelands also constituted a radical about-face for Western communists. Not long before, Maurice Thorez, head of the French Communist Party, had proclaimed that he and his comrades would not fight even if their country were invaded. All that changed when Moscow ordered communists in the Western democracies to spare no effort in rallying national political and military resistance to Hitler.

Although Soviet diplomats and foreign communists labored tirelessly on behalf of collective security, they failed to weld together a powerful alliance capable of deterring or defeating Nazi aggression. Litvinov's entreaties could not transform the League from the powerless debating society it had become into a mighty anti-German rampart. Nor was the foreign commissar any more successful in directly approaching London and Paris for alliances with the USSR. France had signed a mutual defense pact with Soviet Russia, but British opposition, internal frictions within the Popular Front, and French army doubts about the military effectiveness of Russian aid combined to vitiate that agreement. French commanders were never willing to hold the detailed staff talks with their Red Army counterparts that were essential to implementing the pact. The French wanted only a political tie with Moscow, which might intimidate Berlin but would not obligate France to perform any specific military action.

The Soviets were even less successful with England and Poland. Neither country would seriously consider an alliance with the USSR. The Comintern's Popular Front strategy was equally barren of results. Leftist coalitions managed to form governments in only two countries, Spain and France. In the former case, the Frente Popular regime in Madrid provided an excuse for a right-wing insurrection with Italian and German participation. Both the radicalism of the Spanish civil war and the potential danger of widening the conflict frightened people in the Western democracies and made them even more inclined to appease the dictators. After the fall of the Popular Front, the conservative men who led France and Britain in the last years of the decade suspected Moscow of attempting to provoke war in order to foster revolution. Prime Minister Chamberlain said, "I cannot rid myself of the suspicion that they [the Soviets] are chiefly concerned to see the 'capitalist' powers tear each other to pieces while they stay out themselves." French foreign minister Bonnet agreed with this analysis.

Munich fully exposed the fruitlessness of the Soviet campaign for collective security. Without firing a shot, Hitler had undermined the most important bulwark of the Versailles system in Eastern Europe—Czechoslovakia. Moscow could do nothing about it. Chamberlain and Daladier readily agreed to Hitler's demand to exclude Soviet Russia from the Munich Conference. The Munich debacle precipitated a change in Soviet foreign policy. Deputy Foreign Commissar Vladimir Potemkin forecast the shift when he lamented to the French ambassador in Moscow, "My poor friend, what have you done? As for us I do not see any other outcome than a fourth partition of Poland." There were also hints of a change in course in Stalin's speech before the Eighteenth Congress of the Communist Party of the Soviet Union on March 10, 1939. For the first time in years, the Germans and Italians were not singled out as aggressors. Instead, Stalin pictured the current world situation as virtually a state of war among the imperialist powers in which the fascist regimes were trying to get a larger share of the capitalists' plunder from Britain, France, and the United States. He charged that the Western countries appeased the aggressors to divert their main thrust toward the USSR. Stalin warned that the democracies were playing a dangerous game—one that might very well backfire on them.

Even during the heyday of the collective security campaign from 1935 through 1938, the Soviet Union had occasionally made tentative secret approaches to Berlin for a normalization of relations. The Nazis had rebuffed each of these probes. Now in the spring of 1939, the Soviets once again signaled the Germans that a rapprochement was possible, while at the same time warning the British and French to act quickly if they wanted an alliance with Russia. Those messages were also implicit in the dismissal of Litvinov from his post as commissar of foreign affairs at the beginning of May 1939 and his replacement by Viacheslav Molotov. Unencumbered by his predecessor's Jewish background or his image as a champion of collective security, Molotov could deal with Chamberlain or Hitler. Stalin had not entirely given up hope for an alliance with the Western powers against Germany, but his patience was running out.

Moreover, the outbreak of hostilities with Japan on the Soviet-Manchurian border in the summer of 1938 raised the imminent possibility of a conflict in the Far East. If it was to avoid a disastrous two-front war, the Soviet Union needed to reach agreement with either the democracies or Nazi Germany as soon as possible. The Soviets, therefore, mounted a dual campaign. On one hand, they continued their open, high-pressure attempts to come to terms with London and Paris. On the other hand, they began, rather delicately and secretly, to probe German intentions. In April 1939 the Soviet ambassador in Berlin, Aleksei Merekalov, told a German diplomat, "There exists for Russia no reason why she should not live with [Germany] on a normal footing. And from normal, the relations might become better and better." Soon thereafter, previously interrupted Russo-German economic negotiations were resumed, which in turn led to discussions of political cooperation between the USSR and the Reich.

At the same time, the Western powers finally began to show some interest in a coalition with Soviet Russia to check Nazi aggression. Hitler's destruction of Czechoslovakia in March had convinced most Frenchmen that war with Germany was inevitable. Despite their previously negative assessments of Soviet military capability, the French were now anxious for an alliance with Moscow. By May, the British cabinet had also, if reluctantly, concluded that some kind of cooperation with the USSR was desirable. What the Anglo-French and Soviet sides could not agree on, however, was what form their prospective collaboration should take. After debating various possibilities all summer without resolution, military talks opened on August 12 in Moscow.

The British made a poor impression, belatedly sending a low-ranking delegation that was not empowered to conclude an agreement. The conference bogged down immediately over the same issues that had prevented agreement in the previous months. If the USSR were to go to war with Germany in support of the Allied effort to stop Hitler, the Soviets insisted that their military might be brought directly to bear on the enemy. That entailed Soviet troop movements through Poland and Romania. The Russians would not consent to function merely as an arsenal for the Polish army. The Soviet delegation also demanded highly detailed and firm commitments from the Western powers. They wanted precise definitions of what circumstances would precipitate war and what forces Britain and France would commit immediately to the struggle. Finally, Moscow wanted the proposed alliance to respond against indirect aggression in Eastern Europe as well as to overt military attacks. In undermining Austria and Czechoslovakia, Hitler had employed techniques of internal subversion so effectively that a violent assault had not been necessary. The Soviets intended to prevent that sort of bloodless Nazi conquest from occurring in the states along their western border.

The British opposed the Soviet position on each of these issues. They were not even sure that the USSR was worth having as a military ally. Stalin's paranoia caused him to imagine a widespread conspiracy among the Soviet elite and throughout the peoples of the USSR—a "fifth column" waiting to betray the homeland whenever foreign war broke out. These fears caused him to launch the Great Purges of 1937–1938. These purges decimated the Red Army officer corps. More than twenty thousand commanders had been shot or sent to concentration camps. The carnage was especially severe at the highest levels of command. In addition to officers, the purges ravaged cadres of scientists, engineers, aircraft designers, industrial managers, and other groups vital to the defense of the country. The British General Staff told the cabinet that, because of the purges and also the danger of precipitating Japanese involvement, Russian intervention in a European war would more than likely be "an embarrassment rather than a help." The purges also raised a larger political question for the West. Thousands of top Soviet government, party, industrial, scientific, and military leaders had been convicted of spying for Germany or Japan. If the charges were true, it meant that the Soviet elite was riddled with treason. If they were false, the implications were even more horrifying. In either case, the purges diminished the value of Soviet Russia as an alliance partner.

The opposition of Poland and Romania to Soviet troops crossing their territory raised another obstacle. Each of them had taken territory from a devastated Russia in 1918–1920 (parts of Belorussia and Ukraine for Poland and Bessarabia for Romania). Beyond the fear of losing these districts, Warsaw and Bucharest were afraid that if Soviet armies entered their territory they might never leave. France pressed its East European allies to permit Red Army units to cross their lands, but Great Britain refused to pressure Poland or Romania over the issue. As the British foreign secretary, Lord Halifax, put it, "we must not risk offending Colonel Beck. . . . If we had to make a choice between Poland and Russia, it seemed clear that Poland would give the greater value." As the crisis over Czechoslovakia intensified in 1938, the Romanians reconsidered the issue of Red Army passage, but the Poles remained adamantly against it.

Prime Minister Chamberlain was reluctant to meet Soviet demands for transit rights in Eastern Europe and for an ironclad military alliance because his view of the international situation differed fundamentally from Stalin's. The British leader still held out hope that a general European war could be prevented. He feared that pursuit of an aggressively anti-German policy by England might precipitate a conflict that otherwise could be avoided. "Our policy," he told Parliament in 1938, "is not one of dividing Europe into two opposing *blocs* of countries, each arming against the other amidst a growing flood of ill will on both sides, which can only lead to war." The prime minister was determined not to reestablish the system of mutually hostile alliances, which he felt had led to war in 1914. Beyond that consideration, Chamberlain and many of his fellow Conservatives suspected that the Soviet Union actually wanted to see a war break out in Europe that would devastate Germany and the Western democracies, leaving them ripe for communist revolution. Under these circumstances, the British could never bring themselves to offer the sort of binding, comprehensive alliance terms that the Russians sought.

A Pact with the Devil

Hitler suffered from no such qualms. In late May 1939, he told his generals that he would destroy Poland "at the first suitable opportunity," but the Franco-British guarantee to Poland and the possibility of an alliance between the USSR and the democracies upset his calculations. The Führer still believed that England and France, despite their guarantee, either would not fight at all or, at most, would make some feeble gestures in defense of Poland. Still, it was essential to prevent the formation of a new Triple Entente linking Moscow, London, and Paris. That was the one development that could have forestalled Hitler's design for achieving European hegemony piecemeal. German diplomats therefore began to press their Soviet colleagues for an agreement in the summer of 1939. The Nazis were anxious to reach agreement, whereas the Western powers were hesitant. The Germans had no compunctions about offering Russia political and territorial concessions at the expense of other countries, while Britain would not exert the slightest pressure on Warsaw to come to terms with the USSR.

Stalin, always an extremely suspicious man, misread Western timidity and caution as a plot. If Britain and France permitted German aggression, he reasoned, it could not be because of their shortsightedness or weakness but because they wished to encourage Hitler's ambitions in the East. Appeasement, in the Kremlin's view, was a cynical method of deflecting Nazi aggression toward the Soviet Union. After all, as recently as December 1938, Paris and Berlin had signed a declaration of friendship and goodwill. Even more menacing, Göring's representative, Helmuth Wohlthat, was in London during June and July 1939, ostensibly negotiating trade matters but in fact discussing with high government officials the terms on which Britain might support German's claims against Poland. The Russians feared that the Anglo-French military negotiations with the USSR might be only a ruse to entice Hitler into the Western camp. The Soviet leader later characterized these negotiations as "insincere and only for the purpose of intimidating Hitler, with whom the Western powers would later come to terms."

By August, with his projected invasion of Poland just a few weeks away, Hitler was desperate for an agreement with the USSR that would isolate Poland and possibly convince the British and French to dishonor their guarantees to Warsaw. Stalin, moreover, had recently learned from his intelligence sources that the Soviet Union was in less immediate danger of a Nazi attack than he had feared. Soviet spies at the German embassies in Warsaw and Tokyo had reported that after the destruction of Poland, Britain and France were to be Hitler's next victims. The assault on the USSR would come later. Therefore, when Hitler personally pressed the Soviets to receive his foreign minister, Joachim von Ribbentrop, to conclude a nonaggression pact by August 23 at the latest, the Kremlin agreed.

On the evening of August 23, 1939, Molotov and Ribbentrop signed their names to a treaty of nonaggression, which signaled the beginning of the Second World War. The agreement provided that neither country would attack the other or give aid to any third power at war with the other. Significantly, this pact lacked the usual escape clause in such treaties that invalidates the document if either party were the aggressor in a war with some third country. The omission was deliberate. Stalin knew that the Germans intended to attack Poland within a week. Each of the two contracting powers also agreed not to join any alliances directed against the other one. A secret protocol supplemented the nonaggression pact, which divided Eastern Europe into Soviet and German spheres of interest. Eastern Poland, Finland, Estonia, and Latvia were assigned to the Soviet sphere. The rest of Poland and

The Nazi-Soviet Pact Divides Eastern Europe

Lithuania were ascribed to Germany. The USSR reasserted its claim to the Romanian province of Bessarabia, and the Reich expressed its political disinterest in southeastern Europe. Four days earlier, Moscow and Berlin had also concluded a commercial agreement whereby the USSR was to receive a substantial trade credit in exchange for Soviet goods. The trade treaty and nonaggression pact, with its secret protocol, together constituted a quasi-alliance between Stalin and Hitler.

Some historians have argued that Stalin always preferred a deal with Hitler over an alliance with the Western democracies. In this view, the collective security and Popular Front campaigns were cynical operations meant to buy time and pressure Berlin into an accommodation with Moscow. The most radical versions of this interpretation contend that Stalin intended to provoke a great European war so that he could conquer the whole continent![16] These views fundamentally misinterpret Stalin, who was a cautious and opportunistic imperialist, not a reckless gambler like Hitler. Just two weeks after concluding the Nazi-Soviet Pact, Stalin told Comintern chieftain Georgi Dimitrov, "We preferred agreements with the so-called democratic countries and therefore conducted negotiations. But the English and the French wanted us for farmhands and at no cost! We, of course, would not go for being farmhands, still less for getting nothing in return."[17]

These cynical agreements, which neither side saw as more than temporary expedients, were accompanied by an equally hypocritical scene. The same Ribbentrop who had nodded approvingly when Hitler had previously unfolded his plans for invading the Soviet Ukraine now assured the Russians of the German people's deep feeling for them. In response, Joseph Stalin, the self-proclaimed defender of the toiling masses and sworn enemy of fascist oppressors, raised his glass and declared, "I know how much the German nation loves its Führer; I should therefore like to drink to his health."

Hitler now had Stalin's tacit permission to attack Poland. With no serious threat of a two-front war, the Germans were free to crush the Poles while treating the Western democracies with contempt. Hitler dismissed the Anglo-French "guarantee" of Poland, telling his generals, "Our enemies are little worms. I saw them at Munich." Just eight days later, Hitler would do exactly that, thereby opening the European theater of the Second World War.

Notes

1. British historian A. J. P. Taylor has argued that Hitler was a typical German statesman, in the tradition of Otto von Bismarck, who took advantage of opportunities on the international stage but who did not deliberately initiate the Second World War in an attempt to achieve global hegemony. *The Origins of the Second World War* (Greenwich, CT: Fawcett, 1965). Taylor ignores Nazi ideology, a key factor in Hitler's decision-making. For a thorough critique of Taylor's thesis, see Gordon Martel, ed., *The Origins of the Second World War Reconsidered: A. J. P. Taylor and the Historians*, 2nd ed. (London: Routledge, 1999).

2. Quoted in Gerhard L. Weinberg, *Germany, Hitler & World War II* (Cambridge: Cambridge University Press, 1995), 28.

3. Gerhard L. Weinberg, *Visions of Victory: The Hopes of Eight World War II Leaders* (Cambridge: Cambridge University Press, 2005), 8.

4. John Gooch, *Mussolini's War: Fascist Italy from Triumph to Collapse, 1935–1943* (New York: Pegasus, 2020), 33–34.

5. Denis Mack Smith, *Mussolini's Roman Empire* (New York: Penguin, 1977), 153.

6. *Documents on German Foreign Policy* (Washington, DC: Government Printing Office, 1949), series D, vol. VI, no. 433.

7. Winston S. Churchill, *The Second World War*, vol. 1, *The Gathering Storm* (New York: Houghton Mifflin, 1948), 16.

8. Sir Harold Nicolson, *Diaries-Letters* (New York: Atheneum, 1966), 220.

9. Omer Bartov, "Martyrs' Vengeance: Memory, Trauma, and Fear of War in France, 1918–1940," in *The French Defeat of 1940: Reassessments*, ed. Joel Blatt (New York: Berghahn Books, 1998), 61.

10. Peter Jackson, *France and the Nazi Menace: Intelligence and Policy Making, 1933–1939* (Oxford: Oxford University Press, 2000), 171.

11. Peter Fritzsche, *An Iron Wind: Europe under Hitler* (Cambridge, MA: Harvard University Press, 2016), 39.

12. Eugen Weber, *The Hollow Years: France in the 1930s* (New York: Norton, 1994), 11.

13. Henry Pelling, *Britain and the Second World War* (Glasgow: Collins, 1970), 23.

14. Robert Dallek, *Franklin D. Roosevelt and American Foreign Policy* (New York: Oxford, 1979), 166.

15. Churchill, *Gathering Storm*, 175.

16. Examples of this interpretation include Robert C. Tucker, "The Emergence of Stalin's Foreign Policy," *Slavic Review* 36, no. 4 (December 1977): 563–89, 604–7; Tucker, *Stalin in Power: The Revolution from Above, 1938–1941* (New York: Norton, 1990), chs. 3–4, 10–11, 14, 16, 18, 21; Gerhard L. Weinberg, *World in the Balance: Behind the Scenes of World War II* (Hanover, NH: University Press of New England, 1981), 7; R. C. Raack, *Stalin's Drive to the West, 1938–1945: The Origins of the Cold War* (Stanford, CA: Stanford University Press, 1995); and Sean McMeekin, *Stalin's War: A New History of World War II* (New York: Basic Books, 2021). For a discussion of this historiographical debate, see Teddy J. Uldricks, "Debating the Role of Russia in the Origins of the Second World War," in Martel, *The Origins of the Second World War Reconsidered*, 135–54.

17. Ivo Banac, ed., *The Diary of Georgi Dimitrov, 1933–1949* (New Haven, CT: Yale University Press, 2003), 116.

Part II

THE AXIS ONSLAUGHT

CHAPTER 4

Nazi Conquest: Opening Rounds

The European war that broke out in September 1939 differed greatly from the expectations of most military men. According to popular cliché, generals always prepare to fight the last war. It was inevitable that memories of the Great War would dominate discussion of new strategic and tactical ideas during the next two decades. The "lessons" of that war, however, were neither clear nor widely agreed upon. During the interwar period, most professional military officers assumed that a new war would be fought much like the last one. The First World War had been a war of position. Fighting was dominated by defensive strategies that used intricate systems of trenches, barbed wire, fixed machine-gun positions, and massed artillery to repel enemy attacks. Any future continental war, it was widely believed, would again see the means of defensive warfare predominate over offensive strategies. Once again, those nations that had the greatest economic staying power and that could field multimillion-man armies over the duration of a long conflict would enjoy decisive advantages. Yet no one, not even the most belligerent politicians and military men, wanted a repetition of that awful carnage produced by nearly four years of futile but bloody, stalemated warfare.

Military planners searched for new means to break that stalemate, to overcome powerful defensive fortifications, and to restore the offensive. Proponents of strategic bombing imagined (wrongly, as it turned out) that the long-range heavy bomber would transform the nature of war, making all other weapons and tactics obsolete. Another group of visionaries believed that the tank would decisively shift the balance in favor of the attacker. The British invented the tank late in the war as a way of crossing "no-man's-land" in the face of devastating machine-gun and artillery fire. Although the new weapon was little more than an exciting novelty in the First World War, its introduction irrevocably altered the nature of warfare.

After the war, Colonel J. F. C. Fuller, B. H. Liddell Hart (an army captain turned civilian journalist), and a few other British officers continued to develop new theories of high-speed, massed tank warfare. Fuller proposed the creation of large tank units that would operate independently of traditional infantry and artillery formations. These armored shock units would pierce the enemy's front at some weak point in a deep strategic penetration to savage his vulnerable command and supply systems in the rear. Fuller believed that such attacks would disrupt the enemy's operations, spread panic among his troops, and lead to the complete collapse of his defensive network. Movement and offensive punch would thereby be restored to warfare. In contrast to the Great War, Fuller anticipated that the next war would be a short conflict, dominated by tanks, involving relatively few men, and revolving around a handful of brief but decisive battles. Liddell Hart refined Fuller's theories by adding air and infantry components to the tank forces. He projected the employment of ground-attack aircraft (strafing fighters, dive-bombers, and low-level bombers) in support of armored assaults to substitute for conventional artillery, which could not keep up with the fast-moving tank columns. Liddell Hart also foresaw a limited role for small numbers of infantrymen mounted in armored personnel carriers accompanying the tanks to help them exploit their breakthroughs.

In 1927, the British army established an Experimental Armored Force to try out these new ideas of tank warfare. The officers who directed this project were highly enthusiastic about the strategic potential of armor, but they were unable to convince the British high command that tanks could play an independent and decisive role in battle. The dominant belief in the army was that tanks were best suited for reconnaissance and for supporting infantry units. The armored warfare doctrines were too novel, too bizarre to appeal to most officers, and they threatened the powerfully entrenched interests of senior artillery and infantry commanders. Moreover, the clash of personalities and politics further impeded acceptance of the new tactics. Fuller's highly polemical and abrasive style, his association with Oswald Mosley's fascist Blackshirt movement, and his open admiration for Mussolini largely discredited even his more prescient military ideas. Similarly, Liddell Hart's acerbic pen, as well as his status as a civilian "outsider" who nonetheless had the ear of two successive war ministers, served to alienate many career officers.

The situation in France was not much different. There Colonel Charles de Gaulle emerged as the leading proponent of armored warfare. In *Verse l'armée de métier* (Toward a professional army) published in 1934, de Gaulle advocated attacks concentrated on a narrow stretch of the enemy defensive wall by large formations of heavy tanks that would exploit their local tactical success by rapidly driving a wedge into the enemy's rear echelons and thus achieve a major strategic victory. De Gaulle was no more successful at propagating his ideas than were Fuller and Liddell Hart. French military leaders were even more closely wedded to the concepts of defensive war than their British counterparts. French generals relied on densely packed masses of artillery, great hordes of conscripted infantrymen, and the elaborately fortified Maginot Line to create a continuous defensive front from Switzerland to the English Channel. Politics also complicated the tactical debate in France as it did in England. De Gaulle coupled his ideas on tanks with a plea for a smaller, more professional army that would be better prepared to meet the technological demands of modern mechanized warfare. But left-wing and moderate French politicians refused to entrust a long-term-of-service, professional army to an officer corps whose political sympathies were so clearly right of center. They feared that such a force might be employed as readily against the Third Republic as against the Germans.

The Germans reaped the benefits of Anglo-French tank theory. A group of lower- and mid-level German officers eagerly devoured the works of Liddell Hart and Fuller. These officers were fortunate to find some support for their views among senior Wehrmacht officers. More importantly, Hitler seized upon these theories of high-speed armored assault as a means whereby the Anglo-French superiority in defensive position and conventional weaponry might be quickly and cheaply overcome. As early as 1932, Hitler had predicted to Hermann Rauschning that "the next war will be quite different from the last world war. Infantry attacks and mass formations are obsolete. Interlocked frontal struggles lasting for years on petrified fronts will not return. I guarantee that. They were a degenerate form of war."[1] *Blitzkrieg* fit well into the Führer's political thinking. He wanted to avoid the massive bloodletting among German troops and the widespread privations inflicted on the civil population in the First World War. Quick victories cheaply obtained were his recipe for success. "I will never start a war," Hitler said, "without the certainty that a demoralized enemy will succumb to the first stroke of a single gigantic attack."[2]

This style of "lightning war" also fit well into what historian Robert Citino calls "the German way of war" (tracing back to seventeenth-century Prussia), using surprise, rapid movement and flanking maneuvers to annihilate an enemy quickly.[3] Historian Dennis Showalter makes a similar point: "Blitzkrieg was the latest manifestation of mobile war, the historic focus of Prussian/German military planning. . . . In blitzkrieg, the combination of radios and engines made it possible for an army literally to run rings around its enemy."[4] However, the most senior German army commanders were skeptical about this new fad. General Ludwig Beck told a colleague in the summer of 1938, "The idea of a Blitzkrieg . . . is an illusion. One should really have learned from the modern history of warfare that surprise attacks have hardly ever led to lasting success."[5]

Major Heinz Guderian and his colleagues were not merely passive recipients of British tank theories. Modifying and expanding those ideas, they created a totally new concept of warfare—the *Blitzkrieg* (lightning war). Guderian believed that tanks could achieve the maximum effectiveness only if used in combination with infantry and artillery. Whereas Liddell Hart had proposed that small numbers of mobile infantry accompany the tanks, the Germans proceeded to add large units of mechanized infantry to their armored formations. Similarly, artillery received its own motorized transport to keep pace with the speeding tank columns. The result was the powerful panzer (armored) division—a unit able to strike with devastating force, pierce deep into the enemy rear area, and exploit that penetration to the fullest degree. These panzer divisions, when closely supported from the air by the Luftwaffe, proved invincible during the initial stages of the war.

The Conquest of Poland

Poland was the first nation to feel the might of these powerful new panzer divisions. There was never any question in Hitler's mind about the ultimate fate of that nation. As an eastern bastion of the French security system and a strategically crucial avenue for the planned attack on the USSR, Poland had to be destroyed. Moreover, Polish lands were part of the *Lebensraum* Hitler coveted, and the country was populated by despised Slavs and hated Jews. Therefore, soon after dismantling Czechoslovakia, the Führer began to rage incessantly about the status of the ethnically German city of Danzig and about the Polish Corridor separating East Prussia from the rest of Germany. For the previous five years, when it had been expedient to allay Polish fears, Hitler had downplayed the supposedly tragic plight of the Danzig Germans, but now he rose as their champion to intensify the pressure on Warsaw. He offered the Poles a "peaceful solution" to the crisis by which Danzig would be incorporated into the Reich, a German corridor would link East Prussia with the remainder of the country, Berlin would pledge to respect the revised frontiers of its neighbor, and Poland would join the Anti-Comintern Pact. The Polish leaders declined this offer, realizing that its acceptance would reduce their country to Germany's powerless satellite. When the Poles would not voluntarily capitulate, Hitler determined to crush them by force. Nevertheless, he continued to negotiate with his intended victims to mask his own military preparations and to delay the mobilization of the Polish army. While German diplomats continued to talk of a peaceful resolution, the Führer told his generals in secret, "I am only afraid that at the last moment some swine or other will yet submit to me a plan for mediation."[6]

Some of the military leadership advised caution, fearing war with the Western powers while the army still lacked adequate weapons and equipment. Hitler—ever the opportunist and gambler—would not be deterred. He scheduled the attack on Poland for August 26, but repeated assurances from London and Paris that they would honor their commitments to defend Poland momentarily gave him pause. Convinced, however, that the Western powers would not back their firm words with military action, Hitler soon recovered his nerve and rescheduled the invasion for September 1.[7] The failure of negotiations for a new Triple Entente among Britain, France, and the USSR, combined with the signing of the Nazi-Soviet Pact, reassured Hitler and most of his generals that they could overwhelm Poland without being attacked immediately by one or more of the other great powers.

It is unlikely that Hitler went to war against Poland in 1939 because of his supposed fear of internal disruption (even revolution) within the Third Reich, as some historians have argued.[8] However, the sleight-of-hand financing for German rearmament had reached the end of its course. The Führer needed the political capital and the tangible rewards of conquest to justify and sustain his massive weapons program. Moreover, even if those "little worms" in Paris and London honored their pledge to Poland, there was no longer anything to be gained by waiting. Britain, France, and even the United States had all launched rearmament programs. Whatever military advantage Germany had gained in the second half of the 1930s would soon evaporate if Hitler did not strike first. He told his generals in August 1939, "We have nothing to lose; we have everything to gain. Because of our restrictions our economic situation is such that we can only hold out for a few more years. . . . We must act."[9]

Always keenly attuned to the psychological dimension of warfare, Hitler arranged a charade to make Poland appear responsible for the outbreak of hostilities. On August 31, SS men machine-gunned a group of inmates from the Oranienburg concentration camp, who had been dressed in Polish army uniforms. Their dead bodies were then shown to foreign reporters as evidence of an alleged Polish attack on German soil. Later that same day another SS detachment dressed in civilian clothes stormed a radio station in the German border town of Gleiwitz, vandalized the premises, and broadcast in Polish a phony declaration of war on Germany. Finally, they murdered another prisoner and left him at the station to simulate a Polish commando killed in the "battle." Few people abroad were deceived by this ruse, but as the Führer had told his commanders earlier, "the victor will not be asked afterward whether he told the truth or not. In starting and waging a war, it is not right that matters, but victory." Hitler was frustrated that the German people did not greet the outbreak of war in September 1939 with enthusiastic parades and rallies as they had done in August 1914. Their mood was disappointingly somber. Nazi propaganda had done its work, however. Most Germans believed that the Poles had started the war and that British treachery underlay its outbreak.

There was some violence against the German minority in Poland. As the likelihood of war grew, Polish authorities rounded up Germans living in the western part of the country and marched them east. More than two thousand Polish citizens of German heritage were shot or died from exhaustion during this process. In addition, Germans who showed sympathy for the Nazis were attacked by their neighbors. Berlin's propaganda used news of this ethnic violence to convince the German people that its assault on Poland was justified. Most Germans did not need much convincing since there was already widespread prejudice against Poles. Germans commonly referred to Polish affairs as the "Polish muddle" and to any chaotic situation as a "Polish economy." Many would have even agreed with Hitler that the Poles were "more animals than men, totally dull and formless."[10]

The German army skillfully masked the mobilization of some one and a half million men, deployed in more than fifty divisions along the borders with Poland. Yet it was not the quantity but the quality of German forces that assured victory. Of this large force, it was the fourteen modern mobile units—six panzer divisions, four light mechanized divisions (motorized infantry with limited armored support), and four divisions of motorized infantry—plus two Luftwaffe air fleets that proved decisive in battle. The great majority of the German army was neither armored nor mechanized. Its artillery and supplies were hauled by almost six hundred thousand horses. The Germans attacked from three directions. Army Group North straddled the Polish Corridor. Its 4th Army was set to strike eastward from Pomerania, while its 3rd Army was poised in East Prussia to fall on the Poles to the west, south, and east. Army Group South, an even larger force, stood ready to punch deep into central and southern Poland.

The opposing Polish army was large but poorly prepared for modern warfare. It included 280,000 regulars organized into thirty divisions, eleven horsed cavalry brigades, and only two mechanized brigades, backed up by over 1.5 million reservists. The Poles were critically short of tanks, motor vehicles, antitank guns, aircraft, and communications gear. The Polish commander, Marshal Edward Rydz-Smigly, adopted a defensive strategy that played into the enemy's hands. He opted to spread his forces along the entire 1,750-mile length of the frontiers with the Reich, thus making it all the easier for the panzers to break through the overextended Polish lines. No strategy could have enabled the Poles to defeat Germany by themselves, but they might have held out longer, in anticipation of aid from their Western allies, if they had evacuated western Poland and fallen behind a defensive network along the Narew, Vistula, and Sand Rivers. Marshal Rydz-Smigly refused to do this because it meant abandoning major industrial and population centers to the enemy.

The Germans struck in the early morning hours of September 1, 1939. Squadron after squadron of Luftwaffe bombers swarmed above the Polish countryside. First they struck at the fields, hangars, and fuel tanks of the already weak Polish air force. Then they returned to hammer railways and roads. Military assembly points, command centers, and communications facilities were bombed in turn. Because of this disruption, only about half of the Polish reservists called up ever reached their units. Closer to the front, dive-bombers and strafing fighter planes harassed the Polish units and greatly hindered their ability to maneuver. The Stuka dive-bombers were specially fitted with sirens to heighten their terrifying effect. Their bombs inflicted terrible damage, while the awful sound of the Stukas screaming down toward the Polish troops demoralized and spread panic among the ranks. Throngs of Polish civilians took to the roads to escape the violence. A Polish officer noted, "People, seized with panic, were going ahead, without knowing where or why, and without any knowledge of where the exodus would end."[11]

While the Luftwaffe continued its rain of destruction from the skies, the panzer divisions struck the overextended Polish defenders with devastating force. The German plan was to pierce the Poles' defensive screen as rapidly as possible and then penetrate deeply to cut lines of supply and communications and to prevent the bulk of enemy reservists from reaching the front. Polish armies were not allowed to retreat in an orderly fashion to new defensive lines. Rather, they were cut off by the racing German armored columns, trapped in giant encircling pincer movements, and annihilated. Situated on a large plain, Poland was ideally suited to the *Blitzkrieg*. The fall rains usually turned the broad fields and largely unpaved roads of Poland into a quagmire in which tanks could not operate, but this September was unseasonably dry. A relentless sun baked the plains hard for the panzers. The German 4th Army roared east across the corridor, sealing off a Polish corps that had been stationed near Danzig in 1939 for political reasons. The crack Pomorze Cavalry Brigade, which formed a part of that doomed corps, attempted to strike south at their attackers. Their determined assault drove the Germans back briefly. However, the brave but outgunned Poles could not withstand the Wehrmacht's superior firepower for long. Meanwhile, Danzig was already in German hands. SS men, who had previously slipped into town in civilian clothes, donned their black uniforms on the night of September 1 and began to seize key points around the city. The next morning out in the harbor, the old German battleship *Schleswig-Holstein*, which had supposedly arrived to pay a courtesy call, trained its eleven-inch guns on the Polish fortress of Westerplatte and proceeded to reduce it to rubble.

The 3rd Army in East Prussia divided its forces, sending some units west into the corridor, other formations south toward Warsaw, and still others east toward Bialystok and Brest. Meanwhile, Army Group South's 8th Army wheeled northeast so rapidly that it was able to cut off the retreating Poznan Army, pinning it against pursuing German units of Army Group North. The Poles lost nearly a third of their entire military strength in this great encircling operation. The 14th Army drove due east for Cracow, which it took on September 6, and then proceeded to turn the Poles' Carpathian flank. The 10th Army in the center launched the most important attack toward Warsaw. Its panzers raced to the suburbs of the capital in only eight days. Then the offensive stalled temporarily as the Poles barricaded the roads with overturned streetcars and forced the Germans to fight from house to house. On the night of September 5, Marshal Rydz-Smigly gave his hard-pressed troops permission to fall back to the Vistula, but it was too late.

German armored columns and air strikes were quickly cutting the Polish armies into uncoordinated, ineffective segments. The Poles counterattacked fiercely, inflicting defeats on the Germans in some areas. They were unable to take advantage of these local successes, however, because the Polish high command could no longer control, or even keep track of, its scattered and disintegrating formations. Overall, the Polish soldiers had fought bravely, while many commanders of small to medium-sized units had demonstrated great tactical skill—all to no avail. Neither the equipment nor the upper-level leadership of the Polish army were adequate in combat. (However, stories of elegantly attired cavalrymen, sabers gleaming and lances at the ready, flinging themselves on the panzers are myths, promulgated by the Germans themselves.) After only fifteen days of campaigning, German Army Groups North and South converged east of the Bug River, cutting hapless Poland in two. By September 21, the last remnants of Poland's two largest troop concentrations, the Pomorze and Poznan Armies, had surrendered. The fortresses of Modlin, Hel, Warsaw, and Lvov held out for only a few more days.

The Polish government abandoned Warsaw on September 4, followed by the army command three days later. They, and whatever fighting units could escape German encirclement, retreated steadily into eastern Galicia, where they hoped to hold out until an Anglo-French attack on Germany relieved the pressure on them. This last hope collapsed on September 17 when Soviet troops attacked across the Russo-Polish frontier. The extremely rapid progress of the German invasion surprised Stalin and made him fear that, unless he moved quickly, he might have difficulty securing those eastern provinces of Poland defined within the Soviet sphere of interest by the Nazi-Soviet Pact. It was clear to Stalin by this time that the Western powers would take no effective military action in Eastern Europe. Elements of the Soviet army therefore rushed into eastern Poland, overrunning defenses that had been largely denuded of troops at the beginning of the month to meet the German onslaught in the West.

The Kremlin sought to excuse this invasion by declaring that, since the Polish government had disintegrated, the presence of the Soviet army was necessary in eastern Poland to protect the Ukrainian and White Russian populations there. Following some initial difficulties (including some shooting), the German and Soviet occupation forces established a dividing line for their respective zones that ran down from East Prussia just west of Brest-Litovsk and Lvov to the Hungarian border. With the situation now clearly hopeless, the Polish government and many of its troops escaped into neutral Romania on September 18. The last Polish fortress, Hel, was crushed on October 2, and the last field units surrendered at Kock on the 5th. As the situation had deteriorated, the Polish government had called for mass resistance. Some civilians continued to fight, provoking a draconian response from the German army. After its twenty-one-year reincarnation, Poland once again ceased to exist as an independent state. Hitler had won his first great military victory. The Germans declared that the half million Polish war prisoners in their custody could no longer be considered POWs, since there was no Polish state, and promptly reclassified them as forced laborers.

From the beginning, the German invasion was a "total war" on the people of Poland, not merely at attempt to defeat and disarm the Polish army. In Hitler's mind and in the actions of his soldiers, this was not a traditional war for territory but an ideologically driven race war, a *Volkstumskampf*.[12] Declaring even fully uniformed Polish soldiers to be partisans and criminals, the Germans shot or burned alive many prisoners of war. They did the same to captured enemy wounded.[13] Terror bombing of cities, strafing of refugee columns, and shooting civilians was standard procedure. General Bock ordered his soldiers, "If there is shooting from a village behind the front and if it proves impossible to identify the house from which the shot came, then the whole village is to be burned to the ground."[14] *Einsatzgruppen* (special task forces) of the SS Security Service followed German troops to destroy "hostile elements" among the population. Local ethnic German militias carried out widespread massacres of Poles and Jews. About 5,800 ethnic Germans had been killed during the violence preceding the war. Spurred on by lurid stories of Polish atrocities, the Germans would now repay those crimes tenfold. Before the end of the year, they had killed at least fifty thousand civilians, only seven thousand of them Jewish, demonstrating that this ideologically driven campaign of mass murder was directed against the Slavs as well as Jews. A few Wehrmacht officers protested the indiscriminate violence, but their concern was troop morale and keeping rear areas quiet, not humanitarian considerations.

The *Sitzkrieg*

Even if they had followed a sounder defensive strategy and had enjoyed better luck, the Poles' only hope lay with a successful Allied invasion of western Germany. That Anglo-French rescue mission never came. The authorities in London and Paris never intended to send troops to Eastern Europe or even to assault the Rhineland. Their "guarantee" of Poland was supposed to *deter* Hitler from attacking his eastern neighbor; it was a bluff. It was not a promise of decisive military action if the deterrent failed. Even after German troops began pouring across the Polish border, British prime minister Chamberlain continued to cling to the vain hope of peace. The British, using Mussolini and Birger Dahlerus, a Swedish industrialist, as intermediaries, urged the Germans to turn back before it was too late. The escalating conflagration in Poland, combined with mounting pressure from Parliament, finally convinced the British cabinet on September 2 to give Germany an ultimatum, set to expire at 11:00 a.m. the following day. In France, Foreign Minister Bonnet sought to arrange another Munich-style conference through Mussolini, but the cabinet of Premier Daladier repudiated the idea and sent their own ultimatum to Berlin, timed to expire at 5:00 p.m. on September 3. When Hitler failed to respond to these ultimatums, both Britain and France honored their pledges to Poland by declaring war on the Third Reich. Contrary to Hitler's expectations, a major continental war had begun.

Paper declarations of war could not help the Poles, however. French troops manned the Maginot Line, other military units took up positions along the border with Luxembourg and Belgium, and authorities began calling up the great mass of reservists. In England, preparations commenced for shipping the first four divisions of the British Expeditionary Force (the BEF) across the Channel. The Royal Navy quickly established a blockade to deprive the Reich of all its vital seaborne imports, a step that the Allies hoped would soon erode Germany's ability to continue the war. Such naval action, even if successful in the long run, could do nothing for the hard-pressed Poles. Only the French army and the RAF could render the decisive and immediate assistance for which their Polish allies were so desperate. General Maurice Gamelin, the French supreme commander, had promised the Polish generals that if Hitler invaded Poland, the French army would attack Germany with "the majority of its forces" within fifteen days of mobilization.

The French had no intention, however, of mounting a serious offensive on the western front. By September 7, French forces had begun moving into the Saar region of Germany. Some British newspapers hailed the "French Army pouring over the German border," but the relatively small units conducting these probing attacks had orders to advance up to the German defensive line and no farther. The French, haunted by the carnage of the Great War, were anxious to avoid losses at all costs. They overran some twenty deserted villages while pushing about five miles deep into German territory on a front sixteen miles wide. This operation drew not a single Wehrmacht trooper from battle in Poland. The Poles were left to their fate. When they capitulated on September 28, the French evacuated what little German soil they had taken and pulled back to the Maginot Line. The RAF Bomber Command, with its vaunted capacity for strategic destruction, did even less than the French army to help the Poles. German military installations, fuel and ammunition dumps, and supply columns moving eastward all remained unscathed by British air power.

The unwillingness of the Western Allies to provide any significant aid for Poland stemmed both from fear and from mistaken conceptions of military doctrine. The French air force, by far the weakest component of that nation's armed services, did not have much capacity for strategic bombing. The RAF, in contrast, had built a long-range bomber fleet. This force was not employed at the beginning of the war, except to drop propaganda leaflets, because the Allies feared the retaliation that the Luftwaffe might wreak on London and Paris. This excessive fear of bombing provoked the panicked evacuation of thousands of children from London during the first days of the war. One prewar study even predicted as many as a million casualties from bombing in London alone during the first two months of the war. (In fact, the whole of Great Britain suffered just over forty thousand civilian bombing casualties in the entire course of the war!) Given this expectation of horror cascading from the skies, the Anglo-French leaders were unwilling to precipitate an exchange of all-out attacks on German and Allied cities. The Western powers, with an eye to American public opinion, were also anxious to avoid the stigma of massacring civilians from the air as the Germans had already done in Warsaw.

The arguments against a major Allied attack on the ground seemed as compelling as those against an aerial offensive. Believing that the Germans possessed clear superiority in both land and air power, Anglo-French military planners assumed that the Allies would fight on the defensive for the first year or two of the war. Only after they had accumulated overwhelming quantities of men and equipment, knocked Hitler's allies out of the war, mortally weakened Germany with prolonged strategic bombing, and perhaps even procured American assistance did the Western powers contemplate going over to the offensive.[15] After all, the combined output of the British and French economies surpassed that of the Germany and Italy by 60 percent.[16] If these assumptions about German strength and about the superiority of defensive to offensive warfare were correct, then a massive Allied assault at this time would have been premature at the least and possibly even disastrous. The French were also concerned that any attack on Germany would draw Fascist Italy into the war against them. Moreover, in these early months of the war, the British hoped, quite unrealistically, that the German home front might collapse, and with it the Nazi regime.

The Allies' calculation of enemy strength and their defensively oriented doctrines proved entirely wrong. The Western powers probably missed a unique opportunity to inflict a decisive defeat on Nazi Germany in the fall and winter of 1939. Allied generals and political leaders greatly overestimated German military prowess while constantly underrating their own strength. In reality, the balance of power lay substantially in favor of the Western forces. The French army mobilized ninety-nine divisions, most of which, unlike their German counterparts, enjoyed a full complement of men and equipment. French soldiers were supported by more than eleven thousand artillery pieces and well over three thousand tanks. While the French air force was short of modern planes, the RAF could field 566 bombers and 608 fighters in September 1939. To oppose this show of Allied might, the Wehrmacht could deploy only eleven first-line infantry divisions to man the uncompleted defenses of the Siegfried Line. These first-echelon units were supported by thirty-five reserve divisions in varying states of unreadiness. To make matters worse, the Germans could spare virtually no armor or modern aircraft for the western front. General Erwin von Witzleben, the German commander in the West, feared that a French attack might quickly breach the Siegfried Line, encircle and destroy his best units, and soon overrun the great industrial centers of western Germany.

Of course, once Poland capitulated, the Germans began to move the bulk of their forces westward. Even this, however, did not in itself spell disaster for the Allies. Most of the vaunted Panzer divisions were supplied at this time with the panzer Mark I and Mark II tanks. The former was equipped only with machine guns, while the Mark II was armed with a weak 20 mm gun and very thinly armored. Even the Mark III and Mark IV, which began to appear in 1938 and 1939 respectively, were still inferior to the best French tanks. Moreover, the impressive *Blitzkrieg* victory in Poland had not been as easy as Berlin claimed. Polish armor and artillery had knocked out 217 German tanks. Even the weak Polish air and antiaircraft forces had brought down some 160 Luftwaffe planes. The fighting in Poland had exposed critical weaknesses in supply and training.

The German generals knew that their forces were ill prepared to take on the French and British. So great was their fear of imminent defeat that the chief of the General Staff, Franz Halder, sounded out some fellow commanders about a coup against the Nazi regime. The Wehrmacht needed time to rest and replace its losses after its victory in the East. It seems highly probable, therefore, that a determined French assault in the West in September, supported by the massive French superiority in artillery and the full weight of the RAF, could have easily pierced the thin German defensive screen. Anglo-French forces then could have occupied the Rhineland and the Ruhr, thus undermining the ability of the Reich to continue the war. Unfortunately, the Allied leaders had neither the courage nor the will to seize this opportunity. General Edmund Ironside, chief of the British Imperial Staff, later admitted as much in his diary:

> Militarily we ought to have gone all out against the German the minute he invaded Poland. . . . We did not. There were many reasons. We were too prepared for a long war. The French Air Force was so bad that it might be annihilated like the Polish Air Force. We were expanding rapidly in our industry. The British army was crossing to France and passing to the front. All was to our advantage to wait. And so we missed the strategic advantage of the Germans being engaged in the east. We thought completely defensively and of ourselves. We had to subordinate our strategy to that of the French and so didn't let our Air Force in. We missed a wonderful opportunity.[17]

Hitler had taken an enormous gamble, leaving western Germany vulnerable to Allied attack. The Führer could not be sure, but he surmised that his enemies were completely unwilling to seize that opportunity.

The opening of the Second World War bore little resemblance to the beginning of the Great War twenty-five years earlier. In 1914, jubilant crowds in all the capitals of Europe had hailed the outbreak of war. Those scenes were not repeated in September 1939. William L. Shirer, an American journalist in Berlin at that time, described Germans on the street as stunned, astonished, and depressed. Hitler was keenly disappointed that his countrymen showed so little zest for the fight. The stunning victory in Poland, however, coupled with Allied inaction in the West, greatly bolstered Hitler's popularity with the generals and the German people. The British and French public met the declaration of war with acceptance and determination to face the inevitable, but without any real enthusiasm. "Let's get it over with" seemed to be the attitude of many French soldiers. On both sides of the Channel, the deceptively quiet period of "phony war" nurtured false hopes that the conflict might be won bloodlessly by simply outwaiting the enemy until the Allies built up a preponderance of force, or the Americans intervened, or the Hitler regime was toppled from within by some domestic opposition. This climate of wishful thinking justified the Western policy of doing nothing as both humane and militarily prudent.

The failure of the Allies to take the initiative on the western front did not surprise Hitler at all. When he attacked Poland, he was sure that if Britain and France honored their guarantee of that country, it would be no more than a hollow gesture from which no serious military action would follow. Denying any aggressive intent against Britain and France, on October 6 Hitler proposed peace negotiations with the Allies. The Western leaders rejected this gambit that would have sanctioned Germany's conquests without providing guarantees of security for England or France. They would accept no terms from Berlin that did not reestablish an independent Poland and Czechoslovakia at a minimum. The decision to hold out against Germany was easy for Chamberlain, whose public approval rating reached an all-time high of 70 percent in the November Gallup poll.

It was much more difficult for Daladier, who had to overcome strong pacifist and defeatist sentiment to keep France in the war. It mattered little, however, for Hitler's offer of peace was insincere. During the Polish campaign, he had already told his adjutant that he intended to attack the Western powers as soon as he secured victory in the East. Before either Allied leader had responded to his "peace offer," Hitler had already scheduled the invasion of France for November 25. Only continuously bad weather conditions prevented him from launching a major offensive against the Allies in the fall or winter of 1939. The

Führer's "peace offensive" was effective with one constituency—the home front. Most Germans believed that the "counterattack" on Poland had been justified, that Hitler was now sincerely seeking an end to the conflict, and that only malevolent Britain and "the Jews" kept the war going.

Meanwhile, along the Franco-German border the farcical phony war continued. German troops deliberately refrained from any offensive action so as not to shake the Allies from their lethargy. Apart from a few minor raids, the French, too, remained ensconced behind their great fortifications. They made no attempt to prevent the Germans from bringing up more men and equipment or constructing defensive works. The common soldiers grew bored and drank while their officers dined sumptuously on pheasant and pâté de foie gras. The Germans put up large signs promising not to shoot at the French if the French did not fire at them. Nazi propaganda aimed across the lines hammered at two themes—the need to avoid another 1914-style bloodletting and the untrustworthiness of England. Troops of the BEF stationed along the Franco-Belgian frontier could not engage the enemy either, though they maintained better discipline than the French *poilus*. The RAF did bomb a few German coastal cities, with negligible effect, but usually the British bombers carried nothing more lethal than antiwar propaganda leaflets.

While there was little fighting along the front or in the air, the war at sea was anything but phony. Each side hoped to cripple the other's war-making capacity by strangling its seaborne supply lines. Berlin sought to force Great Britain out of the war by cutting off that island kingdom from the support of its overseas imperial possessions. Severing the vital Atlantic sea-lanes to North America was the most crucial objective in that regard. On the first day of the war, a German submarine already on station torpedoed the British liner *Athenia* without warning, killing 112 people, including 28 Americans. During the month of September, Admiral Karl Doenitz's U-boats sank twenty-six British merchantmen. By the end of 1939, German submarines had destroyed over two hundred Allied tankers and freighters.

The damage might have been even worse, but at the beginning of the war, Admiral Doenitz had only twenty-two of the larger oceangoing U-boats available for duty. Of that number, only one-third could be at combat stations at any one time. Nor was it only unarmed civilian craft that went to the bottom. Two weeks after the *Athenia* incident, another Germany submarine sank the aircraft carrier *Courageous* in the English Channel. An even greater blow to British prestige occurred in October when the U-47 threaded its way undetected into the Royal Navy's home base at Scapa Flow off the northern coast of Scotland and torpedoed the battleship *Royal Oak*. Magnetic mines, which the Germans sowed in British sea-lanes, at first caused more damage to Allied shipping than did enemy submarines, until a partially successful method of demagnetizing ("degaussing") the ship hulls by wrapping electrical wires around them was discovered.

The German navy also turned its surface ships against Allied shipping. The Kriegsmarine, under the command of Grand Admiral Erich Raeder, was no match for either the British or the French navies when the war began in 1939. Plan Z, a great naval building program, had been authorized in January but would take years to complete. For the moment Raeder had at his disposal only two battleships, two "pocket battleships" (considerably smaller than normal battleships but very powerfully armed), eight cruisers, and a few destroyers and torpedo boats. It would have been suicidal to challenge the mighty Allied fleets with this modest force, so the German admiral employed many of his ships individually as commerce raiders.

This strategy also had the advantage of forcing the British Admiralty to disperse its vessels throughout the North Sea, the Atlantic Ocean, and the Indian Ocean in search of the Germans. One of these surface raiders, the pocket battleship *Graf Spee*, sank nine merchantmen before encountering three Allied cruisers off the coast of Uruguay in the South Atlantic on December 12. In the ensuing battle, the more heavily armed *Graf Spee* nearly wrecked the British heavy cruiser *Exeter* and damaged the light cruisers *Ajax* and *Achilles*, but the German ship suffered eighteen hits and expended most of its ammunition. The *Graf Spee* withdrew to the nearby neutral port of Montevideo, where its captain ultimately scuttled the ship to prevent its capture by the British. The Royal Navy had avenged the sinking of the *Royal Oak* and provided the public at home with a much-needed morale boost.

The Reich was also vulnerable to the pressure of an economic blockade. At the beginning of the conflict, Germany imported fully 80 percent of its rubber needs, 70 percent of its copper, 65 percent of its tin, 50 percent of its lead, and 25 percent of its zinc. The Royal Navy planned to choke off these desperately needed supplies. With their overwhelming naval superiority, they did not have to rely on hit-or-miss submarine and raider tactics. Instead, the Western powers established a formal blockade of the German coasts to deprive the Reich of all its overseas imports. Allied strategists believed that within two years the blockade would completely disrupt the German war economy and bring Hitler to his knees. In practice, however, the blockade proved to be much less effective than Western planners expected. The Nazi-Soviet Pact enabled Germany to obtain vitally needed stocks of food, fuel, and raw materials from the USSR. Soviet exports to Germany included petroleum, grains, various nonferrous metals, lumber, and cotton. The Russians also willingly procured for Germany on the world market commodities that the Soviet Union could not itself produce. These goods were then transshipped across the USSR to the Reich.

War Comes to Scandinavia

While the western front lay deceptively quiet, war erupted in a most unlikely part of Europe—Scandinavia. There the initial aggressor was not Nazi Germany but the USSR. The secret protocol attached to the Nazi-Soviet Pact recognized Finland, Estonia, and Latvia as part of the Soviet sphere of influence in Eastern Europe. Lithuania lay within the German sphere of interest. By a supplementary agreement of September 28, Berlin ceded Lithuania to the Soviet sphere in exchange for some additional areas of Poland initially within the Russian sector. However much Stalin hoped to appease Hitler temporarily by faithfully provisioning the Nazi war machine, the Soviet dictator realized that ultimately the Third Reich embodied the gravest threat to the security of the USSR. The Soviet Union therefore moved very quickly to bolster its position in the Baltic. In October, Moscow demanded that Latvia, Lithuania, and Estonia allow its troops to establish bases at strategically critical points in their countries. The three weak Baltic republics had no choice but to comply, especially since the Germans advised them to accede to Soviet wishes. The Baltic states had enjoyed independence from Russian control only since 1918. Soviet occupation now fatally undermined that short-lived freedom. Later, in 1940, Soviet pressure subverted the governments of the three states, replaced them with communist regimes, and incorporated them into the USSR. The Soviet Union had thereby acquired an extra defensive glacis along its northwestern frontiers as well as new naval bases on the Baltic.

Finland, in contrast to its three Baltic neighbors, proved unwilling to follow Soviet dictates. The Soviets insisted on pushing the Russo-Finnish border twenty miles up the Karelian Isthmus to protect Leningrad, which lay within artillery range of the existing frontier. Furthermore, the Soviets wanted a lease on the Hango Peninsula at the western end of the Gulf of Finland for naval and air bases. They also demanded several small islands in the gulf and part of the Rybachi Peninsula on the Barents Sea in the far north. In exchange, Finland would receive from the USSR a large but not very valuable portion of the East Karelian wilderness. These territorial changes would have strengthened the USSR against a German attack, but they also would have reduced Finland to a helpless dependency of the Soviet Union. The Finns proclaimed their desire to live in peace with their Russian neighbor and made numerous counterproposals, but they refused to compromise their territorial integrity. Moscow reacted to this show of independence by manufacturing a pretext for war. Claiming that Finnish artillery had bombarded a Russian border village, Soviet troops attacked Finland without warning on the morning of November 30, 1939.

The Red Army command deployed over half a million men supported by thousands of tanks and artillery batteries and hundreds of aircraft against a Finnish force of less than two hundred thousand troops, which was deficient in most types of modern, heavy weapons. The Russians struck at numerous points along their extensive frontier with Finland. In the far north, the Soviet 14th Army launched a drive for Petsamo, an ice-free port on the Arctic Sea, and for the Rybachi Peninsula. In east-central Finland, the 9th Army began a westward offensive toward the Gulf of Bothnia designed to cut Finland in two. Even larger Soviet formations were concentrated in the southeast. General Kirill A. Meretskov's 240,000-man 7th Army began its advance up the narrow Karelian Isthmus. The powerful 8th Army struck from the far side of Lake Ladoga, intending to wheel around the Finnish side of the lake and join the 7th Army. The Soviet air force bombed Helsinki and other cities.

Since the Finns had not voluntarily acquiesced to his demands, Stalin decided to take complete control of their country. On December 1, the USSR announced that it had signed a treaty of friendship with the "Democratic People's Republic of Finland." Stalin appointed the veteran Comintern official and longtime Moscow exile Otto Kuusinen to head the satellite government. When the United States and Sweden offered their services to mediate peace, Moscow dismissed them as unnecessary because the Soviet Union was not at war with Finland, claiming that its troops had entered the country at the request of its legitimate government (i.e., of the Kuusinen puppet regime)! The moribund League of Nations condemned Soviet aggression and expelled the USSR, but its verbal censure was no more effective against aggression in Finland than it had been in Manchuria or Ethiopia. The Soviets anticipated easy going in Finland; they intended to present outraged world opinion with a fait accompli just as Hitler had done in Poland. "We thought that all we had to do was raise our voice a little bit," Nikita Khrushchev later reminisced. "If that didn't work, we would fire one shot and the Finns would put up their hands."[18] What the Finns put up was a very stout defense.

The main Soviet thrust up the Karelian Isthmus made steady progress until it stopped to rest and reorganize in front of the Finns' Mannerheim Line on December 6. This pause gave the badly shaken Finns time to regroup too. The Mannerheim Line was no impregnable fortress like the Maginot Line, but manned by determined Finnish defenders it proved a formidable obstacle to the Russians. It consisted of a series of tank barriers, pillboxes, and concrete gun emplacements blocking every road and open space in the otherwise rough terrain of the isthmus. Meretskov renewed his offensive on December 17 with closely grouped masses of infantry and tanks. The entrenched Finnish gunners slaughtered the exposed Russians in great numbers. Where Soviet tanks broke through the defensive perimeter, Finnish troops displayed exceptional bravery, running among the enemy tanks to jam their tracks with logs or blow them up with small handmade explosives derisively called "Molotov cocktails." The Soviet assault suffered from very poor coordination of infantry, armor, artillery, and air units. After four days, the Soviet commander began pulling back his severely mauled forces.

An even worse disaster befell the 9th Army on the east-central front where its elements were advancing toward Kuhmo and Suomussalmi. The enemy outnumbered the Finnish defenders by as much as five to one, but the Finns still enjoyed several advantages. Snow, ice, extreme cold, and broken countryside largely offset the Soviet advantage in numbers, firepower, and mobility. Beyond that, the Red Army men were not properly outfitted or trained to fight in the frozen forests, while in contrast many of the Finns were experienced woodsmen, good skiers, and expert marksmen. The Finns adopted hit-and-run tactics designed to minimize Finnish casualties and take maximum advantage of terrain and weather. Garbed in white camouflage suits and skiing silently in and out of the dark woods, the Finns hit larger Soviet columns by surprise, cutting them into smaller segments and overrunning them one at a time. When an isolated enemy unit had too much firepower to be stormed, the Finns simply laid siege to it until its soldiers died of exposure. After such battles, Finnish troops often discovered numerous Red Army soldiers frozen stiff in their foxholes or in their tanks. Employing such tactics, the Finns destroyed two Soviet divisions and ultimately decimated the entire Soviet 9th Army. Only on the Arctic coast did Soviet forces experience success. There the 14th Army captured Petsamo by surprise and began descending southward down the Arctic Highway, only to be checked within fifty miles by a Finnish defensive line. Thus, instead of a quickly achieved fait accompli, the Winter War became a major embarrassment for the USSR.

Stalin was enraged, though the disaster was his own fault. Thousands of Soviet casualties were paying the price not only for the high command's underestimation of Finnish resistance but also for the bloody purges by which Stalin had recently deprived the Red Army of many of its best leaders. Of course the officers, not Stalin, were blamed for the losses in Finland. One of them, General A. I. Vinogradov, was executed. Stalin replaced Meretskov with General Semën Timoshenko as overall commander of the operation. Timoshenko reopened the offensive up the Karelian Isthmus on February 11, 1940. This time the Russians did not underestimate their opponents. They massed almost a million troops accompanied by thousands of artillery pieces, tanks, and planes. They also carefully coordinated the assault. The tanks covered each other and advanced together with infantry support. Artillery fire was concentrated against Finnish guns instead of sprayed randomly at the enemy as before. The Soviet air force switched from city bombing to close tactical support of ground troops. The fighting was still tough and costly, but the overmatched Finns could not fend off this powerful Russian attack for long. Running low on manpower and ammunition, Marshal Mannerheim sent a delegation to Moscow on March 6 to sue for peace. Foreign observers of the conflict (especially the Germans) saw the Red Army's difficulties in Finland as evidence of its incompetence and ineffectiveness.

Kremlin leaders sprang at the chance to end the war quickly. This David and Goliath conflict, besides causing deep humiliation for Russian arms, also generated a worldwide wave of revulsion against the Soviet Union. Worse yet, Britain and France were making plans to aid the Finns. Stalin wanted to avoid war with the Western powers at all costs. He even feared that Hitler might take advantage of the Soviet involvement in Finland to strike at the USSR. Stalin therefore agreed to peace terms that were relatively moderate given the military situation. The Soviet Union annexed about sixteen thousand square miles of Finland—somewhat more than had been demanded in October—and leased facilities for a naval base at Hango. The settlement provided no compensation for lost Finnish land. However, Stalin dropped his support for the communist Kuusinen regime and permitted the existing non-communist government to stay in power and retain its army.

The Russo-Finnish war had strange repercussions on the larger conflict in the West. Allied leaders saw in the Winter War a chance to strike a blow against Hitler that they were unwilling to deliver directly across the Rhine. German war industry received a substantial proportion of its high-grade iron ore from the mines in neutral Sweden. The only available Swedish port for shipping the ore to Germany, Lulea on the Gulf of Bothnia, was icebound for part of the year. The most practical route, therefore, was to send the ore by rail to the Norwegian port of Narvik and then by sea south to the Reich. The Norwegian coast was ideal for this purpose. Its shoreline was mountainous and regularly indented by fjords. Offshore, a long chain of reefs and islands screened the entire coastline. Between the shore and the barrier chain lay the Leeds, a 1,200-mile-long deepwater channel that offered the protection of neutral Swedish territorial waters for German ore shipments. As early as September 1939, Winston Churchill, then First Lord of the Admiralty, suggested mining the Leeds and thereby forcing the ore boats out into the open sea where they could be interdicted by the Royal Navy. A mining operation of this sort, however, would have been a violation of Norway's rights as a neutral. The Soviet attack on Finland changed the picture, making it possible to shut off Swedish ore shipments completely under the guise of defending the rights of the small Scandinavian neutral states.

Ostensibly to send aid to the Finns, the Allies planned to seize Narvik, move up the railway that led to the ore fields, leave a substantial number of troops there, and finally send a few units on to Finland. Given the limited resources available and the long distances and difficulties involved, very little aid would have ever reached the Finns, but the Allies would control Sweden's vital ore mines. The British began to accumulate forces for this operation by diverting two divisions scheduled to join the BEF in France. The French readily joined the plan. The foolhardiness of this projected operation is staggering. An attack on neutral Norway and Sweden would have alienated American opinion at a time when the Allies desperately needed assistance from the United States. Moreover, the appearance of Anglo-French troops in Finland easily could have led to a Soviet declaration of war on the Allies. Afraid to attack the German army, the Western powers were about to provoke war with the USSR, a country that possessed an even larger army. The Allies discounted this danger because they believed that the purges and the Soviet debacle in Finland demonstrated the hollowness of Russian military power. In combination with the Scandinavian venture, the French also intended to bomb the Caucasian oil fields in the southern USSR from bases in French-controlled Syria. The Allies also hoped to recruit Greece and Turkey to their cause. Allied reluctance to challenge the Wehrmacht directly by attacking across the Franco-German border led them to contemplate truly bizarre and self-destructive measures. Fortunately for Britain and France, Finland capitulated before the Allies could launch this potentially disastrous operation.

The Allies did not entirely abandon the Norwegian gambit however. News of Finland's defeat caused the fall of the Daladier cabinet in France. Paul Reynaud replaced Daladier as premier. His new cabinet felt considerable public and parliamentary pressure to initiate some military action that would give the Allies a badly needed, morale-boosting victory (though of course no one desired any fighting on French soil). Across the Channel, Churchill and the

British were still eager to cut off German iron ore supplies. They planned to go ahead with the mining of the Leeds on April 8. They also organized a second stroke, the seizure of the ports at Narvik, Trondheim, and Bergen and the airfield at Stavanger. This operation assumed that the Germans would commit some violation of Norwegian neutrality in response to the mining of the coastal waterway. This in turn would justify a greater Allied intrusion into Norway. In addition, Churchill wanted Bomber Command to drop mines in the Rhine while the Royal Navy laid its mines off Norway. Churchill's idea for mining the Rhine was abandoned under pressure from the French, who feared that the Germans might retaliate by bombing their cities, an act from which the Luftwaffe had thus far refrained.

Hitler did not intend to conquer Scandinavia during the preliminary stages of the war, though he was determined ultimately to dominate all of Europe. For the time being, Scandinavian neutrality served Hitler's purposes nicely by protecting his northern flank and facilitating the shipment of raw materials. The German navy did not share the Führer's attitude toward Scandinavia. Admiral Raeder wanted to secure Norwegian bases for his submarines and surface raiders. If the U-boats and raiders could hide in the fjords along the 1,200-mile Norwegian coast, they could more easily avoid the British blockade patrols. Also, Norwegian bases would put them closer to the Atlantic shipping lanes. The time and precious fuel saved would allow the undersea predators to stay on station and savage Allied commerce for much longer periods. It was not his admiral's arguments, however, but the fear that the Western powers might strike first that changed Hitler's strategy for Scandinavia. Between September 1939 and April 1940, various possible British options in northern Europe had been debated publicly in Parliament and in the press. Hitler was therefore aware of the Allied intent to stage some sort of operation in Scandinavia. The Führer's suspicions were further aroused in February when the HMS *Cossack* grappled and boarded the German naval auxiliary *Altmark* in a Norwegian fjord. The incident confirmed Hitler's fear that the Allies soon might take more dramatic action in the north. He decided to seize the initiative from his enemies.

The Royal Navy laid mines in the Leeds just below Narvik fjord on April 8 and, anticipating some German reaction, prepared to ferry British troops to Trondheim, Bergen, Narvik, and Stavanger. Unknown to the Allies, German ships had already left port to launch their own preemptive occupation of Norway, code-named the "Weser Exercise." It was an ambitious coordinated land, sea, and air assault aimed at the same ports targeted by the British plus the additional ports of Egersund and Kristiansand. The German command also intended to capture the Norwegian king and government in Oslo before they could organize national resistance. Fast action and an imposing show of force, it was hoped, would dissuade the Norwegians from fighting. The Oslo government was to be told that the Germans had come only to protect them from a British attack. If the Norwegians would cooperate, they could retain considerable autonomy in their own domestic affairs. Denmark was to be overrun simultaneously to secure communications and additional air bases for the Norwegian campaign. Hitler was taking an enormous chance, risking most of his navy, which might easily be annihilated if detected by the British fleet. The amphibious portion of the operation also required precise timing and good luck to succeed.

On April 9, German troops crossed the Danish border. At the same time, the German ambassador awoke the Danish foreign minister to inform him that unless the Danes surrendered in one hour, Copenhagen would be bombed to rubble. Meanwhile, the German troopship *Hansestadt Danzig* slipped into Copenhagen harbor and proceeded to disembark a thousand-man strike force. King Christian X and his government made the painful decision to capitulate. Throwing the fifteen-thousand-member Danish army against the Wehrmacht would cause needless slaughter without any hope of repelling the invader. By that afternoon, the Luftwaffe was using Danish airfields to fly sorties against Norway.

Farther north, the Weser Exercise encountered considerable difficulty. In the predawn hours of April 9, six separate German naval task forces stealthily approached various points on the Norwegian coast. The heavy cruiser *Blücher* led one group up the Oslo fjord toward the capital. The Germans hoped to take the city by surprise, but just as the *Blücher* slipped into the harbor, shore batteries and the big guns of the ancient Oscarsborg fortress suddenly opened murderous, point-blank fire. The burning cruiser exploded and rolled over in the water. The cruiser *Lützow*, following the doomed flagship, quickly reversed its engines. The German flotilla retreated up the fjord to disembark the assault troops safely. The element of surprise had been lost. Soon German airborne troops overwhelmed the airfields near Oslo and Stavanger and closed in on the capital. Fearing the imminent fall of the city, King Haakon VII and the Norwegian government fled Oslo to rally national resistance in the interior.

At the opposite end of Norway, another German attack team comprised of nine destroyers, each carrying two hundred soldiers, approached Narvik. The destroyers unloaded their troops at various points along the fjord to knock out Norwegian shore batteries and seize a nearby armory. Two antiquated and unwieldy Norwegian ironclad coastal defense ships tried to protect the town, only to be blown out of the water by torpedoes from the destroyers. The German force was soon ashore, seizing strategic points around the city. Its commander and the local German consul persuaded the Norwegian garrison commandant to surrender without a fight. In less than three hours, the strategically crucial port of Narvik was securely in German hands. At Trondheim, the heavy cruiser *Admiral Hipper* and four destroyers sailed into the harbor and debarked 1,700 troops against very light resistance. In Bergen harbor, the cruisers *Königsberg* and *Köln* escorted a flotilla past the port's inept defenders and put an assault force ashore that took the city unopposed. The Norwegian naval base at Kristiansand held off the cruiser *Karlsruhe* with heavy artillery fire until Luftwaffe bombers demolished its batteries. German troops then overran the base.

The German assault on Norway caught the Allies by surprise. Their intelligence services failed to detect enemy preparations for the attack despite uncovering several clues to its existence. Early on the morning of April 7, RAF patrol planes spotted numerous German warships in the North Sea. The Admiralty assumed, falsely, that the Germans intended to break through the Allied blockade with heavy ships and launch a major attack on the north Atlantic shipping lanes. The Royal Navy therefore dispatched a powerful fleet from Scapa Flow to intercept the supposed raiders. The British force sped northward, bypassing the German invasion flotillas. One British destroyer, the HMS *Glowworm*, did encounter the enemy after it became separated from the task force sent to mine the Leeds. Just after 8:00 a.m. on April 8, the *Glowworm* sighted and then attacked two German destroyers off Trondheim, damaging one of the enemy vessels and driving off the other. Soon, however, the German heavy cruiser *Admiral Hipper* arrived on the scene in response to a distress call. Hopelessly outgunned, the *Glowworm* laid down a screen of thick black smoke and turned away as if to escape. The valiant destroyer then wheeled about and unexpectedly broke through the smoke screen to ram the German cruiser. The *Glowworm* sank immediately, but its blow had ripped a 130-foot gap in the enemy ship's armor and left it listing perilously.

Meanwhile the Royal Navy's Home Fleet continued its fruitless search farther out to sea for nonexistent German blockade-runners. Only on the evening of April 8 did the British begin to suspect that the Germans were moving against Norway rather than trying to break into the north Atlantic. Admiral Sir Charles Forbes thereupon divided his forces, sending the bulk of his ships south toward the Skagerrak and the balance north to Narvik. Two days earlier such a deployment would have brought disaster to the German invasion flotillas; now it was too late. The Royal Navy did manage to inflict severe damage on the enemy nonetheless. The cruiser HMS *Renown* encountered the German cruisers *Gneisenau* and *Scharnhorst* in the approaches to Narvik on April 9. The *Renown*'s fire badly damaged the *Gneisenau*, but the *Scharnhorst* escaped into the protective cover of a snowstorm. The next day a squadron of five British destroyers reached Narvik harbor undetected. Launching a surprise attack, they sank two German destroyers and damaged two others at anchor there, as well as sinking eleven enemy merchantmen. On the way out, however, the flotilla was itself surprised by five German destroyers attacking out of adjoining fjords. In the ensuing melee, the British commander was killed, two of his ships were destroyed, and a third was badly damaged. Three days later the Royal Navy exacted its revenge. The battleship *Warspite* and nine destroyers steamed into Narvik fjord to annihilate the remaining German destroyers. Fearing submarines, the *Warspite* and its escorts then quickly left the confined waters of the fjord without attempting to dislodge the German army from Narvik.

The Germans now controlled all of Denmark as well as strategic ports along the Norwegian coast. Their victory was won at a high price to the Germany navy, however. Fully half of the entire German destroyer fleet lay twisted and smoking at Narvik. Three cruisers were sunk, while two more were severely damaged. Some historians have suggested a broader significance of these naval actions. The ships lost would have played a role three months later in Germany's planned amphibious invasion of England.[19] It is doubtful, however, that these craft would have made a significant difference. Even at full strength, the Kriegsmarine was no match for the Royal Navy.

The battle for Norway was not yet over. The Germans had not been able to prevent King Haakon VII and his government from escaping from Oslo and appealing for national resistance against the invader. The six divisions of the Norwegian army began to offer a spirited, if ill-coordinated, defense. The Allies also moved, belatedly, to oppose German control of Norway. Anglo-French forces were dispatched with the objective of retaking Trondheim and Narvik. Yet the German onslaught could not be stopped. The Norwegian army had lost most of its artillery and communications network in the initial German attack. The defenders also lacked air cover, armor, and antitank guns. The enemy, in contrast, employed light tanks to spearhead its advances and enjoyed decisive superiority in the air. The Luftwaffe constantly harassed Norwegian and Allied movements, and just as importantly, it could quickly bring supplies and reinforcements to the advancing German columns. Norwegian resistance was frequently courageous but, constantly pounded on the ground and from the air, three of the four divisions in southern Norway were soon forced to submit. Those defenders still holding out began to retreat northward through central Norway's long mountain valleys, with the Wehrmacht close behind. At best, they could hope only to slow the German advance until Allied help might arrive.

The Allies planned to dislodge the Germans from Trondheim and Narvik, relieve pressure on the hard-pressed Norwegians, and cut the iron ore supply route. They chose not to assault the targeted ports directly but to land forces on either side of the objectives for encircling attacks. It was probably too late to redeem the situation in Norway under any circumstances, but the decision to split the Allied force into four relatively small groups instead of concentrating it for a powerful blow directly against Trondheim undermined whatever chance of success may have remained. In addition, the various land, sea, and air elements of these operations were poorly coordinated under the ponderous direction of a government committee in London chaired by Churchill. A week after the German invasion, Anglo-French forces landed eighty miles north of Trondheim and one hundred miles southwest of that port. To outflank Trondheim and support the Norwegian units in the central valleys, the Allied troops had to slog far inland through the ice and snow still covering the countryside in April. Both contingents were smashed by the Germans, who were strongly reinforced and supported by tanks and aircraft. Allied troops retreated rapidly to avoid annihilation. They could do nothing to assist the beleaguered Norwegian defenders who now were forced to surrender.

Farther north, the campaign to take Narvik and cut the flow of Swedish iron ore to Germany did not fare much better. British troops, later supplemented by French and Polish forces, landed in mid-April at points north and south of Narvik and began to converge on the city. Their progress was slowed by severe Arctic storms and by lack of training for operations in the mountain snows. Norwegian troops also attacked the Germans from the east. Despite the Allies' numerical superiority and supporting fire from the Royal Navy, the advance toward Narvik over rough, snow-covered terrain was agonizingly slow. The port itself was not overrun until May 27. By this time, though, a powerful German relief column was moving northward through central Norway. The capture of Narvik was a fruitless, temporary victory. Allied troops evacuated the Narvik area by sea during the first week in June, leaving the Norwegian forces to negotiate a surrender to the Germans. All of Norway now lay in enemy hands. The ore route to Germany was secure, and Admiral Raeder would have the rugged Norwegian coastline to shelter his U-boats and commerce raiders. The outcome bolstered the prestige of German arms while further sapping the confidence of the Allies.

Even before the evacuation of Narvik, the disastrous turn of events in Norway had undermined the government of Neville Chamberlain. The near rout of British forces in the Trondheim operation brought increasing public calls for new political leadership. The Chamberlain cabinet survived a vote of confidence in Parliament on May 8, but its formerly unassailable majority of well over two hundred votes shrank to eighty-one. Many Conservative members either voted against their own prime minister or abstained. Chamberlain still hoped to maintain his position if he could convince the Labour and Liberal Parties to join a coalition government under his leadership. That proved impossible. Chamberlain's relations with the opposition leaders were too embittered to permit such cooperation and, beyond that, the public had lost confidence in the prime minister.

The political and military situation required the formation of a new cabinet that would unite the Conservatives and the opposition in a government of national unity and buoy up the country's flagging spirits. Labour leaders indicated that they would participate in a new government under either Lord Halifax or Winston Churchill. Chamberlain, most Conservatives, and the king preferred Halifax, but Halifax was reluctant to accept the office. Churchill, in contrast, was eager for the mantle of leadership. He felt himself destined to lead the nation through its supreme ordeal. Churchill was a maverick who had alienated much of his own party by assailing its defense policies and by attempting to block reform in India. Yet his past opposition to appeasement, however unpopular with the party leadership, bolstered his standing among the British people. Ironically, the man who bore a large share of responsibility for the defeat at Norway was now thrust into office as the one candidate who could unite the nation and prosecute the war most effectively. Churchill became prime minister on the evening of May 10, 1940. Britain had a new leader who believed in himself and his people—a leader determined to win the war at whatever cost. Churchill's determination and ability were to be tested immediately. After seven months of *Sitzkrieg*, Hitler launched an all-out offensive on the western front on the morning of May 10.

Notes

1. Quoted in John Lukas, *The Last European War: September 1939/December 1941* (Garden City, NY: Anchor/Doubleday, 1976), 241.

2. John Strawson, *Hitler as Military Commander* (New York: Barnes & Noble, 1971), 39.

3. Robert M. Citino, *The German Way of War: From the Thirty Years' War to the Third Reich* (Lawrence: University Press of Kansas, 2005).

4. Dennis Showalter, *Armor and Blood: The Battle of Kursk; The Turning Point of World War II* (New York: Random House, 2013), 33–34.

5. Quoted in Karl-Heinz Frieser, *The Blitzkrieg Legend: The 1940 Campaign in the West* (Annapolis, MD: Naval Institute Press, 2005), 10.

6. Paul Schmidt, *Statist auf diplomatischer Bühne* (Bonn: Athenäum-Verlag, 1953), 469.

7. Cf. Adam Tooze, who argues that "Hitler was confronted with the near certainty that Britain and France would declare war." *The Wages of Destruction: The Making and Breaking of the Nazi Economy* (New York: Penguin, 2006), 662. Even before signing the Nazi-Soviet Pact, Hitler told the Italian foreign minister that he "was absolutely convinced that the Western democracies would, in the last resort, recoil from unleashing general war." Quoted in Stephen G. Fritz, *The First Soldier: Hitler as Military Leader* (New Haven, CT: Yale University Press, 2018), 76.

8. This is the thesis of T. W. Mason, "Innere Krise und Angriffskrieg," in *Wirtschaft und Rüstung am Vorabend des Zweiten Weltkrieges*, ed. Freidrich Forstmeier and Hans-Erich Volkmann (Düsseldorf: Droste, 1975), 158–88. Also see Timothy Mason, *Nazism, Fascism and the Working Class* (Cambridge: Cambridge University Press, 1995). Cf. Tooze, *The Wages of Destruction*, 321–22.

9. Quoted in Tooze, *The Wages of Destruction*, 316.

10. Quoted in Richard J. Evans, *The Third Reich at War, 1939–1945* (New York: Penguin, 2008), 11.

11. Quoted in Peter Fritzsche, *An Iron Wind: Europe under Hitler* (New York: Basic Books, 2016), 6.

12. Alexander B. Rossino, *Hitler Strikes Poland: Blitzkrieg, Ideology, and Atrocity* (Lawrence: University Press of Kansas, 2003), xiv.

13. Timothy Snyder, *Bloodlands: Europe between Hitler and Stalin* (New York: Basic Books, 2010), 120–21.

14. Nicholas Stargardt, *The German War: A Nation under Arms, 1939–1945; Citizens and Soldiers* (New York: Basic Books, 2015), 38.

15. C. Talbot Imlay, *Facing the Second World War: Strategy, Politics and Economics in Britain and France, 1938–1940* (Oxford: Oxford University Press, 2003).

16. Tooze, *The Wages of Destruction*, xxiii.

17. Roderick Macleod and Denis Kelly, eds., *The Ironside Diaries, 1937–1940* (London: Constable, 1962), 113–14.

18. Nikita Khrushchev, *Khrushchev Remembers* (Boston: Little, Brown, 1970), 152.

19. Evan Mawdsley, *World War II: A New History* (Cambridge: Cambridge University Press, 2009), 115.

CHAPTER 5

Nazi Conquest: The Fall of France and the Battle of Britain

The Fall of France

The strange peace that reigned on the western front could not last indefinitely, for Hitler understood that his ambition to dominate Europe could not be realized before the power of France was broken. As soon as Poland capitulated, the Führer began to press his high command for a plan of attack in the West, but the German generals were not anxious to turn against France so soon after their victory in the East. "The French have some 60 divisions available," General Wilhelm R. F. Ritter von Leeb recorded in his diary. "Our losses will be enormous. . . . An attack against France cannot be conducted like an attack on Poland; it will be longer and much more murderous."[1] Hitler would not be dissuaded, however. He told General Brauchitsch, "I place a low value on the French Army's will to fight. Every army is a mirror of its people. The French people think only of peace and good living, and they are torn apart in Parliamentary life. Accordingly, the Army, however brave and well trained its officer corps may be, does not show the combat determination expected of it. After the first setbacks, it will swiftly crack up."[2] Hitler knew that Germany could not win a prolonged struggle with the richly endowed Allies; only a rapid, crushing blow could secure victory. Under his prodding, the general staff soon came up with a plan, "Case Yellow" (*Fall Gelb*), which consisted of a thrust through Belgium toward Ghent, designed to split the French army from the BEF and to secure air and sea bases on the English Channel for further attacks against Great Britain. This plan was so unimaginative that it might well have led the Wehrmacht to disaster had not the time-consuming difficulties of transferring troops from Poland and continuously severe weather caused a series of postponements. Historian Stephen Fritz suggests that the army leadership produced such an uninspired and limited plan as an indirect way of deterring Hitler from attacking at all.[3] The Führer's seemingly foolhardy aggressiveness caused a few senior commanders, particularly Admiral Wilhelm Canaris of the Abwehr (military intelligence), to consider deposing their leader, but nothing came of it.

Case Yellow was modified subsequently to include a diversionary flanking attack through the Ardennes region of Belgium and France, but it remained an operation of limited objectives with no potential for decisive victory. Moreover, it required the German army to attack precisely where the Allies expected the blow to fall. At this point, a fortuitous accident led to a change in German strategy. On January 10, 1940, a military plane flying between Münster and Cologne lost its way in the fog and eventually made a forced landing at Mechelen, Belgium. The plane's lone passenger, Major Hellmuth Reinberger, was carrying a briefcase full of documents concerning *Fall Gelb*. He had time to burn only a part of these top-secret papers before Belgian soldiers swooped down on him. From the charred fragments, Allied intelligence could discern the German plan, at least in broad outline. Case Yellow was now hopelessly compromised by its disclosure to the enemy. In addition, the Mechelen incident caused the Allies, fearing an imminent German attack, to begin the preplanned, preliminary deployment of their best units along the Belgian frontier. From this movement, German intelligence discovered how well prepared the Anglo-French forces were for a German attack through the Low Countries. The Wehrmacht would have to devise a new strategy for victory in the West.

Even before the Mechelen incident, Hitler was dissatisfied with the battle plan formulated by the high command. Working independently, both the Führer and Generals von Manstein and Guderian had already begun to conceive an alternative plan that would shift the focus of the German thrust from the Low Countries in the north to the Ardennes forest in southern Belgium. This axis of attack avoided both the strong concentration of Allied mobile forces in the north and the virtually impregnable defenses of the Maginot Line in the south. One army and the bulk of the armored forces were now shifted from the north for the Ardennes operation. After punching through this weakly defended sector, these forces were to pivot northward toward the English Channel to cut off and annihilate the British and French armies then moving into Belgium. The Manstein plan, code-named *Sichelschnitt* (Sickle Cut), depended on the devastating striking power and speed of massed armored formations, closely supported by air power. It would surprise the enemy, throw him off balance, outflank him, and pound him into submission before he could reorganize for a counterattack. German studies of Allied tactics, organization, and past behavior led them to believe that the enemy would react slowly to such a surprise.

German general Erich von Manstein, author of the Fall Gelb *plan to defeat the Allies in western Europe.*
Source: *Wikimedia Commons*

Audacious *Blitzkrieg* tactics had succeeded brilliantly in Poland, but would they work against the much larger and more formidable French army? While Manstein's plan was ingenious, it was also highly risky. If the enemy could bring concerted flanking attacks against the racing panzer spearheads, the whole operation might well disintegrate. Many senior German army commanders feared that the *Sichelschnitt* was a plan for disaster. General Fedor von Bock warned:

> You will be creeping by ten miles from the Maginot line with the flank of your breakthrough and hope that the French will watch inertly. You are cramming the mass of the tank units together into the sparse roads of the Ardennes mountain country, as if there were no such thing as air power! And you then hope to be able to lead an operation as far as the coast with an open southern flank 200 miles long, where stands the mass of the French Army![4]

Bock was not wrong. Operation Sickle Cut was a very high-risk roll of the dice. Army Group B in the north fielded only twenty-nine divisions, of which three were panzer units. To provide overwhelming striking power at the decisive point of attack, Army Group A concentrated forty-five divisions, including seven panzer divisions, supported by two-thirds of the Luftwaffe's planes. There were *no reserves* in case the operation failed to achieve decisive results—all the tanks and combat aircraft were committed to the initial attack. Moreover, packing all the resources of Army Group A in one great formation, awaiting the moment of attack, virtually invited the Allies to discover the operation and launch devastating preemptive air strikes. Most ranking generals did not support an all-or-nothing attempt at a knockout blow against France. Their qualms did not matter, however, for Manstein had the backing of the one man whose opinion counted—Hitler.

Allied defense strategy played into German hands. The Allies expected the Germans to repeat the Schlieffen Plan of 1914, that is, to strike at France through neutral Belgium (and perhaps Holland as well). The Maginot Line was so formidable that they expected the enemy to avoid it. Similarly, the Allied planners believed that the inadequate road system, broken terrain, and forests of the Ardennes would preclude a major assault through that region. The Allies therefore assigned the best of the French army as well as the BEF to the Franco-Belgian border. Belgian neutrality prevented these forces from preparing a strong defensive position on Belgian territory before the Germans attacked. The Anglo-French forces therefore had to await the German assault before moving to a defensive line that ran from Antwerp to Brussels along the Dyle River and beyond. In March, General Gamelin, the French supreme commander, revised Allied strategy. Now French troops entering Belgium in response to a German thrust would move much farther than the Dyle Line, all the way to Breda and Moerdijk in the Netherlands. General Henri Giraud's powerful 7th Army was withdrawn from Gamelin's strategic reserve to execute the maneuver. The objectives of this "Breda Variant" were to link up with the Dutch army and to prevent the Germans from securing valuable bases on the coast of Holland.

The heavy commitment of Allied forces to the Low Countries worried General Alphonse Georges, the French commander on the critical northeastern front. He wrote to Gamelin:

> Our defensive maneuver into Belgium and Holland must be conducted with care to avoid . . . engaging on that part of the theater, before a German action which might be no more than a feint, the major part of our available forces. For example, in case of an enemy attack . . . in the center of our front between the Meuse and

the Moselle, we would find ourselves lacking the means necessary for a riposte. It is therefore necessary to act . . . with prudence.[5]

Precisely what Georges feared developed when the Germans attacked. The best Allied armies rushed into Belgium and Holland, leaving weak forces in reserve and covering the Ardennes.

If the Allied cause was to suffer defeat in northern France, it would not be for the lack of men and equipment. In all categories of arms, except air power, the Allies equaled or surpassed enemy strength. French, Belgian, British, and Dutch forces taken together totaled some 134 divisions, opposing 136 German divisions on the western front. Nor were the Allies at any qualitative disadvantage to their opponent. They possessed more well-trained, fully equipped, first-line units than the Wehrmacht. The German generals certainly thought so. After the evacuation of Dunkirk, General von Bock, surveying the equipment left behind by the Allies, commented, "Here lies the *matériel* of a whole army, so incredibly well equipped that we poor devils [i.e., the Germans] can only look on it with envy and amazement."[6] In tanks, the Allies enjoyed both a quantitative and a qualitative edge over Germany. French *Char* B series tanks were by far the most powerful vehicles to see action in this phase of the war. Even the medium-weight French tanks and the British "Matildas" were more than a match for the best German panzer Mark III and IV tanks. Counterpoised to the German army's ten panzer divisions, France fielded three "light mechanized divisions," which were armored divisions equal in striking power to a panzer unit. The French also employed four heavy armored breakthrough divisions that were more powerful than any panzer division. In addition, the French army deployed five tank-equipped light cavalry divisions and thirty-three independent infantry-support tank battalions. A British tank brigade and two Belgian armored divisions augmented these French forces. In total, the four Allies possessed 4,200 armored vehicles compared to the 2,439 tanks of the Wehrmacht. Allied air strength—if it had been fully deployed—outnumbered the Luftwaffe 4,468 to 3,578 combat aircraft.

Yet, even after the lessons of the Spanish civil war and the stunning German victory over Poland, the French still did not grasp the potential of armored warfare. As late as 1939, French army chief Gamelin argued that "armoured divisions . . . can handle local operations, like reducing a pocket, but not an offensive action."[7] Only in the air were the Allies at a substantial disadvantage to the Germans. While the Luftwaffe committed 2,750 aircraft to the battle, the French air force had only one thousand first-line planes available in metropolitan France. The RAF had some four hundred planes based in France at the beginning of May and added a few more squadrons during the struggle, but the British were never willing to commit the bulk of the Royal Air Force to the Battle of France. They retained numerous squadrons in England to protect the home islands and to fly strategic bombing missions over Germany. Besides this significant numerical inferiority, the Allied air forces were neither as thoroughly trained nor as well equipped as the Luftwaffe to carry out tactical attacks against enemy ground troops. This, too, proved to be a serious shortcoming.

In deploying their forces, the Allies allocated great strength to both ends of their line of battle but left its center weakly guarded. Besides the ten garrison divisions manning the Maginot Line, Gamelin left thirty more divisions behind the line to respond to any possible enemy breakthrough. Thus, rather than saving troops for use elsewhere, the Maginot Line absorbed a disproportionate share of available forces. In the north along the Belgian frontier, the Allies assembled their best units for the planned thrust into the Low Countries to join the Belgian and Dutch armies. Closest to the English Channel, General Giraud's 7th Army, with seven crack infantry divisions and one light mechanized division, was set to advance as far as Breda. Next to Giraud, the BEF under Lord Gort would move up to the Dyle River. Below Gort, General Georges Blanchard's powerful 1st Army was assigned to hold the vulnerable Gembloux Gap in Belgium. A Cavalry Corps, consisting of two light mechanized divisions commanded by General René Prioux, would hold the gap while the 1st Army moved into position. In total, some thirty first-line divisions, including all the light mechanized divisions, most of the motorized infantry, and two of the heavy armored divisions, were to be hurled into Belgium.

These heavy concentrations on the northern and southern ends of the Allied defensive line left few resources to plug its center. There General André Corap's 9th Army was to move up to defend the Belgian Ardennes after hostilities began. Next to Corap, the 2nd Army under General Charles Huntziger would protect the French frontier from Sedan to the upper end of the Maginot Line. The 9th and 2nd Armies combined possessed only sixteen divisions, some of which were inferior series B reserve divisions and fortress units. Overcommitted on both wings of his line of battle, Supreme Commander Gamelin retained only thirteen infantry and two armored divisions in strategic reserve. This lack of mobile reserve forces made it extremely difficult for the Allies to respond when the enemy struck unexpectedly at the French center with their most powerful formations. Moreover, the Allied intelligence services failed to evaluate properly the evidence of German troop movements and reconnaissance flights that should have indicated the possibility of an attack through the Ardennes.

The Germans deployed their forces in a very different pattern than the Allies. Across from the imposing Maginot Line, General von Leeb's Army Group C disposed of only nineteen, mainly second-line, divisions and no armor. No serious fighting was anticipated on this front. Leeb's only task was to keep forty-five French divisions pinned down by the possibility of a German attack on the Maginot Line. In the north, Army Group B, under General von Bock, mobilized along the Dutch and Belgian borders. Bock's forces—twenty-four and a half infantry, two motorized, and three armored divisions—were to attack through the Low Countries just as the Allies expected, thereby convincing them to commit their strength prematurely to the northern sector. Meanwhile, the real focal point of the German attack lay through the Belgian Ardennes. Here General Rundstedt's Army Group A would strike with seven armored, three motorized, and thirty-five and a half infantry divisions, supported by more than a thousand aircraft.

Hitler unleashed all this assembled military might early on the morning of May 10, 1940. The first blows fell against Holland to reinforce the Allied expectation that the main German thrust was coming through the north. Göring's Luftwaffe not only hammered Dutch airfields but also mercilessly bombed and strafed The Hague, Rotterdam, and other major cities. Lacking a powerful army, the Dutch defense relied on flooding large areas of their country and blowing up the bridges over Holland's many canals and rivers. The Germans hoped to prevent this by employing terror bombing and an airborne assault on the Dutch capital to force the Netherlands out of the war quickly. At first things did not go well for the attackers. Eleven of thirteen planes carrying German paratroops to take Amsterdam by surprise were shot down by Dutch antiaircraft guns and fighters. Dutch army counterattacks routed the rest of the German airborne force. SS troops in stolen Dutch uniforms tried to take the Meuse bridges at Maastricht, but the defenders destroyed them first. However, at Dordrecht and Waalhaven, the Germans were able to seize key bridges. Even before the enemy had crossed their borders in strength, the Dutch army immediately began to pull back from the Peel-Raam defensive line to defend the big cities of "Fortress Holland." This maneuver undercut Gamelin's Breda Variant, since it was no longer possible for the advancing French 7th Army to make contact with retreating Dutch forces. With its principal cities

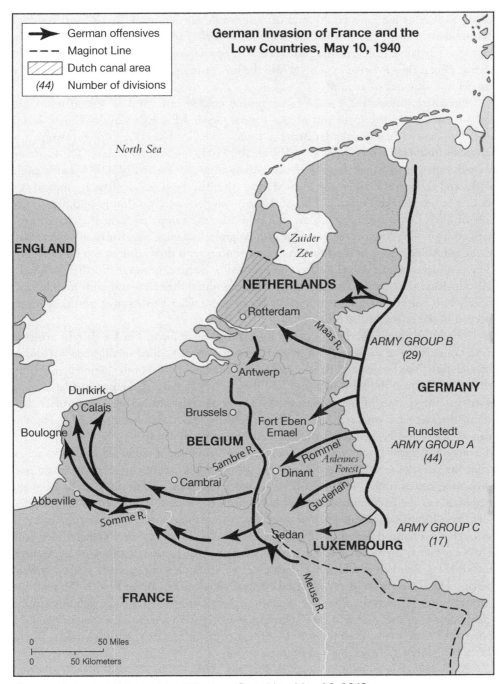

German Invasion of France and the Low Countries, May 10, 1940

Legend:
→ German offensives
- - - Maginot Line
▨ Dutch canal area
(44) Number of divisions

German Invasion of France and the Low Countries, May 10, 1940

suffering under murderous aerial bombardment and German tanks streaming across the Maas (Meuse) River, Holland capitulated within five days.

The Germans' greatest success on the first day of the war occurred in Belgium. There, at the strategically crucial confluence of the Meuse River and the Albert Canal, stood the most powerful fortress in Europe—Fort Eben Emael. Rising a sheer 120 feet above the canal and protected by thick concrete and steel, the fort seemed unassailable. The Allies expected that its big guns could fend off a full-scale enemy attack for at least five days. Rather than attempt a futile direct attack on this mighty fortress, the Germans took it by stealth. They landed a few dozen glider-borne troops on the fort's unprotected roof. These daring raiders then lowered explosives into the turrets and gun casements of the fort. Eben Emael was soon out of action.

Elsewhere, British and French forces moved quickly into the Low Countries to take up positions along the Dyle and Meuse Rivers. General Prioux's Cavalry Corps, racing ahead of General Blanchard's 1st Army to protect the Gembloux Gap, fought two panzer divisions to a standstill on May 12–13. Casualties were high on both sides. The Germans were stunned to discover how well the heavily armored French SOUMA tanks could withstand their fire. Farther north on May 14, the BEF repulsed the first attempt of von Bock's forces to take Louvain. The Allied commanders were cautiously optimistic. The loss of Eben Emael had been a blow, but otherwise the campaign seemed to have begun well enough. The Anglo-French thrust into Belgium had gone smoothly, and the performance of Allied troops in their first major encounters with the Germans was encouraging. The confidence of the Allied leaders soon turned to dismay, however, for they had badly miscalculated the enemy's strategy. They had committed their best and most mobile units deeply into northern Belgium at precisely the moment when those forces were desperately needed in the center of the Allied line.

The Allied command did not detect the main German force. The foe thereby achieved devastating strategic surprise. This was a failure not only of Allied intelligence but also of imagination. The French and British generals could not conceive of the main enemy thrust channeled through the Ardennes, nor had they fully internalized the potential speed and overwhelming punch of massed armored formations. Spearheaded by seven panzer divisions, the Germans smashed into southern Belgium and Luxembourg on May 10. The narrow roads and broken terrain of the Ardennes severely hampered the invaders, but it did not stop them. Long columns of soldiers and equipment stretched back 150 miles, from the point of attack to well beyond the Rhine. Messerschmitt fighters swarmed over this troop concentration to drive off Allied reconnaissance planes and thereby keep the magnitude of the Ardennes operation hidden from the enemy. The German commander, Gerd von Rundstedt, divided his armored forces into three corps, each assigned to break through the French defenses and cross the Meuse at a different point. General Hermann Hoth's armored divisions attacked toward Dinant. Two panzer divisions under General Georg-Hans Reinhart made for Monthermé, while Guderian's panzers slashed toward Sedan. The Germans soon encountered the leading elements of the French 9th and 2nd Armies—four light cavalry divisions and two mounted brigades. These French units gave a good account of themselves in fierce fighting, but they were not strong enough to halt the powerful enemy attack, even though the Ardennes provided many natural barriers. By the 12th, the panzers were rolling into French territory.

As in Poland, so now in France, the *Blitzkrieg* could not be stopped. French observers had studied the Polish debacle, but the French high command still had not adequately prepared for the shattering impact on morale of air and armored assault, or for the devastating speed of *Blitzkrieg*. The Luftwaffe was everywhere in the skies over the battlefield. The psychological effect of the bombing proved even worse than the physical destruction it caused. Soldiers who could withstand the heaviest artillery barrages panicked as the screaming Stukas dived toward them. Allied air power, in contrast, was completely ineffective. Most Allied planes fought in the northern sector; few were available where it really mattered. Neither the RAF nor the French air force had the proper equipment or tactics for close support of ground troops. Luftwaffe fighters and heavy fire from German flak guns savaged Allied bomber formations. At one point, for example, seventy-one obsolete British Fairey Battle light bombers were sent to attack German pontoon bridges across the Meuse at Sedan. Only thirty-one of the planes returned—without having destroyed their targets.

Many of the troops in General Corap's and General Huntziger's commands who bore the brunt of the German onslaught were not up to the challenge. Especially among the raw recruits and overaged reservists of the B-series divisions, the boredom and tense uncertainty of the phony war had seriously undermined morale. Lieutenant General Alan Brooke, a visiting British commander, was shocked by the dispirited and undisciplined men of the French 9th Army.

> I can still see those troops now. Seldom have I seen anything more slovenly and badly turned out. Men unshaven, horses ungroomed, clothes and saddlery that did not fit, vehicles dirty, and complete lack of pride in themselves or their units. What shook me most, however, was the look in the men's faces, disgruntled and insubordinate looks, and, although ordered to give "Eyes Left," hardly a man bothered to do so.[8]

There had been some superficial bravado among the troops, but the grim reality of battle stripped that from them. Confusion and panic soon replaced their earlier boastfulness. These soldiers would not hold their ground when the fighting became intense as their fathers had at Verdun a generation earlier.

Thanks to strong German air cover over the Ardennes, Allied intelligence was slow to assess the significance of developments there. Ninth Army headquarters received some photos of a massive traffic jam in the Ardennes, but commanders there could not believe this was the main enemy thrust. As news began to trickle in of enemy attacks in the region, the Allies assumed that these operations were diversions meant to distract them from the supposedly decisive battle in the Low Countries. By the afternoon of May 11, General Georges began to show some concern over developments in the center of the French line. He instructed two armored, one motorized, and three infantry divisions to move up behind Sedan. Had these orders been carried out energetically, the Battle of France might have ended differently. As it was, the French thought they had days, rather than just hours, to respond to the enemy threat in the Ardennes. This was typical of French reactions to German speed and daring; it was too little, too late. Worse yet, General Huntziger assigned his best units to guard the upper end of the Maginot Line, leaving poorer troops, including the B-series formations, to guard Sedan. Guderian's XIX Corps took Sedan against light opposition on May 12 and prepared to move across the Meuse the following day. The crossing was not easy. French artillery kept up a heavy barrage, while murderous point-blank fire hit the attackers from a line of pillboxes on the other side of the river.

Air power made a crucial difference. The Luftwaffe committed 1,500 planes to the battle, while the Allied air forces were scarcely to be seen above Sedan. Diving Stukas kept the French gunners scrambling for cover while German tanks, as well as antitank and antiaircraft guns, rolled down to the river's edge to fire directly into the French pillboxes. Despite suffering heavy casualties, German assault troops crossed the Meuse in rubber rafts and began to reduce the remaining French fortifications. The French will to resist had already begun to crack. Time after time, small squads of Germans persuaded twenty- to thirty-man French bunkers to surrender without further resistance. By nightfall, three German regiments had carved out a bridgehead four miles beyond the Meuse. Yet no panzers could cross the river, for the French had blown up the bridges. A determined French counterattack at this point would certainly have crushed this weakly held German bridgehead and kept the panzers at bay across the Meuse.

There would be no counterattack. The French high command still did not grasp the seriousness of the situation around Sedan, and Huntziger's troops had lost their enthusiasm for the fight. The dreadful hammering from the air and the mere *rumor* that German tanks had crossed the river caused the French 55th Division to panic. As General Edouard Ruby recalled:

> A wave of terrified fugitives, gunners and infantry, in transport and on foot, many without arms but dragging their kitbags, swept down the Bulson road. "The tanks are at Bulson!" they cried. . . . Officers were among the deserters. Gunners . . . and infantry soldiers . . . were mixed together, terror-stricken and in the grip of mass hysteria. . . . Much worse, commanders at all levels pretended having received orders to withdraw but were quite unable to show them or even to say exactly where the orders had come from. Panic brooked no delay; command posts emptied like magic.[9]

With Guderian's three panzer divisions still on the far side of the Meuse, the only tanks the hysterical French troops could have seen at Bulson would have been their own! Some French units, even among the reservist troops, stood their ground courageously. But far too many French troops threw down their weapons and fled from their first serious encounter with the enemy. Mounting casualties combined with fear and a lack of resolve to defend their homeland undermined French resistance.

The panic of the 55th Division quickly spread to the neighboring units. Meanwhile German engineers spanned the Meuse with a pontoon bridge, and the panzers began to spill into the bridgehead. The French corps commander for the area, General Grandsard, ordered a counterattack by two tank battalions and two infantry regiments. This riposte never materialized. It disintegrated amid the disorganization and fear spreading like a plague throughout Grandsard's X Corps. Guderian's armor was soon pushing west, rapidly expanding the initial bridgehead.

Farther north, this pattern was repeating itself where Hoth's XV Panzer Corps advanced toward the Meuse. One of the corps' two armored divisions lagged behind in snarled traffic, but the other one, commanded by General Erwin Rommel, surged ahead to win a decisive victory. On the night of May 12, elements of Rommel's motorized infantry first crossed the Meuse at Houx. French resistance, even from the A-series troops in this sector, was sluggish. Using his heaviest tanks, two dozen Mark IVs, for covering fire, Rommel forced a crossing at Dinant the following day. Just as at Sedan, the French failed to mount a sufficiently strong counterattack to smash Rommel's bridgehead before his tanks could be brought across the river. The powerful French 1st Armored Division sat idle on the 13th, just twenty-five miles from the enemy's precarious toehold at Dinant, but General Corap thought only to contain the German penetration, not smash it. Another opportunity was missed. By the 14th, the panzers were west of the Meuse and ready to start a decisive breakthrough. Between Guderian and Hoth, Reinhardt's XLI Panzer Corps ran into more determined resistance in its drive to cross the Meuse at Monthermé. Here, well-dug-in French regulars held up the Germans for over two days. Reinhardt's troops also lacked sufficient air support because the Luftwaffe was then concentrating its efforts around Sedan.

The news that enemy forces had crossed the Meuse in at least two places stunned French commanders when they heard it early on May 14. General Georges' earlier fears had now been realized. The Breda maneuver, sending the best Allied troops dashing into the Low Countries, had left the French center fatally weak. Still more unwelcome news awaited the French on the 14th when the Dutch army capitulated.

The German position was still precarious. Guderian's decision to wheel westward after smashing out of his Sedan bridgehead left his overextended forces dangerously vulnerable to counterattack along their flank. His superiors ordered him to halt temporarily to let the infantry catch up, but he disregarded that command. The plan called for all three panzer spearheads to stop and dig in after securing bridgeheads across the Meuse. That would give the infantry time to arrive in support of the next phase of the operation. Both Guderian and Rommel, however, disobeyed these directives in order to take advantage of an opportunity that they sensed but which neither the German nor the French high commands could see. With the 1st and 2nd Panzer Divisions now racing toward the English Channel, Guderian could leave only one infantry regiment and a panzer division at Stonne to guard against a potentially disastrous French counterthrust from the south.

Once more, however, French sluggishness and timidity saved the Germans. Two powerful units, the 3rd Armored and 3rd Motorized Divisions, were available to strike the XIX Panzer Corps' flank, but they did not do so. Huntziger was still confused about the direction the German breakthrough might take. He feared that Rommel intended to curl southward behind the Maginot Line. Huntziger therefore let an equally overcautious corps commander deploy his forces in defensive positions to contain the Germans rather than attack them. The enormous striking power of the 3rd Armored Division was thus wasted, with its complement of superior *Char* B tanks dispersed along a twelve-mile defensive line. Moreover, Huntziger's decision to defend the flank of the Maginot Line entailed pulling his 2nd Army farther away from Corap's 9th Army, thereby widening the gap through which Guderian's forces would burst. By the 15th, they were in Montcornet. Little but open country now stood between them and the Channel. The French eventually did attack the enemy at Stonne, but not with sufficient forces to achieve more than a stalemate in a hard-fought action.

A similar disaster was taking place at Dinant. Early on May 15, General Corap ordered his 9th Army to fall back from the Belgian Meuse to positions on the French frontier. Communications broke down, and instead of executing an orderly retreat, the 9th Army began to disintegrate. At the same time, the French 1st Armored Division was ordered to repulse the German breakthrough. This unfortunate unit, lacking artillery and infantry support, was in the process of refueling when Rommel's panzers struck. Once again, the powerful *Char* B tanks took a heavy toll on the enemy, but without fuel, many of these invaluable machines were destroyed by their own crews to prevent them from falling into German hands. Rommel quickly swung around the immobile French force to the west and broke into open country. The trailing 5th Panzer Division then finished off the 1st Armored in a ferocious engagement. Another of France's irreplaceable armored divisions had been squandered piecemeal.

The French 9th Army now completely buckled under the weight of the German onslaught. Retreat turned into rout. Unit after unit broke up and reeled backward in panic. The collapse of Corap's army doomed the valiant defenders of Monthermé. Two panzer divisions broke through the crumbling enemy lines. Desperate French soldiers began surrendering in droves. An uncomprehending German captain recorded in his diary the incredible spectacle of a French column meekly marching into captivity:

They had, however, no weapons and did not keep their hands up. . . . They were marching willingly without any guard into imprisonment. Behind this first company which I saw followed new groups, ever new groups. . . . There were finally 20,000 men, who here in the sector of our corps, in this one sector and on this one day, were heading backwards as prisoners. . . . It was inexplicable. How was it possible that, after this first major battle on French territory, after this victory on the Meuse, this gigantic consequence should follow? How was it possible, these French soldiers with their officers, so completely downcast, so completely demoralized, would allow themselves to go more or less voluntarily into imprisonment?[10]

In another encounter, some ten thousand French soldiers were captured at a cost of only forty-one casualties among Rommel's troops.[11]

By May 16, all three German armored spearheads had broken through the French defenses and were wheeling westward, beginning their race for the Channel. In the First World War, tens of thousands of men had died in any number of battles just to gain a few hundred yards. Now the panzer columns sped on against light resistance, covering as much as thirty miles a day. General Georges ordered the French 2nd Armored Division forward to help plug the gap, but its units were widely dispersed and unprepared when Reinhardt's panzers smashed through them. Yet another crucially needed armored division had been carelessly committed and therefore wasted.

The Allies were holding their own against the Germans in northern Belgium. The collapse of the French center from Dinant to Sedan, however, caused the Allies to begin a general withdrawal. Their response to the enemy breakthrough was both slow and timid. The throngs of terrified civilian refugees (an estimated eight million people) and demoralized troops that clogged every road hindered Allied redeployment even more than the Luftwaffe's bombing and strafing. Seeking to lessen German air superiority, Premier Reynaud begged the British to send over every available warplane. Air Chief Marshal Hugh Dowding dispatched a few additional fighter squadrons, but he refused to strip England's defenses by shipping the entire Fighter Command to France.

The only remaining hope of avoiding a major Allied defeat in northeastern France lay in the possibility of launching powerful, coordinated attacks from north and south against the flanks of the racing panzer columns. Unfortunately, the French high command still did not understand the situation it faced. The French generals believed that the German offensive would soon lose momentum. Dominated by the World War I continuous front fixation, they continued to pile up reserves along the sides of the German penetration, but they did not attack. First-rate mobile infantry units and tank battalions were stretched out on a defensive line to contain the Germans rather than being concentrated to destroy them. Moreover, the French still had not fathomed the enemy objective. They wasted part of their strength by deploying forces to guard Paris, fearing that the panzers might pivot toward the capital at any moment.

The Allies were also beginning to run out of resources. Three out of four French armored divisions had already been frittered away. Only de Gaulle's newly formed 4th Armored remained. General Prioux's Cavalry Corps, which had fought so well earlier in the Gembloux Gap, had been dispersed along the entire 1st Army front at the insistence of senior infantry commanders. The crack Allied mobile forces in the north were now largely locked in combat with Bock's Army Group B and were therefore unable to disengage and transfer to the critical central zone.

The enemy almost gave the French the reprieve they needed to reorganize and redeploy their forces. The German high command—mainly old infantry generals like their French counterparts—had never really believed that Operation *Sichelschnitt* could achieve decisive results. By May 16, with the panzer divisions ranging far ahead of their supporting infantry and artillery, even Hitler had begun to lose his nerve. The big gaps between the armored spearheads and the rest of the army seemed to invite Allied intervention. On the 17th, Guderian was ordered to halt his advance. Only by threatening to resign his command was he able to get his orders revised to permit at least a "reconnaissance in force." The enterprising, if insubordinate, Guderian thereupon resumed his offensive.

In contrast to Guderian's boldness, what few counterattacks the Allies mounted were scattered and irresolute. De Gaulle's new and still incompletely equipped 4th Armored Division attacked Guderian's flank on the 17th and again on the 19th. Both assaults made good progress initially but, lacking air and infantry support, each was soon beaten back by determined German resistance. General Georges' attempt on the 17th to launch a simultaneous attack from the north simply disintegrated for lack of adequate forces. The German tank commanders grew disdainful of these pathetic Allied ripostes. "The enemy does not represent a very serious danger," General Reinhardt reported, "and his local attacks are nothing more than pinpricks, deprived of any unified command. There is only one mission for the XLI Army Corps: to push on without bothering about either the right or the left." Reinhardt had good reason to discount the danger of a powerful Allied counterstroke. German intelligence had broken the French army field codes, so he and his colleagues knew a great deal about the size and disposition of the enemy units facing them. The Allies had no such advantage. Their efforts to decipher and use German codes were not fully successful until after the Battle of France had been irretrievably lost.

The British did no better than the French. Sir Edmund Ironside, chief of the Imperial General Staff, pressed for a major attack on the northern flank of the panzers in conjunction with a French assault from the south. Lord Gort, the BEF commander, procrastinated and made excuses. When Gort finally launched an armored counterattack southward from Arras on the 21st, he committed a mere two battalions to the battle. Such a light assault force could do no more than win a few local successes and then fall back once more.

Only on the 18th did the French command finally realize that the enemy objective was the English Channel, not Paris. By then the situation in the north was virtually hopeless. The aging Maxime Weygand replaced Gamelin as supreme commander on the 19th, but shuffling generals would not halt the panzers. Like his predecessor, Weygand hoped to stem the enemy tide with counterattacks south from Cambrai and north from the Somme. Such a plan, if executed forcefully a few days earlier, might well have succeeded in blunting the German drive. The Allies could not overcome their own disorganization. By the 23rd, any hope for a successful flanking counterattack collapsed as the German infantry finally moved up to support the panzer columns. The enemy had already reached the Channel. Guderian's armor had crashed through two British territorial divisions on May 20—the only hostile forces between it and the sea—and then had broken through to the coast, cutting off the Allies in Belgium. Soon the panzers were swinging northward along the Channel, attempting to cut off the Allied forces' last route of escape. The Germans had achieved the greatest encirclement in military history. More than 1.7 million Allied troops were caught between Army Groups A and B. Over a million of them would soon be taken prisoner. Success had come not only from German daring and Guderian's brilliant execution of a high-risk plan, but also from an extraordinary amount of good luck and Allied lethargy.

By the evening of the 22nd, Guderian's tanks had reached the gates of Boulogne and Calais, but there they encountered much stiffer Allied resistance. The Germans were now up against the best of the Anglo-French forces. It took three days of hard fighting to take Boulogne and yet another day before Calais was overrun. Army Group B, up to this point merely a decoy to mislead the Allies, now assumed a more significant role in the German strategy. Von Bock's troops increased the pressure on the already exhausted Belgian army, causing it to fall back from the Escaut Line on the 23rd. Meanwhile, Weygand's projected counterattack against the German thrust materialized as nothing more than a few dispersed probes by small British and French units. Yet even these relatively weak sallies alarmed both Hitler and von Rundstedt. Guderian was poised to annihilate the large Allied force apparently trapped between his armor and von Bock's mass of infantry, but Hitler held him back.

The Führer ordered the panzers not to move beyond the Aa Canal, halfway between Calais and Dunkirk. The German armored force had seen almost half of its tanks knocked out of action on its drive from the Ardennes to the Channel. German mobile forces had fought continuously for fifteen days with little food and less rest, sustained only by large doses of amphetamines. Hitler and Rundstedt feared that the remaining panzers would be so badly mauled in the bitter struggle to reduce the encircled Allied pocket around Dunkirk that they would no longer have the strength thereafter to turn south to deal with the rest of the French army. Göring assured Hitler that his Luftwaffe could pulverize the Allies from the air, thereby sparing the precious armored units. Thus, for two days, May 25 and 26, the panzers stood idle. Guderian was thunderstruck, but he dared not countermand a direct order from the Führer. The opportunity to destroy the BEF—virtually all the British army's first-line units—along with large French formations slipped away.

As early as the 19th, Lord Gort was already considering the possibility of abandoning the Continent. Some RAF units, fearing that their bases might be overrun by the panzers, were by now shifting to airfields in England. Gort was convinced that the situation in France was hopeless and that the only sensible course open to him was to save his troops to fight another day by evacuating to Britain. Despite continued discussion among the Allies about a concerted counterattack, Gort was pulling his forces back toward the coast by the 23rd. Hitler's order to halt the panzers gave Gort the time he needed to disengage most of his troops and funnel them to Dunkirk. When Hitler finally unleashed the panzers on the 26th, German armor soon broke through the British defensive line, trapping nearly half of the French 1st Army around Lille. The fierce resistance put up there by French troops enabled the BEF and the remainder of the 1st Army to reach the coast. The British withdrawal left Belgium to its fate. The hard-pressed Belgian army surrendered on May 28.

For the Allies entrapped at Dunkirk, everything depended on holding their bridgehead long enough for the rescue operation, code-named Dynamo, to extricate them. To this end, the British belatedly committed the bulk of the RAF, for the first time winning air superiority over northern France. The Royal Navy and French warships, supplemented by an armada of civilian craft, now began to ferry the Allied soldiers across the Channel to safety. The Luftwaffe, hampered by poor visibility and constantly harried by the RAF, was unable to accomplish Göring's boast that it could "finish the job." In all, some 338,000 Allied troops—including the majority of the BEF and 110,000 French soldiers—were saved. Unfortunately, all their equipment and a thirty-thousand-man French rear guard had to be left behind. For the British, Dunkirk was a glorious and nearly miraculous operation that saved the BEF to defend the home islands. For the French, Dynamo represented abandonment by their ally at the time of France's greatest peril.

France had suffered a calamitous defeat, but it had not necessarily lost the war at this juncture. Large French formations remained intact along the southern perimeter of the German advance. The Maginot Line, backed by large concentrations of troops, was still virtually untouched. Their air force, due to stepped-up production and deliveries from America, was now larger than at the beginning of the invasion. But if the tools to transform defeat into victory were at hand, the spirit was not. Many of the French leaders, much of the army, and perhaps the nation itself had lost the will to fight.[12]

Weygand hurriedly organized a forty-division defensive line along the Somme and Aisne Rivers. Abandoning the continuous front doctrine, Weygand relied on a series of strongpoints, or "hedgehogs," which could continue to offer stout resistance even if surrounded or bypassed by the panzers. Reserves of mobile forces were established behind the hedgehogs to deal with any enemy breakthrough. These reserves were seriously weakened, however, when the French commander squandered most of his remaining armor in futile attacks against the German bridgeheads at Abbeville and Péronne. After the fall of Dunkirk, the Germans gave their exhausted panzer formations several days for rest, repairs, and redeployment. These forces were reorganized into five panzer corps, each consisting of two armored divisions and one motorized infantry division. Then on June 5, three of these corps stormed across the Somme, and on the 9th the other two attacked along the Aisne.

As in the earlier round of fighting, some French units fought with exceptional courage while others simply melted away. There were even incidents of defeatist civilians actively hindering their own troops. Soon the panzers had punched gaping holes in the French line. General Weygand, having lost faith in the outcome of the war, had failed to prepare successive positions to which his troops could fall back to continue resisting. The French government fled from Paris on June 10. Weygand declared the capital an open city, and on the 14th, German troops entered Paris unopposed. The German mobile forces encountered stiff resistance in some places as they advanced to the south, but the French high command failed to organize a coherent defense. The Maginot Line was cut off from the rear by enemy troops on the 17th. Four days later, with the mighty line still unpierced, its four hundred thousand defenders surrendered.

The fighting in Western Europe is sometimes characterized as a "clean" war, conducted by the Wehrmacht according to the widely accepted rules of combat, in stark contrast to numerous atrocities committed by the SS and the army on the eastern front. It is true that, overall, German forces were better behaved in the West than in the East. However, the invasion of neutral states, the terror bombing of large cities, and the murder of thousands of African colonial POWs serving in the French army belie any claim to fighting a "clean" war. The bitter fighting in the Low Countries and France also produced numerous casualties. The Germans lost 49,000 men killed or missing and 111,000 wounded. Panzer formations lost up to half their tanks. The Dutch and Belgians lost over 10,000 troops. The BEF lost about 68,000 men killed, wounded, or taken prisoner, with an additional 2,500 casualties for the RAF. French losses were the most severe—approximately 123,000 killed, 250,000 wounded, and 1.6 million taken prisoner.

Amid this collapse, Premier Reynaud, General de Gaulle, and a few other French leaders sought to hold out against the enemy at all costs. They planned, if necessary, to retreat into Brittany, where, resupplied by sea from England, they might hold out until the tide of war turned against Germany. Failing that, the government could abandon metropolitan France altogether and continue the struggle from French North Africa. Reynaud was opposed by a strong defeatist faction within the government led by General Weygand and by that redoubtable hero of an earlier war, Marshal Philippe Pétain. These men assumed that Britain would soon be conquered too, making their continued resistance pointless. They also grossly underestimated the cost to France of Nazi occupation. Reynaud warned them, but they would not listen: "You are taking Hitler for Wilhelm I, the old gentleman who took Alsace-Lorraine from us, and that was that. But Hitler is Genghis Khan."[13] Moreover, the defeatists had lost all faith in the republic and in the nation. They feared that continued resistance would not only be futile but might also precipitate a leftist revolution in France. Faced with the presumed alternatives of radical revolution or Nazi conquest, they chose Hitler.

The British also had a great stake in the continued resistance of France. Every additional day the French held out gave Britain more time to prepare its own defenses. British leaders were gravely concerned about what might happen to the powerful French fleet if the French government capitulated. In Nazi hands, this fleet might make a cross-Channel invasion of England possible. Prime Minister Churchill therefore frantically sought to stiffen the resistance of his ally. He even went so far, at de Gaulle's suggestion, as to offer a full political union between the French and British peoples if the French would continue to fight. Churchill's gestures, however dramatic, had no effect. After Dunkirk, the British had no influence in French councils.

Under intense pressure from his own defeatist colleagues in the government, Reynaud resigned as premier on the 16th. Marshal Pétain took his place and immediately asked the Germans for a cease-fire. To underscore the symbolic significance of his victory, Hitler forced the French to sign an armistice on June 20 in the same railway car at Compiègne where, at the end of World War I, the German army had surrendered to the Allies. Soon thereafter, to demonstrate German might to the newsreel cameras of the world, the Germans held a triumphant parade down the Champs-Élysées in Paris. The terms of the armistice were lenient by Hitler's standards. Pending a final peace settlement, most of the French army was to demobilize and the navy was confined to its ports. German prisoners were to be released immediately, but French POWs would remain in captivity until peace negotiations were complete. The German army would occupy about two-thirds of France, including the whole Channel and Atlantic coastline. The Germans added all surviving French military equipment to their arsenal. The Reich subsequently incorporated Alsace-Moselle.

The subservient Pétain regime would govern the rest of France from the resort town of Vichy—in cooperation with Berlin, of course. The French fleet and empire would remain (temporarily) under Vichy's control—though the Japanese would quickly pressure Vichy to let them occupy French Indochina. The terms might well have been harsher, but Hitler wanted to ensure that the French would not attempt to fight on from their colonies or turn their fleet over to Britain. Hitler was exultant (though the famous newsreel of him appearing to dance a jig at Compiègne was an invention of Allied film editors). Proclaiming the conquest of France "the greatest battle of world history," the Führer toured Paris in triumph, making a point to have himself photographed at Napoleon's tomb.

Explaining Defeat

The rest of the world was almost as stunned by the victory of the *Blitzkrieg* as were the French themselves. How could the world's most thoroughly trained and best-equipped army crumble so ignominiously after a mere six weeks of fighting? Allied disunity was certainly a part of the problem. Belgium and Holland maintained strict neutrality until attacked by Germany, making it impossible to prepare inter-Allied defenses properly. Once hostilities had begun, the Dutch army rapidly retreated northward into Fortress Holland, thus pulling away from the French army rushing to link up with it at Breda and disrupting Gamelin's strategy at the very outset. Worse still, the Allies had little confidence in each other. Each of them expected to be let down by the other, so each used the anticipated poor performance of its ally as an excuse for its own inadequacies and failures.

British mobilization to flesh out the BEF had been slower than expected. When the Germans struck in May, the BEF fielded only ten divisions, none of them armored. No wonder many people in France gained the impression that Great Britain was willing to "fight to the last Frenchman." This supposed bad faith, even betrayal, provided yet another excuse for a less than resolute defense of France. The British responded in kind. Gort and other British commanders had little faith in the French army and were therefore unwilling to commit the whole BEF to an all-out assault that would have drawn it deeper into France.[14] They never wanted to move very far from the coast. The French, similarly, anticipated a precipitate British evacuation if the military situation grew threatening. This British "treachery" then provided a convenient excuse for not fighting on alone against the Germans.

In addition to these weaknesses within the alliance, there are several strictly military factors that partially account for the Allied defeat. Above all else, the strategy and tactics pursued by the Germans were simply far superior to those of the Allies. Manstein's brilliant strategy, audaciously executed by the panzer commanders, took the fullest advantage of revolutionary developments in weaponry—especially the tank and ground-support aircraft. In contrast, Gamelin's Breda maneuver deprived the Allies of the reserves needed to counter the enemy blow, and thereafter French commanders squandered their excellent armored forces by committing them to static defensive lines or fragmented local attacks. From the outset, the French could never bring themselves to act fast enough or decisively enough to reverse the flow of battle. Fixated on maintaining a continuous front against the panzers racing northward, French commanders never assembled the powerful strike forces necessary to crush the German spearheads. Moreover, inadequate communication and coordination between the Allies further weakened their counterattacks.

The reasons for the rapid and unexpected fall of France have been the subject of intense debate. Politicians and intellectuals scrambled to find the "grave diggers of France."[15] The composition of their various lists of villains depended on the accusers' position along the political spectrum. Marshal Pétain, head of the collaborationist Vichy regime, blamed the defeat on inadequate resources and moral failings: "Too few babies, too few arms, too few allies—these were the causes of our defeat." And later: "Our defeat was due to our laxness. The spirit of pleasure-seeking brings to ruin what the spirit of sacrifice has built."[16] For Vichy, the "grave diggers" were many—communists, socialists, liberals, pacifists, atheists, secularists, and hedonists. Marc Bloch, a French historian who died at the hands of the Gestapo, blamed a self-centered individualism and a moral lethargy that paralyzed resistance among both the nation's elites and its working class.[17] Subsequently, historian Jean-Baptiste Duroselle argued that French society had become too decadent in the 1930s to fight off the Germans as their fathers had done in the First World War.[18] Historian Eugen Weber has judged that "France was not an underdeveloped country, but a developed one in an advanced state of decay. The cascade of scandals and the cat's cradle of political and financial corruption they revealed branded parliament as a kleptocracy, squelched whatever respect the public retained for the country's political personnel, stifled the limited confidence they preserved in their state."[19]

The trend in recent historiography has been to view the defeat of 1940 in predominantly military terms. For example, Julian Jackson argues, "The defeat of France was first and foremost a military defeat—so rapid and so total that these other factors [i.e., social and ideological matters] did not have time to come into play."[20] Similarly, Nicholas Atkin sees as "the principal reason behind the debacle: defective strategy."[21] William Irvine has argued that "it was not decadence that led to 1940; it is 1940 that has led us to view the late Third Republic as decadent."[22] As outlined below, I find these strictly military interpretations far too narrow to explain the scope of the catastrophe. Despite his emphasis on military factors, Jackson has also suggested a more comprehensive way to view the debacle of 1940: "There are many strands to the Fall of France: it was a military defeat, the collapse of a political system, the breakdown of an alliance between two countries, and in the final stages, almost the complete disintegration of a society."[23]

These problems within the alliance and the various military factors can, at best, explain only why the Allies lost a major battle in northeastern France and Belgium. They do not account for the subsequent rapid collapse of all French resistance. The military situation facing France was far from optimal, but it did not absolutely mandate surrender. In comparison, the Chinese had already lost several battles of greater magnitude than the loss suffered by France, but the Chinese continued to resist. During the following year, the Soviet Union would endure still more terrible blows without collapsing. China is larger and the USSR much larger than France, a geography that gave those powers more room to retreat and reorganize a defense. But France is not a small country, like Belgium or Holland, that could be overwhelmed at a single blow.

Moreover, resistance could have continued from the French Empire. The French were defeated after the fall of Dunkirk because they *believed* they were defeated. Weygand went through the motions of organizing a new defensive line and fighting another battle as a matter of national honor, not because he had any faith in his ability to stop the enemy. Nor was it only the leaders who lacked confidence in France. The German assault troops fought their way from the Ardennes to Dunkirk and then to the Pyrenees against numerically superior forces, driving on for days at a time under constant bombardment, with little food and less sleep, often using amphetamines to keep going. Their morale remained excellent. On the French side, while some units fought valiantly, others threw down their weapons and fled at the mere rumor that the panzers were coming. French morale had not seemed terribly low on May 10, but it collapsed almost completely after the first setbacks. Too many Frenchmen had ceased to believe in themselves and their republic; too few were willing to make the sacrifices that all-out resistance entailed.

The phony war—long, tedious, and anxiety ridden—undermined morale. According to Eugen Weber, "testimony about the spring of 1940 paints a somber picture of depression and defeatism among commissioned and noncommissioned officers, as in other ranks. . . . The conclusion is hard to avoid that the long months of inaction during which a great war machine was left to run in neutral sapped what resolution there had been and prepared the rout to come."[24] Historian John Williams suggests that a failure of leadership contributed to this malaise. "Neither the military nor civil leaders were giving the country any moral preparation for the trials to come. Apart from the disappearance of most able-bodied males, civilian France retained an almost peace-time atmosphere in these waiting months."[25] When the fighting started, French casualties were not extreme by World War II standards—much less than those endured by the Chinese and the Russians (even considering the disparities in population size among the three countries). There was little determination to fight to the death for the Third Republic. In 1940, the French lacked what historian Richard Overy has called "the will to win," that is, the determination "to continue through periods of intense crisis, stalemate or defeat, to keep the prospect of victory in sight and to mobilise psychological and moral energies of a people under threat."[26]

The incipient civil war that simmered below the surface of French politics throughout the 1930s further sapped the national will. It robbed Frenchmen of any confidence that the nation could stand together to recover from the initial disaster. It made Frenchmen see saboteurs and "fifth columnists" behind every defeat. There were few actual traitors, either on the extreme right or among the communists, but the sense of cohesion that bound the national community together had been dangerously weakened before the Germans struck. Division, despair, and defeatism doomed the defense of France. Ultimately, the conservative men who dominated the Third Republic's last cabinet—Pétain and his associates—preferred defeat to the specter of revolution. They feared that defeat in 1940 might replay the scenario of 1870–1871 when defeat by the Prussians gave rise to the radical Paris Commune. They did not want France to be defeated, but when defeat seemed likely, they embraced it as a way to destroy the hated Third Republic with its liberalism and pluralism.[27]

For France, the tragedy was just beginning. The Compiègne armistice transformed France from England's partner into a quasi-ally of the Third Reich. There had been considerable friction between Britain and France even while the two countries fought side by side. After the alliance dissolved, a great wave of anti-British sentiment swept over France. Many Frenchmen blamed English treachery for their nation's defeat. Relations between the former allies grew steadily worse.

British authorities were especially concerned that the formidable French fleet might fall into German hands. That dreaded possibility would instantly transform the relatively weak German navy into a serious threat to Great Britain. Powerful French battleships and cruisers, sailing under the swastika flag, might be able to keep the Royal Navy at bay while the Nazi legions crossed the Channel to attack Britain's home islands. The British would go to any length to prevent that eventuality. Admiral François Darlan assured the British Admiralty that the Germans would never gain control of his fleet, but the British hesitated to rely on the French admiral's assurance in so crucial a matter. Therefore, in desperation, they launched Operation Catapult—the neutralization of the French fleet. Beginning on July 3, French ships in British ports and at Alexandria, Egypt, were seized. Most of the French navy, however, was at anchor in its own ports. A British task force (Force H) sailed to Mers-el-Kébir, a major French naval base on the Algerian coast near Oran. Its commander demanded the surrender of all French ships or their internment in neutral ports; otherwise they would face immediate destruction. Complying with the British ultimatum would have violated the Franco-German armistice and might have provoked the Nazis to serious punitive measures against France, so the French refused. Tragedy ensued.

Force H opened fire, sinking the battleship *Bretagne* and badly damaging the battleship *Provence* and the battle cruiser *Dunkerque*. Nearly 1,300 French sailors were killed. In the next few days, the British destroyed or captured several more French warships, but Catapult was far from an unqualified success. Fully two-thirds of the French fleet eluded the British, concentrating at the mighty Toulon naval base. The French government was outraged. The Vichy regime immediately broke diplomatic relations with Great Britain. The former allies were now transformed into virtual enemies. Even after the armistice, Churchill had hoped, by supporting General de Gaulle, to persuade as many Frenchman as possible, especially in the colonies, to continue resisting the Axis. Mers-el-Kébir made de Gaulle's task immensely more difficult. After the incident, most French naval officers and sailors in England abandoned de Gaulle and demanded repatriation. In contrast, Operation Catapult served to boost morale in England and to impress the rest of the world with Britain's ruthless determination to hold out against Germany. Hitler would soon test the strength of that resolve.

The Battle of Britain

Now Great Britain stood alone. Hitler did not expect that he would have to conquer England. After the spectacular success of the *Blitzkrieg* in France, he was sure that the British would realize the futility of holding out against German hegemony in Europe. Hitler therefore initiated peace feelers through Sweden and Spain. "All I have ever asked," he told an American journalist, "is that Germany should enjoy equal rights with Great Britain and receive back its former colonies. It has never been my intention to destroy the empire."[28] He was offering Britain, in effect, a junior partnership in his New Order, though these terms did not reflect his much harsher long-term intentions for the fate of the British people. German military plans and procurement orders at this time indicate that the Führer believed England would voluntarily cooperate in his plans. As early as July 3, Hitler informed his General Staff that their next great campaign would be against Russia. By the end of the month he was also talking about a "battle between the continents"—namely, war with the United States. The construction plan for a great fleet of battleships and aircraft carriers was reinstated. These projects would have to wait, however, because Great Britain stubbornly refused to play the supine role that Hitler had assigned to it.

Britain's leaders briefly debated the possibility of making concessions to Hitler (especially on colonial issues in Africa) in exchange for peace, but they soon came to understand that the proffered Anglo-German partnership would inexorably lead to Nazi domination of England. Lord Halifax, the British foreign secretary, therefore publicly rejected Hitler's peace initiative. The only peace terms London would have accepted at this point were completely unacceptable in Berlin: German withdrawal from all conquered territories and the replacement of Hitler and his regime by a non-Nazi government. Fortunately Britain had now found a man to lead its defiance of Nazi conquest—Prime Minister Winston S. Churchill. During the Battle of France, Churchill had already warned his people that he had "nothing to offer save blood, toil, tears, and sweat." Now, facing the threat of German invasion, he proclaimed: "We shall fight on the beaches, we shall fight on the landing grounds, we shall fight in the fields and in the streets, we shall fight in the hills, we shall never surrender." The prime minister further declared in the House of Commons: "I expect the Battle of Britain is about to begin. . . . Let us therefore brace ourselves to our duty, and so bear ourselves that if the British Empire and its Commonwealth last for a thousand years men will still say, 'This was their finest hour.'" Some of Churchill's wartime rhetoric would become famous, oft-quoted lines. Journalist Edward R. Murrow commented that the prime minister "moblised the English language, and sent it into battle."[29]

These were brave words, but words alone would not halt the Wehrmacht. The miracle at Dunkirk had saved most of the British army. Much of its equipment, though, had been abandoned on the beach. The BEF had left behind 2,500 of its 2,800 artillery pieces and 8,500 of its 9,000 vehicles. General Alan Brooke, charged with organizing Britain's defense against invasion, supplemented the thin ranks of the regular army with a half-million-man Home Guard of civilian volunteers. Shipments from America of millions of World War I vintage rifles as well as machine guns and artillery pieces partially alleviated the shortage of weapons. In desperation, the London authorities even sanctioned the use of poison gas against German assault troops. If the ground forces available to repel an invasion were weak, Britain possessed, in addition to formidable air power, its overwhelming advantage in naval strength. These powerful naval and air forces were especially crucial in facing the possibility of a Nazi amphibious assault on the home islands. Nevertheless, the government was so concerned about the threat of invasion that in late June it quietly began to ship its gold reserves to safety in Canada. It also made secret plans to move the royal family, the government, and key military and scientific personnel to Canada if German conquest seemed imminent.

Great Britain's refusal to capitulate after the fall of France forced Hitler to contemplate an actual cross-Channel invasion, an eventuality he had hoped to avoid. On July 2, he ordered his commanders to begin preparations for Operation Sea Lion. The Germans planned to land in southern England on a broad front from Ramsgate to Lyme Bay. Ten airborne and seaborne divisions would carry out the initial landing. After these assault troops had secured an expanded bridgehead, additional waves of armor and infantry would land to overwhelm British defenses. These ambitious plans amounted to little more than wishful thinking. The Wehrmacht had neither the training nor the equipment for a major amphibious operation. The earlier small-scale landings along the Norwegian coast had not prepared the Germans for the immensely complex assault envisioned for Sea Lion. Lacking the proper combat and landing craft to ferry their troops across the Channel, the Germans commandeered a makeshift fleet of ill-assorted civilian craft—barges, tugboats, fishermen—from the coasts and inland waterways of Europe. Worse yet, crossing the Channel against the murderous fire of the Royal Navy and the RAF would have been a nightmare. The German admirals refused even to consider such an operation unless the British fleet first had been neutralized.

Under these circumstances, everything depended on Göring's Luftwaffe. Fresh from his failure to annihilate the Allies at Dunkirk, the vainglorious *Reichsmarschall* now promised to destroy the British navy and sweep the RAF from the skies of southern England. These foolish boasts reveal a serious underestimation of RAF strength and a gross overestimation of Luftwaffe capabilities. The Luftwaffe had shown itself in Poland and France to be a superb instrument for the tactical support of ground troops. However, the German air force had neither the theory nor the training nor the aircraft necessary for the full-scale campaign of strategic bombing to which Göring had committed it. Crucially, they lacked a heavy bomber capable of carrying a large bomb load for long distances. The Germans attempted to wage strategic air war against the British Isles with dive-bombers and medium bombers that were completely inadequate for the task. The feared Stukas, for example, proved so vulnerable to RAF fighters that they were soon largely withdrawn from the battle. The Luftwaffe also lacked a reliable long-range escort fighter to protect its bombers. The twin-engine Messerschmitt 110, designed for this purpose, had good range but poor maneuverability. It, too, fell easy victim to enemy interceptors. The excellent single-engine Me-109 was a good match for the British fighters, but its effective range was little more than a hundred miles.

Unlike the Germans, the British were reasonably well prepared for the great air battle that was about to begin. Since the mid-1930s, the RAF Fighter Command had operated on the assumption that, contrary to popular opinion, the bomber could indeed be stopped. It had therefore developed a body of tactical theory, trained a corps of pilots, and produced the superior Hurricane and Spitfire fighters. The supply of these fighters fell dangerously low during the Battle of France. The British aircraft industry responded by concentrating its resources on fighter production and quickly doubled the number available. Aircraft production proved critical in this battle. German industry constantly fell short of its goals, so the

Luftwaffe emerged from the campaign with considerably fewer planes than when it started. British industry exceeded its aircraft production quotas, and the RAF not only replaced its losses but grew in strength during the battle. Excellent fighters and well-trained pilots alone might not have been able to stop the Nazi onslaught. Fighter Command fought so effectively because it integrated its interceptors in a sophisticated system of radar stations, observation posts, and command centers. Radar, developed just in time for the Battle of Britain, could pick up flights of enemy bombers coming in over the English Channel or the North Sea. Information from various radar sites and observation stations flowed to regional command posts that plotted the enemy's course, predicted its probable target, and dispatched fighters to intercept its formations.

The British intelligence service made its contribution too. It discovered and subsequently monitored the radio beams that the Luftwaffe used to guide its bombers to their targets in night raids over England. This information was used to predict enemy targeting in advance and also to broadcast interference and thus draw the German planes off course. British cryptographers had broken the main Luftwaffe radio code by this time, so it was sometimes possible to know the enemy's plans as soon as his operational units received them. These feats of scientific intelligence work were of immense value to the RAF defenders. They could not, however, entirely prevent the large German bomber fleets from breaking through Fighter Command's defenses to rain destruction across England.

Göring unleashed his offensive on August 13, code-named *Adlertag* (Eagle Day). The Luftwaffe flew 1,485 sorties that day, losing forty-five planes, while the RAF lost thirteen fighters. Initially the main targets were radar stations, coastal defenses, and communications facilities in the south of England. The Germans hoped to destroy the RAF in the air. In the ensuing days, though, the British shot down two enemy planes for every one they lost. Moreover, the Germans usually lost a whole aircrew every time one of their planes went down, but the British, fighting over their own territory, could often save the pilot even though his plane was lost. The Luftwaffe switched to a more effective tactic on August 24. It began to concentrate massed attacks on Fighter Command's airfields and control centers and on aircraft plants. The Germans intended to smash the RAF on the ground if they could not blow it out of the air. They came perilously close to achieving their objective. Over the next two weeks, the British lost some 450 fighters and over 100 pilots. The RAF could not stand this rate of attrition for long.

Just when it seemed that the Royal Air Force might crumble under this pounding, the enemy shifted the thrust of its attacks. After a few stray bombs fell on London, RAF Bomber Command decided to strike directly against Berlin. These raids on his capital infuriated Hitler, who then ordered Göring to retaliate against London. Indiscriminate terror bombing of British cities had been scheduled to coordinate with the actual invasion, but now the rain of death started earlier than originally intended. Beginning on September 7, the Luftwaffe mounted massive daily raids against the city. Initially the Germans preferred daylight missions, but the heavy toll exacted by Fighter Command persuaded the Luftwaffe to switch almost entirely to night bombing. German bombardiers could not hit precise targets in the dark, so they conducted area bombing. This was not strategic bombing of vital industrial targets; it was terror bombing against the civilian population. The controlled German media reported that the Luftwaffe bombed only military targets, while accusing the RAF of deliberately targeting civilians.

In London, fifteen thousand people were killed, hundreds of buildings were blasted into rubble, and great fires swept the city during the "Blitz." Many Londoners found refuge during those awful nights on the underground platforms of the subway system. The British government organized an extensive evacuation of children from London and other targeted cities. Ultimately, almost four million children and adults were sent to the countryside. The relentless bombing continued night after night throughout September and October, but it failed in its objective. Göring had failed once more—he had failed to disrupt industrial production, he had failed to annihilate the RAF, and he had failed to break the morale of the British people.

Hitler had to concede that the essential precondition to an invasion of the British Isles, neutralizing the RAF, could not be achieved at this time. Operation Sea Lion was postponed indefinitely on October 12. The invasion force gathered in Belgian and French Channel ports was dispersed before the increasingly frequent attacks of RAF Bomber Command could damage it any further. The civilian craft were desperately needed for their normal functions, and the troops began their march eastward. Nonetheless, German air raids continued against England.

On the night of November 14, a force of 450 enemy bombers virtually destroyed the town of Coventry, while in May 1941, during yet another attack on London, the House of Commons was extensively damaged. Gradually, however, the German raids diminished in frequency and intensity. The Nazis drew several unpleasant conclusions from the experience. They learned that the Luftwaffe was not capable of striking decisive blows against the enemy's economic system or the morale of its population. They also discovered that their accuracy in high-altitude bombing, even in the daytime, was not very good. Strategic bombing was an utter disappointment. The Germans realized, too, that they had underestimated British air power. A combination of radar, a coordinated air defense system, good planes and pilots, and an efficient aircraft industry brought victory to the RAF in the Battle of Britain. During the struggle, Churchill commended his fighter pilots (only about one thousand men) with these stirring words: "Never in the field of human conflict was so much owed by so many to so few."

Hitler, of course, had not abandoned his intention to dominate the whole of Europe. If England could not be conquered directly at this stage, he would apply indirect pressure to bring down Great Britain. The British had the courage to hold out against him, he believed, only because they expected decisive assistance from the United States and the Soviet Union in the near future. America lay beyond the Führer's power until the German fleet-building program was completed. However, he had already decided in July to begin preparations to attack the USSR. At that time, Hitler had assumed that Britain would have been humbled long before the invasion of Russia commenced. After the unsuccessful Battle of Britain, he took the fateful decision to continue preparations against the Soviet Union as planned, even though Britain remained unbeaten.

Hitler thus committed Germany to a two-front war—exactly what he had criticized the kaiser for doing in the First World War. This was a desperate gamble to break out of the strategic bind in which he found himself in the fall of 1940. Until that autumn, German forces had smashed everything in their path, but the survival of Great Britain had derailed his strategy for defeating his opponents one at a time. A quick victory over Russia would not only secure *Lebensraum*, a central goal of his program, but would also free Japan from the Soviet threat. That, in turn, would presumably force the United States to retreat into its hemispheric defenses. With the Russians knocked out of the war and the Americans preoccupied by the Japanese menace, Britain could no longer hope for outside aid and would therefore capitulate to the Reich. Such was the fragile chain of reasoning that led Hitler to plunge

Germany into a two-front war against Britain and the USSR at the same time. The attack against Russia could not be launched before the spring of 1941. In the meantime, he would keep up the pressure against England by blockade, bombing, and diplomatic encirclement.

A Mediterranean Strategy?

The stunning German victories in Poland, Scandinavia, and France, together with the Luft-waffe's apparent ability to punish Great Britain at will, greatly strengthened the Führer's popularity at home and enhanced his prestige abroad. In Germany, many professional military men who had opposed Hitler's risky plans at every turn now came to feel that perhaps the Führer was a man of destiny. Covert opposition to the Nazi regime among officers and civilian bureaucrats reached its low ebb. His stock among the general population also rose dramatically, though most Germans were nonetheless anxious for peace. Abroad, the breath-taking string of Nazi triumphs sent nations as diverse as Turkey and Brazil scrambling to improve their relations with Berlin. Hitler sought to capitalize on this diplomatic momentum by welding a broad alliance of states together to encircle Britain and attack its colonial outposts. He planned to overrun Gibraltar, choke off England's Mediterranean supply line, and undermine the British Empire in Africa and the Middle East. Achieving these objectives required the cooperation of Italy, Spain, and Vichy France. There lay the difficulty of a Mediterranean strategy against Britain. Hitler was never able to reconcile his own desires for German colonies and strategic bases in Africa with the various mutually conflicting claims of his erstwhile allies in Rome, Madrid, and Vichy.

The Germans courted Spain briefly in the fall of 1940. Taking the vital British outpost at Gibraltar would be much easier with Spanish cooperation, and Spain could also provide bases in the Canary Islands for attacks against Anglo-American shipping. Assistance from Mussolini and Hitler had been vital to Franco's victory in the Spanish civil war. The Spanish regime was already tied to Berlin by several political and economic treaties. With France defeated and England apparently doomed, General Franco hoped to expand the Spanish Empire at their expense by entering the war on the German side. His price for joining the Axis was high. He demanded Oran, Morocco, and the enlargement of Spanish-held Río de Oro and Spanish Guinea. In addition, Franco asked for great quantities of military equipment from Germany. For Hitler, these were impossible demands. He had already earmarked most of the territories Franco wanted either for Germany itself or for Italy. With an attack on the USSR in the planning stages, there were few armaments to spare for Spain either. Moreover, Hitler was not yet ready to dismantle the French Empire. It was essential not to drive the Vichy regime, and especially its powerful fleet, into Gaullist hands. Hitler met Franco on October 23 at Hendaye on the French-Spanish border, but even the Führer's powers of persuasion could not induce General Franco to enter the war on terms acceptable to Germany. Subsequent negotiations between Franco and the chief of the German counterintelligence service, Admiral Wilhelm Canaris, were no more successful. In fact, Canaris, a longtime covert opponent of the Nazi regime, secretly advised the Spanish dictator not to cooperate with Hitler! The Spanish, despite their greed for colonial territories, were hesitant to join the war before Britain's power to retaliate had been eliminated.

While the Spaniards were reluctant, the leaders of Vichy France were anxious to collaborate with the Nazi war effort. Marshal Pétain and his ministers hoped that cooperation with Germany would win lenient peace terms from Berlin. Such collaboration could include a vigorous defense of the French Empire against Anglo-Gaullist forces, harnessing French industry to German military needs, and even granting the Germans a few bases in French Africa. In return, the Vichy regime expected to regain administrative control of all France, repatriate its POWs, and begin rebuilding its military forces. Most of all, it wanted to preserve the integrity of the French Empire from partition by Germany, Italy, Spain, and Japan. Vichy hopes foundered on Hitler's refusal to treat France as an ally rather than a vanquished enemy. The Führer lusted for the full measure of vengeance against Germany's traditional foe. He intended to abolish the French Empire and reduce metropolitan France to the status of a helpless German satellite. Hitler's only concession was to postpone the final reckoning. He kept his plans for the ultimate fate of France secret so as not to drive every Frenchman into the arms of de Gaulle and the British. He most emphatically did not want to rehabilitate France as a lesser partner in the New Order. Furthermore, as Hitler's attention shifted to the forthcoming attack on Russia, he lost interest in a Mediterranean strategy and, with it, the need to conciliate France.

America: From Neutrality to Nonbelligerence

Hitler could easily push aside the overly ambitious demands of a militarily weak Spain or the entreaties of a defeated France, but it was increasingly difficult for him to ignore the activities of the United States. With mounting anxiety, the Roosevelt administration watched the fall of Poland, then of Norway and Denmark, and finally of France and the Low Countries. For a brief period in the autumn of 1940, it seemed that even England would succumb to the Nazi onslaught. Most of the American public wanted to keep out of the war, but President Roosevelt was convinced that a complete Nazi victory in Europe might doom American efforts to maintain the independence of the Western Hemisphere. FDR hoped to avoid committing the United States to war, but from the beginning of hostilities in Poland, he sought to provide as much aid as possible to the Allies.

The president's desire to support the Allied defense effort, however, ran at cross-purposes to the widespread American belief in neutrality. Nazi aggression finally accomplished what the president's powers of persuasion could not. After the German conquest of Poland, public opinion polls showed that over 80 percent of Americans favored the sale of arms to countries menaced by aggression. Despite a high-pressure campaign by isolationist senators Borah, Vandenberg, Nye, and Clark, and by such influential publicists as Charles Lindbergh and Father Charles Coughlin, in November 1939 the Congress removed the arms embargo from the neutrality statutes. Now the Allies could obtain weapons and ammunition from the United States, so long as they paid cash for them and carried them away in their own ships. By the beginning of 1940, British and French munitions orders were pouring into American arms industries.

In February 1940, Roosevelt sent his undersecretary of state, Sumner Welles, to Germany, Italy, France, and Britain on a "fact-finding" mission to assess possibilities for a negotiated peace. FDR had little confidence that Welles could bring the belligerents to the peace table, but at least the mission would strengthen the president's image as a peacemaker with the American public and thereby help to defuse the isolationist charge that he was a warmonger. Also, American diplomatic intervention might conceivably dissuade Mussolini from entering the war and even cause Hitler to delay launching an offensive in the West, thus giving the Allies time to build up their defenses. The icy reception given Welles in

Berlin by Foreign Minister Ribbentrop laid to rest any slim hopes Roosevelt may have had for a negotiated settlement of the war.

The president therefore turned to building American military might and boosting the level of assistance provided to the Allies. In May, with the German panzers now racing across France, FDR asked Congress for a $1.18 billion supplemental defense appropriation. Thoroughly alarmed over developments in Europe, the Congress proceeded to vote $1.5 billion for defense, $320 million above Roosevelt's request. In July, the Two-Ocean Navy Expansion Act provided for the construction of 210 new warships, including seven battleships and twelve aircraft carriers. The following September, Congress, again prodded by the president, passed the nation's first peacetime military draft legislation. The Selective Training and Service Act required all men between the ages of twenty-one and thirty-five to register, and it initiated the process of expanding the pathetically small US Army into a major force.

Two factors—the need to build up America's own armed might and domestic political considerations—kept President Roosevelt from providing the enormous quantities of war materials the Allies desperately needed. Ironically, American rearmament worked against the short-term interests of the embattled Western democracies. Industry in the United States, not yet fully converted to war production, could not meet the requirements of the rapidly expanding US armed services and at the same time fulfill huge Anglo-French arms orders. Every plane and tank sent to the Allies delayed that much longer America's emergence as a military power that the dictators would take seriously. Moreover, American military chiefs worried that supplies sent to the Allies might be wasted. In mid-1940, with France shattered and a Nazi invasion of England apparently imminent, the US service chiefs feared that no amount of American aid could stave off disaster in Europe. Worse yet, American munitions might well fall into enemy hands after the defeat of England. US combat ships turned over to the Royal Navy, for example, might soon return under the swastika flag to menace America.

Army leaders were especially concerned about the need to defend Latin America. If England were defeated and the Royal Navy placed under German command, the Germans might well invade areas of South America, such as Argentina, where pro-Nazi sentiment was thought to be strong. The prospect of war with Germany in the Western Hemisphere could not be ignored. The menace of Japanese expansion in the Pacific could not be discounted either. Weakening the American military position in the Far East by transferring forces to the Atlantic region might well invite Japanese aggression. Roosevelt faced a cruel dilemma. Once again, however, events abroad helped settle the issue. The Royal Navy's destruction of the French fleet at Mers-el-Kébir demonstrated Britain's resolve not to capitulate, while the victory of the RAF in the Battle of Britain convinced the president that England would make effective use of American supplies.

The domestic political situation also tempered Roosevelt's desire to support England. It was an election year in 1940, and FDR had chosen to run for an unprecedented third term as president. Fortunately, his Republican opponent, Wendell Willkie, was not a rabid isolationist. Both parties pledged to support the democracies, but both also promised to keep the country out of war. Late in the campaign, Willkie, who trailed Roosevelt by several percentage points in public opinion polls, began to accuse the president of leading the country into war. In his public statements on the world situation, Roosevelt had sought to convince Americans that the hope of preserving national security in isolation was "a delusion," but he was also constrained to pledge that, "We will not participate in foreign wars, and we will not send our army, naval or air forces to fight in foreign lands outside of the Americas except in case of attack." Ultimately, however, the danger of war strengthened the president's bid for reelection. Believing that the menacing international scene required FDR's leadership, the voters returned him to the White House in November.

Even before the election, FDR had already pushed the country another step closer to war in support of Great Britain. The German U-boat campaign against British shipping threatened to sever England's supply lines and thereby undermine its defense. The Royal Navy was already stretched to the limit of its capacities. Churchill, therefore, asked Roosevelt to transfer fifty or sixty World War I vintage destroyers to British command. It was, he said, "a matter of life and death" for Britain. Isolationist opponents swarmed to the attack once more, but Churchill and Roosevelt found a formula to disarm the critics. In August the US turned over fifty overaged US destroyers to Britain in exchange for the right to establish American military bases on several British islands in the Atlantic and the Caribbean. Thus, the "destroyers-for-bases deal" was cast as an arrangement that would greatly strengthen American security. In addition, the politically wily president negotiated the swap as an executive agreement, thereby eliminating the need to submit the measure for Senate approval. Isolationist senators were enraged, but they were powerless to block the transaction. Besides the bases, there was also a hidden benefit for America in the deal. The War Cabinet in London secretly reassured the United States that, even if the British Isles were conquered by the enemy, the Home Fleet would under no circumstances fall into German hands.

By the fall of 1940, the United States had departed widely from the requirements of strict neutrality in its efforts to strengthen Allied resistance to Nazi aggression, yet Roosevelt still could not bring himself or the nation to accept the logic of America's increasingly prominent role in the struggle against Hitler's designs—namely, direct involvement in the conflict. The president still favored indirect participation. "There is far less chance of the United States getting into the war," he told the public in one of his "fireside chat" radio speeches, "if we do all we can now to support the nations defending themselves against attack by the Axis than if we acquiesce in their defeat, submit tamely to an Axis victory, and wait our turn to be the object of attack in another war later on. . . . The people of Europe who are defending themselves do not ask us to do their fighting. They ask us for the implements of war." America, he urged, "must be the great arsenal of democracy."

Two further obstacles had to be overcome if America was to become that "arsenal of democracy": an impending fiscal crisis in Britain that would soon make it impossible for that country to meet US "cash-and-carry" requirements for arms, and an escalating German U-boat campaign that threatened to sever England's lifeline to North America. Initially, Allied purchases in the United States had been relatively modest; Anglo-French dollar reserves had seemed more than adequate to cover these orders. During the Battle of Britain, however, a desperate British government abandoned all restraint in ordering American munitions. London now asked for the equipment to supply ten full divisions in 1941 as well as the delivery of twenty-six thousand aircraft. In December, the prime minister informed Roosevelt, "The moment approaches when we shall no longer be able to pay cash for shipping and other supplies." Churchill hoped that the president would find "ways and means" to keep the supplies flowing even when Great Britain could no longer pay cash for them.

The cash-and-carry requirements for arms sales would have to go. While disingenuously disclaiming any desire to repeal the neutrality legislation, FDR engaged his considerable rhetorical skill to do just that. Employing the homely analogy of a neighborhood fire, Roosevelt argued that a man would freely lend his garden hose to a neighbor whose house was on fire to protect his own home from catching fire too. The homeowner would not expect immediate payment for the hose, only its return after the emergency was over. By analogy, without requiring prompt cash payment, the United States ought to provide the implements of war to nations defending themselves against aggression. The United States would neither sell the weapons for cash nor give them to Britain; it would "lend" them. Presumably the munitions would be returned or otherwise be compensated for at some unspecified date after the crisis had passed.

The argument was logically dubious but politically astute. To parry charges that America would be making tremendous sacrifices merely for the preservation of the British Empire, Roosevelt also enunciated a list of noble war aims. The democracies were locked in mortal combat against the forces of aggression, not to maintain imperial hegemony but to establish "a world founded upon four essential human freedoms": freedom of speech, freedom of religion, freedom from want, and freedom from fear. This was a direct ideological challenge to Hitler, Mussolini, and the Japanese militarists, for the president claimed these fundamental rights not just for Americans but "everywhere in the world." FDR's rhetoric, combined with the public's growing apprehension over the Nazi tide of conquest, overwhelmed isolationist opposition. In March 1941, by a vote of 60 to 31 in the Senate and 317 to 71 in the House, Congress authorized the president to dispatch military equipment, without direct payment, to any country whose defense was vital to American security in his estimation. Later that month, Congress appropriated $7 billion to implement the Lend-Lease program. The American "arsenal" was gearing up to throw its full weight behind the Allied cause. Lend-Lease was welcomed by the Allies, but it was not an entirely selfless gift. The program required Britain to give America open access to all of its imperial resources and markets.

US aid, however substantial and generously provided, would have no effect if it did not reach Great Britain. Keeping the trans-Atlantic sea-lanes open was a fundamental problem in 1940–1941. Göring's Luftwaffe, which did not adequately coordinate its activities with the German navy, was never more than a minor annoyance to Allied shipping. German surface raiders, though they caused more damage than the Luftwaffe, were comparatively ineffective as well. The sinking of the German battleship *Bismarck* off the coast of France in May 1941 captured headlines but did not deal with the real threat—the U-boat. In the last half of 1940, Allied shipping losses to enemy submarine attacks jumped from a previous average of 100,000 tons per month to 250,000 tons per month. In early 1941 that figure would double again to nearly 500,000 tons per month—far more than Britain's capacity to replace lost ships.

After failing to bomb the British Isles into submission, Hitler's strategy had switched to strangulation by undersea blockade. Churchill warned Roosevelt that "the decision for 1941 lies upon the seas. Unless we can establish our ability to feed this island, to import . . . munitions of all kinds . . . unless we can move our armies to the various theatres where Hitler . . . must be met . . . we may fall by the way, and the time needed by the United States to complete her defensive preparations may not be forthcoming."[30] The president was slow to respond to the appeal. He feared that the American public was not yet ready to accept the escorting of Allied convoys by the US Navy, a step that would inevitably entail combat with German U-boats. Roosevelt devised an alternative that he hoped the public would perceive as less bellicose. He greatly expanded the area of the Atlantic defined as an American security zone to include Greenland, the Azores, and everything west of twenty-five degrees longitude. In April 1941, the US Navy began patrol duties throughout this broad region with instructions to seek out Axis vessels and radio their positions to the Royal Navy. He also ordered the US Army to occupy Iceland and Greenland to forestall the establishment of German bases on those islands.

President Roosevelt led the country away from the path of strict neutrality in several other ways as well. As 1941 opened, he sanctioned a secret conference of Anglo-American military planners in Washington, which laid the basis for future Allied cooperation. Although the two sides differed on a great many matters, they agreed that, should the United States be drawn into war against both Germany and Japan, the Allies would give priority to defeating Hitler. While such contingency planning was covert, the president took several public steps that directly challenged Berlin. He froze Axis financial assets in the United States, and he ordered Axis merchant vessels in American ports seized and turned over to the Allies.

By August 1941, Roosevelt was ready to meet with the British prime minister for a public declaration of joint aims. Their meeting, known as the Atlantic Conference, took place at sea in Placentia Bay off the coast of Newfoundland. Despite differences on several diplomatic and military issues, the two leaders agreed on a proclamation of objectives, the Atlantic Charter, which included freedom of the seas, national self-determination, collective security, and relatively free international trade. Churchill, however, insisted that these promised freedoms applied exclusively to Axis-occupied territories, *not* to the British Empire. Each side also renounced territorial aggrandizement as a war aim. Roosevelt privately reassured Churchill that he would throw the full weight of American power behind Great Britain even if he could not declare war against Germany. The president hoped that the Atlantic Conference would cause public opinion to shift dramatically in favor of a more active American involvement in the war, but in fact it served only to intensify the already bitter struggle between isolationist and interventionist camps.

By the fall of 1941, Roosevelt, like the British, had reluctantly concluded that the defeat of Nazi Germany would require that America take an active part in the fighting. However, FDR was immobilized, not only by his isolationist opponents but also by his own past rhetoric, having so often assured the American people that he would not lead them into war. He could only hope that the Germans might rashly provide an "incident" that would force the United States to declare war. Conflict between American and German forces in the Atlantic was already escalating into an undeclared naval war. Beginning in September, the president authorized the US Navy to escort Allied shipping from America as far as Iceland, from which point the Royal Navy could take over. Three battleships, a carrier, four cruisers, and various other support ships were transferred from Hawaii to bolster the Atlantic Fleet.

This was a serious challenge to German naval strategy. Either the U-boats would have to allow the convoys unhindered passage across most of the Atlantic or risk the possibility of combat with American forces. The first incident was not long in coming. On September 4 the destroyer USS *Greer*, together with a British plane, stalked an enemy submarine for several hours. After the plane dropped depth charges, the U-boat fired a torpedo at the pursuing destroyer, and the *Greer* returned fire with depth charges. Although the U-boat commander may not have known the destroyer was an American vessel, Roosevelt told a national radio audience, "This attack on the *Greer* was no localized military operation. . . . This was one determined step toward creating a permanent world system based on force, on terror, and on murder." Proclaiming the U-boats "rattlesnakes of the Atlantic," he ordered the navy to "shoot on sight" whenever it encountered enemy warships. Convoy duty would lead to still more serious incidents. On October 16, eleven American sailors were killed during a German submarine attack on the destroyer *Kearney*, and a month later 115 US seamen lost their lives in the torpedoing of the destroyer *Reuben James*.

These incidents did not shake most Americans from their irreconcilable desires to see Hitler defeated but also to avoid direct participation in the conflict. Under these circumstances, Roosevelt shrank from asking for a declaration of war. Instead, he continued to await some unpardonable German provocation or, perhaps, a declaration of war from Berlin. Hitler would not oblige. Although his admirals were eager to strike against the United States, the Führer was anxious to keep America out of the European conflict. His diplomats therefore stressed on numerous occasions that Germany had no aggressive intentions in the Western Hemisphere.

As so often in the past, it suited Hitler to conceal his real ambitions for the time being. The furor over the *Greer* incident had enabled President Roosevelt to push further revisions of the neutrality statutes through Congress—though by very narrow margins. American merchant ships could now be armed and might enter any war zone. Moreover, the navy was now authorized to convoy them all the way to England. This development threatened to undermine German naval strategy completely. England could hold out forever if unlimited American supplies were available. Still, no declaration of war was forthcoming from Berlin, though the U-boats stepped up their attacks on American shipping. America had progressed from neutrality to a pro-Allied nonbelligerence, and then to a state of undeclared war in the Atlantic. For the moment, however, Roosevelt felt himself powerless to take the final, decisive step of declaring war. The president could only wait in hopes that Hitler would lose patience and take the step that FDR could not.

Notes

1. Hans Adolf Jacobsen, ed., *Der Zweiten Weltkrieg: Grundzuge der Politik und Strategie in Dokumenten* (Frankfurt: Fischer Bucherei, 1965), 67.

2. Alistair Horne, *To Lose a Battle: France 1940* (New York: Penguin, 1970), 117.

3. Stephen G. Fritz, *The First Soldier: Hitler as Military Commander* (New Haven, CT: Yale University Press, 2018), 89,

4. Quoted in Horne, *To Lose a Battle*, 197.

5. Quoted in Jeffery A. Gunsburg, *Divided and Conquered: The French High Command and the Defeat in the West, 1940* (Westport, CT: Greenwood, 1979), 132.

6. Fedor von Bock, *Generalfeldmarschall Fedor von Bock: Zwischen Pflicht und Verweigerung, das Kriegstagbuch* (Munich: Herbig, 1995), 143.

7. Quoted in Julian Jackson, *The Fall of France: The Nazi Invasion of 1940* (Oxford: Oxford University Press, 2003), 23.

8. Quoted in Horne, *To Lose a Battle*, 222.

9. Quoted in A. Goutard, *The Battle of France, 1940* (London: F. Muller, 1958), 136.

10. Quoted in Horne, *To Lose a Battle*, 404.

11. B. H. Liddell Hart, ed., *The Rommel Papers* (New York: Harcourt Brace, 1953), 26.

12. Martin S. Alexander demonstrates that at least some French units maintained high morale, fought courageously, and inflicted serious casualties on the enemy. He identifies deficiencies in communication and control as the reasons for the French army's defeat in June. "After Dunkirk: The French Army's Performance against 'Case Red', 25 May to 25 June 1940," *War in History* 14, no. 2 (2007): 219–64. Beyond battlefield issues, however, French military and political elites had lost the will to fight.

13. Quoted in Jackson, *The Fall of France*, 105–6.

14. Gunsburg, *Divided and Conquered*, 239, 276. Cf. Martin Alexander, who argues that the British respected and perhaps even overestimated the power of the French armed forces and that Field Marshal Gort willingly put his BEF under French supreme command. "'Fighting to the Last Frenchman'? Reflections on the BEF Deployment to France and the Strains in the Franco-British Alliance, 1939–1940," in *The French Defeat of 1940: Reassessments*, ed. Joel Blatt (New York: Berghahn Books, 1998), 296–326.

15. Pertinax [pseud. for André Géraud], *The Gravediggers of France* (Garden City, NY: Doubleday, 1944).

16. Quoted in Philip Nord, *France, 1940: Defending the Republic* (New Haven, CT: Yale University Press, 2015), xii, 3.

17. Marc Bloch, *Strange Defeat: A Statement of Evidence Written in 1940* (New York: Norton, 1968).

18. Jean-Baptiste Duroselle, *La Décadence, 1932–1939* (Paris: Impr.-nationale, 1979).

19. Eugen Weber, *The Hollow Years: France in the 1930s* (New York: Norton, 1994), 7.

20. Jackson, *The Fall of France*, 213.

21. Nicholas Atkin, *The French at War, 1934–1944* (Essex: Pearson, 2001), 33.

22. William Irvine, "Domestic Politics and the Fall of France in 1940," in Blatt, *The French Defeat*, 99.

23. Jackson, *The Fall of France*, 4.

24. Weber, *The Hollow Years*, 271–72.

25. John Williams, *The Ides of May: The Defeat of France, May–June 1940* (New York: Knopf, 1968), 93.

26. Richard Overy, *Why the Allies Won* (New York: Norton, 1995), 324.

27. Cf. Irvine, "Domestic Politics and the Fall of France," 85–99; Jean-Louis Crémieux-Brilhac, *Les Français de l'an 40* (Paris: Gallimard, 1990), 1:62. Whatever patriotic rallying to the national cause may have occurred, it must have had very shallow roots for it did not survive the first major defeat in battle.

28. *New York Journal-American*, June 14, 1940.

29. Quoted in Michael Burleigh, *Moral Combat: Good and Evil in World War II* (New York: Harper, 2011), 165.

30. Warren F. Kimball, ed., *Churchill & Roosevelt: The Complete Correspondence*, vol. 1, *Alliance Emerging, October 1933–November 1942* (Princeton, NJ: Princeton University Press. 1984), 103.

CHAPTER 6

Mediterranean War

Hitler was well on his way to mastering the Continent after victories in Poland and western Europe. This impressive series of German triumphs in the first year of the war caused consternation not only in London and Washington but in Rome as well. All Mussolini's talk of a new Roman Empire paled beside the triumphs of the Wehrmacht. Not to be outdone, the Duce launched invasions in North Africa and the Balkans. The failure of those operations soon drew Germany into these theaters of war.

Italy Enters the War

During the early stages of the conflict, President Roosevelt was not the only leader of a great power who hesitated on the brink of war. Mussolini did not join Hitler when Germany attacked Poland in the fall of 1939. Italy at first remained neutral. The Duce vacillated between his desire for military glory and his knowledge of Italy's unpreparedness. The Pact of Steel, signed May 22, 1939, committed Italy to fight alongside the Reich, even in a war where Germany was the aggressor. Moreover, the Duce had often boasted to the Germans of his intent to smash France and create an Italian "*Lebensraum*" in the Mediterranean region. There was an element of social Darwinism in Mussolini's ideology. He told numerous visitors that if Italy failed to become an empire, it would surely become a colony. When the fighting broke out, however, Mussolini excused his inaction by claiming that Italy's military preparations were not yet completed. For once he was telling the truth. Although the Fascist-controlled press bellowed that Italy had large, well-equipped armed forces, in reality the country was completely unprepared for modern warfare. The army was poorly equipped, inadequately trained, and totally lacking in sufficient armored formations and close air support. The air force, despite Italy's reputation as the leading country in aviation, possessed scarcely more than five hundred first-line planes. The navy was somewhat better prepared than its sister services, but even it was not capable of effective action against the British and French fleets. Instead of real strength, Mussolini relied on the illusion of power—on a policy of bluff, bluster, and deceit. By 1939, time was running out for such a policy.

The Italian high command was slow to adopt the insight that modern warfare was "machine war." Italian doctrine held that the numbers of infantry and the spirit of the combatants were the decisive factors in battle. The Royal Army fielded some seventy divisions and would have recruited more infantrymen but for its inability to house, feed, train, and equip additional troops. Bureaucratic complexities and production delays ensured that the infantry lacked sufficient artillery, tanks, and ground-attack aircraft—machines whose quality was inferior to that of its allies and enemies. Many of the Italians' tanks were so lightly armed and armored that their German allies derided them as "self-propelled coffins." The high command was also slow to learn the lessons of Germany's *Blitzkrieg* victories in Poland and France. The inadequate grooming of NCOs and junior officers further hindered combat efficiency. Historian MacGregor Knox condemns the army's senior commanders for "intellectual torpor" and for "self-inflicted" "technological poverty."[1] He identifies the main elements of Italian strategic planning as "myopia, dissipation of effort, passivity, logistical ineffectiveness, and great and ever-growing dependence on the German Reich."[2] The navy largely ignored pathbreaking work on radar by Italian scientists and engineers. The Second World War was a war of machines. Italy failed because it was never able to produce enough of those machines or to secure the fuels and lubricants they required.[3]

Justifying Italy's failure to rush into battle, Mussolini told the Germans that his country could not enter the war unless it received additional supplies from the Reich. He then drew up a list of requirements so long that it would be impossible for Germany to fill. The Duce also affected the statesmanlike pose of a peacemaker. Hitler was not fooled. In private he complained bitterly, "The Italians are behaving to us just as they did in 1914." Berlin was not the only source of pressure for war. After eighteen years of haranguing the Italian people on the glories of conquest, it was difficult for Mussolini to explain his reluctance to fight. He did not wish to appear timid before Hitler or his own people. The stunning success of the *Blitzkrieg* in Poland impressed him greatly, but still he held back. He knew that, despite the propaganda image of overwhelming might, Italy had only ten understrength divisions ready for combat.[4]

If Fascist Italy were to re-create the imperial grandeur of ancient Rome as the Duce proclaimed, war was inevitable. Mussolini intended to postpone that war, however, until Germany had largely destroyed Anglo-French power. Yet the magnitude and speed of German victories were not an entirely pleasant surprise for him. Hitler, he feared, might conquer Europe before Italy's legions had a chance to win glory—and booty—for their master. In that case, Mussolini would never receive the large share of spoils he coveted. Italy might well sink to the status of junior partner in the Axis. German successes required corresponding Italian successes. Hitler's furious assault in the West precipitated a hurried reversal of Mussolini's policy. Mussolini convinced himself that Britain and France were declining societies that could not match the vigor of Italian and German arms—they were finished as great powers. The Duce's only fear was that the Allies might collapse completely before his Fascist war machine could be set in motion. Besides winning conquests and glory, Mussolini also expected war to complete the Fascist revolution. Combat, he thought, would turn the pleasure-loving Italian people into a nation of rock-hard warriors. It would also enable him to perfect his dictatorship by sweeping away the autonomy of the army, the crown, the church, and the rich. This was a fatal self-delusion.

Italy declared war on the Allies on June 10, 1940. The stunning success of the *Blitzkrieg* in France had weakened the resolve of the king and the generals to stay out of the conflict, so Mussolini finally got his war. Because he was so obviously pouncing on an already beaten enemy, the Duce instructed the press to hide the extent of France's collapse so that he could claim victory over a powerful foe. He brushed aside warnings from his generals that the Italian forces were not ready for a major campaign with the brutal retort that he only needed "a few thousand dead" to secure a share of the victors' rewards.

The assault that Mussolini unleashed against France was anything but glorious. In five days of fighting before the armistice, Italian troops overran a mere thirteen border villages without making any dent in the French Alpine Line. The armistice probably saved Italy from a devastating French counterattack. Nevertheless, Mussolini's propaganda machine trumpeted that Italian intervention had precipitated the final collapse of France. This "triumph" of Italian arms did not produce the great rewards that Mussolini expected. He hoped to see France reduced permanently to the status of a second- or even third-rate power. Furthermore, he claimed for Italy extensive acquisitions of French and British territory throughout Africa and the Middle East. Berlin vetoed these ambitions. Hitler was anxious at this point not to drive the French navy and colonies into the hands of de Gaulle and Great Britain. It was necessary, therefore, to mask his real intentions toward France and to make it appear that a Vichy regime that cooperated with Germany might hope to retain most of its empire. Mussolini was unhappy with the Führer's apparently lenient treatment of France, but he was powerless to alter the arrangement. Italy could occupy only Corsica, Savoy, and parts of Provence.

Disappointed though he was over his small share of the booty, Mussolini had now bound his destiny and that of his nation to the fate of Hitler's war machine. Italy, Germany, and Japan forged another link in this ill-starred community of fate on September 27, 1940, by signing the Tripartite Pact. Under its terms, Japan recognized Europe as an Italo-German sphere of influence, while Berlin and Rome acknowledged "the leadership of Japan in the establishment of a new order in Greater East Asia." The participants pledged to assist each other if attacked by a power not currently at war. Since the pact specifically excluded the Soviet Union from its provisions, the obvious intent was to warn Roosevelt that if he intervened in Europe or the Pacific, he would face the combined military might of the Axis. All three of the Axis states were anxious to keep the United States out of the war. They hoped that this show of apparent unity and resolve would deter the American president from entering the conflict. It failed to do so. Far from hindering Roosevelt, the signing of the Tripartite Pact supported his contention that a global conspiracy of aggressors threatened America. Moreover, the pact did not create a tightly unified military bloc. From its beginning, the Axis was always a "hollow alliance."[5] Each of its partners pursued different, often conflicting aims with little regard for the interests of the others, and each undertook major initiatives without consulting its partners.

The fundamental disunity of the Axis was apparent in relations between Rome and Berlin in the latter half of 1940. Mussolini was determined to maintain his independence and prestige and to avoid becoming simply Hitler's protégé. The Duce told his associates that he intended to fight a "parallel war," simultaneous with but not part of the German war effort. The moment seemed opportune for such a venture. After the fall of France, with the capitulation of England seemingly imminent, Mussolini believed that he could easily conquer the great empire he coveted.

War in Africa

The creation of such a great Mediterranean empire required the conquest of all of North Africa. For the moment, however, Hitler's policy of temporary forbearance toward the Vichy regime barred the Italians from seizing French colonial possessions in that region. In contrast, Berlin was eager to foster Italian pressure against Great Britain's African colonies. An offensive began in East Africa early in July 1940. Enjoying a numerical advantage of better than ten to one, Italian forces invaded British Somaliland from Ethiopia and struck at the Sudan from bases in Eritrea. Italian troops soon overran British Somaliland, but in the

Sudan they halted their advance after taking a few border districts. In response, the British began to build up troops in Kenya and the Sudan. They also encouraged various Ethiopian tribes to revolt against their Italian conquerors. They flew exiled emperor Haile Selassie back into the country to serve as a focal point for this resistance. In February 1941, three Kenya-based colonial divisions under General Alan Cunningham swept through Italian Somaliland and quickly wheeled westward into Ethiopia. In March, a British amphibious force from Aden recaptured British Somaliland and continued its drive southward into Ethiopia as well. Cunningham's troops took Addis Ababa on April 6 and within a month reinstalled Haile Selassie in his capital.

Despite the large number of Italian troops in this theater (still three times greater than the British forces that defeated them), Mussolini's warriors put up only weak resistance. Poor leadership at the junior officer level and badly slumping morale led to mass surrenders. Only in Eritrea did Italian troops, led by General Luigi Frusci, fight stoutly. There a determined British assault supported by heavily armored Matilda tanks was required to drive Frusci back into Ethiopia. The end of Italy's short-lived East African empire came on May 19 when the Duke of Aosta surrendered the last of his command. It was a costly defeat for the Duce. Throughout the East African campaign, the British had captured 230,000 Italian prisoners. With the completion of mopping-up operations in the summer and fall of 1941, Ethiopia became the first occupied country liberated from Axis domination.

Meanwhile, an even more important struggle began in North Africa. Flushed with the expectation of quick and easy victory in the summer of 1940, Mussolini was eager to confront England in battle. He even offered to send Italian troops to join the projected German invasion of the British Isles. Although Hitler declined Italian assistance for Operation Sea Lion, the Duce was still determined to play a glorious role in the anticipated defeat of the British Empire. He would conquer Egypt. Marshal Rodolfo Graziani launched the attack from Libyan Cyrenaica. The Italian commander had a formidable force at his disposal—two armies, over three hundred light tanks, seventy medium tanks, nine thousand other vehicles, and three hundred planes. Hitler had offered German troops and equipment to assist in the attack, but Mussolini declined. He needed to achieve a great victory on his own. To oppose this enemy concentration, the British commander in the Middle East, General Archibald Wavell, could spare only two and a fraction incompletely equipped divisions. A determined, well-executed Italian assault at this point would have been disastrous for the British, but the operation that the timorous Graziani undertook on September 13, 1940, was neither. Mussolini expected him to strike deep into Egyptian territory as far as Mersa Matruh, from which the Royal Navy at Alexandria could be bombed. But Graziani moved only about fifty miles into the Egyptian desert against light opposition and then, pleading the need for further supplies and reinforcements, halted at Sidi-el-Barrani behind a screen of widely scattered defensive outposts.

Taking advantage of Graziani's lethargy, the British counterattacked. Portions of a thirty-thousand-man force under General William O'Connor used the dark night of December 8 to sneak unnoticed between two of the fortified Italian camps. The next day they struck the encampments from the rear, moving in behind a line of Matilda tanks whose armor the enemy's antitank guns could not pierce. After overrunning the first camp, O'Connor's men turned northward and attacked the other outposts in turn. The British brought up reinforcements and, after three days of fighting, routed the Italians. The British then mounted their own offensive into Italian-held Libya. O'Connor's tank formations raced across the desert in pursuit of the stunned Italians. Devising their own version of the *Blitzkrieg*, between January

6 and February 9 they stormed Bardia, Tobruk, Benghazi, Beda Fomm, and El Agheila in quick succession. Everywhere, dazed and dispirited Italian troops surrendered in droves. At Beda Fomm, a three-thousand-man British force took some twenty thousand enemy prisoners. In London, Anthony Eden, paraphrasing Churchill's famous line, proclaimed, "Never has so much been surrendered by so many to so few." With all of Cyrenaica now cleared of enemy forces, the way stood open to Tripoli, Mussolini's last stronghold in North Africa.

Looking back on the debacle, Graziani's colleague Marshal Italo Balbo rationalized his army's defeat as a hopelessly unfair contest of Italian "meat" against British "iron." Balbo's self-justifying explanation cannot be taken seriously. While there were some problems with Italian equipment (the planes, for example, had no sand filters for desert operation), it was the British who fought at a substantial disadvantage in both men and matériel. The reasons for the collapse of the Italian military effort lie elsewhere. Most importantly, from top to bottom, Mussolini's officer corps exhibited poor leadership. Graziani was slow and overcautious, forfeiting initiative to the enemy. Many of the lower officers, though fired with Fascist enthusiasm, lacked professional competence. Morale among the troops was a problem too. Far too many of them were raw recruits with very little training. It was characteristic of the Duce's haphazard approach to war that several veteran units had been demobilized shortly before the outbreak of the conflict. Incompetent officers led inexperienced troops to slaughter. Casualty rates sometimes ran as high as ten to one against the Italians. Supply was a critical problem for the Italian forces. They lacked adequate ports on the African coast, while the British sank many of their convoys. No wonder Graziani's men surrendered by the thousands. Moreover, even as the losses mounted in North Africa, the Italians diverted some of their forces to the even more desperate military situation in Greece.

The triumphs of British intelligence also played a crucial role in this desert victory. Even though Hitler had abandoned his Sea Lion plan to invade England in the fall of 1940, the Germans had maintained the pretense that such an invasion was imminent to tie down as many British troops as possible on the home islands. The British intelligence services soon pierced this deception. Information from agents in Europe, airborne photographic reconnaissance, and the interception of enemy radio transmissions indicated that German units assigned to Operation Sea Lion were being dispatched elsewhere. This was confirmed when a key message, decoded by the top-secret Ultra communications intelligence system, revealed that the Sea Lion command staff had been disbanded. With the threat of immediate invasion of the British Isles now past, Churchill could afford to ship vitally needed reinforcements to the Middle Eastern theater.

Unfortunately, the British did not seize final victory in North Africa when it was within their grasp. The poor fighting quality of Italian forces convinced the British that they could crush the remainder of Mussolini's North African empire easily whenever they chose. Instead of marshaling troop strength for a final assault on Tripoli, the British command diverted several units from Wavell's force to other operations in East Africa and the Balkans. An opportunity was lost to liberate all of Africa from Axis control.

Mussolini's endless boasting of his invincible might, without bothering to create the actual economic and military sinews of power, had finally led to an inevitable disaster for Italian arms. Before the North African campaign had gotten underway, Marshal Balbo had requested the addition of some German armored units to his forces. The Duce had quickly vetoed that request. German participation in the conquest of Africa was the last thing Mussolini wanted. Now, however, with his African armies on the verge of extinction, he had no choice. Mussolini had to call on Hitler for assistance. Great Britain would soon have cause to regret its failure to secure all of North Africa easily from the broken remnants of the Italian army.

Italian Disasters at Sea

Misfortune plagued the Italian war effort at every turn. While one debacle unfolded on the North African sands, fresh disasters beset Mussolini's forces at sea. The Italian navy was somewhat better prepared for battle than its sister services were. It possessed some of the most modern and fastest battleships in the world. Italy's admirals, however, proved to be no more capable or aggressive than its generals. In July 1940, a powerful Italian force prematurely broke off an encounter with a British fleet under Admiral Andrew Cunningham off the coast of Calabria. In avoiding a major battle, the Italian naval command squandered two important advantages: its intelligence service had intercepted and decoded Cunningham's orders, thus revealing the enemy's strength and course, and the Italians enjoyed significant superiority in ships and aircraft. Unwilling to risk their beautiful new vessels, the overcautious Italian admirals let slip the opportunity to inflict a decisive defeat on the Royal Navy and thereby cripple Britain's ability to operate in the Mediterranean. Moreover, Italian air power proved ineffective in this encounter, doing as much damage to its own warships as to the enemy fleet.

The British, for their part, did not show the same restraint when an opportunity to destroy the Italian fleet presented itself. Much of that fleet lay exposed, without adequate torpedo netting or antiaircraft defenses, at its base in Taranto bay in southern Italy. Admiral Cunningham designed a bold, carrier-based air strike, code-named Operation Judgment, to smash the enemy's naval power. Twenty-one Swordfish biplanes took off from the carrier *Illustrious* on the brightly moonlit night of November 11. The key to the attack was the newly perfected British torpedo, which could slip under the short Italian torpedo netting to detonate beneath its target without first hitting and exploding on the bottom of the relatively shallow harbor. Skimming just thirty-five feet over the water, the Swordfish launched their torpedoes with deadly accuracy, disabling three of the five enemy battleships in port and damaging several other craft.

The Italians lost yet another round in the continuing struggle for the Mediterranean during March 1941 in the Battle of Cape Matapan. The action began as an Italian raid to cut British supply lines. The Royal Navy was well prepared, however, because British intelligence had intercepted and deciphered orders broadcast to the Italian ships. On the evening of the 28th, Admiral Cunningham's torpedo bombers damaged the battleship *Vittorio Veneto*, and later that night, British naval gunfire, directed in the darkness by radar, sank three enemy cruisers. Although the British victories at Taranto and Matapan did not, in the strictest sense, knock the Duce's navy out of the war, they certainly reinforced his admirals' already pronounced tendency toward excessive caution. Daring Italian midget submarines penetrated Alexandria harbor in December to badly damage the British battleships *Queen Elizabeth* and *Valiant*, but the naval high command in Rome did not show the same courage. The Italian admirals were never again willing to risk their capital ships in a direct confrontation with the strength of the Royal Navy. The Germans had expected the Italian fleet, so impressive on paper, to play a major role in cutting Great Britain's imperial lifeline through the Mediterranean. The failure of the Italian navy to do so was a bitter disappointment in both Rome and Berlin.

The Balkan Tangle

Routed in Africa and defeated at sea, the Italian war effort suffered a still more humiliating setback in Greece. Mussolini had never considered the various Balkan peoples worthy of independent statehood; he intended to incorporate the whole region into his empire. In the summer of 1940, the Duce told his generals to prepare for the conquest of Yugoslavia. Once again, however, Mussolini's ambitions conflicted with those of his Axis partner in Berlin. Hitler did not object to the ultimate destruction of Yugoslavian independence, but he was unhappy with the timing of the operation. The Germans would have preferred that Italy concentrate its efforts in Africa and attack Malta and Crete as well to sap British power in the Mediterranean.

Moreover, a precipitate Italian thrust into the Balkans threatened to undermine the German diplomatic position there. The destruction of Poland and Czechoslovakia followed by the defeat of France had increased Germany's leverage in southeastern Europe tremendously. Previously, French predominance in Eastern Europe constituted a barrier to German penetration and served to constrain the antagonisms each of the nations in this region harbored against its neighbors. With France now prostrate, Germany was free to expand its influence there by direct intimidation and by manipulating the unleashed small power rivalries of the area. Hitler had good reason to exploit that advantage. The region was important to the Führer as a source of foodstuffs, minerals, and, above all else, oil, which could not be cut off by a British naval blockade. Southeast Europe also flanked two vital military operations—the current Mediterranean campaign against England and the projected assault on the Soviet Union.

The Germans moved quickly to establish their dominant influence from Hungary southward to Bulgaria. In the case of Hungary, Budapest's desire for the territory of its neighbors greatly facilitated this task. Hitler had allowed the Hungarians to annex Ruthenia and parts of Slovakia when he dismantled Czechoslovakia. Then in August 1940, a German-dominated court of arbitration awarded them northern Transylvania, taken from Romania. Hungary was inexorably drawn into Berlin's orbit. The authoritarian regime of Admiral Nicholas Horthy joined the Anti-Comintern Pact in February 1939. Soon thereafter, it abandoned the League of Nations and began implementing anti-Semitic measures. The Hungarians also permitted the passage of German troops through their country. Similarly, Bulgaria gravitated toward the Axis camp after a territorial award at Romania's expense—in this case, southern Dobruja. Although King Boris still hoped to maintain neutrality, heavy pressure from Berlin forced Bulgaria to align itself with Germany. Romania, surrounded by enemies and now without the protection of France, had no choice. Having lost nearly a third of their lands, the Romanians had to rely on the protection of Germany to safeguard their remaining territory.

Romania was especially important to the German war effort because of its oil resources. To secure this strategically vital area, Hitler supported the abdication of King Charles II and the installation in Bucharest of a military dictatorship under General Ion Antonescu. By October 1940, German troops were in occupation of the oil fields. The Nazis soon dominated both Romania's army and its economy. The Germans had strengthened their grip on southeastern Europe through largely diplomatic means. They had no interest in precipitating hostilities there. Any such action might well encourage the British to open a troublesome Balkan front, as they had done in the First World War, and it would certainly cause problems with the USSR.

These German successes in Hungary and the Balkans were as unwelcome to Mussolini as they were to the British and the Russians. The Duce was humiliated. He, the senior partner in the Axis, had not even been consulted as Germany extended its dominance throughout a region the Italians considered to be within their own sphere. Once again, Italy seemed to be slipping to the status of a German satellite. That was intolerable for the Duce. He needed a compensating Italian victory in the Balkans. However, he had to abandon the projected Yugoslav campaign because Berlin, anxious to avoid open warfare in the region, had withdrawn its previously promised support and now strongly pressed Rome to drop the plan entirely. But some glorious action, some advance in southeast Europe, was essential to Mussolini's pretensions to imperial grandeur.

An attack on Greece seemed to provide the answer. Such an operation would show the world that Italian Fascism was as dynamic as Nazism, and it would prevent the Balkans from falling completely under German control. At a meeting of the two dictators in early October 1940, Hitler gave vague assurances that Greece would ultimately fall under Italian domination, but the Germans were anxious to keep the Balkans peaceful for now. Yet, in this instance, unlike the Yugoslavian situation, Mussolini believed that he could ignore German reservations. The Italians were confident that they could overrun Greece with little difficulty. The Duce took great delight in the idea of launching a major campaign without informing—and even against the will of—his Axis partner. As he told his foreign minister, Ciano, "Hitler always faces me with a *fait accompli*. This time I am going to pay him back in his own coin. He will find out from the papers that I have occupied Greece. In this way the equilibrium will be re-established."[6]

Mussolini's Balkan adventure was no better planned or executed than the disastrous Italian operations in Africa and on the Mediterranean. The Duce simply assumed that his legions could crush the despised Greeks almost effortlessly. Therefore, no serious thought was given to the difficulties that might be raised by the enemy's defenses, the rugged terrain of Greece, and the inhospitable winter weather that was then setting in. Italian generals, who should have known better, were swept along in this expectation of an easy victory. Just as at the beginning of the African campaign, Italian preparations were hopelessly inadequate. The Duce did not notify his commanders of his final decision to launch the attack until two weeks before its starting date. Raw recruits again were pressed into service, while veteran troops were being demobilized for service in agriculture. No thought was given to providing proper equipment for fighting in rainy or freezing mountain conditions. Cooperation among the army, navy, and air force was almost nonexistent. Fatal overconfidence reigned. All that would be necessary, the Italians believed, was to strike one powerful blow against the enemy and the Greek state would collapse.

The assault began on October 28, 1940, from bases in Italian-occupied Albania. General Visconti Prasca, an incompetent and vainglorious officer, began to push eight divisions, with all their heavy equipment, along the muddy mule trails of the Albanian mountains. The operation was in trouble from its inception. It soon bogged down in the face of murderous enemy artillery fire and determined Greek counterattacks. Large numbers of Albanian fascist irregulars who accompanied the Italians began to desert. The Greeks were forewarned and well prepared. Italian commanders had expected to face a Greek force of no more than thirty thousand. They encountered many times that number. The Greek dictator, General Ioannis Metaxas, rallied his nation to defend its ancient homeland. Mussolini had hoped that the threat of a Bulgarian attack would tie down much of the Greek army on the distant Macedonian frontier. Instead, Turkish pressure kept Bulgaria neutral. The Greek government received large quantities of supplies and munitions from Britain, while its army captured a great deal of equipment from the invading Italians.

By November 14, the Greek army was ready to launch a broad counteroffensive. Greek forces were now more numerous; better trained, equipped, and led; and much more determined than their opponents were. Within four days of sharp fighting, the Italians were reeling back toward Albania across the whole front. With the greatest effort, the Italians at last managed to slow down the Greeks' furious advance, but they could not stop it. At first Mussolini's controlled press hid the debacle from the Italian people. The newspapers reported that the Greeks had welcomed the invaders and shouted the Duce's praises, but the awful truth could not be suppressed for long. At home and before the world, the military prestige of Italian Fascism crumbled into nothing.

Leaders in London and Berlin followed these events in the remote mountains of northern Greece with keen interest. From the moment of the Italian invasion, Churchill was eager to provide the utmost aid to Greece. Beyond just equipment and supplies, the prime minister wanted to dispatch an expeditionary force of British troops. British strategists had already concluded that the best way to weaken Germany was to knock out its Italian ally first. Churchill conceived of southern Europe as the "soft underbelly" of the Axis. The expansion of the war into Greece, with the accompanying opportunity to strike a decisive blow against Mussolini, therefore fit nicely into British plans. Athens was not so anxious to become another element in London's grand design, however. Above all else, Metaxas wanted to avoid provoking German intervention in Greece. He was happy to have material assistance from Great Britain and even some air and naval support, but he feared that the actual presence of Allied troops on Greek soil would be too much for Hitler to tolerate. However, after the death of General Metaxas in January 1941, his successor, Alexander Koryzis, succumbed to pressure from London and allowed British troops to begin a buildup in Greece. Although the British sent only a fraction of the forces they had promised Koryzis, even their limited presence was more than enough to provoke Hitler. Clashing German and Soviet interests in the Balkans also factored into Hitler's decision to fight in southeastern Europe, just as it affected the timing of his long-planned assault of the USSR.

The Duce's plan to fight a "parallel war"—simultaneous with, but not subordinate to, the German effort—had now completely collapsed. Virtually nothing remained of that glorious "Roman Empire" that Mussolini had sought to re-create. East Africa was lost, Italian forces faced disaster in Albania and Libya, and the British navy seemed capable of punishing the Italian fleet at will. Mussolini had run out of alternatives. He could only ask Hitler to save the situation and, thereafter, accept the subordinate position in the alliance that a German rescue mission would entail for Italy. Lacking an understanding of military strategy and operations, Mussolini proved to be an incompetent warlord. The Duce had appointed himself minister of all three armed services and assumed the title of "supreme commander" of all forces. These massive defeats in North Africa and Greece (with another soon to come in Russia) seriously eroded his popularity with Italian elites and the public. His days as dictator were numbered.

Hitler could not watch passively as the Italians were defeated in Africa and the Balkans. Several considerations impelled him to rescue his Axis ally, whatever the cost. The complete collapse of Italian forces in Albania and Libya might very well precipitate the fall of Mussolini. That, in turn, would probably result in Italy abandoning the Axis. It that case, the British might well use Italian naval and air bases against Germany. Therefore, it was vital to ensure the Duce's continued rule. Moreover, the final destruction of Italian power in Africa would have completely undercut Hitler's Mediterranean strategy. It would have eliminated the possibility of cutting Britain's imperial lifeline at the Suez Canal, and it might have jeopardized the loyalty of French African colonies to the Vichy regime.

These were alarming prospects. Also, the highly mechanized German war machine depended in large part on petroleum from Romania. With the establishment of British air bases in Greece, those vital Ploesti oil fields would be well within reach of RAF bombers. Hitler did not believe that fighter and antiaircraft defenses would stop a determined air assault. Only depriving the British of Greek bases by occupying the country could assure the safety of the oil fields. Finally, the British presence in Greece menaced the flank of Hitler's projected invasion of Soviet Russia. He needed to secure the Balkan flank of that momentous operation before proceeding. The logic of intervention in Africa and the Balkans seemed inescapable.

Rommel and the Africa Corps

The situation in North Africa also required prompt attention. The campaign in Greece would have to wait until spring for suitable weather, but the hard-pressed Italians in Libya needed immediate assistance or Africa might be irretrievably lost. Therefore, in February 1941, Hitler dispatched to Tripoli a commander who possessed all the military virtues that his Italian predecessor, Graziani, lacked—audacity, resourcefulness, innovativeness. That man was General Erwin Rommel. The Führer boasted to Mussolini that Rommel was "the most daring general of armored forces whom we possess in the German army." He brought with him to Africa two divisions, one panzer and one infantry, christened the German Africa Corps. Marshal Graziani, who favored a defensive strategy for Axis forces, was dismissed, and the remainder of his troops were placed under Rommel's command. The German army high command intended their troops to defend the Italian position in Libya, but Rommel—on his own initiative—launched a much more aggressive campaign.

The British would soon have cause to regret their failure to press home the advantage over the Italians when they had the chance to clear all North Africa of Axis forces. Instead of maintaining the offensive all the way to Tripoli, General Wavell had been obliged to disperse his strength. Troops were dispatched from his command to assist the Greeks and to help smash Mussolini's empire in East Africa. The need to suppress a dangerous pro-German coup by Rashid Ali al-Gaylani in oil-rich Iraq further diminished Wavell's force. Still more British soldiers were diverted to join Gaullist Free French units in seizing control of Syria from Vichy French troops. As a result, Wavell's commander in the western desert, General O'Connor, had only an Australian division, an Indian motorized brigade, and parts of a British armored division at his disposal. Moreover, German bombing and mining of the Suez Canal further constricted supplies for the British forces in North Africa. The British supply line to Egypt now ran all the way around Africa to the Red Sea.

Ignoring orders from his superiors to play defense, the audacious Rommel planned to smash through the opposing British forces and then drive all the way to the Suez Canal. Wavell anticipated that logistical difficulties would limit German operations until the summer, but Rommel surprised the British by launching an attack before the end of March 1941. O'Connor's troops began falling back at once. Within two weeks, the British had retreated some four hundred miles. El Agheila, Benghazi, Bardia, and Sollum were lost to the Germans even faster than they had been taken from the Italians. In the confused, swirling desert fighting, General O'Connor was captured. All of Cyrenaica was again under

Axis control, except for a strong garrison left behind at the coastal fortress of Tobruk. That British enclave posed a serious problem for Rommel. It threatened the flank of his advance into Egypt and menaced his line of supply from Tripoli. Rommel attacked Tobruk twice in April but was unable to overrun its stout defenses. Each time, the Germans withdrew after experiencing heavy losses in men and tanks.

Rommel's inability to take the fortress exposed a serious weakness. The Afrika Korps was badly understrength for its mission. Reinforcements and supplies that it desperately needed were diverted for the invasion of Russia. Hitler was now repeating the error committed earlier by the British when they let a complete victory over the Italians slip from their grasp. Doubling the size of the Afrika Korps from two to four divisions might have enabled it to break through to the Suez Canal, cutting the most important communication and supply link in the British Empire. Hitler would not divert forces from the eastern front buildup, however. Instead, Rommel could only hope that the high quality of his troops, good intelligence work, and his own ingenuity would compensate for inadequate material support.

The German navy argued for giving priority to Mediterranean operations as a way of defeating Britain by dismantling significant parts of its empire and blocking its "lifeline" to India. Hitler rejected that strategy partly because of the weakness of the Kriegsmarine and the conflicting interests and ambitions of Germany's allies and clients—Italy, Spain, and Vichy France. More importantly, for both strategic and ideological reasons, Hitler had already decided to give absolute priority to an attack on the Soviet Union. The Führer believed that he would have a better opportunity to attack Gibraltar and sweep the British from the Mediterranean *after* he had defeated the USSR.

In contrast, Churchill, who considered the Middle East a vital theater of war, ordered a major reinforcement of men and tanks for Egypt. The prime minister then pressured Wavell to counterattack the Germans. Wavell launched two attacks, one in mid-May and another in mid-June. Both were repelled with considerable loss to the British. Better intelligence work and superior tactics enabled the Germans to triumph in these encounters. British intelligence, which was reading encoded high-level Luftwaffe messages, was able to give Wavell a rough picture of the enemy's overall strategy, but it could not provide battlefield details. The Germans, however, had broken the low-level field ciphers used by Wavell's formations. In addition, the Italians had stolen a copy of the US Army's "Black" code from the American embassy in Rome. Information the British gave to American diplomats was intercepted by the Italians. They shared with the Germans details of the desperate state of British defenses at that point. Rommel enjoyed a reputation as the cunning "Desert Fox" because he frequently knew his opponent's plans in advance.

German successes in the desert also rested on an important tactical innovation in armored warfare. Up to this time, hard-hitting, fast-moving tank columns had swept everything before them. The battles in Poland and France seemed to show that the *Blitzkrieg* could not be stopped. The Germans themselves had discovered, however, that well-placed, powerful antitank guns could stop the armored juggernaut. The German 88 mm antiaircraft gun, pressed into service as an antitank weapon, emerged as the most effective tank killer in the war. The combination of antitank guns, tanks, and resolute infantry provided a formidable tool either for attacks or for defending against enemy armored thrusts. German 88s, dug into the terrain and well concealed, destroyed a great number of British tanks as the unsuspecting vehicles drove toward their hidden positions. These powerful guns could pierce even the thick frontal armor of a Matilda tank at ranges up to two thousand yards. The British had lost nearly one hundred tanks in these engagements to only twelve for the

Germans. Wavell and his commanders were learning the hard way that tanks, unsupported by infantry and mobile artillery, could be quite vulnerable.

Churchill reacted to these defeats by replacing Wavell with General Claude Auchinleck. Britain continued to pour reinforcements into the Middle East, even amid the rising threat of war in the Pacific. Consequently, the British force, soon to be designated the 8th Army, was considerably superior in size and equipment to the Afrika Korps. Auchinleck now had four armored brigades at his disposal, mainly equipped with the new Crusader tanks or American-built Stuart tanks. British tanks outnumbered the panzers by a margin of four to one. The RAF also enjoyed a similar advantage over the Germans in aircraft available for tactical support. Rommel, in contrast, received little additional reinforcement. Apparently operating on the assumption that a mere change in nomenclature could affect fighting power, the high command rechristened Rommel's 5th Light Infantry Division as the 21st Panzer Division, but no extra tanks were supplied from Germany. Rommel also commanded six Italian divisions, one of them armored. Some of these units were of relatively little military value, useful only for garrison duty. Others, however, fought tenaciously under German command.

To the prime minister's great annoyance, Auchinleck would not resume the campaign against the Afrika Korps before he had time to absorb and properly integrate the numerous reinforcements flowing into the Eight Army. Operation "Crusader" did not begin until the middle of November, and it did not go well at first. The British assault, led in the field by General Sir Alan Cunningham, began to fragment immediately. Poor coordination among units was part of the problem, as was failure to learn from the May and June battles how the Germans used their antitank weapons. Once again, the enemy drew the numerous British armor within range of its effectively concealed antitank guns and then commenced the slaughter. Auchinleck and Cunningham had not worked out satisfactory assault tactics either. Their objective was to trap Rommel's armor and, using their four-to-one superiority in tanks, annihilate the panzers. They faced a dilemma, however. If the British tanks went forward with the slow-moving infantry divisions, they could not catch the elusive panzers. If the armor raced ahead without its infantry and artillery support, it fell prey to the enemy's lurking antitank guns. After five days of heavy fighting, Rommel's forces counterattacked. Moving the lighter antitank weapons forward with the panzers, his troops shattered several British units. But it was a costly victory. The Afrika Korps lost over 70 of its 160 remaining tanks.

Under these circumstances, most prudent commanders would have retired to more easily defensible positions. Instead, and against orders from the high command in Berlin, Rommel renewed his offensive. For a moment there was panic among the British. Yet, daring cannot entirely substitute for strength. The Germans simply did not have the necessary weight of men and machines for a decisive breakthrough. Now it was Cunningham's turn to counterattack and Rommel's turn to retreat again. The German commander could not afford a continuous battle of attrition with his better-supplied adversary. The Afrika Korps was still able to administer some stinging blows to the pursuing Allied forces, but it had to continue its westward retreat. On December 4, the long siege of Tobruk was finally lifted. Rommel withdrew his German and Italian forces back to strong defensive positions.

The British seemed once more on the verge of victory in North Africa, but it would again elude their grasp. Several problems plagued the 8th Army. Its large armored formations had pursued the enemy so far, so fast that their gasoline stocks were virtually exhausted. As the distance between the front and support bases deep in Egypt grew longer, the difficulties of supplying such a large force multiplied enormously. (The Germans, of course, experienced the same difficulty going in the reverse direction.) Manpower also became a problem for the Allies. Fierce fighting from May through December had taken its toll of veteran troops. Moreover, the outbreak of war in the Pacific between England and Japan meant that some of Auchinleck's best units, most of the Australians and the New Zealanders, had to return home immediately.

The Allies believed that the Afrika Korps had been fatally weakened, but it was reinforced with new tanks, fresh troops, and an air fleet transferred from the eastern front. The Germans' ability to resupply their troops also improved when Axis forces sank a British carrier and a battleship and badly damaged two other battleships. Instead of awaiting his doom as the British expected, Rommel unleashed another powerful assault in January 1942. This drive would break through the Allied defenses and reach farther into Egypt than any of the previous Axis campaigns—all the way to El Alamein.

The Balkans Overrun

While the 8th Army and the Afrika Korps chased each other back and forth across the desert sands, other German armies overran the Balkans. The invasion of Greece, scheduled for the spring of 1941, would relieve the hard-pressed Italians in Albania and at the same time protect both the Romanian oil fields and the flank of Hitler's projected invasion of Russia from British interference. Berlin had already made careful diplomatic preparations for the military campaigns it intended to mount in 1941. Hungary, Romania, and Bulgaria were drawn into the Axis. On March 1, the Bulgarians permitted the first of 680,000 German troops to enter their country for the assault on Greece. Only the reliability of strategically located Yugoslavia remained questionable. The Germans pressed the Yugoslavs to align themselves with the Axis and accept a much greater degree of economic collaboration with the Reich. The government of Dragiša Cvetkovic preferred to maintain its neutrality, but that was intolerable to Hitler. Under intense German pressure, Yugoslavia adhered to the Tripartite Pact on March 25, 1941. The promise of some Greek territory, Thessaloniki, enhanced the bargain for the Yugoslavs. The alliance was short-lived. Believing that Axis membership was only the first step in a Nazi plan to subvert Yugoslavia, just two days later military officers staged a coup in Belgrade. The Cvetkovic government was deposed, and the head of state, Regent Paul, resigned. Although the new cabinet reaffirmed its friendship with Germany, it also requested an alliance with the USSR. Moscow declined that commitment but agreed to a nonaggression pact. Since the Yugoslavs would not voluntarily accede to his wishes, Hitler determined to crush them.

Powerful Wehrmacht forces attacked Yugoslavia and Greece simultaneously on April 6. Yugoslav army defenses were quickly overwhelmed as large German armored formations poured over the country's long, exposed border from bases in Austria, Hungary, Romania, and Bulgaria. The defenders could not fall back and regroup in the interior as planned because the invaders struck in so many places and advanced so rapidly. Organized resistance soon ceased. Luftwaffe bombers pounded Belgrade mercilessly in the hope of breaking the Yugoslav leaders' will to resist. Seventeen thousand civilians died in the capital. The Nazis used political as well as military weapons in their campaign. They exploited the antagonism of the Croat population toward the dominant Serbians. Croatian cities were spared by the bombers, and Nazi propaganda sought to depict the invaders as liberators of the Croat nation. This sort of ethnic subversion was successful to a degree. Some Croatian units in the army mutinied, and the navy, largely manned by Croat sailors, was immobilized. The Germans reached Belgrade within six days. Yugoslavia's teenaged King Peter and his government fled the country to seek Allied protection. On April 17, the remnants of the Yugoslav army submitted to an armistice.

Greece could not hold out much longer than its neighbor. The Germans swept around strongly prepared Greek defenses in the northeast by striking unexpectedly through Yugoslavia. Soon the two largest Greek armies, one in Thrace and one in Albania, were encircled and neutralized. The panzers also swerved by a blocking British force farther south, threatening its lines of supply or retreat. The Ultra code-breaking system had provided a great deal of information about German strength and plans, but the British did not have enough military resources in the area to take advantage of that knowledge. The British decided to abandon Greece before it was too late. The Royal Navy managed to evacuate most of the expeditionary force, though without much of its equipment. Greek defenders fell back, first to a Mount Olympus line, then to a Thermopylae line, but they could not halt *Blitzkrieg*. By April 23, Greece, too, lay under Axis domination. The swastika flag fluttered over the Acropolis.

An even more spectacular German success soon followed the rapid conquest of Yugoslavia and Greece. When the British sent an expeditionary force to Greece, they also reinforced the Greek-held island of Crete with troops and aircraft. Hitler initially had not intended to attack Crete, but General Kurt Student, chief of airborne forces, persuaded him that a paratroop invasion could neutralize this dangerous enemy base in the Mediterranean. Some fifty thousand Allied troops defended the island. British intelligence gave its commander, General Bernard Freyberg, clear indication of German intentions. Freyberg was doubtful, however, about the prospects of an airborne assault, so he prepared for the more likely possibility of an amphibious invasion.

After a week of Luftwaffe bombing to soften the defenses, three thousand of Student's paratroops descended upon Crete early on the morning of May 20. Their first task was the capture of Maleme airfield to enable landing an additional nineteen thousand Germans. Fierce fighting lasted for eleven days. Although the defenders outnumbered the Germans, a combination of thorough training, high morale, and command of the air carried the day for the invaders. The Royal Navy was able to evacuate only 16,500 men. The rest had to be left on the island—dead or prisoners. Naval losses were severe as well—nine ships sunk and thirteen more badly damaged. German losses were also high, amounting to nearly 30 percent of the invasion forces. Despite the impressive success of this first major airborne assault in military history, Hitler would not try the tactic again because of the toll exacted from his elite troops.

The entire Balkan Peninsula was now secure, and Rommel seemed to be reversing the Axis debacle in North Africa. Hitler was well on the way toward winning the Battle of the Mediterranean, or so it appeared at the time. The Allied position throughout the Middle East was gravely threatened. Britain's oil supply and its communications with its empire in Asia were in jeopardy. The Luftwaffe stepped up its "Blitz" bombing of the British Isles. Churchill had called the autumn of 1940 Britain's "darkest hour," but the situation in the summer of 1941 was every bit as precarious. Hitler's strategic priorities had shifted, however. He no longer focused on Britain, the Mediterranean, and North Africa. Instead, he was now ready to launch his most daring venture yet—an invasion of the Soviet Union. The Germans did not share their planning for this operation with Rome or Tokyo.

Having lost the opportunity to conquer Greece and Yugoslavia—both now occupied by the Germans—Mussolini still projected an ambitious program of conquest. He intended to add Nice, Corsica, Tunis, Malta, the Italian-speaking part of Switzerland, Cyprus, Egypt, Iraq, Djibouti, the Persian Gulf coast of Arabia, and Aden to his imagined great Italian empire. Those goals proved entirely beyond Italy's strength, and in the process of fighting for them, he bound the fate of his nation ever more closely to the fortunes of the Third Reich—a fatal decision for the Duce and for many Italians.

Notes

1. MacGregor Knox, *Hitler's Italian Allies: Royal Armed Forces, Fascist Regime, and the War of 1940–1943* (Cambridge: Cambridge University Press, 2000), 52, 57.

2. Knox, *Hitler's Italian Allies*, 70.

3. That is the theme of John Gooch, *Mussolini's War: Fascist Italy from Triumph to Collapse, 1935–1943* (New York: Pegasus, 2020).

4. In contrast to the view of a reluctant Duce presented by most historians, Ian Kershaw argues that Mussolini wanted to fight, but the cautious king and army leaders held him back. *Fateful Choices: Ten Decisions That Changed the World, 1940–1941* (New York: Penguin, 2007), 136–38.

5. Johanna Meskill, *Hitler and Japan: The Hollow Alliance* (New York: Atherton, 1966).

6. Galeazzo Ciano, *The Ciano Diaries, 1939–1943* (New York: Doubleday, 1946), 300.

CHAPTER 7

Barbarossa

Adolf Hitler's decision to attack the USSR instead of concentrating his forces against the British Empire sprang from a combination of deeply held ideological conviction, strategic considerations, and economic necessity. Nazi Germany and Soviet Russia could not possibly coexist in the long run; according to the Führer's pseudo-Darwinian logic, one inevitably must destroy the other. The Soviet state embodied the principal objects of his hatred—Bolshevism, Jews, and the supposedly "subhuman" Slavs. Nazi racist doctrine taught that communism and the Soviet Union were the central elements in an alleged Jewish plot to undermine and destroy the Germanic "master race." Only fire and the sword, Hitler believed, could eliminate that threat. Beyond that, the western areas of the USSR comprised much of the *Lebensraum* that the Führer coveted.

The Reich must incorporate these lands, he was convinced, to provide the territorial basis for a great expansion of the German population. The acquisition of enormous resources in the East would also permit Germany to compete on an equal basis with the far-flung British and American empires. The increasing likelihood of American entry into the war made the matter even more urgent. Germany needed to knock the Red Army out of the war and acquire the resources of the USSR before facing the American challenge. Thus, Hitler was driven to attack the USSR by the deepest elements of Nazi racist mythology as well as by practical strategic considerations. Much of the fighting up to this point—in Scandinavia, France, the Low Countries, and the Balkans—constituted only preparatory steps for the great racial and ideological crusade against Russia. Hitler told Carl Burckhardt, the League of Nations high commissioner for Danzig, in August 1939, "Everything that I undertake is directed against Russia; if the West is too stupid and too blind to understand this, then I will be forced to reach an understanding with the Russians, smash the West, and then turn all my concentrated strength against the Soviet Union. I need the Ukraine so that no one can starve us out again as in the last war."[1]

Securing Germany's food supply was a key motive for attacking the USSR. Hitler believed that Germany had reached the point of crisis in its food supply in 1941. Britain's ability to hold out against the Germans, combined with the growing American role in the war, presented Hitler with a serious strategic challenge. The Nazi conquests up to this point added little to German industrial or agricultural production. Just the opposite—oil, coal, food, and animal fodder were in increasingly short supply. The prospect of a long war loomed before Hitler, with Britain richly supplied by its empire and the United States, while Germany grew weaker for the lack of key resources. Only the conquest of the USSR, with its abundant agricultural and mineral assets, offered an opportunity to escape that bleak picture. Nazi thinking about *Lebensraum* had evolved from the hope that agricultural abundance would be the reward for victory to the view that the conquest of eastern resources would sustain the war effort.[2] The granaries of Ukraine and western Russia would feed the Wehrmacht and the German civilian population, even if that meant that tens of millions of Soviet citizens had to starve.

Overrunning the oil fields of the Caucasus would also rectify Germany's shortage of petroleum. Economic necessity thus reinforced homicidal ideology. When officials of the Four Year Plan advised that continued trade with the USSR would be more productive for the German economy than conquest and occupation of Russia, Hitler rejected that reasoning out of hand.[3] The prospect of gaining Soviet resources for the German cause may have been an element in the *timing* of the attack on the USSR, but more importantly, destroying the eastern Slavic peoples (along with the Jews) had been fundamental to Hitler's thinking since the early 1920s.

Hitler had criticized the kaiser for entrapping Germany in an unwinnable, two-front war in 1914. In the summer of 1941, the Führer committed the same fatal blunder, plunging the Reich into war against a mighty foe in the East, with an unvanquished England, increasingly aided by the United States, still menacing in the West. Hitler's original and completely unrealistic intent had been to fight a series of smaller wars, defeating each opponent in single combat. First Poland, then France, then England (if it refused to ally with the Reich), then Russia, and finally America were to be conquered in turn.[4] This strategy of limited, serial wars seemed feasibly within the margins of German military and economic power. Hitler also hoped that by quickly subduing his victims one at a time through *Blitzkrieg* tactics he could spare the German people the horrors of total war and thereby maintain his own political popularity. However, the strategy of seriatim conquest had begun to break down when Britain and France honored their pledge to Poland in August 1939. It had collapsed completely with the abandonment of Operation Sea Lion. Under the circumstances, a traditional statesman might well have sought a negotiated settlement with his opponents. That was not an option for Hitler. As he saw it, this war was an inevitable struggle for the survival of the fittest in which the only possible outcomes for Germany were either total victory and global conquest or national extinction. There could be no turning back at this point. Hitler, therefore, had no reservations about plunging his people into a desperate struggle with Russia, even though Britain had not yet been defeated nor the United States neutralized.

The Führer rationalized his decision for a virtually suicidal two-front war in several ways. He rejected any analogy between the situation in 1941 and the two-front war that Germany lost in 1918. This time France lay prostrate and England had been driven from the Continent. America, hindered by isolationism and by the fear of Japan in the Pacific, was still not an active belligerent. Hitler thereby convinced himself that he could conquer Soviet Russia in an isolated campaign, just as he had always intended. If he acted boldly and ruthlessly, he believed, this time Germany could avoid the disaster of a two-front war against a mighty coalition of opponents. The Führer anticipated a quick and easy victory. "We will be in Petersburg [i.e., Leningrad] in three weeks," he told an aide.

Hitler held the Soviet government and its army in absolute contempt. He believed that Stalin's bloody purge of the Soviet officer corps in the late 1930s had completely undermined the Red Army's military capabilities. Its poor performance in the Winter War against Finland seemed to prove the point. Hitler ignored the Soviet army's much better showing against the Japanese in 1938 and 1939; he never let inconvenient facts interfere with his prejudices. He also expected the Soviet system to collapse after a few initial German victories. Presumably the Russian peasants, on whom collective farming had been brutally imposed at a staggering cost of seven million casualties, would rise in revolt against Communist oppression. The national minorities, too, would use the opportunity to throw off Russian domination. He expected the Ukrainians, for example, to greet the German troops as liberators, just as some of them had done in 1915. Beyond the supposed weaknesses of the Soviet military and political systems, Hitler's fatal overconfidence sprang directly from his racist ideology. For him, the Russians and most of their subject minority peoples were simply *Untermenschen*, subhumans who were no match for the warriors of the "master race." A number of senior commanders in the Wehrmacht—including Generals Hoepner, von Manstein, von Reichenau, and von Stülpnagel—also took this radical, race war view of the coming campaign against Russia. After their stunning triumphs in Poland and the West, many senior German commanders caught the same "victory disease" that would soon afflict their Japanese allies.

Hitler misunderstood the complex relationship between Stalin's regime and the Soviet peoples. So have some historians. They have depicted the Soviet people as a restive population of helots awaiting an opportune moment to rise up against their masters.[5] Certainly the people of the territories incorporated into the USSR in 1939 or 1940 had little loyalty to Moscow. Many peasants, as well, would have welcomed the chance to end the collective farm system. Nationalists among the Ukrainians hoped to break free from Moscow. However, as historian Catherine Merridale argues, "the Soviet state commanded real support among large numbers of ordinary citizens. Such people's fundamental motives were more positive than fear, more tangible than hope." "The crucial generation," she adds, "the soldiers who would fight at Stalingrad and Kursk, were born into the Soviet system and knew no other."[6]

Not all of Hitler's generals subscribed to Nazi racial dogma, but most of them shared his low estimate of Soviet military capabilities. The initial German battle plan projected a campaign of from nine to seventeen weeks' duration, ending with the Wehrmacht occupying most of European Russia. The majority of officers agreed with the Führer that the Red Army was "no more than a joke." Most of the generals were now swept up in their master's enthusiasm. For that matter, even Allied officers, who were certainly not under the Führer's spell, were not optimistic about Soviet chances of fending off the *Blitzkrieg*. After only one week of Russo-German fighting, the vice chief of the British General Staff, General Sir Henry Pownall, noted in his diary, "It is impossible to say how long Russian resistance will last—three weeks or three months."[7]

Hitler hoped that the anticipated conquest of the USSR would solve his problems with the English-speaking powers in the West. The fall of Russia would deprive Great Britain of its last hope for a continental ally. Perhaps then the British would come to their senses and accept the partnership with Germany that he offered them. If the Churchill regime remained obstinate, however, the conquest of Soviet Russia would provide the German war machine with vast additional resources and then, free from any threat in the East, enable the Wehrmacht to concentrate its forces against England. Japan also would be freed from the Soviet menace to its rear and thereby be able to move more boldly in the Pacific. That, in turn, would shift American attention to the Far East and hinder Roosevelt's meddling in Europe. Thus, Hitler envisioned the campaign against the Soviet Union as a panacea. It would crush Bolshevism, strike the "Jewish conspiracy" in its heartland, conquer *Lebensraum*, dramatically improve the strategic position of the Reich, and intimidate both the British and the Americans.

Soviet authorities did not provoke the attack by failing to live up to their agreements with Germany. Since the signing of the Nazi-Soviet Pact, Stalin had rivaled Neville Cham-

berlain in appeasing Hitler. Soviet shipments of grain, petroleum, and vitally needed minerals continued to flow into the Reich in massive quantities. German war industries were
dependent on these products. Stalin had misjudged the rapidly shifting balance of power in
Europe. He still thought that England was stronger than Germany, and he worried about
the impact of a German defeat on Soviet security. In November 1940, Foreign Commissar
Molotov even went so far as to express the willingness of the Soviet Union to adhere to the
Tripartite Pact, though only with significant revisions to enhance Soviet security. The USSR
seemed on the verge of formally allying with Germany, Italy, and Japan. In return for joining
the Axis, the Soviets insisted on the evacuation of German troops from Finland, a dominant
influence in Bulgaria, rights to expand into Turkey and Iran, and Japan relinquishing its
claims on Sakhalin Island. At the same time, the Kremlin rebuffed attempts by the British
ambassador, Sir Stafford Cripps, to improve Anglo-Soviet relations. But Hitler had no use
for the voluntary cooperation of a Russian ally. He allowed negotiations for Soviet adherence
to the Axis to languish. Three days after Molotov made his offer, the German army began
war games in preparation for the invasion of the USSR.

Stalin realized that appeasement could postpone Nazi aggression only temporarily. The
overconfident Kremlin dictator bragged to associates, "Of course it's all a game to see who
can fool whom. I know what Hitler's up to. He thinks he's outsmarted me but actually it's
I who's tricked him."[8] Consequently, he attempted to use the period of the Russo-German
quasi-alliance to build up Soviet defenses against a future Nazi attack. Stalin hoped that the
German and Allied armies would exhaust each other. A few days after Britain and France
had declared war on Germany, he told his closest comrades:

> —We see nothing wrong in their having a good hard fight and weakening each
>   other.
> —It would be fine if at the hands of Germany the position of the richest capitalist
>   countries (especially England) were shaken.
> —Hitler, without understanding it or desiring it, is shaking and undermining the
>   capitalist system.[9]

The rapid collapse of France came as a particularly unpleasant surprise. Nikita Khrushchev recalled that "Stalin's nerves cracked when he learned about the fall of France. He
cursed the governments of England and France: 'couldn't they put up any resistance at all?'
he asked despairingly. . . . He too had counted on the French army, with British support, to
grind down the German war machine before it could again turn east. 'Now,' he complained,
'Hitler was sure to beat our brains in.'"[10]

The need to bolster Soviet military strength became even more pressing. The Soviets demanded that Berlin pay for deliveries of Russian foodstuffs and raw materials with shipments
of German military equipment. The Germans were deliberately slow to fill Soviet orders,
knowing that any weapons supplied to the Red Army would be used against them. Stalin also
sought to improve the geographical position of the USSR. At first, locked in combat with
the Western Allies and dependent on Soviet trade, Hitler could only watch in annoyance as
Stalin incorporated the Baltic states into the Soviet Union, attacked Finland, and stripped the
provinces of Bessarabia and northern Bukovina from Romania. The Russians also attempted,
unsuccessfully, to spread their influence in the Balkans at the expense of Germany and to
secure control of the strategically important Danube delta.[11] Subsequently, Moscow protested
vehemently against the movement of German troops into Finland, Romania, and Bulgaria.

Anxious to distract his victim away from the area of the impending invasion, Ribbentrop invited the Soviet foreign affairs commissar to negotiate in Berlin. There the Führer and his foreign minister dangled visions of prizes in the Middle East and Asia before Molotov. They told their Soviet guest that the "natural" avenue of expansion for the Soviet Union was toward the Indian Ocean. England was virtually beaten, they claimed, and the British Empire was ready for a division of spoils among the Axis partners and the USSR. Molotov rejected these far-fetched schemes. He insisted on bringing up the inconvenient topic of the German troop buildup in Eastern Europe. When an RAF attack on Berlin drove the negotiators underground, the blunt-spoken commissar chided his hosts: if England had already lost the war, whose bombs were falling above them? Molotov subsequently informed the Germans that Moscow wanted a German troop withdrawal from Eastern Europe, Soviet bases in Turkey and Bulgaria, and a free hand in Iran and the Persian Gulf. Berlin ignored these demands. Plans for the invasion were already well advanced. Even before the meeting with Molotov took place, Hitler had written in a directive to the high commands, "Political discussions have been initiated with the aim of clarifying Russia's attitude for the coming period. Regardless of what results these discussions will have, all preparations for the East which have been orally ordered are to be continued."[12]

Hitler told his generals in July 1940 to begin planning an attack on the Soviet Union. They code-named the operation "Barbarossa," evoking the memory of the twelfth-century Germanic king Frederick Barbarossa (Red Beard), who had led several successful campaigns in eastern Europe. Production priorities shifted to support the planned assault. The army expanded from 143 to 180 divisions, including a doubling of panzer divisions from ten to twenty. The mobile infantry received more half-tracks, while additional field howitzers and new machine guns significantly increased the firepower of regular infantry divisions. Originally the attack was scheduled for May 1941, but the need to secure the Balkans first, bad spring weather, and logistical difficulties delayed the operation until late June.[13] German preparations—both military and diplomatic—were uncharacteristically lax. The Germans did not prepare Operation Barbarossa with the same thoroughness and precision they had exhibited in planning the conquest of France. From the Führer on down the chain of command, excessive confidence in German arms combined with cavalier disdain for the enemy to reinforce the expectation of a rapid and decisive victory. If the Red Army and the Bolshevik regime collapsed quickly, as expected, no detailed arrangements for a long campaign would be needed.

Berlin's political preparations for the attack on Russia were similarly incomplete. Deputy Führer Rudolf Hess flew to England in May 1941. The unstable Hess, undoubtedly acting without Hitler's authorization, hoped to persuade influential figures outside the Churchill cabinet that Britain's destiny lay in alliance with Germany. His mission was a complete failure. Less dramatic, official German initiatives secured the neutrality of Turkey and the cooperation of Finland, Hungary, and Romania. These East European nations were important for logistical support and staging bases. However, Hitler failed to secure the assistance of the one power whose active collaboration might have made a difference in the outcome of the impending battle—Imperial Japan. The Führer was so confident in the Wehrmacht's ability to overwhelm the Soviet Union with ease that he did not even inform his Japanese ally of his plans. His only interest in cooperating with Japan, looking past the anticipated Barbarossa victory, was for combined operations against the British Empire.

Unlike Hitler, Stalin did not discount the possible role of Japan in any future Russo-German conflict. Moscow had been seeking a nonaggression pact with Tokyo since 1931, but the Japanese had persistently rebuffed Soviet initiatives for such an agreement. Two successive defeats in border clashes with the Red Army in 1938 and 1939, coupled with the rapid deterioration of Japanese-American relations, tipped the balance in Tokyo in favor of those factions that sought an accommodation with the USSR. The result was the Soviet-Japanese Neutrality Pact of April 13, 1941. Article 2 provided that, "in the event of military activity by any other power or powers against either of the contracting powers, the other contracting party shall maintain neutrality throughout the duration of the conflict." This diplomatic coup significantly diminished Soviet fears of a two-front war and subsequently enabled the Kremlin to transfer some of its troops from the far eastern to the western part of the USSR. Once again, two Axis powers were working at cross-purposes. Yet Hitler, supremely confident of victory in the East, was not even aware that he had committed a serious blunder. By 1942, when he realized belatedly that Japanese assistance might be useful in the struggle with Russia, it was too late. Japan was already committed to war against Anglo-American forces in the Pacific.

If German military and diplomatic preparations for the invasion of the Soviet Union were less thorough than usual, in one respect the Führer made his plans for the Russian campaign perfectly clear. Operation Barbarossa would be fundamentally different from earlier battles in Norway and France. It would be a savage race war in which liberal conceptions of humanity, aristocratic codes of chivalry, and international conventions on the conduct of warfare would play no part. It would be a war of annihilation. At the end of March 1941, Hitler gave special instructions for Barbarossa to over two hundred of his commanders. General Halder summarized the Führer's remarks in his diary:

> *Clash of two ideologies.* Crushing denunciation of Bolshevism. . . . We must forget the concept of comradeship between soldiers. A Communist is no comrade before nor after the battle. This is war of extermination. . . . We do not wage war to preserve the enemy. . . .
>
> *War against Russia*—Extermination of the Bolshevist commissar and Communist intelligentsia. . . . Commissars and GPU men [i.e., Soviet political police] are criminals and must be dealt with as such. . . .
>
> This war will be very different from the war in the West. . . . Commanders must make the sacrifice of overcoming their personal scruples.

This so-called commissar order mandated that all Communists who were captured were to be murdered. Another decree removed any violence by German soldiers or police against Soviet civilians from the jurisdiction of army courts-martial and specifically authorized reprisals against whole villages. The more Jews and Slavs killed during the conflict, the better. Hitler wanted to clear the "subhuman" inhabitants from the future German *Lebensraum* to make room for the new "Aryan" settlers. Moscow was to be burned to the ground and the site flooded to create a lake. "The name of Moscow," Hitler said, "will disappear forever." Leningrad, the second-largest city in the USSR, would also be "wiped from the face of the earth."

A few officers protested Hitler's murderous orders, but army chief Walther von Brauchitsch refused to convey their objections to the Führer. Furthermore, the following remarks of Field Marshal von Manstein, made after Operation Barbarossa had begun, convey the extent to which Nazi barbarism had infected even many aristocratic, professional officers:

> The struggle against the Soviet armed forces is not being waged solely according to traditional European military rules. Fighting continues behind the front. Partisans, guerrillas in civilian dress, surprise individual soldiers and small detachments,

seeking to disrupt supply lines by means of sabotage using mines and bombs. . . .
Judaism constitutes the middleman between the enemy in the rear and remaining
fighting forces of the Red Army and Red leadership. It occupies here, more than
in Europe, all key positions of political leadership and administration, of trade and
commerce, and furthermore forms the cause of all unrest and political rebellions.
The Jewish-Bolshevik system must be exterminated once and for all. It must never
again interfere in our European living space.[14]

Barbarossa was to be the ultimate *Blitzkrieg*. Mobility, firepower, and daring would
carry the day, it was hoped, against numerically superior Russian forces. The Germans understood that previous invaders—the Swedish king Charles XII in the eighteenth century
and Napoleon in the nineteenth century—had been drawn ever deeper into the Russian
hinterland until their lines of supply snapped and their troops collapsed from exhaustion.
The brutal winter and the seemingly endless space of the Russian plain had done as much as
the defending tsarist armies to bring these earlier aggressors to grief. This time it would be
different. The Germans were determined not to let the enemy mount a successful defense
by strategic retreat. A prolonged war of attrition would favor the USSR, with its greater
population and natural resources. It would also give the British, and perhaps even the Americans, a chance to intervene in the East. Instead, Germany had to wage "lightning war" for a
quick and decisive victory—or there would be no victory at all. As outlined in the Führer's
December directive, "the mass of the Russian army in western Russia is to be destroyed in
daring operations by driving four deep wedges with tanks, and the retreat of the enemy's
battle-ready forces into the wide spaces of Russia is to be prevented."

The Germans largely stripped the other fighting fronts and the occupied territories of
troops to assemble a force capable of striking a shattering blow against the Soviet Union.
They marshaled 153 German divisions for the attack (supplemented by thirty Finnish and
Romanian divisions), but once again it was the mobile forces—nineteen panzer divisions
and fifteen motorized divisions—that were assigned the decisive role in the assault. Assisted
by the Luftwaffe, they were to tear through the Red Army's defenses, penetrate deep behind
enemy lines, hold open corridors for the pursuing German infantry to fill, and encircle
the Soviet forces before they could retreat and regroup. The overall objective of Operation
Barbarossa was nothing less than the annihilation of the Red Army. German military planners anticipated that the Soviet army would even cooperate in this plan of destruction by
being much slower to initiate a general retreat than Russian forces had in previous centuries.
Presumably the Red Army would be reluctant to abandon its westernmost bases and the
economic infrastructure on which its operational efficiency depended.

Barbarossa was a three-pronged attack. Army Group North, commanded by Field Marshal Wilhelm J. F. Ritter von Leeb and consisting of twenty-nine divisions (including three
armored and three motorized), would strike from East Prussia across the Baltic states toward
Leningrad. At the opposite end of the German line, Field Marshal von Rundstedt's Army
Group South concentrated forty-one divisions in southern Poland. Spearheaded by five
armored and three motorized divisions, it was to drive south of the Pripet Marshes through
Ukraine toward Kiev and the Dnieper River. Army Group Center under Field Marshal von
Bock would launch the main attack. Its fifty divisions (with a total of nine armored and six
motorized divisions) were to punch through Belorussia from their bases in central Poland.
Bock's first objectives were Minsk and Smolensk, but his goal was Moscow. In all, the
Wehrmacht committed 3.2 million men, 600,000 motor vehicles, an equal number of
horses, 3,350 tanks, and over 2,700 combat aircraft to the assault.

The Soviet forces arrayed along the western border of the USSR to meet this German onslaught looked considerably stronger on paper than they were in the field. The 1930s had been a decade of military buildup for the Soviet Union. From nine hundred thousand servicemen in 1934, the Red Army grew to 5.4 million in 1941. The relative success of the Five Year Plans in industry enabled the Soviets to amass an impressive inventory of military equipment. Moscow boasted of its 25,000 tanks and 18,000 military aircraft, but of these inflated numbers, no more than 1,500 of the tanks and 3,700 of the planes were serviceable, modern models. Lack of radios and adequate repair facilities further weakened Soviet armored forces. Soviet designers had produced the best tank then available anywhere in the world, the T-34, but fewer than a thousand of these excellent fighting vehicles were available when the Germans struck. Even that quantity of T-34s would have been a formidable weapon if they had been concentrated in modernized armored divisions instead of dispersed among many units.

The Red Army had pioneered the new forms of armored warfare and "deep battle" in the early 1930s. The purges, however, had left narrow-minded Stalinist officers in charge who had no appreciation for these innovations. According to historian David Glantz, "the bloodletting that ensued tore the brain from the Red Army, smashed its morale, stifled any spark of original thought and left a magnificently hollow military establishment, ripe for catastrophic defeat."[15] Beyond the ravages of the Great Purges, the Red Army's attempts to implement armored warfare in prewar exercises as well as in the Spanish civil war and in smaller engagements against Japan, Poland, and Finland were disappointing.[16] Just at the time when the Wehrmacht was developing the mighty panzer division, the Soviet army was disbanding its pathbreaking mechanized corps. Voroshilov, based on his reading of the Spanish civil war, distributed most of the tanks among infantry units. That decision was reversed in 1940, but by then it was far too late.

Of course, the purge of the officer corps had affected more than just the armored formations. The execution or imprisonment of 22,705 military officers (out of 296,000 officers; a purge disproportionately severe at the highest ranks) weakened the army's leadership disastrously. The purge had consumed 3 of the 5 marshals, 15 of 16 army commanders of the first or second rank, 60 of 67 corps commanders, 136 of 199 division commanders, and all 17 senior political commissars.[17] Of the three surviving senior commanders who controlled the main battlefronts under German attack—Marshals Kliment Voroshilov, Semën Timoshenko, and Semën Budënny—two of them, Voroshilov and Budënny, were incompetent. They owed their survival and their high positions to Stalin's favor, not to any discernible military talent. The Red Army's most able strategist, Marshal Mikhail Tukhachevskii, had been shot. A reinstatement of the old civil war system of dual command, pairing officers with political commissars, accompanied the purges. Moreover, the extremely rapid expansion of the Red Army between 1938 and 1941 meant that most junior officers were inexperienced, while middle- and higher-level commanders had been promoted prematurely. Newly minted Red Army lieutenants had only forty-five to ninety days of training.[18] In June 1941, fully three-quarters of Red Army officers had been on active duty for less than a year!

There were problems in the ranks, too. Despite endless hours of political indoctrination, some soldiers wondered if the cause was worth the risk, as evidenced by these naive remarks from a young recruit: "The fascists have not done a thing to me; I see no point in fighting them. From my point of view, it makes no difference if we have Fascist or Soviet power. It would be better to die or run away than to fight for the motherland."[19] Morale was poor in many Red Army units due to inadequate training (mostly classroom work, with few realistic field exercises) and unrealistic Soviet propaganda that portrayed the Red Army as "invincible," when even ordinary soldiers could see a great many weaknesses.[20] German atrocities would soon convince even such politically naive soldiers that the Nazis were even worse than the commissars. While many peasant soldiers lacked motivation to fight for Stalin's regime and others actually looked forward to its defeat, still other segments of the population responded positively to Molotov's call to arms on June 22, manifesting a surge of patriotism as eager volunteers in every city crowded Red Army recruiting stations.[21] Severe shortages of trucks, radios, mines, and maintenance facilities also hampered Soviet forces. Many units lacked the full complement of weaponry required for effective operations. Yet, for all its defects, the Red Army was still a powerful force in 1941. German disregard for Soviet military capacity evidenced blatant racist disdain for the Slavic peoples, not an objective assessment of the Soviet armed forces' combat capabilities.

Because Stalin never regarded the Nazi-Soviet Pact as anything more than a temporary armed truce, he took several steps to bolster Soviet defenses. Some of them succeeded; some of them backfired. The officer corps reintroduced formal military ranks (banned as too bourgeois after the Bolshevik Revolution) and enhanced the disciplinary power of officers over their troops. At the same time, the power of the political commissars to interfere with command decisions in the army was reduced, though not eliminated. In addition, some capable military officers were recalled from Siberian prison camps. Konstantin Rokossovskii was one such rehabilitated commander who would later win victories over the Germans at Stalingrad and Kursk. Not all of Stalin's decisions worked out so well, however. The Red Army had built a formidable set of fortifications along the Soviet frontier as it existed up to September 1939. Then the Soviet frontier expanded at the expense of Finland, the Baltic states, Poland, and Romania. Stalin thereupon ordered Soviet troops to abandon their existing set of fortifications, move into the newly acquired territories, and build another fortified line along the new borders. To conserve scarce building materials, the army began dismantling the original fortifications. When the Germans attacked, the new line was far from complete while the old line was useless. Similarly, the Red Army's weapons modernization program proved a mixed blessing. In some cases, units had given up their old weapons before their replacements had arrived or before the troops were trained in using the new models.

Stalin insisted on stoutly defending the frontiers of the USSR and carrying the fight onto the aggressor's territory as soon as possible. This meant that the bulk of Soviet forces were stationed much too close to the borders and were therefore more vulnerable to the Germans' encirclement strategy. Soviet doctrine mistakenly assumed that "screening" forces along the border could delay an invader for two to three weeks while the main Red Army concentrations behind these screens prepared a devastating counterattack. A much more effective tactic for the Russians would have been strategic retreat to strongly prepared defenses deeper within the country, but the Kremlin precluded that more sensible alternative.

Stalin's greatest blunder, however, was his failure to see that a German attack was imminent in the summer of 1941 and to take the many last-minute measures necessary to prepare the country for the blow. The Soviet dictator's nearly fatal miscalculation is especially puzzling since he never had any faith in the German promises of peace and friendship. From the fall of 1940 onward, evidence began to flow into the Kremlin that Hitler intended to betray his Soviet ally. Some warnings came from Churchill and Roosevelt. The British and American governments had bits of information about Barbarossa from high-level German informants and from signals intelligence. Stalin dismissed these warnings as provocations since they came from powers that he strongly believed were seeking to provoke Russo-German hostilities. Suspecting a British trap, Stalin told Zhukov, "We are being threatened with the Germans, and the Germans with the Soviet Union, and they are playing us off against one another. It is a subtle political game."[22] He ought to have had more faith in his own intelligence services, especially the "Red Orchestra" spy network in western Europe and Richard Sorge, a Soviet agent at the German embassy in Tokyo. Just four days before the Germans struck, Stalin, faced with a mountain of evidence, shouted at his senior commanders, "You have to realize that Germany on her own will never fight Russia." He warned them that if they provoked the Germans, "heads will roll."[23]

In his desperate self-deception, Stalin even found ways to deny the obvious implications of a three-million-man German troop buildup along the Soviet border. He rationalized that Hitler was only bluffing a war to gain further political and economic concessions from the Soviet Union. Just ten days before the German attack, Stalin prevented full-scale defensive mobilization, telling his commander, "We have a non-aggression pact with Germany; Germany is busy up to her ears with the war in the West and I am certain that Hitler will not risk creating a second front by attacking the Soviet Union. Hitler is not such an idiot and understands that the Soviet Union is not Poland, not France and not even England."[24] Frontier garrison commanders who reported German military preparations always received the same reply from their superiors: "Don't panic. Take it easy. 'The Boss' knows all about it."

Although the Germans tried to mask their actions, Nazi deception efforts were feeble at best. No one should have taken seriously the Berlin-inspired rumors that this extraordinary concentration of strength in eastern Europe was merely a decoy for Operation Sea Lion. Stalin was sure that the Führer would not dare attack the Soviet Union before either defeating or making peace with Great Britain. The Gestapo had a double agent ("Litseist," or O. Berlings) in the Soviet intelligence group in Berlin who fed disinformation to Stalin—fabrications designed to reinforce the dictator's misperceptions. Yet there was so much evidence of German intent that these deceitful ploys should have been winnowed easily from the intelligence report. Stalin dismissed hundreds of German reconnaissance flights over Soviet territory in the spring and early summer of 1941 as more "provocations"—this time presumably by German generals who supposedly wanted to subvert Hitler's policy of cooperation with Russia by provoking a Soviet retaliatory strike against these intrusions. In the days just before the attack, several German soldiers defected to the Soviet side and warned Red Army intelligence of the impending assault. They were not heeded either.

It is worth noting, to put Stalin's mistaken evaluation in perspective, that many officers in the British Foreign Office and intelligence community continued to regard German troop movements in eastern Europe as diplomatic leverage rather than a prelude to war. The possibility that Stalin might allow Hitler to move troops across the northern coast of the Black Sea and into Iraq, thereby flanking the British position in the Middle East, haunted London. The British were so concerned about the specter of a closer Russo-German entente that they made plans to seize Iraq from which to bomb the Caucasus oil fields.[25] Fortunately for the future Grand Alliance, they never carried out that plan.

The question remains, how could Stalin, a man of a pathologically suspicious nature, be so blind? He deceived himself because he clung so pathetically to the hope of peace. Though official propaganda boasted of the Red Army's invincible might, Stalin knew the real weaknesses of the Soviet system all too well. He realized how unprepared for total war the USSR really was. He told the other Soviet leaders in November 1940, "We are not prepared for the sort of war being waged between Germany and England. . . . If in the future our armed forces . . . are not equal to the forces of our enemies . . . then they will devour us."[26] The incursion into Poland and the Winter War with Finland had exposed grave deficiencies in the Red Army. A report in May 1940 by Marshal Timoshenko and General Zhukov found that "the army on the whole did not display particular vigilance, battle-readiness, steadfastness in defence or preparations to repel an armoured invasion."[27] Moreover, the defeats that Russia was likely to experience would expose Stalin's own disastrous failures as a leader—especially the purges, which had devastated the Soviet armed forces, and the Nazi-Soviet Pact that had done so much to strengthen the German war machine. Stalin recoiled in disbelief from these unpalatable truths. Faced with many clear indications that a German invasion was in the offing, he preferred to interpret the data as evidence of Allied provocation, the machinations of a few German generals, or even a ruse by Hitler to gain diplomatic advantage. He even imagined that there might be a peace conference in 1942 at which the Axis powers and the Soviet Union might benefit at the expense of the British Empire and the United States.

The nature of Soviet totalitarianism reinforced Stalin's self-delusion. Once the all-powerful dictator laid down the dictum that there would be no war with Germany and that any apparent indication to the contrary was a British or German trick, it behooved all Soviet intelligence officers—out of concern for their careers and their very lives—to echo that interpretation. The chief of Soviet military intelligence, General Filipp Golikov, reported and analyzed the incoming data in such a way as to make it palatable to his master. He reassured the Kremlin that "it is necessary to assess the rumors and documents which speak of the inevitability this spring of war against the USSR as disinformation originating from British and even perhaps from German intelligence."[28] Similarly, Lavrentii Beria, the NKVD chief, told Stalin just one day before the German assault, "My people and I, Josef Vissarionovich Stalin, firmly remember your wise prediction: Hitler will not attack in 1941!"[29]

Golikov reported just three weeks before the actual invasion that there were more than 120 enemy divisions along the Soviet border. However, misestimating the overall size of the German army, Soviet intelligence thought that this force represented 40 percent of German strength, when the true figure was 60 percent. In addition, Moscow's intelligence apparatus had greatly overestimated the number of German divisions near the USSR in the preceding months, so it missed the significance of the last-minute German buildup. The intelligence picture was clouded, as it always is, by errors in gathering and interpreting data, wild rumors, and German disinformation. Also, Stalin interpreted Berlin's lack of interest in stirring internal dissension among the Soviet population as evidence that a German attack was not an immediate threat. In the same way, Soviet intelligence reports that the German army had not acquired great quantities of winter gear suggested to the Kremlin that a campaign against Russia was unlikely. Yet, despite these uncertainties, the evidence of hostile German intent was there to see if Stalin chose to see it. He did not.

Stalin imposed his bizarre self-deception on the whole Soviet defense establishment. Commanders were warned not to put their troops on alert or move them into the frontier fortifications, or carry out any other preliminary measures to resist an attack, because that would only provoke the Germans. Those few officers with the courage to begin defensive preparations on their own authority received a sharp rebuke and had their orders countermanded. The official Communist Party newspaper, *Pravda*, reassured its readers on June 14 that "the rumors of the intention of Germany to break the Pact and launch an attack against the Soviet Union are completely without foundation, while the recent movements of German troops . . . are connected, it must be supposed, with other motives which have nothing to do with Soviet-German relations." The armed forces were not permitted to prepare for the attack, and the rest of the nation was lulled into a false sense of security. Stalin finally authorized troops in the frontier districts to prepare for action, but he did so only during the night of June 21, so few units received the order before the Germans struck. As a result, Operation Barbarossa achieved virtually complete tactical surprise. One Soviet border outpost, caught between the fury of the Wehrmacht and Stalin's insane order to avoid "provocations," radioed in desperation to its headquarters, "We are being fired on. What shall we do?"

The Nazi attack on the USSR caught not only the Russians by surprise but the German people as well. Hostile propaganda campaigns had preceded previous invasions; this time the German mass media kept up the illusion of German-Soviet friendship so as not to forewarn Stalin of the coming assault. When the battle began, the Nazi press told the stunned German public that the operation was a necessary part of Germany's struggle against "Jewish Bolshevism" and a *defensive* action to preempt an anticipated Soviet attack. German public opinion was already extremely hostile to the Soviet Union. Many people in the Reich equated the Bolshevik regime with widespread rape, murder, and the complete debasement of civilization. Most Germans were ready to accept Hitler's view that it was essential to eliminate the vile Bolsheviks before they could harm Germany.

Some writers, especially Victor Suvorov, accept Hitler's claim, arguing that Soviet forces were caught unprepared to defend the country because they were deploying for an offensive strike against Germany.[30] Numerous scholars have debunked Suvorov's thesis and questioned its documentary basis. Gabriel Gorodetsky has shown that Stalin, realizing the relative weakness of Soviet forces, was desperate to postpone war against Germany, while David Glantz has demonstrated that in 1941 the Red Army lacked the capability for a great offensive against the Germans.[31] In their public utterances, Hitler and other Nazi leaders claimed to fear Soviet aggression, but their private remarks indicate that they had no such concerns. They did not believe the Red Army had any serious offensive capability.

Operation Barbarossa

At 3:15 on the morning of June 22, 1941, lead elements of the 153-division German invasion force (supported by thirty Finnish and Romanian divisions and joined later by Italian, Hungarian, Slovakian, and Spanish units) began crossing the Soviet frontier. Some 150 opposing Red Army divisions were spread along the border from the Arctic Ocean to the Black Sea, while the aggressors were concentrated in three compact masses. The Wehrmacht thus achieved overwhelming numerical superiority in men and armor at the points of attack. The Wehrmacht scored spectacular successes all along the line, bursting through NKVD border troops and smashing into unprepared Red Army formations. Many vital frontier bridges were not properly mined, so the Germans stormed them with ease. The enemy resorted to stealth where explosive charges were in place. At the Koden bridge over the Bug River, for example, German border guards shouted to the unsuspecting Soviet frontier troops to come out onto the bridge to discuss "important business." The Russians were cut down by a hail of machine-gun fire when they emerged.

German sabotage units had already crossed the border or parachuted behind Soviet lines, where they cut telephone and power cables, blew up electrical generators, and otherwise spread havoc. Cutting the phone lines combined with radio jamming left the high command in Moscow virtually blind. It would be days before Soviet leaders had an accurate picture of the devastation along the border. Some of the German infiltrators donned Red Army uniforms to launch surprise attacks on railway yards and military command centers. German heavy artillery and Luftwaffe bombers, relying on detailed photoreconnaissance gained in the previous weeks, savaged their targets with pinpoint accuracy. Göring's air fleets struck first at Red Air Force bases. There they found row after row of Soviet planes parked neatly in the open with no attempt at camouflage or dispersion. By noon, the Luftwaffe had destroyed some twelve hundred enemy aircraft, two-thirds of them on the ground.

Operation Barbarossa: The German Invasion of the USSR

Soviet units were caught by surprise, battered savagely by enemy ground and air forces, and hampered by the paralysis of their own command structure. Commanders of formations near the frontiers tried frantically to get instructions from Moscow. Most of them could not get through; those few who did were told by Marshal Timoshenko, "No action must be taken against the Germans without our consent." When Georgii Zhukov, the Red Army chief of staff, telephoned the Soviet leader with news of the German invasion, Stalin told him, "This is a provocation by the German military. Do not open fire to avoid unleashing wider action"[32] Stalin clung to the "provocation" theory even after Ambassador von der Schulenburg belatedly delivered the German declaration of war.

The morning news broadcast on Radio Moscow carried the usual boasts of Soviet industrial and agricultural triumphs and war news from England and the Middle East, followed by some children's programming and the morning exercises—but nothing about the Nazi assault on the USSR! As reports of the invasion cascaded into the Kremlin throughout the day, Stalin could no longer deny the awful truth. The realization that his policy of appeasing Hitler had backfired and that the continued existence of the Soviet system was gravely threatened left Stalin badly shaken. However, the widely circulated story that Stalin suffered a nervous breakdown, retreated to his suburban villa, and remained out of contact with the Soviet government for more than a week is untrue. A week later, when the magnitude of the disaster was fully apparent after the fall of Minsk, Stalin did withdraw to his dacha, where he remained out of touch for two days in deep depression.

When the state radio finally announced the German attack later on the 22nd, it was Molotov, not Stalin, who appealed to the Soviet people to rally against the aggressor. All citizens, he told them, "must now close ranks behind our glorious Bolshevik Party, our Soviet government, and our great leader, Comrade Stalin." Confusion reigned behind the scenes at the Kremlin and at army headquarters. The Soviet high command (Stavka) was almost completely out of touch with the gigantic battle swirling from the far north to Ukraine. Field commanders were left virtually without operational orders. Several hours after the attack began, Zhukov directed Soviet forces to begin "active offensive operations." Later that day, Timoshenko ordered the Red Army to "surround and annihilate" the enemy. Such directives were of little use to Soviet units along the frontier that were already enveloped and on the verge of destruction.

Well-seasoned German strike forces executed the *Blitzkrieg* strategy to near perfection. Just as in Poland and France, fast-moving panzer columns, closely supported by dive-bombers and strafing fighters, knifed through the Russian defenses. Some Soviet troops fled in confusion before this devastating onslaught; other Soviet units stood their ground in ferocious fighting. All too often, frightened and unprepared officers sent their men, armed only with rifles and bayonets, charging against German tanks. When they met tenacious resistance, the German armored spearheads simply flowed around Soviet strongpoints, leaving them for the infantry to mop up later.

The Wehrmacht had an important advantage over the Red Army—combat effectiveness. Its officers were more experienced, its troops were better trained and maintained a higher level of morale, and its equipment was more reliable mechanically than that of the enemy. In contrast, many Soviet soldiers were inadequately trained recent recruits who were soon demoralized by the enemy's ferocious assault. "Tank panic" and "airplane panic" (i.e., terror at the sight of enemy armor or aircraft) were serious problems in the infantry. Nevertheless, most Soviet soldiers fought the enemy as best they could. There were no mass surrenders of large units like the British at Singapore. Even though the Germans captured very large numbers of Red Army men, most of them were taken in small groups in combat or during breakout attempts. Problems of command, control, and communication account for the massive casualties suffered by the Red Army in these opening battles. In desperation, Stalin issued Order 270 in mid-August, requiring officers to fight their way out of encirclements and forbidding them to surrender. The order equated captivity with desertion to the enemy and mandated punishment not only for offenders but for their families as well.

The Germans were not always able to close the trap because their slow-moving infantry, advancing on foot with horse-drawn artillery and supply wagons, could not keep up with the speeding panzers. Many Red Army soldiers managed to escape encirclement, only to be disarmed and subjected to interrogation ("filtration") for signs of cowardice or treason. Once again, the paranoia of the Stalinist system hindered the defense of the USSR. Yet, much to the Germans' surprise, whenever they destroyed a Russian unit, new Red Army formations materialized in its place. The Soviets created new divisions from the survivors of shattered units, troops transferred from rear areas, and draftees. The universal service requirement meant that Moscow had an available draftee pool of fourteen million men. Casualty rates were high among these green troops, however.

On the northwestern front, von Leeb's armor quickly punched through two Soviet armies stationed on the frontier. German and Soviet armored forces fought a series of swirling engagements in Lithuania on June 23 and 24. Near the village of Raseiniai, 250 Soviet tanks caught the 1st Panzer Division in transit. The Germans were shocked to discover that their antitank shells bounced off the Russian heavy KV tanks. Unfortunately for the Russians, most of their armored vehicles were lighter, obsolete models rather than the formidable KVs and T-34s. The Red Army also blundered seriously by dividing many of its tanks into relatively small formations to avoid air attacks on them. Even the limited number of available KV tanks would have caused the enemy grave problems if they had been concentrated in one powerful unit. After some hard fighting, two German corps broke through the defenders and raced toward the Dvina River, the only major natural obstacle between them and their objective, Leningrad. The Germans took the all-important bridges over the river at Dvinsk by trickery. Using captured Russian uniforms and trucks, a platoon of Germans passed through Soviet lines and seized the main road and rail bridges until reinforcements arrived to secure them. The panzers were soon across the river.

An uprising of local nationalists, led by the Lithuanian Activist Front, assisted the German push through Lithuania. Rebels seized radio stations and attacked withdrawing Soviet troops. They fought to free their nation of Moscow's control and to restore private property. Large-scale arrests and deportations of Baltic people by the NKVD in mid-June sparked resistance. The rebels welcomed the Germans, mistakenly seeing them as liberators. Similar rebellions erupted in Estonia and Latvia. Red Army soldiers of those nationalities deserted en masse and formed guerrilla units to attack the Russians. After the Germans secured the Baltic region, they ordered all partisan units to disband. Berlin intended to incorporate the three Baltic states into the Reich, not grant them independence.

The Red Army launched a series of desperate counterattacks but could not stem the enemy assault. The Soviet command hastily patched together a new defense line centered on the town of Luga, barely one hundred miles from Leningrad. Forty-five thousand civilians dug antitank ditches and built fortifications for the line. To make matters worse, German and Finnish troops attacked from the north on June 25. Two hostile forces were now converging on Leningrad from different directions. Hard pressed for manpower, Soviet authorities formed the Leningrad National Militia Army. Civilians armed only with light weapons and provided with a few days of training faced crack German divisions. Militia losses were appalling. The Soviet high command rushed three more armies northward, but Voroshilov squandered them in premature and indecisive engagements. German forces pierced the Luga line at several points during August. By early September their 240 mm long-range artillery was pounding Leningrad. On the last day of August, they overran the Mga railway junction southeast of the city, thereby cutting the last open supply line to Leningrad. German troops then fought their way north to the shore of Lake Ladoga. The city was now surrounded by Germans in the south, from the Gulf of Finland to the lake, and by Finns in the north, who were attacking down the Karelian Isthmus.

While Army Group North seemed on the verge of achieving its strategic objective, Army Group Center, under von Bock, blasted its way through Belorussia toward Moscow. Bock divided his armored strength into two strike forces: one attacking through Bialystok and Grodno toward Minsk from the northwest and the other striking through Brest-Litovsk toward Minsk from the south. The objective was not merely to seize the capital of Belorussia but, more importantly, to surround and destroy the three Soviet armies defending this stretch of the frontier. The German onslaught hit the Red Army formations with devastating impact. Soviet forces protecting Bialystok began to crumble within a few hours. By the end of the day the Germans had driven a deep wedge between Soviet forces on the Baltic and central fronts. That gap was fully eighty miles wide by the 23rd. While the panzers raced onward, German infantry moved up quickly to fill this enormous hole torn in the Soviet defenses. Guderian's 2nd Panzer Group encountered fierce resistance from the Brest fortress on the frontier. It took a week of pounding with heavy artillery to force the garrison to submit, and even then some isolated pockets continued to hold out. Guderian's armor swept around the obstacle and slashed through the Soviet formations in front of them. His tanks covered 175 miles in the first three days of fighting.

Stalin and the General Staff played into the German strategy by ordering their commander on the central front, General Dmitrii Pavlov, to plunge the bulk of his forces into a counteroffensive toward the border. The result was a disastrous double encirclement. Hoth's and Guderian's panzers closed the trap behind Minsk on June 27. The Red Army took over a bottle works in Minsk to mass-produce Molotov cocktails, but it could not stop the enemy offensive with such weapons. In all, the Germans encircled three Soviet armies in the Bialystok pocket and two more near Minsk. They captured some four hundred thousand prisoners in this operation. The Russians lost seven invaluable tank divisions, six mechanized brigades, and twenty-two infantry divisions. General Pavlov belatedly ordered a withdrawal to avoid encirclement, but the chaos caused by relentless German attacks, a breakdown in communications, and the exhaustion of fuel and ammunition supplies doomed the effort. This was the first great Soviet debacle; it would not be the last. Pavlov himself avoided capture by the enemy only to be recalled to Moscow and shot. The unfortunate general was not alone in suffering for his master's mistakes. The regime executed approximately ten thousand of its own officers and soldiers in the course of 1941. Stalin lamented to his closest associates, "Lenin left us a great legacy, but we, his heirs, have fucked it up."[33] Conversely, things seemed to be going so well for the Germans that on July 3 General Halder noted in his diary, "It is probably no overstatement to say that the Russian campaign has been won in the space of two weeks."[34]

Early in July, Stalin finally spoke to the Soviet people over nationwide radio for the first time since the war began, addressing them uncharacteristically as "comrades, citizens, brothers and sisters . . . my friends." He summoned his people to a "national war in defense of our fatherland against the fascist oppressors . . . [a] war of liberation." The dictator's reappearance was a mixed blessing in many respects. As usual he accepted no personal responsibility but blamed the defeats on others, particularly the ill-fated General Pavlov. Stalin appointed himself commissar of defense and commander-in-chief. He then proceeded to name new front commanders: Voroshilov in the north, Timoshenko for the center, and Budënny in the south. Voroshilov and Budënny proved incompetent, Timoshenko seriously out of his depth. Stalin also reinstituted the system of military commissars (political officers to oversee, and often interfere with, the decisions of Red Army commanders) because he feared treason among his officers.

Stalin and his marshals were determined to contest the enemy for every inch of Soviet soil; that proved to be a serious mistake. They ordered frantic counterattacks on all fronts, which only made it all the easier for the Germans to entrap huge numbers of Russian soldiers. Strategic withdrawal to avoid encirclement was the sensible policy under the circumstances, but Stalin considered any such action treasonable. Besides reinstating political commissars in Red Army units, Stalin assigned some of his closest associates to oversee the main fronts—Nikita Khrushchev in the south, Nikolai Bulganin in the west, and Andrei Zhdanov in the northwest.

The shattering force and lightning pace of the enemy assault continued to keep the Soviet high command off balance. Due to surprise, a widespread communications breakdown, and reluctance to face unpleasant facts, it took Moscow several days to comprehend what had befallen the Red Army. Divisions, even whole armies, were lost to telephone or radio contact with headquarters—some had already been obliterated by the *Blitzkrieg*; others were fleeing in disarray before the panzers. Soviet authorities wasted a good deal of time sending futile "counterattack and annihilate" orders to the dazed survivors of the enemy onslaught. Once the high command realized the magnitude of the German assault, it scrambled to mobilize men and resources. Moscow flung its reserves at first one, then another enemy breakthrough. There was never enough time. The racing panzer columns rendered Soviet plans for counterstrokes or new defensive lines useless before their ink was dry. In desperation, Red Army reserves were thrown into battle before they were fully assembled or completely equipped.

Sufficient men—human cannon fodder—could be dragooned into service, but equipment was a different matter. Antiaircraft guns, ammunition, fuel, antitank guns, radios, and vehicles of all sorts were in critically short supply. Great throngs of civilian refugees choked the roads, hindering the redeployment of forces to meet new enemy attacks. The situation grew increasingly menacing. Red Army units were ordered to hold their ground, no matter what the cost. Commanders whose troops fled or who lost major battles were executed. NKVD troops, stationed behind Red Army units, used their machine guns to discourage unauthorized withdrawals. Moscow also instituted a scorched-earth policy. Anything of value—foodstuffs, fuel dumps, industrial plants—that could not be removed from the grasp of the advancing enemy was destroyed. Stalin was desperate to slow the enemy assault and to show his new Anglo-American allies that shipments of aid to the USSR would not be wasted.

These emergency measures did not stop Army Group Center, however. Timoshenko had seven armies to defend the central front, but not nearly enough tanks and planes. Within two weeks of taking Minsk, the Germans launched another double envelopment operation, this time aimed at taking Smolensk and trapping the Soviet armies west of the city. Hermann Hoth's panzers, already across the Berezina, struck along a northerly route over the Dvina at Vitebsk. General Andrei I. Eremenko counterattacked ferociously with two mechanized corps. His tanks fought the panzers to a standstill until, lacking adequate air cover and antiaircraft guns, the Soviet forces gave way under the pounding of German dive-bombers. At the same time, Guderian's panzer corps broke across the Dnieper River, aiming for Smolensk from the southwest. By July 16, his forward units had reached the city. The following day Hoth's tanks swept down on the city from the north, slamming shut the trap. Timoshenko mounted a series of relief attacks but was unable to break through the panzer ring before the bulk of the German infantry arrived on the scene. Five Soviet armies, caught in the Smolensk pocket, were now hammered into submission. The Soviets lost 340,000 men, killed, missing, or captured. The Germans seized 3,300 Soviet tanks and 1,800 artillery pieces. Among those captured was Stalin's son Iakov. Stalin refused to exchange him for a high-ranking German officer. Army Group Center was now within two hundred miles of Moscow, poised at one end of a serviceable concrete highway that led directly to the Soviet capital.

The Germans' early confidence in an easy, complete victory was beginning to slip away, however. Soviet troops had fought fiercely and inflicted serious casualties on the enemy. The commander of the 18th Panzer Division, who had only a dozen tanks left, noted that casualties must be reduced "if we do not intend to win ourselves to death."[35] Losses sometimes favored the Germans by a ratio of ten to one in these battles, but those losses in men and machines were beginning to take a toll on the Wehrmacht's combat effectiveness. Nonetheless, the situation at this point looked grim for the Soviet regime.

Meanwhile, Army Group South had won victories almost as impressive. Here, as elsewhere, the German objective was to encircle and destroy the Soviet defenders. Rundstedt's forces attacked eastward in the direction of Kiev with the intent of eventually wheeling south toward the Black Sea. The Russians would then be trapped between Army Group South and a supplementary invasion across the Romanian border launched on July 1 by German and Romanian troops. Initially, however, Rundstedt encountered especially tenacious resistance from the men of the Kiev Military District. Their commander, General Mikhail Kirponos, welded together a better-organized and more stubborn defense than the Germans had faced on the other fronts. Rundstedt's forces tore savagely at the Russian lines, pushing them back only slowly and at great cost. One German infantry colonel lamented, "Our ranks got thinner every day. Numberless cemeteries full of our dead appeared along our route." To stop the enemy thrust, Kirponos concentrated his six mechanized corps against Kleist's 1st Panzer Group. Beginning on June 26, for four days the greatest tank battle thus far in the war raged in northwestern Ukraine. Each side employed hundreds of tanks in an all-out test of strength.

Kirponos could not overcome his powerful adversary. Too many of his units were understrength in tanks and fatally deficient in everything from repair facilities to radios to antitank guns. General Rokossovskii, commander of the IV Mechanized Corps, later wrote in his memoirs, "Up to the beginning of the war our corps was up to half of its establishment for personnel, but had not received basic equipment: tanks and motor transport. Here, the stocks were no more than 30 per cent of the authorized strength."[36] The Luftwaffe also controlled the air space over the battlefield. Anti-Soviet partisans of the Organization of Ukrainian Nationalists (OUN) ambushed smaller Red Army detachments and spread confusion. Soviet troops were forced to pull back from the Lvov region toward the pre-1939 border, but they did so in good order, still barring the way against Rundstedt. The pattern continued to repeat itself: the Germans constantly hammering at Soviet defenses, the Russians launching punishing counterattacks, then falling back. By July 8, Kleist's panzers were within one hundred miles of Kiev, capital of Ukraine.

From the beginning of Operation Barbarossa, the SS and the Wehrmacht ruthlessly implemented the "commissar order"—slaughtering military commissars, Soviet officials, and Jews, as well as other civilians and POWs. A few officers protested the murders—especially the killing of women and children—but their superiors overrode their qualms. The killing quickly expanded from "Jewish commissars" and "snipers" to numerous ordinary civilians. The demographic revolution that Hitler intended began immediately, just as it had in Poland in the fall of 1939.

The *Blitzkrieg* Slows Down

In less than a month of campaigning, the Wehrmacht had won a series of impressive victories. Soviet defenses lay in smoking ruins from the Baltic to the Black Sea, the Red Army had suffered well over a million casualties, and Hitler's forces now lay within striking distance of the three largest Soviet cities—Leningrad, Moscow, and Kiev. The reasons for this initial debacle are not hard to fathom. Inexplicably, Stalin had let the enemy achieve strategic surprise. Soviet military doctrine facilitated the Wehrmacht's advance by paying insufficient attention to defensive warfare. Inexperienced junior and middle-grade officers led improperly deployed and inadequately trained troops to slaughter. There were insufficient vehicles to redeploy those units under attack or to bring up reserves. There were not enough rifles or even bullets for all the troops. Artillery fire was inadequate and air support nonexistent. After the *Blitzkrieg* in France, the Red Army command had organized antitank units to support the infantry, but they were often not in the right place to repel such a mobile and unpredictable enemy.

Moscow's forces had more tanks than any other army in the world, by some accounts more than all the other armies combined. Yet many of them were obsolete models, and three-quarters of them needed repair. The Red Army lost tanks in combat with the Germans at a ratio of six to one, while the newly conscripted, barely trained troops panicked with "tank fright" at the sight of panzers charging toward them. There were never enough spare parts, or repair facilities or fuel supplies. Command and control suffered at every level from an entirely inadequate communications system. Hundreds of thousands of Red Army soldiers were now paying with their lives for years of placing political reliability above military competence in the officer corps, as well as for the delusional state of their supreme commander. The surprising thing under these circumstances is not that some units panicked and fled the battlefield while others quickly surrendered, but that so many fought tenaciously to the death. The multiple disasters in the opening phase of Operation Barbarossa profoundly shocked the Soviet public. Moscow had assured its people that the Soviet Union was invincible and that any aggressor would be quickly crushed. Stalin's regime now faced not only the ferocious Wehrmacht but also the corrosive effects of defeatism.

Confident of victory, both military and civilian authorities in Berlin were busy planning what they would do after the fall of the USSR. In mid-July, Hitler shifted industrial production priorities from the army to the navy and Luftwaffe, believing that he had won in Russia and that he could soon carry the fight to Britain and the United States. Yet all was not well for the *Blitzkrieg*. The original battle plan called for the encirclement and destruction of all the major Soviet forces west of the Dnieper. Some German units had already crossed that river, but the war was far from over. Despite staggering losses, the Red Army was still a formidable opponent. It continued to offer fierce resistance on all fronts, and it marshaled, from the German point of view, a truly frightening depth of reserves.

German intelligence had seriously underestimated the enemy's strength. Halder noted in his diary that while he had expected opposition from about two hundred Soviet divisions, by the beginning of August German forces had already encountered 360 enemy divisions.[37] Even that revision missed the mark. By the end of the year, the Soviet army had deployed six hundred divisions on the eastern front. Moreover, the despised *Untermenschen* of the Red Army had shown themselves capable of sustaining combat with the soldiers of the "master race." The 3rd Panzer Group's war diary noted, "The enemy . . . fights tenaciously and courageously to the death. . . . The struggle, as a result, will be harder than those in Poland and the western campaign."[38] German losses, though still far below Soviet totals, mounted alarmingly, while the Wehrmacht's supply of war matériel dwindled rapidly.

Operation Barbarossa had been ill conceived from the beginning. Germany did not have the resources for a war of attrition with the USSR. Success depended on the rapid destruction of the Red Army and collapse of the Soviet regime. That had not happened. Horse-drawn artillery and marching infantry could not keep up with the panzers. There were few armored personnel carriers to keep the infantry on pace. Geography posed a problem, too. Since the Soviet Union was considerably broader at the Urals than on its western frontier, each German advance stretched their battlefront wider and their supply lines longer. The Germans were reaching the point where they could no longer maintain a continuous, all-out offensive on every front.

The *Blitzkrieg* had failed in another way. German planners anticipated that their initial shattering blow against the USSR would provoke the oppressed peoples of the Soviet Union to rebel against their own state. However, the extreme barbarity with which the Germans treated their prisoners of war and the civilian population undermined these possibilities. German forces shot many surrendering Red Army soldiers immediately. Those taken prisoner were frequently deprived of food, medical care, and adequate shelter so that they died in horrific numbers. Civilians were treated brutally, too. Nazi authorities seized most of the food and fuel supplies they could find, while looting and random violence by ordinary German soldiers was widespread. Wherever they even suspected resistance, the Germans burned villages and shot masses of civilians.

Even those Soviet citizens whose loyalty to the Stalin regime was weak were forced by unstinting German cruelty to rally in defense of their Soviet homeland. There was significant popular resistance to the Soviet cause only in the westernmost areas incorporated into the USSR after the Nazi-Soviet Pact. Some accounts of the war on the eastern front condemn Hitler's refusal to cooperate with the ethnic minorities there as a "mistake," implying that the Germans might have treated the non-Russian populations better and thereby gained a significant advantage in fighting the Soviet regime. That assertion is both true and irrelevant. It imagines that Hitler could have been someone other than who he actually was. The concept of *Lebensraum* required enslavement and extermination of the peoples of the USSR. As historian Mark Mazower aptly describes it, Hitler intended to fight "a colonial war of extraction."[39]

All these considerations caused Hitler to make a vitally important strategic decision in mid-July. What made the *Blitzkrieg* strategy so attractive to the Führer was the success of this technique in winning major victories so quickly and at such relatively little cost to the German people. Operation Barbarossa, however, for all its early triumphs, had not brought about the instant collapse of the USSR, while the human and material costs of the campaign grew ever more burdensome to the Germans. The army high command (OKH) now wanted to concentrate its forces for a knockout blow against Moscow, which they thought would force Russia out of the war. Hitler disagreed. Soviet counterattacks on the central front had blunted the German advance and resulted, by German standards, in unacceptable casualties. Instead, the Führer ordered the weight of the Nazi offensive to be shifted to the southern front.

Overrunning Ukraine, Crimea, and perhaps even the Caucasus would harness Russia's vast agricultural, industrial, and energy resources to the German war effort. The likelihood of global war against the United States in the near future made the acquisition of those assets all the more imperative. Simultaneously, a less weighty thrust in the north would permit von Leeb to link up with the Finns and seal off Leningrad securely from the rest of the USSR. Then, with the northern and southern flanks well protected and the resources of Russia fueling the Wehrmacht, it would be time to strike directly at the Kremlin. Halder, Rundstedt, Bock, Guderian, and Hoth disagreed strongly with this strategy. Guderian even traveled to Rastenburg, the Führer's East Prussian war headquarters, to dispute the decision, but to no avail. Contradicting much later criticism, especially in the memoirs of German generals, historian Ian Kershaw suggests, "Strategically and economically, the sweep through the Ukraine with the intention of taking the Caucasus was probably the correct decision."[40]

Army Group Center assumed a defensive posture, with its armored strike forces reassigned to other theaters—Hoth to Leningrad and Guderian to Ukraine. Rundstedt's forces resumed the offensive on the southern front with renewed vigor. Kleist's armor struck hard across central Ukraine. By early August, the 1st Panzer Group had some twenty Soviet divisions pinned against the Axis forces now closing in from Romania. In the Uman region, the Germans took over one hundred thousand prisoners, together with three hundred tanks and eight hundred guns. Farther north, Guderian's 2nd Panzer Group began to hammer on the upper flank of the southern front. At this point, Stalin and some of his senior advisors made a serious error in judgment. They interpreted Guderian's operations below Briansk as the prelude to an imminent drive on Moscow. Zhukov had warned of danger in Ukraine, but Stalin rejected his advice and demoted him to command the Reserve Front. Instead, Stalin pulled back the bulk of his forces in Ukraine behind the Dnieper. Only Kiev and the Black Sea port of Odessa retained substantial Russian troop concentrations. Still concerned more with Briansk and Moscow than with Ukraine, the Soviet high command assigned four armies under Eremenko to attack Guderian. For eight days in early September, fighting raged between Eremenko's forces and the 2nd Panzer Group. The Russian armies, undermanned and already exhausted from earlier battles, could not contain the German armor.

Guderian broke through, but then instead of continuing toward Briansk he wheeled south into Ukraine. The 1st and 2nd Panzer Groups were now converging rapidly to encircle Kiev. Guderian's tanks covered 250 miles in just two weeks, fighting a series of whirlwind engagements as they went. Kleist's panzers faced stronger Russian opposition but still managed to cover 170 miles in the same time. Marshal Budënny finally realized what the Germans were doing. On September 11, he requested permission from Stalin to withdraw from the Kiev salient. In response, Stalin relieved Budënny of his command and ordered General Kirponos to hold fast at Kiev. General Tupikov, Kirponos's chief of staff, wired a grim forecast to Moscow on the 14th: "The beginning of a catastrophe which you know about is only a couple of days away."[41] Stalin denounced him as a panic monger, but Tupikov was right. Two days later the two German armored spearheads converged 125 miles east of Kiev. On September 17, Stalin finally gave permission to evacuate the Kiev pocket, but it was far too late. Both Kirponos and Tupikov died in the breakout attempt. Budënny, Timoshenko, and a future leader of the Soviet Union, Nikita Khrushchev, managed to escape through a small gap in the encirclement. The Germans claimed to have taken 650,000 prisoners. Adding Russian killed and wounded to that figure, the total Soviet loss soared to over a million casualties. Within a month, Odessa had to be evacuated too. The riches of Ukraine now lay open to Nazi exploitation.

While Rundstedt's forces were annihilating the Red Army in the south, von Leeb drew the noose tighter around Leningrad. German armor and air power continued to blast the Russian defenders, pushing them back ever closer to the city. In August, an enemy column reached the Gulf of Finland at a point only a few miles from Leningrad. Voroshilov had lost control of the situation. Stalin replaced the aging marshal with Zhukov, who dismissed several commanders on the Leningrad front and bullied the remainder to stand and fight. He warned them: "All commanders, political workers, and soldiers who abandon the indicated line without a written order from the front or the army military council will be shot immediately."[42]

A series of desperate counterattacks blunted the German offensive temporarily, but within the city the Russians began to prepare for a house-by-house resistance. They laid mines, strung barbed wire, and dug tank traps across the southern entrances to Leningrad. Factory and office workers were organized into a militia, though a shortage of weapons meant that most were armed only with shotguns, pistols, or even shovels. The final enemy assault, for which the Leningraders were so frantically preparing, never came. In mid-September, Hitler decided not to attempt to storm the city. Against Zhukov's tenacious defense, the Germans had suffered many more casualties than expected. Those forces, especially the armor, were now needed for the great offensive soon to be launched on the central front.

Moreover, the Finns, attacking from the north, had slowed their offensive. They were interested only in recovering those territories taken from them by the Soviets in 1940. The Führer therefore ordered Leeb to seal off Leningrad and starve it into submission. This strategy would not only save German lives; it would also ensure that a high proportion of the city's three million inhabitants would die from hunger, freezing, or bombardment. Thinning out the Slavic population was, after all, one of Hitler's primary war aims. Artillery and aerial bombardment rocked the city almost constantly from September onward. The Luftwaffe succeeded in setting fire to the wooden structures of the warehouse district where most of Leningrad's food reserves were stored.

The people of Leningrad were ready to fight an invading enemy to the death, but they were not prepared for a prolonged siege. With all the land routes to Leningrad cut by Germans, supplies could reach the city only by air or by ship over Lake Ladoga. The few planes available could bring in no more than a trickle of provisions. Barges on the lake could carry much more, but still the city received less than half the quantity of food it needed each day. Shipments declined further after the Germans captured Tikhvin, the railhead for the Ladoga route. Strict rationing was instituted. At the beginning of September, officials authorized a six-hundred-gram daily bread ration for workers. Ten days later, it dropped to five hundred grams. By late November, even that meager ration was cut in half. Those who were not manual laborers got still less.

People scoured the city for anything—edible weeds, animal feed, flower bulbs, household pets, even rodents. There was even some cannibalism, though the police shot anyone suspected of the practice. Leningrad was starving to death. Leningraders pursued various survival strategies. Some tried to secure jobs with higher rations or used political connections to get more food. Others bartered precious possessions for food or planted gardens for themselves, or refused to work unless extra food was provided. Nevertheless, one-third of the city's population would eventually die of hunger. The suffering fell disproportionately on women, children, and older people because so many of the men had been evacuated with their factories or drafted into the army or militia.

With so little transport available for food, there was no room for fuel at all. After all the trees in the city were cut down and burned, the people huddled together, shivered, and in many cases froze to death as temperatures plummeted. Without heat, the water pipes burst, and soon there was no running water. The Germans also cut off most of the electricity. Eleven-year-old Tania Savicheva recorded the fate of her family in her notebook:

> Zhenia died 28 December, 12:30 in the morning, 1941. Babushka [grandmother] died 25 January, 3 o'clock, 1942. Leka died 17 March, 5 o'clock in the morning, 1942. Dedia Vashia died 13 April, 2 o'clock at night, 1942. Dedia Lesha, 10 May, 4 o'clock in the afternoon 1942. Mama, 13 May, 7:30 a.m., 1942. All died. Only Tania remains.[43]

Tania died in 1944. The ordeal of Leningrad under siege was to last for 872 days. Although many factories were closed and city services stopped working, theaters and orchestras continued to entertain to keep up morale. The famous composer Dmitri Shostakovich wrote the beginning of his Seventh Symphony (subsequently known as the Leningrad Symphony) in the besieged city. The work became a symbol of heroic Soviet defiance.

Among the litany of disasters rolling over Russia, there was one hopeful note. The USSR would not fight alone; it would have the support of allies. Unlike Stalin, Churchill had not dismissed the mounting evidence of German preparations to invade Soviet Russia, so the British cabinet had formulated a policy in advance to meet that contingency. Veteran anticommunist though he was, the prime minister welcomed the Soviet Union to the Allied cause. "Any man or state who fights on against Nazidom will have our aid," he proclaimed on the first day of the Russo-German war. "Any man or state who marches with Hitler is our foe. . . . It follows, therefore, that we shall give whatever help we can to Russia and the Russian people. We shall appeal to all our friends and allies in every part of the world to take the same course and pursue it, as we shall faithfully and steadfastly to the end."[44] Qualifying that endorsement, Churchill remarked in private, "If Hitler invaded Hell, I would make at least a favourable reference to the devil in the House of Commons."[45]

On July 13, Molotov and British ambassador Stafford Cripps signed an agreement establishing the Anglo-Soviet alliance and pledging the partners never to negotiate a separate peace with the enemy. Stalin was anxious for Allied assistance of all kinds. He asked for the immediate delivery of aluminum, tanks, and airplanes. More urgently, Stalin wanted Britain to open a new battlefront against the Nazis, either in France or perhaps in Norway—one that would draw at least forty German divisions from the Russian front. His request in early September for Allied troops to fight side by side with the Red Army on Soviet soil reveals the full extent of his desperation. Stalin's distress is clear in his message to Churchill: "The relative stabilization of the front, achieved about three weeks ago, has been upset. . . . Without . . . aid the Soviet Union will be either defeated or weakened to the extent that it will lose for a long time the ability to help its Allies by active operations at the front against Hitlerism."[46] Most of these requests were far beyond the capacity of the hard-pressed British government to fulfill. Nonetheless, British supply convoys were soon sailing for northern Russia, with RAF squadrons stationed in Murmansk to protect their sea-lanes.

Like Churchill, President Roosevelt also welcomed Russia to the anti-Nazi cause. He told reporters on June 24, "This country is going to give all the aid it can to the Soviets." After marshaling the necessary public support, FDR extended Lend-Lease assistance to the USSR on November 7.[47] The first American shipment of P-40 fighters, diverted from Britain, arrived by the end of the month. At the time of Russia's greatest peril, however, the Western powers could offer little immediate aid. Britain could spare very little war maté-riel, while for America, aid to the Soviet Union took third priority behind the needs of the rapidly expanding US armed forces and those of England. In the end, Allied aid for Soviet Russia would be substantial, but in the fall of 1941, Moscow had to rely almost entirely on its own resources.

The Drive for Moscow

Those resources were soon taxed to the limit. The Russians knew that the Germans were pulling their armored strike forces out of the Leningrad front in late September. The Soviet high command could not take advantage of this development to lift the siege of Leningrad because all signs pointed to a major new enemy offensive developing in the direction of Moscow. On paper, Soviet defenses along the central front looked formidable—eight hundred thousand men were massed there. This appearance of strength was deceptive. Many of these divisions were physically and emotionally exhausted after so many previous defeats. Some were ragtag formations put together from the survivors of various shattered units. Others consisted of raw recruits or citizen volunteers with virtually no military training. All of them were critically short of equipment. One typical 675-man brigade had a mere nine machine guns, 295 rifles, and some pistols. There were only 770 tanks and 364 planes for the entire front. Against this ragged defense, the Germans marshaled over half the men and tanks available on the eastern front—almost two million troops. General von Bock's Army Group Center recovered Guderian's 2nd Panzer Group from the south and received nearly all the armor from the Leningrad theater as well. The Luftwaffe provided 1,500 planes for close air support. The drive for Moscow, code-named Operation Typhoon, was about to begin.

On September 30, Guderian pivoted his forces ninety degrees and sent them racing toward the Soviet capital from Ukraine. They covered 150 miles in just four days. On October 3, the Germans overran the important communications center of Orel. The speed of the enemy thrust caught the Red Army defenders completely by surprise. Commuters packed on the city trolley cars were horrified to see Nazi armor rumble past them down the streets of Orel. Four days later the strategically important city of Briansk fell to German encirclement. General Eremenko, commander of the Briansk sector, barely managed to escape after enemy tanks had closed to within two hundred yards of his command post. Most of his troops were not so fortunate. Three Soviet armies were now entrapped near Briansk. General M. F. Lukin reported,

> The situation of the encircled forces has worsened sharply. There are few shells, bullets are running out, and there is no food. They eat that which the population can provide and horseflesh. Medicines and dressing materials are used up. All tents and dwellings are overflowing with wounded.[48]

Farther north, the main body of von Bock's forces joined the offensive on October 2. Preoccupied with menacing developments to the southwest, the high command in Moscow was slow to respond. Then on October 5 came a shocking reconnaissance report from a fighter pilot that an enemy armored column twelve miles long was moving up the Smolensk–Moscow highway. The 3rd and 4th Panzer Groups smashed through the Russian defenses quickly to envelop five Soviet armies at Viazma. Confused and savage fighting continued in this area for days. Before it was over the Germans had captured 665,000 prisoners. In desperation, Stalin ordered Zhukov to leave Leningrad and take command on the central front. Zhukov could find only ninety thousand additional reserves, many of them cadets or militia, to bolster the hastily assembled Mozhaisk line just sixty miles from Moscow. Nearly a quarter million civilians, mostly women, dug tank traps and built fortifications. In the capital, demolitions experts began placing explosive charges under bridges and in factories in case the enemy should break through.

Early in October, Stalin seems to have been so shaken by this series of disastrous defeats that he contemplated offering peace terms to Hitler.[49] He was apparently willing to give up the Baltic states, Belorussia, and even Ukraine to save the remainder of the USSR.[50] The Western Allies feared the possibility of a separate Soviet-German peace just as Stalin feared that they might negotiate their own deal with Hitler. Evidence of these top-secret initiatives is contradictory. One Soviet intelligence official later claimed that these efforts were merely disinformation to confuse the enemy.[51] It is also possible that the Soviet side fostered rumors of a deal with Germany as leverage in dealing with the Western powers. Whatever the case, the Germans had no interest in peace at a time when total victory appeared to be in sight. Later, after the course of war had changed dramatically in 1944, Berlin was interested, but Moscow no longer was.[52] Hitler thought that he had won in the East. On October 13, German radio commentator Hans Fritzsche declared that the "military decision of the war has taken place. What remains now is primarily of a domestic and foreign political character. At some point the German armies will stop, and we will draw a new border to guard greater Europe and the European interest bloc under German leadership in the East. . . . This Europe will be economically, industrially and agriculturally completely self-sufficient and practically unassailable militarily."[53]

On the Soviet side, there was fear that the German offensive against Moscow could not be stopped. In mid-October, Molotov told the British and American ambassadors to prepare for evacuation. Lenin's body was moved from Red Square to Tiumen, more than 1,300 miles to the east. Authorities prepared to destroy the capital's factories as well as its electrical power, railway, telegraph, and telephone stations. Three weeks later the sprawling government, party, and economic bureaucracy abandoned Moscow for twenty-one cities located in or near the Urals, hundreds of miles to the east. Panic spread in Moscow. People deserted their factories and offices, the subway stopped working, and many Communists threw away their party cards and badges. Stalin and other top Soviet leaders were scheduled to leave the capital on October 15, but the enemy advance slowed and the panic in the city subsided. Stalin remained in town, involving himself in the details of defending the city.

The Wehrmacht had overrun most of the western USSR and taken millions of prisoners, but the greatest victory, the capture of Moscow, was beyond Hitler's grasp. German forces continued to press the attack after taking Viazma. By October 18, the Germans had reached Mozhaisk. Yet the pace of their advance had slowed to a crawl. The Wehrmacht was near the end of its strength. Having advanced six hundred miles, captured scores of cities, and taken three million Soviet prisoners, the German army desperately needed rest for its weary soldiers and maintenance for its battered vehicles, as well as replacements for the large numbers of troops and equipment lost in combat. The German army began the campaign with 425,000 vehicles of all types. By November, there were only 75,000 operational vehicles.

Moreover, weather was now becoming a serious problem. There were far too few roads leading to Moscow to accommodate the sixty-nine German divisions employed in Operation Typhoon, and most of those roads were unpaved. The heavy October rains turned them into impassable quagmires. The infantry, the horse-drawn artillery, and even the panzers bogged down in the muck. Now creeping rather than racing forward, Hitler's soldiers soaked by day and froze by night. However, ultimately, in the judgment of Richard Overy, "it was not the tough winter conditions that halted the German army but the remarkable revival of Soviet military manpower after the terrible maulings of the summer and autumn."[54] Despite staggering losses, the Red Army grew from 4.9 million men on June 22 to 7.38 million on August 1, 7.7 million on December 1, and 9.8 million by March 1.

Most of the German commanders believed that the time had come to halt the advance, consolidate their gains, and dig in along a defensive line for the winter. Hitler and Bock would not hear of it. It was both a blessing and a curse when the weather turned very cold in November. The armor could roll forward again over the frozen ground, but neither men nor machines were prepared for the Russian winter. Guderian had ordered winter gear for his troops, but his request was denied because it was "not necessary." One German regimental commander lamented that his men were "underfed, overtired, badly clothed" and that their combat effectiveness was "frighteningly slight."[55] Temperatures often reached –22 degrees and sometimes even –49 degrees Fahrenheit. A voluntary "Winter Relief" campaign in Germany netted lots of coats, hats, socks, and boots for the troops. In occupied eastern Europe, giving up such items was not voluntary, but it was not enough. German soldiers paid the price for their leaders' overconfidence. In the subzero temperatures, radiators burst, motor oil congealed, and men froze in their lightweight uniforms. The significance of the Balkan invasions, poor spring weather conditions, and logistical problems, which had caused the postponement of Barbarossa and thus sacrificed a month of fine summer campaigning weather, was now painfully obvious.

Meanwhile, Stalin and most Muscovites had recovered their confidence. Soon stores reopened, public transport began working again, and NKVD troops restored order. As a symbol of Soviet determination to resist, authorities held the traditional military parade in Red Square, marking the anniversary of the Bolshevik Revolution, on November 7, despite the danger of air raids. After the parade, the troops marched directly back to the front. In a speech to Soviet officials, Stalin proclaimed, "If they [the Germans] want a war of extermination, they shall have one." Up to this point, Stalin had been careful not to draw too many troops from the Far Eastern command. In October, however, his principal agent in Japan, Richard Sorge, had confirmed that the Japanese would soon move against Britain and America, not the USSR. Now he ordered half the troop strength in the Far East, including a thousand tanks and a thousand planes, brought to the central front. Zhukov received only a small part of these forces to strengthen the defenses in front of Moscow. Stalin husbanded most of them in his Supreme Command Reserve.

Army Group Center resumed its offensive in mid-November, though now it was staggering rather than smashing forward. Germany's production and logistical systems had reached a crisis point and were no longer able to adequately supply the army.[56] The battle was extremely savage, and casualties were high on both sides. The Germans pushed on through the ice and snow against constant Soviet counterattacks, covering barely forty miles in two weeks of grim fighting. The German 112th Infantry Division, lacking adequate antitank guns, broke and ran under attack from Soviet T-34 tanks. Nonetheless, panzer spearheads penetrated the suburbs of Moscow just twelve miles from the Kremlin walls. Bock's men would get no farther. His troops were completely exhausted, so the offensive ground to a halt. The Germans themselves estimated the combat power of their formations at only 60 percent of normal strength, while the panzer divisions were operating with only 35 percent of their usual tank complement. A steady stream of orders and threats from Berlin could not push Bock's dazed men and battered equipment a step further.

Now, with the Wehrmacht at the limit of its endurance, the Russians struck back, beginning with limited counterattacks on December 2 and escalating to a full-scale offensive three days later. German intelligence did not detect the extensive reserves moving westward from deep in the interior of the USSR. Those carefully hoarded reinforcements—newly formed divisions as well as veteran units from the Urals, Central Asia, and the Far East—now waded into battle. Soviet troop strength in European Russia had increased from 2.2 million to 4 million men. Soviet forces were also fortified in a uniquely Russian way. A new directive ordered that every serviceman stationed in a combat zone should receive one hundred grams of vodka daily.

Zhukov's initial goal was merely to relieve Moscow with a series of counterstrokes, but when he found the enemy giving way everywhere, his plan evolved into a grand encirclement campaign to trap and destroy the German armored formations. The Russians were learning how to fight the Wehrmacht. Zhukov forbade the often-suicidal frontal assaults on heavily defended enemy positions that had characterized Soviet tactics in the past. Instead, he ordered Red Army formations to flow around strongpoints, mounting flanking and rear attacks. On the right flank, he struck with four armies; on the left, he launched two more armies and a reinforced cavalry corps. Zhukov gathered 744 tanks for the blow. For the first time the Red Army employed massed armored assaults.

The Germans were caught off guard. Their intelligence reports assured them that the Red Army was a spent force no longer capable of offensive operations. Exhausted, overextended, and without reserves, the German army recoiled before Zhukov's onslaught. Many of the attacking Soviet troops were Siberians, well equipped for and accustomed to fighting in the bitter cold. Some of the Russian shock forces deployed the devastating new *Katiusha* rockets, another unpleasant surprise for the Germans. For the first time, Guderian saw his crack troops break and flee in panic before the foe. The diarist for the 3rd Panzer Group noted, "Discipline is breaking down. More and more soldiers are heading west on foot without weapons, leading a calf on a rope or pulling a sled loaded with potatoes. The road is under constant air attack. Those killed by bombs are no longer being buried. All the hangers-on (corps troops, Luftwaffe, supply train) are pouring back to the rear in full flight. Without rations, freezing, irrationally they are rushing back. . . . The panzer group has reached its most dismal hour."[57]

By the end of the month, Soviet forces had thrown the Germans back some fifty miles, liberating Kalinin, Klin, Mozhaisk, Kaluga, and Tula. Zhukov's divisions pressed forward steadily, though they were not yet able to strike fast enough or hard enough to entrap the panzers as their commander hoped. The Germans fought stubbornly in retreat and adopted scorched-earth tactics to deny the Russians any useful resources. A retreating German soldier noted this in his diary:

> Precisely at 0230 hours [i.e., 2:30 a.m.], with the civilian population not having any idea at all, the whole village is set ablaze. Within 5 minutes it is engulfed in bright flames. Roused from their sleep and terrified, the inhabitants run outside screaming. All they can do is to save their naked lives. Then we abandon the village, our route taking us through other burning villages. The entire region is lit up bright red; snow reflects the red glow.[58]

Even before the end of December, Stalin assumed personal direction of the operation. Believing that the decisive turning point of the war had arrived, Stalin greatly expanded the focus of the Soviet offensive. He told the British that "the German army is tired out. . . . The German army today is poorly dressed, poorly fed, and losing morale. . . . In the final analysis, the German army is not that strong. Its reputation is highly exaggerated."[59] He now thought it possible to break through all the way to Smolensk and, in the process, annihilate Army Group Center. At the same time, Red Army spearheads were to drive northwest and southwest to smash the enemy concentrations surrounding Leningrad and those occupying Ukraine.

Stalin now committed the same error that Hitler had made earlier—greatly overestimating the capabilities of his forces. This grandiose scheme might possibly have succeeded if all the Soviet units were at full strength in men and equipment, thoroughly rested, and abundantly supplied—but they were none of these things. In planning the operation, Stalin was looking at pins and markers representing formations on a battle map. He was not envisioning the reality of decimated units, exhausted troops, and spent supplies. He ignored Zhukov's advice to consolidate his gains and hold the line. Nonetheless, the Soviet offensive threatened for a while to turn the German triumph into a rout.

As Soviet troops liberated some of the territory previously overrun by the Germans, they found fresh reason to hate and kill the enemy. For example, an eighteen-year-old partisan fighter, Zoia Kosmodemianskaia, was caught setting fire to a stable to deny it to the Germans. After parading her through the village, she was tortured, mutilated, and hanged. Red Army troops retaking that area found her frozen body, still hanging from the scaffold, with one breast cut off. This atrocity, only one of a great many, became a cause célèbre, known to virtually every Soviet soldier and citizen. Visceral hatred of the enemy made this a war of annihilation for the Soviet side, too. Soviet forces sometimes committed atrocities against German prisoners, but these were mostly the spontaneous acts of enraged soldiers, not the official policy of the Soviet government.

Some German generals recommended deep withdrawals, but Hitler insisted that they fight for every inch of conquered Russian soil. Enraged at the setback, the Führer dismissed over thirty of his senior commanders, including Brauchitsch, Bock, Rundstedt, Guderian, and Höppner. He assumed personal command of the Wehrmacht. Hitler never had any sympathy for his beleaguered troops. Privately, he told a visiting Danish diplomat, "If the German people are no longer strong enough and ready to sacrifice their own blood for their existence, they should perish and be wiped out by another, stronger power. They are no longer worthy of the place they have won for themselves."[60] Hitler, of course, never said anything like that in public.

There were some moments of real panic, but Hitler's command that the army fight and, if necessary, die where it stood rather than retreat finally stiffened German resistance. German morale sank dangerously but did not break. Of the 162 divisions deployed in the USSR, 104 were barely able to defend themselves and had no offensive capability.[61] The Russian drive continued throughout January and February. Yet, lacking decisive superiority over the enemy in men and equipment, it began to lose momentum. The Germans organized a formidable defense based on a network of heavily fortified towns they called "hedgehogs." Soviet forces could flow around them without much difficulty, but they suffered prohibitive casualties attacking these hedgehogs. At Stalin's insistence, the Red Army launched still more futile attacks in March and April, but these only resulted in further losses of troops and supplies. The German line held firm.

The *Blitzkrieg* had been halted, Moscow saved, and in some places as much as one hundred miles of previously overrun territory liberated. The enemy, however, still occupied Viazma, Briansk, Orel, and Kursk. The Red Army had lost almost four million men, but the Germans had suffered nearly one million casualties themselves, a quarter of them from frostbite. Much of the Soviet Union's industrial and agricultural capacity still lay in enemy hands: 65 percent of its coal, 68 percent of its iron, 60 percent of its steel and aluminum, 40 percent of its railroad equipment, 40 percent of its grain production, and 40 percent of its population. Elsewhere along the eastern front, the military situation was equally ambiguous. Soviet counterattacks in the north had recaptured Tikhvin, a critically important transport hub, in December. By January, supplies were reaching embattled Leningrad in greater quantities across the thick ice of Lake Ladoga, but it was still not possible to lift the enemy siege of the city. In the south, Soviet forces recaptured Rostov at the end of November, but a subsequent attempt to liberate Kharkov failed. Similarly, a daring but costly amphibious operation temporarily relieved the pressure on Sevastopol, though ultimately the Germans were able to overrun the entire Crimean Peninsula. The Red Army lost 390,000 troops in this futile effort. Stalin's grand design to annihilate Army Group South failed.

Operation Barbarossa was a failure. The Wehrmacht had penetrated as much as six hundred miles into Soviet territory and killed or captured four million Red Army soldiers, but it had not destroyed the Red Army or the Soviet regime. Just the opposite, the Red Army, which had numbered five million men in three hundred divisions when the Germans attacked, had grown by the end of the year to a force eight million strong, fielding almost six hundred divisions. The debate about why Barbarossa failed and if it ever had a chance of succeeding continues to this day. Historian R. H. Stolfi argues that the operation would have succeeded if Hitler had not diverted forces from Army Group Center to Ukraine in August 1941.[62] After the war, numerous German generals claimed in their memoirs that the war would have been won except for the Führer's amateurish meddling in military decisions.[63]

Barbarossa was an extraordinarily complex undertaking. It required numerous operations to be conducted successfully in precise order and in a very short time frame. The famous German military theorist Karl von Clausewitz taught that complex plans can never be executed precisely but are soon shrouded in the "fog of war" and subjected to "friction." In the Russian case, the Red Army, Russia's terrain, and the weather each failed to cooperate. Some historians have suggested that Hitler's ambitious goals were beyond Germany's means to achieve—reflecting arrogance and racism rather than prudent planning.

Historian David Stahel argues that Operation Barbarossa was derailed as early as the late summer of 1941 by a combination of Soviet resistance, Russian distances and terrain, and limited German resources.[64] For a German victory, every assumption of Operation Barbarossa had to prove correct and every move had to be executed perfectly and on schedule. Failing that, the Russo-German struggle would inevitably devolve into a war of attrition in which Nazi Germany was at a serious disadvantage relative to its Soviet and Anglo-American opponents. Surveying the failure of Operation Barbarossa, Hitler (and many subsequent historians) believed that the diversion of German forces to the Balkan campaign in the spring of

1941 had been fatal to the success of the campaign in Russia. Six weeks more of good fighting weather, they argue, would have finished the Soviets before the Russian winter stopped the Wehrmacht's momentum. As discussed above, however, it was the tenacious resistance of the Red Army, more than any other factor, that halted the German advance.

Hitler's intention to destroy the USSR with one rapid, smashing blow had been frustrated. It was not clear in the early months of 1942, however, whether the *Blitzkrieg* had been fatally derailed or only briefly delayed. In Berlin, the German high command was preparing a new operation—a massive blow against Stalingrad and the Caucasus—that the Führer was confident would finally bring total victory in the East. Meanwhile, Hitler's Axis partner, Imperial Japan, had launched its own dramatic assault against British and American possessions in the Pacific. The war had grown to global proportions.

Notes

1. Carl J. Burckhardt, *Meine Danziger Mission, 1937–1939* (Munich: Callwey, 1960), 348.

2. Lizzie Collingham, *The Taste of War: World War II and the Battle for Food* (New York: Penguin, 2011), 32.

3. Gabriel Gorodetsky, *Grand Delusion: Stalin and the German Invasion of Russia* (New Haven, CT: Yale University Press, 2001), 181.

4. Adolf Hitler, *Hitler's Second Book* (New York: Grove Press, 1983), 109ff. Cf. British historian A. J. P. Taylor and German historian Fritz Fischer, who argue that Hitler's ambitions were limited to the domination of Europe. Taylor, *The Origins of the Second World War* (London: Hamish Hamilton, 1961); Fischer, *From Kaiserreich to Third Reich: Elements of Continuity in German History, 1871–1945* (London: Allen & Unwin, 1986). They miss the key point that achieving mastery over Europe was only a step toward the goal of global domination. Beyond Hitler's writings, evidence for the scope of his ambitions is provided by German plans to build a massive surface navy, four-engine trans-Atlantic bombers, and an intercontinental ballistic missile, the A-10, capable of striking the United States.

5. E.g., Sean McMeekin, *Stalin's War: A New History of World War II* (New York: Basic Books, 2021), ch. 18.

6. Catherine Merridale, *Ivan's War: Life and Death in the Red Army, 1939–1945* (New York: Henry Holt, 2006), 33, 48.

7. *Chief of Staff: The Diaries of Lt. General Sir Henry Pownall*, ed., Brian Bond (London: L. Cooper, 1972–1974), 2:29.

8. Quoted in Simon Sebag Montefiore, *Stalin: The Court of the Red Tsar* (New York: Vintage, 2003), 312.

9. *The Diary of Georgi Dimitrov, 1933–1949*, ed. Ivo Banac (New Haven, CT: Yale University Press, 2003), 115.

10. Nikita Khrushchev, *Khrushchev Remembers* (New York: Bantam, 1971), 138–39, 177.

11. Gorodetsky, *Grand Delusion*, ch. 2.

12. Gerhard L. Weinberg, *A World at Arms: A Global History of World War II*, 2nd ed. (Cambridge: Cambridge University Press, 2005), 199.

13. The widely held notion that Germany's Balkan diversion fatally derailed Barbarossa is inaccurate. A prolonged winter and heavy spring rains in Russia made mobile campaigning almost impossible that spring. David M. Glantz, *Colossus Reborn: The Red Army at War, 1941–1943* (Lawrence: University Press of Kansas, 2005), 15.

14. Marlis G. Steinnert, *Hitler's War and the Germans: Public Mood and Attitude during the Second World War* (Athens: Ohio University Press, 1977), 141.

15. David M. Glantz, *Barbarossa: Hitler's Invasion of Russia, 1941* (Stroud, UK: Tempus, 2001), 32.

16. Mary R. Habeck, *Storm of Steel: The Development of Armor Doctrine in Germany and the Soviet Union, 1919–1939* (Ithaca, NY: Cornell University Press, 2003), ch. 7.

17. Roger Reese, *The Soviet Military Experience: A History of the Soviet Army, 1917–1991* (New York: Routledge, 2000), 85–87.

18. Stephen Kotkin, *Stalin: Waiting for Hitler, 1929–1941* (New York: Penguin, 2017), 759.

19. Merridale, *Ivan's War*, 76.

20. Mark von Hagen, "Soviet Soldiers and Officers on the Eve of the German Invasion: Toward a Description of Social Psychology and Political Attitudes," in *The People's War: Responses to World War II in the Soviet Union*, ed. Robert W. Thurston and Bernd Bonwetsch (Urbana: University of Illinois Press, 2000), 187–210.

21. Merridale, *Ivan's War*, 89. Cf. Oleg Budnitskii, "The Great Patriotic War and Soviet Society: Defeatism, 1941–42," *Kritika: Explorations in Russian and Eurasian History* 15, no. 4 (Fall 2014): 767–97, who argues that only "coercion" held the Soviet war effort together.

22. Gorodetsky, *Grand Delusion*, 176.

23. Gorodetsky, *Grand Delusion*, 299.

24. Gorodetsky, *Grand Delusion*, 279.

25. Gorodetsky, *Grand Delusion*, ch. 8 and 286.

26. Banac, *The Diary of Georgi Dimitrov*, 132.

27. Gorodetsky, *Grand Delusion*, 240.

28. Frank Ellis, *Barbarossa, 1941: Reframing Hitler's Invasion of Stalin's Soviet Empire* (Lawrence: University Press of Kansas, 2015), 210.

29. Richard Overy, *Russia's War: A History of the Soviet War Effort, 1941–1945* (New York: Penguin, 1997), 34.

30. Viktor Suvorov [pseud. for V. B. Rezun], *Icebreaker: Who Started the Second World War?* (London: Hamish Hamilton, 1990). Available evidence supports the possibility, though not the certainty, of Soviet intentions to strike against Germany in 1942 or 1943.

31. Gorodetsky, *Grand Delusion*; David Glantz, *Stumbling Colossus: The Red Army on the Eve of World War* (Lawrence: University Press of Kansas, 1998). Also see Teddy J. Uldricks, "The Icebreaker Controversy: Did Stalin Plan to Attack Hitler?," *Slavic Review* 58, no. 3 (Fall 1999): 626–43, for a discussion of revisionist attempts to depict Stalin as the aggressor.

32. Oleg V. Khlevniuk, *Stalin: A New Biography of a Dictator* (New Haven, CT: Yale University Press, 2015), 199.

33. Anastas Mikoian, *Tak bylo* (Moscow: Vagrius, 1999), 390.

34. *The Halder War Diary*, ed. Charles Burdick and Hans-Adolf Jacobsen (Novato, CA: Presidio Press, 1988), 446.

35. Glantz, *Barbarossa*, 82.

36. Konstantin Rokossovskii, *Soldatskii dolg* (Moscow: Olma Press, 2002), 30.

37. *The Halder War Diary*, 506.

38. Stephen G. Fritz, *The First Soldier: Hitler as Military Leader* (New Haven, CT: Yale University Press, 2018), 173.

39. Mark Mazower, *Hitler's Empire: How the Nazis Ruled Europe* (New York: Penguin, 2008), 149.

40. Ian Kershaw, *Hitler* (Harlow: Pearson, 2005), 192.

41. Evan Mawdsley, *Thunder in the East: The Nazi-Soviet War, 1941–1945* (London: Hodder Arnold, 2005), 80.

42. Geoffrey Roberts, *Stalin's General: The Life of Georgy Zhukov* (New York: Random House, 2012), 130.

43. Harrison E. Salisbury, *The 900 Days: The Siege of Leningrad* (New York: Avon, 1970), 557.

44. Winston S. Churchill, *History of the Second World War*, vol. 3, *The Grand Alliance* (Boston: Houghton Mifflin, Brown, 1950), 312–15.

45. Andrew Nagorski, *The Greatest Battle: Stalin, Hitler, and the Desperate Struggle for Moscow* (New York: Simon & Schuster, 2007), 150–51.

46. Andrei A. Gromyko, et al., eds., *Stalin's Correspondence with Churchill and Attlee, 1941–1945* (New York: Capricorn, 1965), 20–21.

47. David Kaiser, *No End Save Victory: How FDR Led the Nation into War* (New York: Basic Books, 2014), 259–62.

48. Glantz, *Barbarossa*, 151.

49. Harold Shukman, ed., *Stalin's Generals* (New York: Grove Press, 1993), 350–51.

50. Nikolai Pavlenko, "Tragediia i triump Krasnoi Armii," *Moskovskie novosti*, May 7, 1989, 8–9; Dmitri Volkogonov, *Stalin: Triumph and Tragedy* (New York: Grove Weidenfeld, 1991), 412–13.

51. Pavel Sudoplatov and Anatoli Sudoplatov, *Special Tasks: The Memoirs of an Unwanted Witness—A Soviet Spymaster* (Boston: Little, Brown, 1994), 175, 177–78.

52. Gerhard Weinberg argues that Moscow sought a separate peace with Berlin as late as the summer of 1943, though at that time insisting on German evacuation of all Soviet territory and perhaps even from half of Poland. *A World at Arms*, 609–11. Evidence for this interpretation is weak at best. See Ingeborg Fleischhauer, *Die Chance des Sonderfriedens: Deutsch-sowjetische Geheimsprache* (Munich: Siedler, 1986). Also see Bernd Wegner, "From Stalingrad to Kursk," in *Germany and the Second World War*, vol. 8, *The Eastern Front, 1943–1944*, ed. Karl-Heinz Frieser (Oxford: Oxford University Press, 2017), 53–61.

53. Steinnert, *Hitler's War and the Germans*, 130–31.

54. Overy, *Russia's War*, 118.

55. Nicholas Stargardt, *The German War: A Nation under Arms, 1939–1945; Citizens and Soldiers* (New York: Basic Books, 2915), 199.

56. Adam Tooze, *The Wages of Destruction: The Making and Breaking of the Nazi Economy* (New York: Penguin, 2006), 493–99.

57. Earl F. Ziemke and Magna E. Bauer, *Moscow to Stalingrad: Decision in the East* (New York: Military Heritage Press, 1988), 77.

58. The diary of Gefreiter [private first class] H. C. von Wiedenbach-Nostitz, in Ellis, *Barbarossa*, 353.

59. Oleg A. Rzheshevsky, ed., *War and Diplomacy* (Amsterdam: Harwood Academic, 1996), 20–21. Stalin also thought the Japanese armed forces might collapse before the end of 1942 (p. 34)!

60. Quoted in Stargardt, *The German War*, 227.

61. Stargardt, *The German War*, 215.

62. R. H. Stolfi, *Hitler's Panzers East: World War II Reinterpreted* (Norman: University of Oklahoma Press, 1991).

63. E.g., Franz Halder, *Hitler as Warlord* (London: Putnam, 1950); Erich von Manstein, *Lost Victories* (Chicago: Regnery, 1958); *The Memoirs of Field-Marshal Keitel*, ed. Walter Görlitz (New York: Stein & Day, 1965); Albrecht Kesselring, *The Memoirs of Field-Marshal Kesselring* (London: Greenhill, 1953).

64. David Stahel, *Operation Barbarossa and Germany's Defeat in the East* (Cambridge: Cambridge University Press, 2009), 2, 20.

CHAPTER 8

From the China Incident to the Pacific War

From Integration and Emulation to Autarky

While Hitler's legions swept from victory to victory in Europe between August 1939 and December 1941, Japanese forces found themselves bogged down in a frustrating, stalemated war in China. Superior mobility and firepower had enabled them to conquer the major cities along the coast and the lower Yangzi (Yangtze) River valley, but by 1939 they faced the unappealing prospect of combat throughout the vast Chinese hinterland. Chiang Kai-shek (Jiang Jieshi) and his Guomindang (Kuomintang) government continued to resist the invaders from their new capital at Chongqing (Chungking) in remote Sichuan (Szechwan) Province. Even in those areas that Japanese troops occupied, they now encountered mounting harassment from GMD and Communist guerrillas. The "China Incident" had turned into a full-scale war on the Asian mainland with no end in sight.

Then, in 1940, developments in Europe seemed to offer Tokyo a new window of opportunity not only to pacify China but also to secure Japan's economic well-being by the creation of a self-sufficient empire in East Asia. Germany occupied France and Holland (whose empires included Indochina and the East Indies), while Great Britain's resources were strained to the utmost defending its home islands against the Nazi menace. The United States had not yet joined the fight against Germany, but its growing support for Britain suggested that America might be too preoccupied with the European conflict to risk war in the Pacific. In these circumstances, the "victory disease" infected many Japanese—that is, the belief that the global balance of power was changing dramatically and that bold, aggressive action would reap great rewards.

As late as 1930, Japan enjoyed a relationship of symbiotic interdependence with the Western powers, both economically and politically. Its economy was dependent on extensive world trade, and the country continued to develop along the path toward parliamentary democracy. Since the Manchurian Incident in 1931, however, those trends had begun to reverse dramatically. A widely shared belief that Japan must control vital markets and natural resources in East Asia began to replace the previous commitment to global free trade. Many Japanese now viewed the authoritarian states with semi-autarkic economies and highly disciplined societies (Nazi Germany, Fascist Italy, and Soviet Russia) as better models for their country than the pluralistic, individualistic Western democracies. Like the Third Reich and Mussolini's Italy, many within the Japanese elites saw their country as a "have-not" nation, discriminated against in the international system by the dominant powers—America, Britain, and France. Berlin, Rome, and Tokyo each called for a "New Order" in which they would get their "place in the sun." Each of them also denounced liberal democracy and capitalist internationalism as cynical masks for the dominance of Washington, London, and Paris. While there was little sympathy for outright fascism among Japan's elites, and none at all for communism, many leaders sought a more harmonious and unified nation, free of the supposedly corrupting influences of big business and party politics.

The influence of the military and the bureaucracy grew, while the power of elected officials and the political parties shrank. Intertwining foreign policy and domestic politics, this process constituted a counterrevolution against individualism, pluralism, capitalist internationalism, and the Washington treaty system. British and American racism as well as the perception that the Anglo-American powers treated Japan unfairly strengthened this shift of opinion. Western criticism of the conquest of Manchuria and Tokyo's subsequent advances in China only served to inflame a great many Japanese with a sense of patriotic defiance.

Although violence and intimidation by the military played a significant role in this process, there was also broad support for it at the imperial court, in the Diet and the press, and among the general population. A growing militarization of Japanese society reinforced this trend. Public schools and apprenticeship programs stressed military training and values, political indoctrination, self-sacrifice, and the supreme duty of absolute obedience to the emperor. The public seemed to have an endless appetite for stories of heroic conquests in Manchuria and northern China and of brave young "martyr" soldiers in Shanghai. The mass media ignored atrocities and at the same time justified killing civilians, including women and children. Most journalists were on the patriotic/imperialistic bandwagon. Those few who were not had reason to fear for their lives and were prudent enough to censor their doubts.

None of this, however, meant that there was unity and harmony throughout the Japanese political system. The armed services underwent a process of radicalization in which less-bellicose officers were pushed out or marginalized. In the navy, for example, a small group of moderate senior admirals was able to keep the militant faction among the naval officer corps at bay for a while. Events in Europe changed that. The fall of France and the weakening of Britain's position tilted the balance in favor of the war hawks. It seemed that Japan now had a unique opportunity to dominate East Asia. Just as in the navy, each of the country's other elites was rent by serious disagreements over strategies and the timing of steps to reach the national goal, but there was now a growing consensus on that goal—an autarkic empire freed of dependence on and subservience to the West. This view found its strongest advocates in parts of the Japanese military. Military spending doubled in the first half of the decade. When Finance Minister Takahashi Korekiyo balked at further increases, ultranationalist radicals hacked him to death. The navy threw off the limitations of the Washington and London treaties and initiated a major fleet expansion program. By the end of the decade, the combined army and navy budgets had risen by 500 percent.

A growing sense of crisis gripped many Japanese leaders, a deep fear that the diplomatic, political, and economic policies of the past would not preserve the nation's security in the future. Ironically, although the Great Depression had been the catalyst in welding these strategic, economic, and political concerns together, Japan emerged from the Depression more rapidly than other countries. However, perception mattered more than reality. A crisis mentality gripped the nation and produced a series of domestic and international measures that propelled Japan toward conflict with the Western powers.

After May 1932, cabinets composed of civilian "experts" and military officers were no longer responsible to the Diet, the political parties, or the electorate. In 1940, Prime Minister Konoe Fumimaro created the Imperial Rule Assistance Association, which replaced the parties altogether and served to mobilize the masses for the national cause. Under pressure from the military, the Diet passed the National General Mobilization Law and the National Regulation of Electricity Law, which gave the government greatly expanded powers over labor, prices, raw materials, capital investment, and even over the limits of political debate. Japanese historian Nakamura Takafusa has compared these measures to the Enabling Act that destroyed the Weimar Republic.[1] Some right-wing civilians and military men hoped to see a Nazi-style revolution in the country, but Japan never became a truly totalitarian state. Political decisions continued to result from infighting and compromise among court, military, bureaucratic, parliamentary, and business elites. Nonetheless, the nation was moving steadily toward full mobilization and war. The widespread perception that this process solved many domestic problems facilitated the slide toward war with both China and the Western powers. Expanding the empire, it was widely believed, would restore national pride, unify the nation, and suppress a host of Depression-era discontents. It would also provide an opportunity for political leaders to expand their powers and for the big industrial combines to enhance their profits.

Before the war widened in China, these trends need not necessarily have led to war with the Western powers, if those states had appeased Tokyo as they had Berlin, but there would be no East Asian Munich. Britain, France, and Holland were determined to maintain their imperial possessions in East Asia. The United States continued to demand an "open door" for its economic activities and influence in the region. Moreover, the Western states seem to have underrated Japanese power (an irony given their consistent overestimation of German might). In this situation, Japan was moving inexorably toward conflict with its former Western allies.

The China Quagmire

When full-scale war broke out in China in 1937, Japanese generals assured the emperor that victory would be theirs within two or three months. By 1939, however, the war had degenerated into a frustrating stalemate that was sapping the nation's resources and sparking confrontation with the Western powers. The Japanese were trapped in a snare of their own making: The longer the war dragged on and the more it cost in blood and treasure, the less possible it became to accept a compromise peace with Nationalist China. Chiang Kai-shek rejected peace terms that would have made China a Japanese vassal. Tokyo thereupon broke relations with the Guomindang government and established a collaborationist regime at Nanjing (Nanking) under the renegade GMD leader Wang Jingwei. In addition to this supposed national government, the Japanese also patronized several regional collaborationist regimes in various parts of occupied China. Leaders in Tokyo had hoped to decrease their war effort in China in order to prepare for conflict with the USSR, which they believed to be inevitable. Instead, the unappealing prospect of a long and bitter war of attrition in China opened before them. However, another strategy suggested itself. The Japanese thought that if the flow of foreign supplies to China ceased, then the Nationalist regime would have to sue for peace. They failed to see that it was not external aid but their own aggression and atrocities that fueled the ferocious growth of Chinese nationalism and resistance.

In 1934 Japan proclaimed the Amau Doctrine, claiming for itself sole responsibility for maintaining the peace in East Asia and opposing all foreign assistance for China, but aid continued to reach the Guomindang from the United States, Britain, France, and the Soviet Union. By 1940, however, the Japanese no longer considered mere diplomatic pressure adequate. Almost half the foreign supplies received by Chiang Kai-shek's regime came through French Indochina, with a large quantity also coming from British-controlled Burma. Smaller amounts were smuggled from the Chinese coast or arrived from the USSR via Xinjiang (Sinkiang). The fall of France presented an opportunity to cut the largest supply route to the Nationalist army. Tokyo demanded that Vichy France halt all deliveries to China and grant military bases for Japan in northern Indochina. The slow and inevitably incomplete victories gained from such diplomacy frustrated the officers of Japan's South China Army. Ignoring orders from Tokyo, the army invaded northern Indochina in September 1940, seizing the capital, Hanoi, and the port of Haiphong, with its rail link to southern China. The Japanese also pressured the beleaguered British government to temporarily suspend shipments to China from Burma and Hong Kong. The Guomindang lost 79 percent of its foreign supplies, but the Chinese kept fighting.

The China Incident intersected at this point with another emerging Japanese goal—expansion into the "South Seas." In 1936, the Japanese government had first expressed its interest in expansion to the south (i.e., Indochina, Burma, Malaya, and the Dutch East Indies) in an internal policy document. Such conquests would secure rice, rubber, nonferrous metals, and, above all, oil. At that stage, however, there was still no consensus on how this was to be accomplished, or even on whether this "southern project" should have priority over the "northern project" (i.e., war against the USSR). Events in East Asia and Europe clarified the issue. The Soviet army taught imperial forces two bitter lessons at Changkufeng and Nomonhan, while the Nazi-Soviet Pact stunned the Japanese. With France and Holland defeated in 1940 and Britain badly weakened, those in the Japanese leadership favoring the southern over a northern advance now gained a decisive advantage. Prime Minister Konoe envisioned a new global order, with the dominance of the Western democracies overthrown and most of the world divided into Japanese, Italo-German, and Soviet spheres of hegemony.

The navy favored this orientation, as did much of the army. The naval planning staff prepared a policy statement in July 1940 that advocated the "establishment of a self-sufficient economic sphere centering upon Japan, Manchuria, and China," which would stretch from the Indian Ocean almost to Australia.[2] An advance to the south would mean war with the now-weakened British Empire and Dutch colonial authorities, though many within the Japanese leadership deluded themselves that the United States could be kept out of the conflict. A few of them, however, including the emperor and Admiral Yamamoto Isorok, realized that war with Holland and England would very likely draw America into the hostilities. Moreover, the navy wanted a confrontation with the United States—to humble its greatest rival in the Pacific and to ensure itself a large share of the military budget.

If the occupation of northern Indochina could be justified entirely by exigencies of the war in China, Japan's next move—into southern Indochina—clearly betrayed much broader ambitions throughout Southeast Asia. The armed forces wanted bases at Cam Ranh Bay and elsewhere as springboards for projected attacks on Burma, Singapore, and the East Indies. In July of 1940, Tokyo bullied the French into submission. Yet, as much as Japan wanted to control East Asia as its own exclusive preserve, its actions there inevitably affected the interests of all the other great powers. The emperor had warned his prime minister that moving into southern Vietnam would provoke a dangerous American reaction, but the new prime minister, Tojo Hideki, ignored that warning.

International Reactions

Nazi Germany inherited a pro-Chinese policy from its Weimar predecessor. Hitler switched to supporting Japan in 1938 to weaken his French, British, and Soviet enemies. At first, Tokyo resisted Berlin's efforts to transform the Anti-Comintern Pact into a real military alliance. By 1940, however, a combination of continuing frustration in China, growing American resistance, and the stunning German victories in Europe had altered Japanese thinking. Prime Minister Konoe and Foreign Minister Matsuoka Yosuke championed the new pro-German orientation. Matsuoka proclaimed, "In the battle between democracy and totalitarianism the latter adversary will without question win and will control the world. The era of democracy is finished and the democratic system bankrupt."[3] Tokyo signed the Tripartite Pact with Berlin and Rome on September 27, 1940. The Axis powers promised to aid each other if any of them were attacked by a power not currently at war—a clear reference to the United States. Both Hitler and the Japanese hoped that the threat of war on two fronts would immobilize the Americans. To embolden the Japanese still further, the Germans shared a critical piece of secret intelligence with them—that the British government had decided that, regardless of what crisis should materialize in East Asia, it could not afford to send additional ships to reinforce its fleet in Asia. The Tripartite Pact was not, however, evidence of a common strategy among the Axis partners. Before Germany's attack on the USSR, Japan had hoped that Berlin would focus its military operations on the destruction of the British Empire. Hitler's priorities were just the opposite: he believed it vital to crush the Soviet Union; Britain's destruction could wait.

Stalin was deeply concerned with developments in East Asia. Although the Soviet dictator still deluded himself that Germany would not attack the USSR before bringing Britain to its knees, it seemed expedient to protect his eastern flank. The Japanese were even more anxious for an agreement with Russia given the growing momentum for a southern advance and, with it, the likelihood of war with England and perhaps America. Significantly, the Germans had given their Japanese ally no hint of their plans to attack the Soviet Union that summer. Therefore, the Japanese signed a Neutrality Pact with Russia on April 13, 1941. Each side pledged to stay out of any war in which the other should become involved. Moscow also agreed "to respect the territorial integrity and inviolability of Manchukuo."[4]

While Germany actively encouraged Japanese expansionism in East Asia, and the USSR grudgingly acquiesced in it, the Western powers opposed any fundamental alteration in the balance of power or in their economic opportunities in the region. During the 1930s, Britain had built up its armed forces at Singapore on the tip of the Malay Peninsula in order to protect its interests in that part of the world. By 1940, however, it was in no position to resist the advances of a belligerent and well-armed Japan. Churchill, for whom the empire was a vital concern, could only press Roosevelt to check the Japanese advance. When FDR first took office, he had "sanctioned a Far East policy of inaction and nonprovocation."[5] That began to change after the outbreak of the Sino-Japanese War in 1937. Neither Roosevelt nor his secretary of state, Cordell Hull, wanted hostilities with Tokyo, but they were unwilling to allow the complete erosion of America's strategic and economic position in East Asia that Japan's projected "New Order" there would entail.

Roosevelt hoped that some combination of diplomacy and economic pressure would deter Japanese aggression, but he was constrained in dealing with the growing crisis in East Asia, just as he was in Europe, by isolationist sentiment and military weakness. His "quarantine" speech in October 1937 condemned belligerence and international lawlessness, but he had to admit at a subsequent press conference that he was launching no specific measures to contain aggression. The following year, FDR appealed to business leaders to honor a "moral embargo" on selling weapons to the aggressors. Congress also approved funding for the fortification of Guam and other Pacific bases. By the end of the decade, public opinion had become markedly hostile to the aggressor powers. *Kristallnacht* in Germany and the rape of Nanjing horrified Americans. They especially disliked the Japanese, as evidenced by the popularity of this Ogden Nash poem, first published in 1938:

> How courteous is the Japanese;
> He always says, "Excuse it please."
> He climbs into his neighbor's garden
> And smiles, and says, "I beg your pardon";
> He bows and grins a friendly grin,
> And calls his hungry family in;
> He grins, and bows a friendly bow;
> "So sorry, this my garden now."[6]

Moving more boldly in 1939, the United States abrogated its 1911 commercial treaty with Japan and granted a loan of $25 million ($542.9 million adjusted for inflation) to the Chinese government. The Tripartite Pact, which was supposed to constrain the United States, had the opposite effect. In the minds of the US administration and the American people, it identified Tokyo more closely with the dictators in Berlin and Rome. In response to the Japanese move into northern Indochina, Roosevelt placed an embargo on the sale to Japan of crucially important scrap iron, steel, and high-octane aviation fuel. The president authorized the establishment of an American military advisory mission in China and consented to the establishment of a corps of volunteer American pilots (the Flying Tigers) to assist the badly overmatched Chinese air force. The US Pacific Fleet moved from its home port in San Diego to Pearl Harbor, Hawaii. After the Japanese occupation of southern Indochina in the summer of 1941, the president froze all Japanese assets in the United States, leading to a de facto embargo on all petroleum exports to Japan. That was an especially serious blow, since the Japanese imported 80 percent of their oil requirements from America. Finally, in August 1941, Roosevelt bluntly warned Ambassador Nomura Kichisaburo that further Japanese aggression would mean war with the United States.

Some of his political enemies at the time and later revisionist historians accused Roosevelt of deliberately provoking war with Japan as a "back door" to war with Germany.[7] That was not the case. FDR sincerely hoped to avoid war in East Asia because it would inevitably draw American resources away from what he viewed as an even graver threat to national security—Nazi expansionism. Nevertheless, the president was not willing to abandon America's strategic, political, and commercial interests in East Asia. Moreover, he and most of his advisors had come to see the Axis as a global conspiracy to destroy freedom and enslave the world. Given this understanding, no accommodation with Japan was possible unless Tokyo reversed its course of conquest and dissolved its alliance with Hitler.

Momentum Builds for War

The unrealistic hope that Japan could attack the British and Dutch empires in Asia without provoking American involvement in the war was rapidly dissipating. Time was a concern among Japanese leaders, just as it was to Hitler. With twelve new American carriers and seven new battleships under construction or on the drawing boards, Japan would soon lose its naval advantage. Officers estimated that the Imperial Japanese Navy currently possessed 70.6 percent of the US Navy's warship tonnage and that in 1942 it would fall to 65 percent, in 1943 to 50 percent, and in 1944 to only 30 percent.[8] The time to strike was now or never. Prime Minister Tojo was convinced that if Japan did not move quickly and decisively to establish regional hegemony, it would fall to the status of a third-rate power. That was a badly mistaken judgment, but it was shared by many of his colleagues. Tojo understood the dangers involved in war with America, but he was fatalistic about them. He commented, "Sometimes a man has to jump, with his eyes closed, from the veranda of the Kiyomizu Temple."[9] Having convinced himself that there were no other acceptable options, he and his country were about to do exactly that—risk their national existence by jumping into a war with America, the outcome of which was uncertain in the extreme.

Emperor Hirohito hesitantly disclosed his fears to the cabinet and military command that the nation was on a path to an unwinnable war with the United States, but they politely ignored his reservations. He told his prime minister, "Continue peaceful diplomatic means as much as possible. Do not pursue war preparations in parallel with diplomacy and put diplomacy first."[10] The Meiji Constitution placed the emperor at the pinnacle of the state, and the cult of devotion to the emperor was widespread, especially among the military. Yet the Showa emperor was anything but sovereign. At meeting after meeting, the civil and military leaders presented the emperor with gloomy scenarios in which war seemed the only option. The military chiefs also assured their monarch that the prospects for victory were bright. His resistance was finally worn down.[11]

Prince Konoe told a friend privately in 1940, "Whenever a new cabinet is formed these days, the emperor warns the new premier on these points: respecting the provisions of the constitution, avoiding any upheavals in the business world, and co-operating with the Anglo-American powers. . . . But politics in Japan today cannot be run in accordance with these imperial wishes."[12] By custom, when the civil and military authorities had reached consensus on a policy, the emperor was not supposed to oppose it. Japanese historian and political activist Ienaga Saburo argues that "the military as a whole had no scruples about disregarding the wishes of their supreme commander, the emperor. . . . The emperor's aide-de-camp made no attempt to convey the emperor's wishes to the military. Instead, he functioned as the military's spokesman at court."[13]

Moreover, Hirohito was carried along, like so many of his countrymen, by the growing tide of chauvinism and anti-Western sentiment in the 1930s. He agreed with the widespread Pan-Asianist belief that Japan had a duty to lead East Asia to independence and progress, but not with the military's perversion of that view into "a brutal ideology of imperialism."[14] Beyond that, he later claimed that in those days he feared for his life if he were to oppose the prowar militants too strongly. In 1946, he claimed that if he had tried to veto the Pearl Harbor attack, "the trusted men around me would have been killed, I myself might have been killed or kidnapped. Actually I was virtually a prisoner and powerless."[15] Certainly, there was no "imperial conspiracy" to attack the United States.[16] Nonetheless, on September 6, 1941, the Imperial Conference (a meeting of top cabinet and military officials in the emperor's presence) endorsed the "Essentials for Carrying Out the Empire's Policies," declaring, "Our Empire, for the purposes of self-defense and self-preservation, will complete preparations for war . . . resolved to go to war with the United States, Great Britain, and the Netherlands if necessary. . . . In the event that there is no prospect of our demands being met . . . through diplomatic negotiations . . . we will immediately decide to commence hostilities."[17] Japan now implemented both tracks of this policy, attempting to reach a diplomatic settlement of the East Asia crisis while at the same time preparing rapidly and secretly for war.

Neither the United States nor Japan wanted war. Both sides negotiated intensely throughout the fall of 1941, but those talks were doomed to failure because each party insisted on a diplomatic resolution of the crisis on its own terms. For the Japanese, that meant that the United States must give them a free hand in China and Indochina, stop all support for Chiang Kai-shek, not augment its forces in the region, end all embargos, restore full commercial relations, and accept Japan's political and economic dominance in East and Southeast Asia. In contrast, the Americans insisted that Japan pull its troops out of China and Indochina, renounce its alliance with Germany and Italy, respect the sovereignty of all its neighbors, and honor the Open Door principle for US commerce and influence in East Asia. Secretary of State Hull hoped that acceptance of these conditions would "regenerate" the Japanese government, leading to a decline in the position of the military and of pro-German civilian leaders.[18] The two positions were utterly incompatible. Through their Magic system of decoding intercepted Japanese diplomatic messages, Roosevelt and Hull knew that the Japanese would not agree to terms acceptable to the United States, but they continued to negotiate anyway so that when the rupture came Japan would bear the onus.

While the diplomats negotiated futilely, Japan's armed forces prepared to attack. They understood that their nation's chances of success were poor in a long war of attrition with a country as large and powerful as the United States. Their plan, therefore, was to strike quickly, destroying the US Pacific Fleet; rapidly overrun the Philippines, Malaya, Burma, and the East Indies (thereby establishing a self-sufficient empire); and finally fortify a chain of strategic islands from the Kuriles in the north to New Guinea in the south in order to create a defensive barrier for that empire. Japanese planners hoped that they then could repulse any Anglo-American counterattack or, better still, that the Western powers might acquiesce in these conquests given their preoccupation with the threat of Nazi Germany. Racism and wishful thinking played strong roles in this fantasy. They imagined that the pleasure-loving, profit-obsessed Anglo-Saxons would recoil from the sacrifices necessary to recapture what Japan had conquered. The Japanese also anticipated that a German victory in Europe would knock Britain out of the war and intimidate the United States into a negotiated settlement favorable to Tokyo. These were the slender reeds of hope on which the Japanese leaders gambled their national existence.

Even the most hawkish among the Japanese militarists intended to wage only a limited war—limited in duration and limited in the resources needed to fight it. Instead, they blundered into a total war that their island kingdom did not have the resources to win. Stark realism sometimes intruded on such illusions, however. Admiral Yamamoto had warned Tojo's predecessor, Prime Minister Konoe, that Japanese forces initially would be very effective against the inadequately prepared Western powers, but if those states then mobilized their vast resources with determination, then the future might be bleak for Japan. "If I am told to fight regardless of the consequences," the admiral warned, "I shall run wild for the first six months or a year, but I have utterly no confidence for the second or third year."[19] Yamamoto understood that the Americans would fight rather than acquiesce. Only the complete destruction of US military power could ensure Japan's success. "To make victory certain," he wrote, "we would have to march into Washington and dictate the terms of peace in the White House."[20] The admiral had little faith in Japan's ability to defeat the United States in a long war of attrition, but the nationalist press quoted these remarks (intended as a sarcastic warning) out of context to whip up enthusiasm for an expanded war.

The Imperial Navy hoped to confront the Americans in one "Great All-Out Battle." At the outbreak of war, the Japanese assumed that the United States would send its entire Pacific Fleet to East Asia. There the massed Japanese fleet would meet and destroy it. This plan assumed the predominance of battleships, with carriers serving them in a supporting capacity. Admiral Yamamoto, however, rejected the defensive, reactive mentality implicit in this strategy. He and Lieutenant Commander Genda Minoru, an expert on naval aviation, devised a daring alternative—a surprise attack that would destroy the US Pacific Fleet at Pearl Harbor before the Americans realized that the war had begun. At first, the Naval General Staff opposed Yamamoto's audacious plan. They regarded the proposed operation as far too difficult and much too dangerous. If it went wrong, Japan could lose most of its naval aviation. Such an operation would also compete for resources with the all-important "southern operation" (i.e., the conquest of a self-sufficient empire in Southeast Asia). Moreover, the staff planners could not ignore the possibility that Japan's next move might be a strike against the USSR if the German assault on Russia should be successful. There was a moment in July 1941 when enthusiasm for an attack on the USSR surged among many Japanese leaders, but stiffening Soviet resistance in August quickly dampened their zeal. Ultimately, Yamamoto's threat to resign if he did not get his way carried the day for the Pearl Harbor attack. The "northern operation" would come only after the southern operation had succeeded in conquering a self-sufficient empire for Japan.

A Naval Revolution

Japan intended to attack Pearl Harbor simultaneously with its assaults on Malaya, the Philippines, and the East Indies. History would repeat itself. The Japanese navy had eliminated the Imperial Russian Pacific Fleet at Port Arthur in 1904 in just such an unexpected raid. This time, however, the decisive weapon would not be battleships, as it had been then, but aircraft carriers—a new weapons system that would revolutionize naval warfare to an even greater degree than the tank had transformed land combat.

For almost sixty years, the giant battleship had been master of the seas, but in the Second World War all but one of the great naval engagements of the Pacific theater would be decided by the power of carrier-based aviation. All the major naval powers began to build aircraft carriers after World War I, yet the strategic potential of carrier aircraft remained largely unrecognized. Most admirals thought of airplanes mainly as aids to reconnaissance. Experiments conducted by General Billy Mitchell and the US Army Air Corps in 1925 began to alter that view. Mitchell's bombers sank a variety of unmanned submarines and surface ships. In 1929, planes from the USS *Saratoga*, involved in war games, theoretically destroyed the Panama Canal. As a result, the US Navy and the fleets of other powers as well began operating independent carrier groups. Newly evolving strategic conceptions called for the employment of large, fast carrier forces as the mainstay of naval warfare, with battleships, cruisers, and destroyers acting in a merely supportive capacity.

The first real demonstration of the carrier's potential had been the British destruction of the Italian fleet at Taranto Bay in 1940. Yamamoto and Genda studied that operation carefully, particularly the way the Royal Navy had solved the problem of using torpedoes in shallow harbor waters. The Japanese planners projected a daring, long-range strike that would destroy the US Pacific Fleet's three aircraft carriers and seven battleships at Pearl Harbor, combined with additional operations to hit American outposts at Guam and Wake Island and to attack Malaya, Burma, Hong Kong, and the Philippines. The destruction of US, British, and Dutch military power in Asia would allow Japan to acquire the resource-rich East Indies and eliminate the interference of the Western powers in the region.

Pearl Harbor

Destroying the US Pacific Fleet would require a much larger operation than the British had mounted at Taranto Bay. Yamamoto committed six of Japan's ten available carriers to the task, along with an imposing array of other warships, under the command of Vice Admiral Nagumo Chuichi. Secrecy was essential. The assault force would have to traverse half the Pacific Ocean (almost 3,800 miles) undetected to achieve success. It would follow an obscure route, far from popular shipping lanes or the flight paths of the few commercial airlines then in operation. The Japanese navy practiced its attack exhaustively, using a mock-up of Pearl Harbor. After the fleet sailed on November 26, it observed radio silence and ran blacked out at night. Back in Japan, signals officers sent out false messages, seemingly from ships of the Pearl Harbor task force, to convince any listening Americans that the fleet was still in home waters.

American military and civilian leaders knew that Tokyo intended to go to war if it could not achieve its objectives by diplomatic means, but they thought a Japanese attack most likely against Singapore or the Philippines. They did not anticipate a spectacularly daring blow at Pearl Harbor. As historian Gordon Prange has suggested, there was a "general underestimation of Japan by the United States in the years before World War II. Americans assured one another that Japan was virtually bankrupt, short of raw materials, and hopelessly bogged down in China. . . . Americans held the average Japanese in utter contempt."[21]

Thus, the Japanese carrier force reached its launch point 220 miles from Oahu undetected in the early morning hours of December 7, 1941. The island had a new radar station, but it was still in training mode. When its technicians spotted a large blip on their screen

American destroyer USS Shaw *exploding during Japanese attack on Pearl Harbor, Hawaii, December 7, 1941.*
Source: Library of Congress

(the incoming Japanese strike force), supervisors dismissed their warning as operator error or possibly a flight of US B-17 bombers from California. The Magic decryption system was of no help either because Tokyo did not share its military plans with its diplomats. The military authorities in Hawaii, Admiral Husband Kimmel and General Walter Short, received only a very general warning that war with Japan might soon break out, but no specific alarm that Pearl Harbor was in imminent danger. Moreover, the American commanders' actions played into the hands of their attackers: Kimmel gave strong priority to training for offensive action at the expense of defensive measures, while Short ordered most of his planes parked together, in the open, without bombs or ammunition, to guard against sabotage. No one thought to patrol the presumably less threatening northern approaches to Hawaii. The Americans underestimated the Japanese and underrated the peril. General George Marshall, the army chief of staff and not normally a careless man, had characterized Pearl Harbor to the president as "the strongest fortress in the world."[22] An attack on Hawaii was unlikely, the general thought, because any enemy force would come under sustained attack as far as 750 miles out from its target.

At 7:48 a.m., the first wave of Japanese bombers appeared over battleship row in Pearl Harbor. The leader of the attacking squadrons, Commander Fuchida Mitsuo, flashed a

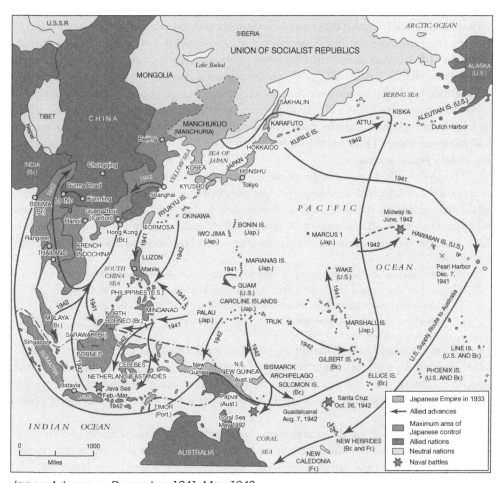

Japan Advances, December 1941–May 1942

coded message—"Tora! Tora! Tora!" (tiger, tiger, tiger)—back to his fleet, indicating that they had achieved complete surprise. December 7 fell on a Sunday in 1941, meaning that many of the fleet's officers were ashore and most of the ships' crews were relaxing. In all, 360 planes—two waves of bombers, dive-bombers, torpedo bombers, and covering fighters—attacked Pearl Harbor as well as Hickam, Wheeler, and other airfields. Through detailed espionage conducted by the Japanese consulate in Honolulu, the Japanese pilots knew the exact locations of the American ships. The *Arizona* and *Oklahoma* were destroyed, while six other battleships were badly damaged, along with eleven cruisers, destroyers, and other ships. Almost two hundred American planes were destroyed easily on their airfields. More than 2,400 Americans died in the attack, and another 1,100 were wounded. In contrast, the Imperial Navy lost only sixty-five men, twenty-nine aircraft, a submarine, and five mini-submarines. However, the Japanese had missed their most important targets—the American carriers—because they were not there. The *Lexington* and *Enterprise* were at sea, along with eight cruisers, while the *Saratoga* had returned to the West Coast for repairs.

Nevertheless, Admiral Nagumo was elated with his stunning victory. Numerous critics have faulted Nagumo for not launching another attack targeting Oahu's dockyards, fuel storage depots, and submarine pens. Fuchida claimed many years later that he had begged the admiral to refuel and rearm his planes for a third strike on these targets. Commander Genda, while unsure about another strike that day, urged Nagumo to remain in Hawaiian waters for several days to hit those secondary targets and to hunt for the American flattops. Nagumo declined both options, however, because he feared that the missing US carriers or the flight of B-17s that some of the Japanese pilots had seen approaching Honolulu might be poised to deliver a devastating counterattack on his fleet at any moment. Moreover, a third attack would have been launched in heavy seas and darkness. Nagumo preferred to keep his carriers safe for the vitally important operations the Imperial forces were about to launch throughout Southeast Asia. The immediate objective of the Pearl Harbor attack had been successful. There would be no interference from the US Pacific Fleet with the impending Japanese attacks.

The Japanese had won a brilliant tactical victory at Pearl Harbor, but it was not the strategic knockout blow they anticipated. Not only had the three carriers survived, but many of the damaged ships that had sunk in the shallow harbor would soon be resurrected and repaired, a task made all the easier by Nagumo's failure to destroy the repair facilities. Samuel Eliot Morison and many other historians have criticized Nagumo severely for this omission:

> One can search military history in vain for an operation more fatal to the aggres-
> sor. On the tactical level, the Pearl Harbor attack was wrongly concentrated on
> ships rather than permanent installations and oil tanks. On the strategic level it
> was idiotic. On the high political level it was disastrous.[23]

In contrast, historian H. P. Willmott argues that "a third strike at this time was never fea-sible." Beyond the perils of a night recovery of aircraft and the danger of counterattack from American carriers, there was not sufficient time after the return of the second-strike wave to refuel, rearm, and (where necessary) repair the planes as well as to debrief and prepare pilots for a third strike.[24]

Far from intimidating the government and people of the United States into inaction, the Pearl Harbor attack unified them in virtually homicidal hatred of Japan. As Admiral Hara Chuichi, one of the carrier division commanders in the attack, later lamented, "We won a great tactical victory at Pearl Harbor and thereby lost the war."[25] That was not the perspective of most Japanese, who, from the naval command staff down to the man on the street, greeted the news of this great victory with jubilation. Meanwhile in America, President Roosevelt proclaimed to Congress and a national radio audience, "Yesterday, December 7, 1941—a date which will live in infamy—the United States of America was suddenly and deliberately attacked by the naval and air forces of the Empire of Japan. . . . No matter how long it may take us to overcome this premeditated invasion, the American people in their righteous might will win through to absolute victory."

The president intended to calm and reassure the public, which was not only angered but also badly shaken by the Pearl Harbor disaster. Hysteria gripped many people, especially on the West Coast. Tom Bradley (a young policeman at that time and later mayor of Los Angeles) recalled:

> Immediately after Pearl Harbor, there was bedlam. Sirens going off, aircraft guns firing. It was panic. Here we are in the middle of the night, there was no enemy in sight, but somebody thought they saw the enemy. . . . They were shooting at random. . . . It was panic that simply overwhelmed us.[26]

In San Francisco, rumors spread that the Japanese had bombed the Golden Gate Bridge. Some intrepid but overly excitable souls grabbed shotguns and hunting rifles and headed for the nearest beach to repel imagined enemy invaders.

Malaya and the Dutch East Indies

While Commander Fuchida's pilots decimated the greatest bastion of American power in the Pacific, other Japanese forces launched a simultaneous campaign against the strongest British military and naval base in the region, Singapore. Tokyo pressured the Thai government to permit troop transit from Indochina across Thailand. On December 8 (December 7 east of the International Date Line), the first Japanese units entered northern Malaya virtually unopposed. At the same time, elements of General Yamashita Tomoyuki's forces landed at five points along the Malay coast, with more landings to follow. Yamashita's troops were supported by 400 guns and mortars, 120 armored vehicles, and over 600 combat aircraft. Ground and air attacks quickly neutralized British airfields in the northern and central portions of the peninsula. Two powerful British warships, the battleship *Prince of Wales* and battle cruiser *Repulse*, raced north from Singapore to disrupt the invasion, but without any air cover. The carrier that should have accompanied them, HMS *Indomitable*, had run aground in Jamaica and was still under repair. Imperial Navy bombers found and quickly sank both ships on the morning of December 10. The faster and more maneuverable Japanese Zero fighter quickly established air supremacy. Even the few British Hurricane fighters available in Malaya were outclassed by the Zeros.

Churchill later wrote, "In all the war I never received a more direct shock. . . . There were no British or American capital ships in the Indian Ocean or the Pacific except the American survivors of Pearl Harbor, who were hastening back to California. Over all this vast expanse of waters Japan was supreme, and we were weak and naked."[27] He was shocked because he believed, like so many in the West, that Japan would never be so foolish as to attack the Singapore bastion unless Britain had already been defeated in Europe.

The British defenders of Malaya outnumbered the Japanese invaders three to one. However, just as in the Battle of France, poor morale, inadequate use of the newest military technologies, and slow-witted generalship led to disaster. Most of the British forces were recently recruited Indian troops who had inadequate training and equipment and who lacked motivation to die for their imperial overlords. To make matters worse, many of their English officers could not speak the Urdu language of their soldiers. In contrast, the Japanese fought with aggressiveness, ingenuity, and tenacity. Japanese troops seized trucks and bicycles from the local population to speed up their attack. They captured supplies and fuel from the retreating British. They also used light tanks effectively, while the defenders had no armor and insufficient antitank guns.

Each time the British fell back to establish a new defensive line, the Imperial Navy out-flanked it by landing troops behind them. Their quickness solved a major logistical problem. Tokyo's soldiers normally went into battle with only a few days' worth of rice and some miso powder or soya sauce in their packs, with little expectation of resupply. Stunned by furious Japanese attacks, the retreating British abandoned great quantities of supplies. The Japanese who dined on them called them "Churchill rations." The widespread view in the West that the Japanese were born jungle fighters was a myth, but Japanese soldiers adapted much more readily to the difficulties of jungle warfare than their opponents, even though they had no prewar training in jungle fighting. In just seven weeks, Yamashita's 25th Army pushed the British down the entire length of the peninsula, some five hundred miles. General Arthur Percival and his troops were now pinned on Singapore Island, but the situation was not entirely desperate. British forces still greatly outnumbered the attackers and, contrary to persistent myth, not all the fortress's heavy guns were fixed in seaward firing positions (i.e., pointed in the wrong direction). Some of them could be rotated or moved, but many were supplied with the wrong sort of ammunition for land combat.

With fewer troops than the British, the Japanese substituted boldness for strength. They struck where the besieged British least expected it, using inflatable craft to cross the narrow Strait of Jahor on February 8, 1942. Within a week, the attackers had captured Singapore's water reservoirs, putting added pressure on a city teeming with refugees. Although the Japanese were running low on both ammunition and food, they launched reckless and costly assaults aimed at frightening the British to surrender. Japanese planes bombed and strafed the city daily. The strategy succeeded. Yamashita later admitted:

> My attack on Singapore was a bluff—a bluff that worked. I had 30,000 men and was outnumbered more than three to one. I knew that if I had to fight for long for Singapore, I would be beaten. That is why the surrender had to be at once. I was very frightened all the time that the British would discover our numerical weakness and lack of supplies and force me into disastrous street fighting.[28]

British morale collapsed. Although Churchill had ordered his troops to fight to the end, on February 15, Percival surrendered Singapore, with its 130,000-man garrison. It was the greatest military disaster in modern British history. The Japanese lost fewer than ten thousand men in the whole campaign. Many Malays initially welcomed Japan's victory as a death blow against their British colonial masters.

Terrible atrocities went unchecked by the Japanese command. At the Alexandria Barracks Hospital, over three hundred staff members and wounded patients were bayoneted. Yamashita's troops committed murder, rape, and pillage throughout the conquered city. Lieutenant Colonel Tsuji Masanobu, Yamashita's chief of operations, ordered his men especially to target Chinese civilians. The atrocities were intended to intimidate the local population into submission and to eliminate as many of the presumably hostile Malayan Chinese as possible. Japanese forces also overran the much smaller British garrison at Hong Kong where, ordered to "take no prisoners," they murdered many of the surrendering soldiers, medical personnel, and hapless civilians who fell under their control. Japan, now freed from any concern over a powerful British or American counterattack, was ready to conquer an empire that would make it self-sufficient and eliminate all Western competition from East Asia.

The Dutch East Indies, a resource-rich, two-thousand-mile-long archipelago, was the prize. The harvest began with a December 16 landing on the British-held portion of Borneo, followed three weeks later by an assault on the larger Dutch section of the island by General Imamura Hitoshi's 16th Army. The defenders received no help from the local population, which had long chafed under European colonial rule. Many younger, educated Indonesians welcomed the Japanese as liberators. Lacking both sufficient troops and adequate air support, Western forces were defeated at one engagement after another. The British surrendered in January, the Dutch in March.

The Allies mounted a more formidable resistance at sea, where they created the ABDA (American-British-Dutch-Australian) naval force under the command of Dutch admiral Karel Doorman. This unit inflicted considerable damage on Japanese supply ships in January and February 1942, but it did not survive its first major encounter with the Imperial Navy. On February 27, Doorman's fleet, comprised of two heavy cruisers, three light cruisers, and nine destroyers, attempted to intercept a Japanese invasion force approaching Java. Doorman's ships were short of fuel and torpedoes. Some of them were seriously damaged from earlier engagements. The ABDA force met a Japanese battle group of about equal strength but equipped with the much superior "long-lance" torpedo (having much greater range and more explosive punch than any Allied torpedoes). In the ensuing Battle of the Java Sea, Admiral Doorman and almost all his fleet went to the bottom. The rest of the major islands of the East Indies were soon overrun by the Japanese—the Celebes in January 1942, Sumatra and Timor in February, and finally the Dutch colonial capital, Batavia (modern-day Jakarta) on Java, fell in March. Another ninety-three thousand Allied troops surrendered. The Southeast Asian treasure trove of oil, rice, timber, metal ores, and rubber had now fallen into Japanese hands.

The Japanese also struck at Burma (modern-day Myanmar), both to destroy one more outpost of British power in Southeast Asia and to sever an important supply link to Nationalist China. The British had only one Burmese division and one Indian division (plus the equivalent of three Chinese Nationalist divisions on the northern border) to defend the country. Moreover, the enemy possessed an advantage in combat aircraft of five to one over the RAF. Planes promised for the defense of Burma were allocated to higher-priority theaters of combat—the Middle East and Britain itself. Like the peoples of the East Indies, the Burmese hated their colonial subjugation to London. A resistance group, under Aung San, was already well developed. During the ensuing campaign, most of the Burmese troops deserted the British force. By March 8, the enemy had taken the capital, Rangoon (Yangon), virtually without opposition. General Harold Alexander, the British commander, retreated into the Irrawaddy valley to establish a new line of resistance. The reinforcements he desperately needed, an Australian division that had been withdrawn from the Middle East to bolster the defense of Burma, was hastily ordered home by their government. News that Japanese troops had landed on New Guinea, that Japanese planes had bombed Darwin, and that a Japanese submarine had been sighted inside Sydney harbor panicked the Australian government.

Meanwhile, Japanese troops drove the shattered remnant of British forces across the Indian border. Only the beginning of monsoon season stopped their pursuit. The Japanese had cut the Burma Road, a vital supply lifeline for Chinese Nationalist forces.

Within hours of their stunning success in Hawaii, Japanese planes also attacked American forces in the Philippines. They intended to strike the two targets simultaneously, but the eighteen-hour time difference between Manila and Honolulu made that impossible. Moreover, heavy fog at their bases on Formosa delayed the Japanese even longer. General Douglas MacArthur, leader of American forces in the Philippines, seems to have been stunned and disoriented by the news from Hawaii. He had convinced himself that the enemy would not strike before the spring of 1942. Although US commanders in Manila had learned about the Pearl Harbor attack at 2:30 a.m. (December 8, Manila time), a Japanese air raid just after noon on that same day caught them by surprise and destroyed almost half of the warplanes available for the defense of the Philippines. During the ensuing days, most of the surviving American aircraft were shot down by the more numerous and more technologically advanced Zero fighters. In addition, most of the ships of the US Asiatic Fleet, normally based in Manila, had joined the doomed ABDA squadron defending the East Indies. Yet MacArthur had substantial ground forces available—over 150,000 troops, outnumbering the invaders three to two. US and Filipino forces lacked adequate artillery and armor, however.

In the preceding months, the US Army leadership in Washington had begun sending B-17 bombers to the Philippine Islands. They were supposed to deter Tokyo's aggression, but they made the Philippines an even more essential target for the Japanese. The American generals' confidence in the "Flying Fortress" proved entirely misplaced. These early models of the B-17 lacked nose and tail guns as well as self-sealing fuel tanks, making them extremely vulnerable to enemy fighters. They also were unable to hit moving targets (such as warships and troop transports). MacArthur had hoped that US submarines could forestall any major amphibious assaults near Manila, but defective torpedoes that often failed to explode undercut that strategy. Although more than twenty American submarines fought in this action, they were able to sink only two small Japanese transports.

After smaller landings in the northern and southern ends of Luzon Island, the main Japanese force of two divisions under General Homma Masaharu came ashore at Lingayen Gulf, northeast of Manila, on December 22. They employed bombers, tanks, and artillery to overwhelm two inadequately trained and lightly equipped divisions of the Philippine army. General Jonathan Wainwright rushed to the scene with the 26th Cavalry Regiment (an American-led Philippine Scouts unit), but his force could only slow the enemy advance and cover the retreat of the shattered Philippine divisions. A second Japanese force landed southwest of Manila in order to hit the Americans from two sides. MacArthur had to face the unpleasant reality that he could not hold the northern and southern ends of the island, nor could he defend Manila itself. He ordered a fighting retreat to the Bataan Peninsula and the fortress of Corregidor in Manila Bay. He hoped that American and Filipino troops could hold out in these redoubts until reinforcements arrived from the United States. But there were few reinforcements to send and, given Japan's mastery of the western Pacific, no safe way to reach the Philippines. In the meantime, MacArthur declared the capital an open city and left it to the mercy of the Japanese. Thinking that the battle had been won and that only mopping-up operations remained, the high command in Tokyo redeployed the crack 48th Division and its air cover to the campaign in the East Indies.

MacArthur's prewar planning for the defense of the Philippines envisioned meeting the enemy on the beaches and driving him back into the sea. Great quantities of equipment and supplies had been stored near the beaches. Now, retreating American forces could retrieve only a limited amount of those vital war materials for the defense of Bataan. That was to prove tragic. Most American and many Filipino troops managed to reach Bataan before the two converging Japanese forces closed the route, but they arrived without much ammunition, food, or medical supplies. Nevertheless, they established a stout defensive line across the peninsula and, in late January, repulsed a major Japanese attack, with very heavy losses to the enemy. They also repelled Japanese attempts to flank their line by amphibious landings behind it. The fighting lulled in February and March because Tokyo gave priority to other campaigns in allocating reinforcements. However, starving, riddled by disease, and almost out of ammunition, the American and Filipino soldiers on Bataan could not keep fighting. MacArthur begged Washington for reinforcements, but the Pearl Harbor warship losses, lack of transport ships, and America's "Europe First" strategic priority made that impossible. What few men and little equipment the United States could spare were sent to Australia, not to MacArthur. Under the circumstances, the loss of the Philippines was inevitable.

MacArthur abandoned the island for the safety of Australia in mid-March, leaving his troops to face an inevitable fate. He proclaimed, "I shall return!" for the newsreel cameras. His genius for public relations and self-promotion made him a hero back in America, but to many of his soldiers he was "Dugout Doug" (meaning that when the fighting got tough, he was sure to be somewhere safe). Still capable of humor, the doomed troops described their plight in the following ditty:

> We're the battling bastards of Bataan:
> No mama, no papa, no Uncle Sam,
> No aunts, no uncles, no nephews, no nieces,
> Nor rifles, no planes, or artillery pieces,
> And nobody gives a damn.

Though unable to defeat the Japanese, MacArthur won the public-relations battle. While Admiral Kimmel and General Short were disgraced for their failure to defend Pearl Harbor, MacArthur emerged as the darling of the press and the hope of the nation.

The Japanese renewed their offensive at the beginning of April. By now the defenders were physically too weak and too poorly supplied to hold back the enemy. Wainwright (MacArthur's replacement) and his Allied forces on Bataan surrendered on April 9. The Japanese then battered the island fortress of Corregidor with bombs and shells until its defenders capitulated on May 6. General Wainwright surrendered on behalf of all the Allied troops in the Philippines, under threat from the Japanese commander that he would butcher everyone on Corregidor if the surrender did not cover all Allied forces. By the end of the first week in June, Allied troops throughout the Philippine Islands had laid down their arms, except for a few who retreated into the jungles to conduct guerrilla warfare. Atrocity followed defeat when the already much weakened defenders of the peninsula were subjected to the Bataan Death March. Their captors marched them to prison camps sixty miles away in blazing tropical heat with no food and very little water. Prisoners who faltered were killed—bayoneted, shot, clubbed with rifle butts, beheaded, run over by trucks. Of the seventy-two thousand American and Filipino POWs who began the trek, only about fifty-four thousand survived. After the war, General Homma was tried and executed for war crimes, including the death march.

Finally, during January and February 1942, relatively small detachments of Japanese troops seized various outposts in the central Pacific. Guam, the largest island of the Marianas group, was weakly defended and easily overrun. On Wake Island, a garrison of only 447 US Marines, with six five-inch guns and twelve obsolete Grumman Wildcat fighters, repulsed an initial Japanese assault, sinking two destroyers and a transport in the battle. The Japanese suffered 407 casualties at a cost of one marine dead. However, a second, much more powerful attack finally overwhelmed the exhausted and depleted defenders. The Japanese forced the survivors to rebuild the island's airfield and then executed them. Japanese troops also took the Bismarck island group. A 5,000-man Japanese force overran the 1,400 Australian defenders of Rabaul on the northern tip of New Britain Island. Subsequently the Japanese built a major army, navy, and air base there.

Japanese forces also landed at Salamaua and Lae on the northeast coast of New Guinea, menacingly close to Australia. Then, in March 1942, Japanese troops occupied the Indian Ocean islands of Nicobar and Andaman. The following month, planes from Admiral Nagumo's 1st Carrier Fleet bombed Colombo and Trincomalee, Ceylon (modern-day Sri Lanka). Learning from his mistake at Pearl Harbor, Nagumo told his pilots to hit oil storage tanks and repair facilities as well as enemy ships. Even the Spitfires and Hurricanes of the RAF found themselves overmatched by the more numerous Zeros, many of them piloted by veterans with more combat flying experience than their British opponents. Blenheim bombers sent to counterattack the Japanese carriers proved entirely ineffective. The Japanese also sank a Royal Navy aircraft carrier, two cruisers, a destroyer, and various support vessels, virtually eliminating the Royal Navy in the Indian Ocean. The surviving ships of Britain's Eastern Fleet quickly made for the safety of the East African coast. Japanese warships and planes were now free to ravage commercial shipping throughout the Bay of Bengal.

These stunning victories—from Pearl Harbor to Singapore to Batavia to Bataan—were made possible by superior Japanese weaponry (the Zero fighter and the "long-lance" torpedo, for example), the extraordinarily thorough training mandated by the Japanese military system, the aggressiveness and flexibility of Japan's commanders, and the resourcefulness and tenacity of its fighting men. Tokyo's warriors won battle after battle by dominating the air and the sea and by mastering the complexities of combined-arms operations, amphibious assaults, and jungle warfare. The defeated Allied powers, in contrast, were overcommitted and underprepared. The British, French, and Dutch could not defend their extensive empires with the resources available to them in 1941. A decade of neglect, inspired by wishful thinking and Depression-era parsimony, had left the military resources of the Western powers in Asia inadequate to meet the Japanese threat. Also, the European imperial powers' domination, and sometimes mistreatment, of their colonial subjects created a spreading disaffection among local populations that played into the hands of the Japanese. Now Tokyo was free to establish its New Order in East Asia.

If overcommitment had been the fatal weakness of the European colonial powers, Japan's series of victories pushed it into the same dangerous position. The army was already overextended in China. Now each of these new conquests required still more troops. Conquest was becoming a self-sustaining chain reaction. As Edward Drea explains it,

> the navy needed Rabaul to protect Truk's southern flank, but then needed Port Moresby to protect Rabaul's flank, and then needed northern Australia to protect Moresby. It needed the Solomons as advance bases for operations against Port Moresby and Australia. And Fiji and Samoa became essential in order to sever the line of communication between Australia and the United States.[29]

Initially, the emperor and even the armed services had hoped to capitalize on Japan's stunning military successes to bring a rapid, diplomatic end to the war, a result that would secure Tokyo's extensive conquests and avoid an unwelcome war of attrition. They sought to mediate the Russo-German war and negotiate favorable peace terms with their battered Western enemies from a position of strength. Three factors foiled these hopes. First, Berlin rebuffed any move to negotiate peace on the eastern front and, in July 1942, even asked the Japanese to enter that conflict (a request Tokyo quickly declined). Second, the Japanese failed to understand the terrible animus that the Pearl Harbor attack had aroused in the American people. Finally, those amazing early successes in battle led the Japanese military leadership and the public to overestimate their martial prowess and underestimate American strength. The "victory disease" was now epidemic.

Some naval officers had begun to think of an expanded defensive perimeter that would run from Australia to Hawaii to India. Having mastered the Indian Ocean, Japanese forces would then link up with the Wehrmacht as it roared through the Middle East. Moreover, the southern operation was to take no more than 150 days so that forces could be redeployed to attack the USSR in the spring of 1942. The Japanese also abandoned any thought of a negotiated peace with China. Overconfidence and best-case scenarios replaced sober analysis. America's will to resist would have to collapse and the Germans would have to find ways to defeat both Britain and the Soviet Union in order to prevent this house of cards from collapsing. For the moment, however, the thrill of victory masked the emergence of these deeper strategic problems. The emperor continued to have doubts about Japan's prospects in a prolonged war, but he did not move effectively to limit hostilities. He remarked to his military aid that "it was easy to start a war but hard to end it."[30]

Hitler Creates the Grand Alliance

The attack on Pearl Harbor not only precipitated the Pacific war; it also transformed wars in Europe and the Far East into an interlinked global conflict. The architect of that transformation was Adolf Hitler. On December 11, in a dramatic speech to the Reichstag, the Führer declared war on the United States. He exulted privately, "We can't lose the war at all. We now have an ally which has never been conquered in 3,000 years."[31] Italy also declared war on the United States. Mussolini again made a rash, unprovoked decision, binding his country ever more tightly to the fate of Germany. Like Hitler, the Duce had come to think of the British and the Americans as degenerate people who could not threaten Italy (amazing given the recent British victories over Italian arms!). His foreign minister, Count Ciano, warned him of America's military and economic potential, but Mussolini did not listen.

America had not posed an immediate threat to Hitler's ambitions before 1939 because President Roosevelt was unable to intervene decisively in European affairs. Hitler had realized by the late 1920s, however, that the United States had the potential to establish global hegemony and that therefore war with America was inevitable. Clouding the picture, Nazi views of the United States alternated between realization of America's enormous industrial (and, therefore, potential military) power and disdain for the nation's ethnic melting pot. Beyond that, the Führer had come to see America as the new center of the "Jewish world conspiracy." Roosevelt and his government were on a collision course with the Reich, Hitler believed, because the president was controlled by his Jewish advisors.

By late 1941, the ability of beleaguered Britain to hold out against Germany and the failure of the *Blitzkrieg* to win quick victory in Russia completely altered Germany's strategic perspective. The Red Army's counteroffensive in front of Moscow drove home the painful realization that the war in the East would be a long, hard struggle. Growing American material and financial support for Britain meant that the island kingdom might resist the German siege indefinitely. The U-boat campaign was meant to starve England into submission, but President Roosevelt's slow escalation of undeclared naval war reduced the effectiveness of that strategy. Hitler resisted pressure from his admirals to engage the US Navy in combat. He did not want to force the USA into the war until the USSR was defeated and Britain was compelled to sue for peace. He therefore prohibited German submarines from hunting in the western Atlantic or attacking American warships. The Führer had always known that time was not on his side. He had to defeat his enemies one at a time before they combined against him in a mighty coalition. Intimidating America into inaction had been the intent of the Tripartite Pact linking Germany and Italy with Japan. Roosevelt had not been intimidated. By 1941, Germany was pressing Japan to attack British and American possessions in the Pacific. Hitler thought, mistakenly, that war in the Pacific would preclude significant American involvement in the European conflict. He was ecstatic over the news of the Pearl Harbor attack.

The terms of the Axis alliance did not require Germany to declare war on the United States because Japan was the aggressor not the victim. However, over the preceding days, Berlin and Tokyo had negotiated a supplementary agreement in which Germany promised to enter the prospective war between Japan and the United States. Both partners pledged themselves not to sign a separate peace (ensuring that Tokyo would not end the war too soon for Hitler's purposes). He knew that war with America was inevitable, that current limitations on the submarine campaign in the Atlantic were hampering its effectiveness, and that his Japanese allies needed reassurance. Hitler was right about the inevitability of war with the United States. Roosevelt had told Churchill in August 1941 that in the north Atlantic he planned "to wage war, but not declare it" in order to "force an incident" that would justify a declaration of war against the Third Reich.[32]

Not waiting for his formal declaration on the 11th, Hitler immediately unleashed his U-boats on American shipping. He had accomplished what all of Roosevelt's political maneuvering could not—the creation of the Grand Alliance of the British Empire, the United States, and the Soviet Union. Hitler had made a fatal mistake. The degree of Hitler's underestimation of US strength was apparent in a letter he wrote to Mussolini just before his attack on the USSR: "Whether or not America enters the war is a matter of indifference, in as much as she is already helping our enemy with all the power she can muster."[33] Much of the Nazi leadership shared the Führer's delusion. Göring told a subordinate that the Americans "can make cars and refrigerators, but not aircraft."[34] Although he and much of the German leadership were jubilant over the opening of hostilities between the Axis and the United States, a few realized the seriousness of Germany's new position. General Walter Warlimont, a member of the Führer's military planning staff, later wrote, "Now the best that could be hoped for was to escape being crushed between two enemies in east and west whose combined war potential was vastly superior to our own."[35]

Notes

1. Takafusa Nakamura, *A History of Shōwa Japan, 1926–1989* (Tokyo: University of Tokyo Press, 1998), 151.

2. Tsunoda Jun, "The Navy's Role in the Southern Strategy," in *The Fateful Choice: Japan's Advance into Southeast Asia, 1939–1941*, ed. James William Morley (New York: Columbia University Press, 1980), 247.

3. Herbert P. Bix, *Hirohito and the Making of Modern Japan* (New York: HarperCollins, 2000), 374.

4. Jane Degras, ed., *Soviet Documents on Foreign Policy*, vol. 3, *1933–1941* (New York: Octagon Books, 1978), 487.

5. Robert Dallek, *Franklin D. Roosevelt and American Foreign Policy, 1932–1945* (New York: Oxford University Press, 1979), 76.

6. Ogden Nash, "The Japanese," in *The Face Is Familiar* (Boston: Little, Brown, 1940), 233–34. Copyright ©1940 by Ogden Nash, renewed. Reprinted by permission of Curtis Brown, Ltd.

7. Charles Beard, *President Roosevelt and the Coming of the War, 1941: Appearances and Reality* (New Haven, CT: Yale University Press, 1948), and Charles Tansill, *Back Door to War* (Chicago: Regnery, 1952). This brand of revisionism continues to be published in spite of the lack of evidence for it. E.g., John Toland, *Infamy* (New York: Doubleday, 1982), and Robert Stinnett, *Day of Deceit* (New York: Free Press, 2000).

8. Den Kotani, "Pearl Harbor: Japanese Planning and Command Structure," in *The Pacific War Companion: From Pearl Harbor to Hiroshima*, ed. Daniel Marston (Oxford: Osprey, 2005), 33.

9. Richard J. Samuels, *Securing Japan: Tokyo's Grand Strategy and the Future of East Asia* (Ithaca, NY: Cornell University Press, 2007), 1.

10. Noriko Kawamura, "Emperor Hirohito and Japan's Decision to Go to War with the United States: Reexamined," *Diplomatic History* 31, no. 1 (2007): 63.

11. Historian Herbert P. Bix portrays Hirohito as a prowar enabler of his aggressive military men rather than a victim of their insubordination in his *Hirohito and the Making of Modern Japan* (New York: HarperCollins, 2000). See the review of Bix's work by Ben-Ami Shillony in *The Journal of Japanese Studies* 28, no. 1 (Winter 2002): 141–46, for a convincing critique of Bix's sources, methodology, and conclusions.

12. Ben-Ami Shillony, *Politics and Culture in Wartime Japan* (Oxford: Clarendon Press, 1978), 37.

13. Saburo Ienaga, *The Pacific War: A Critical Perspective on Japan's Role in World War II* (New York: Pantheon, 1978), 44–45.

14. Rana Mitter and Akira Iriye, preface to Eri Hotta, *Pan-Asianism and Japan's War, 1931–1945* (New York: Palgrave Macmillan, 2007), ix.

15. Kawamura, "Emperor Hirohito," 55.

16. Cf. David Bergamini, *Japan's Imperial Conspiracy* (New York: Morrow, 1971). This author claims that, since the Meiji Restoration, Japan's emperors had pursued a conspiracy for megalomaniacal expansion and had been intensely hostile toward the West. His views ignore or mischaracterize the policies of the Meiji oligarchs and the liberal politicians who succeeded them.

17. Nobutaka Ike, ed., *Japan's Decision for War: Records of the 1941 Policy Conferences* (Stanford, CA: Stanford University Press, 1967), 135.

18. Jonathan G. Utley, *Going to War with Japan* (Knoxville: University of Tennessee Press, 1985), 145–46.

19. Gordon W. Prange, *At Dawn We Slept: The Untold Story of Pearl Harbor* (New York: Penguin, 1981), 10.

20. Prange, *At Dawn We Slept*, 11.

21. Prange, *At Dawn We Slept*, 35.

22. Russell F. Weigley, *History of the United States Army* (New York: Macmillan, 1967), 414.

23. Samuel Eliot Morison, *History of U.S. Naval Operations in World War II*, vol. 3, *The Rising Sun in the Pacific, 1931–April 1942* (Boston: Little, Brown, 1948), 132.

24. H. P. Willmott, *Pearl Harbor* (London: Cassell, 2001), 145–48.

25. Herve Haufler, *Codebreaker's Victory: How the Allied Cryptographers Won World War II* (New York: New American Library, 2003), 127.

26. Studs Terkel, ed., *"The Good War": An Oral History of World War Two* (New York: Ballantine, 1984), 25.

27. Winston S. Churchill, *The Second World War*, vol. 3, *The Grand Alliance* (Boston: Houghton Mifflin, 1941), 620.

28. Peter N. Davies, *The Man behind the Bridge: Colonel Toosey and the River Kwai* (London: Athlone, 1991), 58.

29. Edward J. Drea, *Japan's Imperial Army: Its Rise and Fall, 1853–1945* (Lawrence: University Press of Kansas, 2009), 226–27.

30. Noriko Kawamura, *Emperor Hirohito and the Pacific War* (Seattle: University of Washington Press, 2015), 117.

31. David Irving, *Hitler's War* (New York: Viking, 1977), 352.

32. Dallek, *Franklin D. Roosevelt and American Foreign Policy*, 285.

33. John Ellis, *Brute Force: Allied Strategy and Tactics in the Second World War* (New York: Viking, 1990), 345.

34. Ellis, *Brute Force*, 345–46.

35. Walter Warlimont, *Inside Hitler's Headquarters, 1939–45* (Novato: Presidio, 1991), 203.

Part III

WAR BEHIND THE LINES

CHAPTER 9

Home Fronts: Axis

Before continuing the narrative of combat operations, it is necessary to consider what lies behind the battlefield—home fronts. Many historians contend that Allied victory in the Second World War was inevitable given their great superiority over their Axis opponents in population, industrial base, and natural resources. There is an element of truth in these contentions, but census reports, factories, and oil fields do not fight battles. What happens on the battlefield matters. Otherwise, the French in 1940 and the British at Singapore should not have lost. Poor strategic decisions and low morale among the troops can be fatal, even to an army that appears strong on paper. Conversely, even a well-led, spirited force is unlikely to ultimately prevail against an opponent possessing more resources of every sort in a protracted war of attrition. Many elements are necessary to support a successful, large-scale war: the sagacity of top political leadership, the power of the economy to finance and provision the war effort, the effectiveness of the national mobilization campaign, the ability of the national scientific and technological community to innovate more successfully than the enemy, and the morale of the civilian population (in order to endure the sacrifices of a prolonged, bloody struggle). There was nothing preordained about Allied success.

Home Front Germany

German economic policy during the preparation for and fighting of the Second World War has been the subject of debate among historians. Some scholars have characterized the mobilization policies of the Third Reich as "Blitzkrieg economics." In the view of economic historian Alan Milward, Hitler's planning "involved preparation for a series of short wars which would require no greater degree of commitment of the economy to war than had already existed in 1938." The campaigns were to be short, victorious, and self-financing. That plan seemed to work "until the Blitzkrieg strategy finally failed to achieve its objectives before Moscow in the winter of 1941–42. . . . Little or no economic preparation had been made for a long war because the strategic synthesis was formulated to avoid a prolonged struggle."[1] Hitler's belief that Germany lost the First World War because the home front collapsed mandated that the German people should not be overly burdened in his quest for global domination. Inadequate domestic supplies of many vital resources—oil, rubber, iron, copper, tin, etc.—required brief *Blitzkrieg* campaigns that could be sustained from existing stockpiles. An unflinchingly rational analysis of their war effort was unacceptable to the Nazis because it would have necessitated abandonment of their most cherished ambitions.

Parts of this interpretation are undeniable. The Nazis believed deeply in their own "stab in the back" myth and therefore the need to avoid deep sacrifices of the German people. Hitler hoped to fight his enemies in single combat, thereby avoiding war against a powerful enemy coalition for as long as possible. However, when Hitler spoke of his dedication to the German people, he did not mean the sum of those people living in the Reich under his rule. He meant instead some mythical ideal of the German nation (*das Volk*). As his actions would show, he was more than willing to sacrifice the comfort and the very lives of his unfortunate subjects.

In contrast to Milward's interpretation, Richard Overy contests the theory of *Blitzkrieg* economics.[2] He argues that by 1936, with the appointment of Hermann Göring as economic tsar and the establishment of the Four Year Plan, the Nazis were preparing full mobilization for total war. The Four Year Plan focused particularly on those scarce resources needed for war, especially synthetic rubber and synthetic oil, as well as the use of low-grade iron ore found within Germany. The Nazi Party and state apparatus assumed ever-greater control of the economy, though the administrative chaos of the Nazi party-state and resistance of the business community hindered economic coordination. Overy further suggests that Hitler aimed at total national mobilization for a war of *any* duration against an opponent of *any* size. The Führer understood that the major wars he contemplated would require enormous quantities of raw materials, labor, and industrial output and that some of that burden would fall upon the German people, but he always intended that the countries he defeated would bear most of the sacrifices.

Adam Tooze presents the most compelling revisionist argument. He contends that rearmament was the Reich's economic priority from the day Hitler took power, even though it meant seriously constricting civilian consumption. The Nazi regime dominated the process of mobilizing industry for war.[3] Mobilization for war required considerable sacrifice on the part of consumers because it allocated 20 percent of the gross domestic product to arms production during the years leading up to the war and over a third of GDP to weapons during the conflict. To support this massive military spending, the regime severely restricted the consumer goods and housing sectors of the economy. Tooze argues that the *Blitzkrieg* strategy of quick victory at minimal cost was "not to cushion the civilian population. Its purpose was to allow Germany to fight two wars at once"—against the Red Army and the Western powers.[4]

The Nazi regime survived through a combination of genuine popularity and intimidation. During the years of recovery from the Depression, bloodless diplomatic triumphs, and early military victories, mass popularity buoyed up the regime, though the threat of repression was always present. As the war turned against Germany, fear became a more prominent tool of social control. In April 1942, the Reichstag passed a measure ending all due process and legal protections for German citizens. The regime could now arrest, torture, and execute citizens without hindrance from the legal code or the courts. Death sentences handed out by the courts shot up from 250 in 1939 to 5,336 in 1943. The growing sense of apprehension among almost all Germans by the fall of 1943 came not only from fear of the Gestapo but also from fear of losing the war. Long-held German prejudices combined with Nazi propaganda to produce the horrific specter of "Asiatic hordes" (i.e., the Red Army) despoiling Germany. Moreover, though few would admit it in public, most had come to realize that they personally might suffer for the extraordinary atrocities committed in their name by the SS and the Wehrmacht. Even as any hope of victory receded, fighting on seemed the only possible course of action for many Germans.

Hitler was in a hurry to launch his wars of conquest—both due to concerns about his own mortality and because his enemies would grow overwhelmingly strong if allowed time to rearm completely. He therefore overruled his more cautious generals and economists, launching one campaign after another and allocating huge resources to the military at the expense of the consumer sector. In the months leading up to the attack on France, for example, German armaments production doubled while ordinary citizens had difficulty finding enough coal, food, or housing or any product made of steel or iron. While the Germans fought the early rounds of war against Poland, Norway, and even France with available resources, Hitler anticipated that the later, titanic struggles against the British Empire, the Soviet Union, and the United States would transform the racial consciousness and warrior ethos of the German people so that they would willingly bear any sacrifice to achieve global hegemony. Ultimate victory would enable Hitler to complete the Nazi revolution, dispensing with compromises with traditional elites—officers and businessmen—and achieving a "comprehensive restructuring of German society."[5]

Once the war became global—with the inclusion of the USSR and the United States—Germany fought at a very serious economic disadvantage. Its pool of available natural resources and its industrial output could never match the economic power of the Allies. Except for slave labor and the Czech arms industry, the lands conquered by the Wehrmacht did little to make up the deficit.[6] The Germans drafted millions of enemy POWs and civilians to work in the Reich. Over two million of them died there. The parasitic way in which the German occupiers drained labor, food, and resources from their conquered lands alienated the captive populations but did not solve the Reich's economic problems. Although the economies of the occupied lands were declining, the Reich continued to take an ever-larger slice of that shrinking pie. In the judgment of historian Michael Geyer, "however successful the first two years of the war, the Third Reich never came close to escaping the dilemma posed by the fact that the political and military-strategic costs of expansion continuously outran the benefits of a newly gained hegemonic position."[7]

Germany was subject to an Allied blockade from the first days of the war. The Allies' overwhelming naval superiority kept goods from reaching the Reich from overseas sources. Between 1939 and 1941, Germany received a great many vital commodities from the USSR. What the Russians could not provide, they could buy on the world market and transship to Germany. Hitler's attack on the Soviet Union terminated that valuable relationship. The Allied blockade harmed not only the German war effort but also those countries the Nazis had overrun. Britain blocked food and fuel shipments from reaching the occupied nations. Winston Churchill intended the blockade not only to deprive Germany of vital war materials but also to provoke unrest in the occupied lands. The failure of those occupied lands to produce the quantities of goods anticipated for the German home front, the tightening Allied blockade, and the expansion of the war effort meant that the attempt to maintain the standard of living in Germany was increasingly unsuccessful. Strict rationing of a whole range of consumer goods soon became necessary, as did wage controls. Until the last months of the war, Germans did not suffer the severe levels of food deprivation that they imposed on the peoples they conquered. There were great scarcities, however, especially in meat, dairy products, and sugar. By 1944, starches (bread, potatoes, etc.) comprised as much as 90 percent of the national diet. A black market thrived for those who could afford it.

Germany mobilized its advanced science and technology community to alleviate the effects of the Allied blockade. Their contributions in making synthetic oil and rubber were especially important to the war effort. Another group of German scientists was working to develop an atomic bomb, but that seemed such a distant and expensive goal that the project lost its funding priority and did not come close to achieving its objective. Hitler never supported it. To him it was "Jewish physics." German engineering also developed jet fighter aircraft, the Me-262 as well as V-1 cruise missiles and V-2 ballistic missiles. Ultimately, these marquee projects cost a great deal but came too late to affect the outcome of the war.

The period of cheap and easy German victories ended with the Soviet counteroffensive at Moscow in December 1941. Now Berlin had to face the grim reality that it had blundered into a "total" war against a powerful coalition of Allies whose populations, industrial capacity, and natural resources far exceeded its own. *Blitzkrieg* gave way to a prolonged war of attrition. There seemed to be two answers to this problem. One was to rationalize industry by simplifying production methods, standardizing parts and products, and replacing highly skilled labor working on multipurpose machines with more abundant semiskilled labor working on single-purpose machines.

The second answer was to exploit the populations of conquered Europe even more brutally. Germany was already committing most of its labor and natural resources to the war effort. Part of the problem was low productivity, caused by frequent changes in priority among various weapons systems and the lower efficiency of slave labor. The armed forces interfered with production, constantly stopping assembly lines to introduce minor technical improvements. For example, the Luftwaffe had required eighteen thousand design changes in the Ju-88 bomber by the end of 1942. Moreover, the administrative structure of the Third Reich continued to be a jumble of overlapping jurisdictions and rival prima donnas. Although many historians have criticized the "irrationality" and even "anarchy" of the German wartime economy, Tooze cautions that, for all its weaknesses, "the system was also undeniably effective in shifting huge volumes of raw materials into armaments production."[8]

The expansion of the war in 1941 meant that the army conscripted more German men, even if their skills were vital to the economy. Nazi ideology dictated that women's place was in the kitchen and the nursery, not the factory and certainly not in the armed forces. Nevertheless, fourteen million women worked outside the home (mostly in agriculture) before the start of the war. Employing foreign workers and concentration camp slaves did not fully resolve the severe manpower shortage. The regime modified its view of women's roles in order to include more women in the workforce, though rarely in the Wehrmacht. Between 1939 and 1944, the number of women in the labor force increased by only three hundred thousand (though that figure is deceiving, since a greater proportion of German women were already in the labor force in 1939, compared to women in Britain, France, or the United States). German factories employed fewer women than British plants, but female labor was common in small businesses and farming. Labor conscription for women was introduced in January 1943, but it was not rigorously enforced and was widely evaded, especially by middle-class women who considered factory work demeaning. The regime's unwillingness and ineffectiveness in mobilizing its women resulted in only about a million and a half German women joining the labor force by 1943, the peak year of mobilization.[9] Nonetheless, counting part-time workers, the proportion of females in the labor force exceeded 50 percent in the last year of the war.[10] Ultimately, hundreds of thousands of women worked in the hardest industrial, mining, and agricultural jobs in Germany—but they were not German women; they were conscripted Poles, Russians, and others.

The Wehrmacht inducted eleven million men into its forces during the war. Over four million of them died, and many more were seriously wounded. There were simply too few German men to fill all the necessary positions in the factories and in the army. By the beginning of 1943, fifteen- and sixteen-year-old boys were conscripted into the navy and Luftwaffe auxiliaries—many of them "manning" antiaircraft guns. Worse was to come. By the late summer of 1944, authorities were calling up sixteen-year-old boys for the army. Then in September the regime created a new "people's militia," the *Volkssturm*. It included boys sixteen and even younger as well as men up to age sixty. With insufficient weapons and minimal training, these boys and older men became little more than cannon fodder. Men were transferred from antiaircraft units to serve as infantry, to be replaced by women (breaking a taboo in German culture).

To solve the labor shortage crisis, the Nazis initiated a massive infusion of slave labor from the occupied countries. Virtually all of Germany's major manufacturers—IG Farben, BMW, Siemens, Heinkel, Volkswagen, Daimler-Benz—benefited from the slave system. Millions of slaves worked long, exhausting shifts in unsafe and unsanitary conditions, under draconian discipline, to service Hitler's war machine. The fate of foreign workers in Germany—whether volunteers, POWs, or concentration camp slaves—was often tragic. At the beginning of 1945, there were 7.7 million forced workers in the Reich. As Allied armies closed in from east and west, many of the foreign workers were killed or forced to begin long marches to avoid capture by the enemy—all without any planning for water, food, or shelter.

The expansion of the war into a truly global conflict mandated a sweeping reorganization of production. Now even Hitler, usually disinterested in economic matters, was forced to intervene in favor of industrial rationalization. The ineffective Göring lost his post as "economic dictator," first to Fritz Todt and, after Todt's death in a plane crash, to Hitler's architect, Albert Speer—a Nazi and a close confidant of the Führer. Speer's self-serving memoirs (and the work of historians who relied on them) depict the Speer era as an "economic miracle." He was a talented economic manager, but he was an even more skillful propagandist and self-promoter. His morale-boosting message to the nation was simple: Germany could not lose since it had the best soldiers and a seemingly endless supply of superior weaponry.[11] Enjoying Hitler's direct support, the new minister of armaments overcame the resistance of the army, bureaucracy, and business leaders against the rational allocation of resources and the revamping of industrial practices. However, these efforts to rationalize and increase production were not solely Speer's work but the maturation of programs already in place.

The so-called economic miracle of 1942–1944 enabled German industry to increase production in most categories of weapons, but by the summer of 1943 resource limitations and the Allies' bombing of German industry "brought Speer's 'miracle' to a complete halt."[12] By government fiat, key arms manufacturers received more of the critical resources they required (coal, steel, oil, labor, etc.), at the expense of other industries and consumers. Government ministries colluded with the SS to mount a reign of terror not only against foreign workers and concentration camp inmates but over German workers and managers too. Workers (Germans as well as foreign contract laborers and slaves) now toiled as much as seventy-two hours per week. The productivity of German labor increased dramatically, from an index of 100 in 1939 to 160 by 1944.[13]

Rationalization increased aircraft production tremendously. But here and elsewhere, efforts at streamlining production led to technological obsolescence and sometimes to complete failure. In a life-and-death struggle against stronger opponents, there was little time for the lengthy process of designing and testing complex new weapons systems. For the Luftwaffe, that meant retaining the Messerschmitt 109 and Focke-Wulf 190 as its primary interceptors. They had been excellent fighters at the beginning of the war, but by 1943 they were markedly inferior to the American P-51 Mustang. In some cases, "rationalization" failed altogether. The new Mark XXI submarine was assembled from components (including hull segments) made by various subcontractors instead of being built from scratch in a shipyard. The hull segments leaked badly. Most of these craft were scrapped. The once promising Mark XXI never sank a single Allied ship.

Despite Speer's efforts, German industrial production was never optimized for efficiency and maximum output. Germany under Hitler was still only a partially modernized society.[14] Many historians have described the Third Reich (including the direction of its economy) as chaotic, feudal, and irrational—with rival leaders (Speer, Göring, Himmler, etc.) competing to protect their own fiefdoms. This system "worked" to keep Hitler the decisive authority in every decision, but the Führer was less and less capable of holding it all together in the latter stages of the war. Hitler's physical deterioration in the last two years of the conflict (from heart disease, Parkinson's disease, and other ailments) exacerbated the high-level rivalries and administrative anarchy endemic to the Third Reich. The Führer's lieutenants as well as regional party leaders wrestled for position and, in the case of Himmler and Speer, created their own empires. In the judgment of historian Richard Evans, "the Third Reich was clearly becoming increasingly leaderless on the home front."[15]

The military disasters suffered by Germany in 1943 provoked a further tightening of the system. All adults, women as well as men, were ordered to register at labor exchanges. All businesses not deemed necessary for the war effort were supposed to close. The regime instituted a high-priority Adolf Hitler Panzer Program to turn out new Panther and Tiger tanks. The program greatly increased the production of tanks and made the Battle of Kursk possible, but privileging one weapons system entailed diminished output for the others—more tanks, fewer aircraft and trucks, and less ammunition. The overall German war effort, impressive as it was, was simply not enough.

The Allies hoped that a combination of bombing and battlefield losses would break German morale. That never happened. The Wehrmacht fought fiercely until it was completely crushed by the Allies in the spring of 1945. The home front, too, continued to support the war effort. Morale among German civilians did not crack when the war turned against Germany. Part of the explanation was the threat (and practice) by the Nazi regime of repression against any manifestation of defeatism. Beyond terror, however, Germans were inspired to continue the fight even in the face of repeated defeats because they realized that with Allied victory would come retribution for the crimes their forces had committed throughout Europe. At the beginning of 1944, the public prosecutor for Hamburg reported, "People are becoming increasingly aware that a surrender would not bring relief but rather create a situation compared with which the worst possible terror attacks [i.e., bombing] would only represent temporary bagatelles. Everybody is gradually becoming aware that, in the event of a German defeat, even if individuals manage to survive, Germany would face endless misery and the nation would lose its identity."[16]

Home Front Italy

Italy was the least thoroughly mobilized country of the major belligerents in the Second World War. It mobilized less effectively in 1940 than did liberal Italy in 1915. There was a brief burst of enthusiasm for the war in 1940 among some segments of the public, but that evaporated almost entirely as one defeat followed another. After the disastrous defeat in Greece, the popularity of Fascism, the Fascist Party, and Mussolini personally fell dramatically and never recovered. Moreover, the country entered the war in 1940 with the least developed industrial sector and completely inadequate sources of power (oil, coal, etc.) and raw materials. Only massive coal shipments from Germany partially offset previous overseas supplies, now cut off by Allied blockade. These shortages severely limited Italy's arms industries.

The Fascist Party attempted to rouse the people to an energetic war effort, though its appeals failed to move much of the population. Mussolini's regime was a brutal dictatorship, crushing its liberal and socialist enemies, but it could not dominate Italy's elites. Industrialists and rich landowners frequently schemed to avoid taxes and defraud the government. Rome's feeble efforts to control the economy and channel it for war production largely failed. The nation's factories turned out inadequate quantities of poorly made and often obsolescent weapons. Overall, Italian production peaked in 1939 and declined for the rest of the war. Given the inability of the Italian economy to support the national war effort, it is surprising that Italian soldiers fought so well on some occasions. Mussolini bragged of an army of "eight million bayonets" and an air force that could darken the skies with its massive fleets, but the Italian armed forces fell far short of his boasts. "Mussolini's problem," historian Peter Neville suggests, "lay in separating military fantasies from reality."[17]

Mussolini's regime was forced to modify its stance against women in the workforce. Italian women went to work in growing numbers in the factories and in civil administration, as well as on farms. The rationing of food began in 1939, but hunger was not pervasive before 1942. As elsewhere in war-torn Europe, a black market flourished. Battlefield defeats and worsening conditions on the home front led to a wave of industrial strikes in the spring of 1943.

Allied air raids hit factories hard and further undermined morale. Ultimately, fifty-eight thousand civilians perished in the bombing raids. "In Italy," historian Toby Abse suggests, "bombing raids did not have the effect of unifying the population behind their own government and increasing their hostility toward the war-time enemy."[18] Before the war, many people attributed Italy's problems to Mussolini's subordinates—frequently complaining, "If only the Duce knew!" By 1943, they blamed the Duce directly. Mussolini proved himself to be an incompetent warlord. He "had little if any comprehension of military strategy and none at all of grand strategy."[19] People ceased to believe Fascist propaganda, while many turned to the BBC for accurate war news. Abse argues that the king and Italy's elites turned away from Mussolini not only because of Allied military successes but also because of their fear of revolution.[20]

Mussolini seemed to be declining, both physically and mentally. He gave few big speeches during the war and spent most of his time secluded in his Palazzo Venezia offices. The alliance with Germany was deeply unpopular with most Italians. Mussolini's foolish declaration of war on the United States shredded what little loyalty Italians still felt for their Duce. He had blundered into war with the three strongest powers in the world and brought his native land to the brink of disaster. In response to the Allied conquest of Sicily, the king, the army, the Vatican, and the Fascist Grand Council overthrew Mussolini on July 25, 1943, and prepared to switch sides in the war. A German invasion aborted their clumsy efforts. German commandos rescued Mussolini, and radical Fascists proclaimed a new Italian Social Republic (or Salo Republic)—only nominally under the Duce's leadership. Mussolini was now powerless and entirely at the Führer's mercy. The Germans took the opportunity to annex the South Tyrol, Trieste, and the Trentino. They also disarmed the Italian army and sent many of its men to labor in the Reich. The Italian people overwhelmingly wanted peace, but instead they had to suffer intensified war. In that conflict, most Italians quickly identified the Germans, not the Allies, as the real enemy.

Meanwhile, civil war broke out within German-occupied northern Italy. Fascist radicals were now free to ignite their "second revolution"—rounding up Jews and waging war against the "traitors" who had deposed Mussolini. Foreign Minister Ciano and Marshal de Bono were caught and executed for their part in the plot. The Fascist Party adopted a manifesto that called for abolishing the monarchy, depriving Italian Jews of their citizenship, and weakening the power of the industrialists and big landowners—though not much of this radical rhetoric was ever put into practice. The Germans prioritized stopping the Allied advance up the peninsula and extracting as many human and material resources from Italy as possible, so they blocked any social restructuring that might cause chaos. The Salo regime also revived the anticlericalism of the early days of Fascism. Nonetheless, the church hierarchy condemned resistance and called for obedience to the state.

Resistance groups across much of the political spectrum rose to challenge the Fascists in a brutal civil war. Communist cadres provided the strongest elements in the resistance, while women played a significant role, not only as messengers and spies, but also as armed combatants. Many peasants and some soldiers fled to the resistance to avoid service for the Social Republic or slavery in Germany. Among industrial workers, resistance took the form of widespread strikes. Factory owners colluded with the Germans in deporting strike leaders and militants to the Reich. Peasants risked their lives to shelter downed Allied fliers and escaped POWs. An almost equal number of Italians chose to fight for the new Fascist regime. "What prevailed, therefore, in those who opted for the Social Republic," historian Claudio Pavone explains, "was the fear of losing the identity they had grown accustomed to and the urge to recover it no matter how, both in its version of reassuring order and in its nihilistic version."[21]

The Germans and the Fascist Black Brigades committed particularly brutal excesses, killing forty-five thousand partisans and another ten thousand civilians. The Germans killed groups of hostages to discourage participation in the resistance and sometimes burned whole villages. Pavone argues that German-occupied Italy experienced three overlapping conflicts between 1943 and 1945—a national liberation struggle, a civil war, and a class war.[22] The communists, following Moscow's "united front" tactic, advertised their actions as a struggle to liberate the homeland. Others on the left fought for the social transformation of Italy, while for some peasants and workers the resistance was an anarchistic revolt of the poor against the rich. The resistance mounted a widespread insurrection when German power crumbled in April 1945. As Italy collapsed around him, the forlorn dictator blamed his own people, castigating them as a nation of "sheep." Communist partisans captured and shot Mussolini and his mistress, Claretta Petacci. Their bodies were hung upside down in a public square in Milan, where outraged Italians spat and urinated on them.

Home Front Japan

Given its slender resources compared to those of its enemies, Japan needed to mobilize thoroughly to sustain its war effort. According to Japanese historian Nakamura Takafusa, after the outbreak of war with China in 1937, "the Japanese economy was administered with the sole object of meeting the military demand. Ordinary industry and popular livelihood were sacrificed to that end."[23] New laws allowed the government to allocate both capital investment and commodities, while the military could commandeer factories at its discretion. Between 1940 and 1944, consumer spending fell by almost 30 percent. Production focused on weapons, airplanes, and ships at the expense of consumer goods. By 1938, military spending accounted for 70 percent of the national budget. The National Mobilization Bill passed that year gave the government nominal "total war control" over the country's huge industrial conglomerates.

Despite these efforts, the Japanese economy was never centrally planned or efficiently mobilized. A Total War Resources Institute, created only in October 1944, was never able to implement long-range planning. The Cabinet Planning Board was supposed to mandate annual resource allocation programs but was frustrated in this task by army-navy secretiveness and squabbling. Pessimistic economists, who pointed out dangerous shortfalls, were silenced with accusations of "defeatism." Businessmen fought government control as "communistic" but lost the battle. Yet, even though nominally subservient to bureaucratic and military planners, the large corporations protected their interests and operated at a substantial profit until the intense American bombing of Japanese cities in 1944–1945 destroyed many of their plants.

For all its mobilization efforts, Japan's production rose only by about 25 percent between 1940 and 1944 and declined sharply after that. Allied interdiction cut off most supplies of fuel and raw materials, and then, in the last months of the war, the American bombing campaign destroyed all the nation's industrial cities. Government spending in 1944, mainly for the war, was two hundred times what it had been in 1937! Taxes rose dramatically, but Japan financed its fourteen-year-long war (1931–1945) mainly by borrowing from banks and printing more money. Expanding the money supply in an environment of consumer goods scarcity caused significant inflation (about 20 percent per year), but nothing like the hyperinflation that ravaged the Chinese economy. Wage and price controls failed to stabilize prices. Lack of coordination of its war effort was Japan's Achilles' heel. The political decision-making process required achieving consensus among the government, the military, and the imperial court—a result seldom achieved. Politeness and vagueness papered over the profound disagreements among the three power centers. Deep divisions between the army and navy prevented effective prosecution of the war. General Tojo Hideki, who had already accumulated substantial power in his roles as prime minister and war minister, moved early in 1944 to consolidate his control over the government and both branches of the armed forces, but continuing defeats and mounting internal opposition brought his cabinet down within a few months.

Japan mobilized its labor force less effectively than the other major belligerents. In the fall of 1941, all males between sixteen and forty and all single females between sixteen and twenty-five were required to register for labor service. One and a half million men were drafted for industrial work. Trade unions were disbanded, to be replaced by patriotic industrial associations run by factory managers. Many workers were "frozen" into their jobs (i.e., not permitted to leave). As the war began to go badly after 1942 and more and more men were needed for military service, the regime pressed students (from elementary schools to universities) into the labor force. Except for science and technology majors, all college students were sent to industry or the military. Women's labor was never thoroughly mobilized, except in agriculture. Mainly women, children, and old people worked the fields. The proportion of women in the urban workforce increased by only 3 percent. Traditional attitudes about proper women's work prevented their more effective use. Prostitutes (a legal trade in Japan) had the choice of factory work or serving the military in overseas "comfort stations."

Tanaka Tetsuko, a high school student, worked in a factory making balloon bombs. She lived in an unheated dormitory near the plant and wore a cloth air-raid helmet as well as a headband identifying her as part of the "Student Special Attack Force." She and her fellow students arose at 4:30 a.m. six days each week for a quick breakfast and a long march to the factory. There they worked a twelve-hour shift without lunch or any breaks—aided by amphetamines. After work, they received a bowl of rice with a few bits of spoiled sweet potato in it and a bowl of miso soup without any vegetables. "It wasn't enough," she recalled, "to sustain us at the work we had to do."[24] The regime pressed older people, convicts, prisoners of war, and foreign workers into service. Tens of thousands of Korean and Chinese laborers toiled in the most dangerous mining and construction jobs. Ahn Juretsu, a Korean, was recruited to Japan with the promise of a decent job with high wages, but he became a virtual slave. He helped to build an airfield—working without proper equipment or clothing in cold temperatures, subjected to frequent beatings, and fed only a small plate of rice and a pickle for dinner.[25] The efforts of the Japanese government and its people were never enough. For example, the island kingdom produced 58,822 aircraft during the Pacific war, while in the same period American factories turned out 261,826 planes.[26]

All the mass media—newspapers, magazines, radio, movies—were tightly muzzled by government censorship. The regime and the media referred to the nation as "a hundred million hearts beating as one" (though the population was only seventy million). Prime Minister Tojo admitted bluntly, "The masses are foolish. If we tell them the facts, morale will collapse."[27] The press never mentioned defeats but reported victories that never happened. As the Allies advanced in the central and southwest Pacific, the people were told that Japan was drawing its enemies close for the kill. The government created community councils and neighborhood associations throughout the country to maintain mass support for the war effort and to suppress discontent or defeatism. Those few who voiced criticisms experienced public humiliation, deprivation of rations, and even jail. The police harassed and occasionally arrested "thought criminals" (i.e., those who were in the least critical of the war effort). The authorities denounced foreign influences in general and American jazz in particular, though baseball continued to be popular. Christian students were sometimes asked, "Who is greater, Christ or the emperor?" The regime also created or expanded associations for women, young people, veterans, and many other groups to facilitate the "spiritual mobilization" of the populace.

The message was clear—Japanese "spirit" could defeat Western machines. Female relatives, sweethearts, and even total strangers joined together to make "thousand-stitch belts" for departing soldiers that were to demonstrate home front support and supposedly ward off enemy bullets. The Tokyo regime was authoritarian but not fully totalitarian. There were a few thousand prosecutions and two executions for subversive actions or thought, but nothing like the mass repression and concentration camps in Nazi Germany or Stalinist Russia. General Tojo, who was prime minister from 1941 to 1944, was in no sense the equivalent of Hitler or Mussolini. There was consensus on Japan's need to defeat its enemies and establish a self-sufficient empire in East Asia, but major policy decisions continued to result from a tug-of-war among the politicians, bureaucrats, and military leaders.

With callous disregard for the survival of the nation, in the summer of 1945 the army began to organize a "People's Volunteer Corps" for last-ditch resistance to an anticipated American invasion. Men under age sixty-five and women under forty-five received bamboo spears to face enemy tanks, machine guns, and flamethrowers. Children were taught to throw hand grenades and spear an enemy. Most of the "volunteers" dug trenches, built tank traps, and cleared debris. High school girls were implored: "Even killing just one American soldier will do. You must prepare to use the [carpenter's] awls for self-defense. You must aim at the enemy's abdomen. Understand? The abdomen! If you don't kill at least one enemy soldier, you don't deserve to die!"[28] There was little overt expression of antiwar sentiment, but most people realized the insanity of using spears and awls against Allied firepower.

Japanese agriculture fed the countryside reasonably well but struggled to support the cities. The government extracted food from its newly won empire, causing hunger throughout the region and starvation in Vietnam. Fewer and fewer shipments of overseas food reached the home islands as the American blockade intensified. Government dietitians urged people to eat locusts, insect grubs, rice straw, and other substitute foods. Combined with poor harvests on the home islands in the last three years of the war, the blockade caused widespread hunger in Japan as well as the proliferation of diseases attendant on malnutrition. Rice rationing was introduced in 1940, and subsequently sugar, charcoal, and matches were added to the list. Meat all but disappeared from the Japanese diet, while fresh fruits and vegetables became scarce. The country experienced a food crisis by 1945, with average caloric intake falling below that needed to sustain a hardworking adult. Life became grim in the nation's heavily bombed cities. Dance halls, geisha houses, and most restaurants and bars closed. Theaters were restricted to a few hours of operation each day.

In the last months of the war, pumpkin became the staple diet of most citizens. People resorted to eating acorn flour, thistle, mugwort, and chickweed as well as pulverized mulberry leaves and potato stems. Long waits in line at stores sometimes lasted more than a day. Ordinary citizens experienced great difficulty obtaining most consumer goods, while gasoline was impossible to buy. Metal products, cookware for example, were also unavailable. The regime urged householders to turn in any unused metal objects for recycling. Streetcar rails disappeared from the roads, as did handrails from bridges and bells from Buddhist temples. The increasing scarcity of coal meant that most homes suffered through cold winters. The government told people that "extravagance is the enemy" and urged them to "make do" and to keep working and supporting the war effort.

In 1943, 1.3 million urban children were sent to the countryside to live with relatives or foster families or to stay in Buddhist temples or inns. Heavy US bombing between November 1944 and August 1945 precipitated a wave of adult migration from the devastated cities. Virtually all of Japan's large and midsize cities were demolished by high explosive and incendiary bombs. The state mobilized neighborhood associations for bucket brigades and digging bomb shelters, but their efforts were largely ineffective against the devastating aerial onslaught. The six largest cities lost 58 percent of their population. The Japanese home front maintained its discipline and did not crack under the strain of privation, heavy bombing, social dislocation, and continuing battlefield defeats—but it was a stoic, grim endurance.

Notes

1. Alan S. Milward, *War, Economy and Society* (Berkeley: University of California Press, 1977), 26.

2. R. J. Overy, *War and Economy in the Third Reich* (Oxford: Clarendon Press, 1994), 189, 233–56.

3. Adam Tooze, *The Wages of Destruction: The Making and Unmaking of the Nazi Economy* (New York: Penguin, 2006), ch. 4.

4. Tooze, *The Wages of Destruction*, 667.

5. Tooze, *The Wages of Destruction*, 660.

6. Tooze, *The Wages of Destruction*, 640.

7. Michael Geyer, "German Strategy in the Age of Machine Warfare, 1914–1945," in *The Makers of Modern Strategy: From Machiavelli to the Nuclear Age*, ed. Peter Paret (Oxford: Oxford University Press, 1999), 578.

8. Tooze, *The Wages of Destruction*, 356.

9. Jill Stephenson, "Women in Germany and Britain in the Second World War," in *A World at Total War: Global Conflict and Political Destruction, 1937–1945*, ed. Roger Chickering, Stig Förster, and Bernd Greiner (Cambridge: Cambridge University Press, 2005), 225.

10. Richard Overy, *The Bombers and the Bombed: Allied Air War over Europe, 1940–1945* (New York: Viking, 2013), 289.

11. Tooze, *The Wages of Destruction*, 554.

12. Tooze, *The Wages of Destruction*, 556–57.

13. Overy, *War and Economy in the Third Reich*, 367.

14. Tooze, *The Wages of Destruction*, xxiii.

15. Richard J. Evans, *The Third Reich at War* (New York: Penguin, 2008), 510.

16. Marlis G. Steinert, *Hitlers Krieg und die Deutschen* (Dusseldorf and Vienna: Econ-Verlag, 1970), 436.

17. Peter Neville, *Mussolini*, 2nd ed. (London: Routledge, 2015), 152.

18. Toby Abse, "Italy," in *The Civilian in War: The Home Front in Europe, Japan and the USA in World War II*, ed. Jeremy Noakes (Exeter: University of Exeter Press, 1992), 109.

19. John Gooch, *Mussolini's War: Fascist Italy from Triumph to Collapse, 1935–1943* (New York: Pegasus, 2020), 412.

20. Abse, "Italy," 111.

21. Claudio Pavone, *A Civil War: A History of Italian Resistance* (London: Verso, 2013), 46–47.

22. Pavone, *A Civil War*, 3.

23. Takafusa Nakamura, "Depression, Recovery, and War, 1920–1945," in *The Cambridge History of Japan*, vol. 6, *The Twentieth Century*, ed. Peter Duus (Cambridge: Cambridge University Press, 1988), 480.

24. Haruko Taya Cook and Theodore F. Cook, *Japan at War: An Oral History* (New York: New Press, 1992), 191.

25. Cook and Cook, *Japan at War*, 192–99.

26. Jerome B. Cohen, *Japan's Economy in War and Reconstruction* (Minneapolis: University of Minnesota Press, 1949), 209–10.

27. Quoted in Thomas R. H. Havens, *Valley of Darkness: The Japanese People and World War II* (New York: Norton, 1978), 66.

28. Quoted in Havens, *Valley of Darkness*, 190.

CHAPTER 10

Home Fronts: Allies

Home Front USA

In American memory, the Second World War was the "good war," or even "the greatest war ever." Journalist Tom Brokaw titled his book on the men and women who fought that war *The Greatest Generation*. As historian Michael Adams explains,

> Since then, as America's economic predominance has been challenged and as problems at home and abroad have become less tractable, the war years have come to seem a golden age, an idyllic period when everything was simpler and a can-do generation of Americans solved the world's problems. In this mythic time of the Good War, everyone was united: there were no racial or gender tensions, no class conflicts. Things worked better, from kitchen gadgets to public schools. Families were well adjusted; kids read a lot and respected their elders; parents didn't divorce.[1]

There is certainly some truth in the triumphalist narrative that in World War II the American people were more united than usual in the struggle against an undeniable evil. It is hardly fitting, however, to call a war that resulted in over eighty million deaths "good," though it was undoubtedly a necessary war given the genocidal nature of German aggression and the barbarity of Japanese conquests. Moreover, while in some ways the war drew Americans closer together and improved the quality of life in the United States, in other respects it exacerbated existing tensions and prejudices. America fought the war with three self-imposed handicaps: it failed to rearm and intervene in a timely fashion, its political leaders feared to impose great sacrifices on their people, and prejudices against African Americans, Japanese Americans, and women hindered the full military and industrial mobilization of the country.[2]

The US government strove energetically to maintain public support for the war effort. Its propaganda campaign identified the Four Freedoms as the righteous cause worth fighting for and the Axis as evil incarnate. Journalists seldom reported bad news. Most of them became willing cheerleaders in the war effort, reporting an upbeat, sanitized version of what they saw. Pictures of dead American soldiers did not appear in the press until 1943, and even then many readers protested their appearance. Hollywood did its part, too, most notably in Frank Capra's Why We Fight film series, which portrayed heroic (all-white) Americans fighting for Mom, apple pie, and freedom against the virtually demonic forces of the Axis. Norman Rockwell and other artists created posters bearing similar messages. While the film industry produced mostly escapist romances and comedies, its war movies showed heroism and harmony among troops of different ethnic backgrounds, but never grisly wounds or senseless deaths.

Life was certainly easier on the home front in America than in other belligerent countries. There was rationing of food and some consumer goods, while new cars and automobile tires were virtually unavailable. The standard of living, disposable personal income, and the availability of medical care actually rose for Americans during the war. They did not suffer the serious privations endured by the Russians and the Chinese or even the lesser discomforts borne by the British or the Germans. During the war, American consumer purchases increased by 12 percent. In comparison, British consumption shrank by 22 percent, and Russian consumption dropped by a much larger percentage. Economist John Kenneth Galbraith joked, "In the war years, consumption of consumer goods doubled. Never in the history of human conflict has there been so much talk of sacrifice and so little sacrifice."[3]

Numerous drives to collect scrap metal and other recyclables were more important in making everyone feel a part of the war effort than in contributing to war production. John Blum suggests that for many Americans the real object of the war was to make the world safe for American consumerism. "To most of the American people at home, that advertisement [a Celotex ad touting an affordable "Miracle Home"] symbolized much of what was worth fighting for and, well before the fighting ended, what was worth spending for, whether to satisfy yearnings long unfulfilled or whether just for the fun of spending."[4] The war economy produced a burgeoning and highly materialistic middle class.

As the war clouds gathered in Europe and Asia, the United States possessed an army about the same size as that of Bulgaria. In addition to isolationist sentiment, concerns about how much in new taxes and decreased availability of consumer goods the electorate would tolerate kept the president and Congress from vigorous rearmament. Moreover, initially big business—especially the auto, railway, steel, and electric power generation industries—resisted rapid expansion for war production. Business leaders feared that such growth would lead to excess capacity and renewed depression after the war. Roosevelt could not overcome this opposition before 1942, but once the United States was attacked, government and public opinion forced a change in policy.

Throughout the war, America was determined to use its economic and industrial prowess as its main weapon. President Roosevelt told a radio audience, "In winning this war there is just one sure way to guarantee the minimum of casualties—by seeing to it that, in every action, we have overwhelming material superiority." During the Depression, FDR's New Deal policies had already given the federal government a greater role in the economy. Now the president created a cluster of agencies to spur the mobilization of the nation's industrial and agricultural output. An Office of Emergency Management was installed in the White House in 1939. As historian Gerald Nash suggests, FDR's "political sense persuaded him that he alone should retain the major reins of power over civilian as well as military mobilization."[5] The following year, Roosevelt established a Council of National Defense, under General Motors president William S. Knudsen, to oversee the transition of US industry to war production.

Roosevelt used the Reconstruction Finance Corporation to provide credit for building new factories. An Office of Production Management, under Knudsen and labor leader Sidney Hillman, allocated raw materials and scarce goods. The White House also set up an Office of Price Administration in an effort to limit inflation by controlling prices. These and many other new agencies were staffed by prominent business executives (often "dollar-a-year men," who continued to receive salaries from their corporations), augmented by a few labor leaders. In 1942, two more organizations were added to the list—a War Production Board, under Sears, Roebuck executive vice president Donald Nelson, and the Office of Economic Stabilization, under powerful South Carolina politician James F. Byrnes. The president neither employed a master organizational plan nor appointed an overall mobilization "czar." Instead, the welter of new agencies was created on an ad hoc basis, often with overlapping jurisdictions and personal rivalries.

American factories from Baltimore to Detroit to San Francisco geared up to overwhelm the Axis powers with their productivity. The transition to a full war economy was initially slow, but by 1943 industrial production was double the previous year's total. The Bethlehem Steel Company's Sparrows Point plant in Baltimore produced more steel by itself than Germany, Italy, and Japan combined. The Ford plant at Willow Run, outside Detroit, could complete a B-24 Liberator bomber every sixty-three minutes on its mile-long final assembly line. Each of the four Kaiser shipyards in the San Francisco Bay area could turn out a "Liberty ship" (i.e., a cargo vessel) in as little as seventeen days (down from three hundred days in 1940). Many defense plants went to around-the-clock operation. As historian John Ellis so aptly put it, "many battlefields have been cited as being particularly significant in Germany's defeat in the Second World War. Not the least of them should be Detroit."[6] Ultimately, the war cost the United States $304 billion ($5 trillion adjusted for inflation). Washington raised taxes to pay 45 percent of that sum out of current revenues. It financed the remainder through large loans from banks and the sale of savings bonds to millions of Americans.

Strikes cut into total workforce time on the job by less than 1 percent during the war. The National Defense Mediation Board pressured union leaders to avoid strikes. The wage rates of factory workers increased modestly during the conflict, while their total earnings grew significantly due to working much longer hours. Workers were aware, however, that management and agriculture were profiting from the war to a much greater degree. Moreover, the rush to increase production led to a decline in safety standards throughout industry—particularly in the dangerous coal-mining, munitions, and shipbuilding industries. Injuries and deaths on the job went up dramatically. In the summer of 1941, the

Assembly line of B-24 Liberator bombers at Ford's Willow Run plant outside Detroit.
Source: Wikimedia Commons

workers of North American Aviation, a major defense contractor, went on strike. Roosevelt issued a Declaration of Unlimited National Emergency, condemned the strikers as "fifth columnists," and sent the army to take over the plants. Draft boards canceled the deferments of the strikers as well. The strike was soon broken. Once the men returned to work, the government pressured North American to meet their wage demands. In 1943, an even bigger strike broke out in the crucial coal-mining industry, where injury and death rates had reached five hundred per week. Once again, the president seized the mines and threatened to draft the strikers. The strike collapsed, but the miners subsequently received pay increases and somewhat better safety conditions. The public and troops at the front were overwhelmingly hostile to wartime strikes. "Attempts by businesses to ensure that they did not suffer losses, but indeed profited, during the war were seen as perfectly natural; attempts by workers to ensure that their wages kept up with prices and that they retained the freedom to move jobs were seen as attacking the war effort."[7]

Beyond mobilizing industry, the United States made special efforts to harness the power of science to its war effort. To coordinate that work, Washington established the Office of Scientific Research and Development under Dr. Vannevar Bush. American scientists and engineers made thousands of discoveries and innovations that facilitated the war effort, from advances in weather forecasting to new techniques in combat trauma medicine. Creation of the atomic bomb was the marquee project of wartime American science. Although American military and government officials at first failed to perceive the significance of prewar developments in nuclear physics, a personal appeal from Albert Einstein in 1939 finally persuaded President Roosevelt of both the dangers and the opportunities facing the nation. The British government saw those same dangers and opportunities, but it deferred to the Americans because Washington had the resources and the funding for such a complex endeavor.

The result was the Manhattan Project, a top-secret, crash program under the supervision of General Leslie R. Groves. A giant complex quickly sprang up at Oak Ridge, Tennessee, to produce the U-235 isotope. A plant at Hanford, Washington, synthesized plutonium. The experimental work, under the direction of Berkeley physicist J. Robert Oppenheimer, took place at remote Los Alamos, New Mexico. On July 16, 1945, the world's first atomic device was detonated at Alamogordo, New Mexico. Observers witnessed an intense light and a blast of heat followed by the tremendous roar of a shock wave. A mushroom cloud followed a ball of fire forty thousand feet into the air, and the desert surface fused into glass for a radius of eight hundred yards. The sight reminded Oppenheimer of a passage from the ancient Indian Bhagavad Gita, "Now, I am become Death, the destroyer of worlds." The atomic bomb came too late to be used against Germany, but two of them were dropped on Japan—over the protest of some of the scientists. Ultimately, a host of less dramatic scientific and engineering innovations—new materials for the rapid construction of runways on remote Pacific isles, antibiotics to treat wounds, new aircraft designs, and many more—proved more important in winning the war.

The United States enjoyed an extraordinary level of cooperation with its Canadian neighbor. In 1940, Roosevelt and Canadian prime minister Mackenzie King signed the Ogdensburg Agreement on mutual defense and coordination of war production. Canadian farms, electric power stations, and factories contributed substantially to the US war effort. For example, Alcan's aluminum works in Arvida, Canada, a complex over a mile and a half long and three-quarters of a mile wide, supplied huge quantities of this strategic material to the American aircraft industry. Similarly, Mexico contributed to the US and Allied war effort by supplying oil, forest products, and food.

Table 10.1.   Comparative Production: Axis vs. Grand Alliance

	Steel (in millions of metric tons)	Crude Oil (in millions of metric tons)	Tanks and Self-Propelled Guns	Combat Aircraft	Trucks
Axis	191	50.45	51,845	91,408	594,859
United States	334.5	833.2	88,410	197,760	2,328,311
Britain and Soviet Union	146.2	201.4	133,147	204,571	678,043

Source: Figures derived from John Ellis, *Brute Force: Allied Strategy and Tactics in the Second World War* (New York: Viking, 1990), tables 41, 48, 50–51, 54.

In such critical areas as steel, oil, tanks, combat aircraft, and trucks, the United States and its British and Soviet allies massively outproduced their Axis opponents (see table 10.1). Production of aluminum and synthetic rubber also expanded dramatically. So too did the output of America's farms. Despite the drain of agricultural labor to the armed services and to higher-paying factory work, farm production rose by about one-third. Increased mechanization along with the use of new chemical fertilizers and insecticides offset the loss of farmhands. The number of women working in agriculture tripled. In addition, the bracero program lured two hundred thousand Mexicans across the border to work on farms in the West. Expanding farm output was crucial for feeding American forces and the home front, but also in aiding Britain and the USSR.

Historian William O'Neill argues that American mobilization was inefficient, never fully realizing its potential, because the president failed to enforce clear priorities and was also reluctant to delegate too much authority to any subordinate. "Everywhere in Washington there existed duplication and confusion, overlapping grants of authority, and divided tasks."[8] A large part of the problem, however, sprang from partisan politics and the structural bias toward inaction in the American political system. O'Neill concludes, "It is not on FDR's shoulders that blame should be placed for the holdup and confusion, but rather on American democracy, which he managed so skillfully that it avoided defeating itself."[9] The US economy was never fully mobilized during the war; it did not need to be. By 1943, when production had reached a new high, many factories began cutting back because their output exceeded the nation's requirements.

There was a darker side to America's extraordinary wartime productivity. Most defense contracts went to the biggest corporations, usually excluding and sometimes forcing the closure of smaller businesses. Considerable corruption accompanied both the attaining and the execution of those lucrative government contracts. Harry Truman, then a senator from Missouri, led a Senate committee to investigate this proliferating graft and fraud. Arthur Schlesinger Jr., a future Harvard historian but during the war a lower-level civil servant, lamented, "The home front was not a pretty sight at a time when young Americans were dying around the world."[10]

Wartime mobilization literally changed the face of America. Workers poured out of the South and rural areas elsewhere to factory jobs in the big cities of the Midwest and West. Most notably, the population of California increased by 37 percent. In the factories, workers mingled with people from other regions and of other races to a much higher degree than ever before. The urban population exploded. Rapid labor force expansion and geographic mobility caused social problems. There was never enough housing, public transportation, consumer businesses, or day-care facilities to meet the needs of the burgeoning labor force.

Mobilization of so many men into the armed forces and women into industry created "eight-hour orphans" and a rise of modern "teen culture," along with increases in both juvenile delinquency and teenage prostitution.[11]

The nation had not yet fully recovered from the Depression in 1940, but conversion to war production brought back full employment and boosted personal incomes. The war also changed the political climate of the country. FDR's liberal New Deal reforms had already been under attack in the second half of the 1930s. Now the need to unite the business community behind the war effort and garner support from Republicans and conservative southern Democrats meant that social reform took a backseat to maximizing production. As Roosevelt put it, "Dr. Win the War" replaced "Dr. New Deal."

Because of the lingering effects of the Great Depression, initially there was no labor shortage in the American mobilization effort, for in 1940, nine million men were still unemployed. The United States did not reach full employment before 1943. Thereafter, the government sought to solve the labor shortage by recruiting women, though never as effectively as Britain or Russia. The number of women in the workforce rose by nine and a half million (though 71 percent of working-age American women did not work outside the home).[12]

Government propaganda pictured white, upper-middle-class clubwomen abandoning their salons for war work. However, many women who flocked to the defense plants were leaving low-wage service-sector jobs. A famous poster romanticized "Rosie the Riveter," but women new to the factories faced long hours and often dangerous work, continuing gender discrimination, and inadequate housing, child care, and shopping opportunities. In addition, given prevailing ideas about gender roles, society expected women to work simultaneously as full-time factory hands and full-time homemakers. A majority of Americans continued to oppose the idea of work outside the home for married women. America's

Women wiring a bomber at a West Coast aircraft plant in 1942.
Source: Library of Congress

female workers experienced a significant rise in wages and, in some cases, more advancement opportunities than previously available. However, the widespread perception that women had entered the factories only "for the duration," combined with the need to find work for millions of returning servicemen after the war, meant that many women lost their better-paying factory jobs in 1945. Many were forced to return to low-paid work as maids and cooks. Women served in the military in significant numbers as well—and not just as nurses. The WACS and WAVES and female marines performed in many noncombatant roles as clerks, drivers, and pilots who shuttled aircraft from the factories to bases. Many men were hostile to women entering the factories and regiments. They realized that the employment of women freed them for combat duty.

RACE IN THE AMERICAN WAR EFFORT

The Second World War was, in part, a war against racism, just as it was also, in part, a race war. Americans of African and Asian ancestry faced discrimination and violence at home. American society was not yet ready to extend the blessings of the Four Freedoms to its own nonwhite citizens. Leaders of minority ethnic groups as well as New Deal liberals hoped that the struggle against Nazism would discredit domestic racism and lead to the extension of full civil rights to all Americans. That was not to be. Although it made some progress during the war years, the administration felt constrained to go slowly in challenging American prejudices. In marked contrast, German Americans, who had been victimized during the First World War, and Italian Americans suffered relatively little discrimination. White and fully assimilated, the relatives of Dwight Eisenhower, Lou Gehrig and Joe DiMaggio (New York Yankees baseball team stars), and New York City mayor Fiorello La Guardia were not subjected to the injustices routinely meted out to Asian Americans and African Americans.

Because of pervasive racial discrimination, the mobilization of African Americans for the war effort was halting and controversial. For them, the war was a double struggle against German and Japanese racism abroad and American racism at home. The painful irony of fighting for the Four Freedoms overseas while, for blacks, those very freedoms were denied in the United States, embittered many African American servicemen. Although over a million blacks served in the military, the armed forces were reluctant to use "Negro" troops to their full potential, shunting them into segregated units and employing them mainly for menial tasks as mess men, servants, stevedores, and construction laborers. When urged to banish Jim Crow discrimination from the armed forces, General Marshall responded, "The Army is not a sociological laboratory."[13]

Only late in the war did the armed forces' desperate need for manpower lead to the deployment of African Americans in combat. Examples include the all-black crew (though commanded by white officers) of the destroyer-escort USS *Mason*, which served with distinction in Atlantic convoy duty, and the African American 761st Tank Battalion, which fought courageously, alongside white troops, in the Battle of the Bulge. While the governor of Alabama proclaimed Japanese American soldiers training there to be "honorary white men" for the duration, black troops suffered under segregation and Jim Crow violence. Officers at an Alabama base told their black trainees, "Don't go off the base or you won't come back. You'll be lynched."[14] Black troops suffered discrimination even outside the South. Lloyd Brown, a black soldier, recalled an attempt to eat at a restaurant in Salina, Kansas:

> As we entered, the counterman hurried to the rear to get the owner, who hurried out front to tell us with urgent politeness: "You boys know we don't serve colored here." . . . We ignored him and just stood there inside the door, staring at what we had come to see—the German prisoners of war who were having lunch at the counter.[15]

Sometimes violence erupted on military bases. Dempsey Travis, an African American soldier, recounted what happened when some black troops tried to use the all-white PX (store) at Camp Shenango in Pennsylvania:

> Within minutes a caravan of six trucks loaded with white soldiers in battle-color fatigues . . . drove up and surrounded the area. Cut the street off. The lights went out and they started firing. Firing, firing, firing, just shooting into the goddamn crowd. Everybody started scrambling like hell. I must have run maybe five feet and fell, my friend Kansas beside me. I put my hand on my leg and I could feel something warm running down my pants.[16]

Travis said he saw fourteen or fifteen bodies on the ground when the shooting stopped. Other sources claim that one black soldier died and six others were wounded. A few black units, like the famous Tuskegee Airmen, achieved distinction, but most African Americans in the armed forces endured continuous indignities and occasional violence.

Black Americans faced the same hostility and discrimination in war plants. Many factories at first refused to employ them, while white workers sometimes went on strike because African Americans were hired or promoted. The threat of a massive "Negro" march on Washington pressured the president to issue Order 8802, banning racial discrimination in defense industries and creating the Fair Employment Practices Commission. Unfortunately the FEPC had little enforcement power, so the order was widely ignored. Only the desperate demand for labor in the last years of the war forced reluctant companies to hire black workers. By 1944, more than a million blacks had entered the industrial labor force where they held 7.5 percent of the positions in defense plants, often well-paying, skilled jobs from which they had been barred previously. African Americans were still the last hired, first fired. After the war, many of them were discharged to make room for returning white servicemen. However, their wartime experience of better pay and somewhat better treatment fueled the growing postwar Civil Rights Movement. In historian Ronald Takaki's apt phrase, "the war had given African Americans a taste of the honey of equality."[17]

Outside the factories, hostile race relations continued as before. A major race riot flared in the summer of 1943 on Belle Isle in Detroit, fueled by resident-versus-migrant tensions and racial animus. Thirty-four people were killed, two-thirds of them African Americans, many of them by police and National Guardsmen. Race riots broke out during the war years in Harlem, New York; Mobile, Alabama; Beaumont, Texas; and many other places. Preoccupied with the need to mobilize the white majority in the war effort, the response of the Roosevelt administration to racial injustice was tepid at best.

Hispanic Americans were also the victims of discrimination and violence, especially in the Los Angeles "Zoot Suit Riot" of 1943. There, mobs of club-wielding white servicemen sought out the distinctively dressed teenagers but settled for beating any Hispanics, Filipinos, or blacks they encountered. The military police, shore patrol, and Los Angeles police all looked the other way, while local newspapers blamed the riots on the victims. Only occupation by the military, after a week of rioting, quelled the disturbances. The police just stood by or, worse yet, arrested the victims. Afterward, both police officials and the media praised the rioters for fighting juvenile delinquency.

Racism also devastated the Japanese American population on the West Coast. Unlike German Americans and Italian Americans, who suffered little discrimination during the war, people of Japanese ancestry were labeled an "enemy" population. California governor Culbert Olson made clear the racism underlying this decision: "You know, when I look out at a group of Americans of German or Italian descent, I can tell whether they're loyal or not. . . . But it is impossible for me to do this with the inscrutable orientals, and particularly the Japanese."[18] On February 19, 1942, President Roosevelt signed Executive Order 9066 authorizing the removal of persons of enemy nationalities from areas sensitive to the national defense. The order would affect approximately 120,000 people of Japanese ancestry resident in California, Oregon, and Washington. Not only Japanese citizens visiting the United States on visas but also resident aliens and even US citizens were placed under the control of the War Relocation Authority. General John L. DeWitt, in charge of the Western Defense Command, insisted on the removal of the West Coast Japanese. He argued that "the continued presence of a large, unassimilated, tightly knit racial group, bound to an enemy nation by strong ties of race, culture, custom, and religion along a frontier vulnerable to attack constitute a menace which had to be dealt with."[19]

Initially, the US government intended the internment of Japanese Americans to be a temporary measure in the wake of the Pearl Harbor disaster. In the weeks immediately following Pearl Harbor, the FBI and the military arrested only 3,846 German, Italian, and Japanese visaed aliens and resident aliens, declaring them "dangerous enemy aliens." However, both within the US military and among the American public a clamor arose demanding that the government treat all people of Japanese ancestry in this country as enemy suspects. As the scope of the relocation program grew, its objective changed from a relatively free relocation of Japanese Americans throughout the interior of the country to a policy of imprisoning the evacuees in concentration camps. What had begun as a temporary and limited measure ultimately expanded to include over 120,000 Japanese Americans, of whom over 64 percent were US citizens (either naturalized *Issei* or native-born *Nisei*).

In the racist vernacular of that time, people rationalized that "a Jap is a Jap." Detention became permanent for several reasons. Public opinion strongly opposed the release of Japanese Americans into interior states. The governor of Idaho suggested that "a good solution to the Jap problem would be to send them all back to Japan, then sink the island. They live like rats, breed like rats and act like rats."[20] Beyond that, camp riots broke out in 1942 at Manzanar and other so-called relocation centers. Injustice bred resistance among Japanese American prisoners, and their outbursts of protest were used to justify their continued imprisonment. Suspicion of their supposed disloyalty continued. Loyalty questionnaires given to seventy-five thousand Japanese Americans revealed that 8,700 internees would not unqualifiedly renounce all fealty to the Japanese emperor. While a few of these men may have been fierce Japanese patriots, many of them were reacting bitterly to the injustices inflicted on them. Others, mainly older *Issei*, feared that the United States would soon expel them and, if they renounced the emperor, they would have no country in which to live.

A combination of military misjudgment, fear, hysteria, nativist prejudice, lack of political courage in high places, and greed resulted in the forced expulsion from the West Coast of almost all Japanese Americans, regardless of citizenship. The *Los Angeles Times* told its readers, "A viper is nonetheless a viper wherever the egg is hatched—so a Japanese American, born of Japanese parents—grows up to be a Japanese, not an American."[21] For white farmers, who competed with Japanese truck gardens in California, greed reinforced racism. A white growers' group admitted, "We've been charged with wanting to get rid of the Japs for selfish reasons. We might as well be honest. We do. It's a question of whether the white man lives on the Pacific Coast or the brown man."[22] This expulsion and imprisonment in concentration camps clearly violated Japanese Americans' rights under the Constitution and laws of the United States. Nonetheless, the US Supreme Court initially upheld the legality of the expulsion. Sadly, as historian Ronald Takaki argues, "federal authorities already knew [from internal intelligence reports] that Japanese Americans could be trusted," but the Roosevelt administration was unwilling to buck the military and public sentiment on this hot-button issue.[23] There was very little opposition to relocation and internment. The Justice Department realized the illegality involved but bowed to pressure from the War Department, the White House, and public opinion. Only the American Civil Liberties Union and Quaker groups denounced the process.

The order of expulsion came on relatively short notice. The expellees could bring with them only some clothing, bedding, and utensils. They were forced to settle their family and business affairs very quickly. Under these circumstances, they sold personal property and businesses for pennies on the dollar or simply abandoned them. Japanese Americans lost $6.2 billion ($114.8 billion adjusted for inflation) in property and lost income during the war. Evacuees were taken first to temporary assembly points such as racetracks and fairgrounds. Internee Peter Ota described one such facility: "Santa Anita is a race track. The horse stables were converted into living quarters. . . . The people in the stables had to live with the stench. Everything was communal. We had absolutely no privacy. When you went to the toilet, it was communal. It was very embarrassing for women especially."[24] Eventually the evacuees were sent to permanent concentration camps (dubbed "relocation centers" to avoid the embarrassing comparison with Nazi death camps). Camps sprang up across inland California, Utah, Idaho, Arizona, Colorado, Wyoming, and Arkansas. Most of them were in arid deserts or on swampy land. They consisted in the main of wooden barracks covered with tar paper. These buildings were divided into many one-room apartments shared by a family or by a group of unrelated individuals. Rooms contained only cots and a light bulb. Toilet, laundry, and dining facilities were communal. Facilities for schools, religious observance, and recreation were minimal. Barbed-wire fences enclosed the compounds. Armed troops in watchtowers guarded the camps.

Japanese resident aliens and citizens were interned in Canada as well. Just as in the United States, prejudicial fears of the "Yellow Peril" were common among Canadian whites. At first, all Japanese Canadians were registered and barred from the armed forces. Then, five days after US Order 9066, all Japanese Canadians (citizen and noncitizen alike) were ordered to evacuate the West Coast. Most of their property was confiscated, but only evacuation resisters and Imperial Japanese patriots were interned. Ultimately, 3,964 "disloyal" evacuees were voluntarily or forcibly repatriated to Japan. The rest of the Japanese Canadian population resettled east of the Rocky Mountains.

In contrast to the treatment of Japanese residents of the US mainland and Canada, in Hawaii only a very limited relocation was carried out. Thirty-seven percent of the population there was of Japanese descent—too numerous, too important to the wartime economy, and too influential politically to be mistreated. The military governor of Hawaii, General Delos Emmons, unlike General DeWitt on the mainland, understood that unwarranted persecution of Japanese Americans on the islands would weaken rather than strengthen the island's defense. Moreover, Hawaii was more ethnically diverse and much more cosmopolitan than the population of the US mainland.

By 1943, Army chief of staff General Marshall had come to doubt the necessity as well as the legality and morality of internment. A few thousand internees could leave the camps for jobs in the interior that year, and then many thousands left the following year. Japanese American volunteers also formed the 442nd Regimental Combat Team, which fought in Italy with great distinction and became the most highly decorated army unit in World War II. Others served with the army and marines in the Pacific as translators and interpreters. Order 9066 was rescinded in December 1944. In January 1945, all internees could leave the camps, though about five thousand were still considered dangerous and were banned from the West Coast. In 1968, the US Supreme Court ordered restitution for Japanese American property lost because of the expulsion. President Gerald Ford officially nullified Order 9066 in 1976, and in 1983 the US Congress formally recognized the injustice done to Japanese Americans, authorizing compensation of $20,000 to each still-living victim. A 1982 investigating committee found that internment happened "despite the fact that not a single documented act of espionage, sabotage or fifth column activity was committed by an American citizen of Japanese ancestry or by a resident Japanese alien on the West Coast."[25]

Home Front in Britain and Its Empire

Unlike the United States, which was largely insulated from attack (except for Hawaii and Alaska), the people of the British Isles endured serious bombing from 1940 to 1943, rocket attacks in 1944–1945, the threat of invasion in 1940, and privation caused by the U-boat blockade. Britain inducted almost every able-bodied man between the ages of eighteen and forty into the armed services, except for those engaged in vital industrial or government work. London also mobilized soldiers and sailors from its empire—especially from Canada, Australia, South Africa, and India. A hastily trained and inadequately armed Home Army (or Local Defense Volunteers) of overaged and teenaged recruits augmented their numbers. The government launched a charity campaign to collect rifles, shotguns, and pistols to arm the Home Guard. They freed regular army troops for training and combat by performing such less-demanding tasks as guard duty and dealing with the aftermath of bombing attacks. Other senior citizens served as air-raid wardens, civil defense workers, and enemy aircraft spotters. Women served extensively in noncombat roles in the armed forces. Britain was fully mobilized by 1943, having reached the limit of its manpower reserves.

Depression-era unemployment vanished. With so many men in uniform, Britain mobilized a greater proportion of its women for war work than any other belligerent except the USSR. Fully 70 percent of British women of working age labored full time outside the home (compared to 29 percent in the United States). Women replaced men in the factories, in the civil service, and on the farms. Over eighty thousand women joined the Women's Land Army, replacing men in agricultural labor. Farmland under cultivation increased from twelve million to eighteen million acres during the war. Before the war, Britain had imported most of its food supply. This expansion in cultivated land freed valuable shipping capacity for critical war supplies and raw materials. Most farmers switched from herding and growing various crops to producing wheat and potatoes. Overall, farmers benefited greatly during the war as farm incomes quadrupled.[26]

Strict food rationing was a necessity. The weekly allocation of various foods for each civilian adult in 1940 was:

Butter and lard: 4 ounces
Sugar: 12 ounces
Bacon: 4 ounces
Eggs: 2
Meat: 6 ounces
Tea: 7 ounces

The situation had improved slightly by 1942 when adults received 1.25 pounds of meat, though only two ounces of butter, per week. Rationing continued for eggs, cereals, canned goods, and soap. Cooks used dried egg powder to make scrambled eggs. Coffee lovers often had to make do with "Victory coffee," made of dried, ground acorns. Vegetables, though not rationed, were in short supply. Fruit grown in Britain (apples, pears, strawberries) was available in limited quantities, while imported fruits (bananas, oranges, peaches, etc.) disappeared from the shelves. The Dig for Victory program strongly encouraged people to plant gardens in any spare plot of land. Bread and potatoes remained unrationed and usually available. Those engaged in the hardest physical labor, expectant mothers, and school lunch programs received extra allocations. Despite the government's best efforts, inflation rose steadily. By 1945, food prices reached 170 percent of their 1938 level. A black market thrived for those who could afford it. Wages also rose throughout the war, outpacing inflation, but there were few consumer goods to purchase.

Blackout rules required people to extinguish or cover any light source after dark to foil enemy bombers. Gas masks and bomb shelters became normal parts of life. Beginning in September 1939, one and a half million children were evacuated from cities likely to be bombed. They went to safer suburban and rural locales where they lived with families or in public institutions. During the "Blitz," thousands of Londoners spent uncomfortable nights trying to sleep in the underground stations of the subway system. Under the circumstances, exhaustion, frustration, and a high level of anxiety were common, but the British nation remained determined to defend its islands. Manifold discomforts and deprivation as well as fear and loneliness caused by separation from loved ones affected morale. Rates of divorce, juvenile delinquency, and venereal disease rose. "The worst elements of the bombed streets," Andrew Sinclair tells us, "were the rank smells and rabid cats. A raw and harsh stink pervaded the air, a compound of soot and dust, cinder and the lingering acidity of high explosive. Gas escaping from broken pipes tweaked at the nostrils, and the sweet reek of blood and corpses made the lungs retch."[27]

Prime Minister Churchill is famous for his defiant speeches that galvanized many Britons to endure the dark years of Nazi military victories, the privations of the home front, and the sacrifices that total war entailed. Most historians credit Churchill with pulling together an otherwise divided and dazed nation in 1940. Beyond his undoubted contributions to the British war effort, Churchill's postwar image as an iconic figure emerged in large part because he wrote the most popular memoir-history of the conflict.[28] In the judgment of historian Henry Pelling, "in spite of everything the government was not at all unpopular with the mass of the people."[29] Churchill's personal approval rating among the public reached a high of 70 percent in a Gallup poll early in the war. Battlefield defeats sometimes lowered Parliament's and the public's support for the government, though not their appreciation of the prime minister. Overall, the morale of the British people remained relatively high throughout the war. To that end, the authorities ensured that there was never a shortage of alcohol, cigarettes, or entertainment. The government contemplated taking over the BBC but encountered strong resistance. BBC radio continued reporting both victories and defeats objectively. Official propaganda often failed to inspire, but such popular films as *First of the Few* (retitled *Spitfire* in the United States) and *Henry V* boosted morale. So, too, did the pervasive hope for a better life after the war. Ultimately, however, the widespread understanding of the horror that a Nazi victory would entail kept people working for the war effort.

In May 1940, Winston Churchill formed a coalition government, uniting Conservatives, Liberals, and Labour in support of the war effort. The prime minister brought Ernest Bevin, the best-known British trade union leader, into the government as minister of labor in a further effort to cement "social peace" for the duration of the war. Another Labourite, Clement Attlee, served as deputy prime minister. Churchill kept Neville Chamberlain and Lord Halifax in the cabinet, even though his differences with them were profound, to emphasize the continuity and unity of his administration. Six new ministries were created—Supply, Home Security, Economic Warfare, Information, Shipping, and Food. Parliament continued to function, though an enemy air raid destroyed the House of Commons and no national elections were held until after the defeat of Germany. Government propaganda emphasized that England was fighting for its freedom and for a better future for its people. The 1942 Beveridge Plan (named after the Liberal economist William Beveridge) promised a future in which five "great evils"—squalor, ignorance, want, idleness, and disease—would be eliminated. The plan formed the basis for the sweeping welfare reforms carried out by the Labour Party in the immediate postwar years.

Government control over the economy increased greatly, despite opposition from the business community. A powerful Ministry of Production ensured adequate supplies for the armed forces. Government planning and coordination combined with determined effort by businessmen, trade unions, and the public to produce dramatic results. The output of munitions between 1939 and 1943 grew by an astonishing 600 percent. Britain exceeded German production of aircraft and equaled its production of tanks. The British focused on producing only a few kinds of weapons in each category to maximize production. In the aircraft industry, for example, two fighters (the Spitfire and the Hurricane) and two heavy bombers (the Lancaster and the Halifax) dominated production. Northern Ireland contributed significantly to Britain's output, producing warships, aircraft, tanks, and other war matériel. In contrast, Ireland (Eire) remained neutral, though it offered some limited cooperation with the Allies.

However, the success of Britain's war industries scarcely masked a deep problem. Expenditures for the First World War had seriously weakened England's financial position. The Second World War completed that process. Britain quickly depleted its fiscal reserves and liquidated its overseas investments to meet war expenses. London borrowed heavily to continue the war, resulting in a £3.4 billion ($8.2 trillion in today's dollars) debt at its conclusion. By 1940, the UK depended on American financing of its war effort. The American Lend-Lease program supplied great quantities of food, oil, and military equipment.

Britain, like the United States, sought to mobilize its scientists and engineers in support of the war effort. The government created a Scientific Advisory Committee, attached to the War Cabinet and led by Frederick Lindemann (Lord Cherwell). They pursued what Churchill called "the wizard war." Those wizards made thousands of discoveries and inven-

German "Enigma" cipher machine. British decoding of German messages was the most important scientific achievement during the war.
Source: Getty

tions, from radar technology to the first practical uses of penicillin, that furthered the war effort. The Ultra decoding system was by far the most important of these.

The Wehrmacht encoded its secret messages on a machine known as Enigma. The messages were then broadcast over the radio in standard Morse code. The Enigma device used a system of rotors and electrical switches to change the letters in a plaintext message into other letters, transforming the message into apparent gibberish. The intended recipient typed the gibberish into his machine, which transformed it back into German. Rotor settings changed every eight hours, and each message had its own randomly selected key. The Germans believed their system to be unbreakable. Polish military intelligence had broken an earlier, less-sophisticated version of the system in 1932 and reverse engineered a copy of the machine. Just before the war began in 1939, the Germans upgraded the device, making it ten times more complex. At that point, the Poles turned the project over to their French and British allies.

The British established a top-secret code-breaking center at the Government Code and Cypher School at Bletchley Park, fifty miles northwest of London. The problem was extremely complex—discerning the proper rotor order, rotor settings, and plug-board settings. The possible combinations ran to ten to the nineteenth power. Alan Turing, a brilliant mathematician, led a team of cryptographers, linguists, and engineers who used advanced statistics and mathematical theory to invent an electromechanical cryptanalytical "bombe" device (i.e., the first computer) for replicating the Enigma machine's settings. This was not a onetime victory but an ongoing process of responding continuously to changes the Germans made in their encoding machines.

The extent of the Nazi empire and the often rapid movement of German forces meant that the Wehrmacht frequently had to rely on radio communications, which could be intercepted and decoded. By 1941, the Allies could read at least some of the messages from the army, navy, Luftwaffe, police, and railway system. The information they obtained was invaluable, though it is difficult to assess the overall impact of Ultra intelligence on the Allied conduct of the war. Simply intercepting enemy transmissions and decoding them accomplished little if the messages were not perceptively analyzed, delivered to field commanders in a timely manner, and acted upon effectively. Ultra provided vital data on the U-boats in the Battle of the Atlantic as well as excellent information about the Germans' order of battle on D-Day, but only hints foreshadowing their Ardennes offensive in 1944. Knowing his opponent's strength, disposition, and intent did not propel the cautious Montgomery to dramatic breakthrough and encirclement victories. Moreover, Ultra relied entirely on intercepting enemy radio messages. Wherever the Germans were able to rely mainly on landline communications, as in Sicily, for example, Ultra provided little useful information.

The factors involved in winning a battle are numerous and complex. Knowing the enemy's intent in advance is a great advantage, but it is not the sole key to victory. Nevertheless, after the war General Eisenhower claimed that Ultra was a "decisive" element in the Allied victory. Sir Harry Hinsley, the official historian for Britain's wartime intelligence program, concluded that the war could not have been won without Ultra.[30] Ultra was certainly very important, but that judgment overestimates its value (since the Soviet army defeated the Germans on the eastern front with relatively little Ultra information from its Western allies). London and Washington did not even inform Moscow about this project, though Stalin knew of it from his spies. The operation at Bletchley Park had the highest security protection (hence the label "Ultra Secret") and was kept secret until the 1970s. Just as in the United States, the national emergency did not eliminate labor unrest. According to a team of researchers, "the image of a nation united in self-sacrifice must be heavily qualified: 940,000 working days were lost in strikes in 1940, 3,714,000 in 1944."[31]

Just as on the American West Coast, fear of spies and saboteurs swept much of the British population, especially after the fall of France and during the Battle of Britain. The government interned German and Italian aliens living in England in prison camps, even though most of them were Jews or other anti-Nazi or anti-Fascist refugees. From 1942 onward, the number of US troops in Great Britain began to swell, leading one historian to characterize their presence as "the American occupation of Britain."[32] Britons complained that the "Yanks" were "oversexed, overpaid, overfed, and over here." "War brides," the marriage of English women to Americans, Canadians, and other Allied servicemen, became a common phenomenon.

AN EMPIRE AT WAR

For Churchill, mobilizing for total war also meant bringing the entire empire into play. Three of the four most important constituents of the empire and Commonwealth rallied to the cause with little resistance (Canada, Australia, and South Africa), but India was torn by divisions. Mahatma Gandhi, Jawaharlal Nehru, and most of the leaders of the Indian National Congress condemned fascism and supported the struggle against the Axis. They were angered, however, that the British viceroy for India, Lord Linlithgow, brought the country into the war without even consulting Congress leaders. They offered to support Britain's war effort in return for a promise of independence, but Churchill declined the offer.

Against Churchill's wishes, Chiang Kai-shek visited Gandhi and Nehru in February 1942. Although Chiang hoped for the end of all imperialist domination in Asia, he did not want to see India convulsed by rebellion during the war because he knew how vital the subcontinent was to the British war effort and to the survival of Nationalist China. Indian troops made up a large part (two and a half million soldiers) of British imperial forces. Moreover, at this point India was China's only remaining supply base. The two Indian leaders promised not to hinder British support for China, but they would not unreservedly support the English war effort. Gandhi subsequently wrote to Chiang that, although opposition to British rule must continue, he would "guarantee that all of [his] actions [would] be so calculated as to avoid benefiting Japan in its aggressions against China."[33] Gandhi and Nehru launched the "Quit India" movement, calling for rapid progress toward full independence. The series of humiliating British defeats in Southeast Asia at Japanese hands greatly stimulated nationalist feelings in India. Gandhi demanded the immediate removal of all British and American troops from India, as their presence exacerbated the food crisis and posed a sexual threat to the female population. Not all Indians objected to the "occupation" of the country by British and US troops. Military bases required a great many local workers who earned good wages, while individual soldiers hired manservants for thirty-five cents a week. Prostitution also flourished to service the foreign troops.

British authorities responded to the Quit India campaign by imprisoning over one hundred thousand Congress members, including the party's top leaders. Anger rose in much of the urban population and in some parts of the countryside, especially among students. Demonstrations, strikes, and other acts of civil disobedience proliferated. The 1939 Defense of India Act had given police and the civil service greatly expanded power to crush any opposition. In India and elsewhere in its dominions, "the British Empire used forced labour, broke international law, arrested and tortured without trial or gunned down unarmed protestors, even while (and because of) fighting the 'good' war."[34] Over a thousand rebels were killed and as many as ninety thousand were arrested when the rebellion was crushed by force. Fortunately for Britain, the various Indian princes recognized the importance of the British Raj to their own positions. So too did most of the Indian army, which was vital to British defenses in Asia and North Africa, and so it maintained its discipline and loyalty. "The ideological desire [among Indian soldiers] to defeat the Axis," Khan argues, "was strong especially amongst those who had seen action"[35]

Subhas Chandra Bose, a former president of the Indian National Congress, broke with the other Congress leaders by refusing to denounce the Axis. Instead, he traveled to Nazi Germany in January 1941, participated in the Greater East Asia Conference in Tokyo in 1943, and subsequently led the pro-Japanese Indian National Army. The INA fought alongside Japanese troops in the Imphal campaign. The Rani of Jhansi Regiment was the most radical element in the INA—an all-female unit that fought not only for independence but also for the abolition of all caste, class, religious, and gender discrimination. Bose successfully recruited emigrant Indians throughout Southeast Asia, with whom his violently anti-British message resonated. His radio broadcasts also drew a wide audience in India itself.

A great and partially man-made famine struck the province of Bengal in India from July to November 1943. The previous year a cyclone had depleted the already limited rice supply. Nonetheless, large quantities of grain were exported to feed British imperial forces. "The government," Khan writes, "severely overestimated the Indian peasant's ability to cut back, living as he or she often did on the margins of viable existence in the first place."[36] Calls for "sacrifice" in America meant doing without a new car or bacon every morning. In Britain, it meant eating little fresh fruit and lots of corned beef. In India, it meant famine. Government officials in India responded slowly and ineptly to the crisis. British authorities refused to divert any food shipments to aid the starving in Bengal. Churchill despised the Indians and viewed the food crisis as just punishment for the Quit India movement.

In the judgment of historian Lizzie Collingham, when the war inevitably created food shortages in many parts of the British Empire, "racism was the guiding principle which determined where hunger struck."[37] Approximately three million people starved to death in this famine. There was hunger throughout British colonies in Africa and on Mauritius as well. In Collingham's judgment, "Britain was never as ruthless as Germany and Japan in its exploitation of its empire's resources, nor did it engage in deliberate acts of murder or dispossession, but its officials and politicians did act according to an unspoken food hierarchy which gave the lowest priority to the needs of the empire's colonial inhabitants."[38]

Home Front USSR

"Total war" was no abstract phrase for the Soviet peoples. The war profoundly shaped the lives of all Soviet citizens. No other belligerent state mobilized its population so fully or required so much sacrifice of its people. For almost four years of desperate struggle, most Soviet citizens experienced privation, hunger, and endless toil as well as the tragic loss of numerous family members and friends. Some writers suggest that the Soviet Union won the Great Patriotic War only because it relied on enormous distances and bottomless manpower. That is a myth. The USSR won the war because it successfully mobilized its large, but by no means unlimited, population, effectively restructured its industry, and modernized its army so that it no longer relied solely on masses of men.

Life was unimaginably hard for the Soviet peoples on the home front. The government ordered the mobilization of every able-bodied adult for the war effort. Over thirty-four million people, mostly men, served in the armed forces during the war. Male peasants not inducted into the army were mobilized for factory work. That left mainly women, children, and old people to work on the collective farms. By 1942, women comprised 73 percent of the rural labor force, while children aged twelve to sixteen accounted for another 17 percent of farmworkers. There were few tractors available, and most horses were requisitioned by the army; it was not unusual to see teams of women pulling plows through the fields. The transformation of Soviet agriculture to collective farming since 1929, though it decreased the productivity of the farms, nonetheless enabled the government to extract food from the countryside more effectively than any other combatant. The state took 90 percent of what the farmers produced. Children were required to sacrifice a normal childhood and to instead adopt adult responsibility and discipline. Long hours of arduous labor replaced play. Children paid a high price for their contribution to the war effort—high mortality rates, malnutrition, stunted growth, impaired cognitive ability, many work-related injuries, and emotional damage.[39]

The situation was only slightly better in the cities. Here, too, women and teenagers supplied over half the industrial labor force. Industrial work was arduous—typically eleven or more hours per day, six days per week. The famous physicist Andrei Sakharov described women working in a cartridge factory:

> They sat at the deafening machines hour after hour, in huge, dimly lit rooms, hunched over and perched cross-legged on their stools to keep their wooden shoes

off the cold floor, which was flooded with water and lubricants. Their faces were hidden by kerchiefs but when I caught a glimpse of them, I could see that they were lifeless, drained by fatigue.[40]

Food was strictly rationed (though collective farmers and the unemployed received no ration cards). The rural population depended heavily on potatoes, one of the few foods not rationed. The best-provisioned workers received as much as 2,015 calories per day, while the lowest group (children) got only 944 calories.[41] The bread ration—the staple of the diet—varied by occupational category. Soldiers were supposed to receive nine hundred grams per day, factory workers eight hundred grams, other employees five hundred grams, and dependents and children four hundred grams.[42] A recent study concludes, "No group, with the exception of leading political and economic officials, received enough food through the ration system to cover its biological needs."[43] The diet was monotonous—bread and potatoes, occasionally supplemented by small amounts or meat or fat. Sixteen million urbanites grew their own gardens in courtyards, parks, and along roadways. Collective farmers had small private plots, selling any surplus legally in town markets. Also, those with something to sell—family valuables, pilfered work materials, sex—supplemented their meager diet on the black market. Most factories opened their own canteens to feed workers at least one meal a day to keep up production. Inevitably, some people resorted to theft, embezzlement, and gaming the system to secure more food.

The rationing system involved making some very hard choices because the government did not have enough food available to feed even those with ration cards. The Soviet central planning system worked reasonably well in feeding the military and those engaged in heavy factory labor, but the rest of the population had to rely on whatever local sources of

Soviet fighter pilot aces in front of a Lend-Lease P-39 Airacobra manufactured by Bell Aircraft Company, Buffalo, New York.
Source: Wikimedia Commons

food they could find. Overall, civilian consumption of food and consumer goods fell by 40 percent. Clothing, shoes, and soap virtually vanished from the stores. Malnourishment and overwork made people much more susceptible to disease—especially typhus, typhoid fever, and tuberculosis. Hunger was nearly universal and starvation not uncommon, though not as prevalent as in the German-occupied section of the country. American Lend-Lease aid provided vitally needed canned meat, nuts, dehydrated milk and eggs, fruits, and vegetables for the Red Army and some industrial workers. Nonetheless, most servicemen and civilians were hungry all the time. Overall, the Soviet standard of living fell dramatically. Only a combination of ruthless disciplinary measures, German brutality in the occupied zones, and Allied Lend-Lease aid prevented a collapse of the Soviet war effort in 1942.

The authorities set high production quotas for each worker and tied the workers' food rations to achieving their quotas. Typical factory shifts lasted twelve to sixteen hours, six (sometimes seven) days a week. Although workers were legally bound to their jobs, Wendy Goldman and Donald Filtzer conclude, "repression played a surprisingly small role in the willingness of Soviet workers to endure so much and contribute so mightily to the victory."[44] Millions of men and women, children, and old people were drafted for the construction of defensive fortifications—tank traps, bunkers, pillboxes, trenches, and barricades. The regime released a million prisoners from the gulag prison camps for military service. Millions more inmates worked in Soviet factories and mines, under much worse conditions than the free workers. Housing remained in critically short supply throughout the war. The regime also had to deal with tens of thousands of war orphans and twenty-five million people made homeless by the war.

The food crisis was even worse in those areas of the USSR that were liberated in 1943 and 1944. As they retreated, the Germans took what they could carry and burned or slaughtered the remainder. The Soviet authorities gave top priority to supplying the Red Army and winning the war. There was little food left to spare for hungry people in the liberated zones. Famine was rampant. The government was also slow to resume public services (water, electricity, transportation, and even basic law and order). Even if residents of the liberated territories avoided starvation, they still faced the regime's suspicion for living under German rule. Virtually all the surviving adults underwent a "filtration" process carried out by the NKVD. People had to prove they were not collaborators.

Soviet authorities used civilian militia to supplement the Red Army. Initially, hundreds of thousands of men and women volunteered spontaneously to defend their homeland (which suggests that, contrary to some historical accounts, a great many Soviet citizens were not looking forward to their "liberation" from the Communist system by a foreign conqueror). As many as four million people were enrolled in the militia during the war. Minimally trained and lightly armed, these formations were massacred when thrown into combat. Appalled at the senseless loss of skilled workers, in 1942 the government exempted some of the most highly skilled categories of workers from military service.

Mobilizing the national economy for total war was, in one respect, easier for Moscow than it was for Washington, London, Berlin, or Tokyo. As a socialist state, the Soviet government already had complete control over the economy, though the overcentralization of the war effort caused bottlenecks and inefficiencies. However, Soviet authorities had not prepared to fight a protracted, total war. Stalin had long held the most powerful post in the Soviet system—general secretary of the Communist Party. Just before the war began, he assumed the highest government position—chairman of the Council of People's Commissars. He also became people's commissar of defense, and a month later he assumed supreme command of the armed forces. A State Defense Committee (GKO), also chaired by Stalin, undertook overall direction of the war effort, including management of the economy.

During Operation Barbarossa, German forces occupied the industrial heartland of the USSR. Soviet authorities responded by evacuating some 2,500 industrial enterprises before the advancing enemy could capture or destroy them. For example, they moved a vitally important T-34 tank factory from Kharkov to the distant Ural Mountains in 1941. As much as 10 percent of the Soviet Union's prewar productive capacity relocated to the Urals, the Volga region, western Siberia, and Kazakhstan. Ten million workers, engineers, and managers were sent eastward along with their equipment. Counting refugees, some twenty-five million people were swept up in this human tidal wave. This massive undertaking required eight thousand freight cars to move one large metallurgical complex from Ukraine to Magnitogorsk in the Urals. There had been no prewar planning for mass evacuations because authorities assumed that the Red Army would repulse any attack on the USSR quickly.

The railway system was stretched beyond its capacity in moving troops to the fronts, supplying raw materials to industry, and conveying both equipment and evacuees to the East. Necessary and heroic as it was, the emergency movement of so many people and resources produced chaos in the economy and among much of the population. For example, the Evacuation Council ordered a Moscow tire factory to divide its operations between Orsk, 1,090 miles southeast, and Semipalatinsk in Kazakhstan (782 miles apart). The authorities then decided to move everything to Orsk, only to decide two weeks later to split the enterprise between Petropavlovsk and Chimkent in Kazakhstan. Finally they divided the operation among three widely separate locations, Omsk, Cheliabinsk, and Kirov.[45] In some cases, before an available building could be found or new factories built, equipment was unloaded from the trains and installed on bare ground, while workers lived in dugouts. Evacuated workers and refugees endured a great many hardships and were not always welcomed by the population of their destination. Industrial output declined temporarily in the winter of 1941–1942, but Soviet plants were soon outpacing German ones. For example, in 1942 the USSR built 24,700 tanks while Germany produced only 6,200.[46]

An industrial revolution took place in the Urals, along the Volga, and in Central Asia. Magnitogorsk, Cheliabinsk (known during the war as "Tankograd"), and other Urals cities became industrial boomtowns. The introduction of mass-production techniques also improved productivity. For instance, it took 8,000 man-hours to build a T-34 tank in 1941, but only 3,700 in 1943. While overall industrial production did not recover to 1940 levels until 1944, the manufacturing of weapons and military equipment increased every year until it reached two and a half times the 1940 level in 1944.[47] The proportion of GDP allocated to national defense reached an incredible 55 percent in 1942. Soviet military industries had to produce such extraordinary quantities of equipment because of the unprecedented level of losses in combat. "At the worst, in the winter of 1941–1942, the Soviet front-line forces would be losing one-sixth of their aircraft, one-seventh of their guns and mortars and one-tenth of their armoured equipment *every week*."[48]

The Soviet peoples were the victims of scorched-earth policies carried out by enemy forces and their own government. In 1941–1942, the Soviet authorities deliberately destroyed factories and infrastructure (bridges, railways, etc.) to deny them to the advancing enemy. For instance, Soviet sappers blew up the huge dam and hydroelectric power plant at Dnepropetrovsk on the Dnieper River. Only the Chinese people experienced more devastation at the hands of their own regime. As brutal as these measures were, they kept vital resources, on which the Germans were counting, out of enemy hands. Some Soviet citizens suffered at the hands of their government in yet another way. As German troops advanced in the summer and fall of 1941, the political police (the NKVD) murdered many of their prisoners rather than risk their escape or capture by the enemy. When the tide of battle reversed by 1943, the retreating Germans destroyed everything of value and massacred large numbers of civilians. As Soviet forces liberated the western regions of the USSR, they found only between 13 and 19 percent of factories still intact.[49]

There was considerable panic, drunkenness, rioting, and defeatism in response to the Nazis' early victories. "There was a real danger," Barber and Harrison suggest, "of the state's authority collapsing and society descending into chaos."[50] The response of the Soviet people to German aggression was far from uniform. Even among the mostly Russian residents of Moscow, some people responded patriotically, determined to unite in their nation's hour of peril, while others spread defeatist rumors and even looked forward to a German victory, believing that the Nazis would kill the Communists and Jews but not the Russians.[51] The Soviet regime employed a combination of repression and appeals to patriotism to rally its people to defend their country.

The Germans expected to benefit from widespread disaffection on the part of the oppressed Soviet peoples, but their own atrocious behavior forced Soviet citizens to rally behind the war effort, no matter how much some of them may have disliked Stalin and the Communist Party. While the Nazis alienated the Soviet peoples in many ways, Stalin's regime appealed to powerfully held but non-Marxist values to stimulate national resistance.

The standard injunctions to fight for Stalin and the Communist Party never disappeared, but they were effectively supplemented by appeals to nationalism and religion (two taboo subjects for good Marxists). Moscow characterized the struggle against the invaders not as "the great anti-imperialist war" but as "the Great Patriotic War." Russia's imperial history, previously denigrated as an age of exploitation, was now resurrected to stimulate patriotic resistance to the enemy. One mass-produced poster depicted a Soviet soldier and behind him the silhouettes of a World War I–era Russian soldier, a Napoleonic-era Russian trooper, and a Muscovite warrior. The message was clear—foreigners have often attacked the motherland, but the Russian people have always rallied to defend it.

The military heroes of the Russian past (Aleksandr Nevskii, Dmitri Donskoi, Kuzma Minin, Prince Pozharskii, Aleksandr Suvorov, and Mikhail Kutuzov) reappeared on posters, medals, and postage stamps. Sergei Eisenstein's 1938 film *Aleksandr Nevskii*, portraying the prince's battle against invading Teutonic Knights, which was pulled from theaters after the signing of the Nazi-Soviet Pact, reopened across the country in 1941. This was not a one-way street; there is evidence that the massive outpouring of state-sponsored, patriotic histories, novels, plays, and films found a highly receptive and enthusiastic audience.[52] Red Army soldiers were especially voracious consumers of works glorifying Russia's military history. Those who were reluctant to fight for the Soviet Union rose in defense of Mother Russia. Most historians have explained this rehabilitation of the Russian past as a pragmatic response to the wartime emergency, but Stalin's regime had already begun to curry nationalist sentiment in the 1930s.[53] Historian David Brandenberger calls this phenomenon "National Bolshevism"—an amalgamation of Marxism-Leninism and Russian patriotism in the service of regime consolidation, industrialization, and national defense.

Similarly, having persecuted the Russian Orthodox Church and all religious expression since the Bolshevik Revolution, in 1943 the regime made a truce with the church. Moscow understood that, despite its long campaign to stamp it out, religious belief remained a potent

Wartime Soviet poster with Red Army soldiers and tanks advancing; behind them are images of thirteenth-century Russian prince Aleksandr Nevskii, Napoleonic-era general Mikhail Kutuzov, and Russian civil war commander Vasilii Chapaev.
Source: Shutterstock royalty-free images

motivator for many Soviet citizens. Stalin permitted the election of a new patriarch (a post long vacant) and lessened persecution of the church as long as priests would preach resistance to the invader. Orthodox Church authorities raised 150 million rubles for national defense and promptly excommunicated clergy in the occupied areas who collaborated with the invader. The regime established a new commissariat for religious affairs, which some people irreverently labeled the Narkombog (People's Commissariat for God). The accommodation with the church was unpopular with party activists, but Stalin judged it necessary to rally a segment of the Soviet population less susceptible to regime propaganda and to placate foreign opinion. Why he waited until 1943, when the worst military crises had passed, remains an open question. Historian Steven Miner suggests that the policy shift had more to do with countering religious separatism in Ukraine and that it played a role in pacification efforts in Ukraine and Belorussia after their liberation from the Germans.[54] In addition, legitimizing Christianity was meant to reassure the faithful in Britain and America that the Soviet regime was no longer the godless persecutor of believers.

Many people, especially in the cities, were atheists and believers in the Soviet system. For them, as historian Amir Weiner argues, "the war was universally perceived as the Armageddon of the Revolution, the ultimate clash dreaded yet expected by the first generation to live in a socialist society."[55] Moreover, beyond government propaganda, the war fostered a spontaneous sense of community and purpose among the Russian people. As historian Richard Stites notes, "a community of honest, deep, and shared sorrow as well as the near unanimity in the hatred of the enemy helped to reshape national consciousness—to an extent that the old revolutionary élan could never dislodge."[56]

The regime tightly controlled information about the war disseminated to the public. All privately owned radios were confiscated. The Soviet Information Bureau censored the war news heavily, minimizing German successes and exaggerating Russian victories—though it proved impossible to stop bad news from spreading by word of mouth. The authorities used documentary filmmaking to good effect, too. At first there was nothing positive to show, but after the Battle of Moscow in December 1941, newsreels featured captured German soldiers. More so than in other belligerent countries, Soviet documentaries depicted some of the real horror of war. It was an effective technique in stirring hatred for the cruel enemy and determination to fight him.

Feature films made their contribution as well, after the industry evacuated to the safety of Central Asia. "People craved movies," historian Peter Kenez tells us; "they wanted to be taken away from their everyday miseries; they wanted hope; they wanted their faith in ultimate victory to be reinforced."[57] Prewar films with patriotic messages returned to the theaters, especially *Aleksandr Nevskii*, *Suvorov*, and *Peter the Great*. Movies made during the war emphasized heroism, stoic determination to endure and resist, and the barbarity of the enemy. Audiences found films about the resistance behind German lines, especially by female partisans, particularly moving, as they depicted the bravery of the guerrillas, the evil of the invaders, and the treachery of collaborators. Viewers came away from these films with an urgent desire for vengeance. Most wartime films stressed specifically Russian patriotism, though some movies depicted "the friendship of peoples"—typically showing Russians, Georgians, Latvians, and Central Asians fighting together against a common foe. While the suffering of the Soviet peoples was depicted frequently, the special horror facing Soviet Jews at German hands was largely ignored. The Kremlin did not wish to portray its war effort as a campaign to save the Jews given the extent of anti-Semitism still prevalent in the country.

Cities and towns in the USSR liberated by the Red Army were devastated. Beyond destruction caused by combat, the Germans systematically looted, destroyed, and burned as much as possible. Violent gangs of deserters and orphaned teenagers, often armed with abandoned weapons, roamed the streets. Robberies, assaults, and rapes happened frequently. Infanticide of babies from German fathers was common. Food was scarce. In the countryside, the Germans had slaughtered livestock and burned crops. They had also kidnapped many able-bodied adults to work as slave laborers in the Reich. The civil authorities were slow to reestablish law and order and to provide aid for destitute citizens. Supporting the war effort was the top priority; everything else had to wait. The reestablishment of urban infrastructure—transportation, water, electricity, sewage, medical care, food distribution—took many months.

Economist James Millar argues that "it is clear that the majority of the Soviet population accepted the sacrifices imposed upon it by World War II, and the minority was coerced to go along."[58] Goldman and Filtzer contend that "the state's ability to maintain control through coercion was limited," and "many of these [government] mobilizing efforts would have faltered without broad popular support and participation."[59] However, the use of terror against both real and imagined opponents had always been a part of the Soviet system. That did not change during the war. Many military officers, experienced administrators, technical specialists, scientists, engineers, and others were executed on trumped-up charges of Trotskiism and treason. This was a dysfunctional element of the system that harmed the war effort.

A particularly cruel and tragic aspect of the war years involved the forced deportation of non-Russian ethnic minority peoples. These included the Korean population of the Soviet Far East in 1937; Poles, Romanians, and Baltic peoples in 1939–1941 and again in

1944–1945; Volga Germans in 1941; and the Crimean Tatars, Kalmyks, Chechens, and other non-Slavic groups from the Crimean Peninsula and the Caucasus Mountains region in 1944. Altogether about 3.3 million Soviet citizens were deported to various destinations in Central Asia, Siberia, and the Urals. Although these operations were not designed as extermination campaigns, as many as 43 percent of the deportees died from starvation, exposure, disease, and violence. The expellees lost what few civil rights they possessed under Soviet law. They were replaced in their homelands by Russian and Ukrainian settlers.

The motives for the brutal expulsions were varied. Expulsion of Poles, Romanians, and Baltic peoples from their homelands was selective—meant to eliminate likely sources of opposition in these areas newly annexed by the USSR. Elsewhere, ethnic expulsions arose from a combination of causes: the desire to move potentially "unreliable" populations from areas threatened with enemy attack, misinformation and gross exaggeration about the proportion within each ethnic group that had collaborated with the Germans, long-standing prejudices against the ethnic minorities combined with a growing spirit of chauvinism among the Russian people, and the culture of paranoia and denunciation that pervaded the Stalinist political system.

Whole nations—Volga Germans, Crimean Tatars, Kalmyks, and others—were ripped from their native lands and expelled to remote parts of the country. There had been some instances of active resistance to the Soviet war effort among these peoples. In 1941–1942, many people in the Chechen-Ingush republic evaded the call to military or civil service and began dismantling the collective farm system. An anti-Soviet rebellion flared in Kyrgyzstan in 1942. However, most of the deportees had committed no crime; the regime viewed them as *potentially* guilty. These paranoia-driven operations required large allocations of transport resources (trains, fuel, etc.) even though they were desperately needed elsewhere for the war effort. It was a human tragedy on a massive scale. Most of the deportees were women, children, and older people, because virtually all the able-bodied men were serving in the armed forces. Their destinations were poorly prepared to receive them, already overcrowded with earlier waves of war refugees, and inhospitable, leading to high death rates in the first two years.

Home Front China

The industrially and technologically developed states of Europe and North America mobilized all their resources to compete effectively against their enemies. Underdeveloped China could not meet this challenge. Nonetheless, both Nationalist and Communist leaders strove to maximize the national war effort. The Organic Law for the War of Resistance and National Reconstruction, proclaimed in 1938, identified freeing China from foreign occupation and realizing Sun Yat-sen's Three People's Principles as the primary goals of the war. That was to be accomplished under the leadership of the Guomindang and Generalissimo Chiang Kai-shek. As historian Rana Mitter explains:

> Chongqing became symbolic of a new compact between state and society, namely that in a newly forged China the state should demand much more of its population as it faced a test that could destroy the nation, and that the citizenry should expect much more in return from those who governed them. The underlying compact in Yan'an [i.e., the Communist capital] was similar, but raised to an even greater level with revolution rather than reform at the heart of the Communist project.[60]

Throughout the war years, between eighty and a hundred million Chinese (or between 15 and 20 percent of the population) became refugees. It was, in the judgment of historian Diana Lary, "one of the greatest upheavals in Chinese history. It tore the fabric of society to ribbons. The effect of the refugee flights was that the social and government hierarchy in much of the occupied areas was decapitated. The elite's decisions about whether to stay or flee undermined traditional elite dominance. The *ancient regime* ceased to exist."[61] The Japanese deliberately bombed all the larger market towns within their reach and practiced rape, arson, and indiscriminate killing on a wide scale to terrify the population as well as to hinder Nationalist defense and mobilization efforts. Soon, masses of frightened, hungry, and dirty refugees clogged every road, railway line, and river radiating outward from the enemy axis of advance. The refugees dragged with them whatever possessions they could carry as well as their children and invalids. Journalist Freda Utley witnessed heartbreaking scenes:

> Many [families] had been on the march for weeks, some for months. Families which had set out with five or six children had reached Hankou with only one or two. Small girl children were scarce; when the mother and father have no more strength to carry the little children, and when the smaller children are too exhausted to move another step, some have to be left on the road to die.[62]

Beyond the danger of attack by Japanese bombers or patrols, refugees also had to fear assaults by bandit gangs that proliferated as local government disintegrated. Bands of undisciplined Nationalist army stragglers presented an additional danger. Such massive migrations brought tragedy to many of those involved and had a destabilizing effect both on the areas they left and on the lands to which they fled. Fleeing their homes was especially hard on the Chinese because of their deeply rooted Confucian concepts of family and place. Exhausted and undernourished, many refugees fell victim to epidemic diseases—cholera, dysentery, encephalitis, typhoid fever, and malaria. The Japanese also spread bubonic plague–infested fleas behind Chinese lines.

The Nationalist government developed programs to help feed, house, and find jobs for the refugees, but these efforts were never able to keep pace with the demand for help. By 1938, this veritable human tsunami of refugees overwhelmed Chinese officials at every level. Their failure was inevitable because government revenues had fallen by two-thirds while expenses had risen by a third. Moreover, soaring inflation devalued what money the Chongqing regime could send to its beleaguered counties. In Shanghai, many refugees found shelter in the British-dominated International Settlement and the French Concession, though even there brutal Japanese incursions were frequent. After December 1941, the British, French, and American authorities could no longer protect anyone, since they themselves were now enemy aliens.

Eventually a significant minority of refugees decided to return home, even if it meant living under Japanese occupation. For example, Hangzhou, a city of half a million inhabitants, experienced an 80 percent drop in population as the enemy attacked the city in December 1937. By 1940, however, the city had rebounded to 320,000 residents. Even life under enemy occupation seem preferable to some compared to the miserable refugee experience. Concern for survival sometimes trumped patriotic sentiments.

Political repression was pervasive throughout wartime China. Neither Chiang Kai-shek nor Wang Jingwei nor Mao Zedong was committed to pluralist, liberal democracy. Each of them used state terror to ensure their power and control in the chaos that surrounded them. They employed assassinations, bombings, blackmail, torture, and political repression of rivals and dissidents. A vicious, convert war took place among the intelligence services of the three regimes. Chiang had his rivals, critics, and some of the generals who lost major battles imprisoned or shot. His regime maintained a secret concentration camp in Chongqing where inmates were tortured to death. Wang Jingwei and his Japanese masters sponsored a similar reign of terror in the occupied zones.

Mao Zedong had become the undisputed leader of the CCP by 1940. He imposed "Mao Thought" as the inerrant dogma of the Communist movement. In 1942, Mao launched the Rectification Movement—a purge of comrades who were independent-minded or insufficiently dedicated to his cause. The famous left-wing writer Ding Ling was fired from her job, subjected to intense censure, forced to recant her criticisms, and exiled to hard labor for suggesting that all was not perfect in the Yan'an paradise. Art followed the political line mandated by Mao or it disappeared. Intellectuals were forced to repent their political sins and denounce those colleagues who did not bend completely to the leader's will. Like the bizarre Stalinist purges in the USSR, the CCP security police under Kang Sheng arrested loyal comrades and then tortured them to extract false confessions. Each confession then metastasized into dozens more accusations and arrests. Mao still preached "New Democracy" to the outside world, but party control became ever more rigid in Communist areas.

Artists and intellectuals rallied in large numbers to defend the nation. Short stories and novels, plays and street operas, poetry and songs, as well as wall posters, urged the Chinese people to stand against the invader. Some writers and artists produced works comprehensible by ordinary soldiers and peasants. Such work was, of course, suppressed in Japanese-occupied regions and tightly controlled for political correctness in those areas dominated by the Guomindang or the Communists. There was substantial freedom of expression, however, in some of the warlord-controlled regions. Everywhere there was a common message: Support the united front; oppose the Japanese.

While the United States sought to minimize casualties by using its industrial might to maximize firepower, Nationalist China lacked the manufacturing capacity to pursue this strategy. The situation was made worse when, in the first year of the war, Japanese forces overran those few areas along the China coast and lower Yangzi River that were industrially developed. Chiang Kai-shek's government had anticipated that eventuality and made plans to evacuate some of the factories and their skilled workers to the interior of the country. Over 1,500 companies were evacuated, including industries, mining operations, banks, and transport facilities. More than 150 factories moved from Shanghai and elsewhere in coastal China to Wuhan on the middle course of the Yangzi River. Before that city was overrun by the Japanese a year later, numerous munitions, steel, and textile factories as well as food-processing plants moved still farther inland to Sichuan Province. These efforts may have been small compared to the massive transfer of factories achieved by the Soviet regime, but they were vital to continued Guomindang resistance.

The Chinese could manufacture small arms and explosives during the war, but they were unable to produce heavy weapons and aircraft. At their new base in underdeveloped Sichuan Province, the Nationalists lacked the infrastructure—electric generating capacity, steel production, railroads, and roads—to support a major expansion of war industries. As the Chinese economy and the war situation continued to deteriorate, inevitably industrial production declined as well. One depressing report revealed that Chinese arsenals were producing enough bullets, on average, to supply five per soldier per month.[63]

Instead of using mechanized firepower to meet the enemy, China had to rely on its abundant manpower. At its peak in 1944, the Nationalist army numbered 5.8 million men, with millions more Chinese drafted for labor service. Fourteen million men served in the Nationalist armed forces during the course of the war. In the first years of the conflict, recruitment went relatively well, but in the latter stages of the struggle an increasingly desperate regime and some of its warlord generals resorted to mass kidnapping—often force-marching malnourished men tied together in groups hundreds of miles to training bases. Many died along the way. Not surprisingly, the Nationalist army suffered high desertion rates. Hans van de Ven concludes that China's bitter experience in the war sprang not from "incompetence, a lack of will, corruption, or authoritarianism, but the reality that China was an agrarian society that could not cope with the demands imposed by modern warfare"[64]

Throughout the war, inflation bedeviled both the Chongqing government and the Chinese people. Many factors contributed to steep inflation, including food and consumer goods shortages and declining numbers in the labor force due to mass migration and army recruitment. The central cause of the disaster, however, was the regime's unchecked printing presses. Facing mounting defense expenses and unable to collect enough taxes, the government printed more and more currency. Between 1937 and 1942, consumer goods prices rose sixty-six-fold. In 1937, the government had printed about two billion yuan in banknotes. By 1942, the figure was thirty-five billion yuan.[65] By 1945, government banks were issuing over 462 billion in banknotes. Between 1941 and 1944, prices continued to rise by about 10 percent per month. Even repeated American loans failed to stabilize the Nationalist currency. To a limited extent, the rich could buffer the effect of inflation by buying foreign currency, but most Chinese found their income falling while prices skyrocketed.

Ordinary soldiers suffered badly during the inflation. Their meager pay covered only a small fraction of the cost of living. This shortfall damaged the morale of the army as well as its fighting effectiveness. Soldiers who could not afford enough food or proper medical care were in no condition to put up stout resistance to the enemy. Inflation destroyed the savings of the middle class. Teachers and civil servants found their real incomes (down as much as 85 percent) lagging far behind the spiraling cost of living, making them both less effective and more open to corruption. Food prices provide a good example. In 1937, one hundred yuan could purchase two cows. By 1946, that sum paid for only one egg. Inflation eroded the Guomindang's political support by undermining its natural constituency among the middle classes, merchants, and soldiers. The combination of lowered tax receipts, decreasing harvests, and skyrocketing inflation caused the government to abolish or cut back on many of its programs—including support for the military. In the last years of the war, the majority of Chiang Kai-shek's soldiers (those not in elite, American-supplied units) were ill paid, ill equipped, and ill fed. Some units became militarily ineffective because they spent all their time farming, smuggling, and producing opium to support themselves.

Inflation was even higher in the Communist base areas than in the regions under Nationalist control. Mao's answer was self-sufficiency—people should grow their own food, weave their own cloth, and sew their own clothing. Although the Communists had to tax the peasants to meet their expenses, they exempted the poorest 20 percent of the peasantry. Moreover, Mao did not face the enormous cost of maintaining large standing armies as did Chiang Kai-shek. Most of the Communist forces were guerrilla units that were almost entirely self-sufficient. The Communists bolstered their economy and pursued national liberation and class struggle in a way they did not acknowledge publicly—by growing opium and exporting it to Japanese- and Nationalist-controlled areas.[66]

Hunger was a constant companion throughout the war for most of the population of Free China. By the end of 1938, 20 percent of China's rice-producing capacity and 60 percent of its wheat-producing capability were in Japanese hands. Increasing scarcity led to a 500 percent increase in grain prices in Sichuan during the first half of 1940. Rampant inflation caused large landowners to hoard their grain in expectation of even higher future prices. Numerous "rice riots" broke out, which were suppressed by government troops. Moreover, the Japanese frequently staged raids into the unoccupied areas of China for the sole purpose of seizing grain. The country had been a net importer of grains before the war. After the outbreak of war in the Pacific and the Japanese conquest of Southeast Asia, the importation of foreign grain largely ceased.

The Nationalist government introduced programs to expand the number of acres under cultivation and to spread modern agricultural technology. These measures helped to alleviate famine during the first three years of the war, but harvests plummeted in 1940 and thereafter. The government enacted several measures—price controls and requirements that farmers pay taxes in kind—to secure more grain to feed its army, its bureaucracy, and the public, but corruption and the political clout of big landowners undermined these programs. Big landholders could shift the increasing tax bill for financing the war onto their already hard-pressed tenants. Tenants and independent small farmers were crushed under this burden, provoking anger at the regime and, in some cases, sympathy for the Communists. Native place associations (groups of refugees from the same region) and religious/philanthropic organizations such as the Red Swastika (the Buddhist Red Cross) helped to alleviate some of the misery, but there were too many needy people to feed and shelter. Most Chinese deaths during the war (estimated as high as thirty-five million by one scholar) were not caused by combat or atrocities but by starvation and disease.[67]

The worst disaster occurred in 1942–1943 in the province of Henan, where a combination of drought, increasing grain requisition for the army, and local corruption caused a terrible famine. Grain seizures by the Japanese, Nationalists, and Communists combined with the ravages of war, severe weather, and insect infestations to produce a disaster. Grain production in the province fell from a 1936 high of 11,629 tons to a 1942 low of 2,582 tons.[68] Desperate with hunger, some people committed suicide, sold their children, or engaged in cannibalism. A government inspector reported, "Wherever I went, there were refugees fleeing south, begging for food and those who couldn't move any more just dropped dead by the side of the road. You could exchange a child for a few steamed rolls."[69] Journalist Theodore White reported that "some families sold all they had for one last big meal, then committed suicide."[70] Given the diminished harvests in 1940 and 1941 and increasing government grain requisitions, there would have been hunger in Henan under the best of circumstances. Mass starvation, however, was a man-made tragedy. Counterproductive policies from Chongqing combined with incompetence and corruption on the part of local officials to create a disaster. There were granaries in the province meant to provide relief in times of famine, but many of them were empty because the officers in charge of them had already stolen the grain and sold it for personal profit. There were grain stores available in adjoining provinces, but incompetence and petty rivalries kept those supplies from reaching the needy in Henan. Approximately four million people died in this famine.

The situation was almost as bad, at least initially, in the areas controlled by the Communists. After the GMD-CCP alliance broke down and the Nationalist government stopped sending funds to the Eighth Route Army, but instead sent troops to blockade its base area, Communist forces were in dire straits. The party responded to this crisis with the Great Production Movement. Soldiers, party workers, and teachers were organized to grow their own grains and vegetables. Many Communist military units achieved complete self-sufficiency in food. The peasantry, particularly its poorer strata, were drawn into the movement too. Besides producing more food by this strategy, party leaders also intended it to demonstrate the superiority of their rule to that of the Nationalists.

Chiang Kai-shek was never able to mobilize the resources of China fully because his government lacked some of the strengths characteristic of successful, modern nation-states. Many areas of Free China were under the control of generals wearing Nationalist army uniforms but whose loyalty to Chongqing was conditional at best. They were Chiang's allies, not subordinates under his control. The chaos created by war, enemy occupation, and mass migration made the situation worse. Mitter suggests that the Guomindang regime was fairly well organized and effective in its heartland province of Sichuan, "but the further east one traveled from Chongqing, the harder it became to believe that the Nationalist state had real authority beyond words on paper or devalued banknotes." He suggests that after 1941 the state was "unraveling."[71]

The low regard in which many Chinese held Guomindang officials and Nationalist soldiers also hindered national mobilization. Corruption within the bureaucracy was widespread. Funds for famine relief, public health campaigns, and public works construction were often diverted to the pockets of officeholders. Local officials added various "fees" on top of normal taxes to enrich themselves. Moreover, the traditional Confucian mentality viewed soldiers as the lowest rung of society. Nationalist general Li Zongren told a journalist, "The most important point in the people's war is that . . . troops do not harass the people of the country."[72] In reality, however, poorly supplied and undisciplined Nationalist soldiers frequently took whatever they needed from the peasants without compensation. In Henan Province, the peasants complained of four disasters: "flood, drought, locusts, and Tang Enbo."[73] The latter affliction was a Nationalist general who drafted hundreds of thousands of peasants into forced labor for his army and whose recruiters often used violence and kidnapping to fill the ranks. Communist propaganda successfully emphasized the difference in behavior between CCP troops and those of the government.

Ultimately, the multiple calamities that struck China from 1937 to 1945 destroyed both the Nationalist regime and the traditional Confucian order. The enemy occupied those few sections of the country that were economically and socially "modern." Industries were shattered and trade networks disrupted. Famine blanketed the land. Unimaginable inflation destroyed established wealth overnight. Even more cataclysmically, the invasion triggered a truly massive westward migration that ultimately broke the ancient bonds of China's most powerful institution, the extended family. The collective effect of all these developments was what Lary terms "social deformation." The old elites lost their economic bases of power and, unable to defend their country, their social legitimacy as well. The former hierarchy was replaced by a process of social leveling—"the grim equality of suffering." The Chinese revolution actually began during the first year and a half of the war, though at this stage it had "no ideology, no programme, and no blueprint."[74]

Notes

1. Michael C. C. Adams, *The Best War Ever: America and World War II* (Baltimore, MD: Johns Hopkins University Press, 1994), xiii.

2. William L. O'Neill, *A Democracy at War: America's Fight at Home and Abroad in World War II* (Cambridge, MA: Harvard University Press, 1993), x.

3. Studs Terkel, *"The Good War": An Oral History of World War Two* (New York: Ballantine, 1984), 320.

4. John Morton Blum, *V Was for Victory: Politics and American Culture during World War II* (New York: Harcourt, Brace, Jovanovich, 1976), 104.

5. Gerald D. Nash, *The Great Depression and World War II: Organizing America, 1933–1945* (New York: St. Martin's, 1979), 103.

6. John Ellis, *Brute Force: Allied Strategy and Tactics in the Second World War* (New York: Viking, 1990), 353.

7. John Campbell, ed., *The Experience of World War II* (New York: Oxford University Press, 1989), 168.

8. O'Neill, *A Democracy at War*, 98.

9. O'Neill, *A Democracy at War*, 103.

10. Arthur M. Schlesinger Jr., *A Life in the Twentieth Century: Innocent Beginnings, 1917–1950* (Boston: Houghton Mifflin, 2000), 283–84.

11. Adams defines "teen culture" as the "lack of personal responsibility, broad freedoms enjoyed in separation from the larger, mature society, and a pervasive anti-intellectualism." *The Best War Ever*, 102.

12. Campbell, *The Experience of World War II*, 136.

13. Ulysses Lee, *Employment of Negro Troops* (Washington, DC: Office of the Chief of Military History, US Army, 1966), 140–41.

14. Ronald Takaki, *Double Victory: A Multicultural History of America in World War II* (Boston: Little, Brown, 2000), 29.

15. Blum, *V Was for Victory*, 190–91.

16. Terkel, *"The Good War,"* 150.

17. Takaki, *Double Victory*, 50.

18. Campbell, *The Experience of World War II*, 170.

19. Richard Polenberg, *War and Society: The United States, 1941–1945* (Philadelphia: Lippincott, 1972), 63.

20. Polenberg, *War and Society*, 65.

21. Takaki, *Double Victory*, 146.

22. Takaki, *Double Victory*, 146.

23. Takaki, *Double Victory*, 144.

24. Terkel, *"The Good War,"* 27.

25. Commission on Wartime Relocation and Internment of Civilians, *Personal Justice Denied: Report of the Commission on Wartime Relocation and Internment of Civilians* (Washington, DC: Government Printing Office, 1982), 3.

26. E. M. Collingham, *The Taste of War: World War II and the Battle for Food* (New York: Penguin, 2012), 89.

27. Andrew Sinclair, *War Like a Wasp: The Lost Decade of the 'Forties* (London: Hamish Hamilton, 1989), 60.

28. Winston S. Churchill, *The Second World War*, 6 vols. (Boston: Houghton Mifflin, 1948–1954). Historian David Reynolds demonstrates that, in addition to misreporting numerous key events, Churchill wrote these volumes to defend his wartime actions, establish his reputation as a heroic and indispensable leader, and enhance his prospects in future elections. *In Command of History* (New York: Random House, 2005).

29. Henry Pelling, *Britain and the Second World War* (Glasgow: Collins, 1970), 59.

30. F. H. Hinsley and Alan Stripp, *Codebreakers: The Inside Story of Bletchley Park* (Oxford: Oxford University Press, 1996), 11–13.

31. Campbell, *The Experience of World War II*, 152.

32. David Reynolds, *Rich Relations: The American Occupation of Britain* (New York: Random House, 1995).

33. Jay Taylor, *The Generalissimo: Chiang Kai-shek and the Struggle for Modern China* (Cambridge, MA: Harvard University Press, 2011), 195.

34. Yasmin Khan and Gajendra Singh, introduction to *An Imperial World at War: Aspects of the British Empire's War Experience, 1939–1945*, ed. Ashley Jackson, Yasmin Khan, and Gajendra Singh (London: Routledge, 2017), 7.

35. Yasmin Khan, *India at War: The Subcontinent and the Second World War* (Oxford: Oxford University Press, 2015), 188.

36. Khan, *India at War*, 201.

37. Collingham, *The Taste of War*, 153.

38. Collingham, *The Taste of War*, 124.

39. Julie K. deGraffenried, *Sacrificing Childhood: Children and the Soviet State in the Great Patriotic War* (Lawrence: University Press of Kansas, 2014).

40. Andrei Sakharov, *Memoirs* (New York: Knopf, 1990), 2–3.

41. Wendy Z. Goldman and Donald Filtzer, *Fortress Dark and Stern: The Soviet Home Front during World War II* (New York: Oxford University Press, 2021), 102.

42. William Moskoff, *The Bread of Affliction: The Food Supply in the USSR during World War II* (Cambridge: Cambridge University Press, 1990), 130, 139.

43. Goldman and Filtzer, *Fortress Dark and Stern*, 105.

44. Goldman and Filtzer, *Fortress Dark and Stern*, 262.

45. Larry E. Holmes, *Stalin's World War II Evacuations: Triumph and Troubles in Kirov* (Lawrence: University Press of Kansas, 2017), 133–34.

46. Evan Mawdsley, *Thunder in the East: The Nazi-Soviet War, 1941–1945* (London: Hodder Arnold, 2005), 47, table 2.5.

47. Alec Nove, *An Economic History of the USSR* (New York: Penguin, 1972), 277.

48. John Barber and Mark Harrison, *The Soviet Home Front, 1941–1945: A Social and Economic History of the USSR in World War II* (London: Longman, 1991), 181.

49. Lydia V. Pozdeeva, "The Soviet Union: Phoenix," in *Allies at War: The Soviet, American, and British Experience, 1939–1945*, ed. David Reynolds, Warren F. Kimball, and A. O. Chubarian (New York: St. Martin's, 1994), 156.

50. Barber and Harrison, *The Soviet Home Front*, 63.

51. John Barber, "Popular Reactions in Moscow to the German Invasion of June 22, 1941," *Soviet Union/Union Soviétique* 18, nos. 1–3 (1991), 5–18.

52. David Brandenberger, *National Bolshevism: Stalinist Mass Culture and the Formation of Modern Russian National Identity, 1931–1956* (Cambridge, MA: Harvard University Press, 2002), 146, ch. 10. Brandenberger also suggests that audience selectivity, misunderstanding, oversimplification, and essentializing led to consequences unintended by the regime—the emergence of Great Russian chauvinism and the undervaluing of contributions to the war effort by Soviet Jews, Uzbeks, Azeris, Tadzhiks, and other minorities (pp. 177–78).

53. Brandenberger, *National Bolshevism*, 2.

54. Steven Miner, *Stalin's Holy War: Religion, Nationalism, and Alliance Politics, 1941–1945* (Chapel Hill: University of North Carolina Press, 2003).

55. Amir Weiner, *Making Sense of War: The Second World War and the Fate of the Bolshevik Revolution* (Princeton, NJ: Princeton University Press, 2001), 17.

56. Richard Stites, ed., *Culture and Entertainment in Wartime Russia* (Bloomington: Indiana University Press, 1995), 5.

57. Peter Kenez, "Black and White: The War on Film," in Stites, *Culture and Entertainment in Wartime Russia*, 165.

58. James R. Millar, "Conclusion: Impact and Aftermath of World War II," in *The Impact of World War II on the Soviet Union*, ed. Susan J. Linz, (Totowa, NJ: Rowman & Allanheld, 1985), 286.

59. Goldman and Filtzer, *Fortress Dark and Stern*, 7, 9.

60. Rana Mitter, *Forgotten Ally: China's World War II* (Boston: Houghton Mifflin Harcourt, 2013), 195.

61. Diana Lary, *The Chinese People at War: Human Suffering and Social Transformation, 1937–1945* (Cambridge: Cambridge University Press, 2010), 28.

62. Freda Utley, *China at War* (New York: John Day, 1939), 47.

63. Hans van de Ven, *War and Nationalism in China, 1925–1945* (London: RoutledgeCurzon, 2003), 275.

64. van de Ven, *War and Nationalism in China*, 295.

65. Arthur Young, *China and the Helping Hand, 1937–1945* (Cambridge, MA: Harvard University Press, 1963), 435–37.

66. Peter Vladimirov, *The Vladimirov Diaries: Yenan, China; 1942–1945* (Garden City, NY: Doubleday, 1975), 43, 153–54, 183, 218.

67. Jin Pusen, "To Feed a Country at War: China's Supply and Consumption of Grain during the War of Resistance," in *China in the Anti-Japanese War, 1937–1945: Politics, Culture, and Society*, ed. David P. Barrett and Larry N. Shyu (New York: Peter Lang, 2001), 166.

68. Calculated from Odoric Y. K. Wou, "Food Shortage and Japanese Grain Extraction in Henan," in *China at War: Regions of China, 1937–1945*, ed. Stephen R. MacKinnon, Diana Lary, and Ezra F. Vogel (Stanford, CA: Stanford University Press, 2007), 177.

69. Quoted in Mitter, *Forgotten Ally*, 268.

70. Theodore H. White and Annalee Jacoby, *Thunder out of China* (New York: Da Capo, 1980), 171.

71. Mitter, *Forgotten Ally*, 272–73.

72. Quoted in Mitter, *Forgotten Ally*, 150.

73. Mitter, *Forgotten Ally*, 271.

74. Lary, *The Chinese People at War*, 4, 32, 49.

CHAPTER 11

Life in Occupied Europe

Occupation, Collaboration, Resistance

Occupation, collaboration, resistance—these categories are interdependent and fluid. Preexisting attitudes toward the conquerors held by the defeated population and the severity of the occupation regime determined how extensive collaboration or resistance would be and what forms they would take. Propaganda about cooperation and mutual benefit notwithstanding, the Axis powers, particularly Germany and Japan, treated the areas they conquered in an entirely parasitic fashion. Both the Germans and the Japanese saw themselves as racially superior to the peoples they conquered. Each of them believed that the welfare of their nation, even its very survival, depended on exploiting the countries that they overran.

German Occupation

Nazi propaganda proclaimed that Germany was liberating Europe from "disorder," foreign imperialism, and national degradation. Berlin announced the creation of a Greater European Economic Community, which presumably would benefit all the peoples of the Continent. That was not to be. In theory, the victorious Germans had a choice of how to deal with their conquered lands. They might have imposed a firm but not brutal occupation regime and sought the cooperation of their conquered subjects. In western Europe, among those populations thought racially suitable to participate in the New Order (the Dutch, for example) and those states whose cooperation was at least temporarily important to Berlin (particularly Vichy France), Nazi propaganda paid lip service to the ideal of the victors and the vanquished working together for mutual benefit. In dealing with the defeated peoples, their conquerors had yet another choice to make—whether to patronize the native fascist movements in the conquered nations or to enlist the services of the existing elite (usually conservative, but not fascist). Local fascists found to their dismay that the Nazi authorities preferred to deal with the conservative elites—both because the latter already knew from experience how to keep their countries running and because the Germans wanted subservient minions, not equal comrades.

Alternatively, the Germans could act in a barbarous and entirely parasitic fashion, extorting whatever they needed from their victims without concerning themselves about the human cost of their exactions. Without exception in the East (particularly in the USSR, Poland, and Yugoslavia) and with increasing frequency in western Europe, Hitler and his henchmen chose the latter course. Hitler intended to fight a series of small wars, defeating his opponents one at a time in a series of self-financing conquests. By the end of 1941, Hitler had blundered into a prolonged, total war against a coalition of powerful enemies. The Nazis were anxious to shift the burdens of war from the German people to the conquered nations. People in Berlin and Munich continued to eat reasonably well even if it meant hunger in Amsterdam or starvation in Warsaw. Berlin ransacked the conquered territories for raw materials, manufactured goods, and foodstuffs to fuel the Nazi war machine and maintain the German home front. In 1942, Hermann Göring bluntly told a gathering of Nazi officials charged with extracting food from occupied Europe, "It makes no difference to me in this connection if you say that your people will starve. Let them do so, as long as no German collapses from hunger. . . . I am interested only in those people in the occupied regions who work in armaments and food production. They must receive just enough to enable them to continue working."[1]

Historian Gordon Wright called this process a policy of "smash and grab." The Germans seldom considered the alternative of cooperation with their conquered nations. Brutal extortion was easier.[2] Initially, at least, there was less outright looting of the economies in occupied western Europe than in the East, but the Germans found another way to funnel goods cheaply into the Reich. They set the value of their occupation currency at an artificially high level and then encouraged their troops to buy all the available foodstuffs, clothing, and luxury goods they could find. It was a boon for the consumer-goods-starved German home front. As the war expanded, the Reich experienced a severe labor shortage. Historians have emphasized the Reich's shortage of oil as a key weakness in the German war effort, but another shortage—manpower—was equally significant. Beyond exaction of goods and food, Germany enslaved millions of laborers. The Nazi desire for a "demographic revolution" in Europe (i.e., ethnic cleansing) meant that the death of many of these slaves was of no concern to their German masters, even when such homicidal labor policies were economically counterproductive. By 1944, there were eight million foreign workers in the Reich—some on contract, many more as slaves.

War mobilization set off a food crisis in Europe. Drafting men and requisitioning horses, fertilizer, and feed grains hit agriculture hard. Animal herds dwindled and grain harvests plummeted without these resources. Large grain reserves held by the regime bolstered the food supply in Germany during the first two years of the war, but the situation was much worse in the occupied states. The captive nations of western and northern Europe had to make do with short rations throughout the war, while in the East mass starvation became a tool for ethnic cleansing. The food crisis affected not only occupation politics but foreign policy as well. Dreams of securing the Ukrainian grain basket reinforced the ideological and strategic considerations motivating the attack on the Soviet Union.

While the war still raged, it behooved the Germans to reassure the peoples of occupied northern and western Europe that their national independence would be preserved and to promise them that the conqueror's yoke would be light. The Wehrmacht needed to maximize the number of troops on the fighting fronts and minimize those assigned to occupation duty. Collaborators would serve Berlin's purposes by policing their own people and reorienting their national economy to supply Germany's needs. Very few people in the occupied nations collaborated out of ideological sympathy with the Nazis; more did so for personal advancement, while most of those who cooperated with the Germans did so purely for survival. There were many degrees of collaboration—from those who joined French or Dutch SS units, to political leaders who staffed pro-German governments, to policemen who enforced the occupier's rules (including the arrest of resisters and Jews), to postmen, railway crews, and civil servants who served the Nazis by simply continuing to do their jobs.

Timing played a key role in collaboration. More people collaborated and did so publicly during the early years of the war when the Germans seemed unbeatable. Conversely, more people joined the resistance and took greater risks in defying the occupier during the last two years of the war as Allied victory grew more certain. Resistance took place along a continuum—from partisan groups who battled the Germans, to villagers who hid downed Allied fliers, to workers who engaged in production slowdowns, to ordinary citizens who ignored the occupier's rules whenever they could safely do so. There were relatively few at the two extremes, either identifying themselves heart and soul with the Nazis or joining the armed resistance; most were "passive accommodators" of their Axis occupiers.[3] Most people in the occupied countries engaged in both patterns of collaboration and acts of resistance. Their priority was keeping their families fed and safe in the midst of chaos and death.

Collaboration and Resistance in Vichy France

Beyond German oppression and the struggle against it, the Second World War overlay an incipient civil war in many places—particularly in France, Yugoslavia, Greece, and China—as well as an anticolonial struggle in Asia and Africa. The men who led the collaborationist Vichy regime, Marshal Philippe Pétain and Pierre Laval, were French patriots who were determined to use the opportunity presented by the fall of the Third Republic to "renovate" France—to rid it of the forces they considered evil: Marxism, liberalism, secularism, individualism, atheism, Jewish influence, feminism, hedonism, homosexuality, graft, corruption, and "modernity" itself. They were not fascists, but they were archconservatives on a mission to redress all the wrongs (as they saw them) flowing from the French Revolution. According to Laval, "parliamentary democracy has lost the war. It must disappear and give place to a hierarchical authoritarian regime, national and social."[4] The new regime adopted the motto "Work, Family, Fatherland" (replacing *liberté, égalité, fraternité*), while its operative values were nationalist, Catholic, anticommunist, antiliberal, and antifeminist. Pétain and his cohorts created an authoritarian state to carry out their counterrevolution. Much of the French elite—civil as well as military—were happy to jettison liberal democracy in favor of authoritarianism. The Vichy leaders immediately sought to blame the defeat of France on the "decadence" of the Third Republic and the disloyalty of its political left wing. They created their own "stab in the back" legend. According to them, Leon Blum's Popular Front government had undermined the national will and ability to protect the homeland.

After the stunning defeats on the Meuse and at Dunkirk, most Frenchmen had lost the will to fight on. "There is simply no mistaking the joy and relief," historian Robert Paxton says, "which came flooding after the anguish when Marshal Pétain announced . . . that the government . . . was seeking an armistice."[5] Many people believed that the only alternative to an armistice with the enemy was the complete destruction of France. Some feared that a continuation of the war would only serve the interests of Stalin and the Communists. Above all else, most Frenchmen just wanted to get on with their lives in peace. In Paxton's judgment, "the most elementary promptings of normalcy in the summer of 1940, the urge to return to home and job, started many Frenchmen down a path of everyday complicity that led gradually and eventually to active assistance to German measures undreamed of in 1940."[6]

Vichy initially enjoyed the support of the majority of Frenchmen. The British evacuation at Dunkirk, leaving France to face the enemy alone, and the Royal Navy's attack on the French fleet at Mers-el-Kébir, killing over 1,100 sailors, made it psychologically easier for Frenchmen to shift into the German camp. However, two factors—increasing German brutality and the turn of the war in favor of the Allies—caused that support to diminish steadily. French fascists clustered in German-occupied Paris rather than Vichy, which they despised. They deluded themselves that their homeland might undergo a fascist revolution and reemerge as a proud power within a German-led family of fascist nations. The Reich was the model for what France should become. Both the Germans and Marshal Pétain's administration kept such men at arm's length.

Under the terms of the Armistice of Compiegne, three hundred thousand German troops occupied two-thirds of France, including the English Channel and Atlantic coasts. The French were made to pay the costs of this occupation at a rate so high as to amount to tribute. The collaborationist French government controlled the southern third of the country, including its Mediterranean coast. The enemy kept two million French prisoners of war as forced laborers in Germany to ensure that Vichy officials cooperated with the Reich. The Vichy regime could maintain an army of fewer than one hundred thousand troops, though without heavy weapons, and a *Gendarmerie* (police force) of sixty thousand. In 1943, Vichy also created a paramilitary *Milice* to suppress resistance. French authorities were required to turn foreign Jews and political refugees over to the Nazis. The Germans occupied the remainder of France in November of 1942, after the Allied landings in North Africa.

Most French colonies recognized the authority of the Vichy government, though a few (French possessions in India, Polynesia, and Equatorial Africa) rallied to the "Free French" cause and continued alliance with Great Britain. In France itself and elsewhere in its colonies, hostility to England ("perfidious Albion") seemed greater than any animus toward the German conqueror. When British troops moved to secure French-controlled Syria, they

The head of the collaborationist Vichy French regime, Philippe Pétain (center left), with Reichsmarschall *Hermann Göring (center right), December 1941.*
Source: Library of Congress

met bitter resistance from the Vichy forces there, just as they did in their takeover of Madagascar. Here and elsewhere, bloody struggles took place between Vichy and Free French forces—Frenchmen fighting Frenchmen. The French and British navies fought several minor skirmishes, and French bombers attacked Gibraltar. In 1940, Vichy authorities acceded to pressure from Berlin and Tokyo to allow Japanese troops into Indochina to cut the major supply route to Chiang Kai-shek's armies. Vichy forces also initially opposed the Allied landings in North Africa in November 1942, but the Vichy commander there quickly switched sides and opened the way for the Allied advance. Incentives to cooperate with the Axis grew weaker as the Allied war effort grew stronger.

Hitler ultimately rejected Vichy France as a partner in his grand scheme of conquest, but it was not because the Vichy leaders were unwilling to join the Axis. At first the Führer needed to avoid completely alienating his French clients and balance their claims against the competing ambitions of Mussolini and General Franco of Spain. When Hitler's focus moved from a briefly considered Mediterranean strategy against England to an all-out assault on the Soviet Union, Vichy lost whatever small leverage it had with the Germans. In the end, there was no place for a French empire or even a truly autonomous France in Hitler's New Order.

The Germans were willing, however, to permit Pétain's regime to carry out its domestic counterrevolution. The government began a crackdown on people it considered "undesirable"—Jews, communists, foreign immigrants, Gypsies, homosexuals, and Freemasons. Vichy anti-Semitism was discriminatory and segregationist rather than homicidal, but collaborationist officials proved willing to go along with the more lethal German variety. French police, in both the occupied and "free" sections of the country, launched an operation to identify and label all Jews (citizens as well as aliens). They shared this information with the Germans. A Statute on Jews made Jewish Frenchmen second-class citizens and mandated segregation.

Pétain's regime enacted these laws voluntarily, not at Berlin's insistence. Jews were not made to wear the yellow star in the unoccupied zone, but French officials willingly enforced this requirement in the rest of the country. Beginning in the summer of 1942, the French police started to round up Jews for their transport to Auschwitz and other death camps. Ultimately, about 77,500 Jews (just under 25 percent of the Jewish population in France) perished. Although three-quarters of the Jewish population survived, many of them lost everything—money, possessions, property—in the process. French Jews who were fully assimilated and affluent had a much better chance of surviving than barely literate immigrant Jews. Many Gentile Frenchmen seemed apathetic rather than hostile to their Jewish neighbors, while liberals and socialists opposed persecution of the Jews. Even some conservatives protested. One Paris priest put a yellow star on the baby Jesus in a public manger scene.

The Vichy authorities announced a "National Revolution," by which they meant a fundamental transformation of what prewar France had been. In many respects, theirs was a conservative, even a reactionary vision, though it also included an element of technocratic modernization. They attempted to restore a Catholic moral order of authority, social hierarchy, and charity while rejecting a profit-obsessed capitalist ethic. A virtuous religiosity became an important part of the public image of the Vichy elite. Vichy leaders were especially keen to roll back the militant secularism of the Third Republic. "God" returned to the public schools, and state funding became available to parochial schools. Authorities banned the National Teachers' Union and conducted a purge of teachers, especially targeting Freemasons and Jews. The schools now taught obedience, morality, and patriotism. Within the church, however, there were divisions. Not all Catholics were happy with the authoritarianism of Vichy or its preference for big business. Some Catholic prelates openly denounced the deportation of Jews.

The regime also sought to restore its vision of the traditional family. The only proper place for women was in the home, as obedient wives and prolific mothers. Mothers of multiple offspring received honors and rewards, while women were discouraged from working outside the home. Girls got a different curriculum in school than boys so that they could learn the proper feminine role. Divorces became harder to obtain, and abortion was outlawed. However, as historian Richard Vinen observes, "there was a gulf between Vichy's prescriptions for how women ought to behave—staying at home to bring up large healthy families of children fathered by their husbands—and the reality, in which many found themselves separated from their husbands and forced to work to support themselves or their families."[7]

Xenophobia was part of the Vichy scene too. A powerful backlash arose against foreign workers, political refugees from Spain, and Jews fleeing Germany and Austria. The Vichy regime decreed its authority to intern all foreign adult males and voided the citizenship of thousands of recently naturalized immigrants. These "un-French" sojourners were handy scapegoats for the defeat of France. Racism played a role in this process as zealots sought to "purify" the nation. Also, highly trained technocrats were to replace professional politicians in the provision of social services. They were supposed to sweep away the corruption and inefficiency of liberal, parliamentary government. This counterrevolution began almost entirely at French initiative, without any substantial German prodding. Only when resistance became more serious in the occupied zone in the fall of 1941 did Berlin begin to pressure Vichy to take stronger coercive measures.

For the French and other occupied peoples, collaboration was, as historian Gerhard Weinberg has demonstrated, "a one-way street."[8] So long as it served Germany's immediate needs, Berlin tolerated collaborating allies. Hitler anticipated, however, that after ultimate victory, Vichy and other collaborationist regimes would be swept away in favor of complete German domination and ethnic cleansing. That was the nature of all the Führer's alliances. Vichy leaders, however, convinced themselves—against mounting evidence to the contrary—that cooperation with the occupiers would bring rewards. Laval justified his concessions to the Germans as a way to avoid the "Polonization" of France, that is, mass deportations and direct Nazi rule.

Life was difficult at best for Frenchmen during the occupation. Food was in short supply and tightly rationed—supplying only about 1,300 calories per day per person. Getting extra food, a new pair of shoes, or building materials to repair one's house required expensive and dangerous transactions on the black market. The gasoline supply fell to merely 8 percent of prewar consumption levels. Coal was also scarce, so the French shivered through the winters, while their industry produced only a fraction of what it otherwise might have supplied to its German masters. An early curfew made life difficult, and there was always the threat of violence from the Germans or the French police and paramilitary forces. Countless moral dilemmas arose in daily living, requiring the individual to make painful choices between his loyalty to his country, his love for his family, and the need for survival. Committing an act interpreted by the Germans as resistance could result not only in the death of the individual but also of his whole family. Not informing on the crime of a neighbor or a friend was just such an offense. Committing a flagrant act of resistance might well result in the massacre of a large group of hostages or a whole village.

The peoples of eastern Europe, as outlined below, experienced unstinting barbarity at the hands of the Nazis. In contrast, the Wehrmacht wanted its troops to behave properly toward the French and interact as little as possible with them. There were exceptions, of course, when Nazi ideology or anger got the better of prudent policy—examples include the brutal roundup and deportation of the Jews of Paris in 1942 and the massacre of the whole village of Oradour-sur-Glane by an SS unit in 1944. But overall, in Vinen's judgment, "the French often experienced the occupation as a time of low-level humiliation and the constant threat of violence."[9]

Not all those who helped the Germans were willing collaborators. Between 1942 and 1944, approximately six hundred thousand Frenchmen were sent to the Reich as part of the Service du Travail Obligatoir (or STO, meaning "mandatory labor service"). An additional 250,000 worked voluntarily in Germany, men initially drawn from the ranks of refugees and the unemployed. They cooperated with the enemy for economic, not political, reasons. Tens of thousands more Frenchmen toiled for the enemy in France, at first reopening damaged ports and airports, then building facilities from which to launch an attack on England, and finally constructing defensive works against an anticipated Allied invasion. Work for the Germans, whether freely undertaken or coerced, usually involved exhausting labor, harsh discipline, poor living conditions, short rations, and danger from Allied bombing.

Other young Frenchmen were drawn into more sinister forms of collaboration. In 1943, the Germans began arming the *Milice*, which took an active role in rounding up Jews. Young men joined the militia for a combination of motives, including anticommunism, the lure of adventure, good pay, and the opportunity to loot victims. Another group, the Legion des Volontaires Français contre le Bolchevisme, recruited men to fight in Russia. In addition, several criminal syndicates assisted the Germans with kidnappings and assassinations in the "free" zone and with procurement of black-market goods. In France, as elsewhere in western Europe, major corporations cut deals with German firms to secure profits and prevent blatant looting by the Nazis. Such accommodations supported the German war effort but also preserved French businesses. Even so, the Germans still siphoned off somewhere between a quarter and a third of France's national income as tribute.

Another sort of "collaboration," though distinctly nonpolitical, involved sexual relations between French women and German soldiers. These relationships ran the gamut from deep love affairs to casual sex to prostitution. Many of the women involved with the occupiers desperately sought to escape poverty or mistreatment by violent husbands or fathers. Well over two hundred thousand children were born from these Franco-German liaisons. Women who had sex with Germans—derided as *filles aux boches*—were condemned both by the resistance (as traitors) and by Pétain supporters (as immoral and unpatriotic). After the war, these women were widely vilified—some were prosecuted, and many were beaten and had their heads shaved. A few were murdered. There was a double standard here. Frenchmen working in the Reich were never punished after the war for sleeping with German women. For women, sleeping with the Germans seems to have been regarded as a much graver offense than men's political or even military collaboration with the enemy.

At first there was little resistance either to the German occupiers or to the Vichy government. General Charles de Gaulle, based in London, proclaimed his Free French movement, but initially few colonies rallied to his cause—and no one at all in metropolitan France. No senior French political or military figure stepped forward to champion the cause of France, so de Gaulle, the youngest general in the army, became the leader of the French quasi-government-in-exile by default. The French Communist Party, which later would field the largest resistance force in the country, at this point still followed the Moscow line that the war was an intra-imperialist conflict from which communists should abstain. Stalin needed his comrades in the occupied states to keep quiet to preserve the Nazi-Soviet Pact. Moreover, in the fall of 1940, most Frenchmen thought that the war was over and that the Germans had won. Resistance seemed pointless.

The first resistance groups were small and isolated. After all, one could trust only one's family and close friends, and not always even them. The groups were socially and politically disparate—they came from all walks of life and included anti-Semites, conservatives, liberals, socialists, and Spanish civil war refugees. Only their hatred of the Germans and their growing anger with the Pétain regime bound them together. When Hitler attacked Russia, the Comintern unleashed the French Communist Party, with its skill and experience in covert operations. Many young men who had fled the cities to avoid German labor service found their way into the resistance. Before the labor draft expanded dramatically in 1943, the local population had not always supported the small resistance groups, because doing so drew the Germans' wrath on their towns and villages. Betraying French Jews and foreign refugees to the occupiers had been common. But now, with tens of thousands of young Frenchmen in hiding—and German victory no longer so certain—local support for the resistance surged.

Women played a significant role in the resistance, though paternalism kept women from most leadership posts. Although relatively few of them fought in combat units, women operated safe houses, provided supplies and medical care, hid resistance fighters, served as messengers, and performed many other dangerous tasks. Only in the last year of the war, when Nazi repression grew intense, did women join the armed resistance in large numbers. Paxton estimates that, throughout the course of the war, there were about four hundred thousand active resisters, a number increasing to two million if the most minor and occasional acts of resistance are included. Although most Frenchmen wanted to see their country freed, only a few took up arms against the occupier.[10]

Some resistance units (especially communist-led ones) engaged in small-scale combat with the Germans, assassinated important Germans and French collaborators, and carried out acts of sabotage. Some of them worked with the British Special Operations Executive (SOE) and the American Office of Strategic Services (OSS) to recover downed Allied aircrews and provide valuable intelligence. Still others hid Jews as well as Gentiles avoiding labor conscription in the Reich. Many of them published journals and newspapers to challenge Berlin's and Vichy's versions of the truth, providing global reporting from the BBC. Some wrote the "V" for victory symbol on exterior walls to keep up public morale. Although the military striking power of the resistance was small, their many raids and ambushes "created a psychosis of fear within the enemy . . . giving an impression of numbers and strength which was more illusory than real."[11] It was a difficult and dangerous business; the penalty if caught was torture and death. In June 1943, a secret meeting of top resistance leaders was betrayed to the Germans. All of them arrested, and most were savagely tortured and executed, including de Gaulle's principal agent in France, Jean Moulin. In addition to fighting the Germans, many resistance groups also fought against Vichy's *Milice* and police. Beyond a struggle to liberate their country from foreign occupation, they were fighting a civil war for the future of France. As German power collapsed in France, resistance groups killed over seven thousand collaborators.

General de Gaulle only gradually became the leader of the Free France movement. When he first fled to London, he had barely seven thousand troops at his disposal. Prime Minister Churchill did not recognize him as the French leader-in-exile, while President Roosevelt attempted to work through Vichy, and when that failed he sponsored the leadership of rival general Henri Giraud. Gradually, however, most French colonies recognized de

Gaulle's primacy, ultimately giving him an army of four hundred thousand soldiers. Some of the noncommunist resistance within France also rallied to his cause. In June 1944, his movement renamed itself the Provisional Government of the French Republic. However, when the Allies liberated France in that year, power within the country was divided between de Gaulle's troops, the communists, and other noncommunist resistance forces.

Collaboration and Resistance in Holland

The occupation of Holland presents a special case, since the Nazis considered the Dutch racial kindred and therefore candidates for inclusion in the "master race." Berlin anticipated the ultimate incorporation of the Netherlands into the greater German Reich. Holland also differs from the French experience in that Queen Wilhelmina fled to London to set up a government-in-exile. The occupiers honored Anton Mussert, the local fascist leader, with the title of *Leider* (leader, or Führer), but Artur Seyss-Inquart, German Reich commissar for Holland, chose to rule through the existing Dutch civil service. Civil servants rationalized that remaining at their posts, even under German control, was the best way to protect the Dutch people (though fear and large pay increases also affected their judgment). Similarly, industrialists and businessmen worked to supply Germany's needs. Like the bureaucrats, businessmen reasoned that failing to cooperate with the occupiers would only lead to losing their companies and seeing their workers shipped to Germany.[12]

Given Germany's military hegemony in Europe, most of the Dutch saw some accommodation with the occupier as necessary to preserve as much of normal life as possible. In contrast to the tolerance shown to civil servants and businessmen who cooperated with the occupiers, the Dutch stigmatized women who dated German soldiers as "Hun-whores" and shunned them. German occupation policy in Holland was ambivalent at first. Berlin wanted to extract as many Dutch resources as possible to support its war effort, but it also wanted to encourage the people of Holland to assimilate Nazi attitudes and join the Reich without protest. Wehrmacht troopers were ordered to behave "correctly" when dealing with Dutch civilians.

As the war turned against Germany and the leaders in Berlin grew desperate, the parasitic nature of Nazi conquest became evident. The occupiers immediately outlawed the Communist and Socialist Parties and within a year had banned all political organizations other than the one-hundred-thousand-man Nationaal-Socialistische Beweging, or NSB (National Socialist Movement). As many as twenty-five thousand Dutchmen joined the German army or the Waffen SS, while others joined the Henneicke Column, a paramilitary force that helped the Germans capture a higher proportion of Jews (82 percent) than in any other country in occupied Europe. The Germans also permitted the establishment of the Netherlands Union (replacing political parties), which soon blossomed into an eight-hundred-thousand-member movement. Berlin saw the new group as a vehicle for Nazi ideology, while middle-class, conservative Dutchmen hoped it would rekindle Dutch national spirit. The Germans disbanded the group when it seemed to nurture anti-Nazi sentiment and failed to rally behind Operation Barbarossa.

Except for Rotterdam, the German invasion caused relatively few casualties and little physical damage, so life soon returned to a semblance of normality. People went back to work, refugees returned home, and shops and cafés reopened. Many factories and businesses served German needs, providing the Reich with $3 billion worth of goods throughout the war. At first, most people hoped that German rule would be bearable. Gradually, however, the conquerors tightened their grip, introducing rationing, muzzling the press, closely monitoring all levels of government, and sending workers to the Reich for forced labor.

The Nazis required all public employees (civil servants, teachers, etc.) to swear an oath attesting to their Aryan heritage. Those who could not (especially Jewish Dutchmen) were immediately fired. Jewish university students were expelled. Jews were forced to wear the identifying six-pointed yellow star. They were also banned from cafés, parks, and the public transportation system. The Germans, aided by Dutch collaborators, began the persecution and then the deportation of Jews early in 1942. Jews who lived in the towns and villages of Holland were ordered to move to Amsterdam. The Germans required the Jewish community to create a Jewish Council to facilitate the Nazis' plans. The victims were summoned in groups, purportedly for "work" in the East. The Germans conducted house raids to find those who ignored these notices. Strikes by students and dockworkers to protest the treatment of Jews were brief and ineffective. Over half a million Dutch citizens went to work in Germany, some voluntarily, many by force. Workers from Holland and other Western countries experienced hardship in Germany, but not the hostility and brutal treatment suffered by workers from "the East," whom the Nazis despised and planned to eliminate.

Resistance to the occupation developed only slowly. "In the first two years of the occupation," recalls Dutch survivor Henry Schogt, "resistance was mainly concerned with aiding political fugitives, acts of sabotage, and establishing contact with England and the Dutch government in exile in London."[13] Resistance escalated in response to increasing repression by the occupying forces. It grew from such symbolic acts as wearing orange clothing or flowers (the royal color in Holland), to verbal and written protests, and then to defensive measures (such as hiding people selected to work in Germany), and finally to aggressive acts against the Germans. Resistance was difficult in a small country with a large population and a relatively open countryside. People were frequently under the occupiers' surveillance in the cities of western Holland, though few Germans ventured into rural communities in the eastern part of the country.

Some Dutch Gentiles hid their Jewish neighbors. Anne Frank is the most famous example. Her Jewish-German family fled to Holland after Hitler came to power. To avoid deportation in July 1942, she and some of her family hid in small rooms hidden behind a bookcase in the building where her father worked. Other employees of the firm brought them food. At times the pressures of confinement and the fear of discovery led her to despair. "I've reached the point," she lamented on February 3, 1944, "where I hardly care whether I live or die."[14] Yet she would also write in her diary, "It's a wonder I haven't abandoned all my ideals, they seem so absurd and impractical. Yet I cling to them because I still believe, in spite of everything, that people are really good at heart."[15] The Germans discovered her and her family in August 1944 and sent them to a concentration camp, where she died of typhus. Unlike the German clergy, the Catholic and Protestant churches of Holland protested measures against Dutch Jews from the start.

The turning fortunes of war and the tightening economy bred discontent and then resistance. A 1943 attempt to re-intern Dutch soldiers for labor in the Reich provoked a general strike that the Germans suppressed. Many people fled to the countryside to hide with sympathetic farmers in order to avoid deportation to Germany. Conditions worsened drastically for most Dutchmen in the last two years of the war. By 1944, the authorities were kidnapping people off the streets to feed Germany's insatiable demand for laborers. Dutch communists, who, like their French comrades, already had some experience at underground operations, joined the resistance in June 1941. Responding to acts of sabotage or to assassinations of Nazis or important Dutch collaborators, the Germans staged mass executions of randomly selected victims. Resistance groups also forged ration cards, counterfeited money, and gathered intelligence to share with the Allies. To keep up morale, they scribbled "OZO" (Orange Will Win) on buildings everywhere. There had been some initial criticism of Queen Wilhelmina's flight to England, but as the German occupation grew more repressive, the House of Orange and the government-in-exile became a focus of loyalty within the country. Dutch authorities in London broadcast to Holland daily over the BBC.

Late in the war, when German defeat seemed imminent and the conditions of daily life deteriorated precipitously, many more people committed acts of resistance. Dutch workers shut down the railroad system in support of the Allied offensive to liberate Holland in the fall of 1944. When that offensive failed, the Germans retaliated by cutting supplies of food, water, electricity, and gas. The occupied areas of western Holland experienced severe famine. The death toll reached twenty-two thousand. The Allies dropped food into some of the starving cities during the final days of the war. The German commander in Holland surrendered without a fight three days before the Third Reich's final capitulation. Ultimately there were relatively few heroes or villains. Most people inhabited a middle ground of collaborating as much as necessary for survival and resisting when possible.

Elsewhere in Occupied Europe

In occupied Belgium, King Leopold remained with his people while his cabinet fled to England and formed a government-in-exile there. Because of its strategic location, the Germans opted for direct military administration of the country. The two Nazi-style groups in the country were divided bitterly by ethnic rivalry between Dutch-speaking Flemings and French-speaking Walloons. The most radical of them called for Belgium's incorporation into the Reich, and a number of them volunteered for the Waffen SS. Nonetheless, the Germans preferred to retain the talents of the existing civil service. Some conservative Belgian politicians thought it possible to cooperate with Berlin for mutual benefit, but German behavior soon disabused them of that notion. As in Holland, resistance was difficult and was savagely persecuted by the occupiers. Moreover, the Belgians did not suffer the food crisis endured by most occupied countries. Their farmers adapted to the challenges of wartime agriculture and provided the nation with sufficient food through the black market. Nonetheless, a virtual civil war developed between collaborationists and resisters. Belgian Nazis and some of the Walloon population (hoping for separation from the Flemish majority) helped the Gestapo round up half of the country's Jews.

In Denmark, King Christian X and his government remained in Copenhagen. The Danes were pressured to join the Anti-Comintern Pact and to outlaw the Communist Party. Erik Scavenius, the new pro-German Danish foreign minister, proclaimed his country's willingness "to collaborate, in the most positive and loyal manner, in the building of the continental empire directed by Germany."[16] Although some Danes collaborated enthusiastically and some even joined the SS, most engaged only in passive accommodation. Danish agriculture and industry worked profitably to serve Germany's needs. Young Danish men were subject to neither the military nor the labor draft. The occupiers misplayed their hand, however, by permitting free elections in March 1943 (the only such elections occurring in occupied Europe throughout the war). The Social Democrats won the most votes, while the fascist party garnered only 2 percent of the vote. Labor strikes and acts of sabotage flared, provoking the Germans to dissolve the government and rule by martial law. Neither the king nor most of his subjects were anti-Semitic. At first the Germans delayed any attempt to round up Denmark's Jews. The country was a major supplier of food (especially meat and butter) to the Reich, and the Nazis needed Danish cooperation to keep that supply line open. In September 1943, however, the occupiers planned to deport all of Denmark's Jews, but the Danes, tipped off by a sympathetic German diplomat, managed to smuggle 7,220 of their 7,800 Jewish fellow countrymen across the Kattegat to safety in Sweden.

The Norwegian king, Haakon VII, fled to England and set up a government-in-exile. The king provided his navy and his large commercial fleet to the Allied cause. The Germans disliked the local fascist leader, Vidkun Quisling, but could not find enough cooperation among the country's elites. They made Quisling "minister-president" but took all important decisions themselves. Because of its strategic importance, the Germans kept a three-hundred-thousand-man garrison there. The native fascist movement, the Nasjonal Samling, was quite unpopular and was sharply divided between Norwegian nationalists and those who sought annexation by Germany. A number of Norwegians volunteered for the SS. Although relatively few Norwegians supported the collaborationist regime, resistance initially was limited to helping Jews escape and providing some intelligence to the Allies. Resistance leaders feared that direct confrontations with the Germans would bring brutal retaliation on the Norwegian people. Only later were there some efforts to sabotage enemy heavy water plants (a key element in German atomic research). Norway's mountains and craggy coastline provided plenty of places for resisters to hide and receive supplies and agents from the British. There was little effort to protect the country's 1,700 Jewish citizens. In the judgment of István Deák, "Norwegian collaborators and young Norwegians who volunteered for combat duty on the German side far outnumbered the active resisters."[17]

Resistance grew in all the occupied lands as German oppression intensified and Allied victory seemed likely. Such groups carried out a range of activities to hinder the occupiers and aid the Allies. Most of them, however, put off any plan for general insurrection against the enemy because they were badly outnumbered and outgunned by the Wehrmacht. They intended to coordinate any mass uprising with the arrival of Allied troops in their countries. That fit the plans of the Allies and the governments-in-exile. The Western leaders were aware that, after the USSR joined the Grand Alliance, any successful rebellions in the Axis-occupied countries might benefit the local communists and prevent the return to power of prewar elites.[18]

The Nazis destroyed the Czech state in 1939. The Germans reorganized the Czech lands as the Protectorate of Bohemia and Moravia, with the existing government agreeing to stay in office in a vain attempt to moderate Nazi rule. However, the Germans executed Prime Minister Alois Eliáš when they discovered his covert contact with the London-based Czechoslovak government-in-exile. The next cabinet included Czech fascists and some Germans; it was obviously just a puppet of the occupiers. The first Reich protector, Konstantin von Neurath, planned to make the region wholly German by Germanizing half the Czech population and importing Germans from the Reich to add to the existing German minority. The other half of the Czech nation was to be deported. He would have deported them all if there had been enough German immigrants to replace them. His successor, Reinhard Heydrich, intended to speed up and radicalize this process, but after his assassination his replacement gave priority to increasing economic output for the war effort instead of pressing for immediate ethnic restructuring. Some Czechs lost businesses or farms, without compensation, to

German settlers, though overall the Czech experience of Nazi occupation was less traumatic than that of the Poles or the Russians.

The Central Committee of Internal Resistance coordinated underground activities. After the German invasion of Russia, Czech communists also participated actively in the resistance. These groups were especially important in providing vital intelligence information to Britain and the Czech government-in-exile. Czech agents, who had been flown from England and parachuted into the country, assassinated Heydrich. In retaliation, the Germans burned down the village of Lidice, shooting all its men and boys over age sixteen. Most of its women died in concentration camps. Hitler warned President Emil Hácha that violent resistance would result in massive Czech deportations "to the East." Further widespread pacification efforts substantially suppressed the resistance and limited its operations to small-scale work slowdowns and sabotage. The operation against Heydrich raised an excruciating moral question. Both the British and the Czech government-in-exile knew that assassinating the SS leader would unleash a ferocious Nazi vengeance on the Czech people. Did the benefit to the Allied war effort of killing Heydrich outweigh the terrible cost paid by the Czechs? Such moral dilemmas were common in all resistance work. Most Czechs adopted a stance of passive accommodation toward the Germans, waiting for liberation by the Allies.

The Germans separated the western part of the country, Slovakia, from the Czech lands. Under the collaborationist leadership of Father Josef Tiso, Slovakia became Hitler's most reliable satellite. Slovakia sent troops to fight alongside the Wehrmacht in Russia and implemented severe measures against its Jewish population. The Slovak government offered to pay the Germans to take their Jews on condition that it could seize the victims' property.[19] Resistance did not develop initially in the country, since most people supported the Tiso government. It flared up only as the war turned against Germany. Communist and democratic elements formed a Slovak National Council in 1943. The Soviets also "turned" some of the Slovak POWs who had fought in Russia and parachuted them back into the country as agents. At its largest, the movement boasted some eight thousand partisan fighters. Communists and some Slovak army officers sponsored a premature rebellion against the Germans in 1944 that was crushed. Sixty villages were burned in retaliation, and the remaining resisters were driven into the hills.

Yugoslavia and Greece

Nowhere were the elements of civil war and ethnic cleansing more on display than in Yugoslavia. The Germans immediately dismantled the Yugoslav state. The conquerors occupied the northern two-thirds of Slovenia and deported Slovene intellectuals and professionals. The use of the Slovene language was forbidden in schools and government. German settlers arrived from Bessarabia, Bosnia, and Austria. The region was to be thoroughly Germanized. Italy occupied the southern third of the country, where it followed an only slightly less oppressive occupation policy. Here, too, hostages were shot, villages burned, and property looted. Nonetheless, many Slovenes migrated to the Italian zone. Hungary received the western part of the Voivodina, while the local German minority ruled the eastern section of the province. Most of Macedonia went to Bulgaria, though the western section and the Serb province of Kosovo were incorporated into Italian Albania. Montenegro and parts of Bosnia, Herzegovina, and Dalmatia also came under Mussolini's rule. Ante Pavelič, head of the Ustasha terrorist group, became the dictator of an expanded

Croatia, now including most of Bosnia-Herzegovina. Serbia remained under direct German military rule, even though former Yugloslav army chief of staff General Milan Nedič formed a collaborationist regime.

The Germans unleashed (and even promoted) ethnic conflict within this fractured Yugoslavia. Albanians, Hungarians, and the native German population of the Voivodina massacred thousands of Serbs. In Croatia, the Ustasha launched a thorough ethnic cleansing against Serbs, Jews, and Muslims—with Hitler's full approval. As many as 350,000 Serbs were killed. The Croatian Catholic hierarchy sanctioned the butchery and participated in the forced conversion of surviving Orthodox Serbs. The fighting sometimes took on aspects of religious war, with Catholics and Muslims battling Serbian Orthodox believers and Jews. In Serbia, the German army moved quickly to register all Jews, deprive them of their property, and force them into slave labor. Then the Germans began a campaign to exterminate all Jews, communists, and other designated enemies of the Reich. Unable to contain the growing partisan movement, the Germans resorted to killing numerous hostages each time the guerrillas struck. That process degenerated quickly into a war on the civil population. In areas of partisan activity, all men were to be arrested, women and children expelled, villages burned, and livestock seized.

The mountainous terrain of much of Yugoslavia, combined with the redeployment of most German troops for Operation Barbarossa, facilitated the emergence of primarily Serbian resistance groups. The Chetniks, under Colonel Drazha Mihailovich, were the first to organize. They were loyal to the London-based Yugoslav government-in-exile of King Peter. Fiercely nationalist, anti-Croatian, and anticommunist, they fought the Germans and especially the Ustasha. This orientation appealed to many Serbs but repelled Yugoslavia's other national groups. Lack of discipline and a tight organization hampered Chetnik resistance.

Josip Broz, a Yugoslav communist leader who became famous under the pseudonym "Tito," organized a much larger and more effective resistance movement. Tito fought for three objectives: (1) driving out the German and Italian invaders, (2) re-creating a united Yugoslavia free of ethnic violence, and (3) fostering a social revolution leading to a Marxist state. He chose to downplay the last goal during the war and instead followed the Comintern's united front strategy, appealing to all patriotic forces to ban together against the invaders. The Chetniks believed the Axis occupiers to be undefeatable at the moment and, wanting to avoid unnecessary casualties, husbanded their forces in preparation for a Serbian uprising to coincide with an Allied landing in the Balkans. Conversely, Tito's Partisans attacked the Germans aggressively whenever a favorable opportunity presented itself. The same dynamic that swelled the numbers of Mao's guerrillas in China worked in Yugoslavia. The Germans responded to resistance attacks with unremitting cruelty. They burned villages and executed numerous hostages. Such atrocities motivated still more people to join the resistance. The Partisans fought a savage war, responding in kind to German brutalities.

A civil war soon erupted between the Chetniks and the Partisans. Dragoljub "Draža" Mikhailovich was a Serb nationalist who wanted to re-create the former Serb-dominated Yugoslavia and who intended to reestablish the prewar socioeconomic status quo under the return of the exiled king. Tito promoted a new, federal Yugoslavia with self-rule for each of its nations. Although he did not openly promote a communist revolution during the war, it was clear that he stood for sweeping social and economic reforms. Ultimately, more people were attracted to Tito's mode of active resistance and his vision of ethnic harmony. Moreover, the rise of the communist-dominated resistance movement forced Mikhailovich into tentative collaboration with the Axis.

A German pacification campaign in November 1941 badly hurt both the Chetniks and the Partisans, but with heavy fighting in the USSR and North Africa, Berlin was never able to allocate enough resources to crush the resistance in Yugoslavia. As the war turned against Germany, the Partisan movement controlled large sections of the country through local National Liberation Committees. Hard pressed itself, the Soviet Union was able to send the Partisans very little aid, while the British, realizing that Tito's men were the only active antifascist forces in the country, supplied substantial assistance, even though they continued to recognize the government-in-exile. The collapse of Fascist Italy in 1943 enabled the Partisans to acquire the weapons of several Italian divisions. Heavy fighting ensued between the Germans and Partisan forces. When Soviet troops entered northern Yugoslavia in 1944, they found much of the country already under Partisan control. As German troops retreated from Yugoslavia, the civil war continued, with Tito's fighters crushing collaborationist and ultranationalist forces.

The Axis also truncated conquered Greece. Eastern Macedonia and Thrace went to the Bulgarians, while Albania took the northern section of Epirus. The Wehrmacht controlled the strategically most important parts of the country—Athens, Salonika, the Turkish frontier, and Crete—while Italy occupied the rest of the peninsula. Just as in Serbia, the Germans set up a puppet government in Athens but maintained tight control themselves. There was no significant ethnic conflict in Greece as there was in Yugoslavia, but blatant Axis looting impoverished the middle class and drove up unemployment. The Allied blockade of Greece made the economic situation there even worse. Famine gripped the land by the winter of 1941–1942. Nazi authorities did not seek to starve Greece as they did Poland and the USSR, but the large grain imports that Greece usually received from Canada, the United States, and Australia were cut off. Over half a million Greeks died from starvation or the diseases attendant upon malnutrition.

German occupying forces also committed numerous atrocities in reaction to any manifestation of resistance. In the village of Komeno, for example, a German regiment slaughtered half the population, stole everything of value, and set the hamlet afire. This massacre occurred in response to a report that guerrillas had been seen buying food there.[20] It was not an isolated incident; it was repeated again and again. In contrast, Italian occupation authorities preferred negotiation to massacre of civilians in dealing with the resistance. Repression intensified after the Allied landing in Italy because the Germans feared a second landing in the Balkans.

Privation and oppression stimulated resistance, while the mountainous terrain of the country sheltered it. The communist-controlled National Liberation Front (the EAM) and its military wing, the National People's Liberation Army (ELAS), comprised the largest and most active resistance group. It, too, followed the Comintern strategy of proclaiming an all-class, patriotic resistance to the invaders rather than a sectarian communist revolution. There were other, noncommunist resistance groups—most notably Colonel Napoleon Zervas's National Republican Greek League (EDES)—but none of them attracted mass support. They depended on British aid and even secret collaboration with the invaders.

There was a key difference between the resistance in Greece and Yugoslavia. In the latter, the Allies cooperated with and supplied Tito's Partisans as the only effective anti-Axis forces in the country. In contrast, Britain considered Greece to be of strategic importance to its empire. Therefore, London supported the noncommunist elements of the resistance and fought for the reestablishment of the former monarchist regime in Athens. Realizing this, the communist leaders launched a campaign in October 1943 to control all the territory abandoned by Axis troops. Their superior numbers and acquisition of Italian weapons allowed ELAS to defeat all the other resistance organizations except EDES. By the summer of 1944 when the Germans began to evacuate Greece, the EAM/ELAS controlled at least two-thirds of the country. In the last months of war, in Greece as well as Yugoslavia, collaborationist and noncommunist resistance forces sometimes banded together to combat what they saw as a rising tide of communism. Some prominent Greek officers now joined the German-organized Security Battalions that continued their anti-partisan operations even as Axis forces withdrew. Liberation unleashed civil war between communist and anticommunist forces.

A German Resistance?

There were also resistance groups in Germany, but they were tiny, isolated from each other, and ineffective. Unlike resistance elsewhere, where it was motivated by hatred of a cruel invader, German resistance clearly involved treason to one's country. Prewar purges of thousands of potential anti-Nazis as well as voluntary emigration limited the potential number of resisters. Those few who chose to resist Nazism faced the wrath of a highly effective and ruthless police state. The groups with the greatest potential impact involved senior Wehrmacht commanders. An anti-Nazi group associated with General Ludwig Beck plotted to oust Hitler in 1938 and again in 1939–1940, but Beck could not secure the support of enough officers or of the British government. Another potential node of resistance clustered around Admiral Wilhelm Canaris, chief of military intelligence. Neither group was willing to launch any action against the regime, however, as long as the great majority of military officers and the public supported Hitler.

As the war turned against Germany, some officers did summon the courage to act. The attempted assassination of Hitler on June 20, 1944, at his eastern headquarters, Wolfsschanze (Wolf's Lair), failed when the bomb used in the attempt only slightly injured the Führer. Colonel Claus von Stauffenberg, several generals, and around seven thousand others were arrested. Most of them were savagely tortured and executed. The Allies rebuffed approaches from this group and subsequent contacts from other senior commanders because they did not trust them and because most of these men wanted to keep some of Germany's conquests and continue the war against the USSR. Those plotters also understood that a coup to kill Hitler and overthrow the Nazi regime would not be widely popular among the German people. Too many people stood to lose by the Führer's downfall because many of them were deeply complicit in his crimes. Beyond that, a great many Germans still felt some loyalty to Hitler. In the last years of the war, massive bombing by the Western Allies and the frightening prospect of occupation by the Red Army kept most people working for the war effort. The Allied demand for unconditional surrender (though certainly justified given the nature and crimes of the Nazi regime) also made it more difficult for most Germans to abandon their loyalties to the government.

Small anti-Nazi discussion groups existed around Count Helmuth von Moltke (the Kreisau Circle) and Hans and Sophie Scholl (the White Rose), but they posed no serious threat to the Third Reich. The "military-conservative" orientation of the former group prevented it from appealing either to ordinary Germans or to the Allies, while the tiny White Rose society only managed to propagate its more liberal message when the British received one of its tracts and the RAF dropped thousands of copies over Germany. The Rote Kapelle (Red Orchestra), a group with loose connections to Moscow, provided valuable military intelligence to the Soviets until it was largely destroyed by the Gestapo in 1942. Behind Russian lines, the Soviets organized the National Committee for Free Germany, composed of émigré communists (including the future leader of East Germany, Walther Ulbricht), and a League of German Officers (including General von Seydlitz and Field Marshal Paulus). The latter group broadcast defeatist propaganda at retreating German troops, but it was not very effective due to the pervasive German fear of a Russian conquest of their homeland.

The Christian churches of Germany offered little resistance to the Nazi state. The Catholic Church agreed not to criticize the regime in exchange for protection of its organization and property. That did not stop the Nazis from closing some monasteries and arresting some outspoken priests. Bishop Gehlen of Cologne publicly criticized the program to murder seriously handicapped people, but most bishops kept their moral judgments to themselves. The Protestants were divided between the German Christian movement, which sought to refashion an "Aryanized" Christianity aligned with Nazi racial doctrines, and the Confessing Church, which resisted the corruption of its theology but otherwise had little to say about Nazi atrocities. German Protestants shared some of the Nazis' core values in that they tended to be antimodernist, antidemocratic, and strongly nationalist. The Protestant theologian Dietrich Bonhoeffer is an exception who criticized Hitler and the Nazi persecution of Jews and who was later executed for complicity in the 1944 assassination attempt on the Führer. Martin Niemöller, a militant nationalist and pro-Nazi Lutheran pastor who was later sent to a concentration camp for his opposition to Nazi encroachments on the church, repented for his bad judgment far too late:

> First they came for the Socialists, and I did not speak out—
> Because I was not a Socialist.
> Then they came for the Trade Unionists, and I did not speak out—
> Because I was not a Trade Unionist.
> They came for the Jews, and I did not speak out—
> Because I was not a Jew.
> Then they came for me—and there was no one left to speak for me.[21]

Some Germans committed small acts of resistance—in 1943 a nurse named Hilde bought an onion on the black market to give (illegally) to a badly hurt Russian POW—but such actions were rare. Another nurse remembered that, "more typically, the staff of our hospital stole the food meant for the foreign patients and took it home to their families or ate it themselves. . . . They felt that these Russians, Dutchmen, Belgians and Poles who came into our clinic had been placed on earth to labor for them. To steal a plate of soup from such low creatures seemed not a sin but a perfectly legitimate activity."[22] Some young people, including the Edelweiss Pirates and the "Meuten" group, expressed their opposition to Nazism in assaults on Hitler Youth members, while others devoted themselves to prohibited American swing music and dancing. Given the repressive nature of the regime and its wide popularity, most dissidents limited their "opposition" to "rumors, jokes, unofficial whispering campaigns, [and] news from abroad passed on in confidence."[23] A few brave Germans risked their lives to hide Jewish neighbors. After the war, some 550 were honored by Israel as "Righteous among the Nations."

Historians continue to debate the overall impact of resistance movements on the outcome of the Second World War. Military specialists tend to discount their effectiveness, except for a few special cases such as French resistance activity supporting the Normandy landings. Resistance groups were less aggressive and violent in western and northern Europe where the Germans were somewhat less repressive (except for the mass murder of Jews) and where, by practicing "passive accommodation," most people could survive and even maintain some semblance of a normal life. In eastern Europe, where the occupiers were unstintingly repressive and where the fires of civil war burned even hotter, resistance groups tended to be larger, more violent, and more aggressive. Resistance forces succeeded in hindering the German war effort at several critical moments, tying down hundreds of thousands of Axis troops who otherwise could have been on the fighting fronts, and providing an alternative focus of loyalty to the Axis and the collaborationist regimes. At the same time, however, in many places various resistance factions fought each other in brutal civil wars—neighbor against neighbor, countryman against fellow countryman.

Allies of a Kind

The Axis was a largely ineffective alliance, composed of states with divergent goals and thinly veiled mutual hostility. Most of its members enjoyed some degree of independence from Berlin and thus shared responsibility for Nazi war crimes. Several of them used the war as an opportunity to carry out their own versions of ethnic cleansing among their minority populations.

Finland enjoyed some autonomy. There were never large numbers of German troops in that country until their panicked retreat in 1944–1945, and Finland never formally joined the Axis. Under the authoritarian rule of Marshal Carl Mannerheim, Finland was not a fascist state. Its war objectives were limited to reclaiming the territories that Stalin had taken in 1940. The Finns did not intend to fight beyond those recovered areas in support of the Germans unless the Wehrmacht took Leningrad, thereby crushing Soviet northern front defenses. Beyond that, Mannerheim was not nearly so optimistic as Mussolini and other Axis allies about Hitler's chances of winning the war. Under heavy diplomatic pressure from the United States, he held his forces on the line achieved in 1941. The Finns also resisted German pressure to hand over their Jewish citizens.

Mussolini was the first fascist dictator in Europe and, as such, served as a role model for Adolf Hitler. In 1934, Italian opposition had blocked the German attempt to absorb Austria, while in 1937 the Duce's acquiescence had made the *Anschluss* possible. Hitler felt an obligation to Mussolini and found in him a kindred spirit. The Italian leader intended to fight a "parallel" war, not one subservient to Berlin. By 1940, however, Italy had become a distinctly junior partner in the Axis. Mussolini's pompous blustering could not hide the need for the Wehrmacht to rescue Italian forces in North Africa and Greece. He had also sent 227,000 troops to fight alongside the Germans in Russia. Italy lacked the wealth, a sufficient industrial base, and an efficient national mobilization plan to compete successfully in an era of total war.

Mussolini was constrained to follow the Führer's bidding as the balance of power between Rome and Berlin shifted dramatically in the latter's favor. In 1938, Rome introduced anti-Semitic measures, though not the fully homicidal variety favored in Berlin. Italo-German relations soured further after the Stalingrad defeat. The Italians lost ninety thousand killed and sixty thousand taken prisoner in that debacle, while the Germans blamed their allies for the defeat. The Duce's popularity plummeted. The Allied landing in Italy in 1943 motivated the king, the army, and the Fascist Grand Council to depose and arrest Mussolini. He was rescued by German troops who then occupied most of the peninsula. The Duce remained in seclusion—powerless—until the German position in Italy crumbled in 1945. Under German control, the radical wing of the Fascist Party proclaimed a new Italian Social Republic and cooperated fully with Hitler's plans to destroy the Jews of Italy. The Germans "interned" a million Italian troops and sent over seven hundred thousand of them to the Reich as slave laborers. Berlin also seized the opportunity to annex the South Tyrol, Trieste, and the Trentino. Anti-Fascist Italians captured and executed Mussolini in the spring of 1945.

When a partisan bomb killed thirty-two SS men and wounded many more in Rome, Hitler ordered a hundred Italians executed for every German killed. Fascist militia and the SS murdered thousands more civilians throughout Italy, usually in retaliation for partisan actions. Partisan activity in the German-occupied area escalated dramatically in the summer of 1944 when the Allies broke out of containment in southern Italy. The Wehrmacht's counterinsurgency campaign turned into a broader war against the civilian population. German commanders understood that the use of indiscriminate terror against the populace would be counterproductive in that it would stimulate greater support for the partisans. However, historian Michael Geyer argues that the Germans felt isolated and betrayed by the Italian people. Thus, to them, murderous anti-partisan operations seemed a just punishment for a perfidious ally.[24]

Hungary, Romania, and Bulgaria maintained their nominal independence for a while as Hitler's allies and junior partners in the Axis. In Hungary, the regent, Admiral Nicholas Horthy, felt compelled to collaborate with the Third Reich by its military predominance in east-central Europe as well as the significant fascist movement in the country and a large *Volksdeutsche* (ethnic German) minority population. Hitler rewarded him with lands taken from Czechoslovakia and Romania. Budapest permitted German troops to cross the country on their way to Yugoslavia and Greece. Horthy also sent a large contingent of soldiers to fight against the USSR. The regime readily expelled foreign Jews, but Hungarian Jews, though persecuted, were not shipped out of the country. Horthy attempted to leave the Axis in 1944 because the war had turned against Germany. The Germans responded by occupying the country, replacing Horthy's conservative regime with the fascist Arrow Cross movement, and deporting many of Hungary's Jews, though about 125,000 survived.

In Romania as in Hungary, the Germans preferred to work with traditional, conservative forces rather than the local fascist movement, the Iron Guard. Marshal Ion Antonescu took over the government and established an authoritarian regime that suppressed even the fascists. Widespread anticommunist and anti-Russian sentiment promoted Romania's cooperation with the Germans. Most importantly, the government understood that recovery of Bessarabia and Bukovina (and perhaps also the Hungarian-controlled half of Transylvania) required a German victory over the USSR. Antonescu was enthusiastic about Operation Barbarossa and provided thirty divisions to fight in Russia (far more than any other German ally). Those troops participated in the mass murder of Soviet Jews. The Antonescu regime also launched its own homicidal purge of Romania's Jews and Gypsies. Most Romanians, including Antonescu, had lost their enthusiasm for the eastern crusade by 1943. However, Romania was particularly important to the Germans because its Ploesti oil fields supplied much of the Reich's petroleum. German defeats, Allied bombing of the oil fields and Bucharest, and the rapid approach of the Red Army provoked a royal coup on August 23, 1944, that ousted Antonescu. Romania then declared war on Germany. Soviet troops were soon in control of the country, with the Romanian army now fighting briefly on the Allied side.

Bulgaria, under the leadership of King Boris, maintained semi-independence through quasi-collaboration with the Reich. A royal dictatorship rather than a fascist regime ruled in Sofia. Boris permitted German troops to pass through Bulgaria on their way to attack Greece and Yugoslavia. His government also declared war on the United States and Great Britain, though it never actually fought those opponents. The king avoided going to war with the Soviet Union. Bulgaria benefited from Axis membership by gaining Macedonia and Thrace from defeated Yugoslavia and Greece. Turks and Greeks, not Jews, were the despised minorities in Bulgaria. Under pressure from the public, the authorities canceled the planned deportation of their Jewish population, instead dispersing them to the countryside. That measure saved the Jews of Bulgaria proper, but not those of occupied Macedonia and Thrace.

Life was relatively easy for Bulgarians until late in 1943—their soldiers were not fighting, the country was not bombed, and Germany's need for food was very profitable for farmers. In August of that year, Boris died unexpectedly of a heart attack (though widespread rumors accused the Germans of poisoning him), to be replaced by the six-year-old King Simeon. Allied bombers began striking Bulgarian cities in November. The Soviet Union declared war on Bulgaria on September 5, 1944. Its forces crossed the frontier three days later. The Bulgarian government ordered its soldiers not to resist the Russians and quickly signed an armistice. A left-of-center, multiparty coalition (including communists)—the Fatherland Front—took over the government. Bulgarian troops were soon fighting beside Red Army units against the Germans.

Japan occupied an altogether different position within the Axis compared to Hitler's European allies because of its distant location and its military prowess. Berlin and Tokyo mistrusted each other, and their cooperation was limited. The island kingdom fought not so much a parallel war but an entirely divergent war. Tokyo, along with Rome, pushed Berlin for an early settlement of the Russo-German war. Both of them wanted Germany to focus on the British and American enemies. Neither of them understood Hitler's real war aims. The Führer misunderstood his Japanese ally as well. After the Stalingrad debacle, the Germans pressed Japan to attack the USSR, but by then Japan was fully occupied in China and the Pacific.

Soviet Occupation

During the period of quasi-alliance with the Third Reich from August 1939 to June 1941, the USSR occupied the territories of Lithuania, Estonia, Latvia, eastern Poland, and eastern Romania. The entry of the Red Army into eastern Poland on September 17, 1939, touched off a brief civil war before Soviet authorities suppressed all movements and forces not under their control. Ukrainians, Belorussians, and Jews formed a majority of the population in the lands of eastern Poland, most of which had been taken from Soviet Russia in the Russo-Polish War of 1920. Jews suffered persecution under the Polish state, while many Ukrainians resisted the domination of the Poles. Now, with the Warsaw regime on the verge of collapse, Ukrainian militia groups ambushed retreating Polish soldiers. Polish soldiers and civilians shot up Ukrainian towns and staged small-scale pogroms against Jews. Janusz Bardach, a young Polish Jew, later wrote, "Ukrainian nationalists with pro-Nazi sentiments wasted no time organizing a local militia to loot Jewish stores and homes."[25] Only the forceful imposition of order by Soviet troops prevented full-scale civil war.

Ethnic Poles in the eastern region of the country were almost universally hostile to the Soviet incursion, but some Ukrainians mistakenly hoped that Moscow would allow them to create a truly independent nation-state. A minority of left-leaning Poles and a larger proportion of the Jewish community at first welcomed Soviet intervention. Bardach remembered, "Thousands of citizens and twice as many refugees shouted, danced, sang, and threw flowers to the [Red Army] soldiers on the tanks."[26] Initially Soviet authorities encouraged the non-Polish population to "settle accounts" with the Poles and the rich in general. One Polish survivor recounted a grisly scene: "Ukrainian villages assaulted Polish settlements, such as our hamlet Łeczówka . . . for example. The landowner was tied to a pole, two strips of skin peeled off and the wound covered with salt, and he was left alive to watch the execution of his family."[27]

Stalin intended to effect a thorough social revolution in the lands taken from Poland. Allowing, even provoking, widespread social violence was the first step in this "class struggle." Initially, Soviet forces occupied only the cities and larger towns, leaving country folk to their own devices. A combination of personal vendettas, ethnic and religious hatreds, and greed produced an orgy of killings, beatings, rapes, vandalism, and thefts. Red Army violence targeted mainly Polish officers and NCOs, policemen, local officials, priests, and landowners. The army's sorting process was often quite crude. In some instances, all it took was clean, uncalloused hands to be identified as a class enemy and shot. More than twenty-one thousand captured Polish officers, policemen, and others were executed and buried in the Katyn Forest near Smolensk and elsewhere. There was some looting by Soviet troops, but more frequently the soldiers bought everything in sight—wristwatches, bolts of fabric, bicycles, sausages, etc. Under the Five Year Plans, the USSR had become a great power in heavy industry and arms manufacturing, while light industry and the consumer goods sector atrophied. For these young Soviet conscripts, even backward, impoverished eastern Poland seemed to be a consumer paradise!

Stalin saw these annexed territories as a defensive barrier against future German attack. That objective required an end to anarchic violence and a more thorough and selective purge of suspected "unreliable" elements in the local population. Village committees and militias were organized everywhere, frequently employing sympathetic radicals, the poorest peasants, and known criminals—those with no stake in the status quo. Soon Soviet officials and the village militias began to round up undesirables—not only Polish officials and officers, but also landowners, teachers, and political activists (including socialists). It was not only the big landowners and more affluent peasants whose goods were "liberated," but even many ordinary peasants lost their horses, agricultural equipment, grain stores, and household goods. The Red Army requisitioned large quantities of food without payment. Peasants seized land from big estates, the former government, churches, and even their slightly better off fellow peasants. The redistribution of land among the peasantry was temporary, as the Kremlin did not intend to maintain a system of private property.

Just as Moscow sought to legitimize its invasion of eastern Poland by claiming a mission to protect its Ukrainian and Belorussian population, so now Soviet authorities attempted to justify their annexation of these territories by rigged elections. In October, the much-harassed voters elected representatives to the Ukrainian and Belorussian National Assemblies who duly petitioned Moscow to incorporate their respective lands into the Ukrainian and Belorussian Soviet Republics.

The pace of sovietization now accelerated. During the period from August 1939 to June 1941, about 120,000 residents of the newly incorporated territories were arrested, mainly those who were considered "class hostile" or who resisted sovietization, or people the authorities thought *might* resist. An even larger number, about 320,000 (predominantly Poles and Jews), were deported to remote areas in the Soviet interior. Due to horrendous transport conditions, many died of hunger or exposure en route to their new homes. Some deportees were shipped to labor camps, while others were sent to work in Soviet factories or on collective farms. The remaining population was subjected to intense propaganda and policies designed to destroy the existing network of political, economic, and social relationships. Schools stopped teaching religion as well as Polish history and language. The new schools conveyed a standard Soviet curriculum in Russian, Ukrainian, or Belorussian. Soviet schools strove to undermine traditional sources of authority, especially the church and the family.

A similar fate befell the three Baltic states—Lithuania, Estonia, and Latvia. The Baltic states fell within the Soviet sphere of influence under the Nazi-Soviet Pact and its supplements. In the fall of 1939, Moscow intimidated all three of them into signing mutual assistance agreements that permitted the stationing of Soviet troops on their territories. The Kremlin then accused each of the republics of plotting with foreign powers hostile to the USSR and of provoking incidents with Soviet garrisons stationed in their territories. Under heavy Russian pressure, each republic formed a new government in June 1940 that then requested incorporation into the Soviet Union. As in Poland, there followed large-scale arrests and deportations of "enemies of the people"—government officials, businessmen, clergy, intellectuals, and trade union leaders. Executions and deportations totaled 34,250 in Latvia, 60,000 in Estonia, and 75,000 in Lithuania.[28] This explains why so many of the Baltic peoples welcomed the Germans when they attacked the USSR in 1941. Similarly, on June 26, 1940, Moscow presented the Romanian government with an ultimatum. Bucharest appealed to Berlin for support but was turned away. Soviet troops quickly occupied the easternmost provinces of Romania—Bessarabia and northern Bukovina. They were soon incorporated into the Ukrainian SSR and "sovietized," just as eastern Poland and the Baltic states had been.

Notes

1. Nicholas Stargardt, *The German War: A Nation under Arms, 1939–1945; Citizens and Soldiers* (New York: Basic Books, 2015), 272.

2. Gordon Wright, *The Ordeal of Total War, 1939–1945* (New York: Harper Torchbooks, 1968), 116–17.

3. István Deák, *Europe on Trial: The Story of Collaboration, Resistance, and Retribution during World War II* (Boulder, CO: Westview, 2015), 2.

4. Raymond Aron, *Histoire de Vichy, 1940–1944* (Paris: Fayard, 1954), 130.

5. Robert O. Paxton, *Vichy France: Old Guard and New Order, 1940–1944* (New York: Norton, 1972), 8.

6. Paxton, *Vichy France*, 19.

7. Richard Vinen, *The Unfree French: Life under Occupation* (New Haven, CT: Yale University Press, 2006), 173.

8. Gerhard Weinberg, *Visions of Victory: The Hopes of Eight World War II Leaders* (Cambridge: Cambridge University Press, 2005), 35.

9. Vinen, *The Unfree French*, 132.

10. Paxton, *Vichy France*, 294–95.

11. H. R. Kedward, "Hunters and Hunted, Summer–Autumn 1943," in *In Search of the Maquis: Rural Resistance in Southern France* (New York: Oxford University Press, 1993), 50.

12. Gerhard Hirschfeld, *Nazi Rule and Dutch Collaboration: The Netherlands under German Occupation, 1940–45* (Oxford: Berg, 1988), 319.

13. Henry G. Schogt, *The Curtain: Witness and Memory in Wartime Holland* (Waterloo, ON: Wilfrid Laurier University Press, 2003), 3–4.

14. Anne Frank, *The Diary of a Young Girl: The Definitive Edition*, ed. Otto H. Frank and Mirjam Pressler (New York: Doubleday, 2001), 184.

15. Frank, *Diary of a Young Girl*, 333.

16. Wright, *The Ordeal of Total War*, 131.

17. István Deák, *Europe on Trial*, 130.

18. Mark Mazower, *Hitler's Empire: How the Nazis Ruled Europe* (New York: Penguin, 2009), 509.

19. Laurence Rees, *The Holocaust: A New History* (New York: PublicAffairs, 2017), 261.

20. Mark Mazower, "Military Violence and the National Socialist Consensus: The Wehrmacht in Greece, 1941–1944," in *War of Extermination: The German Military in World War II*, ed. Hannes Heer and Klaus Naumann (New York: Berghahn Books, 2004), 146–48.

21. United States Holocaust Museum, "The Holocaust Encyclopedia," www.ushmm.org.

22. Edith H. Beer, *The Nazi Officer's Wife: How One Jewish Woman Survived the Holocaust* (New York: Morrow, 1999), 1–2.

23. Detlav J. K. Peukert, *Inside Nazi Germany: Conformity, Opposition, and Racism in Everyday Life* (New Haven, CT: Yale University Press, 1987), 53.

24. Michael Geyer, "Civitella della Chiana on 29 June 1944: Reconstruction of a German 'Measure,'" in Heer and Naumann, *War of Extermination*, 200–203.

25. Janusz Bardach and Kathleen Gleeson, *Man Is Wolf to Man: Surviving the Gulag* (Berkeley: University of California Press, 1998), 14.

26. Bardach, *Man Is Wolf to Man*, 24.

27. Jan Gross, *Revolution from Abroad: The Soviet Conquest of Poland's Western Ukraine and Western Belorussia* (Princeton, NJ: Princeton University Press, 2002), 37.

28. John Hiden and Patrick Salmon, *The Baltic Nations and Europe: Estonia, Latvia and Lithuania in the Twentieth Century* (London: Longman, 1991), 115.

CHAPTER 12

Ethnic Cleansing and the Holocaust

Ethnic Cleansing on a Massive Scale in the East

As brutal as Nazi occupation policies were in northern and western Europe, they paled beside the unstinting barbarity of German rule in eastern Europe. Hitler intended to destroy the Czechoslovakian, Polish, and Russian states forever. He envisioned a demographic revolution in eastern Europe. Much of the existing population there would be swept away to create *Lebensraum* for German settlers. Beyond that, two special categories of enemies—Jews and communists—were to be exterminated entirely.

Russia

The Germans showed even less mercy to the peoples of the USSR than they had to the citizens of Poland. They shot many Red Army prisoners immediately upon capture. Still more were allowed to die of starvation, exposure, or disease in prison camps. In all, 5.7 million Soviet troops were taken prisoner; 58 percent of them (or 3.3 million) died in captivity. This death rate contrasts sharply with the experience of British and American POWs. Their death rate in German captivity was only 3.6 percent. About three million surviving Soviet prisoners were forced into slavery for the Germans. POWs identified as communists or Jews were murdered as a matter of policy. German commanders were also authorized to annihilate villages if resistance was even suspected to have come from them or if they impeded the army's advance in any way.

The Germans allowed considerably fewer opportunities for collaboration in the areas of the Soviet Union that they occupied than they did in western Europe. Their goal was to eliminate much of the indigenous population of the USSR to make room for German settlers. They also intended to exploit the resources of the East even more thoroughly and brutally than they did in western Europe. The German administrator in Ukraine, Erich Koch, openly proclaimed, "I will pump every last thing out of this country. I did not come here to spread bliss but to help the Führer."[1] A preinvasion planning document indicated that the Nazis intended to take much of the food production of Russia's rich black earth region for themselves. Germany and the nations of occupied western Europe were net importers of grain. The Germans required a large increase in the grain supply to feed their nine-and-a-half-million-man army and its six hundred thousand horses, as well as the home population. The agriculturally rich Ukraine—the "breadbasket" of the USSR—produced enough to feed the Soviet population but only a small surplus beyond that for export. Soviet cities would have to starve in order to produce the grain "surplus" the conqueror required. The Germans brazenly called this operation their "Hunger Program." They set grain procurement quotas so high—taking even next year's seed grain—that starvation was inevitable. Ultimately, they envisioned murdering as many as one hundred million people.[2] Only their failure to achieve decisive military victory over the Red Army prevented the Germans from fully implementing these plans.

The supply crisis intensified for the Wehrmacht and the German population as it became apparent by September 1941 that there would be no quick *Blitzkrieg* victory in Russia. Hermann Göring ordered the army to "live off the land," that is, to seize food from Soviet farmers, even though that meant widespread famine. In 1942, the Germans killed all the inhabitants of Kamianka and burned the village to the ground as an object lesson to other villages that failed to deliver enough grain. In Belorussia alone, over six hundred villages were massacred. Much to the chagrin of many peasants who expected to be liberated from all things Soviet, the Germans retained the system of collective farms to facilitate seizing most of the harvest. Peasants who refused to work for the Germans or who withheld food were shot. Flogging was introduced to keep the farmers hard at work. The plan also included seizing all the livestock in the region. Except for a few areas such as the oil-producing region of Transcaucasia, the USSR was to be deindustrialized. For the Nazis, Russia was to be a major source of food, natural resources, and slave labor, offsetting the effects on Germany and occupied Europe of the Anglo-American blockade. In the cold words of the Hunger Plan:

> Many tens of millions of people in this area [central Russia] will become superfluous and will die or will have to emigrate to Siberia. Attempts to save the population there from starvation by bringing in surpluses from the Black Earth zone can only be carried out at the cost of supplying Europe. Such measures undermine Germany's resilience in the war and undermine Germany's and Europe's ability to withstand the blockade.[3]

Murder by starvation worked well with captive populations—mainly POWs, Soviet officials, communists, and Jews—but the program failed to starve all the cities in the occupied zone. People survived by resorting to a thriving black market and by abandoning the cities for the countryside. The occupiers could not spare the personnel to keep every city cordoned off.

Unstinting German barbarity soon forced most Soviet citizens to rally in defense of their motherland, no matter how little love they had for Stalin and the Communist system. There were exceptions, however. The Baltic states and those areas of eastern Poland and Romania incorporated into the USSR after the Nazi-Soviet Pact had been subjected to an extremely harsh process of "sovietization." There, many people initially welcomed the Germans as liberators. Non-Russian nationalist movements flared into resistance against everything Soviet and, in the process, sometimes cooperated with the Germans. Non-Russian nationalists were happy to turn over resistance fighters and Soviet officials to the Germans. As many as three hundred thousand Ukrainians and Belorussians joined local police units charged with combating Soviet partisans and participating in ethnic cleansing.[4]

The head of the Ukrainian collaborationist regime, Iaroslav Stets'ko, wrote, "The Jews help Moscow to consolidate its hold on Ukraine. Therefore I am of the opinion that the Jews should be exterminated and [see] the expediency of carrying out in Ukraine the German methods for exterminating the Jews."[5] An ethnic civil war raged within the overarching German reign of terror—Poles fighting Ukrainians and Belorussians, both sides attacking Jews. Even within the Organization of Ukrainian Nationalists (OUN), rival factions frequently battled each other. "Killing was personal," historian Amir Weiner tells us, "with neighbors who had lived together for decades, if not centuries, turning against one another with ferocity that in rare moments of reflection astounded even themselves."[6] Some otherwise loyal Ukrainians and Russians collaborated with the enemy in less dramatic and violent ways simply to protect their families and to secure food or scarce consumer goods.

Outside of the territories acquired by the USSR in 1939–1940, the basic social and political ideas cultivated during more than twenty years of Soviet power remained predominant (except for the partial resurgence of anti-Semitism). Few people became fascists. Soviet values were more deeply inculcated than many historians have realized. Also, the Germans did not proselytize much among their intended slave population. Berlin had only limited tolerance for these nationalist movements. Germany was conquering eastern Europe to exploit its land and peoples, not to liberate them.

On several occasions Hitler forbade the use of Soviet volunteers in German military units, but the severe manpower shortage led the army to ignore that order. Some Soviet POWs volunteered for service in the Wehrmacht to avoid almost certain death in the POW camps; others joined the Germans as a way of striking against the hated Stalinist regime. Most of them worked as noncombatant laborers for the enemy. In all, about a million Soviet citizens served the German army in Russia. Some, however, took up arms to suppress partisans and even to battle the Red Army. For instance, the German 134th Infantry Division was so decimated from the fighting in December and January 1941 that Soviet defectors comprised almost half of the rebuilt division. Eventually the Führer gave in and sanctioned the use of these *Untermenschen*. The Kaminski Brigade, about twelve thousand Soviet volunteers recruited from the prison camps, played a bloody role in the suppression of the Warsaw Uprising in 1944. Later, the Germans blamed these eastern auxiliaries for atrocities committed in Warsaw. One German soldier described them as men who "rape women, cut off their breasts or throw them bodily out of the window."[7] The Germans also had some success in raising troops among Soviet Muslims, Georgians, Armenians, and Volga Tatars. Many Muslims, whose mosques had been closed by the atheistic Soviet regime, came to regard Hitler as a gift from Allah.

The so-called Vlasov Army (or Russian Liberation Army), formed from Soviet POW volunteers, was the best-known manifestation of military collaboration. Actually, the Vlasov Army is something of a myth. Most Soviet citizens who fought alongside the Germans served directly in Wehrmacht units commanded by German officers.[8] General Andrei Vlasov, a Soviet general who had been captured in the battle for Leningrad, was allowed to organize two divisions under his nominal command only in January 1945. Vlasov issued this public appeal to the Russian nation:

> Friends and Brothers! Bolshevism is the enemy of the Russian people. It has brought countless disasters to our country. Enough blood has been spilled! There has been enough starvation, forced labor and suffering in the Bolshevik torture chambers! Arise and join in the struggle for freedom! Long may peace with honor with Germany prevail!

Vlasov led the Committee for the Liberation of the Peoples of Russia that sought a regenerated homeland without Stalin, the Communist Party, or collective farms. Given the strength of the repressive Stalinist regime, these men believed that only a powerful external shock could topple the Soviet dictatorship. They mistook Hitler for their liberator. Ultimately, the Vlasov movement was both militarily and politically negligible.[9] Between two and a half and three million Soviet citizens fought for the Germans during the war. By 1945, they made up 12.5 percent of the German army.[10]

The Germans wanted a docile slave population, not allies to whom they would have to make concessions. Hitler was never enthusiastic about Slavs fighting in Russia on the German side, so he sent many of these troops to fight in Italy and northern France, where they often willingly surrendered to Allied forces. Such prisoners were forcibly repatriated to the USSR after the war. Vlasov and his men were tortured and executed for treason by the Soviet state. Some counterfactual books and films on the war in the East accuse the Führer of making a serious mistake in treating the Soviet minority peoples so badly, suggesting that the war might have been won with the cooperation of disaffected elements within the Soviet population. The problem with such arguments is that they expect Hitler to be someone other than who he actually was—a homicidal racist who intended to destroy the Jewish and Slavic peoples.

Partisan warfare in the occupied sections of the USSR was complicated and brutal. In many places, pro-Soviet Russian, Ukrainian, and Jewish partisan units battled each other for local dominance while also fighting the Germans and their local collaborationist auxiliaries. The Germans reacted savagely, killing any captured partisans and anyone suspected of helping them. They sometimes slaughtered whole villages to intimidate surrounding villages from aiding the partisans. The regular army joined the SS in waging a merciless anti-partisan campaign. Field Marshal Walther von Reichenau proclaimed that the German soldier was the "bearer of a merciless national idea and an avenger of all the bestialities that have been inflicted on Germany and related peoples."[11]

Field Marshal Keitel, chief of the armed forces supreme command, ordered that it was not sufficient to execute the culprit (even if he or she could be found) when a German soldier was killed by partisans, but in addition fifty or even a hundred "communists" should be shot as a deterrent measure. The Germans also forced the appointment of a "village elder" for each community, who was responsible for reporting anti-German activity by any of his villagers or the presence of any strangers. German anti-partisan sweeps were multipurpose affairs, designed to suppress actual partisans, find and kill as many Jews as possible, and kidnap people for slave labor in the Reich. What this meant in practice was that counterinsurgency forces often slaughtered the women, children, and old people of a village (whether suspected of partisan activity or not) and then took away all the able-bodied men for slave labor. However, the Germans were never able to deploy sufficient forces to suppress the growing partisan movement. They could only hope that unstinting terror would intimidate the population on which the partisans depended. That effort failed.

The Holocaust

Hitler always intended to destroy the Jewish people. Before consolidating his political power and rebuilding Germany's military strength, the Führer was constrained in "race policy," just as he was in domestic politics and foreign affairs. He was a careful student of public opinion. Hitler told SS trainees in 1937, "I always know that I must never make a single step that I may have to take back. You always have to have a nose for the situation to ask: 'Now what can I get away with and what can't I get away with.'"[12] Persecution of the Jews escalated as circumstances permitted. There were only about half a million Jewish Germans, and most of them were thoroughly assimilated into the culture and integrated into society. Initially the Nazis ousted Jews from civil service jobs and launched a boycott of Jewish businesses. Two years later, in 1935, the Nuremberg Laws made intermarriage or sexual relations between Jews and non-Jews illegal. They also deprived Jews of their rights as German citizens. Jews were driven out of the professions—medicine, law, higher education, etc. Legalized discrimination required a precise definition of who was and who was not a Jew. For most Germans, "Jew" meant someone who practiced the Jewish faith, but that definition did not fit the Nazis' racialist interpretation of Jewishness. New laws decreed that anyone with two Jewish grandparents was a Jew. Conversion to Christianity, leading an entirely secular life, or even espousing atheism did not matter. In practice, the rules were arbitrarily and inconsistently applied.

Poster for 1940 Nazi film The Eternal Jew, *a grossly anti-Semitic pseudodocumentary about the supposed Jewish plot to destroy "Aryan civilization."*
Source: United States Holocaust Memorial Museum

Storm troopers frequently assaulted Jews. Between 1933 and 1939, almost half of Germany's Jewish population fled the country. Some, however, were reluctant to leave their homeland, and others simply could not afford to do so. Moreover, some countries to which they might have gone, including the United States, sharply limited immigration. Jews did not suffer alone. The Nazis applied similar measures to Gypsies (Romani and Sinti) and to those of German-African parentage. Discrimination also mounted against other objects of Nazi hatred, including gay men and Jehovah's Witnesses. By the late 1930s, Hitler's popularity had soared (because of the recovering economy and his foreign policy successes), and he was able to subordinate his conservative allies in the military and the business community. Nazi radicalism was increasingly unrestrained.

The world learned this in the most shocking way on the night of November 9–10, 1938, during the *Kristallnacht* (night of broken glass) pogrom. Responding to the assassination of a German diplomat in Paris, storm troopers and sympathizers burned synagogues, vandalized Jewish businesses, and attacked homes. An orgy of beatings and rapes spread across Germany. About a hundred Jews were murdered, and twenty-six thousand Jewish men were sent to concentration camps (the first instance of mass incarceration based solely on ethnicity). *Kristallnacht* was the culmination of a wave of violence in the preceding months that was meant to encourage more Jewish emigration. The Nazis were disappointed, however, that most Germans deplored this massive display of public violence. They learned a valuable lesson. Atrocities should be conducted away from the public gaze and, when the opportunity presented itself, outside of Germany altogether.

For a while the Nazis encouraged (and profited from) Jewish emigration, first from Germany and then, after the war began, from Europe. They even briefly considered shipping all European Jews to the distant island of Madagascar. They also contemplated pushing Jews across the border into the Soviet-occupied section of Poland, but Stalin vetoed that idea. This did not mean, however, that Hitler believed that the "master race" could coexist with the Jews if the latter lived sufficiently far away. Emigration was only a temporary expedient based on the Führer's own mythology. Hitler believed the "stab in the back" myth, so he wanted Jews and other potentially disloyal elements out of the country as it prepared for war.[13]

In 1939, the regime launched what would be, in effect, a pilot exercise for its later extermination campaigns, the T-4 program. Designed to eliminate "useless eaters" (anyone who could not contribute to strengthening the Reich), this operation targeted the handicapped, the insane, the feebleminded, and the severely debilitated. Doctors, nurses, hospitals, and asylums selected victims and administered fatal injections or poison gas. News of these killings, including the deaths of decorated heroes from the First World War, leaked out. It distressed much of the public. Roman Catholic bishop August von Galen publicly denounced these crimes from his pulpit. Hitler officially terminated the "Euthanasia Program," but it continued in greater secrecy and expanded to include deformed children. The Nazis did not keep all of their crimes hidden from view. Gerhard Weinberg argues that the mass killing of Jews on Soviet territory in 1941–1942, *which was not kept secret from the home front*, was in part a "trial run" to test the reaction of the German public to genocide.[14] The titanic struggle in the East seems to have hardened people's attitudes toward the mass murder of "enemies."[15] When the program for executing adult psychiatric patients resumed in 1942, neither Galen nor any of the Catholic hierarchy protested—nor did the Protestant clergy. A parallel program forced the sterilization of hundreds of thousands of people defined as racially or socially undesirable (alcoholics, for example).

The outbreak of war in 1939 allowed the Nazis to accelerate and intensify their campaign to destroy enemies and "undesirables." Hitler admitted as much (though, characteristically, he blamed the coming infamies on his intended victims) when he warned in January of 1939, "Should the international Jewry of finance succeed, both within and beyond Europe, in plunging mankind into yet another world war, then the result will not be a Bolshevization of the earth and the victory of Jewry, but the annihilation of the Jewish race in Europe!" Only war could provide the necessary conditions for an extensive, ongoing program of mass murder—heightened fear and hatred, the acceptance of drastic measures to "defend" the homeland, tolerance of brutality. Once the war began and a labor shortage developed, German Jews were forced to work for their oppressors. Edith Hahn, a Jewish Austrian, was assigned to an asparagus farm. "It quickly became clear," she wrote, "that the Germans were interested in using our strength but not in preserving it. . . . We were always ravenous . . . . surrounded by bounty and aching with hunger. . . . The farmers had grown proud and haughty. . . . Like Volkswagen and Siemens, they had slaves."[16]

The people of Poland, both ethnic Poles and Polish Jews, were the first to feel the conqueror's wrath. Hitler had been blunt with his generals about the real objective of the invasion: "The aim of the war lies not in reaching particular lines but in the physical annihilation of the enemy. Thus, so far only in the east, I have put my Death's Head formations at the ready with the command to send man, woman and children of Polish descent and language to their deaths, pitilessly and remorselessly. . . . Poland will be depopulated and settled with Germans."[17] Reinhard Heydrich, head of the Security Service (SD), told his police and SS units that the "nobility, clergy, and Jews must be killed."[18] Intellectuals, teachers, lawyers, scientists, engineers, artists, and writers were added to the list.[19] Polish schools, universities, libraries, museums, presses, and newspapers were shut down. Poles who survived were to constitute a nation of slaves, without leaders or ideas.

Western Poland was incorporated into the Reich, and the conquerors began to deport its non-German inhabitants to the central portion of the country, known as the General Government. Those Poles who remained in the areas slated for immediate Germanization became second-class citizens in their own land—forbidden to use parks, swimming pools, and other public amenities; forced to stand aside for passing Germans; and beaten if they failed to salute anyone in uniform. Tens of thousands of Poles and Jews were shot by German ethnic militias. It was open season on Jews for SS men, party workers, and soldiers. They could be robbed or killed without fear of punishment.

The occupation authorities decreed the confiscation of Polish property without compensation. Hundreds of villages were burned to the ground. The Germans requisitioned much of the country's agricultural production, including most of its meat. By 1941, the official ration for Poles in Warsaw was down to 669 calories per day and only 184 calories for Jews. People bought most of their food on the black market, or they starved to death. Before the end of 1941, more than a million Poles had been sent to work in Germany—POWs as slave laborers and civilians recruited under contract. Even the latter were made to wear a distinctive "P" on their clothing to mark their inferior status, barred from public transportation and entertainment venues, forbidden to socialize with Germans, and executed for having sex with a member of the "master race." Those Poles identified as Jewish were systematically starved and worked to death. Conquering Poland only added to Hitler's popularity at home. Reporter William L Shirer, who was in Berlin at the time, noted, "I have still to find a German, even among those who don't like the regime, who sees anything wrong in the German destruction of Poland."[20]

Hitler intended to replace the Slavic population of Poland (and later the Soviet Union) with members of the "master race." Germans already living in eastern Europe, the *Volksdeutsche*, were to displace many of the Slavic residents, taking over their farms and businesses. Large numbers came from the Baltic states (recently annexed by the USSR) and the Italian Tyrol region. Ethnic Germans abroad were repatriated from Milwaukee, Buenos Aires, Johannesburg, and elsewhere to become settlers in the newly conquered lands. Amazingly, given the Nazis' insistence on the desperate need for *Lebensraum*, there was a serious shortage of settlers to "Germanize" the conquered space! Hitler wanted to see one hundred million Germans colonize "the East," but that was an impossible goal. Relatively few Germans wanted to become pioneers on a hostile frontier.

The views of Liselotte Purper—a German photojournalist assigned to report on and assist in the process of displacing Polish farmers from their land and replacing them with German settlers—suggest the depth of German prejudice against the Poles:

> Sympathy with these creatures?—No, at most I felt quietly appalled that such people exist, people who are in their very being so infinitely alien and incomprehensible to us that there is no way to reach them. For the first time in our lives people whose life and death is a matter of indifference.[21]

Although there was some resistance among the captive population, the Germans were resolved to carry out *Generalplan Ost*—the nearly complete ethnic cleansing of Poland. Those Poles who remained in their homeland were to comprise a pool of exploitable menial labor. A few thousand young Polish children, deemed suitable for "Germanization," were taken from orphanages or families and shipped to the Reich to begin a new life. Hitler appointed Heinrich Himmler, already head of the SS, as Reich commissioner for the strengthening of the German race. He would oversee the massive population transfer. Himmler was clear about German intentions:

> The removal of foreigners from the incorporated eastern territories is one of the most essential goals to be accomplished in the German East. . . . In dealing with members of some Slav nationality, we must not endow these people with decent German thoughts and logical conclusions of which they are not capable, but we must take them as they really are. . . . I think it is our duty to take their children with us. . . . We either win over the good blood we can use for ourselves . . . or else we destroy that blood.[22]

The Germans became ever more brutal as the war dragged on. Indiscriminate shootings and lynchings were commonplace. Hostages were frequently tortured or killed. Numerous villages were massacred in retaliation for any resistance activity. Labor camps and death camps sprouted throughout Poland. In total, between 1939 and 1945, Poland lost over six million people (ethnic Poles and Polish Jews), or 22 percent of its population.[23]

It was not just the SS and soldiers who committed atrocities. Erna Petri resettled near Lvov with her SS-man husband as part of the Germanization program. Both of them routinely beat the Poles who worked on "their" land. One day Erna noticed a group of nearly naked children by the roadside (doubtless Poles or Jews). She took them into the woods and shot each one in the head.[24] Clearly they were "useless eaters" and a potential threat to the "master race." For the German colonists, the East was a kind of "Wild West" where the natives were simply an obstacle to progress.

In the last year of the war, with the Germans in retreat and the Soviet army rapidly approaching, civil war and ethnic cleansing flared again. A Ukrainian Insurgent Army, combining nationalists and former collaborators, attacked German settlements and Polish villages in an effort to create a noncommunist Ukrainian nation-state before the Red Army arrived. Farther west, where Poles predominated, they repaid their Ukrainian neighbors in kind.

While the Poles fared very badly at the hands of their conquerors, Jews suffered still worse. Germans found it even easier to despise Polish Jews and to consider them more animal than human because, in contrast to Jewish Germans, many of them were unassimilated to the majority culture—speaking Yiddish, dressing differently, and the men wearing full beards and side locks. All Jews were ordered to wear a six-pointed yellow star on their sleeves. After the war, most Germans (and ex–army officers in particular) blamed the Nazi Party and the SS for the atrocities committed against civilians. From the beginning, however, the army participated in these crimes.

Historian Richard Evans describes an all-too-common scene: "Groups of grinning German soldiers fired randomly into houses they marched past in the Jewish quarters of the towns they entered, or gathered around Jewish men in the street, forcing them to smear each other with excrement, setting their beards on fire, compelling them to eat pork, or cutting the Jewish star into their foreheads with knives."[25] Sexual intercourse with Jewish women was strictly forbidden to the occupying forces, but rapes were common nonetheless. At a drinking party organized for regimental officers after the fall of Riga, an eyewitness reported that the officers "forced several dozen Jewish girls to come, to undress fully, to dance and to sing. Many of the unfortunate women were raped, then led out into the courtyard and shot."[26]

The Wehrmacht established brothels for its soldiers to avoid the "race pollution" that widespread rape of East European women might entail. When they could not recruit enough German prostitutes to staff the *Einsatzfrauen* (special women) stations, the authorities pressured Soviet, Polish, and Serbian women into sexual service—prohibitions against fraternization with *Untermenschen* notwithstanding.[27]

The almost random acts of violence described above could never accomplish what the Nazis really wanted—a Jew-free Reich in a Jew-free Europe. Only the systematic extermination of the entire population—genocide—could achieve that goal. SS, Security Service, and Order Police units, sometimes assisted by the Polish police, moved in behind the advancing German army to remove the Jews from towns and villages, forcing them into urban ghettos or such newly opened concentration camps as Majdanek and Plaschow. There were also mass executions from the very beginning. German forces would surround a village or ghetto, thoroughly search the area, concentrate all the Jews they found at some central location, and then take them in groups to a more isolated killing ground where they murdered men and women, old people, children, and even infants.

Some of these murders were carried out by SS men who were anti-Semitic zealots and who reveled in the mayhem, though many were committed not by Nazi fanatics but by what seemed to be quite ordinary men. The army and even much of the SS could not be spared for these mobile killing squads, so older men, often from reserve units of the Order Police, were pressed into service. Few of them were party members, and many of them were married with families. Most were working class or lower middle class, and many professed a belief in Christianity. Researchers have found extensive records for one such unit, Battalion 101 from Hamburg. "The fundamental problem," historian Christopher Browning suggests, "is to explain why ordinary men—shaped by a culture that had its own particularities but was nonetheless within the mainstream of western, Christian, and Enlightenment traditions—under specific circumstances willingly carried out the most extreme genocide in human history."[28] It is tempting to assume that in such a brutal dictatorship as the Third Reich, the men had no choice but to obey orders or face the severest consequences, yet that was not the case. Before the first killing operation began, the commander of Battalion 101 excused any man who did not feel up to the task, without repercussions. Once the "action" had begun, more were excused who could not continue, again with no negative consequences. Among the "ordinary men" of this unit, a marked stratification of attitudes toward killing is discernible: some reveled in the savagery, most simply carried out their brutal duties as ordered, while a few evaded or even refused to perpetrate these crimes.[29]

Browning contends that conformity was the key factor in turning "ordinary men" into mass killers. Even though they might have initially been horrified by the barbarity of their assignment, most of them could not bring themselves to "break ranks" and refuse to do their "duty."[30] Another scholar, Daniel Jonah Goldhagen, argues that "eliminationist anti-Semitism" (an especially virulent, homicidal variant produced by German culture) was pervasive among Germans, and this allowed "ordinary men" to commit mass murders willingly, even joyously! "Genocide," he says, "was imminent in the conversation of German society."[31] "By choosing not to excuse themselves from the genocide of the Jews," Goldhagen contends, "the Germans in police battalions themselves indicated that they wanted to be genocidal executioners."[32] Other historians see anti-Semitism as only one factor (and not necessarily the dominant one, at that) in the German consciousness that led to war and genocide. The other significant elements included desperation to reverse their First World War defeat, desire to expand in eastern Europe, notions of their own racial superiority, and militant anticommunism.

At least some of these men displayed no shame or remorse as they proudly displayed photographs of their murderous handiwork or took visiting wives or girlfriends to see their killing grounds. In contrast, Browning notes that members of another Order Police unit in East Upper Silesia, who continued to live in their own homes in relatively normal circumstances, did not exhibit the same degree of hatred and brutality toward the local Jewish population. "This would suggest," he concludes, "that imposing racial imperialism was corrupting. Acting as a 'master race' on occupied territory changed attitudes and behavior, and each step in degrading and mistreating victims made the next step easier."[33] An Austro-German policeman serving in Belorussia (modern-day Belarus) wrote to his wife about the killings:

> During the first try, my hand trembled a bit as I shot, but one gets used to it. By the tenth try I aimed calmly and shot surely at many women, children, and infants. I kept in mind that I have two infants at home, whom these hordes would treat just the same, if not ten times worse. . . . Infants flew in great arcs through the air, and we shot them to pieces in flight, before their bodies fell into the pit and into the water.[34]

Another scholar, Saul Friedländer, dismisses both Goldhagen's claim of a uniquely German, homicidal variant of anti-Semitism and Browning's suggestion that peer pressure pushed otherwise ordinary men to become mass murderers. Instead, he argues persuasively that "the Nazi system as a whole had produced an 'anti-Jewish culture' . . . fostered by all the means at the disposal of the regime and propelled to a unique level of incandescence, with a direct impact on collective and individual behavior."[35] Extreme hatred of Jews was widespread within the German army. A private serving in Poland in 1940 observed, "When

Rounding up Jewish children in the Lodz ghetto (in Poland) for transport to the Chelmno death camp.
Source: Wikimedia Commons

one looks at these people, one gets the impression that they really have no justification for living on God's earth." Similarly, a corporal recounted a discussion among the troops about the "Jewish Question": "To my amazement, everybody agreed in the end that the Jews have to disappear completely from the world."[36]

However conflicted some of the men may have been about their work, Battalion 101 participated in the "Harvest Festival" massacre of November 1943, claiming forty-two thousand victims, which was the largest German killing spree of the war (larger than Babi Yar) and only surpassed by the Romanian murder of over one hundred thousand Jews from the Odessa region beginning in October 1941. SS chief Heinrich Himmler ordered the escalation of killing for several reasons. He was anxious to begin the deportation of German and West European Jews, so he needed to empty the eastern camps and ghettos of their current population to make room for a fresh set of victims. Beyond that, believing the "stab in the back" myth, Hitler and his henchmen feared that any Jews remaining in the fatherland would somehow undermine the current war effort. Also, having lost their illusions of survival, Jewish prisoners in the East were beginning to revolt. Himmler gave absolute priority to the extermination campaign, overriding objections of some factory managers and military officers who protested that they needed at least some of the Jews for vital war work.

Although most of the perpetrators were men, a large number of German women also participated in these crimes. They imbibed the same torrent of Nazi anti-Jewish propaganda as their menfolk. Female teachers in the lower grades purveyed these venomous messages. Some women served as concentration camp guards, nurses, or secretarial personnel. A few of them were particularly brutal. Ilse Koch, wife of the Buchenwald commandant, earned a reputation for sadistic violence toward the helpless inmates. At the all-female Ravensbrück camp, Dorothea Binz frequently chose prisoners at random to be beaten to death or ripped to shreds by dogs. Other women answered the regime's call to join its brutal colonization of the East. Still others denounced their Jewish neighbors (as well as communists, other non-Aryans, and "undesirables") to the authorities and helped the police discover Jews in hiding. Women took part in boycotts of Jewish businesses and street violence against Jews and their property. Many benefited from the Holocaust by stealing the possessions of arrested Jews. Participation in these rites of ethnic cleansing also gave them a sense of empowerment and belonging in a society that otherwise condemned women to subservient positions. Denunciations and other forms of complicity with mass murder often brought material rewards from the regime.[37]

Although the Nazi regime conducted its extermination campaigns as covertly as possible, the crusade to murder all the Jews of Europe was soon an open secret throughout Germany. Awareness of the crimes made many people uneasy but did not motivate them to oppose mass murder. Most Germans did not advocate the physical destruction of all Jews, but their growing apathy toward that process made it possible. As historian Ian Kershaw so aptly put it, "the road to Auschwitz was built by hatred, but paved with indifference."[38] Moreover, most Germans seem to have supported the policies of demographic engineering and ethnic cleansing necessary to construct a German empire in eastern Europe. Those who ordered and carried out the killings were not the only people bearing responsibility for the Holocaust. Mass murder required a massive logistical operation manned by technicians, skilled tradesmen, railway workers, and many others. The Nazis ruled by carrot and stick. News of glorious victories and booty plundered from the conquered lands buoyed up the home front, but those who harbored dissent in their hearts knew that the era of Weimar civil liberties was long past and that the Third Reich was not a state of laws but a criminal regime that held the power of life and death over everyone. As the military situation deteriorated, the regime became even more violently repressive of its own people in a desperate attempt to hold its war effort together.

The guilt for mass murders in Poland does not rest solely on the shoulders of the Germans. In certain places, the homicidal anti-Semitism of the Nazi conquerors fell on soil well prepared to accept it. In 1941, some Poles in the eastern part of the country, previously annexed by the USSR, greeted the German invaders as liberators. Popular prejudice identified all Jews as communists and collaborators with the Soviets. Moreover, Christian anti-Semitism remained strong. A 1941 report from the Polish Catholic Church praised the Germans as agents of "Divine Providence" for their "liberation of Polish society from the Jewish plague."[39]

The German invasion had the effect of "liberating," encouraging, and intensifying the preexisting anti-Semitism of many local inhabitants. Pogroms had occurred there in past centuries and would recur even in postwar communist Poland. In a sense, Nazi criminality and barbarity were contagious. For example, in July 1941, large numbers of Poles in the town of Jedwabne spontaneously and enthusiastically participated in massacring virtually all their Jewish neighbors. In a primitive explosion of violence, the victims were bludgeoned, stabbed, drowned, and burned alive. A surviving witness later described the horror: "Jakub Kac they stoned to death with bricks. Krawiecki they knifed and then plucked his eyes out and cut off his tongue. . . . After various tortures and humiliations, they burned all the Jews in a barn. . . . Local hooligans armed themselves with axes, special clubs studded with nails, and other instruments of torture and destruction and chased all the Jews into the street. . . . Beards of old Jews were burned, newborn babies were killed at their mothers' breasts."[40]

Beyond primitive ethnic hatred, greed for their victims' property motivated some of the culprits. Others participated in the pogrom to curry favor with the Germans. About 1,600 men, women, and children were murdered. Only a few managed to hide or were sheltered by a Polish neighbor who took pity on them. This was not an isolated incident. Similar pogroms took place in several other communities in this region. Nor was this sort of collaboration in genocide unique to Poland. Even before the invading German troops arrived, spontaneously formed militias began to torture and slaughter their Jewish neighbors in Kaunas, Lithuania. Subsequently, German commanders praised the "zeal" of the Lithuanian Security Police in pursuing Jews, Poles, and communists. Friedländer makes a critical point:

> At each step, in occupied Europe, the execution of German measures depended on the submissiveness of political authorities, the assistance of local police forces or other auxiliaries, and the passivity or support of the populations and mainly of the political and spiritual elites. It also depended on the willingness of the victims to follow orders in the hope of alleviating German strictures or gaining time and somehow escaping the inexorable tightening of the German vice.[41]

The initially successful attack on the Soviet Union brought still more Jews under German control. As in Poland, mobile killing squads followed close behind the Wehrmacht to eliminate Jews, communists, and anyone who showed the slightest resistance. Their largest operation slaughtered over thirty thousand Jews and other "undesirables" in a ravine at Babi Yar outside the Ukrainian capital of Kiev. The army, too, killed a great many Jews as well as Russian civilians and POWs. Field Marshal Reichenau told his men that their objective was to destroy the "Jewish-Bolshevik system" and that in executing this task they should show no mercy to "Jewish subhumans."[42] Once again the Germans were able to recruit accomplices from among the disaffected minority peoples of the USSR—Ukrainians, Lithuanians, and others, some of whom fell upon their Jewish neighbors as scapegoats for the hated Soviet system.

By the end of 1941, the leaders of the extermination campaign realized that their current methods were insufficient and problematic for the perpetrators. Shooting defenseless people all day at close range triggered psychological and even physical problems for many men. Leaders from the government, party, SS, and occupation administration met in conference at the Berlin suburb of Wannsee in early 1942 to revamp and codify the Final Solution to the "Jewish problem." They elaborated plans to murder all nine million Jews in Europe, including those in countries not yet under their control such as England, Ireland, Sweden, Spain, Portugal, and Turkey. They also intended to extend their homicidal grasp to Jews outside of Europe. For example, the grand mufti of Jerusalem, Haj Amin al-Husseini, strongly opposed both British control of Palestine and the Zionist project for creating a Jewish homeland there. Although the Nazis had flirted with the idea of sending German Jews to Palestine at an earlier point, during the war the mufti negotiated with Berlin about producing a Jew-free Middle East.[43] Hitler told the mufti that his ultimate aim was to destroy the Jews everywhere in the world.[44] He also told Goebbels that "their [i.e., the Jews'] last refuge is North America; and there, either in the long or the short run, they will have to pay as well."[45] Although Hitler had unleashed the Second World War, he believed that the Jews were ultimately responsible for it. He expected people all over the world to reach the same conclusion, leading to a global tsunami of anti-Semitism.

At Wannsee, the Germans refocused their strategy from mobile killing units to large death camps with gas chambers and crematoria, a labor-saving and cost-effective strategy. Now, instead of bringing the killers to their victims, the victims would come to killing centers (though murders by firing squads, deliberate starvation, and other techniques continued). Hundreds of freight trains packed with Jews from all over occupied Europe fed victims into the camps (despite the logistical burden this imposed on the war effort). Prisoners were seldom provided with food or water on these long trips. The freight wagons, into which the prisoners were packed tightly, lacked toilets and adequate ventilation. Sometimes, because of thirst, stifling heat, or bitter cold, guards at the destination camps found nothing but carloads of corpses.

As ghastly as these crimes were, the Nazis intended the casualty count to be much higher. Besides murdering all Jews, Hitler intended to destroy the Polish and Soviet states, killing tens of millions of Poles, Russians, Ukrainians, Belorussians, and others in the process. Tens of millions more of those populations were to be driven into a perilous exile, while those remaining in their homelands were to be enslaved. Draconian food requisitioning in the conquered lands achieved three objectives: it fed the army, it kept the home front satisfied, and it thinned the population of defeated enemies. "To the most visionary genocidaires," historian Mark Edele suggests, "indeed, the Holocaust was just a dress rehearsal for much more large-scale genocides."[46]

There has been much debate among historians over how the Holocaust came about and Hitler's role in it. Scholars, sometimes known as "intentionalists," contend that Hitler intended the destruction of the European Jews all along and that the Führer's will and commands determined the trajectory of the Holocaust. Their opponents, the so-called "functionalists," deny both that there was any long-term plan to murder the Jews and that Hitler played a dominating role in the mass killings. Instead, they believe that mass murder evolved out of the exigencies and brutalities of the war and that bureaucratic rivalries and the unpredictable course of events established the path of murder rather than any sort of central direction.[47]

Andreas Hillgruber and other intentionalist historians argue that Operation Barbarossa and the Holocaust had been bound together in Hitler's thought for more than two decades.[48] In contrast, German functionalist historian Martin Broszat suggests that German bureaucrats stumbled into mass murder incrementally as they confronted one wartime emergency after another.[49] Intentionalist historian Gerhard Weinberg counters that, "since Hitler expected to win, not lose, the war, there was no urgent need at that moment to decide the matter of timing," and "this program of mass killing was from the beginning a major portion of the whole ideological war planned for the East with its intended demographic revolution."[50] Weinberg also notes that Hitler began talking about the "total extermination" of the Jews as early as April 1920.[51]

The functionalist interpretation emphasizes the absence of planning and execution documents for some aspects of the killing operations. Some of these papers were undoubtedly lost or deliberately destroyed at the end of the war. Moreover, though Hitler and his henchmen were not in the least ashamed to commit mass murder, for political and propaganda reasons they sought to conceal their crimes. They often gave orders verbally rather than committing them to paper. Most importantly, however, this criticism ignores a key aspect of the functioning of the Nazi state. After Hitler consolidated power, he did not need to issue specific orders for mass murder. Knowing his intent, his earnest subordinates rushed to fulfill his murderous plans. Ian Kershaw calls this behavior of Nazi leaders "working toward the Führer." Hitler's ambitious and sycophantic lieutenants strove to outdo each other in assuming their leader's mindset and anticipating his wishes.

Hitler adhered with remarkable consistency to a basic set of strategic ideas (master race, *Lebensraum*, Jewish world conspiracy, etc.) but exhibited extraordinary (and often disingenuous) tactical flexibility in advancing toward his goals. He did not write in *Mein Kampf* that he intended to exterminate all Jews, though he did indicate his desire to expel all of them from Germany. However, in 1922, he told the journalist Joseph Hell, "Once I am in power, my first and foremost task will be the annihilation of the Jews."[52]

Some functionalist historians suggest that the changing nature of the war, after the *Blitzkrieg* faltered in front of Moscow in December 1941, led to a murderous change in policy toward the Jews—a change elaborated at the Wannsee Conference. Many Nazi planning documents envisioned the removal of Jews to remote areas where they would work for the Reich. Yet death was always the intended outcome. The change in 1942 was not from enslaving Jews to murdering them, but from working them to death to killing them more quickly. Moreover, historian Alexander Rossino makes an important point about the careful selection of perpetrators: "The practice of identifying and selecting the proper men for the job [i.e., mass murder] demonstrates beyond doubt that the escalation of violence against Germany's 'racial' enemies did not occur because the war brutalized SS and police personnel. Instead, leading figures in the SS and police apparatus intentionally took steps before the outbreak of hostilities with Poland to sharpen the regime's racial-political policies."[53]

None of these scholars should be confused with Holocaust deniers who claim that there never was a systematic campaign to exterminate Jews and other ethnic groups. Ethnically motivated murders may have happened, they say, but the total of victims was probably only in the tens of thousands, and the crimes were spontaneous, not official Nazi policy.[54] Their work is based on extreme right-wing ideology and anti-Semitism rather than objective scholarly research. Overwhelming documentary and photographic evidence refutes this position entirely.

Murder on an Industrial Scale

The first major killing center opened at Chelmno in December 1941. It used specially designed vans to murder its victims by pumping diesel exhaust into the passenger compartment. After the Wannsee Conference, five more death camps were established, all of them also in Poland—Treblinka, Sobibor, and Auschwitz-Birkenau, as well as Belzec and Majdanek, which already existed as labor camps but were now retrofitted as killing centers. Doomed prisoners were stripped of their belongings and clothing and then ordered to enter "showers," which were disguised gas chambers into which carbon monoxide was pumped. Later at Auschwitz, highly toxic Zyklon B (hydrogen cyanide) pellets were used. Other prisoners were forced to search the victims' clothing and bodies for valuables (including gold teeth) and to throw the corpses into incinerators.

Not all the prisoners were killed immediately. The SS discovered that it could make a handsome profit by leasing slave labor to German industry. Factories sprang up around some of the camps. At Auschwitz, for example, IG Farben, the great German chemical and pharmaceutical conglomerate, built a large synthetic rubber plant. By 1944 there were over seven million slave laborers toiling in a network of some two thousand camps and industrial plants. Prisoners made chemicals, German uniforms, and even V-2 rockets. Although these labor camps were not officially extermination factories, a combination of short rations, hard labor, and abusive treatment meant death for many of the workers. Nazi leaders referred to this process as "extermination through labor." The SS leadership intended to use this same procedure against many of the Slavic peoples of eastern Europe after the war.

Life in the death camps was literally a living hell. Those prisoners not killed soon after arrival were slowly starved to death, forced to do backbreaking labor, and were frequently beaten and tyrannized by sadistic guards and "Kapos" (other prisoners, often criminals, who served the guards). A five-year-old girl in the Ravensbrück concentration camp later recounted this harrowing experience:

> Someone came to get me. And I was given some candy. . . . And I was taken into a building into a small room. . . . There were two men there. And there were some other people in the room. . . . I was put on a table . . . or a tall bed. . . . I was very violently sexually abused. And I remember being hit, I remember crying, and I wanted to get out of there. And I was calling people. And screaming. And I remember . . . one of them told me that they would stand me up on my head and cut me right in half. They wanted me to stop screaming. And . . . I've had nightmares about that for most of my life.[55]

Dr. Josef Mengele and other SS physicians performed ghoulish medical "experiments" on helpless victims. Prisoners wore identifying triangles or stars: green for criminals, yellow for Jews, pink for homosexuals, red for communists, purple for Jehovah's Witnesses, and black for Gypsies and "asocials" (the homeless, mental patients, sex perverts, etc.).

The extreme nature of camp life brought out the extremes of human behavior—deep compassion and self-sacrifice in some, the worst cruelty and treachery in others. Primo Levi, a concentration camp survivor, believed that "here in the Lager [camp] there are no criminals nor madmen; no criminals because there is no moral law to contravene, no madmen because we are wholly devoid of free will."[56] He explains, "The Lager was a great machine to reduce us to beasts," but Levi still maintained that "we must not become beasts; that even in this place one can still survive . . . and that to survive we must force ourselves to save at least the skeleton, the scaffolding, the form of civilization."[57] The camp experience not only destroyed the body, but for many it was soul killing too. Elie Wiesel, sent to Auschwitz as a teenager along with his family, saw his father being beaten with an iron bar by a Kapo. "At first, my father simply doubled over under the blows, but then he seemed to break in two like an old tree struck by lightning. I had watched it all happening without moving. I kept silent. In fact, I thought of stealing away in order not to suffer the blows."[58] The experience of the Holocaust shook his faith to its core. "Why should I sanctify His name? The Almighty, the eternal and terrible Master of the Universe, chose to be silent. What was there to thank Him for?"[59]

Although the Nazis felt pride rather than guilt over this murderous enterprise, they were sensitive to the negative impact that rumors about the camps might have throughout their empire and in the outside world. They built a "model" camp at Theresienstadt in Czechoslovakia that had schools, parks, recreation facilities, concerts, and even a cabaret. Prisoners there were better fed and, for the most part, not subjected to random violence.

There were no gas chambers or incinerators. This camp appeared in widely distributed newsreels. Ultimately, however, the great majority of inmates at Theresienstadt were transferred to other camps and gassed.

In the last months of the war, with the Red Army and the Anglo-American forces closing in from the East and West, the Germans began to evacuate some of the camps before they were overrun by the enemy. Food and water were seldom provided to the marching prisoners, while guards shot any stragglers and prevented local residents from helping the victims. In their weakened condition, these treks proved to be death marches for as many as 375,000 prisoners.

Initially there was relatively little resistance on the part of Jews who were rounded up and sent to ghettos or camps. What resistance there was tended to be passive—running away, hiding, or trying to pass as Aryan. Most people simply could not imagine (or could not bring themselves to believe) the horrors the Nazis had in store for them. The Germans cultivated this illusion with false announcements of resettlement and labor conscription. Surely, many victims reasoned, the Nazis would not kill people performing essential labor for the German war effort.

Their own traditions worked against them as well. In past persecutions, compromise and negotiation had worked better than armed resistance. Beyond that, few of the victims had the training or weapons for active opposition, they were often too debilitated from deprivation and mistreatment to offer physical resistance, and many of them lived among increasingly hostile local populations who would not help them or who aided the Germans in hunting them down. The Jewish historian Emanuel Ringelblum asked, "Why did we allow ourselves to be led like sheep to the slaughter?"[60] His form of resistance was collecting documents and recording atrocities to document the Holocaust in the Warsaw ghetto for posterity. He was later gassed, but his hidden collection survived. Some of the victims even collaborated in the murder campaign. Jewish councils and ghetto police helped maintain order in the ghettos and sometimes selected people for deportation. For some, cooperating with the Germans seemed to be the lesser evil—sacrificing some to save as many as possible. For others, the motive was simply self-preservation.

Life in the ghettos was horrific. A Polish underground publication described the Warsaw ghetto thus: "Groups of pale and emaciated people wander aimlessly through the overcrowded streets. Beggars sit and lie along the walls and the sight of people collapsing from starvation is common. The refuge for abandoned children takes in a dozen infants every day; every day a few more people die on the street. Contagious diseases are spreading, particularly tuberculosis."[61]

As the killing operations intensified, however, the awful truth became undeniable, and resistance occurred more frequently. Some prisoners escaped to join local partisan bands, though not all resistance groups welcomed Jews. Estimates of Jews fighting with resistance groups in eastern Europe run from twenty to thirty thousand. In Poland, for example, many Jews fought in the Home Army. Yet, here as elsewhere, civil war prevented a unified resistance to the Nazis. The Home Army fought not only against the Germans but also against the communist-led People's Guard (or People's Army, which included many Jewish fighters). By 1943, some desperate prisoners began to stage insurrections in the camps.

That spring, the Jews of the Warsaw ghetto rose in revolt when it became clear that most of them were being taken to death camps. The rebels were very poorly armed, with only a few machine guns, rifles, and pistols, as well as hand grenades and Molotov cocktails. They received only minimal help from the Polish resistance movement. Yet these tenacious fighters managed to hold off German counterattack for four weeks before being crushed by overwhelming tank and artillery firepower and by the tactic of burning the fortified buildings in the ghetto one by one. Thirteen thousand Jews died during the uprising, and those who survived its suppression were shipped to the Treblinka death camp. Revolts also took place in the Bialystok and Vilna ghettoes, and smaller prisoner rebellions occurred at Auschwitz, Sobibor, Treblinka, and a few other camps and ghettos. All of them were suppressed by superior German firepower. Thousands of survivors, however, managed to escape the ghettos and join the partisans in the forests.

News of the mass murder campaign began to trickle out to the Allied countries by late 1941. The first indication of mass killings in the East came when Ultra code breakers intercepted and decrypted orders to enemy forces involved in the campaign. That source could not be publicized, of course. More information came from the Polish intelligence service and from citizens of neutral countries who could still travel in Germany and parts of eastern Europe. Jan Karski, of the Polish underground, risked his life to sneak into the Warsaw ghetto and then to bring his firsthand report of German atrocities to London. The USSR published reports of German massacres on its territory. Churchill publicly revealed the mass murders in August 1941, calling them "a crime without a name," but he did not identify Jews as the principal target of the massacres.[62] In June 1942, the British *Daily Telegraph* reported that the Germans had gassed some seven hundred thousand Jews.

Many people in the Western countries doubted these stories. Mass murder on that scale seemed unimaginable, even for the Nazis. Even many Jews in the Allied states could not yet bring themselves to believe it. Beyond that, the apparently discredited Allied propaganda about German atrocities in the First World War made people skeptical about this news.[63] They were ignoring the facts that the Third Reich was clearly a much more homicidal regime than the Kaiserreich of 1914 and that real massacres had occurred in World War I, most notably the killing of a million or more Armenians by the Turks. Many people in authority simply did not want to hear the horrible news. Kurt Gerstein, an SS officer who was distressed about the mass murder of Jews, disclosed the details of the crime to a Swedish diplomat as well as to the Catholic and Protestant bishops of Berlin. He also attempted to inform Swiss and Vatican diplomats. None of them were willing to publicize and protest the fate of the Jews.[64]

Even when increasing evidence made the horrible truth undeniable, Allied governments chose not to emphasize the Holocaust in their propaganda. Given the pervasiveness of anti-Semitism in their countries, London and Washington did not want to portray their war effort as a crusade to save the Jews. After the war, some writers criticized the Allies for doing nothing to stop or at least inhibit the extermination campaign. Western leaders countered that the only real way to end the Holocaust was to defeat Germany, not divert air power to bomb the transports and the camps—measures that were unlikely to end the horror but which would have killed many of the prisoners! Historian Walter Laqueur asked the hard question: Did playing down news of the Holocaust and declining to attempt any measures to hinder it make any difference? "The Jews inside Europe could not have escaped their fate," he concluded; "those outside were too weak to help, and the neutrals and the Allies might not have done more than they did in any case."[65]

Most people in Germany and Nazi-occupied Europe failed to help their Jewish neighbors because they were anti-Semitic themselves, were simply apathetic to the fate of others, or were prevented from extending aid to the victims by fear of Hitler's murderous regime. There were some outstanding exceptions. Raoul Wallenberg, a Swedish diplomat serving in Hungary, saved thousands of Jews by issuing them Swedish passports and by renting thirty-two buildings in Budapest as safe houses for Jews. He declared these structures part of the Swedish diplomatic mission and therefore Swedish sovereign territory. Similarly, Oskar Schindler, a German industrialist (as well as Abwehr agent and member of the Nazi Party!) saved 1,200 Jews by using his connections and large bribes to prevent Jewish workers in his Polish and Czech factories from being sent to death camps. Sugihara Chiune, the Japanese consul in Lithuania, gave passports to several thousand Jews, who were then able to travel across the USSR to Japan and then migrate to Palestine or the United States.

Some victims of the Holocaust could have avoided their fate by fleeing to America, but the United States—a country made by immigration—had largely closed its borders. Since 1924, the total number of immigrants had been limited to 165,000 per year, with lower quotas for specific nationalities. Racism and xenophobia pervaded the government and population. Nonetheless, between 1938 and mid-1942, 150,000 European Jews found sanctuary in the United States. Tragically, however, as the Holocaust intensified, even that trickle was choked off by increasingly onerous rules for admission into the United States.

During the years America was at war, only twenty-one thousand refugees entered the US—that is, less than 10 percent of the legally permitted quota! In one famous case in 1939, 908 Jewish refugees aboard the German passenger liner *St. Louis* were denied entry into the United States. Cuba and Canada declined to accept them as well. The ship was forced to return to Europe, where its passengers settled in various countries, most of which were subsequently overrun by the Nazis. In America, according to historian John Morton Blum, it was "anti-Semitism, the bureaucratic inertia, and the ordering of the government's wartime priorities that prevented any effective effort to save the lives of the Jews of Europe."[66] Similarly, the British refused to permit large numbers of Jews to emigrate to Palestine in order not to exacerbate already serious tensions between native Arabs and Jewish settlers in that region.

The Roman Catholic Church also failed to oppose the Holocaust in any meaningful way. Before the war, the church had negotiated accommodations with both Mussolini and Hitler to protect its organizational integrity and its property. During the conflict, Pope Pius XII saw the Third Reich as a necessary defense against the spread of Bolshevism in Europe. He declined to publicly condemn the Nazis for mass murder because he feared compromising Vatican neutrality. When the issue arose among German bishops, the papal nuncio told them, "It is all well and good to love they neighbour, but the greatest neighbourly love consists in avoiding making any difficulties for the Church."[67] In some places, Catholic priests and believers took grave risks to aid their Jewish neighbors but received little encouragement for their efforts from the church leadership. Similar neglect prevailed among German Protestants.

Some of Germany's client states (France, Slovakia, Croatia, and Romania) enthusiastically rounded up their Jewish citizens for slaughter. Most of the others did so more or less reluctantly under growing German pressure. They disliked the abrogation of their sovereignty, but even after Stalingrad, when it began to seem that Germany might lose the war, they were unable to resist Berlin's menacing demands. In Hungary, extremist elements came to power in the last year of the war and directly participated in mass murder. The Jewish experience in Italy, however, represents a special case in Axis-controlled Europe. Anti-Semitism had not been part of Mussolini's fascist ideology. The Duce proclaimed in 1932, "We too have our Jews. There are many in the Fascist Party, and they are good Fascists and good Italians."[68] Although Mussolini occasionally made comments about Jewish businessmen being "too cosmopolitan," he had a Jewish mistress and appointed Jewish ministers to his government.

After Hitler came to power in 1933, Mussolini criticized the Führer for the barbarity of Nazi racism. There were anti-Semitic elements within the Fascist movement, but the dictator did not encourage them. During the first sixteen years of the Fascist regime, the Jews of Italy continued to live more or less normal lives. They were a highly assimilated group, scarcely distinguishable from their non-Jewish compatriots.

All that changed in 1938. The Duce adopted anti-Semitism as the official policy of the state. A ten-point Manifesto on Race expelled foreign Jews; excluded Jewish Italians from the party, public office, and schools; and banned "mixed" marriages. Italian officials did not enforce the laws rigorously, and the definition of "Jew" was sufficiently vague to allow many to escape penalties. The laws did not mandate physical persecution or interference with religious observances. Nonetheless, many Jewish businesses closed, and some Jewish Italians emigrated—the most serious defection being the renowned physicist Enrico Fermi, whose wife was Jewish. Persecution escalated somewhat once Italy entered the conflict. By May 1942, five thousand Jews had been pressed into forced labor. Nonetheless, during the early years of the war, Mussolini's regime acted to protect Jews in the parts of Yugoslavia, Greece, and southern France that it occupied.

Many historians attribute the sudden espousal of racism in 1938 to the growing Rome-Berlin axis. Fascist Italy was increasingly dragged into Nazi Germany's orbit, and Hitler expected his protégés to share his racist mania. But that is only part of the story. Martin Clark suggests that "the anti-Semitic agitation was . . . part of a more general 'anti-bourgeois' and pro-Empire campaign."[69] Mussolini thought Italians needed to be tougher and to gain a more rigid sense of national identity to exploit their empire. Also, the regime was distressed about the number of Italians who had married or fathered children with Ethiopian women.

The situation turned even worse for the Jews of Italy in July 1943 when the Allies landed in Sicily. The Germans occupied the country and put Fascist radicals, who were genuine anti-Semites, in charge of a new, collaborationist government, the Italian Social Republic. Adolf Eichmann dispatched specially trained German squads to hunt down Italian Jews. A vicious civil war between Fascist and anti-Fascist partisans broke out. The German SS spread terror throughout the country, sometimes wiping out whole villages. They, together with the Italian police and Fascist thugs, rounded up and deported about 7,500 Jews to be murdered in German death camps. There were about 45,200 Jewish Italians living in the country at the time of the German occupation. Of that number, 85 percent survived. They were saved by their neighbors. "Many non-Jewish Italians," historian Susan Zuccotti tells us, "were anti-German, anti-Fascist, and prepared to help all fugitives who came their way. . . . Sympathetic priests and nuns were joined by doctors, lawyers, government officials, peasants, and housewives."[70]

Notes

1. Quoted in Mark Mazower, *Dark Continent: Europe's Twentieth Century* (New York: Viking, 1998), 153.

2. Alex J. Kay, *Exploitation, Resettlement, Mass Murder: Political and Economic Planning for German Occupation Policy in the Soviet Union, 1940–1941* (New York: Berghahn Books, 2006), 203.

3. Quoted in Frank Ellis, *Barbarossa, 1941: Reframing Hitler's Invasion of Stalin's Soviet Empire* (Lawrence: University Press of Kansas, 2015), 59.

4. Martin C. Dean, *Collaboration in the Holocaust: Crimes of the Local Police in Belorussia and Ukraine, 1941–1944* (New York: St. Martin's, 1999).

5. Quoted in Amir Wiener, *Making Sense of War: The Second World War and the Fate of the Bolshevik Revolution* (Princeton, NJ: Princeton University Press, 2001), 260.

6. Amir Wiener, "Saving Private Ivan: From What, Why, and How?," *Kritika: Explorations in Russian and Eurasian History* 1, no. 2 (2000): 321.

7. Nicholas Stargardt, *The German War: A Nation under Arms, 1939–1945* (New York: Basic Books, 2015), 438.

8. "ROA [the Russian Liberation Army] never in fact existed, it was a term coined by the Germans agitating for a change in Nazi policy towards the Soviet Union, and they created a mythical army in order that those Soviet citizens fighting in the ranks of the Wehrmacht should feel some kind of unity and have some concrete aim for which to fight." Catherine Andreyev, *Vlasov and the Russian Liberation Movement: Soviet Reality and Émigré Theories* (Cambridge: Cambridge University Press, 1987), 2.

9. Alfred J. Rieber, "Civil Wars in the Soviet Union," *Kritika: Explorations in Russian and Eurasian History* 4, no. 1 (Winter 2003): 156.

10. Jeffrey Burds, "The Soviet War against 'Fifth Columnists': The Case of Chechnya, 1942–4," *Journal of Contemporary History* 42, no. 2 (2007): 267–314.

11. Ellis, *Barbarossa*, 73–74.

12. Sarah Helm, *Revensbrück: Life and Death in Hitler's Concentration Camp for Women* (New York: Anchor Books, 2015), 68.

13. Gerhard L. Weinberg, *Visions of Victory: The Hopes of Eight World War II Leaders* (Cambridge: Cambridge University Press, 2005), 19. Cf. Christopher Browning, who argues that, before Operation Barbarossa, the Final Solution only meant moving the Jews as far away from the expanding Reich Germany as possible. The invasion of the USSR, he contends, turned this process into a war of extermination. *The Path to Genocide: Essays on Launching the Final Solution* (Cambridge: Cambridge University Press, 1992), 16–17. Mark Mazower offers a similar analysis. *Hitler's Empire: How the Nazis Ruled Europe* (New York: Penguin, 2008), 368–80. Both Browning and Mazower miss the point, made by Laurence Rees, that expelling Europe's Jews to Madagascar or northern Russia would still have resulted in most of them dying. *The Holocaust*, 201.

14. Gerhard Weinberg, "Comments on the Papers by Friedlander, Breitman and Browning," *German Studies Review* 17, no. 3 (1994): 510.

15. Cf. Richard Evans, who argues that "available evidence suggests that, on the whole, ordinary Germans did not approve [of the mass killing of Jews]." *The Third Reich at War* (New York: Penguin, 2008), 561.

16. Edith Hahn Beer, *The Nazi Officer's Wife: How One Jewish Woman Survived the Holocaust* (New York: Morrow, 2015), 84–85, 92.

17. Evans, *The Third Reich at War*, 11.

18. Doris L. Bergen, *War and Genocide: A Concise History of the Holocaust* (Lanham, MD: Rowman & Littlefield, 2009), 105.

19. According to Richard Lukas, "Poland lost 45 percent of her physicians and dentists, 57 percent of her attorneys, more than 15 percent of her teachers, 40 percent of her professors, 30 percent of her technicians, and more than 18 percent of her clergy. Most of her journalists also disappeared." *Forgotten Holocaust: The Poles under German Occupation, 1939–1944* (Lexington: University Press of Kentucky, 1986), 9.

20. William L. Shirer, *Berlin Diary: The Journal of a Foreign Correspondent, 1934–1941* (New York: Knopf, 1941), 173.

21. Stargardt, *The German War*, 138.

22. Norman Davies, *God's Playground: A History of Poland*, vol. 2, *1795 to the Present* (New York: Columbia University Press, 1982), 445.

23. Richard Lukas, *Forgotten Holocaust*, 38.

24. Stargardt, *The German War*, 291–92.

25. Evans, *The Third Reich at War*, 52.

26. Stargardt, *The German War*, 172.

27. Jeffrey Burds, "Sexual Violence in Europe in World War II, 1939–1945," *Politics & Society* 37, no. 1 (2009): 39.

28. Christopher R. Browning, *Ordinary Men: Reserve Police Battalion 101 and the Final Solution in Poland* (New York: Harper Perennial, 1998), 222.

29. Browning, *Ordinary Men*, 168.

30. Browning, *Ordinary Men*, 184.

31. Daniel Jonah Goldhagen, *Hitler's Willing Executioners: Ordinary Germans and the Holocaust* (New York: Knopf, 1996), 449.

32. Goldhagen, *Hitler's Willing Executioners*, 279.

33. Christopher R. Browning, *Nazi Policy, Jewish Workers, German Killers* (Cambridge: Cambridge University Press, 2000), 150.

34. Snyder, *Bloodlands*, 205–6.

35. Saul Friedländer, *Nazi Germany and the Jews, 1939–1945*, vol. 2, *The Years of Extermination* (New York: Harper Perennial, 2007), xx.

36. Friedländer, *The Years of Extermination*, 159.

37. Wendy Lower, *Hitler's Furies: German Women in the Nazi Killing Fields* (Boston: Houghton Mifflin Harcourt, 2013).

38. Ian Kershaw, "The Persecution of the Jews and German Public Opinion in the Third Reich," *Leo Baeck Institute Yearbook*, no. 26 (1981), 261–63.

39. Friedländer, *The Years of Extermination*, 185.

40. Jan T. Gross, *Neighbors: The Destruction of the Jewish Community of Jedwabne, Poland* (Princeton, NJ: Princeton University Press, 2001), 16–19.

41. Friedländer, *The Years of Extermination*, xv.

42. Bergen, *War and Genocide*, 158.

43. Klaus-Michael Mallmann and Martin Cüppers, *Nazi Palestine: The Plans for the Extermination of the Jews of Palestine* (New York: Enigma Books, 2010).

44. Anthony R. DeLuca, "'Der Grossmufti' in Jerusalem: The Politics of Collaboration," *International Journal of Middle East Studies* 10, no. 1 (1979): 125–38.

45. Friedländer, *The Years of Extermination*, 239.

46. Mark Edele, *Stalinism at War: The Soviet Union in World War II* (London: Bloomsbury Academic, 2021), 142,

47. Lucy S. Dawidowicz, *The Holocaust and the Historians* (Cambridge, MA: Harvard University Press, 1981); Otto Dov Kulka, "Singularity and Its Relativization: Changing Views in German Historiography on National Socialism and the 'Final Solution,'" in *Reworking the Past: Hitler, the Holocaust, and the Historians' Debate*, ed. Peter Baldwin (Boston: Beacon, 1990), 146–70.

48. Andreas Hillgruber, *Germany and the Two World Wars* (Cambridge, MA: Harvard University Press, 1981), 51; Saul Friedländer, *Nazi Germany and the* Jews, vol. 1, *The Years of Persecution, 1933–1939* (New York: Harper, 1997).

49. Martin Broszat, "Genesis of the 'Final Solution': An Assessment of David Irving's Theses," in *Aspects of the Third Reich*, ed. H. W. Koch (New York: St. Martin's, 1985), 399–404.

50. Gerhard L. Weinberg, *A World at Arms: A Global History of World War II* (Cambridge: Cambridge University Press, 2005), 192.

51. Weinberg, *Visions of Victory*, 17–18.

52. Gerald Fleming, *Hitler and the Final Solution* (Berkeley: University of California Press, 1987), 17.

53. Alexander B. Rossino, *Hitler Strikes Poland: Blitzkrieg, Ideology, and Atrocity* (Lawrence: University Press of Kansas, 2003), 228.

54. E.g., David Hoggan, *The Myth of the Six Million* (Los Angeles: Noontide Press, 1969); Fred Leuchter and David Irving, *The Leuchter Report: Auschwitz, the End of the Line, the First Forensic Examination of Auschwitz* (Los Angeles: Institute for Historical Review, 1989); and the Los Angeles–based Institute for Historical Review, which published a journal and maintains a website. Also see Michael Shermer and Alex Grobman, *Denying History: Who Says the Holocaust Never Happened and Why Do They Say It?* (Berkeley: University of California Press, 2009).

55. Quoted in Burds, "Sexual Violence," 45.

56. Primo Levi, *Survival in Auschwitz* (New York: Collier, 1993), 98.

57. Levi, *Survival in Auschwitz*, 41.

58. Elie Wiesel, *Night* (New York: Hill & Wang, 2006), 54.

59. Wiesel, *Night*, 33. Wiesel eventually returned to his Orthodox Jewish faith.

60. Quoted in Evans, *The Third Reich at War*, 308–9.

61. Quoted in Wladislaw Bartoszewski, "The Martyrdom and Struggles of the Jews in Warsaw under German Occupation, 1939–1943," in *The Jews in Warsaw: A History*, ed. Wladislaw T. Bartoszewski and Anthony Polonsky (New York: Oxford University Press, 1991), 314.

62. *The Churchill War Papers*, ed. Martin Gilbert (London: Heinemann, 2000), 3:1102.

63. Recent research demonstrates that there were, in fact, numerous German atrocities during World War I. John Horne and Alan Kramer, *German Atrocities, 1914: A History of Denial* (New Haven, CT: Yale University Press, 2001).

64. Stargardt, *The German War*, 252–53.

65. Walter Laqueur, *The Terrible Secret: Suppression of the Truth about Hitler's "Final Solution"* (New York: Penguin, 1982), 10.

66. John Morton Blum, *V Was for Victory: Politics and American Culture during World War II* (New York: Harcourt, Brace, Jovanovich, 1976), 175.

67. Michael Phayer, *The Catholic Church and the Holocaust* (Bloomington: Indiana University Press, 2000), 75.

68. Meir Michaelis, *Mussolini and the Jews: German-Italian Relations and the Jewish Question in Italy, 1934–1941* (New York: Oxford University Press, 1978), 56.

69. Martin Clark, *Mussolini* (Harlow: Pearson, 2005), 222.

70. Susan Zuccotti, *The Italians and the Holocaust: Persecution, Rescue, Survival* (New York: Basic Books, 1987), xvii.

Occupation/Collaboration/ Resistance: Asia

Japanese Occupation

Japan proclaimed itself the liberator of Asia from European and American colonial enslavement. Tokyo envisioned itself as the "father" of a metaphorical Confucian family, with the right and duty to guide other Asian nations to independence, enlightenment, and prosperity. Japan promised the peoples whose lands it overran that they would enjoy the benefits of a Greater East Asia Co-Prosperity Sphere. Japanese propaganda depicted European and American imperialists as depraved, cruel, and avaricious despoilers of Asia. It highlighted the racism of these imperial overlords. It also frequently used pictures of surrendering white soldiers as a weapon against the myth of white invincibility. The rapid defeat and humiliation of British, American, and Dutch forces in the Far East raised hopes for freedom among the colonial peoples. Some Asian leaders rallied to Tokyo's banner, at least initially, but the Japanese soon proved themselves to be even more brutal masters than their white predecessors.

Tokyo did not treat the countries it "liberated" as allies but as colonies. The Japanese set up military governments throughout Southeast Asia to extract that region's rich resources on terms most favorable to Tokyo. The occupied countries were made to pay their occupier's expenses. Everywhere in the empire, occupation regimes printed money to cover their needs. They took huge quantities of food from China, Vietnam, and the East Indies, leaving the local populations hungry. In contrast to the pseudo-liberation of the Dutch and British colonies, the Japanese left Vichy French authorities in nominal control of Indochina, though here, too, real power remained with the Imperial Army. Hunger spread throughout Indochina because Tokyo forced many rice farms to grow cotton and oil-producing plants for its war effort. In March 1945, suspecting a coup, the Japanese overthrew the Vichy colonial regime and proclaimed "freedom" for the Vietnamese. It was certainly not a liberation from hunger, for the Japanese seizure of the rice crop resulted in the starvation of two hundred thousand Vietnamese.

The new colonial masters extorted not just food but human labor as well. In northern China alone, the Japanese forced two and a half million people into virtual slavery. Chinese collaborators often played a crucial role as intermediaries in this human trafficking. These laborers worked in China or were taken to Japan, Korea, or elsewhere in the empire. They toiled on farms and in mines, factories, and construction projects. They were required to do backbreaking, often dangerous labor; were subjected to harsh discipline; and were poorly fed, clothed, and housed. Many died. Prime Minister Tojo bluntly told those supervising slave labor "not to be obsessed with the mistaken ideal of humanitarianism."[1] Beyond government programs for labor mobilization, Japanese soldiers often kidnapped local residents to work for them—for a few hours or days or months. The fortunate ones were released after completing their tasks. The less fortunate were shot or bayoneted. Rather than prosperity, the "Co-Prosperity Sphere" brought the peoples of East Asia repression, exploitation, slavery, inflation, unemployment, and famine.

In Vietnam as elsewhere in Asia, Japanese occupation and brutality sparked resistance. Ho Chi Minh, the communist leader, revived the Viet Minh national liberation movement, ultimately claiming to have mobilized over half a million fighters. Viet Minh guerrillas fought against the Japanese and their Vichy allies for the independence of their homeland. They received support from the United States, the Soviet Union, and Nationalist China. This struggle exposed a rift in the Grand Alliance. The French (both Vichy and the Free French) intended to reimpose colonial domination over Vietnam after the defeat of the Axis. Great Britain was also suspicious of the Viet Minh and all other anticolonial movements throughout Asia. However, the US Office of Strategic Services provided some assistance to the Viet Minh as the only force actively engaging the enemy in Indochina. With the onset of the Cold War, Washington switched its support to France in a losing cause.

When the Japanese overran the Philippines, President Manuel Quezon fled with Mac-Arthur and subsequently established a government-in-exile in the United States. One of his ministers who remained behind, Jose P. Laurel, formed a collaborationist government, the Second Philippine Republic. Laurel had been a critic of US rule in the Philippines. He was a Pan-Asianist with ties to Japan. Under heavy Japanese pressure, Laurel signed a treaty of alliance with Tokyo and declared war on the United States, though he refused to send Filipinos to fight overseas alongside the Japanese. He also represented his country at the 1943 Greater East Asia Conference in Tokyo.

Collaborationist leaders Ba Maw (Burma), Jang Jinghui (Manchuria), Wang Jingwei (China), Tojo Hideki (Japan; host of the conference), Wan Waithayakon (Thailand), Jose Laurel (Philippines), and Subhas Chandra Bose (India) at the Greater East Asia Conference in Tokyo, 1943.
Source: Wikimedia Commons

The occupiers formed a native police force, the Bureau of Constabulary, and secured its halfhearted cooperation by threatening family members. They also organized a six-thousand-man anti-partisan force, the Makapili, or Filipinos Fighting for the Japanese, by promising land for poor men. In general, there was a lower level of collaboration in the Philippines than in Burma and the Dutch colonies. There was also more resistance, but it was fragmented. American and Filipino soldiers who had escaped the Japanese and formed guerrilla groups in the hills comprised the most prominent element in the resistance. These groups supplied valuable intelligence and assisted US forces in liberating the islands in 1944. In contrast, the communist-led Hukbalahap (or People's Army against the Japanese) fought not only to rid the country of its invaders but also to spark a social revolution. Moro Muslim guerrillas on Mindanao and Sulu fought against rule by Christian Filipinos and Americans as well as against the Japanese occupiers. Once again, civil war flared within the world war.

Late in 1942, when the tide of war began to turn against Japan, military and civilian leaders in Tokyo tried to give more substance to their Pan-Asianist rhetoric, hoping to enlist the peoples of Asia to resist the Anglo-American advance. Foreign Minister Shigemitsu Mamoru proclaimed that his country was "liberating great East Asia from the yoke of the United States and Great Britain, constructing a new and just Asian order through voluntary cooperation of Asian peoples, and bringing about Asian stability and prosperity on the basis of equality and mutuality."[2] It was too little, too late. The expanded autonomy given to the collaborationist Wang Jingwei regime in China and to local administrations in Indonesia and Malaya, as well as "independence" for Burma and the Philippines, came with sharp limitations. Each of them had to cooperate closely with Japan militarily, diplomatically, and economically. Malaya and Indonesia remained directly ruled imperial territories.

The Japanese treated Manchukuo somewhat differently than their other conquests. The Kwantung Army and the administration of the South Manchurian Railway dominated the region. Japanese managers and engineers strove to build a model society in Manchukuo—an authoritarian technocracy. The military intended to use the economy of Manchuria, in a form of state capitalism, not only to revitalize but also to transform the stagnant economy of the home islands. Japan invested over nine billion yen there between 1932 and 1944, building factories, opening mines, and expanding the transportation infrastructure.[3] Japanese companies flooded into Manchuria, including the giant Mitsui and Mitsubishi conglomerates. The region became a key source of iron, coal, and other minerals for the home islands. Manchurian production not only financed the Kwantung Army's operations but was crucial to Japan's broader war effort too. The army also profited greatly by the sale of opium.

Japanese penetration of Manchuria had a demographic dimension as well. Tokyo planned to send five million Japanese migrants there. Many Japanese settlers were armed and were allowed to use violence against their Chinese neighbors. Beyond enhancing control over the region, this effort was intended to relieve rural overcrowding and poverty in Japan and also to strengthen defenses against a possible Soviet attack. Ultimately, a coalition linking the army, business groups, ultranationalists, and settlers' organizations formed a powerful voice in Japanese politics supporting imperial expansion.

The pseudo-independent state of Manchukuo and its emperor, Puyi, scarcely masked Japanese domination. There were never enough Japanese troops or civil administrators to rule all of Manchuria effectively, so in many places they relied on the cooperation of local elites. Such collaboration was more a matter of acquiescence than active support and was principally motivated by self-preservation. The occupiers also attempted to create a youthful cohort of collaborationist Chinese and Manchus in the Manchukuo army and civil administration, though most senior positions were held by Japanese. These young men were assimilated as far as possible into the Japanese value system and culture. The Japanese advertised themselves as the "leading race" of Asia while treating Han Chinese, Manchus, and other ethnicities as second-class citizens who were forced to bow to passing Japanese and who were often ill paid and ill fed. The occupation authorities made significant attempts to reach a cooperative accommodation with the peoples of Manchuria, but their need to strip the land of food, labor, and natural resources in the last years of the war undermined those efforts. As guerrilla resistance grew in the countryside, the occupiers forced many villages to consolidate into a small number of fortified hamlets, completely disrupting the rural economy.

Like Germany, Japan was parasitic on its empire. Nonetheless, the imperial experience laid the groundwork in several ways for the postwar decolonization movement in Asia. In many places, civil and military collaborationist experiences served to train postcolonial elites. By forming collaborationist military units and political movements, as well as by viciously exploiting its conquests, Japan gave both positive and negative impetus to the demands of Asian colonial peoples for freedom. In Europe, extensive collaboration with the German or Italian occupiers usually brought disgrace and sometimes punishment after the defeat of the Axis. In contrast (except for China and the Philippines), many of those who led collaborationist efforts in Asia emerged as leading political figures in their postwar, postcolonial societies. At the beginning of December 1943, the Japanese organized a conference in Tokyo to celebrate launching their Greater East Asia Co-Prosperity Sphere. Collaborationist leaders from all over Asia attended—Ba Maw from Burma, Jose Laurel from the Philippines, Wan Waithayakon of Thailand, Subhas Chandra Bose from India, and Wang Jingwei from occupied China. Bose praised his hosts in a public speech: "This is not the first time that the world has turned to the East for light and guidance. . . . In the creation of a new, free and prosperous East, the Government and people of Nippon should play a leading role."[4] The delegates spoke of racial equality among Asians, but the Japanese army's actions in the field belied these noble sentiments.

After the war, some of these same leaders played prominent roles in their newly independent states. In Burma, Aung San served as premier of the British Crown colony (1945–1947) and negotiated his country's independence from Britain, though he was assassinated shortly before the event. Ba Maw, who served the Japanese as head of state in nominally independent Burma, survived the war and returned to Burma to participate in political life. In Thailand, Wan Waithayakon (Prince Wan) was never punished for collaborating with the Japanese, but went on to play important roles not only in Thailand but also in the United Nations, SEATO, and the Bandung Conference. In contrast, Subhas Chandra Bose died in a 1945 plane crash while fleeing arrest by the victorious Allies, though he and the Indian National Army, which he led, were subsequently celebrated as heroes of the national cause. Wang Jingwei, the best-known Chinese collaborator, died in Japan in 1944 from wounds received in an assassination attempt. Soviet forces captured Puyi, the "last emperor," in August 1945 and returned him to China after Mao's victory in 1949. He spent ten years in prison, where he was confronted by numerous victims of Japan's crimes in China, was "reeducated" by the Chinese Communists, and finally repented for his role in supporting Japan. He spent the final years of his life working as a gardener.

Occupation, Collaboration, and Resistance in China

The Chinese people experienced the war in many different ways—those in areas conquered early by the enemy and occupied continuously, versus those in provinces continuously fought over, versus those in relatively secure regions of Free China, as well as those in places where the Nationalists and Communists contested for control. The urban experience was often quite different from life in the countryside. In some of the major cities occupied throughout the war—Beijing, Tianjin, Shanghai, and Guangzhou—some level of collaboration, complying with at least some of the occupier's rules, was essential to find food, hold jobs, and avoid repression.

The Japanese interned Westerners of various nationalities who were living or traveling in occupied China. After December 1941, many were allowed to continue doing business in occupied China, though with significant restrictions. Then in March 1943, the Japanese put most of them in concentration camps. These camps were crude, with few amenities. Food and medical care were in short supply, but the camps were not death camps. The Japanese herded the substantial Jewish community in Shanghai into a ghetto after the victims sold their possessions and businesses for pennies on the dollar. Discipline was harsh. Many of these Jews were forced to work as "coolies" or as prostitutes to avoid starvation. However, the Japanese authorities resisted German pressure to exterminate the whole ghetto.

The Japanese set up several regional puppet regimes throughout occupied China. They needed these collaborationist governments to relieve the Imperial Army of some of the burden of pacifying the occupied zones and to provide civil administration in those areas. Tokyo expected its occupation forces to be self-financing or, better still, to turn a profit for the home islands. The Japanese made extensive use of renegade warlords who feared them more than Chiang Kai-shek. The Reorganized National Government of China, based in Nanjing and founded in 1940 by Guomindang defector Wang Jingwei, provided a semblance of a national government. Wang had been a leader of the left wing of the Guomindang, but he broke with the Communists and moved to the right politically. After the death of Sun Yat-sen, he lost the struggle for leadership of the GMD to Chiang Kai-shek. Soon after the Sino-Japanese War broke out, Wang concluded that resistance to Japan was futile. It would only destroy China and pave the way for Communism. In 1938, he fled Chongqing for Japanese-occupied Hanoi, where he negotiated the formation of his collaborationist regime. Wang based his government on an ideology of Pan-Asianism, anticommunism, and opposition to Chiang Kai-shek. His administration gave the Japanese virtually everything they wanted in China.

After the conquest of Wuhan, Zhang Renli, the Japanese-educated son of a distinguished family, set up a collaborationist regime in the tri-cities. Wuhan became a major Japanese air and army base for operations against the Nationalists. The enemy committed no large-scale atrocities in Wuhan, so its residents lived in relative security until American bombing destroyed much of the area in December 1944. Beyond these pro-Japanese regimes, some Chinese cooperated with the occupiers to gain political and economic advantage, but most people who collaborated did so out of grim necessity. Businessmen in the big cities dealt amicably with the Japanese if they wanted to keep their businesses. Ordinary citizens did whatever the enemy commanded just to stay alive. In many villages within the occupied zone, the Japanese set up Peace Maintenance Committees comprised of collaborators from the local elite. They aided in pacifying the villages and reporting any signs of resistance activity. The proliferation of collaborationist governments made for a kaleidoscopic battlefield. The Nationalist and Communist armies, besides battling each other, were fighting the Japanese and several puppet regimes. All of these forces were also fighting a host of bandit and rebel groups, loyal to no one but themselves. The national liberation struggle was superimposed on and often indistinguishable from an underlying civil war.

The Japanese used ethnic resentments to stimulate collaboration in Inner Mongolia, where they patronized Prince De Wang and his Pan-Mongol movement. Many Mongolians chafed under Chinese rule and saw Prince De as a hero who would liberate them, though the obviously "puppet" status of his government undercut that hope. As elsewhere in their empire, Japanese officers and businessmen treated Mongolia not so much as an ally but as a colony to be exploited. Beyond domestic security concerns, Inner Mongolia was a particularly sensitive area for the Japanese because it bordered Soviet-dominated Outer Mongolia.

As in Europe so also in China, the categories of collaboration and resistance often melded into each other. Though largely illegal, continued trade was necessary to maintain the lives of ordinary people in Free China as well as in the occupied zones. The enemy invasion had disrupted established trade networks. Smuggling on a massive scale took the place of those severed commercial networks, but this entailed making deals with Japanese and Nationalist minor officials as well as various criminals. For many Chinese, the behavior of the enemy undercut any impetus to collaborate. The horrifying Japanese atrocities perpetrated at Shanghai and Nanjing continued to occur throughout occupied China, though on a smaller scale. For instance, in February 1938, Japanese troops attacked the small town of Qiaosi, near Hangzhou, even though there were no Nationalist troops there. As one survivor recalled, "a large Japanese force from nearby surrounded our town. They began what became an inhuman massacre. They stationed sentries at spots along the main street. After that, they set fires and began to kill people."[5] The Japanese intended to intimidate the Chinese people so that they would accept occupation docilely, but the actual results were quite different.

These atrocities and exactions stimulated hatred, political consciousness, and resistance among the population. Many Chinese came to believe that submission to the occupiers would result only in death for many and slavery for most of them. When resistance activities increased, the Japanese responded with an escalation of atrocities—the "three all" policy (kill all, burn all, loot all) in an attempt to frighten the peasantry into submission. One survivor recounted the enemy attack on his village: "On March 30th, 1942, towards evening, five or six hundred Japanese soldiers suddenly rushed in to Shanxitou Village. . . . Fires were lit all over the village. . . . All the grain stored in the houses was taken. . . . At nightfall, the soldiers turned on the women like wild animals, and raped ten or twenty women. Some of the women were unable to move for days after their ordeal. The saddest case was the pretty new wife of Zhang Zhongshun, who was raped to death. . . . Towards dawn the Japanese soldiers cleared out all the valuables in the village."[6] Reactions to enemy brutality varied depending on the individual's immediate situation and psychological makeup. While atrocities provoked resistance, they could also stimulate compliance.

Nationalism had taken root among Chinese students and intellectuals and some of the middle class long before the Japanese conquest of Manchuria in 1931. The onset of full-scale war in 1937 accelerated that process and even motivated some warlords to rally to the national cause. In the face of overwhelming enemy power, higher Guomindang civil officials retreated from north and east China along with the Nationalist army. The Japanese army had neither the desire nor the ability to replace the civil government in much of the territory it nominally occupied. Local, mostly anti-Japanese, governments sprang up throughout occupied rural China. The GMD encouraged its lower officials to maintain local shadow governments in the occupied areas, including sponsorship of local militias. These local regimes, whether established by the Guomindang or provincial elites, were vital to maintaining security in the face of chaos created by the war.

Previously, the identity and loyalty of most Chinese peasants had been familial and local, or regional at best. In the apt phrase of social scientist Chalmers Johnson, up to this point most of the peasantry was "politically illiterate."[7] A combination of Japanese brutality and patriotic appeals by Communists, Nationalists, and others convinced many Chinese of the connection between their personal well-being and the survival of their nation. Johnson argues that the horrendous national liberation struggle against the Japanese welded the vast peasant majority into a cohesive, self-aware nation—to the benefit of the Chinese Communist Party, which proclaimed itself the only champion of that nation.

Social scientist Mark Selden contends that it was the social, economic, and political policies followed by the Communists in response to the wartime emergency that garnered peasant loyalty.[8] Moreover, historian Keith Schoppa argues that truly mass nationalism among the Chinese peasantry developed slowly and only *after* the Second World War. Surveying survivor memoirs from an occupied province, Schoppa found little evidence of deep nationalist sentiment. For most, family security remained the priority.[9] Rana Mitter characterizes wartime Chinese nationalism as "emergent."[10] While some resisted, many others opted for passive acceptance of enemy occupation. They realized that when a guerrilla attack occurred, Japanese wrath came down on the local villagers, not on the guerrillas who had disappeared. Ultimately, Mao Zedong and the Communist Party were the winners in this process, while the Japanese and the Guomindang regime were the losers.

Chinese Communism Reborn

Before the outbreak of full-scale war with Japan in 1937, the Chinese Communist Party had experienced defeat after defeat at the hands of Chiang Kai-shek. Only a small and still beleaguered remnant survived the Long March to reach remote Yan'an. The struggle against the brutal Japanese occupiers gave the CCP the opportunity not only to reemerge as a potent political force but ultimately to triumph in its rivalry with the Nationalist regime. They seized that opportunity by modifying their military and political strategies. Militarily, they adopted hit-and-run guerrilla tactics that allowed them to take credit for fighting the enemy daily but at the same time minimized their casualties. Most of fighting against the Japanese and the preponderance of the casualties were sustained by Chiang Kai-shek's Nationalist armies. The Communists won the propaganda battle, however—painting themselves as the only real defenders of China and castigating Guomindang forces for defeats, retreats, inaction, and failure to cooperate with the Communists in a united front against the invader.

Previously, Mao Zedong had pushed for radical land redistribution and class war not only against landlords but also against "rich" and middle peasants. He abandoned that radicalism, at least partially, during the war. Now CCP social policies focused on reformist measures of rent control and repressing loan sharks. Under orders from Moscow, the party appealed for the formation of a broad resistance coalition of virtually everyone willing to fight the Japanese. However, the Chinese Communists were careful to keep control of the resistance movement in their own hands. There was always tension between the Communist Party's two main objectives—"to substantially improve the poorer peasants' overall living conditions *and* forge a rural united front including all village strata."[11] Party leaders were determined to continue the revolutionary struggle within the national liberation war. Along with Japanese atrocities, the prospect of land redistribution and other measures of social equalization attracted poor peasants and day laborers to the Communist cause. Class struggle was never completely abandoned, neither by the party nor by the rural elite.

While the Japanese were brutal to the peasantry and the Nationalist army sometimes mistreated them as well, Communist forces were ordered not to kill, rape, or steal from the peasants. The size of resistance units was limited so that they would not overburden the local peasantry. In contrast, guerrilla bands associated with the Nationalist government often mistreated and overtaxed the local folk. The Communist guerrillas sometimes assisted the farmers with planting and harvesting when the military situation permitted. While the Communist leadership was not always able to control its irregular forces—who on occasion acted like bandits—they nonetheless gained a reputation for treating the peasants much better than any of the other forces involved in the war. These were winning strategies in the struggle for the hearts and minds of the Chinese peasantry.

The guerrillas depended on the peasants for food, shelter, and information. Mao referred to the guerrillas as fish and to the peasantry as the sea in which they swam. Communist forces could be brutal when it served their interests—for example, assassinating Chinese who collaborated with the enemy or shooting those who disobeyed orders. Overall, Mao and his comrades succeeded in projecting an image of themselves as the group most likely to defeat the invader and create a better society after the war. A lethal dialectic worked in their favor: Communist attacks provoked violent Japanese retaliation, not usually against the guerrillas who had vanished but on the local population. The resultant atrocities motivated many to join the resistance. This escalating spiral of violence continually strengthened the Communists while stretching Japanese resources thin.

The sympathetic American journalist Theodore White described the CCP's approach to recruiting peasants this way:

> If you take a peasant who has been swindled, beaten, and kicked about all his waking days and whose father has transmitted to him an emotion of bitterness reaching back for generations—if you take such a peasant, treat him like a man, ask his opinion, let him vote for a local government, let him organize his own police and gendarmes, decide on his own taxes, and vote himself a reduction in rent and interest—if you do all that, the peasant becomes a man who has something to fight for, and he will fight to preserve it against any enemy, Japanese or Chinese. If in addition you present the peasant with an army and a government that help him harvest, teach him to read and write, fight off the Japanese who raped his wife and tortured his mother, he develops a loyalty to the army and the government and to the party that controls them.[12]

White's romanticized characterization of life in Communist-controlled areas ignored Mao's authoritarianism and the less than egalitarian practices of his regime. Nevertheless, it impressed the peasants that Communist officials were required to grow some of their own food. Mao raised tobacco, while Chu Teh, commander of the army, grew cabbages. Ultimately, peasants rallied under Communist leadership for a variety of reasons, especially their reaction to Japanese brutality and their hopes for a more just postwar order.

Sex Slavery and Biological Warfare

One of the worst infamies perpetrated by Japanese occupation forces throughout their empire was the so-called comfort stations—brothels in which sex slaves (euphemistically known as "comfort women") were forced to serve the erotic and sadistic desires of the Imperial Army and Navy. The Ministry of War claimed that these stations were created to maintain discipline and morale among the troops, to prevent the spread of venereal diseases (since comfort women were examined frequently by doctors), and (ironically) to prevent rape.[13] Ultimately, as many as two hundred thousand victims were enslaved by the Japanese, often with the help of local collaborators. The largest numbers were Korean and Chinese women, but also Taiwanese, Indonesians, and other Asian women, as well as a few European women. In many cases, these young women were kidnapped into sexual slavery. In other instances, naive girls were falsely recruited for nonsexual jobs and then coerced into prostitution. They were often held under appalling conditions, frequently beaten, and sometimes made to "service" as many as thirty or more soldiers in a day. Many of them did not survive this brutal ordeal. Those who did would bear physical and emotional scars for the remainder of their lives.

One survivor from a village near Kuala Lumpur, Malaysia, related this experience: "Two lorries of Japanese soldiers came to our village. . . . Three soldiers with rifles came to our house. . . . They burst in and grabbed me. . . . Then my panties were ripped off and one of the soldiers undid the front of his trousers. While the others held me down, he stuck his thing into me. . . . I was only fifteen and hadn't had my first period. . . . Three soldiers did it to me in turns, and then they took me out and put me in one of the lorries along with some other girls from my village."[14] This woman endured the rest of the war as a sex slave. She survived the ordeal, though not without serious physical and psychological damage. Once imprisoned in the comfort stations, the victims were subjected to multiple rapes and violence daily. Maria Rosa Henson, a Filipina woman who was abducted by Japanese troops at the age of fifteen, described a typical day: "At two, the soldiers came. . . . My work began, and I lay down as one by one the soldiers raped me. . . . . Every day, anywhere from twelve to over twenty soldiers assaulted me. There were times when there were as many as thirty; they came to the garrison in truckloads. . . . I lay on the bed with my knees up and my feet on the mat, as if I were giving birth. . . . Whenever the soldiers did not feel satisfied, they vented their anger on me. . . . Every day, there were incidents of violence and humiliation."[15]

Once a sex slave became too sick or too injured to be useful in these brothels, she was typically murdered or ransomed back to their families. One fifteen-year-old Chinese girl remembered, "Japanese troops raped me every day. . . . The torture made my private parts infected and my entire body swollen. The pain in my lower body was excruciating to the point that I could neither sit nor stand. Since I could not walk, when I needed to go to the latrine I had to crawl on the ground. What a living hell!"[16] Since she soon became useless to her captors, they let her father ransom her by selling his entire goat herd. Other ill or maimed comfort women were not so fortunate. Female Chinese POWs were treated with especial harshness as the following report indicates: "The supply of condoms to the frontline troops was scant, so many of these women who were raped by soldiers without condoms became pregnant. The pregnant women were continually raped as long as they were useable. When they were no longer usable they were taken out of the strongholds and tied to standing timbers so new soldiers could practice using their bayonets."[17]

The establishment and maintenance of comfort stations were the official policy of the Japanese military and government (even where civilian contractors did the recruiting and managed their operation). Students in the Imperial Army's accounting school studied the "endurance" of comfort women and the rate at which they would "wear out." Their existence reflects values common in Japanese society at that time. Japan had long had a system of legal, licensed prostitution, typically employing some Japanese women but also many Koreans and other Asians. Impoverished peasants sometimes indentured female children into this system. Moreover, in Japan prostitution did not have the moral stigma that it bore in the United States. Japanese scholar Yoshimi Yoshiaki contends that modern Japanese "culture sanctioned male sexual self-indulgence—that is, the fulfillment of male sexual desire regardless of the dignity and human rights of women."[18] This statement by a Japanese soldier illustrates this negative, utilitarian view of women: "During the battle, which lasted about fifty days, I did not see any women at all. I knew that as a result of (being without access to women), men's mental condition ends up declining, and that's when I realized once again the necessity of the special comfort stations. This desire is the same as hunger or the need to urinate and soldiers merely thought of comfort stations as practically the same as latrines."[19]

Beyond the need for sexual gratification for the troops, these barbaric institutions served a psychological-political purpose. Historian Timothy Brook suggests that "women of child-bearing age were raped or forced into prostitution because they were, or stood in for, the body of the nation. So, rape was widely performed as a gesture of conquest, but not simply as a release for male sexual starvation; it was an act of humiliation. Japanese soldiers performed this act on the bodies of Chinese women, but the target of the humiliation was Chinese men; it was proof of their impotence in all ways."[20]

Mass murder and rape were not the only atrocities committed in China by the Japanese. There was also involuntary medical experimentation on human subjects carried out by the infamous Unit 731 (euphemistically labeled a section of the Epidemic Prevention and Water Purification Department of the Kwantung Army) as part of their biological and chemical warfare program. As many as twelve thousand Chinese civilians (including women, children, and even infants), as well as captured guerrilla fighters, Koreans, Russians, and a few Western POWs, were injected with smallpox, cholera, bubonic plague, botulism, and other infectious agents. Many of these victims were then subjected to vivisection without anesthetic to remove their organs to study the effects of the pathogens. The Japanese conducted this experimentation at a large covert facility near Harbin, Manchuria, under the direction of Lieutenant General Ishii Shiro. One of the program's research assistants explained the need for vivisection: "Unless you dissected them quickly [i.e., while they were still alive], extraneous bacteria would intrude." This forced human experimentation seemed acceptable to him because "we were already implanted with a narrow racism, in the form of a belief in the superiority of the so-called 'Yamato Race.'"[21] It was acceptable to subject members of these supposedly inferior races to excruciating tortures and death to promote the victory of the superior Japanese.

These military officers and medical scientists sought to weaponize the pathogens. In one case the victims "were tied to stakes in the ground. Then anthrax-filled bombs were exploded nearby."[22] This particular series of tests failed to develop an effective delivery system for anthrax. In addition to bacterial bombs, the scientists tested spraying jellied bacterial compounds and infected insects from airplanes, disease-carrying balloons, infected food and vaccines, and diseased rats, birds, dogs, and horses as vectors for biological attacks. The program also examined the effects on humans of lethal but nonbiological conditions, including hypothermia and frostbite, dehydration, malnutrition, drastic air pressure changes, and the introduction of animal blood into people's circulatory systems.

The Japanese employed the poisonous fruits of this scientific research in military operations. Major General Kawashima Kiyashi testified at the Soviet war crimes trial at Khabarovsk in 1949, "There was one instance in 1941 and another in 1942 when Detachment 731 expeditions employed lethal gas as a weapon against Chinese troops in Central China."[23] The Japanese army also launched large-scale germ warfare attacks in Yunnan and Shandong Provinces. "Plague literally rained down upon people's heads," reports investigator Daniel

Barenblatt, "sprayed from special bio-war air team planes of the military; cholera, typhoid, dysentery, anthrax, paratyphoid, glanders, and other pestilences infected their food, drinking wells, crops, and livestock."[24] Beyond their use against Guomindang forces, these biological attacks were intended to destroy the will of the Chinese people to continue fighting. Hu Xian-zhong, a survivor of such an attack, recalled:

> I am the sole surviving member of a family exterminated by germ warfare carried out by Unit 731. . . . In the end of October 1940, Unit 731 aircraft flew low over Ningbo and hovering over downtown Kai ming jie, dropping plague-infected fleas along with wheat and corn. . . . The first victim of the plague was my sister, Hu Ju Xian. At the start of November, she started complaining of headaches and developed a fever. Her face was completely red and the lymph nodes in her thighs were swollen. She lost consciousness. . . . Barely 10 days after my sister's death, my brother, then my father and mother, passed away infected with the plague. . . . I became an orphan.[25]

As a final atrocity, before they fled from Manchuria in August 1945, the Japanese released rather than destroyed rats that had been inflected with bubonic plague as part of their research program. More than thirty thousand people subsequently died from this plague outbreak. Chinese investigators believe that the total number of victims of Japanese medical experimentation and these attacks may be 580,000 people. At the end of the war, those Unit 731 staff members who were caught by the Russians or the Chinese were tried and punished, but many of the top officers and scientists in the program, who were then in Japan and thus under American control, escaped punishment in exchange for sharing their research with the US military.

Notes

1. Michael Burleigh, *Moral Combat: Good and Evil in World War II* (New York: Harper, 2011), 561.

2. Akira Iriye, *Power and Culture: The Japanese-American War, 1941–1945* (Cambridge, MA: Harvard University Press, 1981), 117.

3. S. C. M. Paine, *The Wars for Asia, 1911–1949* (Cambridge: Cambridge University Press, 2012), 27.

4. John H. Boyle, *China and Japan at War, 1937–1945: The Politics of Collaboration* (Stanford, CA: Stanford University Press, 1972), 23.

5. R. Keith Schoppa, *In a Sea of Bitterness: Refugees during the Sino-Japanese War* (Cambridge, MA: Harvard University Press, 2011), 2–3.

6. Diana Lary, *The Chinese People at War: Human Suffering and Social Transformation, 1937–1945* (Cambridge: Cambridge University Press, 200), 145.

7. Chalmers A. Johnson, *Peasant Nationalism and Communist Power: The Emergence of Revolutionary China, 1937–1945* (Stanford, CA: Stanford University Press, 1962), 3.

8. Mark Selden, *China in Revolution: The Yenan Way Revisited* (Armonk, NY: M. E. Sharpe, 1995).

9. Schoppa, *In a Sea of Bitterness*, 135–36.

10. Rana Mitter, *China's Good War: How World War II Is Shaping a New Nationalism* (Cambridge, MA: Harvard University Press, 2020), 34.

11. Dagfinn Gatu, *Village China at War: The Impact of Resistance to Japan, 1937–1945* (Vancouver: UBC Press, 2008), 5.

12. Theodore H. White and Annalee Jacoby, *Thunder Out of China* (New York: Da Capo, 1980), 201–2.

13. George Hicks, "The 'Comfort Women,'" in *The Japanese Wartime Empire, 1931–1945*, ed. Peter Duus, Ramon H. Myers, and Mark R. Peattie (Princeton, NJ: Princeton University Press, 1996), 310.

14. George Hicks, *The Comfort Women: Japan's Brutal Regime of Forced Prostitution in the Second World War* (New York: Norton, 1994), 12.

15. Maria Rosa Henson, *Comfort Women: A Filipina's Story of Prostitution and Slavery under the Japanese Military* (Lanham, MD: Rowman & Littlefield, 1999), 38–40.

16. Peipei Qiu, *Chinese Comfort Women: Testimonies from Imperial Japan's Sex Slaves*, with Su Zhiliang and Chen Lifei (Vancouver: UBC Press, 2013), xviii.

17. Peipei Qiu, *Chinese Comfort Women*, 48.

18. Yoshimi Yoshiaki, *Comfort Women: Sexual Slavery in the Japanese Military during World War II* (New York: Columbia University Press, 2002), 200.

19. Yoshimi, *Comfort Women*, 199.

20. Timothy Brook, *Collaboration: Japanese Agents and Local Elites in Wartime China* (Cambridge, MA: Harvard University Press, 2007), 23–24.

21. Haruko Taya Cook and Theodore F. Cook, *Japan at War: An Oral History* (New York: New Press, 1992), 164–65.

22. Sheldon H. Harris, *Factories of Death: Japanese Biological Warfare, 1932–45, and the American Cover-Up*, 2nd ed. (New York: Routledge, 2002), 89.

23. *Materials on the Trial of Former Servicemen of the Japanese Army Charged with Manufacturing and Employing Bacteriological Weapons* (Moscow: Foreign Languages Publishing House, 1950), 260.

24. Daniel Barenblatt, *A Plague upon Humanity: The Hidden History of Japan's Biological Warfare Program* (New York: HarperCollins, 2004), xii.

25. Barenblatt, *A Plague upon Humanity*, 138–40.

Part IV

THE ALLIED VICTORY

CHAPTER 14

The Eastern Front:
A Shifting Balance

The outcome of the Second World War was largely determined on the eastern front.[1] It was there that the Wehrmacht deployed three-quarters of its troops, and it was there that the German army was bled white. The enormous scale of combat there dwarfed that in any other theater of operations. Casualty figures tell the story. In the summer of 1944, the German army was losing about eight thousand men per month fighting the Western Allies in France, while it was losing up to two hundred thousand troops per month on the eastern front. Even Winston Churchill admitted in March 1944: "Not only have the Hun invaders been driven from the lands they had ravaged, but the guts of the German Army have been largely torn out by Russian valour and generalship."[2]

After a disastrous beginning to the war, the Red Army rebounded to defeat Hitler's vaunted legions. Soviet forces had to master a steep learning curve to recover from their initial battlefield disasters and fight effectively against an enemy both ruthless and skilled in the techniques of modern warfare. The tuition for those brutal lessons could only be paid in blood. Dmitrii Krutskikh, a Red Army platoon leader, put it bluntly: "Learning in combat means losing people. It must be said—our experience was earned through a lot of blood. In my unit, I practically had to replace everybody."[3] Stalin's initially inept performance as war leader inflated that fearful price. He was overconfident in his own judgment, largely ignorant of the latest advances in military strategy, and determined to make all the important decisions himself. He also relied too heavily on cronies who had fought alongside him in the Russian civil war but who were seriously out of their depth fighting against the Wehrmacht.

A great many of the Soviet people would have perished in the fight against Germany even with the best leadership, but how many of the twenty-seven million wartime Soviet deaths are attributable to Stalin's amateurish generalship, paranoia, and ruthlessness remains an open question. The lives of his people simply did not matter to him. The Soviet dictator eventually did find new commanders who could meet the German challenge, and he learned to delegate at least some decision-making authority to those leaders. There is no escaping the conclusion, however, that the USSR's victory over Germany cost several million more Soviet lives than necessary due to the deficiencies of Stalin personally and of the brutal system of rule that he created.

Soviet Winter and Spring Offensives, 1942

Soviet success in the fighting in front of Moscow in December 1941 convinced Stalin that the balance of power between the Red Army and the Wehrmacht had shifted decisively in his favor. Against the advice of his senior commanders, he ordered offensive operations along the whole eight-hundred-mile front. The Soviet press and radio began touting "complete defeat of the Hitlerite forces in the year 1942." In March he informed Churchill, "I feel entirely confident that the combined efforts of our troops, occasional setbacks notwithstanding, will culminate in crushing the common enemy and that the year 1942 will see a decisive turn on the anti-Hitler front."[4] The Soviet dictator now repeated the mistake the Germans had made by thinking that he could smash his enemies in one rapid, overwhelming blow. Based on incomplete and sometimes inaccurate intelligence reports, but even more on his own instincts, Stalin now ordered attacks along the whole front.

Soviet forces continued to attack German Army Group Center in front of Moscow on a broad front stretching 340 miles until the spring mud season brought the offensive to a halt. Some of Hitler's generals recommended a further retreat of fifty to seventy-five miles, but the Führer demanded "fanatical resistance" where they stood. The Soviet high command (Stavka) hoped to encircle and destroy all enemy formations on the central front. In February 1942, Georgii Zhukov's Western Army Group pushed ahead, while to his north, General Ivan Konev's Kalinin Army Group punched through the thinly defended enemy line to sweep west of Rzhev and link up with Soviet spearheads attacking from the southeast. The surrounded German forces fought fiercely and eventually escaped encirclement. At the same time, the Red Army used paratroopers and horsed cavalry to harass the enemy rear and temporarily cut communications.

Hitler finally modified his "no retreat" order, allowing German troops to fall back to the more defensible Königsberg Line. The Germans replaced exhausted commanders and reorganized their defense, plugging gaps and stabilizing their perimeter. Both at the front and in Berlin, the sense of panic began to subside. Elements of three Soviet armies were now trapped behind enemy lines, though they continued to fight. Minimally supplied by air and backwoods trails, some of these troops reached their own lines, but most of them were killed or captured. The Stavka ordered Zhukov to resume his offensive in the Rzhev-Viazma sector, but the campaign made little progress against a strengthened enemy defense.

Stalin also hoped that the German defeats west of Moscow would enable him to relieve Leningrad. That besieged city had seemed on the verge of collapse in October 1941. The Volkov Army Group, under General Kirill Meretskov, attempted to destroy the enemy forces surrounding Russia's second-largest city. Soviet troops within the city were so debilitated at this point that they did not have the strength to strike outward in support of their own liberation. Meretskov's units made some initial progress, but poor coordination of forces, enemy air superiority, and powerful German flanking attacks foiled the operation. The Germans encircled and destroyed General Andrei Vlasov's 2nd Shock Army, capturing the unfortunate commander. The Soviets lost ninety-five thousand men in this campaign. Leningrad would continue to freeze and starve. The Germans refused to permit any of the starving population to cross their lines. South of Leningrad, the Northwestern Army Group drove a hundred miles into occupied territory, cutting off ninety-five thousand enemy troops at Kholm and the village of Demiansk. The Germans stood their ground in heavy fighting, with the Luftwaffe supplying and reinforcing them by air. Relief columns lifted the siege in March. The Soviets lost another ninety thousand soldiers in a failed effort.

The Russians also launched major operations in the far south. The Wehrmacht had broken into the Crimean Peninsula at the end of September 1941 and laid siege to the Soviet military and naval concentration at Sevastopol. They had also taken the Kerch Peninsula on the eastern end of the Crimea in November, potentially giving them access to the oil-rich

Caucasus region. Stalin was determined to reverse those disasters. The Soviets launched the first major Allied amphibious operation of the war in late December 1941, striking at Kerch. General Erich von Manstein abandoned his siege of Sevastopol to organize a successful counterattack against the Russians. Moscow poured in reinforcements and broadened the scope of the operation to recapture the whole of the Crimea. Manstein, now reinforced with armor and air power, struck back decisively, capturing 170,000 prisoners, 1,100 artillery pieces, and 250 tanks. The Germans killed Soviet defenders holding out deep in limestone quarries with poison gas. Freed from the threat to his rear, Manstein now redoubled his attack on the Sevastopol fortress, bringing in huge siege artillery. A Soviet survivor of the battled described the ghastly scene:

> About 2,000 guns and mortars kept firing at our positions without a moment's interval. Shells shined overhead and exploded on all sides. The thunder of guns merged into a deafening roar, splitting our eardrums. . . . German aircraft were in the air above our positions all day long. We could not hear their engines in the continuous thunder of guns and shell explosions. . . . A whirlwind of fire was raging at all our positions. The sky was clouded by smoke from thousands of bombs and shells. . . . An enormous dark grey cloud of smoke and dust rolled higher and higher and finally eclipsed the sun.[5]

The defenders fought tenaciously but soon ran out of ammunition. Hitler promoted Manstein to field marshal for his triumph. The Crimean debacle cost the USSR another 390,000 troops.

Soviet military planners also intended to liberate the great Ukrainian industrial city of Kharkov. Marshal Semën Timoshenko launched a broad offensive in January that reached points twenty-five to thirty-five miles from the city by May. He intended to destroy the occupying forces by a two-pronged encirclement from the east and southeast. The Germans, alerted to Soviet plans by their intelligence service, launched their own preemptive encirclement campaign, soon trapping much of the Soviet 6th Army. Red Army losses exceeded 171,000 men. Once again, the Russians lost because they underestimated enemy capabilities, because their command and control was too slow to recognize and respond to fast-moving battlefield developments, and because the Luftwaffe's control of the air gave the Germans a decisive advantage. Beyond the massive defeat itself, the disaster at Kharkov left a huge gap in the Soviet defensive line—one which the Germans would exploit to attack the Caucasus and Stalingrad.

These defeats came because the Soviets were now overextended and exhausted. Moreover, much of the rebuilt Red Army consisted of hastily trained conscripts, while Soviet industry, still reeling from the Barbarossa onslaught, had not yet produced enough replacement weapons. Beyond that, Soviet leaders still had not fully absorbed the bloody lessons about how to fight the Germans. Boris Gorbachevskii, who was in officer candidate school at this time, was taught that "the officer must precisely follow the Field Regulations on the attack and on defense, in winter and in summer, while on guard, and so forth. All of us, both instructors and cadets, know that the field regulations we are learning are outdated, based largely on the experience of the Russian Civil War, with no regard for the experiences and understanding of contemporary warfare."[6] Because so many Soviet junior and mid-level officers had been lost in combat, inexperienced and inadequately trained replacements commanded far too many units. Aleksandr Bodnar, a junior officer, describes one disaster caused by poor tactical leadership during the 1942 offensive:

> I went one or one and a half kilometers behind our combat formation and sud-
> denly saw a field dotted with our dead and wounded soldiers. Young guys, with
> Guards badges, in brand new uniforms. . . . A German machine gunner sat in a
> pillbox and wiped out our soldiers. This was such an inept surmounting of the
> no-man's-land. The soldiers were ready for anything, but the commanders did not
> know how to attack properly. They needed to bring up the mortars, some artillery,
> suppress this machine gun, but no, the commanders urged, "Onward! Onward![7]

Stalin and his generals had opened themselves to a potentially devastating enemy counteroffensive. By their foolishly aggressive tactics, they had squandered their resources for
minimal gains. Total Soviet losses for the first half of 1942 exceeded 1.4 million troops,
while the Germans lost 188,000 men. Stalin believed that powerful Soviet offensive operations early in 1942 would consume enemy reserves and prevent the Germans from mounting
major attacks that year. He was wrong.

Hitler Resumes the Offensive

For 1942, the Kriegsmarine wanted to commit all of Germany's resources to a "war of the
continents" against Great Britain and the United States, but Hitler and the army leadership
insisted that the eastern front remain the top priority. The Führer needed to seize Russia's
food and oil and drive the USSR out of the war before turning against his maritime enemies.
Now that the war had become a global conflict, Hitler and the army high command (OKH)
understood that an all-out offensive in the East was a high-risk, all-or-nothing gamble.
Failure would leave Germany too weak to resist its three powerful opponents. At this point,
the Germans were no longer strong enough the launch offensives along the entire front as
they had done the preceding year. The army fielded 625,000 fewer troops on the eastern
front than it had when Barbarossa began, and it was not yet able to replace the majority of
combat vehicles destroyed in earlier fighting. Hitler's generals advocated a renewed drive on
Moscow, believing that the fall of the capital would finally crack Soviet morale. The Führer
had other plans. He focused on the southern front, with the objective of depriving the enemy
war effort of resources, particularly oil, and seizing those resources for himself.

Rommel's capture of Tobruk in North Africa, Japan's stunning victories in the Far
East, and the successes of the U-boat campaign in the north Atlantic raised the possibility
of a death blow to the Grand Alliance. Hitler had thought in 1941 that he had no need of
Japanese assistance to destroy the Soviet Union. By July 1942, he had changed his mind,
but Tokyo now declined to enter the war against Russia since its forces were fully committed
against the Americans, British, and Chinese. Nonetheless, he thought success in southern
Russia might allow Axis forces to link up in the Middle East and Indian Ocean, fatally undermining the defenses of the British Empire and the Soviet Union. If those two enemies
could be defeated before America was fully mobilized for war, the chances for an Axis victory
would improve dramatically.

For Operation Blue (*Fall Blau*), the Germans diverted much of the infantry and nearly
all the armor and air power to the campaign in the south. They and their allies would strike
with almost two million troops—eighty-nine divisions, including nine panzer divisions. Almost two thousand aircraft supported them. Hitler pressed his Italian, Hungarian, and Romanian allies to provide additional forces. Those units were less well trained and equipped

than Wehrmacht divisions. They were used to guard the flanks of German offensives. The operation was scheduled to begin in May, but delays in the Crimean campaign and supply difficulties pushed the start date back to the end of June. Army Group Center was to hold in place, merely threatening a renewed assault toward Moscow, while Army Group North would finish off Leningrad only after the anticipated victory in the south.

Soviet forces were less prepared for the German summer offensive than they should have been because, once again, Stalin's suspicions trumped verifiable intelligence information. The Germans attempted to prepare their operations in secret, but the British passed along Ultra intercepts that betrayed their intent. In addition, Soviet intelligence obtained detailed information on enemy dispositions and battle plans when, on July 19, a German light plane carrying that information crashed behind Soviet lines. It seemed to the ever-suspicious Soviet leader that such an intelligence windfall had to be a deliberate disinformation ploy. An enemy deception effort, Operation Kreml (Kremlin), involving fake preparations for attacking Moscow, may have influenced Stalin as well—illustrating the point that deception operations work best when their intended victim is predisposed to believe them. Stalin insisted—and many of his generals concurred—that the main German blow would fall against Moscow. He therefore kept 2.53 million men, 4,260 tanks, and 1,400 warplanes on the central front, compared to less than half that number of troops and fewer tanks and planes on the southern front.

Stalin still thought that German forces were too depleted for a major offensive. Believing that an attack in the south might catch the enemy by surprise, he ordered an assault on the Izium bridgehead along the west bank of the Donets River. Although the operation caught the Germans off guard, they soon recovered their composure and enveloped the attackers. They killed or wounded 267,000 Soviet troops, took 240,000 more as prisoners, and destroyed or captured 1,200 tanks and 2,600 artillery pieces.[8]

Fall Blau got underway on June 28. The ensuing Battle of the Don Bend was a gigantic confrontation, fought across a 350-mile front. The Germans—once again spearheaded by armor and ground-attack aircraft—smashed through the defending Soviet forces. As Soviet resistance crumbled, morale plummeted, defeatism swelled, and many soldiers deserted. The Red Army lost a staggering 370,000 men and 2,500 tanks, though many survivors managed to escape the enemy encirclement that had so often befallen Soviet forces the previous year. At the northern end of the front, Axis forces captured Voronezh on July 5. The Wehrmacht soon overran the rich Donbass (Donets basin) coal-mining and industrial region. The Germans recaptured the city of Rostov almost unopposed on July 23 because panicked soldiers fled in disarray, leaving only a few NKVD troops to fight to the last man. Capturing Rostov also allowed the Germans to cut the vital pipeline connecting the oil fields of the south with central Russia. With army discipline seemingly on the verge of collapse again, Stalin issued Order Number 227: "Not one step backward! This must now be our main slogan. It is necessary steadfastly, to the last drop of blood, to defend each position, each meter of Soviet territory, to hold every patch of Soviet soil, and to hold it as long as possible."

While Stalin was in a virtual state of panic, Hitler was elated. He thought that the victory that had eluded him in 1941 was now within his grasp. On July 20, Hitler exclaimed to General Halder, "The Russian is finished!" Halder agreed. Overconfident, but also fearing British and American attacks in western or northern Europe, Hitler diverted several powerful SS panzer divisions to the West. He sent more units to bolster the Leningrad front. Neither the Führer nor his generals understood that the recent Red Army retreats to avoid encirclement (compared to the "stand and fight" tactics of 1941, which made encirclement so effective) were a tactic to preserve Soviet forces, not evidence that the Russians were completely beaten and fleeing in disarray.

The Nazis' hatred of the Soviet system and their disdain for the Slavs as fighting men led them to conclude that the Red Army was a spent force, no longer capable of serious resistance. Operation *Blau* had originally envisioned a massive drive in stages, first to occupy the west bank of the Volga River and then to push south into the oil fields of the Caucasus Mountains. Now, suffering from fatal overconfidence, Hitler split his forces. The main effort, undertaken by Army Group A under Field Marshal Wilhelm List, was to strike into the Caucasus toward those all-important oil wells near the Caspian Sea. Army Group B, comprised of General Friedrich Paulus's 6th Army and large Italian, Romanian, and Hungarian forces, would launch a secondary attack, driving toward the major city of Stalingrad on the Volga River.

Paulus's forces were to secure the flank of Army Group A while it moved into the northern Caucasus region. His forces initially made steady progress in open country against relatively light opposition. Lack of provisions hindered Soviet units. The Germans had now cut the railway lines from central Russia. The Western Allies sent some supplies across the Caspian Sea. As the invaders approached the Caucasus Mountains, however, the terrain began to favor the defenders, slowing the German advance. The enormous distances involved—eight hundred miles from the attackers' starting point to their objective—meant inevitable fuel shortages. The Germans mounted a supplemental amphibious operation from the Crimea in early September, but progress was still slow. Frustrated, Hitler dismissed List and took over direction of the Caucasus fighting himself. The 1st Panzer Army neared Ordzhonikidze (modern-day Vladikavkaz) in early November, but its offensive stalled in the face of stubborn Soviet resistance. Hitler's adjutant, visiting the scene, observed:

> Troops more or less at the end of their tether. . . . Caucasus south of Krasnodar and Maikop only negotiable . . . by mountain troops with mules. No possibility of . . . a decisive attack. . . . Operations off roads and paths totally out of question because of primeval-type jungle. . . . A Panzer division is totally out of place there. Tough Russian resistance in the mountains, heavy casualties.[9]

Finally, in late November, the Führer let Army Group A—exhausted and now threatened by possible Soviet encirclement—withdraw from the Caucasus. Those much-needed oil fields remained beyond his grasp.

Meanwhile, Army Group B moved steadily eastward across the open steppe toward the Don and Volga Rivers. This flat countryside was perfect for German armored tactics. Originally planned merely to cover the flank of Army Group A, this thrust developed into one of the great battles of the Second World War. General Paulus's 6th Army fought its way through serious enemy opposition at Kalach and crossed the Don on August 21. German forces managed to entrap much of the Soviet 62nd Army, taking fifty-seven thousand prisoners. Then on August 23, lead elements of the 14th Panzer Corps dashed all the way to the Volga River north of Stalingrad. This was a narrow penetration. The main body of Army Group B still lay almost forty miles behind this spearhead. Alarmed, Stalin named Zhukov deputy supreme commander-in-chief with overall command of the southern front. The fighting had been costly for the Red Army. General Chuikov lamented that, of the ten-thousand-man 35th Guards Division, only 250 were fit for duty by the second week of September.

Hitler and his generals shared a sense of imminent victory. Paulus thought that he would have Stalingrad within a few days. The 4th Panzer Army joined the operation to give the drive more punch. The bulk of Paulus's forces had reached the outskirts of the apparently doomed city in late August. The Luftwaffe launched an all-out blitz on the town, reducing much of it to rubble and killing forty thousand civilians (because residents were ordered to shelter in place to keep the roads open for military traffic). Work continued in those factories not completely devastated, while employees from the destroyed plants hastily formed a "Workers' Militia." Civilians dug trenches and built defensive works. Stalin at first insisted that there be no civilian evacuation but then relented because the decreasing food shipments into the city could not support the population. Continuous Luftwaffe attacks on the slow-moving barges crossing the Volga made leaving almost as dangerous as staying in the beleaguered city. Citizens caught by the enemy faced a grim fate. The Germans executed several thousand civilians and enslaved many more.

Stalingrad was an industrial city of about half a million inhabitants that stretched for almost forty miles along the western bank of the Volga. It had three main districts—"old town" in the south; a modern development of public buildings and department stores in the center, as well as the highest point in the city, the three-hundred-foot Mamaev Hill; and the factory district in the north (dominated by the huge Dzerzhinskii Tractor, Barrikady, and Krasnii Oktiabr factories). Stalingrad was a strategically important city for the Soviets, both for its war industries and as a transit hub for oil supplies and Allied aid coming through Iraq. Because the town was named for the Soviet dictator, it became an objective of psychological importance to both Stalin and Hitler well beyond its strategic significance. When Hitler changed the status of Stalingrad from a secondary to a primary objective, he ordered that all the men of the city be killed and its women and children enslaved. This urban symbol of communist industrial development was to be eradicated from the earth. Moreover, the Anglo-American invasion of North Africa occurred during the Stalingrad battle, putting added pressure on Hitler to achieve some signal victory that might allow him to reach a temporary settlement with either his enemy in the East or those in the West. Otherwise, he faced a strategic impasse—his enemies were growing in strength while German power declined.

Moscow received more bad news during the German advance. Commissar of Foreign Affairs Viacheslav Molotov had traveled to London and Washington in May and June to secure pledges that Russia's allies would open a second front in Europe later in 1942. Soviet forces desperately needed the British and Americans to take some of the pressure off of them on the eastern front. Joint Allied communiqués reassured the Soviet public that "full understanding had been reached on the urgent task of creating a Second Front in Europe in 1942." In August, Winston Churchill (accompanied by Averell Harriman representing Roosevelt) traveled to Moscow to tell a very angry Joseph Stalin that the Western Allies could not invade any part of Europe that year. The only Allied landing would be in North Africa (which, when it happened, drew no Axis divisions from the eastern front). Britain also suspended its Arctic Ocean supply convoys to the USSR because its losses were prohibitive. American Lend-Lease aid to Russia had begun, but it was still only a token of what it would become in 1943–1945. In 1942, Soviet soldiers would fight and die against the common enemy without any significant aid from their allies.

Stalin was not only angry; he was also suspicious. His ambassador in London, Ivan Maiskii, reported that, while the Western powers certainly did not want to see an Axis victory in eastern Europe, the prospect of *both* a weakened Germany *and* a weakened Soviet

Union appealed to them.[10] Stalin suspected that Churchill and Roosevelt were willing to fight to the last Russian. The Soviet leader's deepest suspicions surfaced in a telegram to Maiskii: "All of us in Moscow have formed the impression that Churchill is intent on the defeat of the USSR in order to then come to terms with . . . Hitler . . . at our expense."[11]

Meanwhile, General Paulus was ready to administer the coup de grâce to Stalin's city. The Germans deployed 170,000 men, 500 tanks, 3,000 artillery pieces, and 1,000 combat aircraft against Stalingrad. Soviet defenders within the city were about half that strong. Fighting in the confines of a largely destroyed city took away some of the advantages the German army had enjoyed up to that point. There would be no sweeping armored maneuvers, nor could the Luftwaffe provide as much close air support when the front lines were so entangled in very close fighting. Adding to the destruction caused by bombing, German heavy artillery pounded the city constantly, creating a landscape of rubble that provided endless cover for resolute defenders. Large parts of the city caught fire. The Germans destroyed the municipal water system, so the fires burned uncontrollably. Soviet crews struggled to restore vital electricity, water, and bakery services, only to have the repaired facilities blown up again. Factories continued to operate until they were destroyed or overrun by the enemy. The tanks and artillery they produced went directly into battle. Stalin dispatched three reserve armies to drive the enemy back from the approaches to the city, but German firepower, especially control of the air, smashed the effort.

The Soviet 62nd Army, commanded by General Vasilii Chuikov, and 64th Army, under General Mikhail Shumilov, defended the city. On the outskirts of the city, overwhelming German firepower repulsed successive Red Army counterattacks, with the Ju-88 bombers doing especially great damage against Soviet armor. In the city itself, the Soviet 62nd Army fought tenaciously from house to house, from within destroyed buildings, and from behind piles of rubble. Soviet artillery on the east bank of the Volga fired at German positions in the city. Chuikov ordered his men to stand and fight, with no retreat allowed. He used intimidation to bolster their determination. "On September 14," the general later told interviewers, "I shot a commander and commissar of one regiment, and a short while later I shot two brigade commanders and their commissars. This caught everyone off guard. We made sure news of this got to the men, especially the officers."[12]

Typically the Germans used firepower and air support to make small but costly advances each day, while at night Soviet troops stole back into enemy positions to reclaim them in vicious hand-to-hand fighting. German soldiers began calling this ordeal a *Rattenkrieg*, or "rats' war." This style of combat was the very opposite of the *Blitzkrieg*. It was slow and extraordinarily costly in human lives. Alexander Werth, a British war correspondent at Stalingrad, recorded this grisly impression of the aftermath of such brutal hand-to-hand combat:

> At the bottom of the trenches there lay frozen green Germans and frozen grey Russians and frozen fragments of human shapes, and there were helmets, Russian and German, lying among the brick debris. . . . How anyone could have survived was hard to imagine.[13]

Russian soldiers believed that the life span of an infantryman in Stalingrad was about ten days. The 62nd Army defending the city fielded just twenty-thousand soldiers and ninety tanks by September 12. It pressed cooks and mechanics into service as infantrymen; by then there was little food to cook and few vehicles to repair. The Soviet high command continued to feed reinforcements into the besieged city, though they could not calculate precisely the minimum number of additional troops required just to hold on, as some historians have

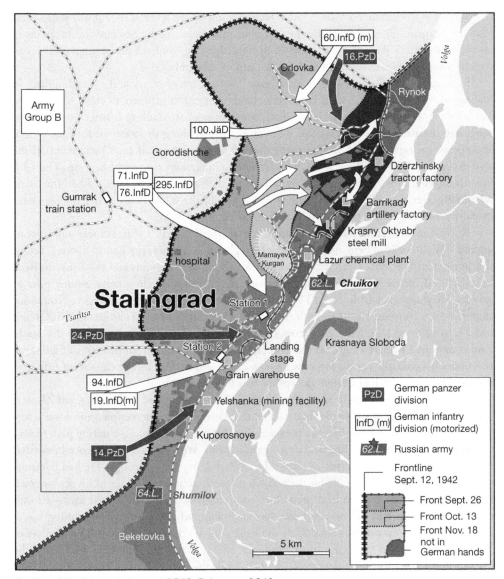

Battle of Stalingrad, August 1942–February 1943

suggested. Soldiers who attempted to desert or even showed signs of wavering were shot to keep the rest at their posts, but the widely held assumption that Russian troops fought only because they were coerced is inaccurate.

A great many Soviet soldiers faced almost certain death because of their aroused patriotism and their deep hatred of a cruel enemy. For example, in the south of the city, approaching Germans ran into heavy resistance from a grain elevator. The defenders beat off attack after attack for six days before they ran out of ammunition and water. When the enemy finally overran the elevator, they found only forty dead Soviet soldiers. One member of the German assault group, Wilhelm Hoffman, complained in his diary, "The elevator is occupied not by men, but by devils that no flames or bullets can destroy." After still more bitter fighting, he added, "Soldiers are calling Stalingrad the mass grave of the Wehrmacht. . . . Every soldier sees himself as a condemned man."[14] Such tactically important spots as the railway station and Mamaev Kurgan hill were taken by the Germans, reclaimed by the Soviets, and taken again by the Germans in ferocious back-and-forth fighting. The southern and central districts of the city were largely in German hands by the end of September.

In desperation, Stalin ordered his troops "to turn every street and every building in Stalingrad into a fortress." Chuikov's men (and women) continued to fight tenaciously, but by the end of October the enemy had taken most of the factory district in the north, squeezing the Russians into a sixteen-mile-long corridor along the west bank of the Volga, at some places only a few hundred yards deep. The Germans had even penetrated all the way to the river in a couple of spots. The Soviets had taken an enormous beating. The 13th Guards Division, for example, began the campaign with ten thousand men. When the battle was finally over, only 320 survivors remained. Overall, the 62nd Army suffered 75 percent casualties, but they continued to fight with grim determination.

In November, Hitler had told an audience in Munich that Stalingrad was all but conquered. "We have it. There are only a few tiny places [left in enemy hands] there." Yet, at this point, German forces were badly worn down. Both the Germans and the Russians lived in cellars and the shells of burned-out factories. They fought at close range among piles of rubble. They ate what little could be brought to them and often went hungry. Numerous snipers were a constant threat to both sides. The most famous Soviet sniper, Vasilii Zaitsev, had 242 confirmed kills. Men fought on, even when wounded. This was a fight to the death. Paulus mounted his last attack on November 11 and reported that 90 percent of Stalingrad was under his control. Yet his forces were now exhausted and no longer capable of offensive action. The two sides had beaten each other to a bloody standstill.

Stalin had wanted to pour more reinforcements into Stalingrad in October, but Zhukov and General Aleksandr Vasilevskii had argued that committing reserves piecemeal was a losing strategy. They devised an alternative scenario—Operation Uranus—a daring plan to save the embattled city by encircling and destroying the 6th Army. Soviet intelligence knew that Paulus did not have any reserves to respond to a Red Army breakthrough. He had committed all his forces to Stalingrad. This time Stalin chose to accept the advice of his senior commanders and not force them into premature counterattacks. The key was to *wait*—to wait until the Germans had exhausted themselves in Stalingrad and until overwhelming forces could be brought up on the east side of the Volga. That strategy required the defenders of Stalingrad to hold out for four months while the enemy slowly ground them into dust. The prewar Soviet army had been destroyed in 1941, while the new Red Army, hurriedly cobbled together during that disaster, was now also largely destroyed. However, to the Germans' surprise, the Soviets built a third-generation Red Army during 1942.

The Japanese attack on Pearl Harbor gave Stalin the courage to pull elite units from the Far East, and one hundred thousand sailors were pressed into service as infantrymen after the loss of the Baltic and Sevastopol meant they no longer had ships to man. Soviet factories turned out large numbers of the formidable T-34 tank as well as new and improved combat aircraft. Secrecy was another key to the projected operation. German overconfidence plus the waning of Luftwaffe strength, combined with growing Soviet air power, prevented the enemy from detecting the massive reinforcements now piling up behind the Volga. On November 8, numerous squadrons of German Air Fleet 4 were withdrawn from the Stalingrad sector to deal with the Allied landings in North Africa. Rough winter weather helped mask growing Soviet strength as well. The Russians cleared civilians from staging areas to make the penetration of enemy scouts harder. The main forces for the coming offensive reached their start positions only at the last moment. The Soviets managed to hide a force of over a million men, fourteen thousand artillery pieces, almost a thousand tanks, and 1,350 planes! German intelligence had some inkling of the Soviet buildup, but, trapped in Stalingrad, the Germans had few resources to deploy against possible flank attacks.

General Paulus stationed the forces of his allies—Italians, Hungarians, and Romanians—to guard his flanks at Stalingrad. These troops had fought well in some earlier engagements, but they were not as well equipped or as motivated to die for the "master race" as were German soldiers. The Soviet blow fell on November 19. Their forces smashed through the surprised Romanian 3rd Army north of Stalingrad. Massed armor with close air support, followed by fast-moving mobile infantry, shattered Romanian resistance within hours. Another powerful Soviet armored assault force crushed the Romanian 4th Army south of the city. German units behind the Romanians put up somewhat better resistance but could not stop the Soviet assault. Within four days, the two Red Army columns met near Kalach, far behind Paulus's now-encircled 6th Army. Soviet troops soon opened a hundred-mile gap between Wehrmacht lines to the west and the Germans at Stalingrad. More than 330,000 Axis troops were now trapped. General Paulus's first instinct was to attempt a breakout, but Hitler ordered him to hold his position at all costs. Though often criticized, Hitler's decision may have been irrelevant. Fully engaged in Stalingrad and lacking adequate fuel reserves, the 6th Army stood little chance of a successful escape.

Göring promised to supply the encircled army by air, while Manstein organized a relief operation. The Soviet command anticipated that response. Manstein's drive, launched on December 12, ran straight into sixty Red Army divisions and one thousand tanks waiting for it. The relief column fled before it too was entrapped. The German rescue attempt nonetheless disrupted a Soviet follow-up campaign—Operation Saturn—which sought to retake Rostov and trap German Army Group A. Meanwhile, the remainder of the 6th Army was now alone, without much ammunition, fuel, food, or hope. Göring could not keep his promise. The Soviets surrounded the German pocket with fields of antiaircraft guns, while the much-improved Red Air Force swarmed to attack Luftwaffe cargo planes. The 6th Army received only 20 percent of its minimum needs, even less after severe winter weather set in. German troops received only two and a half ounces of bread and half an ounce of sugar per day, supplemented by occasional meat when a draft horse died or when they could catch a cat or a rat. They shivered in subzero temperatures while Russian artillery, rockets, and bombers battered them continuously. Exhaustion and resignation replaced their earlier confidence.

The Russians offered surrender terms, which the Germans promptly refused. The largest artillery bombardment of the war followed. The Red Army cleared the approaches to the city within three days, but then resistance stiffened. Soviet commanders discovered from POW debriefings that they had trapped not 80,000 enemy soldiers as they had expected but 250,000 Axis troops. Chuikov's 62nd Army, now reinforced and resupplied, attacked from the riverbank. Once more, there was brutal house-to-house fighting involving close-range tank fire and flamethrowers to root out stubborn enemy defenders. Some German soldiers surrendered, while others retreated and fought on, killing their wounded as they fell back. Most German troops willingly fought to the very end because they believed the Soviets would execute them if captured; and, as Omer Bartov argues, because of their deep belief in National Socialist ideology, they were willing to "sacrifice themselves for the Führer."[15]

On January 26, Soviet forces attacking from the west linked up with Chuikov's men, splitting the Germans into two encircled groups. Hitler still insisted on resistance to the last man. Despite the increasingly hopeless situation, Paulus rejected several Soviet offers to halt the fighting. German historian Bernd Wegner suggests that Paulus's continued refusal to surrender reflected not only a sense of obligation to obey the Führer's orders but also the degree to which Nazi radicalism had infected senior Wehrmacht commanders.[16] However, neither honor nor fanaticism could hold off the Red Army. Hitler promoted Paulus to field marshal to stiffen his commander's resolve. The gesture failed in its purpose—the newly minted field marshal surrendered. Western historians used to attribute the outcome of the Battle of Stalingrad to mistakes committed by Hitler and his generals, but more recently the trend among both Russian and Western researchers is to emphasize the improvements in and successes of the Red Army as the key to victory at Stalingrad.[17]

The 6th Army ceased to exist. More than 147,000 had died, and 91,000 more were taken prisoner. Over a hundred thousand Italian, Romanian, and Hungarian troops surrendered as well. For the first time in German history, a field marshal was captured. In Moscow, Stalin made himself a marshal of the Soviet Union, crediting this great victory to his "military genius." The Red Army had paid a high price for its triumph—the lives of more than a million men. Soviet forces still suffered from inadequate coordination among units and lack of discipline, but they were gradually correcting those problems. The Soviet victory at Stalingrad marked the critical turning point in the war. From this point on, the Soviets would campaign with rising confidence, a greatly enhanced arsenal of high-quality weapons, and growing support from their Western Allies. Much hard fighting lay ahead, but victory on the eastern front now seemed assured.

The myth of German invincibility also died at Stalingrad. Moreover, on a global scale, Stalingrad, in combination with the British victory at El Alamein, the Allied landings in North Africa, the Japanese defeat at Midway, and the US conquest of Guadalcanal, indicated a fundamental shift in the balance of power between the Axis and the Grand Alliance. Axis forces were in retreat all around the globe (except in China). The Stalingrad debacle also sent an alarming message to Hitler's allies—especially to the Italians, Romanians, and Hungarians who had lost so many troops in Russia. The German army no longer seemed invincible—not to its enemies or its allies. Perhaps an Axis victory was not inevitable after all. Perhaps the fate of their countries should not be tied so closely to that of the Third Reich.

Beyond all those considerations, Hitler's grand strategy for 1942 had failed completely. Germany could not drive either the Soviet Union or the British Empire out of the war before America mobilized its industrial and economic might. The Stalingrad defeat had a significant impact on the German home front as well. Hitler had taken personal command of the German army. Now, for the first time, people began to question the Führer's alleged military genius. In Berlin, Propaganda Minister Joseph Goebbels told the German people to gird themselves for "total war."

The German disaster at Stalingrad also endangered Army Group A as it retreated from the Caucasus. The Stavka hoped to trap that force, too, but Soviet units in the region were not strong enough to hold back the Germans struggling desperately along the Black Sea coast. Stalin, once again overly excited by the prospect of victory, hoped to push the enemy entirely out of Ukraine. The Soviet offensive, which began on January 13, 1943 (even before the final collapse of Stalingrad), shattered the Italian 8th Army and the Hungarian 2nd Army. The Italian army had deployed 229,000 men along the Don River. It lost 60 percent of this force in the Stalingrad disaster. The Germans scapegoated the Italians, blaming them for the Stalingrad defeat.

From Kharkov to Rzhev to Leningrad

Hitler ordered Kharkov held at all costs, but the SS Panzer Corps occupying the town abandoned it to avoid encirclement and destruction. The Russians were overextended, however. Soviet intelligence mistakenly concluded that the enemy had no reserves and intended to retreat to the Dnieper River. The Germans brought significant reinforcements, including a Waffen SS panzer corps, from France and Germany. Manstein counterattacked, driving Soviet forces from Kharkov once again. He stabilized a new front approximately where the Wehrmacht had begun its ill-fated offensive in the summer of 1942. The audacious general had hoped to fight defensive battles that would annihilate large numbers of Soviet troops. Hitler "gave Manstein some freedom of action, but denied him the necessary strength to attain potentially significant results."[18] Hitler was not the only warlord to make serious battlefield errors. In the view of historian David Glantz,

> during the winter campaign of 1942–43, Stalin and his *Stavka* began displaying strategic and operational habits that would endure to war's end, the most important of which was their tendency to test the Red Army's operational limits during virtually every strategic offensive operation. After the Red Army's victory at Stalingrad, throughout the remainder of 1943, and into 1944, the *Stavka* routinely and often deliberately assigned the Red Army strategic tasks that were clearly beyond its capability.[19]

Stalin and his commanders had begun to think in much larger terms, anticipating complete victory throughout the USSR. They envisioned a cosmic sweep that would encircle and destroy German Army Groups South and Center—naming their projected operations Mars, Jupiter, Saturn, and Uranus. While the battle for Stalingrad still raged in November 1942, Marshal Zhukov launched yet another two-pronged assault against the German salient at Rzhev on the central front. The enemy brought up five panzer divisions and stopped the Soviet offensive cold. The Germans possessed strongly constructed defenses, air superiority, and excellent communications. Mars wasted a great deal of Soviet manpower for no gain—100,000 killed, 235,000 wounded, and 1,600 tanks lost.[20] The loss was made worse by the persistent use of frontal assaults against well-entrenched enemy positions. Boris Gorbachevskii, who fought in this battle, lamented, "Shell bursts, shell fragments and bullets are sweeping away the infantry lines. . . . The remnants of former companies and battalions have turned into a senseless mass of onward-charging desperate men."[21] He was bitter about the unwarranted sacrifices imposed on him and his fellow infantrymen:

> Our soldiers christened the battles for Rzhev the "Rzhev meat grinder," into which Stalin, Zhukov, and Konev fed division after division. Forty-two mass graves in the Rzhev soil contain the remains of servicemen and women from more than 140 rifle divisions, 50 separate rifle brigades, and 50 tank brigades. The tragedy of this battle consisted not only of the unparalleled sacrifices but also the lack of success of these operations. . . . The Germans at Rzhev had qualitatively better equipment, more experienced officers, much superior command and control over their forces, extensive combat experience, and professional soldiers. . . . To offset these German advantages, the Red Army had only numbers.[22]

Despite its enormous investment in blood and treasure, the Red Army would not occupy the Rzhev-Viazma sector until the end of March 1943 when Hitler finally authorized his troops to withdraw to shorten their defensive lines. Adopting a scorched-earth policy, the retreating Germans left only ruins behind them and forced as many as 190,000 local residents to move west with them. The experience of the Rzhev "meat grinder" taught Red Army commanders valuable lessons—the need for better coordination of offensives, for greater battlefield flexibility, and for exploiting successes rather than reinforcing failures.[23]

While these titanic battles raged on the southern and central fronts, a smaller but still significant struggle erupted on the northern front. Like Stalingrad, Leningrad seemed to have a psychological significance for both the Germans and the Russians beyond any strategic importance. It was the cradle of the Bolshevik Revolution. Hitler's plans for 1942 included a campaign in the north that would finally take Leningrad, allow German and Finnish forces to link up, and facilitate an expanded effort to interdict the northern ports of Arkhangelsk and Murmansk. Manstein planned to assault the Soviet second city in the fall. The Red Army preempted that operation, attacking in mid-August. Manstein's troops fended off the Russian thrust, but after heavy losses they no longer had the strength to launch their own campaign.

In January 1943, the Soviets initiated another attempt to rescue Leningrad, Operation Spark. The Red Army attacked the besieging German forces from the southeast and from the Leningrad side. The Germans rallied to stop the offensive, but not before the Russians had opened a narrow corridor along the southern shore of Lake Ladoga and quickly built a railway line there. Leningrad was not yet liberated, though its supply situation improved significantly. The Russians made yet another attempt to free the besieged city in February and March 1943—Operation Pole Star. Employing three army groups (or fronts), Pole Star aimed to encircle and destroy German Army Group North. However, the Germans withdrew to more defensible positions and repulsed the Soviet assault. The Red Army lost 250,000 troops killed, wounded, or captured, and the Leningrad front stabilized again.

As the balance of offensive power shifted from the German to the Russian side, the nature of the war changed dramatically for German soldiers. The high rates of attrition suffered by the Wehrmacht in both men and machines, at the same time that the Red Army was fielding more and better tanks and aircraft, led to what historian Omer Bartov terms the "demodernization" of the German army.[24] Even though total war mobilization in Germany produced greater numbers of tanks and planes, this increase could not keep pace with the terrible loss rates on the eastern front, nor with the enemy's rapidly growing arsenal. More and more, not just infantry divisions but panzer divisions as well were digging in and fighting First World War–style trench warfare in an attempt to hold back the Soviet offensives. German soldiers lived in unheated dugouts, ate short rations, and suffered terribly from disease and frostbite.

The Improving Red Army

There are several reasons why Soviet forces turned the tide against the Nazis in the winter of 1942–1943. The emphasis in the memoirs of German generals and the works of some German historians on errors and possible alternatives reflects a continuing disdain for the fighting qualities of Soviet forces. Many Western historians have credited Soviet victories to sheer numbers and the role of Russian winter weather. These judgments fail to acknowledge the rapidly improving abilities of Soviet forces. By the second half 1942, the Red Army was markedly better trained, better equipped, and better led than it had been in 1941. In contrast, the Wehrmacht was now overcommitted, undermanned, and at the end of a long and tenuous supply line. The Germans at Stalingrad did not lose a battle through errors and the Führer's interference that they might otherwise have won; they were defeated by a superior Soviet force.

Stalin learned to listen to and sometimes defer to his better generals. Zhukov noted, "During the second phase of the war, Stalin was not inclined to be hasty in making decisions and usually listened to reports." Marshal Konev later wrote that "less and less often he imposed his own solutions to individual questions on Front commanders."[25] At the senior level, officers who were incompetent or, at best, beyond their depth—Voroshilov, Kulik, Budënny, Timoshenko—were retired or transferred to posts where they would do no harm. Highly capable senior strategists—Zhukov, Vasilevskii—as well as talented battlefield commanders—Rokossovskii, Malinovskii, Vatutin, Konev, Chuikov—were promoted. Throughout the army, officers were now encouraged to shoulder responsibility and take initiative (though never to the degree common in the Wehrmacht). The authority of officers expanded, while the power of political commissars declined. The introduction of officers' epaulettes and gold braid symbolized the growing status and professionalism of Soviet commanders. As Glantz and House suggest, "by 1943 Soviet doctrine, organization, and expectations were much closer to battlefield reality than were those of the senior German leadership."[26]

The reborn Red Army was reorganized around tank corps. Each of these elite mobile units had 168 tanks, its own antitank and antiaircraft artillery, and *Katiusha* rockets. Two of these tanks corps plus an infantry division comprised a tank army. The army also developed mechanized corps, which possessed fewer tanks but more mobile infantry and self-propelled artillery. The Soviets formed twenty-two of these mechanized corps and forty-three tank corps during the last two and a half years of the war. Both the armored and infantry units received more and better communications gear, while many infantrymen traded their old rifles for more effective submachine guns. The Red Air Force received much-improved aircraft of all types, better communications equipment, radar, and supporting infrastructure. Now better led, better equipped, better trained, and better supported, Soviet troops were able to mount large-scale combined-arms operations at the same level of sophistication and with the same punch as their German opponents.

Such elite mobile units represented about 20 percent of Red Army strength. The remainder of Soviet forces still marched on foot with horse-drawn transport for their artillery and supplies. While Soviet mobility increased dramatically, that of the Germans declined. Guy Sajer, a German soldier, describes himself as "plodding" along the Konotop–Kiev highway "at the rate of three miles an hour," fleeing from the advancing Red Army. "Our mobility, which had always given us an advantage over the vast but slow Soviet formations, was now only a memory, and the disproportion of numbers made even flight a doubtful prospect. Moreover, the equipment of the Red Army was constantly improving, and we often found ourselves pitted against extremely mobile motorized regiments of fresh troops."[27]

Soviet Women at War

Women played a role in the fast-improving Red Army, not just as nurses, clerks, drivers, and relay pilots, as they did with British and American forces, but also in combat as snipers, sappers, bomber pilots, and even regular infantry. Aleksandra Samusenko, for example, a tank commander/gunner at the Battle of Kursk, received a medal for destroying three Tiger tanks. Women filled all positions in the 46th "Taman" Guards Night Bomber Aviation Regiment. These "Night Witches," as the Germans called them, flew dangerous, low-level, nighttime bombing missions in obsolete, plywood-framed, open-cockpit Polikarpov Po-2 biplanes. Women learned to deal with the horrors of combat just as their male comrades had. Nadiia, a night bomber pilot, recalled:

> And when I got up in the air, I could see the front line marked by green, red and white tracer lights, where skirmishes continued throughout the night. I followed the lights towards the accumulation of enemy troops. Suddenly, the plane in front of mine got caught in three and later five projector lights, which blind pilots. I watched them fall to earth right in front of my eyes and saw the explosion of flames below. I flew towards the enemy lines, thinking I must help my friends. Irrational thoughts . . . I knew they were dead. We dropped the bombs on the dots of light below.[28]

Even those women serving in nominally noncombatant roles, like sixteen-year-old medic Olga Omelchenko, experienced the terror of hand-to-hand combat on the front lines. She told an interviewer, "That was awful. . . . It isn't for human beings. . . . Men strike, thrust their bayonets into stomachs, eyes, strangle one another. . . . Howling, shouts, groans. It's just terrible, even for war."[29] Another female soldier, Sergeant Klara Tikhonovich, commented, "A young person recently told me that going off to fight was a masculine urge. No, it was a human urge. . . . That was how we were brought up, to take part in everything. A war had begun and that meant that we must help in some way."[30] Soviet paramilitary training in the 1930s had given some women both the skills and a sense of martial empowerment that enabled them to fill combat roles.

Prejudice against women in leadership and combat roles permeated Soviet society. Nevertheless, many Soviet women believed that they had both the right and the duty to fight alongside the men. General Chuikov later wrote, "Remembering the defense of Stalingrad, I can't overlook the very important question . . . about the role of women in the war, in the rear, but also at the front. Equally with men they bore all the burdens of combat life and together with us men, they went all the way to Berlin."[31] At Stalingrad, women had "manned" most of the antiaircraft batteries, fighting against the Luftwaffe and depressing their barrels to destroy panzers.

In all, some eight hundred thousand Soviet women served at the front. By 1943, severe combat losses forced the Red Army to recruit many more women, but it did so "with considerable hesitation, mistrust, contempt, and even hostility."[32] Moreover, the army was not well prepared to meet the needs of female "servicemen." Uniforms, cut for men, were ill fitting, while bras and sanitary napkins were unavailable. Although women played a significant role in the Red Army, the Soviet regime chose to downplay women's military contribution to victory. By 1944, with that victory now assured, the army began to demobilize women, sending them back to the factories and the farms and, above all else, to conceive a new generation of children to replace the country's staggering losses.

Beyond the normal hardships of military life and the rigors of combat, women in the Red Army frequently suffered discrimination and sometimes endured sexual abuse from their male comrades in arms. The official rhetoric of gender equality seems not to have penetrated very deeply into Soviet society, not even within the Communist Party. Patriarchal attitudes and gender stereotypes dominated at every level of the regime and its army. The 1st

Separate Women's Volunteer Rifle Brigade, a rare all-female infantry unit (with some male officers), was shunted into construction and guard duties rather than combat, even though the army was desperate for more frontline troops.

Many male soldiers respected their female comrades once they saw the heroism of women combat medics and infantry—referring to them as "sisters" or "daughters." However, some male officers misused their authority to coerce the sexual services of lower-ranking women. In the Women's Volunteer Rifle Brigade, a Lieutenant Morosov pressured four successive female sergeants to live with him in camp. Atypically, Morosov was reduced in rank and expelled from the party.[33] Most male sexual predators got away with their offenses. The situation was still worse for female partisans, who had even fewer opportunities to appeal to higher authorities. Sometimes women became "mobile field wives" to ranking officers to protect themselves from pervasive sexual harassment in their unit. The Main Political Directorate of the army ruled that commanders should not be punished for sexual relationships with female subordinates.

Help from the Allies

The role of Lend-Lease aid in the Soviet victory over Germany has been a controversial subject. During the Cold War, Russian writers tended to ignore Allied aid, while Western historians stressed its centrality to Soviet survival. Aid from Britain and the United States was important in the transformation of the Red Army, but it was only one of several factors that accounted for the Russian victory. Among the more important items supplied by the Western Allies were aircraft, radios that greatly enhanced Soviet command and control, and 275,000 vehicles—Jeeps and Studebaker trucks that helped to make the Red Army as mobile as its opponent. The United States sent a total of $12.5 billion (over $170 billion adjusted for inflation) in assistance to the USSR. Perhaps the most important commodity was food. America supplied approximately one pound of "concentrated ration" per Soviet soldier per day![34] In his memoirs, Nikita Khrushchev remembered American Spam fondly: "Without Spam we wouldn't have been able to feed our army."[35] While glad to have the food, Soviet soldiers referred sarcastically to the cans of Spam as the "second front." Marshal Zhukov wrote that "the Americans shipped over to us materiel without which we could not have equipped our armies held in reserve or been able to continue the war."[36]

Barber and Harrison estimate that "Lend-Lease may have amounted to one-fifth of the Soviet national product in 1943, and only fractionally less in 1944. . . . Without Allied aid, the authorities would have been compelled to withdraw major resources from fighting in 1943 in order to stabilize the economy."[37] Certainly the war would have been longer and even bloodier for the Soviet people without Western aid. Domestic sources of supply enabled the Red Army to fight from Operation Barbarossa through the Stalingrad victory, but equipment and food supplied by the Western Allies played a key role in its offensives from that point on.

Partisan Actions

In his speech to the Soviet people on July 3, 1941, Stalin called for all-out partisan war. However, Soviet authorities were not prepared to support partisan activities at the beginning of the war. Few weapons and little communications gear were available, and there had been no planning for guerrilla warfare behind enemy lines. Moreover, the Bolshevik leaders distrusted the spontaneous, uncontrollable, and potentially disloyal autonomous partisan groups. They feared the potential for anti-Soviet civil war in the western and southern borderlands.[38] Nevertheless, Moscow reported that it had eighty-seven thousand fighters behind enemy lines in the fall of 1941. That number plummeted to thirty thousand the following spring. The hardships of partisan life caused many to abandon the cause, while enemy antiguerrilla campaigns killed still more. Initially, most partisans were "shareholders" in the regime, that is, people who were part of and drew the most benefits from the Soviet system.

Most Soviet citizens in the German-occupied zone adopted a stance of neutrality, simply keeping their heads down and hoping the war would pass them by. Few people wanted to take the risks involved in helping the guerrillas, and most were opposed to partisan attempts to destroy local infrastructure so that the Germans could not make use of it. Partisan effectiveness improved in 1942 as more Red Army stragglers cut off behind enemy lines and escaped POWs joined the resistance movement. The Germans' ruthless treatment of the civil population, combined with a growing belief that the USSR would survive the enemy onslaught, brought still more volunteers and much greater material support to the partisans. Soviet authorities used airdrops and small landing strips carved into the forests to bring in supplies.

The Germans fought a particularly cruel campaign against the partisans. Their antipartisan operations easily morphed into a "war of extermination" against the general population—though the escalation of German violence toward the civil population *preceded* rather than followed increasing resistance activity.[39] The Order Police and the army committed brutal acts of repression. "The 12th Infantry's standard reaction to partisan attacks on its units," Omer Bartov writes, "was to burn down the villages in the vicinity of the attack, shoot all the male inhabitants, and leave the remaining women and children to fend for themselves in winter conditions without any shelter."[40]

Large-scale counterinsurgency campaigns brought devastation to whole districts. For example, the 18th Panzer Division conducted an "anti-partisan" operation in May 1943 that resulted in 1,584 executions, 1,568 additional arrests, the expulsion of 15,812 remaining inhabitants from the district, and the burning of all their villages. Civilians were shot not only if they were *suspected* of aiding the partisans but also even for *failing to prevent* "terrorist" attacks. Such operations also served Berlin's objective of reducing the Slavic population. Soviet civilians in the occupied area walked a tightrope. The slightest gesture of support for the partisans brought the Germans' wrath upon them; the smallest token of cooperation with the occupiers provoked partisan fury. Often, survival required the villagers to be proGerman during the day and pro-Soviet at night.

In all, these anti-partisan sweeps killed approximately 345,000 civilians and 30,000 fighters. Given this barbarity, the number of insurgents soon swelled to 115,000, while Moscow created a Central Staff of the Partisan Movement to coordinate their activities. Many more joined the partisan ranks as the tide of battle turned decisively against the invaders. By 1944, guerrilla forces numbered over a quarter million men and women. Still others joined the movement to avoid conscription as slave laborers by the Germans. Late in the war, many joined the insurgency to demonstrate their political loyalty as the Soviets reestablished control in the formerly occupied regions.

In the face of these brutal German counterinsurgency campaigns, partisan life required extraordinary self-discipline and sacrifice. The tale of one female partisan is particularly tragic:

Somebody betrayed us. . . . The Germans found out where the camp of our partisan unit was. They cordoned off the forest and the approaches to it on all sides. We hid in the wild thickets, we were saved by the swamps where the punitive forces didn't go. . . . For days, for weeks we stood up to our necks in water. Our radio operator was a woman who had recently given birth. The baby was hungry . . . It had to be nursed . . . But the mother herself was hungry and had no milk. The baby cried. The punitive forces were close . . . With dogs . . . If the dogs heard it, we'd all be killed. The whole group—thirty of us . . . You understand?

The Commander makes a decision . . .

Nobody can bring himself to give the mother his order, but she figures it out herself. She lowers the swaddled baby into the water and holds it there for a long time . . . The baby doesn't cry anymore . . . Not a sound . . . And we can't raise our eyes. Neither to the mother nor to each other.[41]

Some women took part in combat operations alongside their male comrades. Others undertook dangerous missions as saboteurs or scouts. Willingly or not, some women became "camp wives," while most female partisans were relegated to stereotypically female roles of cooking, cleaning, and nursing. Lingering prejudices against non-Slavic ethnic groups in the USSR, particularly Jews, and against women often hindered the effectiveness of guerrilla units. Sometimes Jews were forced to form their own separate partisan units. Partisan life was hard. In addition to the omnipresent danger of enemy pacification sweeps, resistance fighters often lacked adequate food, clothing, and shelter, as well as supplies and medical care. They gleaned most of their food and supplies from surrounding villages (which were already impoverished) or took them from the enemy.

Many of the fighters experienced a sense of isolation and the pervasive fear of betrayal. Partisans also lived with the painful knowledge that their operations were likely to bring down the Germans' wrath on local villages. Despite the hardships, partisan bands ultimately proved their worth in sabotage and intelligence gathering. For example, partisan groups launched 2,092 attacks against German railway supply routes during the Battle of Kursk.[42] Their most important function was to maintain a Soviet shadow state within the German-occupied zones.

The Germans had to retreat from forested regions to defensible urban areas by 1944, leaving the surrounding countryside under partisan control. When the Red Army liberated zones of partisan activity, some party members and commanders became local administrators, while most of the units joined the army. Historian Kenneth Slepyan concludes that the partisan movement diminished the Germans' ability to control the territory they conquered, caused the enemy severe logistical problems, and forced the Wehrmacht to divert significant forces from the front to the anti-partisan campaigns.[43]

The partisans fought a savage and brutal war not only against the invader but also against Soviet collaborators. A Wehrmacht report covering a forty-four-day period behind the lines of the 2nd Panzer Army makes the point—partisans killed 33 Germans and over 238 Russians. "The war in the occupied territories was indeed a civil war in the bitterest sense of the term," Slepyan explains. "Collaborators and partisans from the same family seemed to have little compunction about killing one another."[44] The partisans were involved in a civil war in yet another sense—fighting against separatist forces in Ukraine, the Baltic states, and elsewhere. They sought to reestablish Soviet institutions and remind the local population that the Soviet system would soon be fully restored.

Many of the insurgents manifested a "partisan ethos." Insofar as possible, they resisted tight control from the center and strict military discipline. When not fighting, they cherished a bohemian life of "wine, women, and song." They identified with some of the famous "social bandits" of Russia's past, and they administered a rough-and-ready "justice" in the areas they controlled. Not surprisingly, the Moscow authorities saw such behavior not as necessary autonomy but as dangerous anarchy, which they sought to rein in.

Why Soviet Soldiers Fought

Given the unprecedented German victories and horrendous Soviet losses in 1941 and again in 1942, why did the soldiers of the Red Army continue to fight and to sacrifice themselves in extraordinary numbers? Why did they not collapse like the French in 1940 or British resistance in Malaya? One answer is the harsh discipline imposed upon them by the Stalinist regime, but this is only a partial reason at best. Order 227 forbade any retreat without authorization from superior authorities. Punishment for "cowards" and "panickers" could be quick and severe—execution or assignment to a "punishment unit" (often for virtually suicidal operations such as frontal attacks on strongly held enemy positions or clearing minefields without proper equipment). The Red Army executed 158,000 of its own troops during the war, a total that far exceeded the number of Wehrmacht executions of its own soldiers—21,000 (compared to a total of *one* such execution for desertion in the US Army).

Throughout the war, authorities arrested over four million soldiers for desertion, straggling, draft evasion, or deliberately wounding themselves to avoid combat. However, only 8.6 percent of those caught were punished by the military judicial system.[45] Many men found absent from their units without authorization were simply returned to their unit or reorganized into new units. The Soviet draft evasion and desertion rate of 8.6 percent, though higher than the 3 percent rate experienced by the Western Allies, seems relatively low considering that 44 percent of Red Army soldiers were wounded and 25 percent were killed or permanently missing. The number of "blocking detachments"—army or NKVD units behind the front lines meant to prevent any unauthorized retreats—also increased sharply. Contrary to the prevailing myth, blocking forces returned most of the men they intercepted to their units. Opening fire on deserters occurred infrequently.

After Stalin's death, Marshal Zhukov criticized Order 227 as a "disgraceful" attempt to shift blame for defeats from Stalin's mistakes to ordinary soldiers, though some troops thought that draconian order an unavoidable necessity. Boris Gorbachevskii, a junior officer, wrote, "I think instead that the issuance of this order was both a timely and necessary step. The order was not aimed at reprisal against individual officers and soldiers; it threatened only those who permitted themselves and others to retreat without orders. . . . Stern measures were necessary at the time, so that officers and soldiers understood their personal responsibility for the fate of the nation."[46] Based on a large-scale study of soldiers' letters, diaries, and interviews, historian Roger Reese concludes, "Thus, coercion was a far less important factor in maintaining effectiveness than it has been made out to be."[47] Unstinting Nazi barbarity and the perilous military situation required a stern, fight-to-the-death mentality to prevent defeat. However, the harshness of discipline and the overwhelming suspicion prevalent in the Red Army (and broader Soviet society) were sometimes counterproductive. For example, for accidentally overturning his tank during a difficult river crossing, Janusz Bardach was court-martialed for treason and sentenced to ten years at hard labor.[48]

White-hot anger over German atrocities soon pervaded the Red Army and Soviet society as a whole, sparking fanatical resistance. Soldiers learned of the Nazis' mass murder of POWs and Soviet civilians. Those who participated in the liberation of territory west of Moscow in the winter of 1941–1942 saw with their own eyes the brutalities of Wehrmacht occupation in Russia. One veteran, Boris Ol'shanskii, later wrote about the experience of returning to his native place:

> Many found only carbonized debris. "They have all perished. Our hut was burned down as a reprisal. Father and mother were shot. Little sister has been taken to Germany for slave labor. Brother was hanged for cooperation with the partisans. My wife was beaten with a stick by order of the German commandant on account of allegedly lack of respect towards a policeman. Soon after that she died on consequence of the beating. The children were taken by other people. I do not know where they are now."[49]

Similarly, a female veteran recalled, "One of our nurses was captured. . . . A day later we took back that village. . . . We found her: eyes put out, breasts cut off. They had impaled her on a stake. . . . It was freezing cold, and she was white as could be, and her hair was all gray. . . . She was nineteen years old."[50] Essentially, the Germans gave Soviet soldiers no choice. They could either fight or be killed or enslaved along with their families. Revenge became a major motive for many Soviet soldiers.

Mansur Abdulin's unit liberated a village only to find that the enemy had murdered every resident—old men, women, and children. They also discovered the body of one of their scouts horribly mutilated by the Germans. Abdulin later wrote, "I was consumed by the idea that while alive, I would have my revenge on the Germans in advance: for I never expected to survive that slaughter. Once, on my initiative, we shot no less than 200 wounded Nazis in some vegetable store."[51] The Nazis had come to Russia to fight a war of extermination—the Red Army would repay them in kind.

Soviet troops sometimes committed war crimes of their own—usually, but not always, in response to German atrocities. At times they killed prisoners, even when battlefield conditions made taking captives possible. However, historian Mark Edele concludes, "the murder and mutilation of prisoners by the Soviets was less common than Germans at the time and some later historians believed."[52] There was no Soviet equivalent of the German "commissar order," which mandated the execution of some categories of prisoners. Both the Supreme Soviet and the Red Army issued instructions on the care of POWs, and Soviet forces took 4.1 million enemy prisoners during the war (though 15 percent of that number died in captivity). The regime sent mixed messages, however. Stalin, in his speech of November 6, 1941, called on his soldiers "to exterminate each and every German who has forced his way as an occupier onto our homeland." Some soldiers took those words as a license to slaughter prisoners until their commanders issued a corrective. Moscow's propaganda directed toward its soldiers was pervasive, powerful, and flexible. Thousands of journalists, writers, artists, photographers, and cinematographers hammered home the message that the barbarous enemy was determined to enslave and kill the Soviet people.

Mobilizing Beliefs and Ideologies

The Soviet regime modified its previous hostility to nationalism and religion in a further effort to spur combat motivation. If some of the population were disinclined to fight and die for Stalin and communism, they might well do so for Holy Mother Russia. As long as the

Russian Orthodox Church preached resistance to the demonic invader, it was tolerated. Iuri Belash, a poet and combat veteran, expressed the significance of religion for some soldiers:

> To be honest about it
> In the trenches the last thing we thought about
> Was Stalin.
> God was on our minds more.
> Stalin played no part at all
> In our soldiers' war.[53]

The regime also fostered explicitly Russian (as opposed to Soviet) patriotism. In Reese's view, "the Stalinist state astutely and successfully used the war to reinvent its image. It dropped its revolutionary rhetoric and attached itself to the legacy of historic Russia, thereby establishing a more durable legitimacy."[54] In 1944, a new national anthem, which praised "Great Russia," replaced the socialist Internationale. Soviet propaganda could be flexible, also appealing to the nationalisms of some of the minority peoples of the USSR—though tirelessly reminding those ethnic groups that they were part of the Soviet "family of nations." It is significant, however, that in a speech in November of 1944 marking the twenty-seventh anniversary of the Bolshevik Revolution—at a point when the USSR had been completely liberated and the Red Army was advancing in Eastern Europe—Stalin chose to credit the Soviet system, not Mother Russia, for defeating the Third Reich.

Marxist-Leninist ideology also played a part in the regime's strategy for motivating its soldiers. It exhorted its troops and its home front to defend the *socialist* motherland, to defend the gains of the revolution, and to make sacrifices in the name of Stalin. For example, Stalin's speech on the anniversary of the Bolshevik Revolution in 1941 condemned German National Socialism as false socialism and held up Soviet-style socialism as the only hope, not only for Russia but also for the world's working class. For a significant portion of the troops, the Soviet experiment was a cause worth fighting for. "The cement that the Red Army command used to bind together diverse soldiers and motivate them to fight," argues historian Jochen Hellbeck, "was ideology."[55]

By the end of the war, soldiers' membership in the Communist Party had quadrupled to almost three million. Constant ideological bombardment had trained many soldiers to "speak Bolshevik." Even though some of them may have parroted back what their political commissars wanted to hear, the pervasive inculcation of language and concepts cannot have failed to affect attitudes and understanding. Most frontline troops had lived under the Soviet system their entire lives—educated in Soviet schools, indoctrinated by Soviet propaganda. It should not be surprising that they were ready to defend the only social system they had ever known, even while criticizing some of its faults. Moreover, historian Amir Weiner argues that, "simply put, the relentless and harsh experiences of collectivization, famine, and terror produced a tough people who could and did endure difficulties which had defeated others."[56]

Still other motivations played a role in arousing resistance to the enemy. Some men joined the armed forces in search of political rehabilitation. The regime had classified many people as potential enemies not because of their actions but only because of their class. For example, during the collectivization campaign of 1929–1933, Soviet authorities labeled *kulaks* (meaning "rich" peasants, in reality not rich at all but only slightly better off than their neighbors) as class enemies. Some men in this category collaborated readily with the enemy, while others sought political redemption in the Red Army.

Many citizens, though unhappy with the current Soviet regime, fought the enemy in hopes that their enormous sacrifices would lead to significant change in the postwar era—especially an end to political repression, the dissolution of the collective farms and distribution of land to the peasants, and an end to the prolonged period of suffering and privation endured by the Soviet people. Surely, after these years of hardship and loss borne by so many people, the USSR would become a freer, more prosperous, and happy place after the war. Those who thought so were to be disappointed.

The relationship among soldiers also affects combat motivation. If larger political and ideological issues seem remote in the heat of battle, concern for the welfare and opinion of one's "buddies" is often an immediate concern. Small-unit cohesion fostered military effectiveness in most armies—certainly among the British and the Americans, as well as the Germans. This phenomenon played some role among Soviet troops, but perhaps not as great a role as it did in other armies. In his memoir-history of the Rzhev battles, Gorbachevskii has curiously little to say about the buddy phenomenon. While he produces a few examples of small-unit bonding, most of the soldiers he commanded were strangers to each other—separated by ethnicity, religion, ignorance, and fear. Catherine Merridale argues that "the Red Army does not readily fit the mold. . . . When the rates of loss were high, when the average front-line tour of duty for an infantryman before he was removed by death or serious disability was three weeks, the small groups seldom lasted long."[57] Beyond that, the Soviet military system distrusted rather than encouraged close relationships among the troops. Reese offers a contrary opinion, at least regarding the smallest units (squads and platoons): "The overwhelming majority of Soviet soldiers managed to contain their fear and fulfill their duties; of the several things that helped them . . . the primary group was probably the most significant."[58]

Like soldiers in other armies, the experience of combat created among Soviet soldiers a sense of estrangement from their noncombatant countrymen. Civilians, they believed, could not possibly comprehend the real face of battle. Although that feeling was a nearly universal phenomenon among fighting men of all countries, the Soviet system intensified this alienation among Red Army troops. "By setting soldier against civilian, by raising fears of spies and stool pigeons, by setting the *frontovik* [i.e., the frontline soldier] against the whole community of military 'rats' who did not fight," Merridale suggests, "the war had shattered, not united, the Soviet people."[59]

After initially faltering against the 1941 German assault, Soviet troops fought with courage and determination even though the national political leadership and their own commanders often squandered men and equipment recklessly. There were differences in levels of commitment and willingness to sacrifice among the soldiers of the Red Army. Fear of defeat in 1941–1942 caused more troops to waver in combat, while the growing likelihood of victory in 1943–1945 raised morale greatly. In 1941, desperate Soviet authorities had thrown barely trained and minimally equipped recruits into the slaughter. Stalin's soldiers fought much more effectively in the later years of the war because they were more extensively and realistically trained, they were much better equipped and led, and they had a cause most of them believed worth fighting for. Russians (and within that group, factory workers and college students as well as Communist Party and Komsomol members) volunteered more readily for military service and exhibited greater determination to defend the Soviet regime. Peasants, who made up the majority of the Red Army during the war, volunteered less frequently but became effective fighters with proper training and equipment. Members of the non-Slavic minorities of the USSR also volunteered less frequently, and some of them hoped for national freedom from Russian domination.

German Combat Motivation

As many students of the war have noted, the German army manifested greater "fighting power" than did any of its opponents, and, as one component of that power, its soldiers displayed great skill and tenacity in combat.[60] Military historian Colonel Trevor N. Dupuy concludes,

> [The] record shows that the Germans consistently outfought the far more numerous Allied armies that eventually defeated them. . . . On a man for man basis the German ground soldiers consistently inflicted casualties at about a 50 percent higher rate than they incurred from the opposing British and American troops under all circumstances. This was true when they were attacking and when they were defending, when they had a local numerical superiority and when, as was usually the case, they were outnumbered, when they had air superiority and when they did not, when they won and when the lost.[61]

The casualty rate differential was even higher on the eastern front. Why were German soldiers so highly motivated to fight, sometimes under appalling conditions? Also, why did they willingly commit systematic atrocities? For the Germans, morale and combat motivation were high from 1939 through the summer of 1941. Sweeping victories in those years buoyed morale and, along with sound training and good leadership, contributed greatly to the Wehrmacht's military effectiveness.

That string of apparently easy triumphs ended in the fall of 1941. Although German troops would continue to win some battles, they now encountered bitter resistance from the Red Army, escalating casualties, and horrendous living conditions in the winters. Their fighting prowess did not slacken even after the Stalingrad disaster and into 1944 when it became obvious that the Third Reich would lose the war. German troops may have been initially better, man for man, than their opponents, but that margin of superiority narrowed each year as Allied combat effectiveness improved while material support for the German army decreased.

Why did German soldiers continue to resist stoutly even when all hope of victory was gone? The answer lies in a combination of several factors. Martin van Creveld argues that the German army's organizational structure, its culture, and its emphasis on operational skill fostered military efficiency, though Allan R. Millett and Williamson Murray suggest that this narrowness of view led to inadequate attention to "grand strategy in industrial war."[62] Social scientists A. Shils and Morris Janowitz stress small-unit cohesion as key to the German army's continuing effectiveness.[63] The German high command worked to strengthen this sense of group loyalty by recruiting on a territorial basis so that young soldiers in each unit would speak the same dialect, have similar formative experiences, and might even have known each other previously. The army wanted each soldier to feel that his unit was his "family." Historian Nicholas Stargardt suggests that "male honour became entirely bound up with military service, comradeship and calmness under fire; so much so that 'war neurotics' [i.e., PTSD victims], cowards and deserters were seen as neither honourable nor real men."[64]

However, Omer Bartov demonstrates that the extraordinary casualty rates suffered by the Wehrmacht on the eastern front destroyed most of these "primary groups." Scrambling to replace massive losses, the authorities cobbled together units from diverse sources—younger, older, and less than fully fit men. They also pulled battalions out of the divisions occupying western Europe and combined the remnants of shattered formations into new units. A division chaplain noted, "This is no longer the old division. All around us are new faces. When one asks where this or that man is, one is always given the same reply: dead or wounded. Most of the infantry company commanders are new, most of the old ones are gone."[65] Yet after this small-unit cohesion was shattered, the German army demonstrated its fiercest resistance as the Red Army battered it toward Berlin.

Instead of primary group loyalty, Bartov contends that the German army's cohesion and fighting effectiveness were based on two factors—brutal discipline and ideological commitment. Troops who failed to fight fiercely faced long prison terms or even execution. At first, soldiers accused of dereliction of duty faced courts-martial, but as the situation on the eastern front deteriorated for the Germans, soldiers deserting or showing panic in battle were shot immediately. Military prisoners (and sometimes civilian criminals as well) were formed into penal units for particularly dangerous, high-casualty assignments. These harsh methods led not only to stout resistance against the enemy but also to innumerable atrocities. "Under permanent threat of draconian punishment by his superiors if he shrank away from the lethal realities of the front, the individual soldier's compensation was his ability to wield the same destructive power against enemy civilians and POWs."[66] German soldiers had license to plunder, rape, and murder the civilian population with impunity. Gruesome atrocities, such as the burning out of eyes, torture with hot pokers, and setting captives afire, happened all too frequently.

The remarkable penetration of Nazi ideology throughout the Wehrmacht constituted the other key element in German combat motivation. Most German soldiers had grown up under the Third Reich, had undergone indoctrination in its schools and the Hitler Youth organization, and had learned to worship the Führer. They accepted the racist, social Darwinist, anticommunist, and imperialist tenants of Nazi ideology more easily because those ideas were already prevalent in less radical form in German society. The army picked up where the schools and Hitler Youth left off, subjecting its men to frequent doses of Nazi dogma. National Socialist leadership officers joined every unit in 1942. A typical homily emphasized core racist and anti-Semitic beliefs:

1. Asia has never defeated Europe. We will break the Asiatic tidal wave this time too.
2. A rule of Asiatic subhumans over the West is unnatural and contradicts the sense of history.
3. Behind the flood of red mobs sneers the distorted face of the Jew. His craving for power will be broken, as it was once broken in Germany.[67]

A captured German officer told his Soviet interrogators: "To us officers it's clear that the war came about because of the Jews, who seized leadership roles in the governments of all nations except for Germany."[68] Defeats drove the German army more closely into the arms of the National Socialists. Like the Japanese, the Germans now hoped that "spirit" could triumph over the enemy's material superiority. Hitler told his officers, "He who fights with the purist will, the bravest belief and the most fanatical determination will be victorious in the end."[69]

Hitler asked his soldiers to fight a quasi-religious crusade, not a limited war with rational objectives. These ideological warriors therefore saw Jews as implacable enemies of Germany, and they viewed Slavs as subhuman brutes, not fellow human beings. When the war turned against Germany, they fought still harder, even in an obviously hopeless cause, because they believed they were defending their homeland and civilization itself from the hordes of "Judeo-Bolshevik" barbarism.

Their own crimes in the occupied lands gave German troops further incentive to fight tenaciously, fearing the revenge the Russians would surely exact if Germany lost the war. Gerhard Nebel, a German soldier, wrote in his diary that eastern front veterans "assure us that we have to win the war under all circumstances. Because if we lose and are treated anywhere near to how we have treated the populations in the East, it will be our downfall."[70] Timothy Snyder suggests that the horrendous treatment of Soviet POWs was intended "to ensure that German soldiers would fear the same from the Soviets, and so fight desperately to prevent themselves from falling into the hands of the enemy."[71] Many senior commanders shared this radical view of the war as an all-or-nothing racial conflict, even though they spent their formative years under the Kaiserreich and then served the Weimar Republic. Generals von Küchler, Hoepner, von Reichenau, Hoth, von Manstein, Guderian, and many others saw the war on the eastern front as a sacred crusade to eliminate Jewish and "Asiatic" barbarism.

The common view that the Red Army was ideologically driven while the German army was "professional" and above politics is simply wrong. Soviet troops were subjected to a great deal of propaganda, but similar German efforts seem to have been even more effective. After examining many letters and diaries of German frontline soldiers, Stephen G. Fritz argues that "these ordinary men, to an extent far greater than previously acknowledged, were ideologically motivated and participated in grievous atrocities for racial and ideological reasons."[72] However, he is not so quick to dismiss the bonding power of small units. "For the Landser [the German soldier], life in the midst of terror and uncertainty often seemed bearable only because of the intense feeling of camaraderie forged in the fire furnace of battle."[73]

In addition to thorough training, skilled leadership, and pervasive ideological indoctrination, drugs enhanced the fighting spirit of German soldiers—most commonly Pervitin, a methamphetamine. The Wehrmacht supplied massive quantities of the drug to its troops throughout the war. This drug enabled soldiers to fight on beyond the normal limits of human endurance, and it made them significantly more aggressive.

For decades after the war, many German historians attributed the mass rape, torture, and murder of millions of civilians to the SS. The German army, they suggested, had fought a tough but "clean" war. It is now clear, however, that the regular army participated in atrocities together with the SS. From 1933 onward, the Wehrmacht leadership willingly and systematically shaped the reborn German army as a tool of Nazi extermination goals.[74] Stargardt suggests that "the winter retreat [of 1941–1942] bound the German Army in the East (*Ostheer*) together in a common culture marked by mass slaughter." Even those soldiers who previously had some reservations about the criminal treatment of POWs and civilians now steeled themselves for a merciless struggle. "The retreat quickened this process," Stargardt writes, "reshaping the entire outlook and self-understanding of the eastern front."[75]

Notes

1. For a different perspective, see Phillips P. O'Brien, *How the War Was Won: Air-Sea Power and Allied Victory in World War II* (Cambridge: Cambridge University Press, 2015). He makes a spirited, though ultimately unconvincing, argument that Anglo-American naval and air power played a much greater part in bringing down the Axis than such big battles as Stalingrad, Kursk, and El Alamein. Paul Kennedy has it right: "Victory at sea and victory in the air, as critical and absolutely necessary as they were, simply were not enough." *Engineers of Victory: The Problem Solvers Who Turned the Tide in the Second World War* (New York: Random House, 2013), 209. The Allies had to smash the Wehrmacht on the ground. Evan Mawd-

sley offers a more balanced judgment: "Sea power, *along with* land power and air power, was crucial in the European and the Asian struggle" (italics in original). *The War for the Seas: A Maritime History of World War II* (New Haven, CT: Yale University Press, 2019), 477.

2. Winston S. Churchill, "The Hour of Our Greatest Effort Is Approaching," in *Dawn of Liberation: War Speeches* (London: Cassell, 1945), 41.

3. Roger Reese, *Why Stalin's Soldiers Fought* (Lawrence: University Press of Kansas, 2011), 36.

4. Andrei A. Gromyko, et al., eds., *Stalin's Correspondence with Churchill and Attlee, 1941–1945* (New York: Capricorn, 1965), 41.

5. J. S. A. Hayward, *Stopped at Stalingrad: The Luftwaffe and Hitler's Defeat in the East, 1942–1943* (Lawrence: University Press of Kansas, 1998), 96–97.

6. Boris Gorbachevsky, *Through the Maelstrom: The Red Army Soldier's War on the Eastern Front, 1942–1945* (Lawrence: University Press of Kansas, 2008), 11.

7. Reese, *Why Stalin's Soldiers Fought*, 204.

8. Stephen G. Fritz, *The First Soldier: Hitler as Military Leader* (New Haven, CT: Yale University Press, 2018), 250.

9. Quoted in Fritz, *The First Soldier*, 259.

10. "New Documents about Winston Churchill from the Russian Archives," *International Affairs* (Moscow), 47, no. 5 (2001): 133.

11. Andrei Gromyko et al., eds., *Sovetsko-Angliiskie otnosheniia vo vremia Velikoi Otechestvinnoi Voiny, 1941–1944* (Moscow: Izd. Polit. Lit., 1983), vol. I, doc. 147.

12. Jochen Hellbeck, *Stalingrad: The City That Defeated the Third Reich* (New York: PublicAffairs, 2015), 273.

13. Alexander Werth, *Russia at War, 1941–1945* (New York: Avon, 1964), 519.

14. Vasilii Chuikov, *The Beginning of the Road* (London: MacGibbon & Kee, 1963), 248ff.

15. Omer Bartov, *Hitler's Army: Soldiers, Nazis, and War in the Third Reich* (New York: Oxford University Press, 1991), 166–67.

16. Bernd Wegner, "The War against the Soviet Union, 1942–1943," in *Germany and the Second World War*, vol. 6, *The Global War*, ed. Horst Boog et al. (Oxford: Clarendon Press, 2001), 1163.

17. Earl F. Ziemke, *Stalingrad to Berlin: German Defeat in the East* (Washington, DC: Center for Military History, 1987), 80, is a good example of the former emphasis, while David M. Glantz, *Colossus Reborn: The Red Army at War, 1941–1943* (Lawrence: University Press of Kansas, 2005), chs. 2 and 3, exemplifies the current trend.

18. Fritz, *The First Soldier*, 275.

19. Glantz, *Colossus Reborn*, 45.

20. David M. Glantz, *Zhukov's Greatest Defeat: The Red Army's Epic Disaster in Operation Mars, 1942* (Lawrence: University Press of Kansas, 1999), 308.

21. Gorbachevsky, *Through the Maelstrom*, 113.

22. Gorbachevsky, *Through the Maelstrom*, 432–33.

23. Dennis Showalter, *Armor and Blood: The Battle of Kursk; The Turning Point of World War II* (New York: Random House, 2013), 11.

24. Bartov, *Hitler's Army*, 12.

25. Oleg V. Khlevniuk, *Stalin: New Biography of a Dictator* (New Haven, CT: Yale University Press, 2015), 239.

26. David M. Glantz and Jonathan M. House, *The Battle of Kursk* (Lawrence: University Press of Kansas, 1999), 269.

27. Guy Sajer, *The Forgotten Soldier: The True Story of a Young German Soldier on the Russian Front* (London: Phoenix, 2000), 302.

28. Shelley Saywell, *Women in War: From World War II to El Salvador* (New York: Penguin, 1986), 139.

29. John Erickson, "Soviet Women at War," in *World War 2 and the Soviet People*, ed. John Garrard and Carol Garrard (New York: St. Martin's, 1993), 62.

30. Svetlana Alexiyevich, *War's Unwomanly Face* (Moscow: Progress, 1988), 156.

31. Chris Bellamy, *Absolute War: Soviet Russia in the Second World War* (New York: Vintage, 2007), 520.

32. Susanne Conze and Beate Fieseler, "Soviet Women as Comrades-in-Arms: A Blind Spot in the History of the War," in *People's War: Responses to World War II in the Soviet Union*, ed. Robert W. Thurston (Urbana: University of Illinois Press, 2000), 222.

33. Roger D. Marwick and Euridice Charon Cardona, *Soviet Women on the Frontline in the Second World War* (New York: Palgrave, 2012), 199–200.

34. Herbert P. van Tuyll, *Feeding the Bear: American Aid to the Soviet Union, 1941–1945* (Westport, CT: Greenwood, 1989), 117.

35. Nikita Khrushchev, *Khrushchev Remembers* (New York: Bantam, 1970), 239.

36. Quoted in Albert L. Weeks, *Russia's Life-Saver: Lend-Lease Aid to the U.S.S.R. in World War II* (Lanham, MD: Lexington Books, 2004), 1.

37. John Barber and Mark Harrison, *The Soviet Home Front, 1941–1945: A Social History of the USSR in World War II* (London: Longman, 1991), 192.

38. Alfred J. Rieber, "Civil Wars in the Soviet Union," *Kritika: Explorations in Russian and Eurasian History* 4, no. 1 (Winter 2003): 140–41.

39. Hannes Heer, "The Logic of the War of Extermination: The Wehrmacht and the Anti-Partisan War," in *War of Extermination: The German Military in World War II*, ed. Hannes Heer and Klaus Naumann (New York: Berghahn Books, 2004), 95–103, 107–10.

40. Bartov, *Hitler's Army*, 91–92.

41. Svetlana Alexievich, *The Unwomanly Face of War* (New York: Random House, 2017), xxxiii–xxxiv.

42. Niklas Zetterling and Anders Frankson, *Kursk 1943: A Statistical Analysis* (London: Frank Cass, 2000), 22.

43. Kenneth Slepyan, *Stalin's Guerrillas: Soviet Partisans in World War II* (Lawrence: University Press of Kansas, 2006), 4.

44. Slepyan, *Stalin's Guerrillas*, 80–81.

45. Reese, *Why Stalin's Soldiers Fought*, 174–75.

46. Gorbachevsky, *Through the Maelstrom*, 97.

47. Reese, *Why Stalin's Soldiers Fought*, 306.

48. Janusz Bardach and Kathleen Gleeson, *Man Is Wolf to Man: Surviving the Gulag* (Berkeley: University of California Press, 1998), ch. 4.

49. Quoted in Reese, *Why Stalin's Soldiers Fought*, 180.

50. Alexievich, *The Unwomanly Face of War* (US edition), 123.

51. Mansur G. Abdulin, *Red Road from Stalingrad: Recollections of a Soviet Infantryman* (Barnsley: Pen and Sword, 2004), 109.

52. Mark Edele, "Take (No) Prisoners! The Red Army and German POWs, 1941–1943," *Journal of Modern History* 88, no. 2 (June 2016): 346–47.

53. Richard Overy, *Russia's War: A History of the Soviet War Effort, 1941–1945* (New York: Penguin, 1997), 213.

54. Reese, *Why Stalin's Soldiers Fought*, 311.

55. Hellbeck, *Stalingrad*, 22.

56. Amir Weiner, "Saving Private Ivan: From What, Why, and How?," *Kritika: Explorations in Russian and Eurasian History* 1, no. 2 (Spring 2000): 313–14.

57. Catherine Merridale, *Ivan's War: Life and Death in the Red Army, 1939–1945* (New York: Metropolitan Books, 2006), 16, 134.

58. Reese, *Why Stalin's Soldiers Fought*, 218.

59. Merridale, *Ivan's War*, 233.

60. Martin van Creveld defines "fighting power" as a combination of "discipline and cohesion, morale and initiative, courage and toughness, the willingness to fight and the readiness, if necessary, to die." *Fighting Power: German and U.S. Army Performance, 1939–1945* (Westport, CT: Greenwood, 1982), 3.

61. Trevor N. Dupuy, *A Genius for War: The German Army and General Staff, 1807–1945* (Englewood Cliffs, NJ: Prentice-Hall, 1977), 34–35.

62. van Creveld, *Fighting Power*, 163–66; Allan R. Millett and Williamson Murray, eds., *Military Effectiveness*, vol. 3, *The Second World War* (Cambridge: Cambridge University Press, 2010), 212.

63. E. A. Shils and Morris Janowitz, "Cohesion and Disintegration in the Wehrmacht in World War II," *Public Opinion Quarterly* 12 (1948): 280–315.

64. Nicholas Stargardt, *The German War: A Nation under Arms, 1939–1945; Citizens and Soldiers* (New York: Basic Books, 2013), 140.

65. Quoted in Bartov, *Hitler's Army*, 41.

66. Bartov, *Hitler's Army*, 71. Cf. Karl-Heinz Frieser, who downplays ideology and argues that German fighting prowess sprang from a combination of technical proficiency and desperation caused by fighting against much more powerful enemies. "Concluding Summary," in *Germany and the Second World War*, vol. 8, *The Eastern Front, 1943–1944*, ed. Karl-Heinz Frieser (Oxford: Oxford University Press, 2017), 1220.

67. Bartov, *Hitler's Army*, 135.

68. Hellbeck, *Stalingrad*, 408.

69. Quoted in Jürgen E. Förster, "The Dynamics of Volksgemeinschaft: The Effectiveness of the German Military Establishment in the Second World War," in *Military Effectiveness*, vol. 3, *The Second World War*, ed. Allan R. Millett and Williamson Murray (Cambridge: Cambridge University Press, 2010), 207. Cf. van Creveld who contends that ordinary German soldiers "did not as a rule fight out of a belief in Nazi ideology—indeed, the opposite may have been nearer the truth in many cases." *Fighting Power*, 163.

70. Peter Fritzsche, *An Iron Wind: Europe under Hitler* (New York: Basic Books, 2016), 20.

71. Timothy Snyder, *Bloodlands: Europe between Hitler and Stalin* (New York: Basic Books, 2010), 175.

72. Stephen G. Fritz, *Frontsoldaten: The German Soldier in World War II* (Lexington: University Press of Kentucky, 1995), viii.

73. Fritz, *Frontsoldaten*, 156.

74. Manfred Messerschmidt, "Foreign Policy and Preparation for War," in *Germany and the Second World War*, vol. 1, *The Build-up of German Aggression*, ed. Wilhelm Deist et al. (Oxford: Clarendon Press, 1990), 546–47.

75. Stargardt, *The German War*, 207–8.

CHAPTER 15

The Eastern Front: Red Army Triumphant

The Slaughter Continues

Soviet forces had been battered and depleted in their overly ambitious offensives after the Battle of Stalingrad, but so too were the Germans. By the spring of 1943, the eighteen panzer divisions serving in Russia possessed only six hundred tanks. With so many vehicles destroyed, motorized units were marching to their destinations and moving their supplies by horse-drawn wagons. Most divisions were understrength by 20 to 50 percent. Reinforcements were coming, though exhausted veterans needed rest, and fresh recruits required more training and assimilation into their units. New and better weapons were in the pipeline as well, but the troops needed time to train with them and to repair their first-production-run glitches.

The Battle of Kursk

The fighting in the winter and spring of 1943 left the front lines uneven. On the northern end of the central front, the Germans pulled back from Rzhev and Demiansk, greatly shortening—and therefore strengthening—their lines. On the southern end, Manstein's counterattack had retaken Belgorod and Kharkov. That left a Soviet-occupied "bulge" south of Orel and north of Kharkov. The Kursk salient, 150 miles wide, protruded some 60 miles into the enemy defensive line. Army chief of staff General Kurt Zeitzler wanted a major operation to preempt any Soviet offensive in the summer of 1943. Hitler was enthusiastic too, but General Alfred Jodl, chief of the OKW operations staff, and other officers worried about committing more resources to the eastern front when Anglo-American forces seemed poised to invade Italy.

Zeitzler and Hitler got their way because trying something seemed preferable to just waiting for inevitable defeat. The Wehrmacht needed a big victory to reverse the tide of battle on the eastern front as well as to recover its prestige and its confidence. Hitler needed a dramatic triumph to ensure the now-wavering loyalty of his allies and to restore his reputation as a military genius. In addition, given the severe shortage of workers in the Reich, the Germans hoped to net a huge catch of prisoners for slave labor.

In 1941, Stalin doubtless would have ordered an offensive if he had been confronted with this situation. By the summer of 1943, the Soviet leader and his generals had learned a great deal, both about their own capabilities and about the propensities of the enemy. The Soviets anticipated that this large salient filled with Russian troops would tempt the

Germans to launch attacks at the northern and southern sides of its "neck" in order to surround and destroy the Red Army forces there. Moscow's calculations were confirmed by intelligence—Ultra information forwarded by a Soviet spy at Bletchley Park, reports from partisan units behind enemy lines, and radio intercepts. Zhukov advised Stalin not to attack precipitously but to wait for the Germans to strike first. This time the dictator listened to his generals.

A great tank and artillery duel between the elite forces of both sides was about to develop. Behind the battle lines, designers and engineers on both sides fought their own tank war. The sturdy Soviet T-34 had become the Red Army's main battle tank by the winter of 1941–1942. With sloping armor to deflect enemy shells, a strong 76 mm gun, a powerful diesel engine, and suspension that enabled relatively high speeds, the T-34 outclassed the panzer *Kampfwagen* IIIs and IVs it faced. The Germans responded in 1943 by introducing the Panther tank, with stronger armor and a heavier gun, as a "T-34 killer." They also produced a new heavy tank, the Tiger, with an 88 mm gun and 110 mm armor, as well as a self-propelled, sixty-five-ton Ferdinand assault gun. The Tiger's 88 mm gun had a much longer range than the T-34, which, when combined with excellent optical gunsights, allowed it to engage Soviet tanks before they were in range to respond.

However, there were fewer than 200 Panthers and only 138 Tigers at Kursk, and they initially suffered from serious reliability problems. Tigers and Panthers would spearhead the attack, but the Germans relied on the Pzkfw IV as the mainstay of their armored operations at Kursk. The Soviets, in turn, upgraded the T-34 with numerous innovations, including a lethal high-velocity 85 mm gun mounted in an improved turret, though this version was not available in quantity until 1944. During the course of the war, Soviet factories produced fifty-seven thousand of these formidable fighting vehicles. At Kursk, the Russians would rely on greater numbers and the bravery of tank and antitank gun crews to reduce German technical superiority by fighting at extremely close range.

The Soviet high command, with Stalin's approval, chose a defensive strategy for the anticipated battle at Kursk. They would let the Germans take the offensive, let the enemy forces wear themselves out battering against strongly prepared Red Army defenses, and then launch their own devastating counteroffensive. General Rokossovskii on the north edge of the bulge and General Vatutin on the southern side prepared a deeply echeloned defense, with eight barriers, one behind the other (the Germans would never get farther than the third). Thickly planted minefields, a dense network of artillery positions (one gun every ten meters in the most important sectors), and well-dug-in infantry protected each of these "belts." Behind each of them, mobile armor and antitank guns stood ready to plug any breakthrough.

The Red Army deployed 1.9 million troops, 5,128 tanks, and 25,000 artillery pieces and mortars in and behind the salient.[1] A German tank commander later described it this way: "What happened at Kursk was unbelievable. I've never experienced anything like it in war, either before or since. The Soviets had prepared a defensive system whose extension in depth was inconceivable to us. Every time we broke through one position in bitter fighting, we found ourselves confronted with a new one."[2] Local inhabitants dug trenches and constructed tank traps. Then all civilians were evacuated to a depth of twenty-five miles behind the front line. It was, in the view of historian Dennis Showalter, "the most formidable large-scale defensive system in the history of warfare."[3] General Konev marshaled huge reserve forces more than a hundred miles behind the front lines, ready to launch a powerful counteroffensive once the Germans had been weakened fatally by Soviet defenses.

The German plan, Operation Citadel, called for powerful attacks on the northern and southern necks of the salient, just as the Russians anticipated. The Wehrmacht committed over 780,000 troops, 2,928 tanks, 10,000 artillery pieces, and 2,000 airplanes to this assault. Field Marshal Walther Model's 9th Panzer Army would conduct the northern operation. He had no Panthers and only a battalion of Tigers, plus two battalions of Ferdinands. In the south, an even more powerful force, the 4th Panzer Army under General Hermann Hoth, prepared to strike the Red Army. Hoth commanded nine armored divisions, including three Waffen SS panzer divisions. His forces included two hundred Panther and forty-two Tiger tanks. They sought to encircle and destroy Soviet forces within the salient and thereby shorten their defensive line—a necessity for an army whose manpower shortage was acute. Army Detachment Kempf (commanded by General Werner Kempf), with three panzer divisions, protected Hoth's right flank. In the weeks before Operation Citadel began, the Luftwaffe mounted several raids against the Soviet rail network. Russian fighter aircraft were inferior to German fighters, but there were now a great many of them and their pilots were determined to stop the enemy. The Germans abandoned daytime bombing missions after particularly severe losses in early June.

The Germans intended to begin their campaign in the spring, but disaster in North Africa and the impending threat to Italy required further transfers of forces to the West. Hitler also insisted on waiting until the strike forces could be equipped with the new "super" tanks. After the war, some German commanders claimed that the operation might have succeeded if started earlier. That is unlikely. They did not know what large and powerful forces the Russians had already deployed behind the central front in the spring.

Model's attack in the north was to begin early on July 5. Soviet intelligence learned the start date and time, so the Red Army launched a massive preemptive artillery bombardment and air strike just as the enemy offensive was about to begin. The Red Air Force had also hit Luftwaffe bases in the area repeatedly in the days before the attack. Heavy Tiger tanks and self-propelled Ferdinand guns led the assault. The Tigers' 88 mm guns blasted Russian bunkers, while lighter Mark III tanks, infantry, and flamethrower units struggled to root out entrenched enemy infantry. Soviet artillery, antitank guns, and *Katiusha* rockets put up a virtual wall of fire. Red Army infantrymen, hidden in ditches and foliage, popped up to shower enemy tanks and vehicles with Molotov cocktails and grenades. Soviet ground-attack planes, led by the highly effective Iliushin Il-2 Shturmoviks, swarmed over the enemy. Model's forces suffered thirteen thousand casualties in the first two days alone. The German commander ordered more tanks and reserves forward, but his attack ground to a halt no more than seven miles into the salient.

Hoth's offensive to the south of the bulge was more powerful than the Soviets anticipated. In two days of tough and very costly fighting, his tanks covered twenty miles but were then stopped by the Soviet 1st Tank Army. Hoping to bypass the heavily entrenched defenders, Hoth swung his forces northeast toward Prokhorovka, a small railway junction—a "fatal" error according to Glantz and House.[4] Between July 9 and 13, a great tank battle took place in the rolling fields outside this little town. The Soviet command quickly brought up General Pavel Rotmistrov's 5th Guards Tank Army along with the 5th Guards Army from its reserves. German intelligence did not discover this massive Soviet tank deployment. Hoth and his commanders believed that Soviet forces were badly battered and were either just hanging on or even preparing to retreat. The SS divisions at Prokhorovka should have been supported by the III Panzer Corps coming from the south. That force, however, was unable to fight its way through an increasingly tenacious Soviet defense. Many accounts

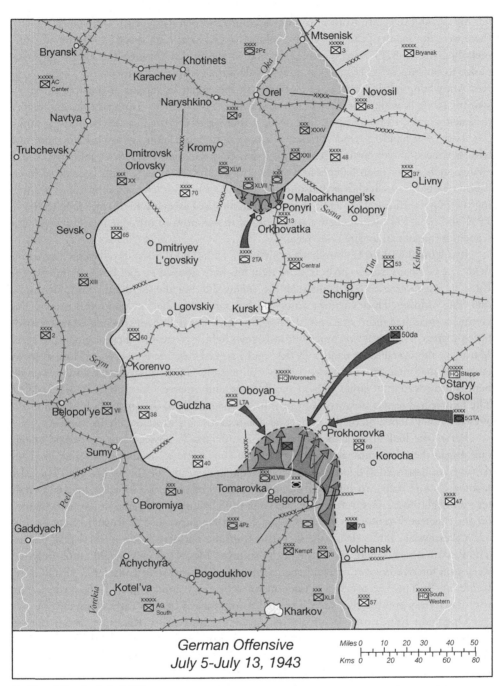

German Offensive
July 5–July 13, 1943

Miles 0   10   20   30   40   50
Kms 0   20   40   60   80

Battle of Kursk, July 1943

suggest that between 1,500 and 2,000 tanks participated in this great battle, but the actual number was about 850—250 panzers against 600 Soviet tanks.[5]

Soviet artillery and bombers pounded the enemy at Prokhorovka. Then the T-34s struck. Unlike 1941, Soviet tank units now fought in a much more coordinated fashion, with better radio communications and air support. A German captain reported, "What I saw left me speechless. . . . In front of me appeared fifteen, then thirty, then forty tanks. Finally, there were too many of them to count, rolling toward us at high speed."[6] A Luftwaffe raid, including the Ju-87G "tank-busting" version of the Stuka, thinned the attacking Soviet ranks. Rotmistrov's T-34s were less powerful than the Germans' Panthers and Tigers, so the Red Army adopted the strategy of closing with the enemy as rapidly as possible to fight a swirling battle in which the Soviet tanks could fire at the less well-armored sides and rear of the enemy tanks. In many cases, infantrymen rode on or followed closely behind the tanks.

There was hand-to-hand combat, not only with submachine guns and rifles but also with bayonets, knives, and entrenching spades. Both German and Soviet soldiers boarded enemy tanks to pry open hatches and throw in grenades. The combatants became so intermixed that both sides had to stop using artillery and ground-attack planes for fear of destroying their own vehicles. The "tank fright" that had caused so many Red Army men to flee in 1941 and even 1942 when enemy armor closed in was now an infrequent occurrence. The scene was one of extraordinary carnage.

By nightfall on July 12, hundreds of shattered tanks and thousands of bodies littered the field. The Germans tried to pivot left and right but were stopped by mobile Soviet forces. The Russians lost more men and tanks than the enemy did, but the Germans could not sustain their rate of losses. Hoth's panzer army had lost more than half its tanks and troops. The Germans attempted more attacks in the next few days, but their badly decimated forces made little progress. There was no choice but to begin a fighting retreat to their original start lines. Manstein, the overall commander in the south, argued that the Russians had lost so many tanks and men that a German victory was still possible.[7] Hitler disagreed, fearing an imminent Allied invasion of either Italy or the Balkans, and ordered Operation Citadel canceled. The Führer had reason to worry. On July 10, in the middle of this great clash of armor, the Western Allies landed on Sicily. Hitler was about to lose his strongest ally in Europe.

Before the Red Army launched its great counterattack, Soviet partisans behind enemy lines began their own campaign against German communications and transportation. They damaged or destroyed 298 locomotives, 1,233 freight cars, and 44 railway bridges.[8] They also sabotaged more than two hundred thousand sections of track and killed many train crews (even though those crews were mostly Russians and Ukrainians). Operation Kutuzov (named for the nineteenth-century general who had chased Napoleon out of Russia) began on July 12. Rokossovskii's forces struck the Germans from the northern sector of the Kursk pocket. The Russian attack caught the Germans by surprise. Model's troops fought stubbornly but were soon forced to retreat to avoid encirclement. The Wehrmacht considered Army Group Center an "inactive" sector. It was undermanned by raw recruits and shell-shocked veterans withdrawn from combat elsewhere. The Red Army reached Orel by early October.

Operation Rumiantsev (named after an eighteenth-century Russian general) opened on the southern side of the salient on August 3. Rotmistrov's battered 5th Guards Tank Army (which had lost 80 percent of its armor at Prokhorovka), reinforced by Konev's large reserves, attacked toward Belgorod and Kharkov. Massive artillery and rocket barrages, along with strikes by ground-attack planes, devastated German reinforcements and supplies moving toward the front. Soviet forces liberated Kharkov on August 23. Red Army losses were high once more, but the Soviet casualty rate was declining while the German rate increased dramatically. Soviet civilians were paying the price, too. The retreating Germans conducted a brutal scorched-earth campaign, burning or blowing up anything of value—crops, houses, towns, infrastructure of all sorts—and forcing the civil population to move west with them. Manstein wanted the advancing Russians to reconquer nothing but "rubble."

Both the outcome and the overall significance of the Battle of Kursk, and within it the engagement at Prokhorovka, have been a matter of contention among historians. Some historians see Prokhorovka as a Soviet defeat because the Russians lost far more men and tanks in the engagement than the Germans. Others contend that neither side won, since neither achieved its objectives. Still others argue that the Soviets won decisively at Prokhorovka. From this point on, the Soviets, not the Germans, were on the offensive. According to Dennis Showalter, "the Battle of Kursk was the Eastern Front's transition point—and its point of no return." Even though "the German army was neither bled white nor demodernized by Citadel's human and material losses," and despite the fact that "the Waffen SS won a tactical victory on July 12," nonetheless the Red Army "took what the Germans had left to give. Citadel's turning point was not July 12, but July 13, when the Germans flailed desperately and vainly . . . to regain even the local initiative."[9] In Showalter's view, Kursk was the key turning point not just on the eastern front but in the Second World War as a whole.[10]

The grim realization of impending defeat was beginning to set in throughout the Wehrmacht. After the Battle of Kursk, the Germans were never again able to launch a strategic offensive in the East. The Luftwaffe, having endured grave losses against the Anglo-American bombing campaign in western Europe, also lost more than a thousand planes in the Kursk operation. Much heavy fighting still lay ahead, but the Red Army had taken its first major step on the road to Berlin. Its commanders had demonstrated for the first time their ability to coordinate large-scale strategic operations and to defeat the Wehrmacht's best forces even without the help of winter weather.

Following the great battle at Kursk, Soviet forces went on the offensive in the south, aiming to recover the rest of the Donbass. This time Manstein could work no miracles. He bluntly told Hitler that without twelve fresh divisions he could not hold the enemy back, but, pressured on the central front and now in Italy as well, there were no new divisions to send. The Red Army took Taganrog and Stalino and continued racing toward the Dnieper River. Farther south, they drove the Germans out of the Kuban region. On the northern sector of the central front, Kluge's Army Group Center pulled back to better defensive lines, allowing the Soviets to liberate Smolensk in Belorussia on September 25.

So, what happened to the previously ever-victorious Wehrmacht in Russia? Showalter suggests that three elements account for the German army's decline. First, a campaign intended to be a *Blitzkrieg* devolved into a bloody war of attrition. The Germans could not recruit enough men or produce enough equipment to replace their enormous losses on the eastern front. Second, now caught up in an attritional struggle they had not anticipated, German commanders focused on operational objectives without seriously rethinking strategic capabilities and priorities. Third, Showalter contends, "and arguably most serious in the long run, was a culture, a mentality, that had developed into something combining convenience and indifference, embedded in a matrix of 'hardness.' . . . It was a mind-set particularly enabling the brutal expediency that is an enduring aspect of war and was underwritten and nurtured by Nazi ideology."[11]

Liberating the Western USSR

In 1944, Soviet forces reversed what the Wehrmacht had done to them in 1941. They struck the enemy along the whole line from the far north to the Black Sea, though not simultaneously. They finally carried out the "deep operations" that Soviet military theorists had envisioned in the 1930s. The Stavka reorganized the Red Army to accomplish this task. It created five tank armies capable of carrying out powerful combined-arms operations. These forces were to punch holes in German defenses and penetrate deep into the enemy rear to encircle and destroy his formations. Tank regiments, deploying upgraded models of the T-34, and mobile artillery gave the infantry armies breakthrough power. The Red Air Force received greatly improved new aircraft. Moreover, the resources of the Wehrmacht, already severely depleted by combat on the eastern front, were stretched to the limit first by the Anglo-American bombing campaign over Germany and then by the long-delayed invasion of France by the Western Allies. By April 1944, the Luftwaffe had barely five hundred aircraft on the eastern front facing over thirteen thousand Soviet planes.

In the wake of shattering defeats at Stalingrad and Kursk, the Wehrmacht attempted to consolidate a new defensive barrier, the East Wall, stretching from the Gulf of Finland to the Sea of Azov. The Germans forced thousands of Soviet civilians to dig entrenchments for this barrier. Hitler and his high command hoped that concentrating their troops in a shortened, fortified defensive line would finally enable them to stop the enemy advance. The Red Army was even more determined to breach that line and drive the invaders from Soviet territory. The most important assault took place in the south—the Second Battle of Ukraine, lasting from August 1943 to April 1944. Moscow committed five army groups (almost two and a half million men) to shattering German Army Group South. First the Russians pushed the enemy back to the Dnieper River, liberating the Donbass region and establishing a few bridgeheads across that river. The Stavka authorized a paratroop assault on the western side of the Dnieper to speed up the advance, but that ended in disaster. Lacking complete dominance in the air and sufficient numbers at the point of attack, barely half of the unfortunate paratroopers were able to fight their way back to their own lines.

The Soviets had hoped to maintain a rapid offensive to keep the Germans from digging in and from destroying valuable resources as they retreated, but the difficulties of ferrying large numbers of armored vehicles across the river slowed their drive. Nonetheless, Soviet forces commanded by General Vatutin retook Kiev on November 6 and pressed on as far as ninety miles west of the Ukrainian capital. A German counterattack pushed the Russians back temporarily, but Vatutin's and Konev's armies cooperated to encircle two enemy corps near Korsun. Konev's troops plunged ahead, driving across the Bug, Dniester, and Prut Rivers to the Romanian frontier. The reconstituted German 6th Army suffered severe losses, barely managing to escape encirclement. Odessa was liberated on April 10. Then the front in the southern Ukraine stabilized along the Dniester for four months.

Zhukov took direct command of operations in northern Ukraine after Vatutin was killed by nationalist guerrillas. His forces struck southward to the Carpathian Mountains, cutting the last remaining railroad line connecting Army Group South with Germany. The "fortified places," which Hitler had ordered to be held at all costs, were overrun one by one. Furious over the rolling collapse of his eastern empire, the Führer dismissed Hoth, Kleist, and Manstein. Once again, shuffling commanders could not halt the Red Army's momentum. Against the advice of some of his generals, Hitler insisted they hold the Dniester line, even though it was militarily indefensible. Unquestioned loyalty to Hitler and Nazi ideology became the key qualification for command. The generals argued with each other and with their supreme commander. The army high command (the OKH, responsible for the eastern front) fought bitterly with the armed forces high command (the OKW, responsible for western and southern Europe) over the allocation of increasingly scarce resources. Some generals argued for a mobile defensive strategy, involving some retreats. Instead, Hitler ordered them to hold in place.

The official Wehrmacht history insists that "Hitler's 'stand firm' mania had disastrous consequences. He repeatedly brought about a fiasco by his constant refusal to withdraw in time."[12]

Facing severe labor shortages, the Führer and his high command created new divisions by decreasing the size of existing divisions and using the "surplus" troops to form new units. By the last months of the war, most German divisions were barely a quarter of their normal strength. Neither Hitler's misguided decisions nor his commanders' mistakes made much difference. At this stage of the conflict, the Wehrmacht was no longer strong enough to hold back its powerful opponent. Soviet forces attacked the Crimean Peninsula from the winter of 1943 to the spring of the following year, launching an amphibious operation from the west and a larger invasion from the north. The Red Army greatly outnumbered the German and Romanian defenders in both men and equipment. Sevastopol finally fell on May 12 as the Germans evacuated 130,000 troops by sea and air.

At the opposite end of the eastern front, the Stavka amassed 1.25 million troops, 1,590 tanks and self-propelled guns, and almost 1,400 warplanes to assault the outnumbered German Army Group North near Leningrad. Hitler insisted, once again, on defending an indefensible area. Stubborn German resistance and the early onset of the fall mud season slowed the Soviet advance, but the long ordeal of Leningrad finally ended on January 16, 1944, when the Moscow–Leningrad railway line reopened. Although it suffered significant casualties, Army Group North was able to retreat in good order some one hundred miles back to the *Ostwall.*

Meanwhile, Soviet troops attacked the Finnish forces holding the Karelian Isthmus. This was a vastly more potent force than the Russian army that had bungled the Winter War against Finland in 1939–1940. It soon pushed back the overmatched Finns. The Finns asked for peace terms and left the war. Finland would lose some territory and pay an indemnity but keep its independence. Peace did not come so quickly, however. The Finns now had to fight to oust their German "guests." Subsequently, Soviet troops cleared the Arctic region of German forces that had blockaded the Arctic port of Murmansk.

Having liberated Karelia and driven Finland from the war, Soviet armies moved to clear the Germans from the Baltic states—Latvia, Estonia, and Lithuania—which had been forcibly incorporated into the USSR in 1940 but lost in 1941. Two Soviet armies drove into Estonia in September, forcing the Germans to abandon their hopeless position there. The fighting in Latvia and Lithuania was more intense, but a tank army and five infantry armies under General Bagramian finally cut their way through to the Baltic coast, trapping Army Group North at Kurland. The encircled German force held out until the end of the war, losing half of its four hundred thousand troops in the process. The USSR reabsorbed the three Baltic republics, while the Red Army regrouped for its next offensive into East Prussia.

Operation Bagration

The biggest and most important campaign of 1944 took place in Belorussia. During the winter of 1943–1944, German Army Group Center had given ground steadily but had successfully resisted any enemy breakthrough. It would not be able to resist the truly massive offensive that the Stavka organized to liberate Belorussia—Operation Bagration (named after an Imperial Russian general who had fought Napoleon at the Battle of Borodino). Launched just two weeks after the Allied D-Day landings, the carefully planned operation deployed enormous resources: 1.67 million men, 5,818 tanks, 32,968 guns and mortars, and

7,790 warplanes divided among four large army groups. The Soviets faced fifty Wehrmacht divisions in Belorussia; in comparison, the Western Allies initially encountered only nine German divisions in Normandy. Zhukov and Vasilevskii were in overall command. In the days before the operation began, thousands of Soviet partisans attacked German communications, transportation, and supply operations throughout the region.

The Germans did not anticipate such a powerful onslaught in the center of the eastern front. They expected the Russians to devote most of their forces to following up their earlier success in Ukraine. The Germans also believed that the presumably impenetrable Pripet Marshes adequately protected their southern flank in Belorussia. Guided by local partisans, Soviet engineers built wooden plank roads through the marshes, allowing Rokossovskii's tanks and self-propelled guns to attack the enemy suddenly and unexpectedly. Using successful deception techniques and radio silence, the Russians achieved complete surprise.

Soviet Operation Bagration, June 22–August 19, 1944

Soviet forces hit Bobruisk, Mogilev, Vitebsk, and Orsha with extraordinary force. Hitler had designated all four as "fortified places," which were supposed to hold out even though enemy spearheads flowed around them. Ordered to fight rather than withdraw, the defending units were soon encircled and neutralized.

The Red Army continued to advance rapidly, covering three hundred miles in just five weeks and liberating Minsk on July 3. German Army Group Center, a force of over eight hundred thousand men, largely ceased to exist at this point, with Soviet spearheads pursuing its survivors. Lacking mobile forces and sufficient tanks for any sort of counterattack, German defense efforts were doomed. It was the largest defeat the German army had ever suffered. As usual, the Soviets endured more casualties than the Germans, but the Soviet ratio of killed and wounded compared to the total number of troops involved in the campaign decreased significantly—both because the Russians had learned to fight the enemy more effectively and because the power of German resistance was also diminishing. Stalin celebrated the victory by marching fifty-seven thousand captured Germans through Moscow.

In 1939–1940, the all-conquering Wehrmacht could not imagine defeat. But by the end of 1944, defeat had become a certainty. German forces were fatally overstretched in their attempt to slow the Soviet juggernaut in the East and deal with the Allied invasion of France, while also fighting a holding action in Italy. The RAF and American bombing campaigns were destroying the military industries on which the Wehrmacht depended. Hitler hoped to hold the line on the eastern front, redeploy strong forces to the West, throw the Anglo-American invaders back into the English Channel, and then rebound to defeat the Red Army. This was a fantasy. Soviet forces were now poised to sweep the Germans from eastern Europe and invade the Reich itself.

Into Eastern Europe

The nature of the war was about to change for the Soviet Union. Up to this point, Moscow had been reclaiming its own territory; from here on it would be liberating large parts of eastern and central Europe from German domination. Stalin intended to carry the fight all the way to Berlin, both because he realized the necessity of destroying the Nazi regime and because he wanted to create a large Soviet sphere of influence throughout eastern Europe. To acquire that security zone and to extract reparations from defeated Germany, he needed to occupy eastern Europe and Prussia before the Western Allies got there or before a negotiated settlement left regimes in power that were hostile to Soviet Russia.

For the Russians, Poland was the most important theater of combat from mid-1944 to early 1945—both because it was the shortest route to Berlin and because the fate of postwar Poland was a particularly sensitive issue for the Kremlin. The Red Army launched two campaigns against the Germans in the summer of 1944, the Lublin-Brest operation in the north and the Lvov-Sandomierz operation farther south. Russian troops reached the Bug River (i.e., the 1939 Soviet-Polish border) on July 20, by coincidence the same day as the attempted assassination of Hitler at his eastern front headquarters in Rastenburg, East Prussia.

The 1st and 2nd Belorussian Armies, under Rokossovskii and Zhukov, respectively, surged into northeastern Poland, entering Lublin on July 23 and liberating the nearby Majdanek concentration camp. Three days later they reached the Vistula River. Meanwhile, Konev's powerful 1st Ukrainian Army Group took Lvov on July 27. The enemy fought hard for the city, but when another Soviet spearhead penetrated to the Vistula threatening to encircle them, the Germans abandoned Lvov. Near Brody, however, Soviet forces surrounded and destroyed eight German divisions. Both Rokossovskii's and Konev's troops managed to established bridgeheads across the Vistula, though they were barely able to hold them against strong enemy counterattacks. The Red Army was beginning to experience some of the same problems the Wehrmacht had faced in 1941. Their rapid advance meant that the men were exhausted, their equipment needed repair or replacement, and their supply lines were growing ever longer.

At this point, with lead elements of the Red Army just on the other side of the Vistula, General Tadeusz Bor-Komorowski's Home Army (underground forces loyal to the London-based Polish government-in-exile) launched an insurrection in Warsaw. The rebels fought to liberate the capital city and establish an independent, nationalist government *before* Soviet forces arrived. They held out for two months of brutal street fighting but, short of arms and ammunition, they were crushed by SS units. More than two hundred thousand civilians died during the fighting, and Warsaw was virtually reduced to rubble. An angry Hitler ordered the city completely obliterated.

During the Cold War, Western politicians, journalists, and historians blamed the failure of the Warsaw Uprising on Stalin's supposedly callous unwillingness to unleash Soviet troops in support of the insurrection. The situation was more complicated than that. Of course, the Soviet dictator had no love for the "London Poles" and their Home Army. As Deputy Foreign Minister Ivan Maiskii wrote in January 1944, "in the past Poland was almost always an enemy of Russia."[13] An independent, nationalist Poland had been consistently hostile to the USSR throughout the interwar period. Nonetheless, military realities are as important as political considerations in understanding the Red Army's inability to support the Warsaw Uprising. After a long campaign across two-thirds of Ukraine and well into Poland, the Russians needed considerable time to bring up reinforcements and replenish supplies. Stalin dismissed the uprising as "a reckless and fearful gamble."[14]

Moscow at first denied American requests to use Soviet air bases to airlift supplies to the insurgents, though the Soviet air force eliminated German air cover in September. Reversing prior policy, in mid-September the Soviets offered to cooperate with the Western Allies in supplying the Warsaw rebels, and they began their own airdrops of weapons and food. Certainly Stalin shed no tears over the demise of Polish resistance forces that were as hostile to the Russians as they were to the Germans. The Soviet leader was determined to keep the Belorussian and Ukrainian sections of prewar Poland, occupied by the Red Army in 1939, and he intended to see a government friendly to the Soviet Union installed in Warsaw. Toward that end, the Russians established a Polish Committee of National Liberation (led by Polish communist émigrés from Moscow) in Lublin and armed pro-Soviet Polish forces under General Zygmunt Berling.

Relations between Moscow and the London-based Polish government-in-exile had soured well before the Warsaw Uprising. In 1943, the Germans had publicized the discovery of the mass graves of over twenty thousand executed Polish officers and had blamed the Russians for the atrocity. The Soviet government denied the crime. Roosevelt and Churchill supported the Soviet denial, accusing the Germans of having committed the crime and then lying about it in an attempt to weaken the Grand Alliance. Even as evidence to the contrary trickled in, US and British leaders were compelled the defend Moscow for the sake of Allied unity. The "London Poles" requested an investigation by the Red Cross, whereupon the USSR severed diplomatic relations with them. Intent on recovering his 1940 borders and on covering up the Katyn massacre, Stalin would only deal with the pro-Soviet "Lublin Poles."

Fighting broke out all over Poland between the Home Army and pro-Soviet Polish forces loyal to the Lublin government—a civil war simultaneous with the battle against Germany.

By January 1945, Zhukov's and Konev's armies, now strongly reinforced, were prepared to drive the Germans out of the remainder of Poland. The German defenders, in contrast, were weakened by earlier combat losses as well as by the redeployment of some of their troops to fight in Hungary and in the Ardennes offensive in the West. German intelligence presented Hitler with accurate information on the Soviet buildup, but the Führer refused to believe it. He ordered German troops to fight to the death, yet they gave way rapidly under the powerful Red Army assault. Replacing their commander with the fanatical Nazi, Field Marshal Ferdinand Schörner, could not save the situation. While the 2nd and 3rd Belorussian Armies attacked East Prussia, Zhukov's and Konev's forces raced across western Poland, bypassing enemy strongpoints. Zhukov's lead elements soon reached the Oder River in Germany, just sixty miles from Berlin. As the Germans retreated, where possible they emptied the concentration camps, sending the inmates westward on foot—operations that often turned into death marches. On January 27, Soviet troops entered Auschwitz, where they found 7,600 sick and starving prisoners as well as mountains of corpses.

While resistance crumbled in Poland, farther south the 2nd and 3rd Ukrainian Army Groups swept into Romania against weakened German and Romanian opposition. The Germans were taken by surprise, once again underestimating the strength and speed of the Russian assault. As the Russians encircled large Axis forces, a military coup toppled the pro-German regime of Marshal Antonescu, and Soviet troops took Bucharest at the end of August 1944. The Romanian army switched sides, now fighting alongside the Red Army, particularly in the drive into Hungary where the Romanians had territorial claims. The Red Army also occupied the Ploesti oil fields, though American bombing had already rendered them useless. Soviet pressure soon produced a coalition government dominated by communists. Stalin saw Romania, like Poland, as crucial to the Soviet Union's postwar security.

Dividing Southeast Europe

In October 1944, during Churchill's visit to Moscow, the British and Soviet leaders reached an unofficial agreement on spheres of influence in southeastern Europe. According to Churchill's memoir-history, he outlined a division of the region on a sheet of paper (Romania 90 percent, Bulgaria 75 percent, Hungary and Yugoslavia 50 percent Soviet influence; Greece 100 percent British influence) and passed the sheet to Stalin who put an approving check mark on the "document."[15] All this transpired in the absence of any US representative. The Americans rejected this deal, subsequently known as the Percentages Agreement, when they learned of it.[16] It was not a binding and enforceable treaty. Except for Greece, Stalin would take more than his allotted share when his troops controlled most of the region.

Crumbling enemy resistance in Romania opened the way into its southern neighbor, Bulgaria. That country had joined the Axis, permitted German troop movement and bases on its territory, and declared war on Britain and the United States, but not on the USSR. Soviet Russia declared war on Bulgaria on September 5 and promptly invaded the country. Although the Bulgarian Communist Party was small, it forged a coalition, the Fatherland Front; seized power in Sophia; and ordered Bulgarian forces not to resist the Soviet incursion. Soviet troops and their new Bulgarian allies soon crossed into Yugoslavia. There they found much of the country already under the control of Marshal Tito's Partisans. German troops had already begun pulling out of Greece, Yugoslavia, and their smaller holdings in the Mediterranean in October. Soviet and Partisan units jointly liberated Belgrade before the end of the month. However, Soviet forces involved in this operation were needed for higher-priority attacks on Hungary and the Reich itself. The Russians supplied Tito's Partisans with large quantities of equipment so that they could deal with the remaining Axis strongholds.

Unlike the relatively easy victories in Romania, Bulgaria, and Yugoslavia, the struggle for Hungary was long and hard fought. Hitler considered Hungary to be of greater strategic importance than the Balkan states, so he sent German troops to occupy the country and took measures to prevent a Hungarian departure from the Axis. The Führer pressured Admiral Horthy to install a new government compliant to German wishes. It remained loyal to Berlin and handed over Hungary's four hundred thousand Jews (a step the Hungarians had resisted up to this point). The Soviet 2nd and 3rd Ukrainian Army Groups, supported by troops from their new Romanian, Bulgarian, and Yugoslavian allies, fought through the Carpathian Mountains barrier and spread out onto the Hungarian plain in October 1944.

Despite his assurances to Hitler, Admiral Horthy negotiated peace with the Russians and signed on armistice with them on October 15. SS commandos, led by Otto Skorzeny, staged a coup in Budapest, overthrowing the Horthy government and installing a native fascist Arrow Cross regime. Some Hungarian army commanders declined to fight the Red Army or even went over to its side, but most senior officers remained loyal to their Axis partners. Some of them feared the atrocities that Soviet troops might inflict on the Hungarian population, but most were concerned that the Romanians would take Hungarian territory. The Soviet offensive faced the determined resistance of three German and two Hungarian armies.

After much heavy fighting, General Roman Malinovskii's troops finally reached Budapest on December 26 and laid siege to the capital. Few civilians had been evacuated when Soviet artillery bombarded the city. Hitler once again refused permission for the encircled defenders to break out. Nonetheless, the desperate German commander, SS general Karl Pfeffer-Wildenbruch, attempted to break through the encirclement. His effort failed, and the Russians took 110,000 enemy prisoners. The Germans attempted to reverse their defeats in Hungary by launching Operation Spring Awakening (the last German offensive of the war). The 6th SS Panzer Army and the 6th Army (reorganized once again after having been destroyed twice) attempted to retake Budapest in March 1945. The attack failed due to lack of fuel, muddy ground, and powerful Soviet resistance. A Provisional National Government signed a peace treaty taking Hungary out of the war.

Having taken most of Hungary, Malinovskii's 2nd Ukrainian Army turned northward toward Bohemia, while General Fëdr Tolbukhin's 3rd Ukrainian Army drove toward Vienna. The Red Army's campaign to liberate Czechoslovakia was both long and frustrating—a nine-month ordeal hindered by difficult terrain and stubborn German resistance. Some units of the Slovak army rebelled against the Germans and their own collaborationist government, but the Germans quickly crushed the uprising. Soviet forces did not take Prague until May 9—after the fall of Berlin, the death of Hitler, and the German surrender on the western front (May 8). When the fighting finally ceased in Czechoslovakia, the Russians took 719,000 German prisoners.

Crushing the Third Reich

The Red Army had now liberated all of eastern Europe, but at a terrible price. The fighting from Poland in the north to Yugoslavia in the south took 1.1 million Soviet lives. German losses amounted to 447,000 killed or missing. In contrast, the Western Allies lost only one hundred thousand men during the fighting in France, Belgium, and Holland. In November 1944, Stalin declared, "Now for the Red Army there remains one last and conclusive mission: to complete, together with the armies of our allies, the destruction of the German-fascist army, to kill the fascist beast in its own den, and to hoist over Berlin the banner of victory."[17] That mission would be longer and bloodier than anyone anticipated.

Though battered on the eastern and western fronts, the Wehrmacht still had several million men under its command, supplemented by the creation of the *Volkssturm* (older men and teenagers with minimal training and weaponry). Amazingly, despite the Allied bombing campaign, munitions production in Germany had increased during 1944. Hitler, the Nazi Party, and the German army were determined to defend the fatherland to the death. One Hitler Youth member who survived the ordeal later wrote, "My mind was filled with Nazi propaganda assuring certain death for all of us if the enemy won the war."[18]

Himmler, Göring, Ribbentrop, and Speer sought peace terms from the Allies in the closing months of the war (more frequently from Washington and London than from Moscow). However, Hitler, Goebbels, and many other German leaders, especially in the military, were adamant not to repeat the capitulation of 1918 but instead to fight to the end. That determination sprang from a variety of motives. First, there existed a widespread understanding in the army and among the civil population that German forces had committed vast atrocities against the Jews, Poles, and Soviet peoples. By 1944 a great many Germans had reached the same conclusion that Goebbels recorded in his diary in 1941:

> The Führer says: right or wrong, we must win. It is the only way. And victory is right, moral and necessary. And once we have won, who is going to question our methods? In any case, we have so much to answer for already that we must win, because otherwise our entire nation—with us at its head—and all we hold dear will be eradicated.[19]

The Nazi elite and senior Wehrmacht commanders believed—quite reasonably—that they would be held responsible for those atrocities. The Allies' "unconditional surrender" demand reinforced that conviction. Clearly the enemy intended to impose a thoroughgoing regime change on Germany. There was also a widespread fear among the German population that they too might have to pay for the horrors committed in their name.

Germany was gripped by an even more pervasive fear—caused by a mixture of guilt and racism—that the "Asiatic hordes" (i.e., the Red Army) would murder, pillage, and rape their way through Germany. Mixed with these fears, however, there was also hope. Hitler continued to believe that new superweapons—jet fighters, cruise and ballistic missiles, and super submarines—would yet turn the tide of battle in favor of the Third Reich. There was also a widespread (though premature) expectation that the Grand Alliance would break apart, to be replaced by a new Western coalition of Britain, the United States, and Germany against the USSR.

German troops fought on during the hopeless last weeks of the war for a variety of reasons—simply obeying orders or to hold back the "red tide," or because they could not imagine life without the Third Reich, or in hopes of capture by the Western Allies. In addition, the regime took brutal measures to keep its people fighting. Anyone who hindered the war effort in any way was subject to immediate execution. There would be no negotiated settlement as the Prussians had made in 1871, nor a German collapse as had happened in 1918. This would be a fight to the death. As early as 1941, Hitler had contemplated the possibility of defeat: "In this, too, I am as cold as ice. If the German people proves no longer strong enough, or sufficiently self-sacrificing, to pay for its existence with its own blood, then let it perish and be destroyed by another, stronger power . . . then I shall shed no tears for the German people."[20]

Having reached the line formed by the Oder and Neisse Rivers in January 1945, the Soviet offensive stalled because of severe supply problems (especially the destruction of the transport infrastructure in Poland), the spring thaw that made the movement of heavy armored vehicles difficult, and the remaining danger of enemy flanking attacks. The latter problem materialized in the form of a counterattack against Zhukov's northern flank from Pomerania in mid-February. It took the Red Army until the end of March to destroy the enemy forces in Pomerania and reach the Baltic coast. At the same time, General Chuikov's 8th Guards Army established a bridgehead over the Oder, while Rokossovskii's forces took Danzig (present-day Gdansk). There were other flanking attacks along the Soviet perimeter, but they were pinpricks, easily brushed off by the Red Army. There was a political dimension as well to the Soviets' slowed advance toward Berlin. Stalin wanted the Red Army to complete the conquest of East Prussia as soon as possible so that he could annex part of it, including the port of Königsberg (now Kaliningrad), to the USSR. Farther south, the armies of Malinovskii and Tolbukhin drove through southwestern Czechoslovakia and into Austria, finally securing Vienna on April 13.

While American and British forces crossed the Rhine and began to overrun western Germany, the Red Army launched its final drive in mid-March to capture Berlin. It was a powerful three-pronged assault: Rokossovskii's 2nd Belorussian Army Group (or Front) attacking north of Berlin, Zhukov's 1st Belorussian Army Group striking directly at the Nazi capital, and Konev's 1st Ukrainian Army Group driving to its south. In all, the Soviets deployed 2.5 million troops, 6,250 tanks and self-propelled guns, 41,500 artillery pieces, and 7,500 aircraft in their campaign to capture Berlin and overrun eastern Germany. General Gotthard Heinrici commanded 100,000 German troops, supported by 1,200 tanks and guns, dug into the Seelow Heights, some fifty-five miles east of Berlin. The battle raged four days, but inevitably the superior weight of Zhukov's forces broke through these defenses on April 19. Despite bitter German resistance along all the approaches to the capital, Zhukov's and Konev's armies encircled Berlin by April 25.

At the same time, the RAF bombed Berlin almost every night. Hitler's capital might well have been sealed off and bypassed at this point, leaving it to starve or surrender, but Stalin ordered its conquest. Russian artillery began to shell the city intensively, keeping up the barrage until the last resistance was extinguished in the demolished capital. Zhukov was determined to get credit for taking the Nazi capital. He issued a directive for his armored spearheads to find ways to dash to its suburbs and a further order to report the triumph not only to Stalin but to the world press as well. The Red Army repulsed German attempts to relieve the besieged city from the south and north. Hitler, who had issued numerous unrealistic orders for impossible counteroffensives, seems finally to have realized the hopelessness of his situation on April 22. He ranted that the war had been lost because of the incompetence and faithlessness of his generals.

Soviet forces completely sealed off the doomed city the following day. Savage house-to-house urban warfare was to follow. General Helmuth Weidling had just forty-five thousand regular army and SS troopers to defend Berlin, supplemented by a ragtag assortment of policemen, Hitler Youth, and *Volkssturm*. The battle for Berlin soon deteriorated into a series of local engagements. Soviet artillery demolished the buildings from which the defenders fought but did not quash their resistance. The Germans kept fighting from the rubble. Russian

Red Army soldiers raise the Soviet flag over the Reichstag building in Berlin, May 2, 1945.
Source: Library of Congress

troops assaulted the old Reichstag building on April 30. They secured it, after bitter room-to-room fighting, only on May 2. It was there that two Soviet soldiers planted the Soviet flag on the Reichstag roof for a photograph that became the most famous icon of the eastern front. Once again, Soviet leaders—not just Stalin, but his generals too—cared more about dramatic results than the lives of their soldiers. Zhukov's desire to be the conqueror of the enemy capital (before Konev's forces could get there) led him to squander soldiers' lives. Over 360,000 Soviet and Polish troops died in the campaign for Berlin.

As the Red Army closed in around him on the 29th, Hitler wrote his last will and testament, naming Admiral Karl Dönitz as Germany's new president and commander-in-chief. He then married his mistress, Eva Braun. The next morning the newlyweds committed suicide. Their bodies were cremated, but Soviet investigators were able to make a positive identification from the dictator's dental records. Hitler died believing that the German people had failed him. A few days before his death, he had ordered the destruction of Germany's remaining industry, transport system, and food supplies. Known as the "Nero Order," this command was widely ignored by economic managers and military commanders. Hitler thought the German people would be better off dead than under the heel of the Allies. He had told one of his adjutants, "We will not capitulate, ever. We may go down. But we will take the world down with us."[21] More than a third of all German soldiers killed during the war died in its last four and a half months because of Hitler's nihilistic refusal to surrender.

Advancing from all sides, the Russians pushed the remaining German defenders into the center of the city. General Hans Krebs attempted to secure surrender terms from the Soviets, but Goebbels blocked his efforts. When surrender, nevertheless, became inevitable, Goebbels and his wife murdered their children and then killed themselves. The surviving German soldiers in the city center attempted to break out on the night of May 1, but few managed to get through the concentric rings of Soviet forces surrounding the city. The next day the Red Army took the Reich chancellery, whereupon General Weidling surrendered to General Chuikov. Elsewhere in eastern Germany, Russian troops suppressed various remnants of the once-proud Wehrmacht. Hostilities on the eastern front finally ceased on May 9. Hitler's "thousand-year Reich" had crumbled into dust in just twelve years.

Taking Revenge

The sequel to the Red Army's heroic conquest of the Nazi heartland was less than glorious. Soviet soldiers engaged in looting and acts of violence not only in the foreign countries they overran but also on Soviet territory they liberated. Historian Mark Edele blames a "culture of violence" in the Red Army.[22] Generals hit, threatened with guns, and sometimes executed their subordinate officers; the officers did the same to troops under their command. Ordinary soldiers took out their anger and violence on defenseless civilians. Anger at the Germans and the thirst for vengeance motivated many murders, assaults, rapes, and robberies as the Red Army entered the Reich.

Every Soviet trooper knew in grisly detail what the Germans had done in Russia. They had seen it with their own eyes, heard the gruesome tales of their comrades, and been exposed to endless hate propaganda by the Soviet regime. As they liberated western Russia and Ukraine, Red Army men frequently encounter buildings blown up, villages burned to the ground, crops incinerated, herds slaughtered, corpses of men tortured and murdered, and the bodies of women raped and killed. The enemy had not spared old people or children, either. The Nazis had made the struggle a race war—a war of extermination. Entering the Reich, the Red Army instructed its men that "on German soil there is only one master—the Soviet soldier, that he is both the judge and the punisher for the torments of his fathers and mothers, for the destroyed cities and villages. . . . 'Remember your friends are not there, there is the next of kin of the killers and oppressors.'"[23] Many Soviet soldiers were ready to repay the enemy in kind. Timothy Snyder suggests that "Soviet soldiers may have understood the rape of German women as a way to humiliate and dishonor German men."[24] As many as two million German women were raped, many of them repeatedly.[25] Sometimes husbands, fathers, brothers, or other male family members were made to watch the rapes to drive home their humiliation.

The famous Russian author Aleksandr Solzhenitsyn later wrote about his experience as a Red Army officer in East Prussia:

> Zweiundzwanzig, Höringstrasse
> It's not been burned, just looted, rifled.
> A moaning, by the walls half muffled:
> The mother's wounded, still alive.
> The little daughter's on the mattress,
> Dead. How many have been on it?
> A platoon, a company perhaps?
> A girl's been turned into a woman.
> A woman turned into a corpse.[26]

Envy motivated the violence as well. Many soldiers were outraged to learn that the evil people of the Third Reich lived so much better than the heroes of the Soviet Republic. Appropriating wristwatches, bicycles, and anything else of value seemed like simple justice. Boris Suris, a Soviet soldier, rationalized the "liberation" of German consumer goods this way: "They [the Germans] stole and extorted enough from our country; now we will steal and extort."[27] The Soviet government never officially authorized looting, but it tacitly sanctioned these thefts. In 1945, it allowed soldiers to send five-kilo parcels home each month without charge, facilitating looting. Sometimes, however, the soldiers' rage led to smashing rather than stealing the enemy's luxury goods.

Elsewhere, including Yugoslavia, which was in the process of becoming a communist state, inadequate discipline in the ranks, negative attitudes toward women, and, in the case of some soldiers, a criminal background fostered Red Army crimes. Stalin was informed of the mass rapes taking place in Germany, but he trivialized these crimes as merely "misbehaving with women"—in his mind an entirely understandable, venial sin for men who had endured so much in combat. In Germany, Marshal Zhukov issued a strict order prohibiting crimes against civilians, but Stalin thought the order went too far and had it rescinded. Only when this orgy of violence caused difficulties for Soviet occupation authorities and provoked foreign criticism did Stalin signal that the military anarchy should end. Looting and assaults continued, however. It was hard for many Soviet soldiers to understand the transition from a race war in which all Germans were the enemy to the new concept of a class war in which non-Nazi Germans were potential comrades in building a socialist society. The threat of rape continued until the winter of 1947–1948, when Soviet soldiers were confined to their camps.

Notes

1. David M. Glantz and Jonathan M. House, *The Battle of Kursk* (Lawrence: University Press of Kansas, 1999), 336–37.

2. Richard J. Evans, *The Third Reich at War* (New York: Penguin, 2008), 486–87.

3. Dennis Showalter, *Armor and Blood: The Battle of Kursk; The Turning Point in World War II* (New York: Random House, 2013), 61.

4. Glantz and House, *The Battle of Kursk*, 146.

5. Russian historian Valeriy Zamulin provides an even lower figure: 368 tanks and self-propelled guns for the Russians versus 150 tanks and assault guns for the Germans participating directly in the engagement at Prokhorovka. *Demolishing the Myth: The Tank Battle at Prokhorovka, Kursk, July 1943: An Operational Narrative* (Solihull: Helion, 2011), 528. Also see Nikolas Zetterling and Anders Frankson, *Kursk 1943: A Statistical Analysis* (London: Frank Cass, 2000), 105–7. Richard Evans and Karl-Heinz Frieser contend that the great Prokhorovka tank battle was largely mythical and that the outcome was a disaster for the Soviets. Evans, *The Third Reich at War*, 488; Karl-Heinz Frieser, "The Battle of the Kursk Salient," in *Germany in the Second World War*, vol. 8, *The Eastern Front, 1943–1944*, ed. Frieser (Oxford: Oxford University Press, 2017), 118–38. Frieser suggests very low German losses, only 3 tanks, against 522 destroyed Soviet tanks (p. 132).

6. Showalter, *Armor and Blood*, 203–4.

7. After the war, Manstein depicted himself as a warrior of insight and daring who might have won the war but for the timidity of his fellow generals and his Führer. See Erich von Manstein, *Lost Victories: The Memoirs of Hitler's Most Brilliant General* (Novato: Presidio Press, 1993).

8. Chris Bellamy, *Absolute War: Soviet Russia in the Second World War* (New York: Vintage, 2008), 587.

9. Showalter, *Armor and Blood*, 268–69.

10. Showalter, *Armor and Blood*, 272.

11. Showalter, *Armor and Blood*, 34–35.

12. Karl-Heinz Frieser, "Concluding Summary," in *Germany and the Second World War*, vol. 8, *The Eastern Front, 1943–1944*, ed. Frieser (Oxford: Oxford University Press, 2017), 1215.

13. G. P. Kynin and I. Laufer, eds., *SSSR i germanskii vopros, 1941–1949: Dokumenty iz arkhiva politiki Rossiskoi Federatsii* (Moscow: Mezhdunarodnye Otnosheniia, 1996), 1:341ff.

14. Andrei A. Gromyko, et al., eds., *Stalin's Correspondence with Churchill and Attlee, 1941–1945* (New York: Capricorn, 1965), 254.

15. Winston S. Churchill, *The Second World War*, vol. 6, *Triumph and Tragedy* (Boston: Houghton Mifflin, 1953), 227.

16. Mark A. Stoler, *Allies at War: Britain and America against the Axis Powers, 1940–1945* (London: Hodder Arnold, 2005), 187–88. Cf. Robert Dallek, who claims that Roosevelt readily accepted the agreement. *Franklin D. Roosevelt and American Foreign Policy, 1932–1945* (New York: Oxford University Press, 1979), 479–80.

17. Evan Mawdsley, *Thunder in the East: The Nazi-Soviet War, 1941–1945* (London: Bloomsbury, 2005), 361.

18. Ursula R. Mahlendorf, *Shame of Survival: Working through a Nazi Childhood* (University Park: Pennsylvania State University Press, 2009), 198.

19. Fred Taylor, ed., *The Goebbels Diaries, 1939–1941* (London: H. Hamilton, 1982), 415.

20. Frieser, "Concluding Summary," 1225.

21. Nicolaus von Below, *At Hitler's Side: The Memoirs of Hitler's Luftwaffe Adjutant, 1937–1945* (London: Greenhill Books, 2001), 223.

22. Mark Edele, *Stalinism at War: The Soviet Union in World War II* (London: Bloomsbury Academic, 2021), 166.

23. Norman M. Naimark, *The Russians in Germany: A History of the Soviet Zone of Occupation, 1945–1949* (Cambridge, MA: Harvard University Press, 1995), 72.

24. Timothy Snyder, *Bloodlands: Europe between Hitler and Stalin* (New York: Basic Books, 2010), 317.

25. For comparison, American troops committed about 1,500 rapes in their occupation zone during 1945. Ian Buruma, *Year Zero: A History of 1945* (New York: Penguin, 2013), 39.

26. Alexander Solzhenitsyn, *Prussian Nights* (New York: Farrar, Strauss & Giroux, 1977), 7, 39.

27. Brandon M. Schechter, *The Stuff of Soldiers: A History of the Red Army in World War II through Objects* (Ithaca, NY: Cornell University Press, 2019), 212.

CHAPTER 16

The Western Allies Strike

Allied Strategy

The Grand Alliance, the mightiest military combination in world history, came into being slowly and fitfully. President Roosevelt saw the mortal danger to American security posed by the Third Reich, but powerful currents of isolationism, both in Congress and among the public, hampered his efforts to deter or defeat Nazi aggression. FDR could only move to rearm the United States and aid Britain and France as American public opinion gradually shifted in response to German and Japanese atrocities. In contrast, British prime minister Churchill established an alliance with the USSR soon after the German assault on Russia. Britain no longer stood alone.

Leaders in London understood the importance of their new Soviet ally. The British chiefs of staff admitted frankly in October 1942, "The Russian army is, today, the only force capable of defeating the German army or, indeed, of containing it."[1] The Japanese bombing of Pearl Harbor, together with Hitler's declaration of war on the United States, finally propelled America into the conflict and established the Grand Alliance. The "Big Three" never signed a binding treaty of alliance. Roosevelt refused to do so, and the British objected to some of Stalin's demands. Instead, they issued the "Declaration by United Nations" at the beginning of 1942 in which each promised to assist the other and not to make a separate peace. Signed by the US, the USSR, Great Britain, China, and twenty-two other governments, the declaration reaffirmed the political goals previously stated in the Atlantic Charter (though both Britain and Russia interpreted the self-determination clause to suit its own interests). Yet, for all their differences, the three Allies cooperated with each other to a much higher degree than did their Axis opponents.

From its beginning, however, differing strategic conceptions and mutual suspicions divided the coalition. Stalin feared that his new Western partners were willing to fight to the last Soviet soldier and that they anticipated the destruction of *both* Germany and Russia. The Soviet Union desperately needed Anglo-American forces to establish a second front in western Europe as soon as possible, which Stalin hoped would draw off forty Wehrmacht divisions from the eastern front. The USSR also needed as much material support from its partners as possible—food, trucks, radios, warplanes, etc. Strained to the limit by its own defense requirements, Britain had little material support to offer Moscow, but it would send the Russians what it could as a token of their partnership. The United States began to meet some of Moscow's needs through the Lend-Lease program, though not in substantial quantities before the tide of battle had already turned in 1943.

In addition, Stalin wanted his Western allies to recognize the incorporation of the Baltic states, eastern Poland, eastern Romania, and parts of Finland into the USSR as well as to accept a restructuring of eastern Europe that would establish states friendly to the Soviet Union. Stalin also desired an ongoing arrangement with his allies to keep Germany weak and to divide Europe among them into spheres of influence. The USSR's distrust of all capitalist states, which had informed Soviet foreign policy since the 1917 revolution, did not dissipate during the war. Stalin continued to fear that that his Western allies would betray him by signing a separate peace with Germany. In the fall of 1942, he wrote to his ambassador in London, "All of us in Moscow are getting the impression that Churchill is sustaining a course toward the defeat of the USSR in order to come to terms with the Germany of Hitler or Brüning at the expense of our country."[2]

Churchill, a staunch anticommunist, was no supporter of Soviet expansionism, but Britain's desperate position required some compromises with Moscow. London would recognize the 1941 borders of the USSR because this was a nonnegotiable Soviet demand. The postwar fate of eastern Europe was another matter, however, which would later play a key role in the dissolution of the Grand Alliance. Unlike Churchill, Roosevelt rebuffed Stalin's demands for recognition of his wartime gains. They conflicted with America's basic war aims. Moreover, FDR realized that by the end of the war the United States would be in a much stronger negotiating position, so putting off such decisions served American interests.

The second-front issue tested Anglo-Soviet relations severely. Determined to avoid a repetition of the massive bloodletting of the First World War, British leaders advocated a "peripheral strategy" of fighting on the fringes of the Axis empires and relying on blockades, bombing, and the fomenting of resistance movements to weaken Germany. They planned to assault the Reich in its heartland only *after* these peripheral tactics had fatally weakened Germany. British defeats at German hands in Norway, France, and Greece seemed to require that caution rather than audacity should inform strategic decision-making. England would rely on its strengths—the Royal Navy and the RAF—while delaying a frontal confrontation with the Wehrmacht as long as possible. Only with Allied command of the seas and the air and with the full mobilization of American strength would British strategists contemplate a direct blow against Germany. Even when those conditions existed in 1943–1945, the prime minister sought to deflect ground operations from France to the Balkans, a strategy that would have met three of his desires: avoiding combat with large German formations, preventing Soviet penetration of the peninsula, and protecting the "lifeline of empire."

For Churchill, the preservation of the British Empire was a high priority, second only to the protection of the home islands. He famously proclaimed in the House of Commons in 1942, "I have not become the King's First Minister in order to preside over the liquidation of the British Empire." For the prime minister, the noble promises of the Atlantic Charter did not apply to England's colonies (nor to those of other European states). He told an American diplomat, "Nations live on their traditions or die. . . . As long as I am here, we will hold to them and the Empire. We will not let Hottentots by popular vote throw the white people into the sea."[3] The prime minister held to that position even though many in his government realized that the empire in its prewar form could not continue and that there was waning support for it among the British people. Churchill's fixation brought him into conflict with the Americans, who insisted from the outset that they were not fighting to preserve the old colonial order. The British Empire's "imperial preference" system, which disadvantaged trade with countries outside the Commonwealth, also contradicted the American desire for

Soviet premier Joseph Stalin, US president Franklin D. Roosevelt, and British prime minister Winston S. Churchill at the Tehran Conference summit meeting in 1943.
Source: Wikimedia Commons

global free trade. In addition, the American wish to see a strong, united China conflicted with British, French, and Dutch colonial interests in Asia.

For Roosevelt and his liberal advisors, the Second World War was as much an ideological conflict as it was for Hitler. The Four Freedoms declaration was not just propaganda for them. America would fight for liberal democracy, capitalism, and free trade. Critics of US foreign policy argue that, given America's virtually hegemonic economic position at the end of the war, the demand for free trade was a vehicle for American "open door imperialism."[4] The anticolonialist thrust implicit in the doctrine of self-determination caused conflict with America's British and Free French allies (and later with the USSR as well), but while the threat of Nazi conquest still loomed large, those issues were suppressed for the sake of Allied unity. Moreover, in the war's last year, the perception of a Soviet threat emerging in East Asia began to soften the anticolonial thrust of US policy.

The Americans also clashed with their British colleagues over a prospective second front. Churchill and Roosevelt agreed on a "Europe First" policy because they knew that the German threat was far more menacing than that posed by the Japanese. That decision pleased Stalin and the US generals, but not the US Navy and the American public, who wanted to punish Japan immediately. The two Western leaders agreed to pursue the "unconditional surrender" of the Axis states. They intended that declaration to reassure Stalin and Chiang

Kai-shek of their allies' determination to fight through to total victory and to prevent another German "stab in the back" myth after the war. It was also politically useful to Roosevelt because it allowed him to put off consideration of divisive Allied territorial claims
until after the war. Some writers have criticized the unconditional surrender policy as poor
strategy, but it is hard to deny the necessity of rooting out fascism and Japanese militarism.

The US Army leadership believed that they could defeat Germany only by a major assault on Nazi-occupied western Europe combined with continuing Red Army pressure in
the East. They envisioned the creation of a 215-division army to engage the Germans (a
goal never reached). To the horror of the British, the American generals advocated action
as soon as possible—in 1942 or 1943 at the latest. General Alan Brooke, chief of the Imperial General Staff, noted in his diary, "The [American] plans are fraught with the gravest
dangers. The prospects of success are small and dependent on a mass of unknowns, whilst
the chances of disaster are great and dependent on a mass of well-established military facts."[5]
The Americans were at a disadvantage in dealing with the British on this issue because they
were only in the process of creating the forces that their strategy required. In addition, the
two allies doubted each other's military effectiveness. The British were hesitant to rely on
freshly recruited US divisions and untested American commanders. The Americans in turn
wondered if British arms, which had been defeated in France, Malaya, and Africa, would
fare any better in the future.

Historians Williamson Murray and Allan Millett argue that "the British were entirely
right. None of the preconditions for a successful landing on the coast of France yet existed.
The Battle of the Atlantic was not over; the Luftwaffe had yet to be defeated; the logistical
infrastructure for the immediate support of the invasion did not exist; and Allied air forces
were not capable of interdicting the landing area and preventing the Germans from moving
rapidly against the invasion."[6] The disastrous defeat of a premature Allied invasion might
well have turned the British and American public against continuing the war. The Dieppe
disaster, an attempted raid on a German-occupied French port on the English Channel on
August 19, 1942, demonstrated the dangers involved. Enemy fire and obstacles trapped six
thousand Canadian and British troops, fifty US Army Rangers, and a tank battalion on the
beaches or in their landing craft. Sixty percent of the troops were killed, wounded, or captured, while 106 aircraft and one destroyer were lost. This was to have been a trial run for
a full-scale invasion. Instead it became a bloody lesson in the difficulties of that enterprise.

Given the life-and-death struggle on the eastern front, the Soviets had little patience
with Western excuses for postponing a second front in western Europe. Moscow also tended
to underestimate the immense complexities of such a massive amphibious operation. American general John Deane cabled to Washington from Moscow in November 1943, "Belief
current here that cross-Channel operations involve same problems as river crossing. Soviets
actually believe Channel no more difficult than Dnieper [River]."[7]

The Americans insisted on the creation of a unified Allied command in order to use
resources efficiently. Despite the differences between the British and the Americans (as
well as disagreements within each country's armed forces), Great Britain and the United
States established a remarkably integrated command during the war. The Combined Anglo-
American Chiefs of Staff met almost continuously in Washington, under the chairmanship
of Field Marshal Sir John Dill, who reported directly to Churchill and Roosevelt. A thoroughly integrated team of British and American commanders conducted the biggest operation launched by the Western Allies, the invasion of France in 1944. Coordination with
the Soviet armed forces was much looser, but it still surpassed the almost total lack of co-

operation among the Axis powers. Anglo-American collaboration extended to the very top. Churchill and Roosevelt developed a strong bond, their differences notwithstanding. FDR cabled the British leader in 1942, "It is fun to be in the same decade with you."[8] Churchill had courted the American leader assiduously. For him, "the natural Anglo-American special relationship" was the key to British survival. Nonetheless, the British tended to look down on their American allies. Churchill was sure that his judgment was superior to Roosevelt's, while most British generals regarded their US counterparts as incompetent.

Churchill and Roosevelt also had to deal with a host of difficulties among lesser members of the anti-Axis coalition. Two antagonistic generals, Charles de Gaulle and Henri Giraud, vied with each other over control of Free French forces, while communist-led and noncommunist resistance groups in occupied France struggled with one another for supremacy. Governments-in-exile in London (especially the Polish, Greek, and Yugoslav governments) were frequently at odds with some of the resistance groups in their countries. Alliance politics often exacerbated these tensions: Roosevelt backed Giraud, while Churchill favored de Gaulle; the two Western leaders supported the "London Poles," while Stalin backed (having virtually created) the "Lublin Poles." The American president recognized de Gaulle, whom he despised, as the leader of liberated France only in August 1944, while the division over Poland would become one of the key issues in the dissolution of the Grand Alliance after the war. Similarly, in the Asia-Pacific theater of war, the British were highly suspicious of nationalist (and therefore anticolonial) resistance movements, while the Americans supported them.

The loss of a "mere" 3,600 troops at Dieppe did not impress Stalin. The hard-pressed Red Army needed help immediately. Roosevelt's broken promises of a second front in 1942 and again in 1943 angered the Soviet dictator. The Western Allies' invasions of North Africa in 1942 and Italy in 1943 did little to assist the Soviet war effort. When the Soviet leader learned that the Allied invasion of France would be delayed until 1944, he warned the Western leaders, "I must tell you that the point here is not just the disappointment of the Soviet Government, but the preservation of its confidence in its Allies, a confidence which is being subjected to severe stress."[9] Emphasizing his displeasure, he recalled his ambassadors from London and Washington. To overcome this growing rift in the alliance, Churchill and Roosevelt met Stalin at a summit conference in Tehran, Iran, in late 1943. There the two Western leaders promised Stalin that Britain and the United States would launch a major invasion in western Europe during the coming year. They still feared that if Stalin lost confidence in them he might conclude a separate peace with Germany. London and Washington also realized that, to avoid the Red Army penetrating deeply into western Europe, they needed to project their own forces onto the Continent as soon as possible.

As a gesture of appeasement toward his Western allies, Stalin dissolved the Communist International in June 1943. He meant to reassure Churchill, Roosevelt, and Western public opinion that the Soviet Union did not intend to use the chaos of total war to foster global revolution. Dissident Spanish communist historian Fernando Claudin has suggested that scrapping the Comintern (the global organization of Communist parties) amounted to a deal with Stalin's Western partners whereby he sanctioned the reestablishment of liberal, democratic capitalism in western Europe in exchange for their recognition of a large Soviet sphere of influence in eastern Europe.[10] Beyond these diplomatic considerations, terminating the Third International also gave foreign Communist parties somewhat more flexibility in building "united front" resistance coalitions with noncommunist forces. Nevertheless, the Kremlin still wielded substantial control over most Communist parties because of the preeminence of Stalin and the USSR and because some of the Comintern's apparatus continued to operate surreptitiously. Stalin's partial rehabilitation of the Russian Orthodox Church in 1943 was also in part a gesture of appeasement toward his Allies, meant to counter Western criticism of Soviet persecution of Christianity.

The Battle of the Atlantic

The Western Allies enjoyed a massive material advantage over Germany and Italy—greater population, larger industrial base, and more abundant natural resources. That advantage, however, would materialize on the battlefield only if those resources arrived securely in England and on the front lines in Europe and North Africa. Germany and Italy were determined to strangle that Allied lifeline—with good reason. Britain depended on overseas shipping for half of its food supply and two-thirds of its raw materials. The German navy (or Kriegsmarine) was tiny compared to the mighty British and American fleets. Initially it employed a few surface raiders against Britain's supply lines, but with minimal effect. Germany had used submarines (U-boats) with some success in the First World War, but when war broke out in 1939, the Kriegsmarine had only eighteen of these undersea predators, and they could reach the Atlantic shipping lanes from their bases on the North Sea only with great difficulty.

Failure to prepare for a large-scale submarine campaign before the conflict began was a critical mistake of the German war effort. Churchill thought so, too: "The U-boat attack," he said, "was our worst evil. It would have been wise for the Germans to stake all on it."[11] Yet, even with these limited resources, the U-boats were able to do some damage—sinking over a million and a half tons of shipping in 1940. Almost six thousand British, Indian, and African seamen perished in that year. These losses forced the British to divert incoming ships from the south coast of England to ports on the west coast. The Royal Navy sank no enemy submarines in 1939 and only four in 1940 because it lacked sufficient destroyers and patrol aircraft as well as sophisticated techniques of antisubmarine warfare. The "destroyers-for-bases deal" in 1940 brought fifty older US destroyers to the Royal Navy, but they required substantial refitting before they could operate effectively.

After many attempts, Grand Admiral Erich Raeder, head of the German navy, and Admiral Karl Dönitz, chief of its submarine service, finally convinced Hitler that interdicting Allied freighters, oil tankers, and troopships was a strategic imperative for Germany. The Führer authorized a crash program for building submarines. By the end of 1941, the Kriegsmarine had almost three hundred U-boats. A year later the number was nearly four hundred, though seldom were more than a third of that number on patrol in the Atlantic at any one time (with the remainder traveling to or from station, in port for refitting, or assigned elsewhere). The capture of Norway and the fall of France provided much better bases for the U-boats. The Germans also cracked the British naval code, allowing U-boat captains to know the course of enemy convoys.

Even with these advantages, the U-boats still had difficulty finding and attacking their targets. German submarines of this era were much slower than surface ships (only between 3 and 7.4 knots) when running submerged on electric power. They had to surface frequently, running on diesel engines at seventeen knots, to recharge their batteries. While underwater, U-boat commanders had very limited vision through their periscopes. Long-range patrol aircraft were much better at finding enemy convoys, but few were available because, by the spring of 1941, the Luftwaffe had allocated most of its resources to Operation Barbarossa.

The life of a German submariner was hard. Crews of about fifty lived in extremely cramped quarters, gave up bathing and shaving for the duration of the cruise, and, by 1942, lived in constant fear of attacks by Allied warships and planes. The intense camaraderie among U-boat crews made up for some of these hardships. Lieutenant Helmut Dauter described it this way:

> The life aboard our Atlantic operational boats was very hard because of the constricted space and the proximity of the sea; even on the bridge we were only five metres above the water. As every man on board was visible to everyone else and regardless of rank and position exposed to severe hardships, sacrifices and dangers, there had to clearly quickly be a strong feeling of togetherness, of sharing the same fate. It fulfilled us completely even when we were not at sea. It was our whole life. We had been put into it with all its glory and terror and we accepted it, often with anxiety and fear, often with joy and enthusiasm.[12]

The British organized their shipping into convoys escorted by Royal Navy destroyers. These warships used underwater sound detection equipment, known as ASDIC (or sonar), to locate submerged U-boats. The Germans responded by launching night attacks, with their submarines running on the surface, invisible to ASDIC and to lookouts on Allied destroyers. At the beginning of the war, many escort vessels were equipped with an early and not very effective version of long-wave (metric) radar. The Germans developed a device (Metox receivers) to detect those signals and use them to home in on enemy targets. The U-boats operated in groups, known as "herds" by the Germans and "wolf packs" by the Allies, in order sink many more ships in each convoy. They could stay out on patrol longer because the Germans employed supply submarines to replenish fuel and torpedoes for the attack boats. When Italy joined the war in May 1940, more than a hundred Italian submarines went into action against Allied shipping in the Mediterranean. Luftwaffe bombers joined in the hunt as well.

For a while, the Anglo-American war effort hung in the balance. German submariners described the period from June 1940 to February 1941 as the "happy time" when they sank over 270 Allied ships. Few seamen survived when their ship sank. Dönitz ordered his crews to "rescue no one and take no one with you. Have no care for the ships' boats. . . . Care only for your own boat and strive to achieve the next success as soon as possible. We must be hard in this war."[13]

After America's entry into the war, U-boats prowled the US eastern coastline with impunity. The Americans had not yet organized their shipping into convoys, while bright lights from cities along the coast made it easy for German submarines to pick off ships one by one. The US Navy ignored the bitter lessons of Britain's experience with the U-boats. Even as Allied defenses improved along the English west coast and the US east coast, the U-boats still thrived in a mid-Atlantic kill zone beyond the range of Allied patrol planes. In March 1943, thirty-eight U-boats attacked two large convoys, sailing close together and totaling ninety-one ships, escorted by only two destroyers and five smaller corvettes. The Germans sank twenty-one of the merchantmen while losing only one submarine. Nature sometimes aided the enemy. In the winter of 1942–1943, severe north Atlantic storms sank almost a hundred Allied ships.

Efforts to bomb the large, heavily reinforced U-boat pens at bases along the French coast failed, though many civilians were killed in the process. The Allies did not have the necessary accuracy or sufficiently powerful bombs. The balance in this naval struggle gradually shifted in the Allies' favor, however, due to their ability to manufacture extraordinary numbers of ships and aircraft, technological breakthroughs, and better organization of the antisubmarine campaign. British, Canadian, and American shipyards began to pour out hundreds of freighters, tankers, and warships—producing ships much faster than the Axis could sink them.

At the Casablanca Conference in January 1943, Roosevelt and Churchill assigned top priority to the war against the U-boat. The Allies produced long-range aircraft capable of finding and attacking enemy submarines even in the mid-Atlantic. They also introduced the escort carrier—a smaller aircraft carrier, typically with only eighteen planes—which provided air cover for a convoy all the way across the Atlantic. A new weapon, the hedgehog (a multiple-firing mortar), allowed warships to shower submarines below with a wide pattern of explosive charges while keeping the target fixed on radar. Allied planes now had powerful searchlights, enabling them to find and destroy surfaced U-boats at night. Allied ships and planes also deployed new homing torpedoes and much-improved depth charges. The Allies achieved a major advantage late in 1941 when they broke the German naval code. From that point on, controllers directed convoys away from the wolf packs, while Allied air-sea hunter-killer groups sped toward them. However, there were occasional lapses in Ultra intelligence whenever the Germans made modifications to their Enigma encoding machines. It took time for cryptographers to adjust to the changes.[14] The Allies also developed more effective, undetectable shortwave (centimetric) radar, and they used high-frequency direction-finding equipment (HF/DF, or "huff-duff") to locate U-boats by their radio transmissions.

Just as in the Battle of Britain, an integrated systems concept was crucial to exploiting all of these advantages. Antisubmarine control centers in England and the United States plotted the courses of U-boats and convoys, gathered all the intelligence reports, and directed the deployment of warships and airplanes to maximum effect. The Allies won the Battle of the Atlantic in 1943. In 1940 and 1941, U-boats sank more merchantmen than the Allies built. That comparison drew almost even in 1942. The following year Britain and America launched almost 15.4 million tons of shipping, while enemy submarines sank only 3.2 million tons. In 1944, almost 13 million tons of ships were commissioned, while only just over a million tons were sunk.[15]

Now it was the U-boats that were endangered. In 1942, the Allies sank just sixty-five enemy submarines in the Atlantic. In 1943 that total increased to 237 and then to 261 the following year. The Germans were losing U-boats faster than they could replace them. The attrition rate for German submariners reached 75 percent. Dönitz's own son was killed when Allied bombers sank his U-boat. He tried to shame his wavering crews, telling them, "If there is anyone who thinks that combating convoys is no longer possible, he is a weakling and no true U-boat captain."[16] However, even Dönitz realized the growing imbalance in the battle, lamenting, "The enemy holds every trump card, covering all areas with long-range air patrols and using location methods against which we still have no warning. . . . The enemy knows all our secrets and we know none of his."[17] The admiral had to pull his submarines back to their bases or risk losing them all. Surviving German U-boats still operated occasionally when they found favorable situations, but they no longer had a significant strategic impact on the war.

The Allies won the battle at sea not only in the Atlantic but in the Mediterranean as well. Initially, German and Italian submarines virtually closed British shipping lanes in the Mediterranean, forcing London to use the 12,500-mile route around southern Africa and into the Red Sea. The same improved equipment and integrated systems concept of antisubmarine warfare that won the Battle of the Atlantic allowed the Allies to prevail in the Mediterranean and launch successful amphibious attacks in North Africa, Sicily, and Italy. Only on the very difficult convoy route through the Arctic Ocean to bring supplies to the USSR did British efforts meet defeat. Here the Germans had every advantage. With air and submarine bases in northern Germany, Norway, and, after the success of Operation Barbarossa, on the Baltic coast as well, they could savage the convoys with little fear of retaliation. German attempts to use surface ships to disrupt British convoys to the USSR were less successful. RAF bombers flying from bases in northern Russia sank the battleship *Tirpitz*, while Royal Navy ships sank the battle cruiser *Scharnhorst*. Nonetheless, losses grew so severe on this route that the British suspended convoys twice and shifted to a route through Iran.

Historians disagree about the strategic significance of the Battle of the Atlantic. Richard Overy suggests that "no Allied strategy was possible across the Atlantic Ocean without the defeat of the submarine."[18] In contrast, John Ellis argues that the U-boat menace was never quite the mortal threat to the Allied cause that most historians have thought.[19] Both have a point. Allied material superiority could never be brought to bear in the war without securing the shipping lanes in the Atlantic (and the Mediterranean and Pacific as well). At the same time, Britain was never really in danger of being starved into submission. Most ships crossing the Atlantic were never attacked, and the Allies managed the invasion of North Africa in 1942 and the even larger buildup for Operation Overlord in 1944 without significant Axis interference.

Driving the Axis from North Africa

After the collapse of the Italian offensive in 1940, Erwin Rommel's Afrika Korps and Claude Auchinleck's 8th Army pushed each other back and forth across the sands of North Africa. German attacks foundered for lack of adequate reinforcements and supplies. British offensives, though enjoying superiority in men and equipment, failed for lack of coordination and an inadequate understanding of combined-arms operations. Rommel, having received more troops and aircraft and a promotion to field marshal, launched a series of attacks in May and June of 1942 that pushed the British back into Egypt, though with serious losses of men and equipment on both sides. The important port at Tobruk fell to the Germans on June 21. For a while there was panic in Egypt. Government workers burned documents and prepared to flee to Palestine. Rommel was not able to amass a decisively powerful force because he lacked sufficient reinforcements and supplies.

The British attacked German and Italian supply lines across the Mediterranean, using air power, submarines, and surface ships guided by Ultra intelligence. Churchill, unhappy over the British army's poor performance in North Africa, brought in General Sir Harold Alexander as theater commander and General William Gott as head of the 8th Army, but Gott's plane was shot down before he could take up his duties, so the prime minister had to settle for his second choice, General Bernard Law Montgomery. Montgomery, though prickly and conceited, would finally succeed in ousting Axis forces from North Africa. "Monty" wore a dashing beret, affected a confident air, and visited his troops often in a successful effort to bolster the 8th Army's sagging morale. His approach to combat was cautious, conservative, and methodical.

The British established a strong defensive line near El Alamein, sixty miles from Alexandria, Egypt. Rommel won his earlier battles by outflanking opponents. That would be impossible this time, with the Mediterranean on one end of the British line and, only forty

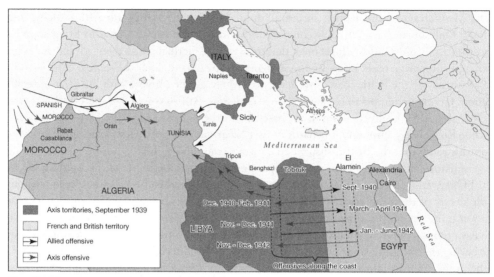

The Fighting in North Africa, 1940–1943

miles to the south, the Qattara Depression (a salt marsh impassable by heavy armor). Protected by geography as well as by dense minefields and effective antitank weaponry, Montgomery amassed superiority over the enemy of between three and four to one in men, tanks, and aircraft. The RAF finally gained air superiority over the Luftwaffe, savaging Rommel's supply lines and providing direct support to the troops on the ground.

The Afrika Korps attacked the British position on the Alam el Halfa Ridge on August 30, 1942, but the defenders repelled this offensive. Montgomery's forces (British, Australian, New Zealand, South African, Indian, Polish, and Free French troops) struck the German and Italian lines in late October at a particularly inopportune time for them—Rommel was convalescing in Germany, and his replacement, General Georg Stumme, suffered a fatal heart attack as the assault began. Montgomery used artillery fire, tanks with flails mounted in front, and handheld acoustic mine detectors to clear the thick minefields protecting the Axis lines, and then poured armor and infantry through the open corridors (including three hundred Sherman tanks just arrived from America). The Germans managed to beat back the initial attacks only at the cost of most of their armor. The decisive moment came at the beginning of November when Montgomery's armor blasted a four-mile-wide hole in Italian infantry defenses and then wheeled northward to attack two depleted panzer divisions. Down to just thirty tanks (against almost six hundred for the British), Rommel ordered retreat, only to be countermanded by Hitler's command to hold fast. The British suffered an unfavorable loss rate of four to one in tanks, but unlike the Germans they were able to replenish their losses and move forward. After absorbing further heavy losses, the Germans finally broke contact and retreated into Tunisia.

Montgomery has been widely criticized for his sluggishness in not destroying the badly depleted German force at this point.[20] He allowed the Germans and Italians to escape, even though Montgomery knew of their weakened condition from multiple intelligence sources. The vaunted Afrika Korps was now just a shell of its once powerful self. Rommel wrote that the battle had been "like a mill. Everything that went into it, regardless of quantity, was ground to dust. . . . Anyone who has to fight, even with the most modern weapons, against an enemy in complete command of the air, fights like a savage against modern European troops, under the same handicaps and with the same chances of success."[21] In March 1943, Montgomery's troops finally shattered the remainder of Rommel's German and Italian forces on the Tunisian-Libyan border. By June, British troops were in Tripoli, a thousand miles from their start point. They had finally eliminated the Axis threat to Egypt, the Suez Canal, and Britain's supply lifeline. Events elsewhere were also going badly for the Germans. Allied forces landed in Morocco and Algeria on November 8, while on the 19th the Russians sprang their trap at Stalingrad.

Operation Torch

The Anglo-American amphibious assault on North Africa, Operation Torch, under the command of General Dwight Eisenhower, involved three separate attacks along the Moroccan and Algerian coasts. Despite American diplomatic wooing of Marshal Pétain's French regime, Vichy authorities in North Africa resisted the Allied invasion (while they let German forces enter Tunisia without protest). The Allies hoped that Vichy's soldiers would obey Free French commander General Henri Giraud, but they ignored his orders. Vichy troops fought hard against the Allies, but they were not equipped or supplied well enough to stop such a force. Even so, the American invaders had difficulty pushing aside this weak resistance because the inexperienced US troops were still mastering the complexities of amphibious assault. In three days of fighting, the French lost 3,000 men, while 2,225 of Eisenhower's troops fell. The Allies finally negotiated a cease-fire with the commander of all Vichy forces, Admiral François Darlan—a much-criticized arrangement that left the collaborationist admiral in charge of all French military forces and civil administration in North Africa. Only after Darlan's assassination in December by a young French monarchist did Giraud take control in the region.

Lacking sufficient forces, Rommel and the German high command wanted to abandon North Africa, but Hitler insisted that it be held. This was a political as well as a strategic decision. He feared that a catastrophic defeat in North Africa would undermine Mussolini's regime and expose the southern flank of Axis-occupied Europe. Therefore the Germans rushed paratroopers to Tunisia, followed by infantry and panzer reinforcements—eventually building up to a quarter million troops. The Germans also moved into the previously unoccupied portion of Vichy France, while French admirals scuttled their fleet at Toulon (rather than give it up to the Germans or defect to the Allies). Air Marshal Albert Kesselring served as commander of the Mediterranean theater, while Rommel continued to lead the Afrika Korps and General Jürgen von Arnim commanded the reinforcements pouring into Tunisia.

Rommel and Arnim planned a preemptive operation to destroy Allied supply bases in Algeria, though their rivalry prevented close coordination of their attacks. Nonetheless, they inflicted stinging local defeats on green American troops and their incompetent commander, General Lloyd Fredendall. Axis forces wiped out the US 168th Infantry Regiment at Sidi bou-Zid in Tunisia. An even worse disaster occurred when veteran German and Italian armored forces attacked weak and inexperienced American troops at Kasserine Pass in February 1943. A US artillery spotter recalled, "It was murder. They [US tanks] rolled right into the muzzles of the concealed eighty-eights and all I could do was stand by and watch tank after tank blown to bits or burst into flames or just stop, wrecked. Those in the rear tried to turn back but the eighty-eights seemed to be everywhere."[22] Two hundred US tanks were destroyed. The Americans had to withdraw from their positions, leaving much of their heavy equipment and suffering the loss of six thousand troops (over one thousand dead and many more captured).

This defeat was an important learning experience for the Americans. Eisenhower reorganized his forces, changed some of their operating procedures, and replaced Fredendall with General George Patton—a skilled (even if frequently obnoxious) commander. Patton's lack of self-control (notoriously exhibited in his widely reported slapping of two GIs suffering from malaria and "shell shock") and his inability to avoid publicly criticizing his superiors almost cost this talented general his command. Both the Germans and the British drew the same faulty conclusion from the initial US military defeats—that American troops were inadequately trained, poorly led, and short on fighting spirit. Eisenhower's forces would have to show their enemies and their allies that they could deal with the mighty Wehrmacht. After the Kasserine disaster, stiffening Allied resistance repulsed further German offensives. Rommel had failed to destroy the Allied army to his west or to take the well-stocked American supply bases. The westward offensive had been another desperate German gamble to escape an impossible situation. He now had only minimal rations and fuel for his forces, while Montgomery's 8th Army was closing in from the east.

However embarrassing it was for the Americans, the debacle at Kasserine Pass merely delayed the inevitable for the Germans. Allied fliers now achieved dominance in the air over the Mediterranean. Berlin had to end convoys across the sea because Allied air strikes were devastating them. The Germans switched to airfreight, even though planes could transport only a small fraction of what the ships had carried. That failed, too, because Ultra told Allied fighter pilots when and where enemy transport planes would fly. Some German officers suspected that the Allies were reading their messages, but the high command could not believe that their highly complex Enigma encoding system had been broken. German troops in North Africa lacked replacements, equipment, and supplies. Allied forces began closing in on the doomed German garrison at Tunis—Montgomery's 8th Army from the east and US, British, and Free French units from the west. Italian and German troops resisted as best they could, but with no possibility of retreat and dwindling supplies of ammunition, the Axis pocket at Tunis collapsed in early May. The Allies killed or captured 290,000 enemy soldiers. Victory came at a price. The Allies suffered thirty-six thousand British, eighteen thousand US, and sixteen thousand French casualties.

Some American generals at the time and some historians subsequently have criticized the Allied invasion of North Africa as a strategic mistake, a diversion from the decisive invasion of western Europe. Operation Torch may not have been a military necessity for the Allies, but it was a political necessity for Roosevelt. FDR needed American troops to engage the German enemy as soon as possible, thereby building American public support for the war in Europe and fending off the clamor for a "Pacific First" strategy. In 1942, only North Africa could serve that purpose.

Difficulties in Italy

The Allies differed over what to do next. Still adhering to his "peripheral" or "Mediterranean" strategy, Churchill argued that invading Italy and knocking that country out of the war should receive top priority, followed by a possible strike in the Balkans. The Americans objected strongly, characterizing Mediterranean operations as a "sideshow" and even threatening to shift their priorities to the Pacific if the British would not commit to a major cross-Channel invasion of France. The balance of power had shifted in the Anglo-American relationship, since the United States was now providing most of the troops and funding. Churchill had to accept the American position, on condition that the Allies undertake at least a limited effort to defeat Italy. The prime minister abandoned his opposition to a cross-Channel operation only at the end of 1943 at the Tehran summit conference where both Roosevelt and Stalin pummeled him into submission. Churchill continued to fear a disastrous outcome for the invasion of France, telling Eisenhower of his nightmares of "Channel tides running red with Allied blood."[23]

The Allies therefore launched their amphibious assault on the island of Sicily. It opened with an extensive bombing campaign against Axis air bases on Sicily and southern Italy and with a successful deception operation that convinced the Germans to redeploy substantial ground and air forces to Greece. British troops under Montgomery and US units commanded by Patton landed on July 10 (while the Battle of Kursk raged on the eastern front). British, Canadian, and American units assaulted the Italian and German defenders of the island with overwhelming force—the equivalent of two armored divisions, two airborne divisions, seven infantry divisions, a two-to-one advantage in the air, and devastating naval gunfire. The Italian 6th Army (three hundred thousand men) and two German mechanized divisions defended the island. Although the initial airborne operation went badly, dropping some men into the sea and scattering others all over southeastern Sicily, Axis forces could not repel the amphibious landings. The British drove northeast while the Americans looped northwest to meet at Messina on the northeastern tip of Sicily. British troops quickly captured Syracuse, while American forces repulsed a counterattack by a panzer division. Montgomery's ponderous 8th Army made slow progress, forgoing the opportunity for decisive engagement on favorable coastal terrain in exchange for indecisive flanking attacks in much rougher (and more easily defended) inland country. Nonetheless, many of the Italian units melted away, though some of them fought and were slaughtered where they stood. The two German divisions and some reinforcements from the mainland were pushed back steadily, absorbing heavy casualties. Allied forces reached Messina on August 17, only to find that the Germans and Italians had evacuated to the mainland.

Although the outcome of the battle for Sicily was never in doubt, from the infantryman's perspective the fight was tough. American journalist Richard Tregaskis wrote about the experience of enduring enemy artillery fire:

> Then the German artillery began to fire at us. We heard the screech of the approaching shell, but it was so quick that we did not have time to hit the deck. I saw a splash of earth forty or fifty yards away, and then the blast of the explosion came almost directly over us. By that time, I was lying down, and I found myself next to a sergeant. Almost immediately we heard the crying of a wounded man, a bubbling sort of attempt at "Help, help," which had the strangely liquid sound of a voice under water. I had heard similar cries of the wounded in the Pacific.
>
> A man hobbled down the hill with his hands over his face, blood running down his shirt. The sergeant called out, "Jimmy, you hit?" Jimmy nodded, made no sound. Another man sat on the ground, one hand holding his back. The captain called, "Medics here!"
>
> I suddenly realized that the burst must have gone off just over my head, for two men had been hit, on each side of me, neither more than fifteen feet away. Then I, too, began to feel the increasing breathlessness, that almost unbearable tension of waiting for the next shell.

> Then it came. We heard the rustling of a shell suddenly swelling into a screech, then bursting with a blast that shook the air and filmed our vision over with concussion. Again, here was the breathless moment of waiting for the cries of the wounded, wondering if you, too, had been hit, thinking that you should look and see, not daring for a moment to make the effort. Again the wounded screamed, and we looked up higher on the hill, where, apparently, the shell had done most damage. Up there someone cried out, "Medics, medics!" It was the same desperate sound I had heard on Guadalcanal, only the word was "corpsman."[24]

The Allies suffered over 16,000 casualties in the battle for Sicily, while 132,000 Italians and 32,000 Germans were killed, wounded, or captured. Conquest of the island and the destruction of Axis air bases on the mainland greatly facilitated Allied shipping in the Mediterranean.

The Allied invasion of Sicily led quickly to the fall of Mussolini, the German occupation of northern and central Italy, and the transfer of several Wehrmacht units from the eastern front to Italy and the Balkans. King Victor Emmanuel at first procrastinated and then bungled Italy's transition from the Axis to the Grand Alliance. The Allies intended to send an airborne division to hold Rome with the support of the Italian army, but the failure of the Italian leadership to organize any resistance enabled German forces to flow quickly into the country and disarm Italian units. The Germans overran and executed those few Italian units that did resist. The majority of surviving Italian soldiers were forced to work in Berlin's slave labor empire.

Berlin's response to the Anglo-American invasion of Italy was robust, even at a point when the Wehrmacht desperately needed every soldier and tank deployed on the eastern front. The Red Army was inflicting far larger disasters on the Germans at about the same time at Kursk and Orel. Strategic and ideological concerns motivated the Führer's decision to fight stubbornly in the Mediterranean. The defection of Italy from the Axis and the Allied invasion of the peninsula threatened southern Germany directly. Moreover, the campaign in the West was as much an ideological crusade as the war for *Lebensraum* in the East. In Hitler's view, President Roosevelt was the stooge of "Jewish Wall Street" and the "Jewish media." Beyond a war against Bolshevism, Nazi Germany's campaign was a struggle against the prospect of American hegemony and, in Hitler's mind, the triumph of the "Jewish world conspiracy."

The Allies next turned their attention to Italy itself. The Italian Peninsula is long, relatively thin, and mountainous—ideal terrain for defensive warfare and very difficult for the attacker. The Allies were overly optimistic, thinking that the collapse of the Fascist regime would allow them to conquer the whole country easily, or at least its southern half. They were wrong. Montgomery's 8th Army landed on the southernmost tip of the peninsula on September 3 but made slow progress because the Germans had destroyed all the bridges in the area. Six days later, elements of Mark Clark's US 5th Army and the British X Corps stormed separate beaches at Salerno, 150 miles farther up the west coast of Italy. They met fierce German resistance on the beaches and much stronger opposition from the Luftwaffe than anticipated. Only the devastating support of naval gunfire allowed them to establish beachheads.

Kesselring, in charge of Italy's defense, dispatched a panzer division and two mobile infantry divisions to the Salerno-Naples area. The Germans exploited the gap between the British and US landings to attack the Americans' left flank. They did considerable damage to US forces, but the Allies' overwhelming firepower and their ability to bring in reinforcements quickly defeated the enemy counterattack. The battle had cost the Allies fifteen

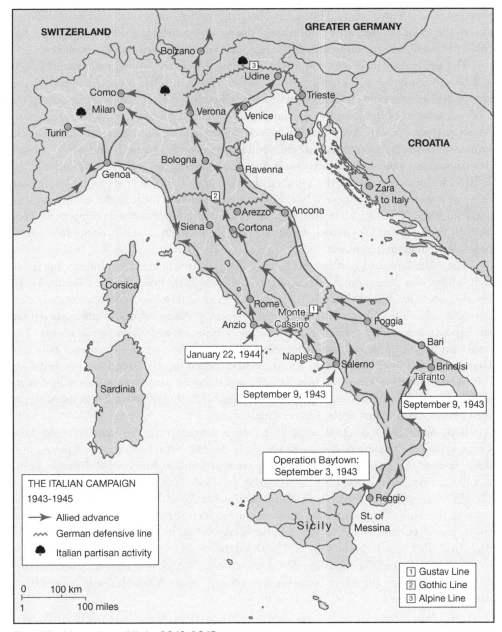

The Allied Invasion of Italy, 1943–1945

thousand troops—the Germans lost only half that many. Beyond quantitative superiority, American forces were improving steadily, both in their determination to stand and fight and in their tactical ability. Meanwhile, an antifascist uprising in Naples fought the Germans to a standstill before the arrival of British forces.

Kesselring's surviving troops retreated to a stronger defensive position, the Gustav Line, stretching from the Rapido River in the west, across the Apennine Mountains, to the Adriatic Sea in the east. Hitler and his high command had planned to retreat all the way north to the Po River, but the Americans' shaky performance at Salerno convinced them to defend the peninsula much farther south. The onset of bad fall weather—rain, mud, and snow—further slowed the Allied advance, as did outbreaks of disease (pneumonia and other respiratory infections, dysentery, and trench foot), which accounted for more casualties than combat.

The pattern for the Italian campaign was now established. Allied troops would fight a slow and costly battle over difficult mountainous terrain, often in rough weather, and always against determined German resistance. Churchill had championed attacking the "soft underbelly" of southern Europe, but General Clark described it as "a tough old gut." Moreover, the Western Allies did not possess the overwhelming numerical advantage in ground troops in Italy that they had enjoyed in North Africa and Sicily and would achieve in France, mainly because the British and Americans never agreed on the significance of the Italian campaign. On paper, the number of Allied and Wehrmacht divisions facing each other in Italy seemed about even, but the German units were badly understrength in men and equipment. The difficult terrain, without much possibility of Allied flanking maneuvers, partially compensated for German weakness. The Allies also enjoyed superiority in numbers of artillery, tanks, and airplanes.

The Allies hoped to outflank the Gustav Line by launching an amphibious operation well behind it at Anzio, on the west coast of Italy, just forty miles south of Rome. To assist that operation, General Clark "organized" a series of disjointed and inadequately supported attacks on the Gustav Line that failed completely. American troops stormed German strongpoints repeatedly, at Clark's insistence, only to be mowed down by the enemy. The Anzio landing, in contrast, caught the enemy completely by surprise—a colossal failure of German military intelligence. Some historians have argued that the Americans frittered away this opportunity by taking time to establish a well-fortified beachhead rather than driving rapidly for the Alban Hills south of Rome and thereby cutting off the main supply route to the German forces manning the Gustav Line.

Both Alexander and Clark, as well as their commander on the scene, General John Lucas, approved the conservative approach. After their near-run experience at Salerno, prudence seemed the better part of valor. They were probably right. A rapid drive on Rome would have exposed the operation to punishing and likely fatal counterattacks on its flanks. Caught by surprise, the enemy reacted quickly to the Allied landing. In little more than a week, elements of eight German divisions surrounded the Anzio perimeter. A series of strong attacks pounded the American and British defenders, but once again Allied firepower decimated the German assault groups. Hitler ordered more fruitless attacks that only served to deplete his forces. The fighting often devolved into World War I–style trench warfare. Ultimately, however, the Anzio operation was a costly failure. A British doctor, James Ross, described the awful scene at an Allied aid station:

> The wounded lay in two rows, mostly British but some American as well in their sodden filthy clothes . . . soaked, caked, buried in mud and blood; with ghastly pale faces, shuddering, shivering, with the cold of the February night and their great wounds . . . some (too many; far too many) were carried in dying, with gross combinations of shattered limbs, protrusions of intestines and brain from great holes in their poor frames torn by 88-millimetre shells, mortar and anti-personnel bombs.[25]

In an attempt to take some of the pressure off their besieged troops at Anzio, the Allies attacked the Gustav Line again at Cassino. German defenders, in well-situated mountaintop defensive positions, repulsed attack after attack, inflicting great casualties on the attackers. An Allied air strike against the Benedictine monastery atop Monte Cassino only served to destroy a historic treasure and give the defenders still better cover amid the rubble. Many military historians have been critical of Allied strategy at this point. Ellis, for example, argues that "the attempt to breach the Gustav Line, and the ensuing four battles of Monte Cassino, constitute an especially depressing saga and one which reveals the Allied commanders as being quite unable to adapt their tactics to the terrain in which they were fighting."[26]

The Allies renewed their offensive in mid-May. The British 8th Army replaced the Americans besieging Monte Casino, with the mission of taking the German stronghold and breaking through to the Liri valley. At the same time, the US 5th Army was to break the German investment of Anzio while the six American divisions in that pocket fought their way out. The overall objective of these operations was to cut off the lines of supply and retreat for all German forces in southern Italy. Despite intensive Allied firepower (including hitting enemy lines with 1.2 million artillery shells as the operation began), both offensives bogged down against heavy resistance. Surprisingly, however, four Free French colonial divisions broke through in the mountainous sector between the two major Allied assaults. Then French and American troops poured through the gap into the Liri valley. US forces in the Anzio pocket finally fought their way out on May 23. The theater commander, General Alexander, ordered the US 5th Army to strike toward Valmontone to trap the German 10th Army in the south. However, Mark Clark defied his superior's orders and struck directly toward Rome to win the glory of liberating that ancient city. A critic suggested that Clark's "reading of Clausewitz's famous dictum was that war was the pursuit of publicity by other means."[27] Most of the Germans escaped to fight again. Clark's troops and their vainglorious commander (accompanied by a platoon of photographers) liberated the undefended capital on June 4.

Allied success in central Italy did not break enemy resistance throughout the peninsula, though the Germans had suffered heavy casualties. Troops serving under General Heinz Greiner at Anzio composed this bit of doggerel:

> This Division of Greiner
> Gets chopped ever finer
> Till roll-call's a one-liner
> Which simply reads Greiner.[28]

Despite their losses, the Germans retreated northward to the Gothic Line, just below the Po River valley near Florence. Then the withdrawal of three US divisions and six French divisions from Italy for the invasion of southern France (Operation Dragoon) lessened what little chance the Allies had for a breakthrough in the north. Allied forces renewed their attacks toward the Po at the end of August. Canadian troops drove a wedge into enemy defenses near the Adriatic, though the British 8th Army responded too slowly to take advantage of this opening, which the Germans were quick to plug. In September, Clark's 5th Army began an attempt to take Bologna. German defenses held firm. Clark continued a series of unimaginative attacks that resulted in a great many American casualties but very little progress. German resistance in Italy began to crumble only in April 1945 when the Red Army and the Western powers were already crushing the Reich itself. Italian partisans launched a general uprising on April 25. German forces in northern Italy finally laid down their weapons on May 2. In Ellis's judgment, "the [Germans'] Italian campaign must rank as one of the greatest defensive achievements in the history of warfare."[29] The fighting in Italy cost the Allies 312,000 casualties.

In retrospect, some military historians have condemned the entire Italian campaign as a fruitless waste of men and resources. It was a long, bloody, costly struggle that ultimately was not decisive in defeating the Third Reich. It did occupy twenty Wehrmacht divisions that otherwise might have fought on the eastern front or against Operation Overlord. The critics respond that the mere *threat* of an Allied invasion of Italy would have forced the Germans to deploy substantial forces there. The establishment of air bases in Italy also allowed the Allies to bomb southern Germany and the Ploesti oil fields for the first time. Most importantly, the Italian campaign was a matter of alliance politics. It substituted for a major second front in France in 1943, which Anglo-American forces were unable to launch until the following year. It drew some enemy forces from the eastern front and was meant to reassure Stalin that his Western partners really were committed to fighting on the Continent.

Allied Bombing Offensive

The advocates of strategic bombing theory expected that long-range strikes by great fleets of heavy bombers would be decisive in any future war. They were sure that massive air strikes would cripple an enemy's industry and destroy the morale of his civilian population at the outset of any conflict. Their theory assumed that there could be no effective defense against strategic bombing, that bombers could hit their targets with accuracy (or even "precision"), and that the effects of such bombing would be so devastating as to force the early surrender of any country exposed to it. Beyond that, since the Western Allies could not fight the Germans on land before late 1942, air and naval war constituted the only means of inflicting damage on the enemy. The apparent lessons of the Spanish civil war, especially the devastating bombing of Guernica, appeared to prove the case. The Japanese bombing of Chinese cities seemed to drive home the point. However, each of these assumptions proved to be wrong—at least in the pre-nuclear era.

The bombing carried out by the Germans in Spain, the Italians in Ethiopia, and the Japanese in China had been widely condemned throughout the Western world on moral grounds. Defenseless civilians were not supposed to be slaughtered. The Second World War so brutalized human values that the Allies also came to accept the grim logic of massive attacks on cities. If war was to be truly "total"—the whole of society mobilized for the war effort—then everything and everyone was a military target.

None of the Axis powers developed large fleets of long-range heavy bombers. The extraordinary expense of producing large numbers of four-engine bombers and the competition of other weapons systems in the budgetary process kept Berlin, Rome, and Tokyo from launching such air armadas. Hermann Göring promised Hitler that his Luftwaffe could bring England to its knees in the Battle of Britain, but he never had the equipment to fulfill the prophecies of the air power theorists. The Luftwaffe became a very effective ground-support air force, but defeating the RAF and knocking Britain out of the war proved beyond its capabilities. Moreover, the outcome of the Battle of Britain undermined all three basic assumptions of strategic bombing theory. High-quality fighters manned by well-trained pilots and directed by a coordinated air defense system could gravely damage bomber fleets. Bombing from high altitude, often in bad weather and against determined fighter resistance, was not very accurate. The Luftwaffe inflicted a lot of damage, but it did not break the British people's will to fight.

Despite these early warnings, the commanders of the RAF and the US Army Air Forces (USAAF) clung to strategic bombing theory as dogma. Much of the British and American political establishment shared that faith—in large part because relying on air power seemed to offer a way to avoid the horrendous bloodletting of First World War–style ground combat. Moreover, the Allies thought—mistakenly—that the German economy would collapse quickly under sustained bombing. Even though the RAF was committed to strategic bombing, it lacked the necessary equipment to fulfill that mission when war broke out in 1939. RAF Bomber Command had only 488 bombers, some of them obsolete, most of them only light or medium bombers, and none of them capable of carrying large bomb loads into the heart of Germany. They also lacked good bombsights, adequate navigation equipment, and sufficient armor and armaments to fend off fighter attacks.[30]

Initially, Prime Minister Chamberlain and his French ally refrained from attacks on German cities, both on moral grounds and on the realization that the Luftwaffe might retaliate strongly against Allied cities. That changed when the Churchill cabinet took office in 1940. The new prime minister had no scruples about bombing cities, and with the Battle of France going badly, it seemed the only way to strike back at Germany. In reporting to the government, RAF commanders greatly exaggerated the damage they could do to the enemy economy and to Germany's supposedly fragile morale. British authorities claimed throughout the war that the RAF only attacked military targets, to avoid the invidious comparison with Nazi "terror bombing," but a line had been crossed. The definition of "military targets" grew to include almost everything in Germany *and the lands it occupied*. Civilian "collateral damage" was accepted as a necessary evil. The RAF launched sporadic attacks against Germany throughout 1940 but caused little damage, an unsurprising outcome given its lack of planes and its inability to hit or even find targets.

The RAF's fleet of heavier bombers expanded slowly in 1940–1941, in part because so much of the country's aircraft production went to build fighters to protect the home islands. Rapid training programs resulted in numerous accidents, losses that sometimes exceeded the number of planes lost in combat. The desperate battle against the U-boats in the Atlantic also drew off some of Bomber Command's resources. The RAF attacked targets in the heavily industrial Ruhr region, but mostly with medium bombers. Accuracy was a problem, since relatively few bombs fell close to their intended target.

The British learned that bombing at night gave the aircrews a much better chance of surviving and that concentrating many planes in the general *area* of a target produced better results than trying to bomb specific targets with some precision. In practice, this meant that even though the primary target—a factory or an oil tank farm—might be missed, the bombs scattered in the area would do great damage to the working-class communities surrounding such facilities. Civilian laborers now had the same status as enemy combatants. Bomber Command also learned that using incendiary bombs caused greater damage than high explosives alone. Historians have severely criticized the British area bombing campaign. It killed six hundred thousand Germans (mostly civilians), while costing Bomber Command almost sixty thousand crew members, yet it failed to cripple the German economy or break the morale of the German people.[31] Even though these raids by the RAF early in the war accomplished little of value, they served to raise British morale and to give Churchill credibility with Roosevelt and Stalin.

The RAF began to receive heavy bombers in late 1941 and 1942 with the appearance of the four-engine Stirling, Halifax, and Lancaster aircraft. The Lancaster became Britain's main strategic bomber. It had a top speed of 287 miles per hour and a range of a thousand miles, and it could carry twenty-two tons of bombs. The RAF now had a plane capable of strategic bombing, but not enough of them. Germany countered with an air defense system including radar, powerful searchlights, night fighters, antiaircraft artillery, and an effective blackout system. Berlin claimed to have brought down 764 British bombers in the first nine months of 1941.

America's entry into the war in December 1941 did not immediately increase the supply of heavy bombers. Although the US Army Air Forces were committed to the idea of strategic bombing (as was President Roosevelt), it lacked a fleet of four-engine bombers at the outset. The United States had developed a long-range bomber, the B-17, but few of these were available in 1942. The slow buildup of both British and US bomber fleets limited the effectiveness of raids and frustrated the leadership and the public in England and America. The chief of Bomber Command—Air Marshal Harris—determined to launch dramatic one-thousand-plane raids in 1942 to bolster morale and to prevent his independent, strategic bomber force from being reallocated to tactical support roles for the navy and army.

In May and June, he launched big raids against Cologne, Essen, and Bremen. Cologne was badly hit (with over five thousand casualties, eleven thousand buildings destroyed or damaged, and almost sixty thousand residents made homeless), but the other two raids caused far less damage and the Germans shot down 123 bombers in the three attacks. However, these operations forced the Germans to divert substantial resources from the eastern front and North Africa to defend the homeland. Overy is critical of the RAF, particularly of Harris, for insisting on an independent strategic bombing campaign when the resources for success in that effort were not available and when those limited assets could have been put to better use in the Battle of the Atlantic and in North Africa.[32]

The US 8th Air Force, based in England, grew rapidly, from only eighty operational bombers at the beginning of 1943 to over two thousand a year and a half later. This expansion required enormous effort, not only to build all the necessary fighters and bombers but also to construct extensive supply and repair facilities, as well as to recruit large numbers of air and ground crews.

London and Washington had very different ideas about how to use long-range heavy bombers. British Bomber Command continued to mount mostly nighttime raids, with the objective of hitting the general area in which a target was located. Their intent was to destroy large cities and thereby cripple the enemy's war effort. In Operation Gomorrah (a reference to the fiery destruction of the Old Testament city), the RAF launched large raids on Stuttgart, Dortmund, Krefeld, and other German cities. The worst damage occurred in the large port city of Hamburg, which Bomber Command struck over three consecutive nights beginning on July 24. Raging fires set by incendiary bombs completely overwhelmed the local firefighting forces. The conflagration killed 40,000 people, destroyed or severely damaged 315,000 homes and apartments, and drove approximately 900,000 terrified refugees from the city.

In contrast, the Americans committed their force to daylight "precision" bombing of selected targets, though given the frequently cloudy skies over Germany, there were few days when the bombardiers could see their targets well. The 8th Air Force first targeted the German air defense system and then hit objectives they believed would facilitate an Allied landing in Europe. Neither the RAF nor the 8th Air Force was able to bomb with much accuracy, and both suffered increasing losses as German defenses stiffened. Bombing from high altitude, frequently in severe weather, while avoiding enemy flak and fighters, made accuracy virtually impossible. A study found that, in daytime attacks in clear weather, on average bombs missed their intended target by 450 yards. In poor weather, the margin of error was 1,200 yards. For night bombing, the figure was three miles![33] Moreover, even when the bombers scored direct hits, German repair efforts frequently reopened plants in a few weeks if not days.

Throughout 1943, the air war was essentially a stalemate. The bombers did considerable damage to German cities, but many of the planes were shot down. On August 17, 376 B-17s attacked the important ball-bearing plant at Schweinfurt and the Messerschmitt aircraft factory at Regensburg. Ball-bearing and fighter production were temporarily reduced, but at a cost of 187 bombers brought down and many more damaged. A second raid on Schweinfurt the following month saw the loss of 65 of the 229 bombers employed. RAF bombers struck the rocket research station at Peenemünde on August 17–18. They did substantial damage to the rocket program and inadvertently killed five hundred Polish slave laborers, while losing forty aircraft. Such loss rates were unsustainable. At this stage in the war, Allied fighters were unable to escort the bombers to targets deep within Germany. Both the British and the Americans suspended deep raids, concentrating instead on more accessible targets along the German coast and in France.

The work of the aircrews was dangerous, difficult, and demanding. They endured eight- to ten-hour flights, often in bone-chilling temperatures. High winds, storms, and heavy cloud cover made it hard to find their targets. Over Germany, they dodged fighters, antiaircraft fire, and searchlights. They flew in relatively tight formations to maximize their firepower against enemy fighters while trying to avoid colliding with each other or letting their bombs drop on another plane below them (though both of those things happened on occasion). Their casualty rates were high—both from combat and from accidents. The US 8th Air Force lost over ten thousand crewmen in 1943 alone; the RAF lost well over fifteen thousand. Besides deaths and severe wounds, bombing operations took a psychological toll on the crews. Crewmen realized that they were unlikely to survive numerous missions. One flier remembered, "I was scared all the time, but I was more scared of letting the rest of the crew see."[34] An Australian lieutenant described the precarious situation of the bomber fleets before they had long-range fighters to protect them: "Coming back from the target we didn't need a navigator, because the [German] fighters were all along the route . . . they were picking us off like anything. . . . They were forty-four odd planes shot down. You just had to follow the burning planes on the ground to take you out over the coast and back to England. That was a horrific show."[35]

In the last months of 1943 and the first half of 1944, Allied commanders redirected much of their bomber force from strategic attacks throughout Germany to tactical assaults on the transportation and communications systems in western Germany and northern France. Their objective was to slow any German response to the Allied landings in Normandy planned for the following June. Heavy and medium bombers hit bridges and towns that were major transport hubs, while fighter-bombers swooped down on freight trains. They mauled Luftwaffe bases in the region as well.

The air war turned decisively in the Allies' favor in 1944. American bombers based in England and Italy focused on destroying the Luftwaffe as an essential preliminary to successful strategic bombing and to the invasion of northern France. The key to success in the air lay in developing long-range fighters that could accompany the bombers anywhere over the Reich and that would outclass the Messerschmitt and Focke-Wulf fighters employed by Germany throughout the war. American air force commanders and the designers of the B-17 had thought that the heavily armed bombers, flying in disciplined formations to increase their firepower, could defend themselves adequately. After all, the plane was nicknamed the "Flying Fortress." German fighter pilots had proven them wrong. Now new generations of US fighters—the P-38 Lightning, the P-47 Thunderbolt, and the P-51 Mustang—often flying with droppable extra fuel tanks, could escort the bombers deep into Germany and take on the Luftwaffe's best fighters.

The Mustang proved to be the Luftwaffe killer. Originally with an aerodynamically superior airframe mated to an underpowered Allison engine, the P-51 evolved into an air supremacy fighter when it received a much more powerful Rolls-Royce Merlin engine. It could outfight the best enemy interceptors and reach well beyond Berlin, even to Vienna and Prague. American fighter tactics became more aggressive, not just passively protecting the bomber formations but actively seeking out German fighters. Allied bombers were improving, too. They carried new electronic navigation devices that helped to find targets and even allowed them to "fly blind" in bad weather.

In response, the Germans shifted most of their fighters and much of their antiaircraft artillery to the defense of the homeland, at the expense of supporting the ground troops on the eastern front and elsewhere. They had to devote almost a third of their artillery production to antiaircraft guns. The Germans built tall flak towers, with multiple guns, large bomb shelters, and even hospital facilities, to defend key cities. They also rationalized their air defense system (based on the British model) and developed more sophisticated radar that could ignore "window" radar-jamming distractions. For a while, the Germans were able to sustain rapid production of fighters despite Allied bombing, but the growing attrition among fighter pilots led to a marked decrease in pilot quality, giving their better-trained British and American adversaries a significant advantage.

In the last quarter of 1943, the German Fighter Command lost 967 planes in combat and another 1,052 to accidents. The Germans had to withdraw their best weapon against the bombers, the less than agile twin-engine Me-110, in March 1944 because Allied fighters decimated them. They introduced a jet-powered interceptor, the Me-262, but there were too few of them and they came too late in the war to have a decisive impact. Increasingly, antiaircraft defense depended on artillery, though here too the shortage of manpower led to decreasing efficiency. The Germans resorted to using Soviet POWs, Italian Fascist volunteers, less seriously wounded Luftwaffe personnel, women, and Hitler Youth to operate the guns. Other important measures to reduce the effectiveness of Allied bombing included dispersing production facilities widely and building underground factories for such high-priority weapons as fighter planes and V-2 rockets. The regime drew on slave laborers from the occupied lands to offset the disruption of the labor force by Allied bombing.

The Luftwaffe experienced unsustainable losses not only in the air war over western Europe but on the eastern front as well. German air ace Adolf Gallant later wrote, "The Eastern Front held Luftwaffe units in its clutches . . . and methodically ground them down. Luftwaffe effectiveness became really nothing more than air support of ground forces on a numerically inadequate scale."[36] With attrition rates skyrocketing on both fronts, even the German "production miracle" of 1944 could not keep sufficient planes in the air.

Under the direction of General Carl Spaatz, the USAAF stepped up its counterforce campaign against the Luftwaffe. By the spring of 1944, aircraft, pilots, and crews were flowing from America in great numbers. Big US bomber formations were virtually bait to force German interceptors into action, where they were overwhelmed by superior numbers of modern American fighters. US bombers continued to hit German airplane plants and began to strike Germany's fuel sources as well—the 15th Air Force attacked the vital Ploesti oil fields in Romania, while the 8th Air Force hit synthetic oil production in Germany. US forces also bombed communications and transportation targets throughout southeastern Europe in support of the advancing Red Army.

The Allies were determined to use this superiority to launch a final crushing blow that would drive Germany out of the war. After the war, some critics condemned these last big air raids as unnecessary and immoral given that Germany was already on the brink of defeat, its major cities ravaged. At the time, however, British and American leaders were still concerned about the potential of German superweapons as well as the possibility of suicidal German resistance to the bitter end that would have been extremely costly in Allied lives. They also hoped that major bombing raids in eastern Germany would aid the Red Army in its advance on Berlin. A thousand-bomber American raid on Berlin on February 3, 1945, with almost as many fighters, killed 2,890 people and left 120,000 homeless. They hit Chemnitz, Leipzig, Dessau, and other cities as well. The most dramatic and deadly attack struck Dresden on February 13 and 14 when both Bomber Command and the 8th Air Force carried out major raids. They targeted the center of the city with incendiary bombs. In dry weather with low humidity, the many fires lit by the bombs soon combined into a massive firestorm. Twenty-five thousand people died, and fifteen square miles of the city burned. One survivor of the raid recalled:

> Never would I have thought that death could come to so many people in so many different ways. . . . Never had I expected to see people interred in that state: burnt, cremated, torn and crushed to death; sometimes the victims looked like ordinary people apparently peacefully sleeping; the faces of others racked with pain, the bodies stripped almost naked by the explosive blasts; there great boiling clouds of smoke that thundered upward from the flaming carnage, smoke that momentarily obscured from view the fire, but could never hide the deep, angry, glowing, fearful red. It was as though the men looked down upon the surface of a planet still in its throes of creation, still lashed and whipped by the fury.[37]

Although Allied bombing was never very accurate, over 350,000 Germans died, while many more suffered wounds and still more lost their homes. There were never enough bomb shelters in the cities. Shelter construction competed for scarce building materials with military needs and other high-priority projects. Heavy conscription into the army depleted the ranks of German firefighters. Foreign workers and women replaced them. By the fall of 1944, some 275,000 women toiled in this dangerous service. The Nazi Party organized a program for evacuating children from endangered cities, either to live in Hitler Youth camps or with relatives in the countryside. By 1944, when one thousand plane raids blasted numerous urban areas, hundreds of thousands of refugees—not just children—fled the cities. The regime made efforts to house and care for the refugees, but there were never enough resources.

After the war, British and American studies of strategic bombing concluded that "city busting" and area bombing had been largely a failure. Moreover, the Nazi economy was more resilient than Allied planners thought. The Germans found ways to substitute products for those in short supply and to retool undamaged factories for war work to replace those destroyed by bombing. In addition to dispersing industrial plants around the country and camouflaging them, the regime built dummy factories, identical to real industrial complexes, to fool Allied aircrews into dropping their bombs in harmless locations. The output of munitions, armor, artillery, aircraft, and U-boats increased in 1943 and again in 1944.[38]

Shortages of weapons and supplies that began to appear in all branches of the German armed services from mid-1943 resulted from greatly increased combat losses rather than the effects of Allied bombing. While many historians doubt the effectiveness of Allied bombing, Adam Tooze argues that the RAF's massive campaign against Ruhr industries in the spring of 1944 stopped the Reich's armament expansion in its tracks.[39]

Bombing caused a significant increase in rumors and also some grumbling about the authorities by the German people, but never any sign of defeatism or significant opposition to the regime. The devastation of their homeland and the continuous flow of bad news from the eastern front may have made many Germans silently critical of the Nazi regime, but it did not cause them to abandon the war effort. Large-scale bombing made them more dependent on the regime for survival and thus less likely to rebel against it.[40]

Strategic bombing had not obviated the need for the Red Army and the Western Allies to conquer the Nazi empire on the ground. However, the elimination of the Luftwaffe as an effective fighting force, as well as attacks on Germany's oil resources and its transportation system, had seriously undermined the Reich's defenses. In addition, the tactical bombing campaign against transportation and communications in western Germany and northern France had made the Normandy invasion possible. Though air power did not win the war by itself, as some air force generals had anticipated, it played a significant role in the Allied victory.

Italy was also the target of a large-scale bombing campaign. The prospect of hitting irreplaceable artistic treasures and important religious sites (especially the Vatican) gave the Allies pause, but ultimately their perception of military necessity prevailed. There were relatively few raids in 1940 and 1941. The operation accelerated rapidly in the following two years. Besides tactical support for the Allied invasion, bombers struck at Italian factories working for the Germans and at the transportation system that supplied enemy defenders of the peninsula after they occupied it in 1943. Allied fighters were able to suppress most Axis interceptors, so the attackers could bomb from lower altitudes, improving accuracy somewhat. Nonetheless, over sixty thousand civilians were killed and many more wounded—partly because Italian civil defense was even less well organized than its German counterpart. The Allies hoped that a combination of bombing and propaganda leaflets would inspire the Italian population to overthrow the Fascist regime and abandon their alliance with Berlin, but the rapid German occupation of Italy foiled those plans. Moreover, the mounting civilian casualties from the bombing made more Italians hostile to the Allies.

The saddest chapter in the Allied air war concerns the bombing of some of Hitler's victims—the occupied peoples of France, Belgium, Holland, Denmark, and Norway. The Allies made the decision to fight the Germans in any area they occupied and to destroy anything that helped the enemy war effort. From 1940 to 1942, Allied bombers struck occupied western Europe more frequently than Germany itself, mainly because the former was easier to reach and less stoutly defended. Allied propaganda hoped to raise disaffection and spark resistance among the captive peoples, but bombing sometimes undermined that effort. RAF and American bombing were no more accurate in the occupied countries than in Germany. A series of large US raids on the French port of Nantes in mid-September 1943 hit an aircraft plant and a locomotive factory, but also killed almost 1,300 French civilians.

The Germans organized the evacuation of children, mothers, and old people from the most likely bombing targets along the coasts of France. In 1944, with the prospect of an Allied invasion ever more likely, they forced a more radical evacuation of most of the population from the northern coastal towns. Many French families were reluctant to let their children leave or to abandon their homes and businesses. As Overy suggests, "the French population faced an inescapable dilemma that made it difficult to know how to respond to the raids: they wanted the Allies who were bombing them to win, and they wanted the Germans who protected them to lose."[41]

Allied propaganda depicted the bombing of France as necessary to liberation, while the Germans and the Vichy regime condemned it as terrorism. The fate of downed Allied fliers reflected the cruel dilemma faced by Frenchmen. On one hand, the French resistance rescued two to three thousand Allied airmen. On the other hand, at times enraged mobs killed downed crewmen or turned them over to the Germans. Over twenty-five thousand civilians died in bombing raids on northern France during the four months leading up to the D-Day landings. Tactical low-level bombing by light bombers and fighter-bombers did much more damage to key targets and much less harm to civilians, while for the high-altitude heavy bombers, the outcome was reversed. Over fifty-three thousand Frenchmen died under Allied bombing. Allied propaganda urged people in the occupied countries not to work in war plants. There were serious disincentives to following that advice, however: skilled workers needed jobs to support their families, and if they refused to work, the Germans might well seize the equipment and draft the workers to the Reich. As the Allies liberated parts of western Europe, these areas came under German air assault. With the liberation of Belgium, the port of Antwerp became a major Allied transportation hub. The Germans targeted it with their new V-1 cruise missiles and V-2 rockets.

Notes

1. Alex Danchev, "Great Britain: The Indirect Strategy," in *Allies at War: The Soviet, American and British Experience, 1939–1945*, ed. David Reynolds, Warren F. Kimball, and A. O. Chubarian (New York: St. Martin's, 1994), 4.

2. *Sovetsko-angliiskie otnosheniia vo vremia velikoi otechestvennoi voiny, 1941–1945* (Moscow: Politizdat., 1983), 147.

3. Robert Dallek, *Franklin D. Roosevelt and American Foreign Policy, 1932–1945* (New York: Oxford University Press, 1970), 430.

4. William Appleman Williams, *The Tragedy of American Diplomacy* (New York: Delta, 1962); Mark Stoler, *Allies in War: Britain and America against the Axis Powers, 1940–1945* (London: Hodder Arnold, 2005), 167.

5. *War Diaries, 1939–1945: Field Marshal Lord Alanbrooke*, ed. Alex Danchev and Dan Todman (London: Weidenfeld & Nicolson, 2001), 407.

6. Williamson Murray and Allan R. Millett, *A War to Be Won: Fighting the Second World War* (Cambridge, MA: Belknap, 2000), 299.

7. Theodore A. Wilson, "Coalition: Structure, Strategy, and Statecraft," in Reynolds et al., *Allies at War*, 95.

8. Warren F. Kimball, ed., *Churchill and Roosevelt: The Complete Correspondence* (Princeton, NJ: Princeton University Press, 1984), 1:337.

9. Andrei A. Gromyko et al., eds., *Stalin's Correspondence with Churchill and Attlee, 1941–1945* (New York: Capricorn, 1965), 188.

10. Fernando Claudin, *The Communist Movement: From Comintern to Cominform* (New York: Monthly Review Press, 1975), 1:303–4.

11. Winston S. Churchill, *The Second World War*, vol. 4, *The Hinge of Fate* (Boston: Houghton Mifflin, 1951), 107.

12. John Keegan, *The Price of Admiralty: The Evolution of Naval Warfare* (New York: Viking, 1988), 235.

13. Keegan, *The Price of Admiralty*, 229.

14. E.g., during the second half of 1942, "Bletchley Park lost its capacity to read enemy messages." Paul Kennedy, *Victory at Sea: Naval Power and the Transformation of the Global Order in World War II* (New Haven, CT: Yale University Press, 2022), 210–11.

15. John Ellis, *Brute Force: Allied Strategy and Tactics in the Second World War* (New York: Viking, 1990), 157.

16. Paul Kennedy, *Engineers of Victory: The Problem Solvers Who Turned the Tide in the Second World War* (New York: Random House, 2013), 49.

17. Robert Goralski, ed., *World War II Almanac: A Political and Military Record* (New York: Bonanza Books, 1981), 293.

18. Richard Overy, *Why the Allies Won* (New York: Norton, 1995), 45.

19. Ellis, *Brute Force*, 158–61.

20. John Ellis, *Brute Force*, 283–84; Correlli Barnett, *The Desert Generals* (London: William Kimber, 1981), 300.

21. B. H. Liddell Hart, ed., *The Rommel Papers* (New York: Harcourt Brace, 1953), 285, 334.

22. Evan V. Westrate, *Forward Observer* (Philadelphia: Blakiston, 1944), 109–17.

23. Danchev, "Great Britain," 3–4.

24. Richard Tregaskis, *Invasion Diary* (Lincoln, NE: Bison Books, 2004), 37–38.

25. John A. Ross, *Memoirs of an Army Surgeon* (London: Blackwood, 1948), 209.

26. Ellis, *Brute Force*, 331.

27. David Hunt, "After Husky," *Times Literary Supplement*, June 8, 1984, 634. What Clausewitz actually said was, "War is the continuation of politics by other means." Carl von Clausewitz, *On War* (Princeton, NJ: Princeton University Press, 1984), 87.

28. Ellis, *Brute Force*, 326.

29. Ellis, *Brute Force*, 342.

30. Richard Overy, *The Bombers and the Bombed: Allied Air War over Europe, 1940–1945* (New York: Viking, 2013), 38–39.

31. Ellis, *Brute Force*, 219.

32. Overy, *The Bombers and the Bombed*, 104–6. John Ellis also argues even more strongly that area bombing was a mistake that unnecessarily prolonged the war and thereby cost thousands of Allied lives. *Brute Force*, 185–92.

33. Ellis, *Brute Force*, 175.

34. Quoted in Overy, *The Bombers and the Bombed*, 163.

35. Interview with Noel Sanders, 463 Squadron, RAAF, Australians at War Archive, http://australiansat warfilmarchive.unsw.edu.au.

36. Adolf Galland, "Defeat of the Luftwaffe," in *The Impact of Air Power: National Security and World Politics*, ed. Eugene M. Emme (New York: Van Nostrand, 1959), 256–57.

37. David Irving, *The Destruction of Dresden* (New York: Holt, Reinhart & Winston, 1963), 189.

38. Overy, *The Bombers and the Bombed*, 278.

39. Adam Tooze, *The Wages of Destruction: The Making and Breaking of the Nazi Economy* (New York: Penguin, 2006), 597.

40. Overy, *The Bombers and the Bombed*, 316.

41. Overy, *The Bombers and the Bombed*, 384.

CHAPTER 17

Western Allies Assault Fortress Europe

Assaulting Hitler's Fortress Europe

Neither the prolonged agony of the Italian campaign nor the massive Anglo-American bombing offensive defeated the Third Reich. It could only be conquered on the ground, in its heartland—by the Red Army crashing through Poland into Prussia and by the Western Allies landing in France and pushing on past the Rhine. The major "second front," which Stalin had long demanded and which Churchill had tried to avoid at all costs, finally opened on June 6, 1944—D-Day (Operation Overlord). By that time, even the reluctant British understood that, with Soviet forces smashing their way toward Berlin, the Western powers needed to establish a major presence on the Continent if they were to have any voice in the reconstruction of liberated Europe.

The Germans certainly realized the imminence of an Allied attack in the West. As early as November 1943, Hitler had written to his commanders:

> The danger in the East remains, but a greater danger threatens to the West—the Anglo-Saxon landings. In the East, in the worst scenario, the vast size of the territory allows a loss of ground even on the large scale without delivering us a mortal blow. But it is different in the West! . . . It is there that the enemy has to attack, there—if we are not deceived—that the decisive landing battles will be fought.[1]

Fortunately the Nazis did not know where—in Norway, in France at the Pas de Calais or Normandy, or along the Mediterranean coast—or when the blow would fall. The Allies chose Normandy because the enemy's opportunities for rapid reinforcement and counterattack would be more limited than at Calais. Hitler had a hunch that Normandy might be the choice, but the Allies undertook an extensive deception operation that succeeded in confusing the German military. They fed false information to German spies (the Double-Cross System). They flew as many bombing raids and reconnaissance missions over the Pas de Calais as they did over Normandy. They set up a fake army positioned to assault the Pas de Calais region, commanded by their most audacious general (Patton), with fake barracks, tanks, and landing craft. They flooded the airwaves with fake messages seemingly from this "army."

This deception campaign worked so well because it fit German expectations. The Germans anticipated that valuable channel ports, mainly in the Pas de Calais region, would be the primary Allied objectives. Unsure where the attack would come, the Germans had to commit forces to defend Norway, the south of France, and Calais, as well as Normandy. They also believed that, even if the Allies attacked Normandy, a second, larger invasion would strike the Pas de Calais soon thereafter. Even after the Allied landings started, the Germans did not release their reserves, thinking that the Normandy assault might be a diversion masking a main attack elsewhere. Twenty days after the invasion, half a million German troops remained in the wrong place.

Operation Overlord was the largest amphibious assault in history. On D-Day, five battleships, twenty-three cruisers, and hundreds of lesser warships escorted 1,400 troop transports and landing craft, under a protective umbrella of 3,700 fighter aircraft. The Allies jammed German radar to prevent them from detecting the approach of this massive fleet. The impact of Allied air supremacy cannot be overestimated. The Luftwaffe had suffered such terrible attrition in the Allied bombing campaign over Germany that it offered virtually no resistance to the invasion—neither did the Kriegsmarine. U-boats and E-boats (small, fast assault craft) sent against the invading armada were destroyed or driven off. Only the pressure-sensitive German "oyster" mines sank a few Allied ships.

An enormous naval bombardment and swarms of fighter-bombers pounded German defenses on and near the beaches. Five divisions assaulted a fifty-mile stretch of the Normandy coast—British and Canadian forces at beaches designated Sword, Juno, and Gold, and on their right flank, Americans at Omaha and Utah beaches. An additional British division and two more US divisions preceded these landings, parachuting or landing in gliders behind German lines to protect the flanks of the operation. An American, General Dwight Eisenhower, served as the overall Allied commander at SHAEF (Supreme Headquarters Allied Expeditionary Force) in London. Air chief marshal Sir Arthur Tedder served as Eisenhower's deputy and directed the Allied air armadas. Bernard Montgomery oversaw the battle once the troops landed in Normandy.

Murray and Millett credit Eisenhower with supreme diplomatic skill in holding the Allied war effort together: "If Ike deserves the accolade of 'great,' it rests on his performance in managing the generals under his command, as fractious and dysfunctional a group of egomaniacs as any war had ever seen."[2] Eisenhower presided over a collection of strong-willed, egocentric generals, each of whom wanted personal credit for winning the war. Montgomery became more and more anti-American as US predominance in the war effort increased. He and his American rivals fought a cold war against each other with press conferences and information leaks. The hostility between George Patton and Montgomery was particularly intense. The outspoken Patton was often his own worst enemy in this duel. Though a brilliant battlefield commander, his views on politics, race, and the "Bolshevist-Zionist" conspiracy would have been better suited to the German army.

Allied engineers invented an array of specialized equipment to facilitate the assault. Tanks were modified to carry flails (chains on rotating drums to beat the ground) for exploding mines, bulldozer blades to crash through obstacles, rolls of metal or wood segments to bridge ditches and tank traps, and flamethrowers to clear enemy bunkers. Not all the engineers' imaginative creations were effective. The "panjandrum" was a spectacular but unsuccessful rocket-propelled, explosive-carrying wheel meant to roll over the beach and destroy mines. It resembled an out-of-control fireworks display.

The key to victory for the Allies lay in their ability to expand beachheads and then pour in troops faster than the enemy could bring up reinforcements. If they failed in this vital requirement, they might be thrown back into the sea. Beyond the deception campaign to keep German troops elsewhere, Allied bombers devastated French railways, roads, and bridges in Normandy during the weeks before the invasion. By D-Day, traffic on railroads

Allied supreme commander Dwight D. Eisenhower (front left) and British general Bernard Montgomery (front right).
Source: Wikimedia Commons

in the region was down to 30 percent of its previous volume. When the invasion came, the Germans were uncharacteristically slow to respond to it. They thought the weather in early June too bad (rain, wind, and rough seas) for a major invasion. They had not detected the short break in the otherwise unsuitable conditions that Allied meteorologists had seen. Field Marshal Gerd von Rundstedt held overall command in western Europe, while General Erwin Rommel led Army Group B in charge of defending the Channel coast. Both of them expected the Allies to attack the Pas de Calais, but they disagreed on how to meet that threat. Rundstedt wanted to hold his reserves well back from the coast to launch a counterattack once the location and direction of the enemy assault was determined. Rommel, fearing that Allied air power would decimate reserves in the rear, wanted to destroy the Allied landings on the beaches. Hitler did not resolve the dispute, but he did order the armored reserves not to move without his permission.

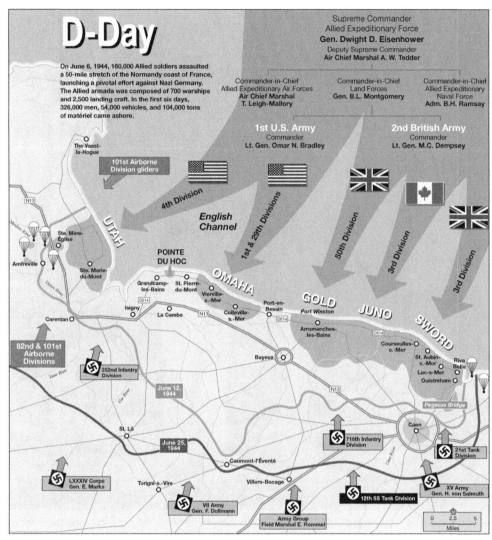

D-Day: The Allied Invasion of Nazi-Occupied France, June 6, 1944

By not committing the bulk of available forces to one strategy or the other, Hitler weakened German defenses in northern France. Meanwhile, Rommel prepared his defenses—laying millions of mines in the water and on land, placing thousands of metal obstacles on the beaches to hinder landing craft and tanks, building thousands of bunkers, and littering open fields with metal poles (known as "Rommel asparagus") to deter glider landings. The Allies were aware of German defensive plans and troop dispositions thanks to Ultra. The French resistance played a role too, constantly sabotaging enemy telephone lines so that the Germans were forced to use radio communications that Ultra could intercept. Although the Germans had fifty-nine divisions in western Europe, only six of them were guarding the two-hundred-mile-long Normandy coast. When the Allied attack began at 5:50 a.m. on June 6, Rommel was in Germany celebrating his wife's birthday, while the Führer was sound asleep. Because he had been up until 3 a.m. that morning, his adjutants declined to wake him.

When Hitler finally arose, he still thought that the events in Normandy were a diversion. Only at 4:00 p.m. did he authorize two more armored divisions to join the two panzer divisions already on the scene. Twenty-four German divisions, including five panzer units, were within 120 miles of the Allied landings, but they continued to await the "real" attack along the Pas de Calais. This typified the German reaction to the Allied landings—sending in reinforcements belatedly and piecemeal. Constant Allied air attacks as well as operations by the French resistance continued to slow German movement toward the Normandy beaches. Rommel later wrote:

> Even the movement of the most minor formations on the battlefield—artillery going into position, tanks forming up, etc.—is instantly attacked from the air with devastating effect. During the day fighting troops and headquarters alike are forced to seek cover in wooded and close country in order to escape the constant pounding of the air. Up to 640 [naval] guns have been used. The effect is so immense that no operation of any kind is possible in the area commanded by this rapid-fire artillery, either by infantry or tanks.[3]

Moreover, many of the German divisions in northern France were second-tier units, which included poorly motivated troops recruited from Soviet POWs.

Overlord began on June 6 because that date fell within a very small window of opportunity in which the weather and tides were suitable for a major amphibious operation. An armada of C-47 transport planes began disgorging two American paratroop divisions (more than thirteen thousand men) over the Cotentin Peninsula in the first dark hours of D-Day. Dense cloud cover and heavy antiaircraft fire caused many of them to drop their men far from their assigned zones. The paratroopers' work was difficult and dangerous in the extreme. Some were hit by enemy flak while still in their planes or during their descent. The parachutes of others failed to open in time, smashing them into the ground. Burdened with enough equipment to double their normal body weight, some drowned when they fell into lakes, ponds, or streams. Most paratroopers survived the drop but found themselves separated from their units and unsure how to find them. Many radio sets were damaged or lost during the drop, adding to the confusion. A combination of sleep deprivation, nervous exhaustion, and sleep-inducing airsickness pills caused many of the troopers to find cover and collapse for hours. Only the inexplicably lethargic German reaction to the airborne assault prevented disaster that night.

Officers spend all night and a good part of the next day rounding up stragglers, often forming mixed formations of men from different units. Some of these groups completed their missions, others failed for lack of personnel or equipment, and still others simply vanished, never to be seen again. The one positive result of the widely dispersed paratroop drops was the confusion it caused the Germans. In contrast to the chaos prevailing among the American paratroops, a British airborne division, landing at the opposite end of the invasion beaches by glider as well as parachute, arrived relatively intact and captured or destroyed a series of bridges to prevent enemy counterattacks against the invasion beaches.

Lead elements of seven Allied divisions began hitting the beaches at 6:30 a.m. The assault went well on four of the five beaches. British landings on Sword and Gold beaches and the Canadian landing on Juno beach overcame German defenses and penetrated inland, though neither reached their initial object, the city of Caen. The Americans hitting Utah beach—aided by paratroopers attacking German defenses from the rear—managed to cross the beach and establish a lodgment inland. US Army Rangers scaled the one-hundred-foot cliffs of Pointe du Hoc, a promontory between Utah and Omaha beaches, while under fire—only to find most of the gun emplacements empty.

While Allied troops elsewhere achieved considerable success, American forces at Omaha beach barely escaped disaster. Practically everything went wrong. Allied bombing and shelling had failed to take out German artillery on the high bluffs behind the beach. The British and Canadians had launched their landing craft within six miles of the beaches, but the Americans launched theirs as far as twelve miles from shore amid heavy swells. Waves swamped and sank some of the landing craft and most of the amphibious tanks. More soldiers drowned who almost reached the beach but stepped off the landing craft into deeper water than expected and were dragged down by the sixty-eight pounds of equipment they carried. Because of the winds and tides, virtually no unit landed at its intended location. Those who made it to the beach walked into a storm of fire from German artillery and machine guns. "We hit the sandbar," a navy crewman remembered, "and then all hell poured loose on us. The soldiers in the boat received a hail of machine-gun bullets. The Army lieutenant was immediately killed, shot through the head."[4]

The terrain gave the German defenders a huge advantage. As historian Stephen Ambrose describes it:

> No tactician could have devised a better defensive situation. A narrow, enclosed battlefield, with no possibility of outflanking it; many natural obstacles for the attacker to overcome; an ideal place to build fixed fortifications and a trench system on the slope of the bluff and on the high ground looking down on a wide, open killing field for any infantry trying to cross no-man's-land.[5]

The general in charge, Omar Bradley, ignored both intelligence reports about a larger number of defenders than originally anticipated and the lessons from the Pacific theater about assaulting well-defended coastlines. The operation hung in the balance for several hours. Surviving soldiers clustered behind the seawall or rock formations or behind ruined vehicles, seeking shelter from the murderous enemy fire. Officers patched together assault groups of men from various shattered units and led attacks against the well-defended draws that were the only exits from the beach. They used Bangalore torpedoes (explosive charges at the end of long poles) to detonate mines and break through wire entanglements. Destroyers moved in close to shore to provide naval gunfire. Once off the beach, the men attacked the trenches, bunkers, and pillboxes housing the German defenders. A sergeant of the 16th Regiment later recounted that he had told his men "that we had to get off the beach and that I'd lead the way. . . . I scurried and scratched along until I got within ten meters of the [enemy] gun position. Then I unloaded all four of my fragmentation grenades. When the last one went off, I made a dash for the top. The other kids were right behind me and we all made it. I don't know if I knocked out that gun crew but they stopped shooting."[6] Finally, heavy naval gunfire and the persistence of the attackers (though enduring horrendous casualties) enabled them to break through German defenses. The Germans were also running out of ammunition. The Allied air forces' interdiction campaign made rapid resupply all but impossible for the Germans.

By nightfall on D-Day, more than 155,000 Allied troops had landed in France. Although they had failed to meet their objective of linking their separate landings by that evening, all of them were connected and expanding by June 12. The invaders also were to have taken the nearby towns of Caen, Saint-Lô, and Bayeux by the end of the day, but those targets remained beyond their grasp. Eisenhower had anticipated that the landings would be difficult—so much so that he had prepared a press release in advance taking personal responsibility for the failure of the operation. Fortunately, he never had to broadcast it.

Victory on the Normandy beaches required not only great heroism but also unprecedented logistical prowess. To win, the Allies had to pour in more men, equipment, and supplies than the enemy could bring up to reinforce his defenses—and do so without the services of a major port. By D+5 (June 11), the Allies had landed more than 326,000 men, 54,000 vehicles, and 104,000 tons of supplies. By D+24 (June 30), those figures rose to over 850,000 troops, 148,000 vehicles, and 570,000 tons of supplies. Compensating for the lack of deepwater ports, the Allies created two prefabricated harbors (code-named Mulberries) and towed them across the English Channel. The worst storm to hit the Normandy coast in forty years destroyed the Mulberry at Omaha beach on June 19, though the other harbor continued to function with only minor damage. The Allies also laid a fuel pipeline under the English Channel. They expected to overrun some small ports along the Normandy coast quickly. That was not to be. Rather than evacuate them as the Allies advanced, Hitler ordered their garrisons to fight to the last man. Lack of adequate port facilities combined with the damage the Allied bombing campaign had done to railways, bridges, and roads in northern France seriously limited Allied operations for five months.

The Germans belatedly and only partially recognized the significance of the Normandy landings and attempted a series of counterattacks. These were stifled by powerful naval gunfire (the battleships' big guns could reach fifteen miles inland) and by swarms of bombers. It became almost impossible for the Germans to bring in reinforcements and supplies in a timely manner. Rocket-firing British Typhoon and American Thunderbolt fighter-bombers destroyed masses of tanks, trucks, and personnel carriers almost unopposed. The Germans now began to experience the same gruesome attrition of men and equipment in the West that they had already suffered in the East. The Reich could not replace these losses. The Wehrmacht lost 117,000 troops killed, wounded, or missing in the first eighteen days of combat, but received only about 20,000 replacements—and many of them were raw recruits, Luftwaffe ground crews pressed into service as infantry, or poorly motivated Soviet POWs serving in the German army. In response to Operation Overlord, the Germans began moving some divisions from the eastern front, but that movement soon stopped. Honoring his earlier promise to his allies, Stalin launched Operation Bagration on June 22. This massive, 1,670,000-man offensive blew a 250-mile-wide hole in the Germans' lines, ensuring that there would be no further transfer of Wehrmacht forces from the East to oppose Overlord.

Once Allied troops were able to break out from the beaches, General Montgomery had two main objectives—the capture of the port of Cherbourg and the town of Caen, a vital transportation hub. He anticipated that the Germans would defend Caen stoutly, perhaps freeing the Americans on his flank to sweep through presumably less well-guarded northwestern France and encircle the enemy. He told his subordinate British and American commanders that he expected them to act aggressively at all times and keep the enemy on the run. That is not what happened, but historians disagree about the cause of the Allies' slow progress. John Ellis blames the British commander for overcautious, unimaginative generalship. "What Montgomery was proposing was authentic mobile warfare. . . . Unfortunately, he was probably the Allied general the least able properly to orchestrate this mode of warfare."[7] Voicing the opposing view, Richard Overy argues, "The delays to the breakout were unavoidable. . . . British and Canadian forces fought against the bulk of German armoured divisions in France, against bitter resistance and with a declining rate of reinforcement. But when the breakout finally came, the long weeks of attrition around Caen bore out Montgomery's aims."[8]

The Allies made use of their command of the air and massed artillery both to savage enemy positions before an assault and to decimate German attempts to retake that ground. The objective was to minimize Allied casualties and maximize those of the enemy. The Wehrmacht could not win this attritional battle. At times, Allied forces still suffered significant losses, not only because of stubborn German resistance but also because difficult terrain (hills, forests, etc.) and weather (heavy cloud cover, storms) reduced the effectiveness of their advantages in tanks, artillery, and air power. Infantrymen and tank crews suffered casualties disproportionately because they were the sharp end of the spear. In some units, infantry comprised only 20 percent of the complement but endured 80 percent of the casualties.[9]

British troops had not been able to move immediately against Caen as planned, allowing time for Rommel to move substantial forces, including five panzer divisions, to protect the town. In the face of the Allied onslaught, Rundstedt wanted to begin a fighting retreat to more defensible positions, but Hitler ordered his troops to hold in place. British and Canadian troops fought a desperate battle with the enemy for forty-four days, with heavy casualties on both sides, before securing Caen on July 20, a process that destroyed the town and killed many of its inhabitants. The fighting in the drive for Caen was as savage as that in any other theater. A British artillery officer recounted one brutal encounter:

> There was a bloody battle where infantry, tanks and self-propelled guns, ours and the Germans', were at times inextricably mixed. At one point, in a rift on the ground . . . I brought my four guns into action in the midst of hand-to-hand bayonet fighting between a Scottish company and some panzer grenadiers, which I watched (and almost had to take part) as a horrified spectator.[10]

The British used flame-throwing Churchill Crocodile tanks to suppress enemy infantry. They were much feared by the Germans but, unfortunately, in short supply.

Montgomery had another reason for moving slowly apart from his propensity toward caution and elaborate preparation for battles. Great Britain was nearing the end of its resources, including manpower. If Britain were to continue playing a significant role in the war—and in the postwar era—Montgomery needed to minimize casualties, though he failed in that objective at Caen because of fierce German resistance. Political necessity reinforced "Monty's" conservative propensities. His army was "conceptually unsuited" to daring breakout operations, John Buckley argues, "because it had adopted operational and tactical methods that emphasized risk aversion, where possible only committing to battle when the weight of allied resources and firepower could reduce the likelihood of heavy casualties."[11]

Like Montgomery, most British and American commanders relied on "blunt-force" tactics that could not fail to win, given the Allies' overwhelming material advantages. Only after heavy artillery bombardment and powerful air strikes were most of them willing to commit their infantry and armor to assaults. The German generals, though in awe of Allied material superiority, were unimpressed by their enemy's generalship. One of them commented, "In contrast to the Eastern theatre of operations, in the West it was possible to still straighten out seemingly impossible situations because the opposing Armies there . . . despite their enormous material superiority, were limited by slow and methodical modes of combat."[12]

The Allies were learning how to fight the Germans, however. For example, when British armor attacked, the enemy targeted the most lethal Sherman Firefly tanks (recognizable by their longer gun barrels). In response, the British began to lead their armored assaults with standard Shermans and let the Fireflies pick off German tanks and antitank guns once they had exposed themselves by firing at the lead tanks. Sometimes a problem was readily identified but the solution proved elusive. Deadly enemy mortar fire accounted for a high proportion of Allied infantry casualties. British and American officers tried various methods, including radar, to improve their ability to locate and destroy German mortars. Their success was partial at best.

While British forces battered their way to Caen, American units to Montgomery's west were delayed by the slow trickle of supplies and ammunition needed to support major operations. Dense *bocage* (hedgerows as much as ten feet thick on elevated banks) separating fields in this part of Normandy created a situation difficult for attackers but ideal for defenders. An inventive sergeant devised the solution of welding steel "teeth" onto the front of Sherman tanks to cut through the hedgerows. A tank equipped with "rhino" teeth cut through the hedgerow and fired white phosphorus shells to suppress enemy machine-gun pits in the next hedgerow. The tank then fired its .50-caliber machine gun while mortarmen lobbed shells at the German infantry behind that next hedge. American infantry then followed the tank across the open ground between the two hedgerows, continually moving and firing. It was slow progress, and not without significant casualties, but the troops were moving again.

Having broken out of its beachheads, the American 1st Army under General Bradley launched Operation Cobra on July 25, driving south toward Avranches. It overcame initially stiff German opposition in the Saint-Lô area by intensive bombing of enemy strongpoints and artillery positions. Bradley intended to secure the Cotentin Peninsula, with its port at Cherbourg, and then drive westward into Brittany. While Allied air superiority contributed greatly to the advance of their ground forces, inaccurate bombing sometimes led to "friendly fire" casualties. The use of heavy bombers, flying at high altitude, was particularly problematic. For example, on July 24–25, massive raids by the 8th Air Force against German formations resulted in the death of 101 US troops, including General Lesley McNair, and the wounding of many more. Subsequently, American units used distinctive ground markings and radar beams to signal their location to the planes overhead, though some bombs still fell on US forces.

Obeying the Führer's order to hold their ground, German troops fought stubbornly against the American advance, but their opponent's overwhelming firepower had cost them dearly. General Fritz Bayerlein, commander of the Panzer Lehr Division, responded sarcastically to Field Marshal von Kluge's order to hold the line against the Allied advance: "Out in front everyone is holding out. Everyone. My grenadiers and my engineers, and my tank crews—they're holding their ground. Not a single one is leaving his post. They are lying silent in their foxholes for they are dead."[13]

The Falaise Pocket

General Patton, now free from his phantom command of a nonexistent army, led the real 3rd Army against light resistance west into Brittany as far as the Loire River. Patton told his troops, "I want you men to remember that no bastard ever won a war by dying for his country. He won it by making the other dumb bastard die for his country."[14] Patton then wheeled eastward to swing behind enemy forces fighting against the British and Canadians. The Germans faced encirclement, with British forces pressing them from the north and Patton's troops racing eastward across Normandy. A withdrawal would have been sensible, but Hitler ordered a counterattack to divide the enemy forces. Against his better judgment, von Kluge sent five understrength divisions toward Mortain. Forewarned by Ultra, Allied air power decimated them. The Canadian 1st Army and Patton's forces had now caught the battered remnants of three German armies between them. The combination of battlefield losses and the attempted assassination of the Führer on July 20 left the German high command in crisis. Hitler had fired Rundstedt for failing to stop the Allied invasion (and even telling the Führer that he needed to "make peace" in the West) and replaced him with Kluge. Rommel had been seriously wounded by an Allied air strike. Both Kluge and Rommel were implicated to a degree in the plot against Hitler—both committed suicide. In mid-August, Field Marshal Walther Model took command of the western front.

It took Model only a few hours in his new command to realize the hopelessness of the situation and authorize a withdrawal before the Allied trap slammed shut at Falaise. Estimates vary, but between eighty and one hundred thousand Germans were caught in the pocket, while between twenty and fifty thousand managed to escape, though without their heavy equipment. Eisenhower later wrote:

> The battlefield at Falaise was unquestionably one of the greatest "killing fields" of any of the war areas. Roads, highways, and fields were so choked with destroyed equipment and with dead men and animals that passage through the area was extremely difficult. Forty-eight hours after the closing of the gap I was conducted through it on foot, to encounter scenes that could be described only by Dante. It was literally possible to walk for hundreds of yards at a time, stepping on nothing but dead and decaying flesh.[15]

The paths to Paris and to the Franco-German border were now open to the Allies. Some historians have criticized Montgomery and/or Bradley for not closing the gap fast enough and catching the entire German force.[16] Ellis condemns the British commander for abandoning mobile warfare for a war of attrition—"for doggedly accepting enormous armoured casualties in the knowledge that the enemy's own losses, though smaller, would have a much greater impact on his ability to fight on."[17] Nevertheless, Falaise was a disaster for the Germans. In Normandy, they had lost seven hundred tanks and thousands more vehicles and suffered 450,000 casualties (forty divisions shattered). The Allies had stormed Hitler's "Fortress Europe," driven the enemy out of most of France, and inflicted massive casualties on the Germans, but those triumphs came at an agonizing price. By the end of the year, the seven British infantry divisions that fought in northwest Europe had lost nearly three-quarters of their initial strength. Some American units had even higher replacement rates.

The Bridge Too Far

Eisenhower planned to advance through France on a broad front, even though that meant slower progress.[18] That strategy angered some of his fractious generals. Patton and Montgomery each thought that their campaigns should receive absolute priority for scarce supplies (especially of gasoline) and that the other commanders should remain on the defensive. Montgomery wanted a much narrower and more rapid assault to hit the northern end of the German defensive line, penetrate Holland, and then pivot into Germany itself. Churchill and his senior commanders strongly supported Montgomery's plan because it promised an end to the war in 1944—a necessity for Great Britain because it was rapidly running out of resources to continue the war. Much to the annoyance of the American commanders, Eisenhower bowed to this pressure and authorized Montgomery's offensive.

In Operation Market, one British and two American airborne divisions were to drop behind enemy lines to capture key bridges over the Maas (Meuse), Waal, and Neder Rijn Rivers. In Operation Garden, British ground forces were to break through to Eindhoven, Nijmegen, and Arnhem, relieving the paratroopers holding the bridges and allowing Allied armor to pour into Germany and overrun the important Ruhr region. The path of this campaign lay on flat ground, facilitating an armored offensive, and constituted the short-est route to Berlin. Launched on September 17, Market-Garden proved a costly failure. Planners assumed incorrectly that the two panzer divisions in the Arnhem area had been mauled too severely in previous fighting to be a real danger. They also underestimated the Germans' ability to assemble forces quickly in the path of Operation Garden's ground as-sault. Consequently, the attack began without enough men or antitank guns. Compounding the problem, bad weather and heavier than expected enemy flak prevented both adequate air support and bringing in reinforcements and supplies.

British paratroopers reached Arnhem and sent a small detachment across the bridge there, but a powerful enemy counterattack stopped them. A Polish parachute brigade dropped in support of the British at Arnhem, but the Germans quickly surrounded them as well. The Allied ground forces were not able to break through to the trapped paratroopers. British tanks had to travel on an elevated road (soon dubbed "Hell's Highway") because the soft Dutch soil in the area would not support heavy armor. That made them easy targets for the German artillery. The enemy also had the advantage of finding the plans for Market-Garden in a downed Allied aircraft. The whole operation collapsed, with over seventeen thousand Allied casualties. The large allocation of men and resources for Market-Garden may have prevented Patton from crossing the Rhine farther south before German defenses stiffened. Montgomery called the operation "90 percent successful" and, though admitting a few mistakes on his part, blamed its collapse on the Allied high command's failure to al-locate enough resources to him. Ellis suggests that the whole operation was so defective that it had no chance of success.[19]

A serious bottleneck in the supply system caused the Allied advance in western Eu-rope to slow dramatically after the failure of Operation Market-Garden. The successful Allied air campaign, which destroyed railways and bridges in northern France and thereby prevented the Germans from responding more forcefully to the Normandy landings, now limited the shipment of critical supplies to the advancing Allied armies. Moreover, the retreating Germans had thoroughly wrecked Cherbourg and the smaller ports the Allies had captured. Montgomery's decision, with Eisenhower's acquiesce, to attempt a dash into Germany, rather than liberate the major port of Antwerp, ensured that the supply crisis would continue.

British troops finally captured Antwerp with its port intact on September 4, but it was not useful until Canadian forces secured the critical Scheldt estuary connecting it to the sea by November 8. That operation involved fierce fighting, amphibious landings, and serious casualties. The first Allied convoy reached Antwerp at the end of that month. Keegan con-demns Montgomery's failure to secure the estuary sooner as "the most calamitous flaw in the post-Normandy campaign."[20] The Allies counted on material superiority to defeat their enemy. That strategy put greater burdens on the Allied supply system. Whereas a typical German division needed about two hundred tons of supplies per day, an Allied division required seven hundred tons per day! Antwerp became the most important port channeling vital supplies to the Allied armies. The Germans attacked it with V-1 and V-2 missiles, doing considerable damage but never stopping the torrent of supplies.

A series of poor decisions by Allied political leaders and commanders also contributed to stalling their offensive. The United States had planned to create 250 army divisions, but in 1944 it fielded only 89. This manpower shortage meant that US units often lacked the necessary punch to sustain offensives and that divisions which suffered considerable attrition in combat could not be withdrawn for a significant period of rest and refitting. In addition, the US Army allocated a far larger number of men to support roles than necessary. This was true in all theaters of war but was especially serious in Europe. Overall, the United States inducted 16.3 million men and women into its armed services, but no more than eight hundred thousand of them experienced extended combat.[21] The British, too, were reaching their manpower limit.

American generals also decided to retain the Sherman tank as the mainstay of their armored forces rather than replacing it with the new and more powerful Pershing tank. The Shermans were no match for the Germans' Panther and Tiger tanks. The British were using a modified version of the Sherman tank known as the Firefly, mounting the much more potent seventeen-pounder antitank gun. By mid-1944, the Americans had fitted some of their Shermans with a more powerful, high-velocity 76 mm gun that could penetrate the frontal armor of their Panther and Tiger adversaries. In the fall, US forces also added the M-36 tank destroyer, with a formidable 90 mm gun. Still, in armored clashes, the Allies counted on massed artillery barrages and air strikes to even the playing field.

There were tactical mistakes as well. The US 1st Army, under General Courtney Hodges, took Aachen, the first German city to fall, in October. It was brutal, house-to-house urban warfare in which Allied advantages in air power and artillery were significantly diminished. Beginning in September, US forces attacked into the Hürtgen Forest, near the border of Belgium and Germany. American generals failed to recognize the tactical significance of German-held dams on the Roer River south of the forest. The Germans could easily neutralize any American breakthrough in the forest by opening the dams and flooding the area. Also, dense vegetation, uneven terrain, and bad weather limited the use of US armor and air power. The Americans fought for three months and suffered thirty-three thousand casualties for no significant gain. The higher command's lack of detailed knowledge about specific conditions at the front caused problems in the forest and elsewhere along the line.

Because of this shortage of men and supplies, as well as poor command decisions, US casualties in November more than doubled monthly totals since June. German defenses seemed to be crumbling after the initial breakout in Normandy, leading some Allied generals to anticipate a rapid collapse of the Third Reich. The Allies' slow progress in the fall of 1944 gave the Germans a chance to reorganize and strengthen their West Wall barrier. The fall of Antwerp caused some panic both among German officers and among ordinary soldiers. The Germans resorted to Soviet-style methods to force dispirited troops to fight. They executed deserters immediately, reorganized stragglers into punishment battalions, and forced reluctant troops back into the front lines at gunpoint.

The supply situation began to improve slowly after the Allied invasion of southern France—Operation Dragoon—on August 15. That campaign had been scheduled to coincide with the Normandy landings, which would have provided the Allies with a great strategic advantage, but the lack of enough landing craft for both Overlord and Dragoon (together with the island-hopping campaign in the Pacific) forced postponement of the latter operation. After a heavy naval bombardment and enjoying dominance in the air, American and French troops landed at beaches along the Côte d'Azur. The initial forces numbered 151,000 men, later built up to over half a million troops. They faced the much-weakened German Army Group G, which had lost some of its units to other fronts and which included many *Ostlegionen* troops (i.e., poorly equipped volunteers and draftees from the occupied East Europe). The Allies pushed the Germans to the Vosges Mountains. Most of southern France was liberated in just four weeks. The capture of the port of Marseilles, the naval base at Toulon, and the Rhône River valley, with its intact railroads, provided an enormous boost to the Allied supply system. General Jacob Devers's 6th Army advanced rapidly along the Rhône valley and within less than a month linked up with Patton's 3rd Army. Hitler allowed his forces to withdraw from an untenable situation in the south of France.

French troops, supported by American units, liberated Paris on August 25. Eisenhower had ordered his forces to bypass the city, but General Jacques Leclerc ignored that command in order to free the French capital. Free French resistance groups had begun an uprising on the 19th, and bitter fighting ensued in which resistance forces suffered 2,500 casualties. Leclerc's 2nd Armored Division arrived on the 24th. Hitler ordered all-out resistance to the Allied assault and the destruction of Paris, but the German commander on the scene, General Dietrich von Choltitz, surrendered the city within a day. Sporadic fighting continued for a few days between Vichy loyalists and Free French forces. De Gaulle arrived soon after the city's liberation to set up a Provisional Government of the French Republic. Free French units combed the city to arrest collaborators. They frequently shot people deeply involved in aiding the Germans. Women accused of "horizontal collaboration" (i.e., sexual relations with Germans) were publicly shamed by having their heads shaved, and in some cases they were beaten by angry mobs.

The Battle of the Bulge

Pressed now by advancing enemies in both western and eastern Europe, Hitler decided on a desperate gamble in December 1944—Operation Autumn Fog (also known as Operation Watch on the Rhine). He gathered all his reserves to attack the center of the Allied line on the western front, with the objectives of driving a wedge between the British in the north and the Americans farther south and of seizing the Allies' key port at Antwerp. Hitler believed that if he could inflict a sufficiently punishing defeat on the Western Allies, he could force them to conclude a negotiated peace. Then he could transfer the bulk of his forces in the West to the eastern front. Hitler's generals doubted the prospects for success. Waffen SS general Josef "Sepp" Dietrich complained privately, "All Hitler wants me to do is to cross a river, capture Brussels, and then go on and take Antwerp. And all this in the worst time of the year through the Ardennes when the snow is waist deep and there isn't room to deploy four tanks abreast let alone armoured divisions. When it doesn't get light until eight and it's dark again at four and with re-formed divisions made up chiefly of kids and sick old men—at Christmas."[22] Dietrich failed to mention that the mobile units would have only about 25 percent of the fuel they needed.

Hitler marshaled thirty divisions, comprised of two hundred thousand men and six hundred tanks, for this offensive that would strike through the forested Ardennes region, where German arms had achieved such a great victory in 1940. This powerful assault would hit a weak point on the American line, manned by only four divisions (about eighty thousand men) spread along a seventy-mile front. Severe weather and German radio silence prevented the Allies from detecting this enemy buildup. There were some indications from Ultra intercepts of gathering enemy strength, but Allied commanders believed that Germany was no longer capable of staging a major offensive. The Germans achieved complete tactical surprise by launching their attack in severe weather conditions on December 16. They sowed further confusion among the stunned US troops by infiltrating English-speaking commandos dressed in American uniforms. Within just a few days, the enemy had blasted a "bulge" forty miles across and sixty miles deep into the Americans' defenses. In the process, German SS troopers committed an infamous atrocity during their offensive, killing 107 American prisoners at Malmedy (only one of several mass murders of Allied POWs in northwestern Europe).

Despite its initial successes, Operation Autumn Fog never had a real chance of reaching its objectives. Though some American units panicked and fled the battle, most of the initially shocked US forces soon regrouped and mounted a tenacious defense. Eisenhower sent in two divisions of paratroopers (by truck in this bad weather) to stiffen the resistance. The German offensive slowed. At the Belgian town of Bastogne, a vital road junction, troops of the US 101st Airborne Division and the US 10th Armored Division held off the attackers even though they were surrounded. In response to a surrender demand, their commander, General Anthony McAuliffe, famously replied, "Nuts!"

Eisenhower ordered counterattacks from the south by Patton's 3rd Army and from the north by Montgomery, now commanding the US 1st and 9th Armies. Stalin, responding to a request from Churchill, moved up the date of a Soviet assault in Poland to prevent the Germans from moving any more troops to the western front. The weather cleared on December 23, and Allied air power struck the attackers hard. A German tank captain characterized the air blitz as "psychologically fantastic. Airplanes everywhere. Thousands. Shitting all over us. I didn't see a single Luftwaffe plane."[23] C-47 transport planes dropped much-needed supplies into Bastogne and other American outposts. This "Battle of the Bulge" was the costliest battle fought by American troops in Europe, one in which they suffered 89,000 casualties. Estimates of German casualties run from 67,600 to 125,000 men, 600 to 800 tanks and assault guns, and 800 warplanes. The Germans retreated, leaving most of their vehicles, their dead, and many of their wounded. Some American commanders issued verbal orders not to take SS prisoners in retaliation for the Malmedy massacre. On January 1, 1945, soldiers of the US 11th Armored Division shot seventy-nine German prisoners at Chenogne, Belgium. Informed of the matter, Patton wrote in his diary, "I hope we can conceal this."[24]

The Wehrmacht emerged from the battle so weakened that it no longer possessed any offensive capability in the West. Ambrose suggests that, from the Allied point of view, the enemy's Ardennes offensive was a stroke of luck. "The Germans were out of their fixed fortifications, out in the open where American artillery, American tanks, American infantry, American fighter-bombers would be capable of destroying them."[25] Hitler's last offensive had run out of gas—both figuratively and literally—as did a smaller attack against General Devers's forces in Alsace that was intended to immobilize Patton's troops. There, French and US troops blunted the enemy advance and then drove the Germans out of Alsace. After these battles, Montgomery publicly claimed credit for stopping the Germans, an assertion that outraged the Americans. The Battle of the Bulge had delayed the Western Allies' advance across the Rhine only briefly, but at the cost of starving the German defense in the East of vitally needed reinforcements. During this period, the Germans assembled eighteen new divisions and 2,299 new tanks and assault guns in the West, while only five divisions and 921 tanks were sent to bolster the badly outnumbered *Ostheer* (Eastern Army).

British and American commanders fighting in western Europe have frequently been criticized for their inability to replicate the German generals' bold armored offensives of 1940 and the summer of 1941. That complaint has some validity, but it misses a critical point. The nature of warfare had changed. The Wehrmacht's early successes depended not only on daring tactics but also on facing defenders who were less than fully resolute (especially in France in 1940) and who had not yet worked out methods to stop deeply penetrating armored thrusts. The Germans themselves developed the techniques to halt tank attacks during the African campaign. Thereafter, there was little chance for a rapid breakthrough and exploitation against well-prepared enemy defenses, with antitank weapons echeloned in depth.

An American corporal in Normandy registered his surprise at the changing nature of the conflict: "We were stuck. Something dreadful seemed to have happened in terms of the overall plan. Things had gone awry. The whole theory of mobility that we had been taught, of our racing across the battlefield, seemed to have gone up in smoke."[26] Tanks, infantry, and antitank guns had to advance together—supported by massed artillery fire and air power—laboriously reducing the enemy's strongpoints. Most German casualties resulted from the Allies' massive superiority in artillery and ground-attack aircraft. Yet bombardment and bombing did not eliminate the need for infantry and tanks to root out stubborn defenders. Casualty rates for US infantry divisions that experienced prolonged combat in western Europe ran between 15.6 and 19.2 percent of their troops killed and between 45.3 and 65.1 percent wounded.[27] Abundant manpower and industrial production replaced tactical brilliance as the keys to victory.

The "Real" War—The Soldier's Experience

For the Allied high command at SHAEF, the war was a matter of maps, reconnaissance photographs, and statistical reports; for ordinary American "GIs" and British "Tommies," the war was an entirely different experience. Unlike Germany or Japan, America did not have a highly militarized culture. It had to create an army of "citizen-soldiers" from its independent-minded and creature-comfort-loving civilian population. The war required, according to John Keegan, the subjection of individualistic Americans "to a system of subordination and autocracy entirely alien to American values."[28] Beyond inculcating the discipline necessary for coordinated military operations, that process of subordination all too frequently involved subjecting soldiers to a stream of unwarranted petty injustices—or "chickenshit." Literary historian and veteran Paul Fussell defines "chickenshit" as:

> behavior that makes military life worse than it need be: petty harassment of the weak by the strong; open scrimmage for power and authority and prestige; sadism thinly disguised as necessary discipline; a constant "paying off of old scores"; and insistence on the letter rather than the spirit of ordinances. Chickenshit is . . . small-minded and ignoble and takes the trivial seriously. Chickenshit can be recognized instantly because it never has anything to do with winning the war.[29]

Most American servicemen never saw combat, but the experience was transformative for those who did. The superficial bravado inculcated in training did not survive the first taste of battle. Boredom and terror formed the opposing poles of military life. For noncombatant servicemen as well as for combat troops between engagements, boredom was a central fact of life, "hurry up and wait" a common occurrence. For many soldiers, alcohol provided relief from that tedium as well as from the terrors of combat. In Fussell's apt phrase, military life involved "drinking far too much, copulating too little." John Garcia, who fought in the Pacific, later admitted, "I was drinking about a fifth and a half of whiskey every day. . . . It was the only way I could kill."[30]

Sex was certainly on the lonely soldiers' minds. Fully 80 percent of unmarried soldiers and 50 percent of married soldiers admitted to having had casual sex. Many desperate European women found the food, cigarettes, candy, and nylons that GIs had to offer irresistible. These encounters were not always consensual. US forces committed eighteen thousand rapes (almost half of them gang rapes) in Europe alone.[31] Similar crimes occurred in American-occupied Japan. *Time* magazine admitted in 1945 that "our own army and the British army along with ours have done their share of looting and raping. . . . We too are considered an army of rapists."[32] According to historian Mary Roberts, First World War tales of France as a sexual playground combined with American soldiers' growing sense of power in the liberated lands to unleash "a veritable tsunami of male lust."[33] The army sought to protect its image by blaming rapes on the supposedly "primitive instincts" of black soldiers and by letting very little information about these crimes reach the home front. Although African Americans made up only 10 percent of US forces in Europe, they accounted for 87 percent of defendants in courts-martial for rape. The penalty for those found guilty on the sketchiest of evidence (or none at all) was often death by hanging. American and French racism reinforced each other in frequent miscarriages of justice.

Recruits were told that they were the best-trained, best-armed troops in the world and that victory was assured. The experience of combat soon dissolved that superficial bravado. All armies prefer to induct young men, not only because they are physically fit but also because they tend to believe that they are immortal. Herman Melville wrote during the Civil War, "All wars are boyish, and are fought by boys, The Champions and enthusiasts of the state."[34] That innocence did not last long. Soldiers in combat experienced a steep learning curve that jolted their view of themselves and their world. Troops soon learned just how fragile their hold on life had become. As Fussell explains it, infantrymen go from believing that their intelligence, ability, and training will prevent their death, to the awareness that they could be killed if they are not much more careful, and finally to the realization that death on the battlefield is often a matter of chance which no amount of training, skill, or care can prevent.[35] "The average combat soldier," historian Gerald Linderman tells us, "thus lost his sense of invulnerability—and discovered how accessible he was to death. He lost too his sense of control over battle—and discovered his helplessness in the face of shellings and minefields."[36]

For some men, the extreme stress of combat was psychologically shattering. They suffered "combat fatigue"—that is, posttraumatic stress disorder. As many as 30 percent of US casualties were psychological. Most men found ways of coping with the fear and tension. Still, prolonged engagement in combat challenged the sanity of even the strongest individuals. Although there was no marked religious revival during the war, superstition played a role in the lives of many men. Some believed that wearing a St. Christopher medal or carrying a small New Testament in the pocket over their heart would protect them from injury. American servicemen knew that they were in the war for its duration. The US Army did not routinely rotate combat divisions out of action but kept them in the line, sending individual replacements for those killed or wounded.

In as few as three months of protracted combat, a division might suffer a 100 percent casualty rate. Even periods between battles could be exhausting and stressful. Audie Murphy, a soldier who went on to become a Hollywood star, recalled, "My eyeballs burn; my bones ache; and my muscles twitch from exhaustion. Oh, to sleep and never awaken. The war is without beginning, without end. It goes on forever."[37] Not all troops recoiled from the horrors of combat. Some soldiers actually enjoyed the experience because it provided both an extraordinary adrenaline rush and an opportunity to "prove their manhood." Most, however, adapted to the task of killing as a grim necessity. It was kill or be killed on the battlefield. It was a "job" to be done before they could do what they most wanted—go home.

Sometimes exhausted or angry Allied soldiers committed atrocities. They executed prisoners when they did not have the time or extra personnel to manage their captives or when they were simply too tired to deal with them. US troops shot seventy-three unarmed German and Italian prisoners at Biscari, Sicily, because they were enraged over the combat deaths of their buddies. General Patton attempted to cover up the incident, but some of the perpetrators faced trial and punishment. "That some men under stress lost the fine distinctions should not surprise us," Adams argues. "What is more remarkable is that most retained their sense of humanity and pulled back from the abyss of savagery."[38]

The American people hoped that US technology (the B-17 and its Norden bombsight, the Jeep, etc.), along with extraordinary American industrial productivity, would somehow make victory come easily and painlessly. For soldiers, that illusion dissipated rapidly in combat. People on the home front wanted to believe in the myth of easy victory. Their government did everything possible to shield them from the cruel realities of war. Moreover, US and British commanders sought to minimize casualties wherever possible by employing massive firepower—preferring tactical bombers and heavy artillery to bayonet charges.

Historians have disagreed sharply about the combat motivation of US and British troops. Fussell argues that American soldiers fought the war in an "ideological vacuum." "For most of the troops," he writes, "the war might just as well have been about good looks, so evanescent at times did its meaning and purpose seem."[39] President Roosevelt proclaimed the Four Freedoms as a key Allied objective in the war—preserving them in democratic countries and expanding them to other lands. Frank Capra's government-sponsored Why We Fight film series cast the war as an epochal struggle between a "world of Light and a world of Darkness," between a "slave world" and a "free world." Although all inductees saw these films in basic training, social scientists discovered that soldiers remembered very little about them a few months later.

Moreover, the Western Allies could never draw the distinction in sufficient detail between their societies and those of the Axis powers because their regimes were imperialist and their societies were racist too. Rather than any ideological motivation (which was important to German and Japanese soldiers), Fussell asserts that US troops fought mainly to defend their country from the vicious Japanese who had attacked it at Pearl Harbor and from Tokyo's dastardly Nazi ally. It was simply a nasty job that had to be done and gotten over with as soon as possible. He quotes an American private at Anzio: "If we killed we could go on living. Whatever we were fighting for seemed irrelevant."[40] That essentially negative motivation, self-defense, was bolstered in the heat of battle by another—the desire to support one's buddies and not to be shamed in front of them. Combat created tight peer groups—men whose very lives depended on each other and who shared experiences that those at home could never fully comprehend.

Historian Stephen Ambrose condemns Fussell's claim that the war was ideologically vacuous for Western soldiers as "preposterous." He argues, "Citing examples of Allied wrongdoing does not destroy any Allied claim to a moral superiority over the Nazis and

Japanese."[41] Linderman suggests that many soldiers fought pragmatically, mainly to end the war so that they could go home, but he also thinks it likely that democratic and humanitarian values were so deeply and pervasively held that they did not require constant repetition by government propagandists.[42] Most GIs understood that they were fighting for freedom and democracy without any patriotic slogans to remind them. In the heat of battle, however, small-group loyalties and the imperative of kill or be killed took precedence.

Initially, few American soldiers held any animus toward the Germans. Only 6 percent of recruits surveyed expressed a hatred of and desire to kill Germans, though the rigors of combat soon drove that figure up to 41 percent. Even then, only 20 percent of US troops admitted hatred of German civilians. They were much more likely to draw a sharp distinction between the Nazi leadership and ordinary German soldiers and civilians.[43] It was different in the Pacific, where most GIs and marines harbored a deep, visceral hatred of the Japanese.

American soldiers learned to fight and fight well, but they were seldom as effective as their German opponent. Studying the Normandy campaign, Colonel Trevor N. Dupuy concluded that despite massive Allied superiority, US troops were outfought by the Germans, suffering 50 percent more casualties.[44] Historian Martin van Creveld finds the source of this disparity in contrasting command cultures. The Wehrmacht rewarded aggressiveness and initiative, while the US Army allowed its junior officers and noncoms too little independence.[45] Moreover, the US Army developed a huge "tail." It took a great many more support troops behind the lines to keep one American soldier in action than it did for the German army. Draconian discipline and much more thorough ideological indoctrination in the German forces also help explain the differences in combat efficiency.

Invading the Nazi Heartland

The Ardennes disaster severely depleted the ranks of the German army on the western front. Most units had only a fraction of the men and equipment they normally would have possessed. Some "divisions" had as few as one thousand men. Some panzer divisions had only a few tanks or none at all. The Luftwaffe had practically disappeared from the skies. During the first three months of 1945, the Germans were able to supply their forces in the West with only 644 replacement tanks and assault guns to face the overwhelming strength of their Allied opponents.[46] Scraping the bottom of the manpower barrel, Hitler ordered the creation of twenty-five new *Volksgrenadier* divisions. These were smaller than normal divisions, armed mainly with submachine guns and handheld *Panzerfaust* antitank weapons and thus only suitable for defensive assignments. These units included older men as well as "unemployed" Kriegsmarine and Luftwaffe personnel and soldiers who had recovered from their wounds. Some of these divisions fought fiercely, while others disintegrated almost immediately in combat, but none of them could stand up to the crushing weight of Allied air power, artillery, and tanks. The unbroken litany of defeats undermined morale, and desertion rates began to rise. The regime responded brutally, executing anyone even suspected of dereliction of duty and threatening to arrest and punish family members of deserters.

Despite German weakness, Allied progress continued to be slow. By early March 1945, eight British, Canadian, American, and French armies held the west bank of the Rhine. The Allied forces included eighty-five divisions containing over four million men. Montgomery procrastinated at the northern end of the Allied line. He was still wedded to the concept of elaborate preparation for a set-piece battle. When US general William Simpson asked permission to force a crossing of the Rhine between Düsseldorf and Duisburg, Montgomery vetoed the idea. Ellis suggests that a combination of overcautiousness and a desire to have British troops lead the charge into the enemy's heartland motivated his refusal. In the opinion of one German general,

> there was no doubt that Allied strategy was not on a high level at this period of the war; it was rigid, inflexible and tied to preconceived plans. The whole German defence on the lower Rhine was collapsing, but the Allied leaders would not allow their subordinates to exploit success. Everything had to wait until Montgomery had prepared an elaborate setpiece attack and was ready to cross the river according to plan. Thus Field Marshal Model's Army Group B was given a new lease on life and the long agony in the West was prolonged for a few weeks.[47]

Eisenhower planned to cross the Rhine at multiple points in a grand offensive involving amphibious and airborne operations. By chance, on March 7, the US 9th Armored Division found an unguarded railroad bridge over the river at Remagen, south of Cologne, and quickly established a bridgehead on the eastern side. Farther south, Patton's forces stormed across the river near Oppenheim on the 22nd of that month. British and Canadian units then attacked toward Homburg, while American forces encircled the Ruhr district, capturing 325,000 enemy troops. General Model, their commander, committed suicide. Simultaneously, Patton's 3rd Army plunged onto southern Germany. In some places, Allied troops encountered stiff resistance from remnants of SS units and Hitler Youth groups, while elsewhere they pushed aside *Volkssturm* (militia) formations comprised of boys and old men. They also came upon numerous death camps, labor camps, and other evidence of German atrocities.

Liberating Bergen-Belsen, Dachau, Buchenwald, and Mauthausen, soldiers were shocked and appalled to find mountains of corpses and handfuls of cadaverous survivors. Lead elements of the US 9th Army reached the Elbe River (the agreed-upon dividing line between Soviet and Western forces) on April 11. Soviet and US troops famously linked up at Torgau and, twenty miles farther south, Lorenzkirch, along the Elbe, on April 25. There was still more mopping up of scattered enemy forces to do, but for all practical purposes German resistance had ceased. On May 7, General Alfred Jodl formally surrendered unconditionally to the Western Allies at SHAEF headquarters in Reims, France. Hitler's "thousand-year Reich" collapsed after only twelve years.

Notes

1. Nicolaus von Below, *At Hitler's Side: The Memoirs of Hitler's Luftwaffe Adjutant, 1937–1944* (London: Greenhill Books, 2001), 184.

2. Williamson Murray and Allan R. Millett, *A War to Be Won: Fighting the Second World War* (Cambridge, MA: Harvard University Press, 2001), 416.

3. B. H. Liddell Hart, ed., *The Rommel Papers* (New York: Harcourt Brace, 1953), 476–77.

4. Stephen E. Ambrose, *D-Day, June 6, 1944: The Climactic Battle of World War II* (New York: Simon & Schuster, 1994), 326.

5. Ambrose, *D-Day*, 321.

6. Ambrose, *D-Day*, 358–59.

7. John Ellis, *Brute Force: Allied Strategy and Tactics in the Second World War* (New York: Viking, 1990), 375.

8. Richard Overy, *Why the Allies Won* (New York: Norton, 1995), 170–71.

9. John Buckley, *Monty's Men: The British Army and the Liberation of Europe, 1944–5* (New Haven, CT: Yale University Press, 2013), 87.

10. Buckley, *Monty's Men*, 79.

11. Buckley, *Monty's Men*, 298.

12. Quoted in Ellis, *Brute Force*, 380–81.

13. Max Hastings, *Overlord: D-Day and the Battle for Normandy, 1944* (New York: Simon & Schuster, 1984), 256.

14. Andrew Roberts, *The Storm of War: A New History of the Second World War* (New York: HarperCollins, 2011), 400.

15. Dwight D. Eisenhower, *Crusade in Europe* (Garden City, NY: Doubleday, 1948), 296.

16. E.g., Chester Wilmot, *The Struggle for Europe* (London: Collins, 1952), 424–25; Hastings, *Overlord*, 353, 369; Russell F. Weigley, *Eisenhower's Lieutenants: The Campaigns in France and Germany, 1944–1945* (Bloomington: Indiana University Press, 1981), 204–14.

17. Ellis, *Brute Force*, 377.

18. Ellis suggests that the broad front strategy was mandated by alliance politics. Eisenhower could neither offend American public opinion by allocating the bulk of Allied resources to Montgomery nor affront Churchill by prioritizing American forces for operations farther south. Ellis, *Brute Force*, 413.

19. Ellis, *Brute Force*, 409.

20. John Keegan, *The Second World War* (New York: Penguin, 2005), 437.

21. Gerald F. Linderman, *The World within War: America's Combat Experience in World War II* (Cambridge, MA: Harvard University Press, 1997), 1.

22. Keegan, *The Second World War*, 441.

23. Ambrose, *Citizen Soldiers: The U.S. Army from the Normandy Beaches to the Bulge to the Surrender of Germany* (New York: Simon & Schuster, 1997), 225.

24. George S. Patton Papers: Diaries, 1910–1945, Library of Congress, October 3, 1944–February 5, 1945, 110. An investigation into the matter was sidetracked and eventually dropped.

25. Ambrose, *Citizen Soldiers*, 200.

26. Hastings, *Overlord*, 248.

27. Ellis, *Brute Force*, 538–39.

28. John Keegan, "Britain and America," *Times Literary Supplement*, May 17, 1984, 544.

29. Paul Fussell, *Wartime: Understanding and Behavior in the Second World War* (New York: Oxford University Press, 1989), 80.

30. Studs Terkel, *"The Good War": An Oral History of World War Two* (New York: Ballantine, 1984), 21.

31. Michael C. C. Adams, *The Best War Ever: America and World War II* (Baltimore, MD: Johns Hopkins University Press, 1994), 69.

32. *Time Magazine*, September 17, 1945.

33. Mary Louise Roberts, *What Soldiers Do: Sex and the American GI in World War II* (Chicago: University of Chicago Press, 2013), 9.

34. Herman Melville, "The March into Virginia Ending in the First Manassas," 1861, http://poetryfoundation.org/poems/45904 (accessed June 10, 2017).

35. Fussell, *Wartime*, 282.

36. Linderman, *The World within War*, 19.

37. Audie Murphy, *To Hell and Back* (Blue Ridge Summit, TN: TAB Military Classics, 1988), 46.

38. Adams, *The Best War Ever*, 84.

39. Fussell, *Wartime*, 129.

40. Quoted in Fussell, *Wartime*, 140.

41. Stephen E. Ambrose, review of *Wartime*, by Paul Fussell, *American Historical Review* 96, no. 3 (June 1991): 844.

42. Linderman, *The World within War*, 264.

43. S. A. Stouffer et al., *The American Soldier: Combat and Its Aftermath* (Princeton, NJ: Princeton University Press, 1965), 2:34, 158–59.

44. Adams, *The Best War Ever*, 55.

45. Martin van Creveld, *Fighting Power: German and U.S. Army Performance, 1939–1945* (Westport, CT: Greenwood, 1982), 163–71.

46. Ellis, *Brute Force*, 424.

47. Ellis, *Brute Force*, 438–39.

CHAPTER 18

The China, Burma, India Theater

Most accounts of the Second World War relegate the fighting in China to the level of secondary or even tertiary importance. However, China was the key issue in the outbreak of hostilities between Japan and the Western powers. Moreover, the fighting in the Middle Kingdom played a significant role in the outcome of the war. The China theater occupied most of the Japanese army. In 1939, Tokyo had thirty-five divisions, comprised of 1.1 million troops, in China. In contrast, the Imperial Army used just ten divisions and three brigades in its 1941–1942 conquest of all British, American, and Dutch possessions in East Asia. China remains, in the apt description by historian Rana Mitter, "the forgotten ally."

By 1939 the nature, though not the significance, of the war in China was changing. Although the Imperial Army had won almost all its major battles and conquered the richest parts of China along the coast and the lower Yangzi (Yangtze) River valley, Tokyo had failed to knock the Guomindang regime out of the war. It now found itself locked in a seemingly limitless struggle in the vast Chinese hinterland. The Japanese had fallen into a morass of their own making. They could not define their objectives, nor could they devise a strategy to terminate this endless conflict. The exorbitant costs of this crusade were skyrocketing. By the end of 1938, 70 percent of Japan's national budget went toward the war in China.

In contrast, the Nationalist army had lost most of its battles. Most of Chiang Kai-shek's elite forces had been decimated. He was now dependent on the troops of provincial military commanders (in some cases just the old warlords in new Nationalist army uniforms) and, to a lesser extent, on his fragile alliance with the Chinese Communists. In the view of historian Hans van de Ven, "the lack of military unity and the desire of commanders to preserve their forces again and again crippled China's efforts to resist Japan."[1] Chinese forces lacked sufficient mobility, forcing them to rely too much on static, positional warfare and thus playing into the hands of their much more agile opponent. Also, the enemy had conquered the most economically developed parts of the country, which were the core of Guomindang political strength. Appeals to the Western powers for aid against Japanese aggression had produced little beyond sympathetic words. Limited quantities of weaponry, supplies, and money continued to flow from the Soviet Union; but during his own urgent rearmament campaign, Stalin had little to spare, and he flatly rejected Chiang's call for the USSR to join China in fighting the Japanese. Worse still, before the end of the year Moscow signed the Nazi-Soviet Pact with Germany and began courting Tokyo for a nonaggression treaty.

Thus, both Tokyo and Chongqing were locked in a stalemated war that neither had the resources or a viable strategy to win. The Chinese had plenty of men available but lacked the aircraft, artillery, armor, communications, mobility, and logistics necessary to defeat their opponent. China's soldiers were using mainly pistols, rifles, machine guns, and grenades to fight against an enemy employing bombers, tanks, artillery, and poison gas. To offset their enemy's superior weaponry, the Chinese relied on fighting at night, mass assaults, and closing with the enemy as tightly as possible. Their handful of victories and some of their stout defensive stands (even in losing operations) had instilled new confidence in Chinese troops and their leaders.

Yet there was no obvious way to defeat the invader. Some within the Guomindang regime counseled negotiation with (essentially surrender to) the Japanese, but given the enemy's frequent atrocities, that was not an acceptable alternative to Chiang or to most of the Chinese people. Chiang's only option at this point was to wage a protracted war of resistance. That, however, was not a strategy for victory. It was only a technique for holding on until something else in the situation changed—perhaps a decline in the enemy's will to fight due to problems on the home front, or the entry of the Western powers or the USSR into the war. None of that seemed likely in 1939–1940. China was fighting alone.

Unlike the Chinese, the Japanese had an arsenal of powerful weaponry. Their problems were manpower and money. Their initial strategy had been to strike fast and hard—to destroy the Nationalist army in a few decisive blows. Although the Imperial Army won many battles, that overall strategy had failed. Now the Japanese faced the unappealing prospect of protracted war—of being bled white with no clear path to victory. There were just too many Chinese, too much China. Tokyo had to change its strategy. There would be no more large-scale military campaigns until 1944.

Employing limited military operations combined with diplomacy, Japan sought to strangle the Guomindang regime by choking off its external sources of supply and by fostering collaborationist alternatives to the Nationalist government. Perhaps then Chiang Kai-shek would realize the hopelessness of his situation and surrender. That strategy seemed even more promising in 1940 when France was defeated and Britain was besieged by an apparently unstoppable Germany. Now Tokyo could cut the most important supply routes to Chongqing by occupying northern Indochina and pressuring London to close the Burma Road. These actions hindered the Nationalists' war effort, but they did not address the heart of Japan's strategic problem. The longer the Japanese stayed in China and the more of the country they occupied, the more they oppressed the Chinese people. That in turn angered and politicized that most populous nation as never before. Japanese brutality was the key factor in galvanizing a powerful Chinese war effort and mobilizing the nation to oppose the invader.

Chiang Kai-shek and His Allies

The Japanese attack on Pearl Harbor was a godsend for Chiang Kai-shek, just as it was for Churchill and Stalin. There had been no clear path to Nationalist victory, but American entry into the war changed that prospect dramatically. Chiang could now be certain that ultimately Japan would be defeated. That did not mean, however, that Nationalist China could stop fighting. To justify American aid and secure China's status as a postwar power, as well as to protect as much of the country as possible from the ravages of a cruel enemy, the Chinese needed to keep fighting.

Beyond that, Chiang feared that after the defeat of Germany, Britain and the United States might sign a negotiated settlement with Japan, leaving parts of China under Imperial control. Chongqing formally declared war on Japan as well as its Axis partners. Then it joined the US, Great Britain, and the USSR in signing the United Nations Declaration. At

President Roosevelt's insistence, Nationalist China was now recognized as one of the "Big Four" Allies.[2] At this stage of the war, American strategists expected China to be a major theater of operations against Japan. Roosevelt also envisioned a united Nationalist China as the anchor of postwar American policy in East Asia. A strong Guomindang regime would also provide a useful counterweight to the USSR in that part of the world.

There were substantial disagreements among the Allies, however. Chiang Kai-shek disliked and distrusted Great Britain as an imperialist power committed to maintaining its empire after the war. He told his new allies that he expected an end not just to Japanese but also to Western incursions on Chinese sovereignty. Chiang demanded the end of extraterritoriality and all special privileges for foreigners in China. Beyond recovering Manchuria and Taiwan, he also sought the return of Kowloon from the British, the regaining of control over Tibet, and the return of Outer Mongolia from Russia.

British leaders doubted Chongqing's ability to play the role of a major ally, and they did not share the American desire to see China emerge as a strong power in postwar Asia. Stalin valued whatever resistance the Nationalists could mount as a way of deflecting Japanese aggression from the vulnerable Soviet Far East, but he shared British doubts about China as a great power. Beyond appreciating China's role in tying down six hundred thousand enemy troops, Roosevelt also supported Chiang's goal of a strong and fully independent China. Nonetheless, even the United States failed to treat China as a true equal in the alliance. "China was," in the view of historian Hans van de Ven, "a bargain-basement ally of whom much was demanded, but to whom little was granted."[3] The Allies' "Europe First" policy did not sit well with Chiang. Few resources would reach China given the Americans' emphasis on Europe and on their own thrust across the Pacific. In 1942, for example, as disaster loomed in the Middle East, the Americans transferred to that theater the bomber formations that they were assembling in India, even though the Nationalist army desperately needed air support.

Roosevelt and Churchill invited Chiang to meet with them at the Cairo Conference in 1943, but they excluded him from the important Casablanca, Tehran, Yalta, and Potsdam summit meetings. Part of the reason for China's exclusion lay in the Soviet Union's unique position within the Grand Alliance—at war with Germany and Italy but not with Japan before August 1945. Under those circumstances, Stalin could not publicly negotiate with Chiang Kai-shek without compromising Soviet neutrality in East Asia. China was excluded from the most important Allied organizations—the Combined Chiefs of Staff, the Munitions Assignments Board, the Combined Food Board, and the Combined Raw Materials Board. The Western powers agreed, however, to end the unequal treaty system and restore full Chinese sovereignty in Shanghai after its liberation from Japan. To gain some leverage with his powerful allies, Chiang warned that if they did not send more support, China would lose the war. More ominously, he occasionally threatened to negotiate a settlement with the enemy. Chiang attempted the latter strategy a few times, but Tokyo's terms were always unacceptably harsh.

China was now included in Lend-Lease Act funding, so both money and equipment began to flow to China in greater quantities. Though very welcome, American aid was never adequate in Chinese eyes. The United States assigned China a low priority for scarce resources (behind America's own military needs and assistance for Britain and Russia). The arduous supply route from India over "the Hump" also constricted supplies for China. Pilots flew over the fourteen-thousand-foot peaks of the Himalayas, sometimes enduring winds of 125–200 miles per hour and temperatures of −40 degrees Fahrenheit. Allied forces lost over one thousand men and six hundred aircraft on this grueling course—a few to Japanese fighters, but most to oxygen deprivation, bad weather, and looming peaks. Initially China received only about five hundred tons of aid per month. Less than 2 percent of Lend-Lease aid went to China before 1944. Moreover, much of the material shipped to China went to the growing American presence there. A greater infusion of American assistance came only in the second half of 1944 when the Allies reopened a land route to the Nationalist base areas.

Chiang Kai-shek was named Allied commander-in-chief for the China theater. Roosevelt sent Lieutenant General Joseph "Vinegar Joe" Stilwell to serve as his representative in China and as Chiang's chief of staff. The relationship between the prideful and sensitive Chinese leader and the acerbic, insensitive American general was thorny. The generalissimo soon came to regard his nominal chief of staff as incompetent and a danger to his own political power. Stilwell viewed Chiang and his Guomindang regime as ineffective, corrupt, and unwilling to confront the enemy. As van de Ven suggests, the American general possessed an "orientalist disdain for most things Chinese."[4] In private he referred to Chiang as "the Peanut" and even "the little dummy." Beyond the clash of egos, Stilwell and the American military establishment disrespected Chiang for his emphasis on defensive warfare.

The Sino-American alliance was troubled from its inception. Each side held unrealistic expectations of the other. Stilwell believed that Chiang wanted America to defeat Japan while he hoarded US weaponry and supplies for the impending civil war with the Communists. While not so critical of Chiang personally, Stilwell's predecessor as chief foreign advisor to Chiang, Soviet general Vasilii Chuikov, shared Stilwell's assessment of the Nationalists' reluctance to fight the Japanese and their preoccupation with the impending civil war.[5] He had much the same thing to say about Mao Zedong. "I came to the conclusion," Chuikov admitted, "that Mao and his associates were not much interested in working with the Nationalists but were intent instead on building up their strength for the eventual struggle for power in China."[6]

"Vinegar Joe" also complicated Chiang Kai-shek's relationship with his own generals. The reliability of provincial commanders continued to be a problem. In 1943, the GMD intelligence service uncovered a plot by some of the younger Guomindang generals to kidnap Chiang. That threat was quickly aborted and the participants severely punished. An even greater danger arose in the south, where General Li Qishen and other regional commanders formed a cabal to replace Chiang if the opportunity arose. Many of these insubordinate officers had been in contact with Stilwell or his assistant, Colonel Frank Dorn. Even if Stilwell was not directly involved in anti-Chiang plotting, his negative opinion of the generalissimo was widely known among senior regional commanders, and they probably believed that they would have American support in a move to oust their supreme leader. At one point Stilwell and Dorn themselves prepared a plan to assassinate Chiang Kai-shek![7] In addition to contacts with Stilwell, some unreliable Nationalist commanders, including General Bai Chongxi and his Guangxi Clique, also maintained a liaison with the Communists, not out of any sympathy for socialism but as an "insurance" policy in case the Guomindang did not prevail.

Fighting in Burma

China immediately joined the Allied struggle for the defense of Burma (modern-day Myanmar) by providing three armies, including the remainder of its best German-trained divisions, and the full strength of the Flying Tigers (only about seventy-five fighters), under the command of General Stilwell. Stilwell sought to recover northern Burma so that he could open a reliable supply route to China, enabling the Nationalist army to launch a major offensive against the Japanese. Chiang strongly doubted that this commitment to Burma was the best use of these elite troops, but he needed to demonstrate China's value to his allies.

Stilwell planned an aggressive campaign to retake Rangoon. The American general had seriously underestimated enemy strength in Burma. Given Japan's absolute air and naval superiority, the continuing reinforcement of its forces in this theater, and the apparent tendency of British troops to retreat rather than stand and fight, Chiang thought prudence preferable to boldness. "The best strategy in Burma," he told Stilwell, "is to hold an east–west line at Mandalay."[8] As historian Jay Taylor reports, Chiang "was risking his best armies with a man he had quickly come not to trust, someone who had never actually led troops in combat or planned and executed a real multidivisional battle."[9]

The American general assured the generalissimo of his compliance, but noted privately that he intended to blunt the enemy drive at Toungoo, 150 miles north of Rangoon, and then launch a powerful counteroffensive to recapture the Burmese capital. The Japanese, however, did not wait for Stilwell and Chiang to resolve their differences. They launched at attack on Toungoo, causing the British to pull back their Indian and Burmese troops. The enemy soon all but encircled the 1st Burmese Division near the Yenangyaung oil fields, exposing the flank of the Indian 17th Division. The Allies rushed in two Chinese divisions and a British armored brigade. After three days of heavy fighting, they managed to extricate most of the Burmese troops, though without their equipment. British colonial forces were rapidly losing their will to fight. Stories of Japanese atrocities—burning Indian prisoners alive and using captured British officers for bayonet practice—accelerated their demoralization. The enemy soon punched through one of the weaker Chinese divisions, causing the whole 6th Army to retreat in panic.

Disagreements between Chiang and his American general intensified. The generalissimo believed that Stilwell's dispatch of the 200th Division to Yenangyaung had fatally weakened the position of the 6th Army. He therefore instructed his field commanders *not* to execute Stilwell's orders without prior approval by the Chinese War Ministry. In contrast, Stilwell blamed the disaster on Chiang's interference and the poor performance of Chinese generals. Ultimately, superior Japanese forces crushed China's only fully mobile division. By April 25, Allied troops were in full retreat. Four days later, the Japanese seized Lashio, raising the fear that all Allied forces might be cut off. Chiang ordered Stilwell to move west to Myitkyina. Inexplicably, Stillwell chose to go by road rather than plane, an odyssey that turned into a four-day ordeal. During the trip, he concluded that the military situation was hopeless and that he should abandon Burma for Imphal across the Indian border. Stilwell also ordered his Chinese commanders to retreat into India.

Stunned that his American advisor had fled Burma, Chiang countermanded Stilwell's orders, but the situation could not be saved. Retreating Chinese forces were ravaged by malaria, dysentery, hunger, and Japanese ambushes. Chiang ordered six divisions to mount a counteroffensive from Yunnan Province to rescue as much of his expeditionary force as possible, but he could not prevent the enemy from cutting the vital Burma Road. The Burma campaign was a disaster not only for the British and their colonial forces but for the Chinese army as well, which lost over twenty-five thousand of its best soldiers and most of its artillery and trucks.

The Chinese had fought relatively well in Burma, considering their deficiencies in logistics, communications, and intelligence. However, they were not able to cooperate closely with British units since the British did not respect or trust the Chinese and were themselves infected with defeatism. Defeat in Burma and the closing of the supply route to China badly hurt morale among the Chinese and permanently soured the relationship between the generalissimo and his American chief of staff. Chiang wrote in his diary that Stilwell's "abandonment of his troops" proved that he "lacked the virtue and vision of a commander." Stilwell blamed Chinese incompetence and irresolution for the defeat in Burma. Misinformed and badly in need of good news, the American press reported "invading Jap force crushed by Stilwell" and portrayed the general's flight to India as courageous and resourceful.

The British attempted a limited offensive in northwest Burma (the Arakan region) beginning in December 1942, but the Japanese soon repulsed it, with significant Allied casualties. British and Indian units employed in this operation had neither the numbers nor the proper training in jungle warfare to defeat a seasoned and numerous enemy. In February 1943, three thousand "Chindits" (a special forces unit trained in the techniques of jungle combat), commanded by British general Orde Wingate, crossed into Burma. Once more, the Japanese responded forcefully, killing or capturing two-thirds of the British-Indian force.

Soon after the initial string of Japanese victories, the Doolittle Raid on Tokyo served to raise American morale, but it ultimately had the opposite effect in China. The enraged Japanese launched punitive attacks on those sections of coastal China where villagers had rescued US fliers. Chiang bitterly informed Roosevelt that "the Japanese slaughtered every man, woman, and child in these areas." The Chinese committed thirty-four divisions to the ensuing battles of Jiangxi and Zhejiang, where they lost thirty thousand troops. Stilwell and other Americans had already begun to criticize the Nationalist war effort as passive—virtually a facade for garnering American equipment and supplies for the impending civil war with the Communists after the United States defeated Japan. Chiang was astounded by these criticisms given the enormous loses the Chinese had just sustained in Burma and elsewhere. He wanted to have Stilwell replaced, but he could not risk alienating President Roosevelt or the chairman of the American Joint Chiefs, George Marshall (a friend of Stilwell's).

Stilwell made some of the same reform proposals that Chiang had received from his previous German military advisors. He thought the existing Chinese army much too large—logistically unsupportable, impossible to coordinate, and of poor combat quality. The average Nationalist division, while it might have seven to nine thousand men on its roster, seldom fielded more than three thousand riflemen, supported by perhaps 140 machine guns, a few mortars, and a few small-caliber antitank weapons. Most divisions had no artillery or armor, few trucks, and inadequate communications equipment. Many units suffered from malnutrition and sparse medical care. Widespread sickness and hunger drastically curtailed mobility. The Chinese themselves understood all too well that it took several of their divisions to equal the combat power of one Japanese division (only partially because Japanese divisions tended to be twice as large as Chinese divisions).

Stilwell suggested a new army of only ninety divisions, to be trained and equipped by the Americans. Using India as a base, he planned to retrain and rearm a nucleus of troops who had escaped from Burma. Eventually growing to thirty divisions, this contingent reemerged as X-Force. Another cluster of twenty divisions in south China was to be transformed similarly as Y-Force. Chiang authorized the creation of these units, but he shrank from the military and domestic political consequences of demobilizing more than two hundred existing divisions. He also may have feared that the commanders of these new, well-equipped units would pose a serious political challenge to him. Moreover, General Claire Chennault, now commander of the US 14th Air Force in China, opposed Stillwell's project.

He promised that if he received priority on the single, inadequate remaining supply route, he would crush the Japanese invaders by air power alone—an idea that Chiang supported. By the middle of 1942, President Roosevelt and General Marshall had come to support that idea too. Developing a major American bombing campaign against Japan from bases in China seemed more cost effective than rebuilding the entire Nationalist army.

Bombing Chongqing

During the initial air battles over China in 1937–1938, the Nationalist air force had experienced some success in attacking enemy formations. Japanese bombers at first flew without fighter escorts, and the Curtiss Hawk III interceptors flown by the Chinese were superior to most enemy fighters and bombers. By 1939–1940, however, that situation had changed. The Japanese introduced new and much-improved aircraft, while attrition wore down the small Chinese air force to fewer than a hundred planes. After the Zero fighter made its appearance in 1940, the Japanese gained absolute air superiority in China. They implemented a new strategy in 1939, terror bombing of Nationalist cities, particularly the provisional capital at Chongqing.

Beyond disrupting the operations of the GMD government, Tokyo expected that massive damage to civilian life and property would undermine popular support for Chiang Kai-shek and his war effort. Imperial Navy bombers began a sustained campaign against the capital on May 3, 1939. They returned frequently, using a combination of high explosive and incendiary bombs to smash buildings and set raging fires. Much of the city was reduced to a blasted, burned-out ruin. One survivor recalled that enduring these air raids "was like being in a tiny boat, constantly shaking. . . . Outside, bomb shrapnel was flying, window glass was shattering and falling to the floor. . . . The whole sky was lit up by flames, and the surrounding buildings were collapsing one by one. Our beloved homes were being flattened and turned into a sea of fire."[10] More than eight thousand people were killed in the first two days of bombing. Many more were injured, and more still were made homeless.

For all the devastation it wrought, the Japanese terror bombing campaign never brought the Chinese to their knees. Heavy fog, which shrouded Chongqing half of each year, limited operations to the clear months, and Japan lacked the large fleets of heavy bombers that air war against the civil population required. Moreover, the Chinese fought back with both active and passive measures. The Nationalists created an effective early-warning system that relied primarily on human observers. They signaled commanders in Chongqing almost as soon as Japanese bombers took off from their bases in the Wuhan region, six hundred miles away. Chinese fighter pilots, augmented first by Soviet and then by volunteer American fliers, and Nationalist antiaircraft batteries harassed the attackers. The Chinese also dug a network of air-raid shelter tunnels in the limestone on which Chongqing was built. The shelters were mostly primitive and could be wet, dark, and suffocating, but, with advance warning of impending raids, they saved hundreds of thousands of lives. However, during one tragic raid in June 1941, thousands suffocated in one of those densely packed tunnels. Departments of government and some factories were moved underground. Sections of the city were bull-dozed to create firebreaks. A quarter million residents were evacuated. This terror bombing failed to undermine the resistance of China's government or its people. Contrary to expectations in Tokyo, bombing civilians, combined with continuing atrocities committed by the Japanese army, only strengthened the Chinese will to resist.

From the summer of 1941 onward, Japanese attacks on Chongqing diminished dramatically as the Imperial Navy, responsible for bombing in central and south China, began moving most of its planes for impending operations in Southeast Asia and the Pacific. Imperial Army aviation, previously engaged almost entirely in the north, was spread too thin to cover the entire country. American entry into the war soon reversed the balance of power in the air. General Chennault and his American Volunteer Group (or Flying Tigers) were absorbed into the new US 14th Air Force. Even though loss of the Burma Road and reliance solely on the air route from India over the Himalayas to Kunming slowed progress, the Americans built a network of bases in south and central China and brought in Curtiss P-40 fighters and B-25 medium bombers. The United States also began to supply planes and training to rebuild the Chinese air force. By 1943, Allies had regained air superiority over southwestern China. On November 25, 1943, American bombers flying from Sichuan launched their first attack against naval targets on Taiwan. Now not only Taiwan but also the Japanese mainland itself was threatened with destruction from the air. Japanese army air squadrons attempted to strike back at the US bases in China but failed.

Nationalists, Communists, and the United Front

The "united front" between Nationalist and Communist forces formed after the Xi'an Incident was not entirely illusory. For a while the Nationalist government refrained from attacking Communist formations and even sent monthly cash subsidies to Yan'an. The relationship was a difficult one, however, because each side distrusted and hated the other. Both Chiang Kai-shek and Mao Zedong were playing a zero-sum game in which one would emerge completely victorious and the other would be destroyed. Mao insisted that 25 percent of his forces always remain near his command center to guard against a surprise attack by Nationalist troops. Mao never intended to subordinate his forces to Nationalist control.

Moreover, he never lost sight of his Marxist goal. The war against Japan did not mean a suspension of revolutionary struggle, only a different strategy of pursuing it. "While conducting a joint war of resistance [with the Guomindang] against Japan," Mao wrote, "we need to combine the national and social revolutions."[11] Necessity born of weakness, plus orders from Moscow, pushed the Communists to ally with their mortal enemy, while the Nationalists accepted the alliance under very strong public opinion pressure to unite China against the Japanese. Stalin had decreed at a 1937 meeting with CCP representatives in Moscow: "*The fundamental thing* for the Chinese Communist Party at present: to merge with the common national wave [of defense against Japan] and take a leading part. . . . *The main thing now is the war*, not an agrarian revolution, not confiscation of land."[12] Mao Zedong was forced to accede to the Soviet dictator's wishes. Many in the party leadership cadre, including Zhou Enlai, wanted a closer degree of cooperation with the Guomindang, but Mao either persuaded them to accept his position or destroyed them politically.

Chiang Kai-shek wanted Communist troops completely integrated into his National Revolutionary Army, but Mao feared that such a move would deprive them of all power and lead to their destruction. The Communists renamed their main force the Eighth Route Army (dropping the name Red Army and following the nomenclature of the Nationalist army), while a smaller concentration of troops in the south was christened the New Fourth Army. From the beginning, Communist forces employed guerrilla tactics rather than seeking the sort of large, frontal confrontations with the Japanese that had so damaged the Nationalist army.

They attacked the enemy from the flanks and the rear, ambushing small contingents of Japanese troops when the opportunity arose. Such small-scale operations could not defeat Japan, but they did tie down many enemy troops and provoked the Japanese into retaliatory atrocities that only aroused the Chinese people to greater resistance. Even orders from Moscow in 1940–1941 to attack the main Japanese troop concentrations did not move the Communist forces to alter their strategy. The Comintern criticized Mao, but he did not submit on this issue. In van de Ven's judgment, "in transforming the CCP during the 1937–1945 Sino-Japanese War from a defeated, demoralized, and divided party oriented toward Moscow into an organization with a strong ethos, a clear sense of a separate Chinese identity, and a powerful army, Mao domesticated, militarized, and nationalized revolution in China."[13]

The Eighth Route Army recruited its swelling ranks from the local peasantry. Communist leaders dampened their radicalism, emphasizing rent control and loan shark suppression as well as defense against the invaders. Brutal treatment of the civil population by the Japanese occupiers ensured that many would join the guerrillas. The Communists insisted that all Chinese forces operating within their area of control join the Red Army. Those who refused were eliminated.

Only once did the Yan'an high command deviate from its emphasis on smaller units employing guerrilla tactics. The Communists' ability to expand their forces and the areas under their control as well as a string of successful raids against Japanese weak points provoked the enemy into a major "bandit" suppression operation in north China. In response, Communist forces launched their Hundred Regiments Campaign in the summer of 1940. More than forty thousand troops attacked the Japanese communications network—roads, bridges, railroad lines, etc.—all over the region. Even this operation was more a series of diverse engagements rather than a large, centralized campaign.

Ultimately, however, Mao's forces were no match for the enemy's firepower. The Eighth Route Army lost twenty thousand men and much of the territory previously under its control. The Imperial Army's response was savage. The Japanese destroyed some villages in the combat area—all their inhabitants killed, all their animals slaughtered, all their buildings burned. This was the first and last major Communist offensive of the war. Mao directed his forces to return to guerrilla tactics. Communist troops had more success fighting against Chinese soldiers of regional collaborationist (or "puppet") regimes, who were less well armed and less strongly motivated than Japanese troops. Historian Yang Kuisong explains, "Communists set ambushes, exploiting the 'green curtain' of tall crops and the cover of darkness to attack small detachments of Japanese and puppets on the march. They would launch a brief but fierce attack with automatic rifles and hand grenades and then swarm forth like bees to engage in hand-to-hand combat."[14] Communist squads also undertook a campaign of assassinations against collaborationists.

The contending forces in north China were locked in a brutal dialectic of Communist ambush and Japanese retaliatory strike. Eighth Route Army units usually melted back into the countryside after an operation, but that was not always possible. In 1941 and 1942, the Japanese undertook a massive pacification campaign, employing the "three all" (kill all, burn all, loot all) tactic to deprive the guerrillas of peasant support. Their biggest success came in 1942 in Hebei Province, where their operations killed ten thousand Communist soldiers and many times that number of civilians. The population of the Communist base areas shrank from forty-four million to twenty-five million people. Mao's troops continued to suffer serious losses (and increasing desertions) until the latter part of 1943, by which time Tokyo began pulling some divisions out of China to meet the American advance in the Pacific. The following year, still more units were diverted from north China for the *Ichigo* offensive in the south. Taking advantage of this situation, Yan'an continued to increase the size of its army and to expand the area under its control. However, they still did not have the heavy weaponry or training in conventional warfare required to push the Japanese out of their strongpoints. They went over to larger offensives against the enemy only in the spring of 1945 when the Japanese Empire was collapsing.

The united front, never a love match, soon began to fray. Chiang Kai-shek sent four hundred thousand troops to blockade the Communist base area in north China at the beginning of 1939. The Nationalist army did not attack the Communist forces, but its presence served to prevent their further expansion. The blockade badly hurt the economy of the Communist-dominated region, an effect made worse by the ending of GMD subsidies to Yan'an and the poor harvests of 1939 and 1940. (Though Stalin replaced the $180,000 monthly subvention from the Nationalists with Soviet payments of $300,000 per month.)

Worse still, by 1941 large-scale fighting had broken out between Nationalist and Communist forces. Elements of the Communist New Fourth Army had moved south of the Yangzi River into areas prohibited to them by Chiang Kai-shek. The generalissimo ordered them out of the region and authorized GMD troops in the area to use force if necessary. Bitter fighting soon broke out between Nationalist and CCP units. Over nine thousand Communist soldiers were killed, and their commander, Xiang Ying, was captured and executed. Nationalist commanders were angry because in the previous year the New Fourth Army had annihilated a large GMD force operating behind Japanese lines.

This breakdown of the united front angered public opinion all over China. Stalin pressured both Mao and Chiang to renew their cooperation. Chiang was forced to end his campaign against the Communists, though smaller-scale clashes between GMD and CCP troops continued to occur. This "New Fourth Army Incident" marked a temporary setback for the Communists, though in the end it proved a public-relations boon. It added credibility to their claim that they were the real defenders of China against the Japanese, while the Nationalists preferred to kill other Chinese.

The Nationalists were not always the aggressors in this incipient civil war. In 1939 in Hebei Province, the Communist Eighth Route Army crushed GMD guerrilla forces that would not submit to its authority. CCP troops also repeatedly ambushed shipments of arms and money to Nationalist units in remote locations. By the middle of 1943, posters in Yan'an depicted the generalissimo together with Tojo, Hitler, and Mussolini, while Communist soldiers were urged to "struggle against Japan *and* Chiang Kai-shek." Zhou Enlai launched a program to "turn" Guomindang officials into covert Communist agents. Clearly both sides were preparing for the inevitable postwar confrontation.

That was not the impression that Americans got. When US journalists were finally allowed to visit Yan'an, Mao disingenuously told them that the Chinese Communist Party "never wavered from its policy of supporting Chiang Kai-shek" in his effort to oust the enemy invaders.[15] Many Americans came to view Chiang as a brutal dictator who expected US servicemen to fight and die while he preserved his forces for the coming civil war. In contrast, some observers saw Mao by as a benign "agrarian reformer" whose troops were carrying the fight to the Japanese. Initially, General Stilwell, some of the junior American diplomats, and the OSS were enthusiastic about drawing Communist forces more deeply into the struggle against Japan. The OSS even promised to arm and equip twenty-five thousand guerrilla fighters.[16] In July 1944, the US Army Observer Group (or "Dixie Mission"), comprised of army officers, diplomatic personnel, and OSS agents, traveled to Yan'an. "In the beginning," historian Carolle Carter suggests, "it was responsible for exploring means of cooperating more closely with the Communists. Increasingly this focus gave way to an emphasis on intelligence gathering as cooperation with the Chinese Communists went out of political favor."[17]

John Service, a young US Foreign Service officer who took part in the Dixie Mission, was impressed by the Communists. Although he admitted that if they won they might revert to undemocratic and socialist policies, he gave an ecstatic report of what he saw. "There is no criticism of Party leaders . . . there is no tension in the local situation . . . there is no feeling of restraint or oppression . . . there is no hesitation in admitting failure . . . there are . . . no beggars, nor signs of desperate poverty . . . [there is] total . . . unity of army and people." "Simple democracy," he declared, "is their policy . . . much more American than Russian in form and spirit."[18] The young American misjudged the Chinese Communists in several ways. For example, factional politics were not limited to the Guomindang. From 1941 to 1944, Mao pursued a "Rectification Campaign" to neutralize rivals and opponents within the CCP. Moreover, Service, his colleague John Paton Davies, and others tended to agree with Stalin that the Maoists were not real Marxists but only "radish" communists (i.e., red on the outside, white on the inside).

Mao had developed real talent for appeasing his American guests. A US Marine colonel, Evans Carlson, reported to President Roosevelt, "I had two long talks with Mao Tse-tung. He is a dreamer, of course; a genius. . . . He replied that the class struggle and the agrarian revolution as such would be given up—until the nation has passed through the preparatory stage of democracy. He felt that the state should own the mines, railways and banks, that cooperatives should be established, and that private enterprises would be encouraged. About foreign capital he felt that those nations which are willing to meet China on a basis of equality should be encouraged to invest. He was very friendly and cordial."[19] These Americans saw the "vigor and popularity" of the Communist regime but seem to have missed its ruthlessness. Mao's courting of Westerners alarmed one of his Soviet advisors, Piotr Vladimirov, who feared that he was on the verge of making a deal with the Americans and British that would decrease his reliance on Moscow.[20] Vladimirov need not have worried. Mao and his closest associates never intended to align themselves with the Western imperialists. Vladimirov complained, "Mao would have me believe talks with the Americans were an attempt, if not to fool them, then in any case to blackmail Chiang Kai-shek."[21] In this instance, Mao was telling the Comintern representative the truth.

These interactions with Americans reflected Mao's theory of "New Democracy." He taught that China's backwardness required the Communist Party to preside over a fully democratic, multiclass coalition with a mixed economy. Socialism would only come much later. This pleased his American listeners and served as good propaganda among the Chinese people given the Guomindang's increasingly authoritarian tendencies. However, that is not what Mao did when he came to power in 1949. While some officers and reporters on the scene were taken in by Mao's charade, that was less true of senior officials in Washington. Roosevelt wanted a strong, united postwar China that would be pro-American and serve as a buffer to the expansion of Soviet influence in the Far East. In Barbara Tuchman's view, "in the absence of coalition [between the GMD and CCP], we feared the Russians might use their influence, when they entered the war, to stir up the Communists and increase the possibility of a disunited China afterwards."[22]

American policy was, in the judgment of historian Robert Dallek, "reliance on Soviet force to fight the Japanese in Manchuria and intimidate Chiang into domestic political compromise; and a Soviet treaty of alliance with Chiang to compel Communist agreement to coalition rule."[23] It seems likely that Washington's real goal for the Dixie Mission was to gain leverage with Chiang Kai-shek by making it appear that America might give some support to Yan'an. US policy in China lacked coherence. What was the primary American objective in the Middle Kingdom? Was it to fight the Japanese; build China into a strong, modern power; or support Chiang Kai-shek's regime? President Roosevelt never saw fit to lay down a clear and consistent set of prioritized objectives.

When the new American ambassador to China, General Patrick Hurley, finally visited Yan'an, he presented a five-point peace plan to Mao: the GMD and CCP were recognized as equals; the CCP would participate in the Nationalist government; Communist military units would remain separate, but under Nationalist command; and Communist forces would receive Western aid. Hurley offered these terms to improve joint GMD-CCP resistance to the enemy, not because he was at all sympathetic to the Maoist cause. Privately he anticipated that the "Communist rebellion" would be suppressed after the war was over.

Chiang and Mao were not the only parties negotiating in something less than good faith. While some lower-level American officers and diplomats as well as some journalists regarded Yan'an positively, anticommunism prevailed in the corridors of power in Washington. Mao agreed to Hurley's generous terms and promised that he would support and follow the leadership of Chiang Kai-shek. Not surprisingly, the generalissimo refused to take the Communists into the Guomindang government unless they fully integrated their forces into his Central Army. Both sides continued to negotiate for the rest of the war but could not reach agreement. Meanwhile, Mao Zedong ordered his cadres to prepare for a struggle against Chiang and America.

The Stalemate Continues

In 1942, after their stunning series of victories over Britain, Holland, and the United States, the Japanese believed that they could finally destroy the Chinese Nationalist government, while they still contemplated an attack on the Soviet Far East. The Imperial Army planned Operation *Gogo*, a powerful strike into Sichuan Province that would capture Chongqing and Chengdu and crush the Guomindang regime. They transferred eighty-nine thousand troops to China from the home islands and Southeast Asia for this purpose. However, continuing uncertainty about the outcome of the Russo-German conflict and the unexpected American victories at sea and on Guadalcanal forced Tokyo to cancel these plans and transfer three divisions, scheduled to participate in *Gogo*, to the Southeast Asian and Pacific theaters.

During this period, the Japanese initiated some military operations for the sole purpose of resupplying their troops without burdening the national economy. In March 1941, they raided five cities along the Guangdong coastline to seize quantities of food and gasoline. Raids to capture food and other supplies from the opponent were so much a part of Japanese strategy that the Chinese referred to the Imperial Army as the "locust army." In May, Japanese forces began a major offensive in southern Shanxi Province. They committed one hundred thousand troops and 172 aircraft with the objective of destroying the two hundred thousand Nationalist troops in the area. They split their forces into two columns, attacking the target from north and south. Japanese infantry and cavalry soon encircled and annihilated many of the Chinese. In September, four Japanese divisions drove for Changsha, battering the Nationalist units in front of them. Lead elements of the enemy strike force entered the city on the 27th. Having achieved their objective of smashing Chinese forces in the area, the Japanese high command ordered a withdrawal from Changsha.

GMD troops reoccupied the city and harassed the retreating enemy. Chinese generals reported a great victory over the Imperial Army, but that was hardly the case. The Nationalists suffered seventy thousand casualties while the Japanese lost ten thousand men. Independent-minded provincial generals had not attacked the retreating enemy as vigorously as they might have. If not a victory, the battle for Changsha was telling in another way. The looming war against the Western Allies in the Pacific and Southeast Asia limited what the Japanese could accomplish in China. They could hold strongpoints and, to an extent, the communications channels connecting them, but they were overextended. In late December, the Japanese struck at Changsha again and, after fierce fighting, managed to retake the city. Nationalist forces counterattacked in January and, after more bitter combat, reclaimed Changsha yet again. In the fall of 1941, the Nationalist army planned a major offensive to retake Yichang as a preliminary to the reconquest of Wuhan. The plan called for employing two hundred thousand troops and almost 250 artillery pieces. However, local commanders, fearful of heavy combat losses and therefore of losing their political influence, committed only a fraction of those numbers to the battle. The offensive soon ground to a halt.

Back to Burma

Although Stilwell and other Americans continued to disparage Chiang Kai-shek for his alleged unwillingness to confront the enemy, Chiang strongly supported the idea of a major campaign to recapture all of Burma in 1943. Such an operation would require large numbers of Chinese and Indian troops executing both overland and amphibious assaults, British naval control of the Bay of Bengal, and powerful American air cover. Churchill opposed this plan from the beginning, both because he thought it a wasteful diversion from more important objectives and because he did not want Chinese troops liberating Burma. The British proposed a much smaller operation to retake only part of northern Burma. Chiang Kai-shek thought he had won approval for the larger operation at the November 1943 summit conference in Cairo, but within a month Roosevelt and Churchill backed away from this commitment because of the enormous requirements of the impending Operation Overlord. Chiang had to accept FDR's postponement of a major Burma offensive for a year.

Meanwhile, Japanese forces had established themselves at Songshan mountain where a key bridge spanned the Nujiang (Salween) River in western Yunnan Province, thus blocking any possible reopening of the Burma Road. Nationalist troops crossed the river in May 1944 and attacked the deeply entrenched enemy. When several frontal assaults failed, the Chinese tunneled into the mountain to blow up an enemy citadel and shatter the defensive position. Over 7,600 Chinese and 3,000 Japanese soldiers died before the GMD secured the area.

Only smaller Allied operations continued in northern Burma. The Chinese New First Army under Stilwell pushed slowly down the Hukawng Valley, while British troops attacked from India down the Arakan coast. On March 8, however, the Japanese launched a devastating counterattack against the British with three divisions. They soon surrounded sixty thousand British and Indian troops on the Imphal plain. This enemy advance also threatened to overrun the American air bases flying the Hump route, thereby depriving Stilwell's Chinese forces of their supplies. Chiang quickly sent two additional Chinese divisions into northern Burma, but he resisted sending his new, elite, American-equipped Y-Force until compelled to do so by strong pressure from Roosevelt.

Meanwhile, Stilwell's Chinese troops and an American special forces unit, Merrill's Marauders, battled both the Japanese and the monsoon to close in on Myitkyina. Another special forces unit, Wingate's Chindits, landed behind Japanese lines in gliders to cut them off from their supply base at Myitkyina. By this time, not only the Chindits but also all British and Indian troops had much better training in jungle fighting, and they attacked in much greater numbers than previously. In June, however, the attempt by the Chinese Y-Force to break through Japanese defenses on the Salween line failed when a determined counterattack by a mere 1,500 enemy troops drove back a Chinese division in panic.

Although Allied forces greatly outnumbered their opponents in this theater of war, the Japanese had one significant advantage. They had captured a Chinese Army codebook and cipher table, enabling them to read most of the enemy's communications. Despite the Japanese attack already underway from north China, Chiang sent two more armies south to support the Allied effort in Burma. In late January 1945, Y-Force, fighting its way east, linked up with X-Force, which had attacked from India. There were simply too few Japanese troops, pulled in too many directions, to defend northern Burma successfully. Indian and Chinese forces reduced the enemy garrisons in north Burma one by one. At some of those garrisons, the desperate defenders launched suicidal *banzai* charges when they could hold out no longer. This campaign was, in the judgment of historian Zang Yunhu, "the first in which Chinese forces took the offensive and won a decisive victory."[24]

Allied forces eventually recaptured enough of northern Burma to make the reopening of the Burma Road and the construction of the Lido Road (linking Assam in India with the Burma Road at Lashio) possible in early 1945. This objective had dominated the Allied war effort in East Asia and had cost the Chinese tens of thousands of casualties. It was scarcely worth the effort. During its first month of operation, the Lido Road brought in 1,111 tons of cargo, while pilots flying C-47 Dakotas over the Hump route delivered more than 71,000 tons of supplies. Most of that quantity went to support the thirty thousand Americans stationed in China.

Ultimately, neither the campaign in Burma nor the opening of the Burma and Lido Roads contributed much to the defeat of Japan. However, in the later stages of the war, the American and Chinese war efforts were mutually supportive. Beyond American supplies for the Nationalist army, US air and sea power interdicted supplies for Japanese forces in China, while the Chinese continued to hold down a large portion of the Imperial Army. On balance, American pressure on Chiang Kai-shek to commit his best forces to the Burma campaign was a mistake, especially in view of the crushing offensive the Japanese launched in China during 1944.

In late 1944 and early 1945, the British 14th Army commanded by General William Slim continued to push southward down the length of Burma by both overland and amphibious assaults. Allied forces now enjoyed substantial superiority in both men and matériel over their opponent. They recaptured Mandalay on March 20, 1945. Soon thereafter, the Burma National Army defected from the Japanese to the Allied side. Nonetheless, British and Indian troops still faced stiff enemy opposition, but overcame it with powerful tank and mechanized infantry attacks. Paratroop and amphibious assaults finally took Rangoon (Yangon) at the beginning of May.

Imphal and Kohima

While Chinese forces struggled in northern Burma, the decisive battle took place at Imphal and Kohima, where the Japanese committed 120,000 troops to bring the war to India. Responding to raids in 1943 by the Chindits, General Mutaguchi Renya, commander of the Japanese 15th Army, launched an assault across the Indian frontier designed to cut Allied communications with their north Burma front and forestall a British attack from Imphal. Having read that Chinggis Khan took cattle on his campaigns to provision his troops, Mutaguchi attached twenty thousand head of cattle to his force. The animals also carried the army's provisions. A great many of the cattle died while crossing rain forests, rivers, and mountains, leaving the Japanese without sufficient food or transport. The Allied command had four divisions and two regiments of mixed British, Indian, and Gurkha troops near Imphal. Mutaguchi struck in early March 1944 with three divisions and other mixed units, supported by Subhas Chandra Bose's anti-British Indian National Army. He also attacked Kohima to block Imphal's supply route.

The Japanese commander did not expect British forces to fight effectively given their poor performance in defending Malaya and Burma in 1942. He imagined his troops marching all the way to New Delhi with ease. He planned to surround the widely scattered British units, cut off their sources of resupply, and decimate them. Japanese forces were to move fast and "live off the land." Mutaguchi also believed that the enemy would be unable to employ tanks in the jungles and steep hills surrounding Imphal, so he left his most effective antitank guns behind. Virtually all his calculations proved wrong. He had not anticipated how difficult terrain and bad weather would impede his forces. Moreover, the Allies did use tanks effectively, frequently destroying the lighter enemy armor. Japanese troops ran short on supplies, while the British, now with command of the air, resupplied their surrounded units with parachute drops.

Mutaguchi did not encounter the same poorly led, disorganized Indian army of raw recruits that he had routed in 1942. Under the leadership of General William Slim, the Indian army was reborn as a determined, well-led, well-trained, well-supplied fighting force.[25] British forces now fought with a skill and determination not seen in 1942. By the beginning of May, the Japanese had lost almost half their troops; the remainder were exhausted and starving. Once again, poor logistics doomed a Japanese operation. The British commander, Admiral Lord Mountbatten, brought up large ground and air forces to punish the enemy and lift the siege of both towns. The Japanese began a general retreat after suffering fifty-five thousand casualties. This was the largest defeat Imperial forces had suffered thus far in the war.

It was at this point, with the situation improving in Burma, but with Japanese forces mounting a powerful new attack from north China, that the always difficult relationship between Chiang Kai-shek and "Vinegar Joe" finally exploded. Acting on outdated and misleading information supplied by Stilwell, in September of 1944 President Roosevelt sent an uncharacteristically insulting and demanding letter to the Chinese leader. Even though Chiang had already agreed to the main demands of the letter—Stilwell's appointment as commander of Chinese forces and reinforcing the Burma operation—Stilwell still insisted on delivering to Chiang the demeaning message (which he characterized as "hot as a fire cracker"). The jubilant general later composed this bit of doggerel to celebrate his "triumph."

> I've waited long for vengeance—
> At last I've had my chance.
> I've looked the Peanut in the eye
> And kicked him in the pants.
> The old harpoon was ready
> With air and timing true,
> I sank it to the handle,
> And stung him through and through.
> The little bastard shivered,
> And lost the power of speech.
> His face turned green and quivered
> As he struggled not to screech.
> For all my weary battles,
> For all my hours of woe,
> At last I've had my innings
> And laid the Peanut low.
> I know I've still to suffer,
> And run a weary race,
> But oh! The blessed pleasure!
> I've wrecked the Peanut's face.[26]

Stilwell was ecstatic for the moment, but he had overplayed his hand. The insulting tone of the letter deeply offended Chiang. He told Hurley he could work with Stilwell no longer and that he would not negotiate with the United States until it replaced the obnoxious general. Beyond wounded pride, Chiang feared that accepting such insults and agreeing to abridge Chinese sovereignty might lead discontented elements in the Guomindang to oust him from power. Roosevelt moderated his approach to the generalissimo, rejecting suggestions from General Marshall and Secretary of War Stimson to cut off all US aid to Nationalist China. He appointed General Albert C. Wedemeyer, an officer acceptable to Chiang, to replace Stilwell, and there was no more talk of an American officer being in command of all Chinese forces. Firing Stilwell and not giving his replacement command over any Chinese troops was not just a matter of appeasing Chiang. Given the *Ichigo* debacle, Washington worried that China might collapse. The Roosevelt administration wanted no responsibility for that looming disaster, especially in an election year. Wedemeyer also developed a negative impression of the generalissimo and his army, but he treated Chiang with much more tact than his predecessor and he admired the "tenacity and endurance" of Chinese forces resisting the enemy.

The *Ichigo* Offensive

Chiang and General Chennault feared that committing the best remaining Nationalist forces to Burma would expose Nationalist China to a potentially devastating enemy attack from the north—all the more so since Operation Overlord signaled to Tokyo that the Allies' main thrust in 1944 would be in western Europe. The Chinese leader warned President Roosevelt of the danger. Stilwell, however, dismissed that possibility, but once again he had underestimated the Japanese. Heavy American pressure, including Roosevelt's threat to cut off US aid, forced Chiang to send some of his best troops to Burma. Meanwhile, responding to losses in the Pacific, in September 1943 the Japanese high command defined an "Absolute

National Defense Perimeter" that gave priority to the Pacific, Southeast Asia, and Manchuria, leaving China proper in a secondary status. Forces there were to conduct essentially a holding action. Over half the troop strength in China was to be transferred to other fronts. Then the accelerating shipping losses inflicted by the American air and submarine interdiction campaign caused a drastic reassessment. The *Ichigo* offensive, lasting from April 1944 to February 1945, was the most significant departure from Tokyo's policy after 1938 of pacifying occupied areas, promoting Wang Jingwei's collaborationist alternative government, and blockading the Nationalist regime in Chongqing.

It was the largest operation the Japanese army had ever undertaken, employing over half a million troops, fully 80 percent of the forces available in China. It focused on the Beijing–Wuhan, Wuhan–Guangzhou, and Hunan–Guangxi railroad lines, with the triple

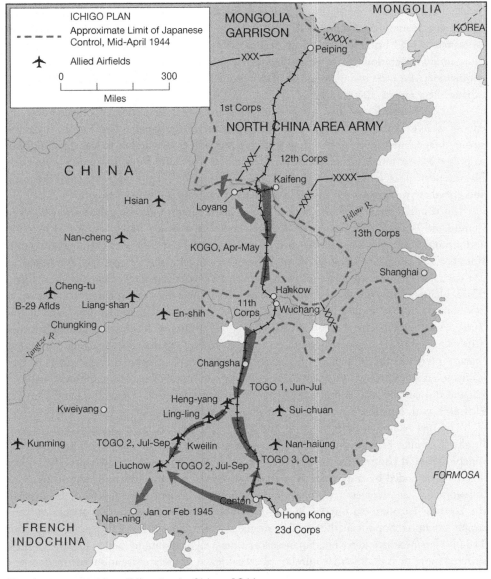

The Japanese Ichigo *Offensive in China, 1944*

objectives of annihilating the Guomindang army, destroying American air bases in China, and opening the Chinese segment of a primarily land-based supply route from Southeast Asia to the home islands. The campaign was fought on a nine-hundred-mile axis stretching from the Yellow River in north China southward to the Vietnamese border. The war in the Pacific was going badly for Japan at this point. Guadalcanal had been lost, and the Allies were reducing Imperial garrisons on New Guinea one by one, while Admiral Nimitz had begun his advance against Japan's central Pacific island outposts.

Already in the fall of 1943, an army General Staff study had demonstrated that no conceivable strategy held any reasonable prospect of victory for the empire. However sound it may have been, that was an unacceptable conclusion. Planners now imagined that they could find some way to halt the American advance across the Pacific, protect the homeland from bombing, and open an alternative to the seaborne supply route that US air and naval power had blocked. These accomplishments in turn would make it possible to launch a decisive counterattack across the Pacific in 1946. The *Ichigo* campaign was the silver bullet that, they fantasized, would bring all this about. Prime Minister Tojo and the emperor approved a more limited operation just to neutralize the American air bases. Once launched, however, commanders on the ground used the always available excuse of "operational necessity" to expand the scope of their mission.

Chiang Kai-shek and his generals initially misjudged the scale and objectives of the enemy assault. Once they understood the magnitude of the Japanese operation, there was strong disagreement within the Chinese high command over whether to stand and fight or to preserve their forces for another day. Under heavy pressure from domestic opinion and his American allies, Chiang committed to all-out resistance. He pulled forces from the north and elsewhere to amass seven hundred thousand troops to confront enemy.

In the initial phase of the operation, the Japanese fought to control the railway between Beijing and Wuhan. The Japanese 6th Army launched a major attack, supported by tanks and armored cars, into Hunan Province, supplemented by smaller units striking the target from bases in Guangzhou and Vietnam. Flying three to four missions per day, the American 14th Air Force pummeled the invaders, but also experienced staggering casualties themselves. Neither Chiang Kai-shek nor General Stilwell supported the defense of the province as resolutely as they should have. Chiang, fearing that the local commander, General Xue Yue, was disloyal to him, suspended shipments of supplies to the suspect general's forces. Stilwell happily went along with that decision. Jay Taylor believes that the American general "clearly preferred that Chiang suffer a serious defeat in Changsha and elsewhere in East China to enhance his own prospects of taking over command of the entire Chinese Army."[27] Chiang did support the commander defending Changsha itself, General Zhang Deneng. However, with Japanese forces closing in, Zhang fled the city. Chiang had him shot.

The first enemy assaults in April and May went well. A large Japanese force, spearheaded by tanks, crossed the Yellow River and attacked toward Luoyang. Three hundred ninety thousand Chinese troops, under General Tang Enbo, were spread across the region. The city, defended by only three Nationalist divisions, fell after thirteen days of fighting. Subsequently, at Hengyang (a major railway junction ninety miles south of Changsha), the Japanese encountered bitter Chinese resistance as well as American air attacks on their supply columns. Seventeen thousand Nationalist defenders held out for six weeks against 110,000 Japanese attackers. The Japanese lost almost eight thousand men, while the Chinese suffered more than double that number of casualties. A desperate situation was made worse by the refusal of both Chiang and Stilwell to send additional supplies to the besieged city.

For Stilwell, Hengyang was merely leverage in his struggle for power with Chiang Kai-shek. The town was finally overrun on August 8. After this string of victories, the Japanese might well have turned west to attack the Nationalist capital at Chongqing, but the need to position major forces against an anticipated American landing on the southeast China coast (an invasion that never came) foreclosed that option.

Chinese forces faced an additional and surprising enemy at this point—their own civilian population. Tired of the war and angry over soldiers mistreating them, the local people attacked some of the Nationalist military units. General Jiang Dingwen recorded that:

> During this campaign, the unexpected phenomenon was that the people of the mountains in western Henan attacked our troops, taking guns, bullets, and explosives, and even high-power mortars and radio equipment. . . . They surrounded our troops and killed our officers. We heard this pretty often. . . . At the same time they took away our stored grain, leaving their houses and fields empty, which meant that our officers and soldiers had no food for many days.[28]

Clearly, in some areas, such as famine-ravaged Henan, there had been a fundamental breakdown of trust between the regime and its people. This bruising series of defeats badly damaged Nationalist army moral as well. When the enemy attacked Guangxi Province southwest of Hunan, resistance began to crumble. Desertions escalated. Chiang Kai-shek ordered senior commanders shot, but that did not stop the panic. Deserters sacked the large city of Guilin and then burned it down to cover evidence of their own looting. Once again, great streams of refugees fled the devastation. They were strafed from the air or caught by pursuing Japanese forces who slaughtered many of them. Still other Chinese died at Allied hands. American bombers devastated the Wuhan complex because it was a vital enemy transport hub.

The long and costly *Ichigo* offensive seemed to have achieved its objectives. The Nationalist army lost about three-quarters of a million troops. US air bases at Hengyang, Guilin, Liuzhou, Nanning, Suichuan, and Nan-hsiung were overrun. Japanese forces also secured an overland supply route through China to Indochina. Yet they failed to achieve the larger objectives of reversing both the precipitate decline of Japan's war effort and the tide of battle in the Pacific. Though battered by serious loses, Chiang Kai-shek still maintained major armies in the field and did not capitulate. The Japanese success in occupying more of China meant that their forces were spread more thinly than ever. The Americans reestablished air fields farther into the interior of China, well behind Nationalist army lines, and they began supplementing their medium-range B-25 bombers with long-range B-29s. They were soon not only devastating Japan's overland supply routes but also striking targets in the homeland itself. For all its battlefield victories, Operation *Ichigo* was a strategic failure.

Chiang Kai-shek and his Guomindang regime were, of course, losers in the *Ichigo* campaign. In addition to the loss of 750,000 troops, the Nationalist government lost half of the territory previously under its direct rule and a quarter of its remaining industrial resources. It also lost the confidence of its American allies. Beyond that, moving so many troops from north China—forces that had been blocking Mao Zedong and his Eighth Route Army—opened the door for Communist expansion in that region. Thus, less than a year before the outbreak of civil war between the Nationalists and the Communists, the *Ichigo* campaign resulted in greatly weakening the former while strengthening the latter. Hans van de Ven suggests that the real motive for both the Imphal and the *Ichigo* offensives was the Japanese desire to win one last big victory, thereby forcing "the USA and Britain, facing a difficult campaign in Europe, to the negotiation table."[29] That strategy failed as well.

After the *Ichigo* offensive, in the spring of 1945 General Okamura Yasuji launched a new attack aimed at Hubei Province. He intended to forestall a Chinese campaign designed by General Wedemeyer to retake Hunan and Guangxi Provinces as well as Guangzhou and Hong Kong. Now, however, the Japanese no longer had the margin of superiority over their Allied opponents that had made them practically invincible earlier. The Chinese mustered sixty-six divisions, with powerful air support, to blunt and then drive back the enemy operation. The Americans had built new air bases at Lahekou and Zhijiang, which the Japanese intended to destroy. The Japanese 20th Army succeeded in knocking out the Lahekou airfield, but when it marched on the Zhijiang base, it met five fully modernized Chinese divisions supported by fifteen partially modernized divisions and two hundred American warplanes. The Chinese repelled the enemy attack, inflicting heavy Japanese casualties. By the spring of 1945, Imperial forces began to retreat from some of their *Ichigo* conquests to shorten their defensive perimeter and to prepare for an anticipated American landing on the China coast (though US officials had already dropped earlier plans to use their own troops on the mainland).

Even while the offensive continued, Tokyo made new peace offers to Chongqing. After Tojo's dismissal, the new cabinet offered to withdraw Imperial troops from China proper, but the Nationalists would have to recognize Japanese control of Manchuria, Mongolia, and Xinjiang; come to terms with Wang Jingwei's collaborationist regime; oust all American and British forces from the country; and become a virtual ally of Japan. Those were unacceptable terms.

August Storm

Stalin had agreed at the Tehran and Yalta Conferences to Allied requests that the USSR enter the war against Japan within ninety days of Germany's defeat. At Yalta, Roosevelt, Churchill, and Stalin had agreed—without Chiang Kai-shek's participation or even knowledge—that the USSR would receive the Kurile Islands and recover the southern half of Sakhalin Island after the war. They also guaranteed Moscow's existing control of Outer Mongolia and its "preeminent interests" in Manchuria. The USSR was authorized to lease Port Arthur as a military base and use the port at Dalian. In return, Stalin promised to respect China's territorial integrity, evacuate Manchuria as soon as possible, and not interfere in Chinese domestic politics. While Chiang was left temporarily in ignorance, Stalin immediately briefed Mao. The Chinese Communist leader may not have liked the violations of Chinese sovereignty contained in the Yalta Accords, but he was wise enough not to protest—and he was delighted that the Red Army was on its way. Beyond these territorial gains, Stalin wished to eliminate Japan as a great power in East Asia. He feared that his Western allies might prove too soft, allowing the rapid recovery of German and Japanese strength and thereby threatening Soviet security.

Moscow had already notified Tokyo on April 5, 1945, that it would not renew its 1941 Neutrality Pact. Soon Red Army forces in the Far East grew from forty to eighty divisions. Fearing that the war might end too soon for his purposes, in July Stalin pressured his commanders in Siberia to begin their invasion earlier than planned. On August 9, the USSR launched a three-pronged attack, code-named August Storm, across the Manchurian and Inner Mongolian borders. The Red Army struck with 1.5 million troops, 3,704 tanks, and 1,852 self-propelled guns. It caught the Japanese almost completely by surprise. Although the invaders met strong resistance in a few places, the once formidable Kwantung Army had been drained of troops and equipment for the *Ketsu-Go* operation to defend the home

Emperor Hirohito was revered as a descendant of the gods, but he had remarkably little influence on the formulation of policies.
Source: Wikimedia Commons

islands against an anticipated American invasion. Much of the Japanese force remaining in Manchuria consisted of briefly trained and inadequately equipped recent recruits. Most crucially, they lacked any weaponry capable of stopping the massive armored assault unleashed by the Soviets. Only the repeated need to stop for more supplies and fuel slowed the Russian advance. The Soviets suffered thirty-six thousand casualties in the operation, while eighty thousand Japanese were killed. Soviet forces took over 640,000 prisoners. Apparently the fight-to-the-death ethic had eroded in the Kwantung Army.

The Japanese government surrendered soon after the Americans dropped atomic bombs on Hiroshima and Nagasaki and the Soviets invaded Manchuria. Emperor Hirohito called on his troops throughout the empire to lay down their arms. General He Yingqin, acting on behalf of Chiang Kai-shek, took the Japanese surrender in Nanjing on August 9, 1945.

Conclusion

It has become a staple of Western historiography to depict Nationalist China as dictatorial, reactionary, incompetent, corrupt, preoccupied with the menace of Chinese Communism, and essentially sitting out the war after American entry ensured ultimate victory. Barbara Tuchman's bestseller *Stilwell and the American Experience in China*, and journalist Theodore White's widely read *Thunder Out of China*, as well as memoirs by US Foreign Service officers and other Americans, indict Chiang and the Guomindang as incapable and unwilling to fight Japan. At the same time, they mythologize Chinese Communist resistance as heroic, more reformist than revolutionary, and much larger in scale than it actually was.[30] Tuchman declares that "from first to last Chiang Kai-shek had one purpose: to destroy the Communists and wait for foreign help to defeat the Japanese."[31]

There are elements of truth in this interpretation. Wartime China was no democracy, and the common people sometimes suffered at the hands of their own government. Chiang could be ruthless, and he was compelled to play a delicate political game within the Guomindang as well as with regional military commanders and with the Chinese Communists. Yet, as the above account has demonstrated, Nationalist forces continued active resistance to the enemy throughout the war, often on a very large scale. Hans van de Ven concludes, "The Nationalists were determined to resist the Japanese. . . . For China itself, the Sino-Japanese War was all. China would either outlast Japan or be destroyed as an independent nation or even a culture."[32] Moreover, most Americans of that time did not understand that, for Chiang Kai-shek and for Mao Zedong, their rivalry was implacable—a fight to the death for supremacy.

Notes

1. Hans van de Ven, "Campaigns in China, 1937–1945," in *The Cambridge History of the Second World War*, vol. 1, *Fighting the War*, ed. John Ferris and Evan Mawdsley (Cambridge: Cambridge University Press, 2015), 263.

2. Roosevelt knew that China was not a great power at this point. His insistence on elevating China's status sprang from the country's potential, American public opinion, and the necessity of keeping China fighting. Robert Dallek, *Franklin D. Roosevelt and American Foreign Policy, 1932–1945* (New York: Oxford University Press, 1979), 329.

3. van de Ven, "Campaigns in China," 267.

4. Hans van de Ven, *China at War: Triumph and Tragedy in the Emergence of the New China* (Cambridge, MA: Harvard University Press, 2018), 164.

5. Vasilii I. Chuikov, *Mission to China: Memoirs of a Soviet Military Advisor to Chiang Kaishek* (Norwalk: EastBridge, 2004), 65.

6. Chuikov, *Mission to China*, 17.

7. Frank Dorn, *Walkout; with Stilwell in Burma* (New York: Crowell, 1971), 75–79; Michael Schaller, *The US Crusade in China* (New York: Columbia University Press, 1979), 153.

8. Jay Taylor, *Generalissimo: Chiang Kai-shek and the Struggle for Modern China* (Cambridge, MA: Harvard University Press, 2011), 199.

9. Taylor, *Generalissimo*, 200.

10. Rana Mitter, *Forgotten Ally: China's World War II, 1937–1945* (Boston: Houghton Mifflin Harcourt, 2013), 3.

11. Alexander V. Pantsov, *Mao: The Real Story* (New York: Simon & Shuster, 2012), 314.

12. Georgi Dimitrov, *The Diary of Georgi Dimitrov*, ed. Ivo Banac (New Haven, CT: Yale University Press, 2003), 67.

13. Hans J. van de Ven, "War, Cosmopolitanism, and Authority: Mao from 1937 to 1956," in *A Critical Introduction to Mao*, ed. Timothy Cheek (Cambridge: Cambridge University Press, 2010), 87.

14. Yang Kuisong, "Nationalist and Communist Guerrilla Warfare in North China," *The Battle for China: Essays on the Military History of the Sino-Japanese War of 1937–1945*, ed. Mark Peattie, Edward Drea, and Hans van de Ven (Stanford, CA: Stanford University Press, 2011), 323.

15. Taylor, *Generalissimo*, 274.

16. Maochun Yu, *OSS in China: Prelude to the Cold War* (New Haven, CT: Yale University Press, 1996), 187.

17. Carolle J. Carter, *Mission to Yenan: American Liaison with the Chinese Communists, 1944–1947* (Lexington: University Press of Kentucky, 1997), 13.

18. John S. Service, *Lost Chance in China: The World War II Dispatches of John S. Service* (New York: Random House, 1974), 179–86, 196–97, 271, 312.

19. Evans F. Carlson, *Evans F. Carlson on China at War, 1937–1941* (New York: China and US Publication, 1993), 37–38.

20. Peter Vladimirov, *The Vladimirov Diaries: Yenan, 1942–1945* (Garden City, NY: Doubleday, 1975), 225, 227–30.

21. Vladimirov, *The Vladimirov Diaries*, 282. Mao also assured Vladimirov, "No matter what form the contacts with the Americans will take, our revolution will eventually turn against the imperialists" (p. 233).

22. Barbara Tuchman, "If Mao Had Come to Washington: An Essay in Alternatives," *Foreign Affairs* 51, no. 1 (October 1972): 47.

23. Dallek, *Franklin D. Roosevelt*, 523.

24. Zang Yunhu, "Chinese Operations in Yunnan and Central Burma," in Peattie, *The Battle for China*, 386.

25. Raymond A. Callahan, *Triumph at Imphal-Kohima: How the Indian Army Finally Stopped the Japanese Juggernaut* (Lawrence: University Press of Kansas, 2017), 50.

26. Joseph W. Stilwell, *The Stilwell Papers* (New York: W. Sloane, 1948), 263–64.

27. Taylor, *Generalissimo*, 273.

28. Mitter, *Forgotten Ally*, 320.

29. van de Ven, *War and Nationalism in China*, 48.

30. Barbara Tuchman, *Stilwell and the American Experience in China* (New York: Bantam, 1972); Theodore White and Annalee Jacoby, *Thunder Out of China* (New York: William Sloane, 1946).

31. Tuchman, *Stilwell*, 213.

32. Hans van de Ven, "The Sino-Japanese War in History," in Peattie, *The Battle for China*, 464–65.

CHAPTER 19

The Allies Strike Back in the Pacific

The Aftermath of Japanese Victory

In the relatively brief period from December 1941 to May 1942, Imperial Japanese forces had won a stunning series of victories, taking possession of the riches of Southeast Asia and the East Indies; humbling the British, French, and Dutch Empires; and driving the Americans out of the Philippines and gravely damaging the US Pacific Fleet. Admiral Yamamoto's prediction to former prime minister Konoe had been correct; he had run wild for almost six months. The Japanese had conquered a supposedly self-sufficient and defensible empire in East Asia. Only in China did victory continue to elude the Imperial Army. Taken together with Germany's extensive conquests throughout Europe and North Africa, this period marked the high tide of Axis advance. The emperor hoped that Japan might soon be able to negotiate peace with the Western powers. Not only the emperor but also many at the court, in the government, and in the military believed that if Britain and the United States did not immediately sue for peace after the disasters of Pearl Harbor and Singapore, then one more major Japanese victory would surely crush their fighting spirit. They badly underestimated the resolve of their enemies.

Moreover, each Japanese conquest raised new strategic challenges. The flanks and supply lines of the newly acquired territories required protection. Potential bases for enemy counterattacks had to be neutralized. A host of tantalizing strategic opportunities now presented themselves. With Britain strained to the limit defending its home islands and its position in the Middle East and with American power in the Pacific dramatically reduced, the way seemed open to even greater Japanese triumphs. The "victory disease" spread unchecked. Japanese advances had come so quickly and easily, often against numerically superior foes, that it seemed as if Imperial forces were invincible while their opponents were weak and cowardly. While the navy General Staff thought it best to rest and replenish the Combined Fleet, some of the more aggressive admirals began to envision a vastly expanded perimeter (beyond the already established 14,200-mile outer limits!) for their Greater East Asian Empire—one running from Hawaii to Australia to India. That would deprive the Americans of the bases needed to push back Japan's advance and allow Imperial forces to link up with the Wehrmacht (now presumably about to roar through the Middle East toward the Red Sea and the Indian Ocean). In that event, Britain's war effort would be fatally undermined and the United States forced to conclude peace on Tokyo's terms. President Roosevelt feared exactly that possibility, particularly if Chinese resistance collapsed.

These dreams would founder on two serious deficiencies in the Japanese war effort—inadequate resources and an entirely dysfunctional decision-making apparatus. As impressive as the Japanese armed forces were, there were simply not enough troops, ships, or planes to conquer Australia, Hawaii, and India, while also bringing the "China Incident" to a successful conclusion. Moreover, there was no authoritative source of strategic decision-making in Tokyo—no equivalent to Hitler or Stalin, Churchill or Roosevelt. The emperor did not provide strong leadership, the army and navy often worked at cross-purposes, and factions battled one another within each branch of the armed services. Thus, the navy could not take advantage of Britain's weakness in the Indian Ocean and still conduct the offensives that some of its officers demanded in the central and south Pacific.

For example, Japanese naval officers contemplated seizing the Vichy French–controlled island of Madagascar, but the British beat them to it. Royal Marines stormed the island on May 5 and secured its capital after three days of tough fighting against the Vichy garrison. Had Japan taken the island, it could have severed vital British supply routes to India and the Middle East as well as facilitated a link with advancing German forces. Similarly, the navy had to abandon its ambitious plans to overrun Australia because the army, still focused on China and a possible attack on the USSR, refused to provide enough troops. There was no one at the center of the political system, certainly neither the emperor nor even Prime Minister Tojo, who could impose a coherent strategy and a rational set of priorities on the national war effort. The Imperial General Headquarters–Government Liaison Conference should have provided overall coordination, but in practice each service retained complete autonomy, while such powerful field commanders as Admiral Yamamoto sometimes forced their views on the central authorities.

American strategic planners faced complex challenges as well, though they did not lack clear lines of authority. President Roosevelt and the Joint Chiefs of Staff could and usually did enforce their strategic decisions and priories. Nonetheless, there were serious differences over strategy between the army and the navy as well as heated rivalries among ambitious senior officers in each of the services. Army leaders wanted the earliest possible confrontation with the Germans in Europe, while navy commanders gave priority to battling the Japanese in the Pacific. Within the Pacific theater, General MacArthur demanded absolute priority for his projected advance from the southwest toward the Philippines. Admiral Chester Nimitz, commander of the Pacific Fleet, countered that a drive through the central Pacific (with operations controlled by the navy) would be a much more effective use of limited resources.

After the Pearl Harbor disaster, Roosevelt and Churchill reaffirmed the "Europe First" doctrine. Realizing that Nazi Germany was by far their most dangerous Axis opponent, the two Western leaders intended to give priority in allocating men and equipment to the European theater of operations. Japan's conquests could be liberated after the Third Reich had been defeated. In practice, however, several factors combined to dilute this resolve. Lack of adequate shipping to transport large American armies to Europe and supply them there delayed major operations on the Continent. The terrible U-boat danger in the north Atlantic during 1942–1943 magnified that problem.

The British also strongly opposed any direct assault on Nazi-occupied Europe in 1942. Churchill still hoped to find some "peripheral" route to victory. In addition, American commanders, even with their limited resources and options at this point, were anxious at least to harass the Japanese and keep them from strengthening their defensive perimeter. Therefore, more US troops, ships, and aircraft were assigned to the Pacific than originally planned. As late as the end of 1943, there were more American forces in the Pacific than in Europe and Africa, though crises in the Mediterranean and North Africa in the latter months of that year required a reassertion of the Europe First priority. Yet American forces in the Pacific were still substantially weaker than their opponent in 1942—especially in numbers of battleships and aircraft carriers and in quality of warplanes.

Churchill and Roosevelt also agreed on a division of their respective responsibilities in this now global war. The Atlantic and western Europe would be a joint Anglo-American assignment. The Mediterranean, the Middle East, and the Indian Ocean were to be under British control, while the United States would lead the campaign in the Pacific. Washington divided this latter theater into two separate commands. It gave MacArthur control of the Southwest Pacific Area, which included Australia, New Guinea, the Solomon Islands, the Philippines, and most of the Dutch East Indies. The remainder of the Pacific, dubbed the Pacific Ocean Area, fell under the jurisdiction of Admiral Nimitz. This unusual division of the Pacific into two theater commands violated the principle of concentration of force, introduced logistical inefficiencies, and of course generated a great deal of friction between rival commanders. The Pacific theater of operations was a vast region, so some subdivision of commands was probably inevitable.

Moreover, launching two separate axes of advance—southwestern and central—greatly complicated the problems facing the Japanese. The most important reason for this division, however, was political. MacArthur's immensely successful self-promotion campaign had convinced most Americans that he was the indispensable savior of the nation's then tenuous military position in the Pacific—an irony, since any other general who had so bungled the defense of the Philippines would have lost his command. Public opinion demanded that he play a leading role in driving back the Japanese. Beyond that consideration, MacArthur thought that he should command all US forces. He even had presidential ambitions. Both the army and the Roosevelt administration wanted the troublesome general as far away from Washington as possible. A separate southwest Pacific command, based in Australia, served that purpose.

Japan Strikes in the South and Central Pacific

Beyond the victory disease, a series of relatively minor American raids in February and March of 1942 also pushed the Japanese to expand their perimeter still farther. US carrier-based aircraft surprised and angered the enemy by striking Kwajalein, Rabaul, Wake, and Marcus islands as well as Lae and Salamaua on New Guinea. Then on April 18, sixteen army B-25 Mitchell bombers, flying from the carrier *Hornet* and under the command of James Doolittle, launched a daring raid on Tokyo and three other cities.

From the American perspective, this small raid was essentially a morale-boosting exercise for a public yearning for some symbol of retaliation, but it had an effect on the Japanese entirely disproportionate to the limited physical damage inflicted. It spread panic among the civil population and, more importantly, deeply embarrassed the military. Army leaders were finally convinced to provide more troops for operations in the central and southwest Pacific, even if it meant drawing forces from a projected attack on Chongqing in China. Although grand campaigns to conquer Australia and Hawaii were beyond Japan's capabilities, the army and navy agreed on smaller operations to take Tulagi, in the Solomon Islands chain, and Port Moresby, near the southeast tip of New Guinea. These operations were to block American communications with Australia and foil Allied counterattacks.

In undertaking their plan (code-named Operation MO) to capture Port Moresby and other key bases in the region, the Japanese enjoyed a significant advantage in numbers of warships and planes, but they lacked any knowledge of the enemy navy's position or intentions. Conversely, code breaking, radio traffic analysis, aerial reconnaissance, and the reports of Australian "coast watchers" (civilians equipped with binoculars and shortwave radios scattered throughout the region) provided the Americans with a rough picture of their opponent's plans. Action began on May 3, 1942, with a Japanese landing on Tulagi (unopposed because the small Australian garrison had already departed). Planes from the carrier USS *Yorktown* attacked the ships supporting the Tulagi invasion, sinking or damaging six of them.

This encounter initiated the Battle of the Coral Sea (May 4–8), the first engagement in naval history in which the opposing sides never saw each other or exchanged direct gunfire. The Japanese were now painfully aware that one or more American carriers were operating in the area. Each side searched for the other. On the morning of May 7, a Japanese scout plane spotted and misidentified the destroyer *Sims* and the oiler *Neosho* as two US carriers. A dive-bomber attack quickly destroyed them both. Later that morning, planes from the *Yorktown* and the carrier *Lexington* found and sank the enemy light carrier *Shoho*. The next day each side searched for and attacked the other.

The Americans struck first. Torpedo planes from the *Yorktown* failed to hit their target, while the dive-bombers scored only two hits on the fleet carrier *Zuikaku*, temporarily preventing any more aircraft from launching. Planes from the *Lexington* attacked the fleet carrier *Shokaku*, but once again all the torpedoes missed and only three bombs found their mark, damaging its flight deck. The Japanese had already launched their own planes against the US carriers. Dive-bombers hit the *Lexington* hard. A series of internal explosions forced abandonment of the ship before an American destroyer sank it deliberately. The attack also seriously damaged the *Yorktown*. Both fleets quickly retired from the battle because of the damage each sustained. In terms of ships lost, the Battle of the Coral Sea was a tactical victory for Japan. In the broader strategic sense, however, the Americans benefited from the outcome. Both of the Imperial Navy's heavy carriers returned to Japan—*Shokaku* to repair extensive damage and *Zuikaku* to replace more than half of its planes and pilots lost in this ferocious engagement. Unwilling to continue Operation MO without their carriers, the Japanese canceled the invasion of Port Moresby. For the first time, the Allies had repulsed a Japanese advance.

The Midway Disaster

Meanwhile, Admiral Yamamoto was planning an even larger operation in the central Pacific. While not immune to the victory disease, the admiral still believed that Japan could not win a protracted war with the United States. Victory could be secured only by provoking a decisive engagement with the US Pacific Fleet as soon as possible, a battle that he was sure his much stronger Combined Fleet would win. Surely then Washington would see the wisdom of a negotiated peace favorable to Japan. Yamamoto identified an attack on Midway, 1,300 miles west of Hawaii, as the provocation that would lure the American ships to their doom. The Naval General Staff strongly opposed this plan, but a combination of the Doolittle Raid, which deeply humiliated the Japanese military, and the prestigious admiral's threat to resign overcame all opposition. He mobilized an imposing armada—seventy-one powerful warships, including four fleet carriers—for the operation (code-named MI). He also sanctioned a diversionary raid on Dutch Harbor and the occupation of Kiska and Attu in the Aleutian Islands in the far north.

Unlike the attack on Pearl Harbor, which was painstakingly planned and practiced, the Midway operation bore the marks of overconfidence and carelessness. Yamamoto and the commander of his carrier strike force, Admiral Nagumo, launched the operation without adequate knowledge of the strength and location of enemy naval forces. They believed that both the *Lexington* and the *Yorktown* had been sunk in the Coral Sea. Previously, submarines had monitored US warships at Pearl Harbor, but the presence of the *Yorktown* was missed because the submarines' refueling station at French Frigate Shoals had been taken by the Americans. The Japanese dispatched a picket line of submarines to detect any approaching enemy vessels, but too late. Two US Navy carrier task forces had already entered the operational area before the submarines reached their stations. The Japanese thought they would catch the Americans by surprise once again.

There were additional mistakes beyond these deficiencies in intelligence gathering. The Aleutian diversion served only to dissipate Japanese strength. The two light carriers assigned to that operation would be sorely missed in the coming Battle of Midway. The Americans were not distracted. Admiral Nimitz concentrated his forces against the approaching Combined Fleet. The Japanese also allowed the five battle groups of the Combined Fleet to separate from each other by as much as five hundred miles. Once the action started, quick response of one group in support of another was impossible. Finally, launching what they expected to be the decisive showdown with the US Pacific Fleet, when four Japanese carriers usually with their fleet were unavailable, betrayed a serious underestimation of enemy strength and aggressiveness. Although Yamamoto appreciated the value of carrier-based air power, he still expected the awesome power of his battleships, especially the super battleship *Yamato*, to dominate the final confrontation with the US Pacific Fleet. The *Yamato* was by far the largest battleship in the world, a seventy-three-thousand-ton monster bearing nine massive eighteen-inch guns.

Admiral Nimitz, in contrast, suffered neither from overconfidence nor from lack of good intelligence about his adversary. The Americans had begun to break the Japanese JN-25 naval code. The Japanese had intended to change that code at the beginning of April (i.e., before the Coral Sea and Midway battles), but the difficulties of getting new codebooks to all the elements in their now far-flung empire caused a two-month delay in this process, giving US forces an invaluable window of information at this critical turning point in the Pacific war.

The Americans anticipated a major Japanese attack in the central Pacific, though they did not know the specific target of the assault. They solved that problem by a clever ruse. Suspecting that the location, code-named "AF" in intercepted messages, might be Midway Island, they broadcast a fake, unencoded message that the water treatment plant on the island had broken down. A subsequent Japanese transmission to field commanders about a water shortage at the target confirmed that "AF" was Midway. The Americans enjoyed yet another advantage—radar. Midway Island and the US Navy's major ships all had radar, while Nagumo's four carriers had none.

Nimitz was determined to defend the approaches to Hawaii as well as the line of communication with Australia, even though the naval forces under his command were significantly weaker than those deployed by the enemy. He counted on the element of surprise to equalize the fight. The three carriers available to him, organized in two task forces, hid northeast of Midway, out of range of carrier-based Japanese scout planes, while longer-range American reconnaissance aircraft, flying from Midway, searched for the Combined Fleet. Even fielding three American carriers required a near miracle. Nimitz could deploy the *En-*

terprise and the *Hornet* (the latter recently transferred from the Atlantic), but the *Yorktown* had been badly mauled in the Battle of the Coral Sea. Engineers estimated that repairs would take ninety days, but hundreds of workmen swarmed over the stricken ship to perform only the most essential, temporary repairs in just over forty-eight hours! The ship could fight, but given its compromised structural integrity, any further damage might be fatal.

The Japanese began the operation on June 3 with an air raid on US military installations at Dutch Harbor in the Aleutians. The attack destroyed all the oil storage tanks at the base and damaged a barracks and a hospital. The Japanese then occupied the barren, almost unpopulated islands of Kiska and Attu without opposition. Tokyo announced another "victory," but by any realistic measure the operation was a failure and a waste. It was supposed to draw off American strength from the Midway battles and prevent the United States from using the Aleutians as a base for bombing or a route for invading Japan. The former purpose failed, while the latter was never a serious possibility. The only positive outcome of the operation benefited the Americans. They shot down a Zero fighter, which crash-landed without extensive damage. US forces recovered the plane, studied it intensively, and used that knowledge to create a new generation of American fighters (especially the Grumman F6F Hellcat) that would outperform the Zero.

The real action began later that same morning when a US flying boat (a seaplane that could land directly on the water) spotted the Japanese invasion force headed for Midway. B-17 bombers attacked these ships without effect, and flying boats equipped with torpedoes scored only one minor hit on a transport. The next morning American air patrols sighted the enemy carriers, which had already launched their first attack toward Midway. Over the island, US fighters rose to meet enemy, but Zeros shot down most of these obsolete planes. The attacking bombers blew up the power-generating station and some oil storage tanks, but the runways were still usable and most of the island's big guns still firing. The commander of the Japanese attack force radioed to his carrier that another attack would be necessary to soften Midway's defenses before the assault troops came ashore. At the same time, an American attack launched from Midway against the carriers failed completely. Old and slow US dive-bombers were massacred, while B-26 bombers could not hit their targets.

The need for a second strike against Midway caused Admiral Nagumo to make a fateful decision. All his bombers not used in the first wave against the island had been loaded with torpedoes and armor-piercing bombs in case enemy ships were sighted. Now the admiral ordered those planes lowered to the hangar deck and rearmed with high explosive bombs suitable for attacking targets on the ground. Soon a Japanese scout plane discovered US ships in the area, but the pilot did not recognize carriers among them. Nagumo reaffirmed his decision to continue preparations for a second strike on Midway. Moreover, as historian Gordon Prange has suggested:

> Another reason why the Nagumo staff made no change of tactics at this moment was that the experience of the past six months had imbued these men with a bone-deep contempt for American naval aviation, a contempt which the land-based attacks now under way did nothing to dispel. The individual American airman was brave, but seemingly could not hit a Japanese ship from the inside with the hatches closed.[1]

At this moment, after his crew had rearmed the second-wave bombers, the unfortunate admiral finally received word that spotters had identified at least one carrier among the American ships sighted. To compound matters, the planes of the first wave returning from

Midway, low on fuel and some damaged by antiaircraft fire, were approaching and needed to land soon. Nagumo ordered the second-wave planes lowered back to the hangar deck and hurriedly rearmed with torpedoes. Normal safety procedures were ignored in that chaotic process. Fuel lines and dismounted bombs remained in the open rather than safely stored. Some commentators have severely criticized Admiral Nagumo for his decision to rearm his second-wave bombers. Historian Paul Dull calls it "the most crucial miscalculation of the war."[2] Gordon Prange, however, has argued that, "under the circumstances of the moment, Nagumo took the logical, sensible course."[3]

It was at that point that the Americans struck. When US search planes reported sighting enemy carrier forces earlier that morning, Admiral Raymond Spruance (Task Force 16) ordered the immediate launching of all his planes, even though the enemy targets were at the absolute range limit of the American torpedo bombers. Planes from the *Hornet* could not find the enemy, but those from the *Enterprise* did. The American attack was uncoordinated and, at first, unsuccessful. Lacking any US fighter escorts, the torpedo bombers dove in first and were once again slaughtered without inflicting any damage on their targets. Zeros drove off torpedo planes from the *Yorktown* before they could do any harm.

The sacrifice of many torpedo planes was not entirely in vain. They distracted the Japanese fighter cover from the American dive-bombers high above, and they disrupted Japanese flight deck operations. Those dive-bombers struck without serious fighter opposition. One of their bombs hit the flight deck of the fleet carrier *Kaga*. Crowded with planes readying for takeoff, the deck became an instant inferno. Another bomb penetrated the hangar deck below where it detonated planes that had just been rearmed and refueled. One plane after another exploded until the whole deck was engulfed in fire. The same fate befell the fleet carrier *Akagi*, which, in the words of one surviving Japanese officer, turned into "a burning hell." Dive-bombers from the *Yorktown* found the fleet carrier *Soryu* and scored three quick hits, which caused a series of internal explosions.

Thus far, the fourth Japanese fleet carrier, *Hiryu*, had escaped the attention of the American strike force. It now launched its planes to counterattack the US carriers. Three of their bombs struck the *Yorktown*, but its damage control crews managed to contain the fires and keep the ship operational. Then a torpedo penetrated the ship's fuel tanks, cut all electrical power, and stopped the vessel dead in the water, forcing its abandonment. Meanwhile, Admiral Spruance launched his planes again. This time they found *Hiryu* and hit the doomed carrier four times in quick succession. When this disaster—the loss of all four Japanese fleet carriers—was reported to Yamamoto, the admiral initially ordered his battleships and cruisers to press forward to find and attack the American task forces, but, calculating the risk, he soon turned his ships around and canceled the invasion of Midway. The Imperial Navy had never experienced a debacle of that magnitude. Beyond the four carriers, Japan had lost 332 planes and 2,155 highly skilled pilots, aircraft technicians, and other specialists, as well as one cruiser sunk and another out of action for a year.

The navy suppressed news of the defeat and even claimed a victory. It informed the emperor but hid the disaster from the army and the public. Though no one in Tokyo would admit it, Japan had lost the strategic initiative in the Pacific war. Doubtless, Yamamoto and Nagumo had made serious errors, but historians Jonathan Parshall and Anthony Tully suggest a deeper cause for the disaster beyond the errors of individuals. In their view, "it is clear that it wasn't just Yamamoto or Genda who failed at Midway—in several important ways, the entire institution of the Japanese Navy was to blame as well."[4] These researchers contend that the root cause of the Midway catastrophe was the multiple failures of the Imperial Japanese Navy, as a culture, to learn from the past, anticipate future developments, and adapt quickly to the changing battlefield situation.

Guadalcanal

After taking Tulagi, the Japanese discovered a suitable location for an airfield on the nearby island of Guadalcanal (a rare find given the rough topography of islands in the Solomons). Admiral Ernest King had already ordered Nimitz to begin offensive operations in the lower Solomons. Nimitz planned attacks, code-named Watchtower, on Tulagi and two adjacent small islands. Now he added Guadalcanal to the list. After preliminary air and sea bombardments of that island, marines stormed ashore unopposed on August 7. The six-hundred-man Japanese construction battalion and more than two thousand conscripted laborers immediately fled into the surrounding jungle. Within two days, marines captured the partially completed airfield. In contrast, the marines who landed on Tulagi, Gavutu, and Tanambogo met fierce resistance from enemy combat troops. Japanese tactics included entrenching themselves in dugouts and coral caves, allowing the lead element of marine forces to pass through their lines unmolested, and then ambushing the main body of the unit. They also employed numerous snipers and savage nighttime counterattacks.

Lieutenant Colonel Merritt Edson characterized Japanese resistance on Tulagi as essentially suicidal:

> The Nip defense was apparently built around small groups in dugouts with no hope of escape. They would stay in there as long as there was one live Jap. . . . We pulled out thirty-five dead Japs from one dugout. In another we took out thirty. Some of these people had been dead for three days. But others were still in there shooting. . . . In none of these places was there any water or food. . . . In one case there were three Japs cornered. They had one pistol. They fired the pistol until they had three shots left. Then one Jap shot the two others and killed himself.[5]

Though suffering casualty rates exceeding 20 percent in some units, the marines cleared the three smaller islands within four days. The Japanese high command was stunned. They had not thought the Americans capable of mounting offensive operations before late 1943.

American forces came to see their enemy as devious and despicable. The marines captured a Japanese sailor soon after landing on Guadalcanal. He said that there were others in his crew who might surrender as well. Lieutenant Colonel Frank Goettge, an intelligence officer, led a twenty-five-man patrol to find these potentially informative sailors. The ill-fated patrol came under fire and was virtually wiped out. It is not known whether there was any connection between the sailor and the troops who attacked the Goettge patrol, but every American believed that the unscrupulous Japanese had perpetrated a fake surrender leading to an ambush.

The Imperial Navy moved quickly in an attempt to choke the American assault by attacking its shipping. On the moonless and foggy night of August 8–9, Admiral Mikawa Gunichi slipped his strike force of seven cruisers into the approaches to Guadalcanal and Tulagi, completely undetected by the Allied warships guarding the area. Although the Allied ships outnumbered and outgunned their opponent, superior Japanese doctrine, training, and equipment for nighttime encounters, combined with considerable disorganization and miscommunication by the Allied vessels, led to the destruction of one Australian and three US cruisers, with extensive damage to two more cruisers. The Imperial Navy suffered no ship losses in this one-sided engagement, though one of its cruisers was sunk by a US submarine on its return voyage to Rabaul. Mikawa's victory in this Battle of Savo Island was incomplete, however, because he chose not to proceed with an attack on the Allied transports, fearing an assault by carrier-based enemy bombers. He did not know that Admiral Fletcher, afraid of raids by Japanese land-based planes, had moved the carriers out of operational range, leaving the marines and their supply ships unprotected. A flight of land-based Japanese bombers failed to attack the transports the next day, instead sinking a US destroyer. In both cases, the Japanese manifested their strong preference for battling enemy warships rather than merchantmen.

In these clashes on and around Guadalcanal, the Americans lacked one key advantage they had enjoyed in the battles of the Coral Sea and Midway—the ability to read enemy encrypted messages. The Japanese had finally changed their codes. Other radio intercept techniques (traffic analysis and location analysis), aerial reconnaissance, coast watchers, and information from friendly natives partially compensated for this deficiency, however. To secure their battlefield radio communications, American forces employed Navajo and other Native American marines to transmit messages in their native languages, which the Japanese could not understand.

Constructing and defending an airfield was both the objective of the marines' mission and the key to their survival. Navy construction battalions (or Seabees) used captured Japanese equipment to build an airstrip because there had not been time to unload their own equipment before the transports made a hasty departure. By August 18, a rough landing strip was ready. They named it Henderson Field after an aviator who died in the Battle of Midway. The first planes, nineteen Wildcat fighters and twelve dive-bombers, arrived two days later. The Cactus Air Force, as the squadrons at Henderson Field were called, was never very large, but it played a crucial role in the struggle for Guadalcanal.

The Imperial Army failed in its initial attempt to dislodge the Americans on land. Although there was disagreement in the high command about the size and purpose of the American presence on Guadalcanal, they committed troops on the assumption that the enemy attack on the island was only a small-scale raid. After an ineffective air strike, they dispatched a nine-hundred-man detachment commanded by Colonel Ichiki Kiyonao. Not realizing that he faced the 1st Marine Division in well-prepared defensive positions, Ichiki launched a frontal night assault that resulted in the annihilation of most his force. On August 24–25, a Japanese convoy approached Guadalcanal with two thousand troops, under the protection of two heavy and one light aircraft carriers. They were challenged by a three-carrier American task force. In the ensuing battle, the light carrier *Ryujo*, a destroyer, and a transport were lost, while several other Japanese transports and warships were damaged. The reinforcement mission was aborted. The *Enterprise* was hit badly enough that it had to return to Pearl Harbor for repairs. At the end of August, a submarine-launched torpedo hit the carrier *Saratoga*, putting it out of action for two months and reducing American carrier strength in the region to two.

Beyond the courage and tenacity of the fighting men on both sides, logistics largely determined the outcome of the struggle for Guadalcanal. The vast distances involved, the scarcity of shipping, and the vulnerability of transports to enemy interdiction made supplying and reinforcing their troops enormously difficult for each side. For the Americans, the distance was more than seven thousand miles from San Francisco to ports in Australia or New Zeeland, and then more than 1,300 miles to Guadalcanal. For the Japanese, the route

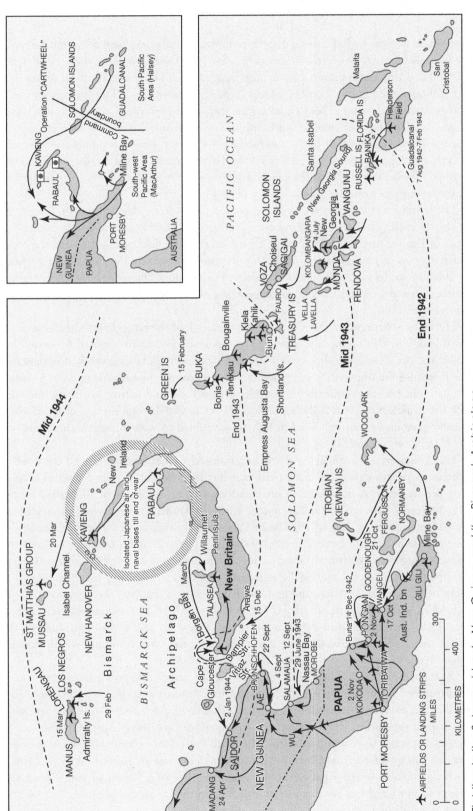

Fighting in the Solomon Islands, New Guinea, and the Bismarck Archipelago

to their bases at Truk or Rabaul was over three thousand miles and then down the 665-mile New Georgia Sound (known to marines as "the Slot") to the island. After the sinking of the *Ryujo* and aborting the transport convoy, the Japanese could only reinforce and resupply at night without suffering dive-bomber attacks from Henderson Field. This meant they could no longer use merchantmen, because such slow ships could not travel the Slot in one night. Instead, they had to load troops, ammunition, and food onto destroyers or even submarines, but those vessels could not accommodate the troops' heavier equipment (especially artillery). The Japanese resupply line (called the Tokyo Express by the marines) was severely constricted for the remainder of the campaign, a factor that proved fatal in their attempt to oust the Americans from the island.

The battle for this island established a pattern for fighting throughout the Pacific. As historian Eric Bergerud suggests, "the nature of ground combat in the South Pacific was unique in this century. . . . Because the dense jungle battlefield greatly lessened the tactical effectiveness of modern weapons, the war became a ferocious slugging match between light-infantry armies at extremely close quarters. Furthermore, the radical battle ethos of the Japanese initiated a vicious circle of violence where no mercy was asked or given, creating a war of annihilation."[6]

Throughout September and October, the outcome of the struggle for Guadalcanal remained in doubt. During the day, American transports and warships operated freely to bring supplies and occasionally to shell enemy positions. Before nightfall, however, they departed quickly because the Imperial Navy owned the waters around the island after dark. Japanese destroyers and cruisers frequently shelled Henderson Field and marine positions. Air raids struck the Americans almost daily but seldom did extensive damage because coast watchers and radar gave ample warning. Wildcat fighters scrambled to meet the attacks, and bombers flew off to be out of harm's way.

The American commander on the island, General Archer Vandegrift, did not confine his forces to passive defense of their perimeter but launched numerous probes to disrupt enemy deployments. A major assault on Henderson Field could not be forestalled indefinitely, however. Major General Kawaguchi Kiyotake launched three-pronged attacks on the nights of September 12 and 13. The first assault disintegrated as the attackers struggled through dense jungle and came under heavy shelling. The next night, however, in the Battle of Bloody Ridge (also known as Edson's Ridge), Japanese troops penetrated marine lines at several points. The assault was finally repulsed by devastating artillery fire, bombing, and strafing by the Cactus Air Force and by fierce hand-to-hand combat. The Japanese lost 850 troops killed while the marines suffered 104 casualties. This bitter and entirely unexpected defeat finally forced the army high command in Tokyo to realize the magnitude of the problem they faced on Guadalcanal and to understand that they could not simultaneously conduct major campaigns on the island and in New Guinea.

On the same day that Edson's men repelled the last desperate enemy assaults, the Americans dispatched major reinforcements for Guadalcanal, accompanied by two carriers and a battleship. En route to the island, the carrier *Wasp* and a destroyer were torpedoed and sunk by a Japanese submarine, while the recently commissioned battleship *North Carolina* was so damaged that it had to be withdrawn from the south Pacific for major repairs. Now only one American flattop (*Hornet*) remained in this theater of operations (compared to six carriers potentially available to the Japanese). Once again, the Imperial Navy had won a great victory over enemy warships, but that was of little help to the Japanese soldiers on Guadalcanal because none of the US troopships had been stopped.

Guadalcanal was a miserable place to fight. The marines and their Japanese adversaries had to contend with short rations, foul weather, terrible terrain, and incapacitating disease. Supply problems put the marines on a repetitive diet of only two meals a day. It was much worse for the Japanese, who subsisted on just a third of their normal ration—mainly rice and soybeans, supplemented by whatever they gathered from the jungle. Travel through dense jungle and fetid marshes or over steep ridges tired out units before they reached their objectives. Debilitating heat and humidity alternated with torrential rains (up to ten inches of precipitation in a single day) exhausted men and hindered operations. Fatigue and diarrhea were the soldiers' constant companions. Dengue fever and malaria were epidemic for both sides. Some Allied units had a malaria infection rate of 85–95 percent. Marine Bud DeVere later recalled the misery of fighting on Guadalcanal: "Fatigue was extraordinary. I don't recall sleeping a night through on any island that was under fire. If there wasn't some kind of incoming fire, you'd have guard duty. Or torrential downpours. There was more rain there than anywhere I've ever seen. Constant rain. Everything was mud. I had an extraordinary case of trench foot. It was caused from being constantly in water. There was water in all of the foxholes or dugouts. Some of the nights when they had all-night bombardments or attacks you'd sit in a foxhole with just your head out of the water."[7]

Weakened by exposure and malnutrition, the Japanese lost more men to disease than to marine guns. Their troops began calling Guadalcanal "Starvation Island" and "the Island of Death." Japanese soldiers on the island lost an average of forty pounds, while marines typically lost eighteen pounds.[8] Logistics, especially food supply, was a pervasive weakness of the Japanese war effort. Japanese troops carried very little food with them into battle. If they ran short, they were expected to forage for it or capture it from the enemy, or even grow it themselves. Throughout the war, of the 1.74 million Imperial soldiers and sailors who died, 60 percent succumbed to starvation rather than combat wounds.

Both sides determined to bring in large-scale reinforcements in parallel efforts to break the bloody stalemate on Guadalcanal. The Americans landed an army regiment on October 13, protected by the carrier *Hornet*, the battleship *Washington*, and five destroyers. This naval force arrived on the night of October 11–12 to discover a group of three Japanese cruisers and two destroyers. The Japanese were caught by surprise because, up to this point, the US Navy had not ventured to challenge them in night operations. In the ensuing action, known as the Battle of Cape Esperance, the Imperial Navy lost a cruiser and a destroyer, with another cruiser and destroyer heavily damaged. The Japanese commander was killed, and his mission to bombard Henderson Field had to be abandoned. A US destroyer was sunk, and another destroyer plus a cruiser were damaged. The Americans did not find the enemy reinforcement convoy, which delivered its troops and equipment unmolested. The next morning, however, Cactus Air Force planes sank two destroyers escorting that convoy. The Americans called the stretch of water between Guadalcanal and Florida Island "Iron Bottom Sound" because so many ships had been sunk there.

Henderson Field received its worst bombardment ever on the 13th—slammed by newly arrived enemy artillery, pummeled by more bombing, and pounded by almost a thousand shells from two battleships. The attack cratered the main landing strip, destroyed much of the fuel reserves, and put most US bombers out of action. Mechanics worked feverishly around the clock, cannibalizing parts from unsalvageable planes to patch together those less damaged. They siphoned gas from aircraft that would never fly again to launch a handful of planes, soon supplemented by bombers from the *Hornet*. US pilots found plenty of targets, for the large raid on Henderson Field was timed to coincide with the largest enemy convoy yet—now including six transport ships. The Americans managed to sink half the merchantmen, but not before they had disgorged almost five thousand troops and two-thirds of their supplies.

The Japanese commander, General Hyakutake Harukichi, now had twenty thousand troops at his disposal, though most of the men who had been on the island for more than a month were weakened by fatigue, malnutrition, and disease. Nonetheless, higher authorities pressed him to launch a second major assault on Henderson Field. The Japanese underestimated American strength (now at twenty-three thousand men) by 50 percent, and they assumed that the southern perimeter of the US enclave, surrounded by dense jungle, was weakly defended. The operation began on October 23 with a feint along the coast against the west side of the US position, employing all the heavy artillery and tanks available to convince the enemy that this was the real axis of attack. Meanwhile, seven thousand troops had to cut their way undetected through miles of almost impenetrable jungle to the south.

In addition to his own equipment, each man carried an artillery shell on his back, and the artillerymen each lugged a heavy piece of their disassembled field guns. Units strayed off course in the trackless vegetation, communications broke down, and the troops were exhausted by the time they reached the American perimeter. US artillery fire crushed the diversionary attacks on the west side of the base, destroying all the Japanese tanks. Due to poor communication, confusion, and exhaustion, Japanese troops were committed piecemeal to the main line of attack on the south side, only to be mowed down as they staggered from the jungle into intense fire from the American defenders. The fighting on all perimeters was savage and personal. Marine sergeant Mitchell Paige described one intense engagement:

> The first Japanese wave swarmed into our position. It was a confusing struggle lit up by flashes from machine-gun fire, grenades, and mortars. Dark shapes crawled across the ground. Men fought on the ground with bayonets and swords, shouting curses at each other. In the flickering light I saw three Japanese charge our number-two gun. I shot two of them but the third ran through one of my gunners with a bayonet, and actually lifted him into the air. I shot him too. The Japs swarmed into another gun position and killed or wounded four men. It was so confusing that I think the Japs didn't really know I was there. One took a swipe at me with a bayonet, which I warded off with my hand. Someone had shot him that instant and he dropped at my feet dead.[9]

Overall, Japanese losses exceeded 2,500 troops, while the Americans lost fewer than 90 men. Once again, the Japanese dogma that "spirit" (meaning discipline and determination) could overcome superior enemy firepower proved disastrously wrong.

The day after the battle ended on land, another major naval engagement erupted near Santa Cruz Island. The new and aggressive American naval commander in the south Pacific, Admiral William "Bull" Halsey, ordered his forces, spearheaded by carriers *Hornet* and *Enterprise* (just returned from repairs in Hawaii), to search for Japanese ships approaching Guadalcanal. Elements of Admiral Yamamoto's Combined Fleet were in the area too, and they found the Americans first. Bombers from carriers *Shokaku*, *Zuikaku*, *Zuiho*, and *Junyo* sank the *Hornet* and severely damaged the *Enterprise*, but not before the US ships had launched their own strikes, which damaged *Shokaku* and *Zuiho* and the cruiser *Chikuma*. Halsey ordered US warships to withdraw before suffering any more losses. The Imperial Navy was the clear winner in this engagement in terms of ships lost or damaged, but the Japanese experienced very high losses of experienced aircrews.

Even after their costly losses at Bloody Ridge and Henderson Field, Japanese commanders continued to believe that they could win a decisive victory over the Americans in the struggle for Guadalcanal. This confidence sprang from misinformation. They thought that they had sunk four US aircraft carriers and a battleship at the Battle of Santa Cruz Island and that their forces had come very close to breaking the marines' defense line south of Henderson Field. Therefore they continued to plan for another big offensive on the island, but the difficulties of reinforcement and supply undermined their efforts. Meanwhile, the Americans reinforced the long-suffering marines on the island with fresh army units and expanded the Cactus Air Force. In November, US forces launched attacks on Japanese defenders depleted by malnutrition and disease, inflicting heavy casualties.

Sea battles continued unabated as well. In the second week of November, Admiral Yamamoto dispatched eleven transports carrying seven thousand troops and protected by two battleships, a cruiser, and eleven destroyers. The big guns of the battleships were to bombard Henderson Field, preventing US planes from attacking the convoy. Allied intelligence learned of the operation, and Admiral Nimitz ordered five cruisers and eight destroyers to disrupt the enemy. In the ensuing melee (a rare, close-quarters gun battle between surface ships), the Japanese lost the battleship *Hiei* and two destroyers, while the Americans lost two cruisers and four destroyers. As a result, Yamamoto postponed shelling the airfield and landing the reinforcements.

The price for this "victory" was high for the United States. Two admirals and 1,437 sailors were killed. In a tragedy that gripped all of America, five Sullivan brothers died serving on one of the cruisers. The next day a Japanese cruiser and destroyer shelled Henderson Field but failed to stop an air operation that sank the cruiser and seven of the approaching transports. Late that night, US battleships *South Dakota* and *Washington* and several destroyers intercepted the four surviving transports, protected by a battleship, two cruisers, and nine destroyers. Once again, sharp-eyed Japanese lookouts spotted one of the American ships before US radar identified the enemy. The *South Dakota* was so damaged that it had to withdraw. At the same time, the *Washington* approached undetected and wrecked the battleship *Kirishima*. The four transports beached themselves, but American artillery and bombers destroyed them before much of their cargo was unloaded. The Japanese were forced to cancel the major assault they had planned to recapture Henderson Field.

Attempts to use only submarines to resupply Japanese forces on the island proved completely inadequate and led to a food crisis by late November. At best, the Japanese troops were getting only one-third of their normal ration. To address this problem but preserve their dwindling number of destroyers, the Imperial Navy developed a new supply method. They packed provisions in oil drums and then pushed them over the side near the shore so that the destroyers spent minimal time in the dangerous waters around Guadalcanal.

Given the already large and still growing disparity on Guadalcanal between American and Japanese troop strength (fifty thousand versus about fifteen thousand), warplanes, and resupply capability, the Imperial General Headquarters took the painful decision at the end of December to withdraw from the island. They masked the evacuation process with a highly skillful and ultimately successful deception campaign. Until they discovered that almost all the Japanese had left the island, US commanders continued to believe that the increased destroyer traffic down the Slot was bringing in reinforcements for a renewed enemy offensive. Ultimately, 10,652 (mostly those still able to walk), out of over thirty thousand who had served on the island, were evacuated. Those survivors unable to walk but still strong enough to fire their weapons were ordered to continue resisting the enemy. Those who could do neither were expected to commit suicide.

Historian Richard Frank argues that, "quite simply, Guadalcanal was the literal turning point of the war in the Pacific."[10] The combination of Midway and Guadalcanal snuffed out any hope for a quick Japanese victory and transformed the conflict into a war of attrition that the island nation could not win. The decision to defend a vast arc from Burma to New Guinea to Wake Island to the Aleutian Islands meant that Japanese forces were spread very thin. Initiative now passed to the Allies, who could determine which point on that perimeter to attack with decisive local superiority. Strongly defended Japanese bastions would be bypassed and isolated. Their garrisons were left to die of starvation or disease. Unfortunately, the indigenous peoples of those islands often shared the same fate. The defeats at Midway and Guadalcanal also shattered the myth of Japanese invincibility, a crucial factor for the morale of US troops and the American home front. The campaigns on Guadalcanal and New Guinea taught the Allies how to fight the Japanese successfully and, as in North Africa and Italy, enforced a brutally Darwinian process of selecting combat officers with the skills and temperament required to defeat tenacious opponents.

The Guadalcanal landing was also an important learning experience for American forces in amphibious assaults and combined-arms engagements. It should have taught the Japanese a lesson, too. The brutal and bloody fighting on the island disproved a fundamental assumption underlying Tokyo's approach to the war—namely, the belief that the Allies could not endure the sacrifices necessary to reclaim Japan's recent conquests. Japanese leaders, however, chose to ignore the implications of that unpalatable truth. According to British field marshal William Slim, "the fundamental fault of [Japanese] generalship was a lack of moral, as distinct from physical, courage. They were not prepared to admit that they had made a mistake, that their plans had misfired and needed recasting."[11]

For all its apparent strengths, the Japanese army suffered from numerous weaknesses that the Allies learned to exploit. Japanese soldiers manifested high morale and excellent combat skills, and they possessed good light-infantry weaponry. They were led by excellent noncommissioned and lower-grade officers. Their small-unit tactics were exceptional. However, their logistics, planning, interservice coordination, and intelligence were woefully inadequate. The inability to supply its forces adequately was a fatal flaw. In Bergerud's judgment, "Ultimately, the Allies' ability to come to grips with this supply nightmare, and Japan's failure to do so, proved crucial to the Allied triumph."[12]

The New Guinea Campaign

Cancellation of the amphibious assault on Port Moresby did not mean that the Japanese had lost interest in that strategically valuable town. They landed sixteen thousand troops at Buna, on the east coast of New Guinea, on July 21–22 to secure that important coastal area and take Port Moresby by crossing the Owen Stanley mountain range along the Kokoda Trail—a narrow, sixty-mile path over extremely rugged terrain. MacArthur had underestimated the Japanese. He assumed, wrongly, that a small force at Milne Bay and a thin screen of troops at the crest of the Kokoda Trail could hold off the enemy while he prepared his own counteroffensive. By mid-September, Japanese troops had reached the end of the trail, within thirty miles of their objective, but they could advance no farther. A combination of stiffening Australian resistance and the impossibility of pushing adequate supplies up the

Kokoda Trail halted their drive. Only a quarter of the six thousand troops who had begun this operation remained combat effective, due not only to battle casualties but also to disease and malnutrition. Moreover, reinforcements, initially intended for this battle, were diverted to the desperate struggle on Guadalcanal. Supplied with fresh troops, the Australians began to push the exhausted Japanese back down the trail. In early November, Australian forces inflicted a shattering defeat on the Japanese.

Meanwhile, Japanese naval infantry attacked the airstrips the Allies had built at Milne Bay on the southeast tip of New Guinea. The Japanese seriously underestimated the defenders' strength, and an Allied air raid sank a third of their transport barges. Nonetheless, a determined attack initially punched through Australian defenses to reach the nearest airfield, but then Australian reinforcements and Allied air support repulsed the Japanese, forcing them to abort the entire operation. General MacArthur then determined to eliminate the main enemy beachheads in the Buna-Gona area, but he badly underestimated both the number of defenders and the strength of their fortifications. A three-pronged Allied attack in mid-November, lacking artillery and tanks, was stopped cold with heavy casualties. Terrible jungle conditions and tropical disease further hindered the Australian and American troops. One veteran of this campaign later wrote:

> The men at the front in New Guinea were perhaps among the most wretched-looking soldiers ever to wear the American uniform. They were gaunt and thin, with deep black circles under their sunken eyes. They were covered with tropical sores. . . . They were clothed in tattered, stained jackets and pants. . . . Often the soles had been sucked off their shoes by the tenacious, stinking mud. Many of them fought for days with fevers and didn't know it. . . . Malaria, dengue fever, dysentery, and, in a few cases, typhus hit man after man. There was hardly a soldier, among the thousands who went into the jungle, who didn't come down with some kind of fever at least once.[13]

The Japanese endured similar agonies. One survivor later remembered:

> I was suffering from malaria and malnutrition, so weak I could only carry a pistol. . . . Soldiers sat like mummies in front line foxholes. . . . Because of malnutrition, after dark we had trouble seeing. . . . Enemy patrols freely penetrated our front lines. Everyone had malaria or amebic dysentery and there were many nervous breakdowns or shell shock. . . . The enemy attacks intensified and it seemed like we're bombed every day as the seriously wounded begged the battalion surgeon to kill them.[14]

The combatants were not the only ones to suffer. On New Guinea and elsewhere in the Pacific, hungry Japanese soldiers stole produce and livestock from the villages and sometimes forced native people to work for them. The Allies bombed native villages. Both the Japanese and Allied troops sometimes raped native women.[15]

MacArthur blamed the defeat at Buna-Gona on poor leadership and replaced the local commander with Lieutenant General Robert Eichelberger. He ordered Eichelberger "to take Buna or not come back alive."[16] Finally, supplied with tanks, artillery, and air support, the Allies captured Gona in December and broke the remaining Japanese resistance in January 1943. This success came at a very high price. MacArthur had told reporters that he always sought to minimize Allied casualties, but his blunt-force, frontal assault tactics resulted in three times the number of Allied deaths compared even to the bloody fighting on Guadalcanal. When the operation was over, a "MacArthur Communiqué" credited the victory solely to the general's tactical brilliance.

After clearing Buna-Gona, the Allies launched a series of amphibious operations, gradually pushing along the northeast coast of New Guinea, though they did not eliminate the Japanese presence on the island until 1945. Growing American air, naval, and amphibious capabilities, together with the advantages of breaking Japanese codes, enabled MacArthur to make a virtue of necessity in these coast-hopping assaults (since he did not have the strength to drive the enemy before him in one continuous sweep). The Japanese intended to reinforce their New Guinea costal garrisons, especially at Lae, but the rapidly growing Allied air power made that impossible.

The Battle of the Bismarck Sea on March 2–4, 1943, demonstrated this dramatically. The Japanese marshaled a 6,500-man force on eight transports headed for Lae. Allied code breakers discovered this mission, which was then attacked repeatedly by American and Australian bombers. Up to this point, bombing of ships by Allied land-based aircraft had been relatively ineffective. Now, however, under the leadership of General George Kenney, new bombing tactics were implemented that produced much better results. All eight enemy transports were sunk. Only about a sixth of the Japanese reinforcements reached Lae. Japanese air power declined as America's grew. A Japanese soldier noted the effects of US bombing: "We saw the skeletons of our aircraft littering graveyard airfields; we saw the countless masts of our sunken ships sticking out of the water; we knew no ships would ever again come to this port."[17]

Having the strategic initiative allowed MacArthur's forces to attack tactically important but more lightly defended targets along the nine-hundred-mile New Guinea coast while isolating and bypassing Japanese strongpoints. Exceptions occurred at Biak (May 27 to August 17, 1944) and Wakde-Sarmi (June 14 to September 1, 1944) when Allied forces engaged larger concentrations of well-entrenched enemy troops, making very slow progress and experiencing heavy casualties. Biak could have turned into an Allied disaster because the Japanese intended to send major reinforcements there along with two super battleships, but the American landing on Saipan forced them to divert resources back to the central Pacific.

The central and southwest axes of Allied advance reinforced each other by stretching enemy resources too thin to be effective. Japanese soldiers on New Guinea continued to fight as fiercely as their emaciated bodies permitted. By the summer of 1944, they ate little more than starch from sago palms. The food situation deteriorated to the point that in December their commander ordered them not to eat the flesh of dead comrades but permitted the consumption of dead Allied troops.[18] When the once-proud Japanese 18th Army surrendered at the end of the war, only 10,000 men remained of the 140,000 deployed to New Guinea.

MacArthur was anxious to avoid delays as had happened at Biak and Wakde-Sarmi. He was in a hurry. For him New Guinea was just a stepping stone to his real goal—returning to the Philippines. Historian Stephen Taaffe gives MacArthur's direction of this campaign a mixed evaluation. "As a military commander, MacArthur had both significant strengths and weaknesses. In New Guinea, many circumstances beyond the realm of personal leadership—Ultra intelligence, material and technical superiority, and Japanese strategic errors—helped counterbalance his military failings and contributed greatly to his victory. MacArthur's ultimate success in the campaign and as a commander, however, was due to his self-confident ability to recognize and take advantage of the American military assets."[19]

Japan lost its greatest naval hero, Admiral Yamamoto, at this time. Responding to a series of Japanese defeats, the admiral organized a morale-boosting tour of the northern Solomons. American radio intercepts revealed the details of this plan, and President Roosevelt authorized an ambush of the architect of Pearl Harbor. On April 18, American P-38 Lightning fighters intercepted and shot down Yamamoto's plane, which crashed in the New Guinea jungle. His death was universally mourned throughout Japan.

Meanwhile, MacArthur intended to strike directly at the main enemy base in the region, Rabaul, but Washington vetoed that risky plan. The ensuing compromise, Operation Cartwheel, called for attacks in stages up the coast of New Guinea and northward along the Solomons. In July 1943, green US Army troops suffered significant casualties and made slow progress against well-entrenched enemy defenders on the island of New Georgia. They finally overcame the Japanese by using light tanks to blast enemy pillboxes and fortifications. The marines and the army were learning to fight the Japanese effectively, but at a steep price in the lives of young men. The sharpest fighting occurred in November and December 1943 when a US Army division and a marine division landed on Bougainville Island where the Japanese had built several airfields and had a good anchorage, manned by over forty-five thousand troops, to protect the approaches to Rabaul. Forewarned by radio intercepts, the US Navy beat off an attempt by the Imperial Navy to disrupt the invasion, while the American forces established a beachhead and defended it against vigorous counterattacks. Two subsequent American air raids on Rabaul extensively damaged Japanese warships and planes there, forcing an end to operations against the Bougainville landings.

On Bougainville, the grim pattern of warfare established on Guadalcanal and New Guinea was repeated—vicious jungle fighting made worse by the need to battle terrain, weather, and tropical disease. Casualties were once again high. The two American divisions initially employed in the invasion had to be replaced by the end of the year. A major Japanese counterattack in March 1944 was repulsed with severe enemy losses. The remaining Japanese forces withdrew deep into the interior of the island to continue a protracted and bloody resistance. As their control over the island expanded, the Allies constructed several airfields from which to bomb Rabaul and other Japanese bases.

The planned assault against that enemy stronghold was never launched. At the Quadrant Conference in Quebec in August 1943, Roosevelt, Churchill, and the Combined Chiefs (British and American) decided to isolate and bypass the powerful Japanese base at Rabaul, suppressing it by frequent air raids. Here was the fatal flaw in Tokyo's strategy of defending an extensive Pacific perimeter (with much more open space than strongpoints) and depending on attrition to wear down the opponent's will to fight. The Allies, now possessed of superior air and sea mobility, flowed around and sealed off major Japanese island bases, cutting their lines of communication and supply and leaving their large, trapped garrisons impotent. Imperial Army and Navy commanders, however, refused to see the grim truth now facing them. As historian Gerhard Weinberg suggests, "the leaders in Tokyo displayed a bankruptcy of strategic thinking."[20]

Having been battered in the Allies' first wave of attacks, the Japanese military resolved in late September 1943 to create a more manageable inner defense zone running from the Kuriles through the mid-Pacific, western New Guinea, Sumatra, and Burma. They planned to increase aircraft production greatly and repulse further enemy advances along this strategic "barrier." They also continued to entertain dreams of destroying the Nationalist regime in China and conquering India, after which they could then reassign those forces to the Pacific theater. The plan was hopelessly unrealistic. Japanese industry could produce only a fraction of the fifty-five thousand planes the military demanded. It also failed to consider that American strength in men, ships, and aircraft continued to grow at an astonishing pace. Moreover, their plans for China and India far exceeded their operational capacity.

A War of Cruelty and Annihilation

The campaigns on most of the Pacific island battlegrounds were small in scale compared to the massive operations carried out in Europe, but for intensity and ferocity of combat, only the savage fighting between the Wehrmacht and the Red Army on the eastern front matched the unrelenting hatred and brutality of the struggle between the Japanese and the Allies. Each side hated the other passionately and intended to destroy its opponent without remorse or compassion.

When the war expanded in late 1941, Emperor Hirohito enjoined his troops to treat prisoners of war with the "utmost benevolence and kindness," a command reinforced by the orders of several senior army commanders. The Japanese armed forces had no history of mistreating prisoners. In the Russo-Japanese War and World War I, the Japanese, for the most part, had respected international agreements on the treatment of captives. However, in the 1930s and 1940s, Imperial troops routinely tortured and killed Allied prisoners (just as they had already done for years in China). Combat veteran Samuel Grashio noted that it was "commonplace to find the bodies of one's comrades, tightly bound, obviously tortured, disemboweled, with their severed genitals stuffed in their mouths."[21]

Just as in China, these atrocities in the Pacific theater cannot be explained as merely the explosions of individual soldiers or small groups of men stressed beyond their breaking point in combat. Japanese troops on Guadalcanal were told that the marines were monsters and homicidal maniacs especially recruited from prisons and insane asylums. Surrender was never an option for Imperial forces. Besides being a crime against the military code, the act of surrender profoundly disgraced not only the individual but also his family and community. The handbook issued to all soldiers enjoined them: "The Destiny of the Empire rests upon victory or defeat in battle. Do not give up under any circumstances, keeping in mind your responsibility not to tarnish the glorious history of the Imperial Army with its tradition of invincibility."[22] Japanese troops fought to the death rather than surrender, no matter how hopeless the situation. They also readily sacrificed their lives if they could take one or more enemy soldiers with them. Historian Louise Young suggests that Japanese society in the 1930s cultivated not only an ethic of self-sacrifice but also a culture of death—merciless death to the enemy and glorious death for one's self.[23] Under these circumstances, the Allied campaign in the Pacific became a war of annihilation.

Allied troops (and the public) came to see the Japanese as subhuman, as vicious animals. While many Americans made a distinction between Nazis and "good Germans," they condemned all Japanese as savage beasts. The famous war correspondent Ernie Pyle was struck by the sharply differing attitudes of GIs toward their German and Japanese enemies. "In Europe we felt our enemies, horrible and deadly as they were, were still people. But out here I've already gathered the feeling that the Japanese are looked upon as something inhuman and squirmy—like some people feel about cockroaches or mice."[24] Admiral Halsey reflected the passions of his countrymen when he said publicly, "The only good Jap is a Jap who's been dead for six months."[25] A January 1942 memorandum from Admiral William Leahy bluntly stated, "In fighting the Japanese savages all previously accepted rules of warfare must be abandoned."[26]

Eugene Sledge, a marine mortarman, describes the battlefield origins of such intense hatred:

> The Goettge patrol incident plus such Japanese tactics as playing dead and then throwing a grenade—or playing wounded, calling for a corpsman and then knifing the medic when he came—plus the sneak attack on Pearl Harbor, caused Marines to hate the Japanese intensely and to be reluctant to take prisoners. . . .

> My experiences on Peleliu and Okinawa made me believe that the Japanese had mutual feelings for us. . . . This collective attitude, Marine and Japanese, resulted in a savage, ferocious fighting with no holds barred.[27]

American fighting men knew that the Japanese sometimes tortured their prisoners cruelly before killing them. US troops at times responded in kind. Some American servicemen collected enemy body parts (ears, for example) as souvenirs of their kills—others did far worse. Sledge reported the following gruesome scene:

> I noticed a Marine near me. . . . He came up to me dragging what I assumed to be a corpse. But the Japanese wasn't dead. . . . The Japanese's mouth glowed with huge gold-crowned teeth, and his captor wanted them. He put the point of his kabar [knife] on the base of a tooth and hit the handle with the palm of his hand. Because the Japanese was kicking and thrashing about, the knife point glanced off the tooth and sank deeply into the victim's mouth. The Marine cursed him and with a slash cut his cheeks open to each ear. He put his foot on the sufferer's lower jaw and tried again. Blood poured out of the soldier's mouth. . . . Such was the incredible cruelty that decent men could commit when reduced to a brutish existence in their fight for survival amid the violent death, terror, tension, fatigue, and filth that was the infantryman's war. . . . The fierce struggle for survival in the abyss of Peleliu eroded the veneer of civilization and made savages of us all.[28]

Beyond the hatreds and savagery generated by the horrors of the battlefield, historian John Dower argues that the Pacific campaign was an unstintingly brutal war of annihilation because at its core it was a race war. Each side saw the other in terms of racist stereotypes that dehumanized the opponent and justified violence against him. "War words and race words came together in a manner which did not just reflect the savagery of the war," Dower contends, "but contributed to it by reinforcing the impression of a truly Manichaean struggle between completely incompatible antagonists. The natural response to such a vision was an obsession with extermination on both sides—a war without mercy."[29]

Japanese propaganda portrayed the Western powers as greedy, immoral, hedonistic, racist parasites who sought world domination. A 1942 cartoon in the government humor magazine *Manga* showed a woman combing dandruff out of her hair, with the caption "Purging one's head of Anglo-Americanism." Another widely circulated cartoon depicted Roosevelt and Churchill as devils, with horns and long claws on their three-fingered hands and three-toed feet, under attack by a culture hero from Japanese mythology dressed in samurai garb.[30] Conversely, the Japanese leadership and press always characterized their nation as unique, pure, and possessed of a holy mission to liberate Asia.

They stressed the divine origins of the emperors as well as the supposed racial purity and cultural homogeneity of the Japanese population. Individualistic Westerners were said to be focused entirely on their own personal pleasure and advancement, while the superior Japanese sacrificed themselves for the collective good. The war itself and its attendant sacrifices were seen as a national ritual of purification. As part of that process, the authorities called upon all Japanese to rid themselves of foreign influences, live austerely, and be prepared to fight and die for the emperor. In a perversion of Confucian ideology, Japanese propaganda claimed their "Yamato race" to be superior and destined to preside over a hierarchy of freed nations in East Asia, each of which would understand its "proper place" under Japanese tutelage. Tokyo intended to punish its Western enemies for 140 years of Asian humiliation at the hands of the imperialist powers.

Allied propaganda replied in kind, depicting the "Japs" or "Nips" as apes, insects, snakes, or rats. As Imperial forces advanced down the Malay Peninsula in January 1942, the British

Allied anti-Japanese poster. British and American propaganda often depicted the Japanese as monkeys, rats, or insects.
Source: Shutterstock royalty-free images

satirical magazine *Punch* published a cartoon showing a horde of monkeys swinging through the jungle on vines, each wearing a helmet and carrying a submachine gun. Similarly, the Marine Corps magazine *Leatherneck* featured a cartoon depicting the Japanese as an infestation of lice ("*Louseous japanicas*"). Its caption suggested, "The breeding grounds around the Tokyo area must be completely annihilated."[31] The Japanese were said to have no respect for life and would stoop to any despicable trick. In this view, the enemy was scarcely human, but instead an infestation, a mindless swarm that required extermination. A vicious cycle thus emerged in this poisonous ideological environment. "Race hatred fed atrocities and atrocities fanned the fires of race hate."[32] It is not surprising that US troops viewed the Japanese in negative, racial stereotypes, given that most American servicemen came from a profoundly racist culture that deeply conditioned their perception of the enemy and his actions.

While the Allies often portrayed the conflict as a race war to their home audiences, they endeavored to avoid that image in propaganda directed toward the other peoples of Asia. Fearing the appeal of Japan's "Asia for the Asians" message, American propaganda emphasized the alliance with Nationalist China. In this view, the US war effort sought to free East Asia from Japanese oppression.

Notes

1. Gordon W. Prange, with Donald M. Goldstein and Katherine V. Dillon, *Miracle at Midway* (New York: Penguin, 1983), 225.

2. Paul S. Dull, *A Battle History of the Imperial Japanese Navy, 1941–1945* (Annapolis, MD: Naval Institute Press, 1978), 149.

3. Prange, *Miracle at Midway*, 215.

4. Jonathan B. Parshall and Anthony P. Tully, *Shattered Sword: The Untold Story of the Battle of Midway* (Washington, DC: Potomac Books, 2007), 402.

5. Richard Tregaskis, *Guadalcanal Diary* (New York: Random House, 1943), 83.

6. Eric M. Bergerud, *Touched with Fire: The Land War in the South Pacific* (New York: Penguin, 1997), xii.

7. Bergerud, *Touched with Fire*, 101.

8. Mark D. Roehrs and William Renzi, *World War II in the Pacific* (New York: Routledge, 2004), 112.

9. Bergerud, *Touched with Fire*, 312.

10. Richard B. Frank, *Guadalcanal: The Definitive Account of the Landmark Battle* (New York: Random House, 1990), 614.

11. William Slim, *Defeat into Victory: Battling Japan in Burma and India, 1942–1945* (New York: D. McKay, 1961), 446.

12. Bergerud, *Touched with Fire*, 61.

13. E. J. Kahn, *G.I. Jungle: An American Soldier in Australia and New Guinea* (New York: Simon & Schuster, 1943), 121–22.

14. Edward J. Drea, *In the Service of the Emperor: Essays on the Imperial Japanese Army* (Lincoln: University of Nebraska Press, 1998), 70.

15. Hank Nelson, "*Taim Bilong Pait:* The Impact of the Second World War on Papua New Guinea," in *Southeast Asia under Japanese Occupation*, ed. Alfred W. McCoy (New Haven, CT: Yale University Press, 1980), 256.

16. Michael Schaller, *Douglas MacArthur: The Far Eastern General* (New York: Oxford University Press, 1989), 71.

17. Quoted in Drea, *In the Service of the Emperor*, 106.

18. E. M. Collingham, *The Taste of War: World War II and the Battle for Food* (New York: Penguin, 2012), 297.

19. Stephen R. Taaffe, *MacArthur's Jungle War: The 1944 New Guinea Campaign* (Lawrence: University Press of Kansas, 1998), 237.

20. Gerhard L. Weinberg, *A World at Arms: A Global History of World War II*, 2nd ed. (Cambridge: Cambridge University Press, 2005), 344.

21. Gerald F. Linderman, *The World within War: America's Combat Experience in World War II* (Cambridge, MA: Harvard University Press, 1997), 147.

22. Samuel Hideo Yamashita, *Daily Life in Wartime Japan, 1940–1945* (Lawrence: University Press of Kansas, 2015), 136.

23. Louise Young, "Ideologies of Difference and the Turn to Atrocity: Japan's War on China," in *A World at Total War: Global Conflict and the Politics of Destruction, 1937–1945*, ed. Roger Chickering, Stig Förster, and Bernd Greiner (Cambridge: Cambridge University Press, 2005), 347–52.

24. Ernie Pyle, *Ernie's War: The Best of Ernie Pyle's World War II Dispatches* (New York: Random House, 1986), 367.

25. Linderman, *The World within War*, 178.

26. John W. Dower, *War without Mercy: Race and Power in the Pacific War* (New York: Pantheon, 1986), 141–42.

27. E. B. Sledge, *With the Old Breed at Peleliu and Okinawa* (Novato, CA: Presidio Press, 1981), 34.

28. Sledge, *With the Old Breed*, 120–21.

29. Dower, *War without Mercy*, 11.

30. These two cartoons and similar examples are reproduced in Dower, *War without Mercy*, 181–200.

31. Reproduced in Dower, *War without Mercy*, 191, 198.

32. Dower, *War without Mercy*, 11.

CHAPTER 20

Defeating Japan

Carrying the War to Japan—The Central Pacific

MacArthur's advance along the New Guinea coast and eventually into the Philippines continued to the end of the war, but by 1943 the focus of the Pacific war shifted to the central Pacific theater under Admiral Chester Nimitz. Early in that year the US Pacific Fleet had only one carrier still operational, the *Saratoga*. Soon, however, the dramatic increase in American industrial output produced numerous new ships, planes, and landing craft. The new *Essex*-class carriers coming into service boasted radar detection and fire control systems, armored handlers, space for ninety to one hundred planes, and powerful engines capable of propelling them at thirty knots. The Allied decision in 1943 to postpone any cross-Channel invasion of Nazi-occupied Europe until 1944 meant that equipment and troops could be reassigned, at least temporarily, to the Pacific. Allied strategy called for the capture of bases in the Mariana Islands from which to attack Japan directly, but first US forces had to overcome Japanese bastions in the Gilbert and Marshall Islands. This entailed an island-hopping campaign punctuated by a series of amphibious assaults on Japanese bases.

Fortunately the US Navy and Marine Corps were already in the process of developing the methodology and equipment necessary for successful amphibious operations. Powerful carrier task forces provided air support for these assaults while also fending off attempts by the enemy's navy to break up those operations. US Marine tacticians worked out the enormously complicated process of getting combat troops, with all their necessary equipment, to hostile beaches in the right order and at the right time. Finally, engineers designed a wide range of hardware to facilitate amphibious attacks—from the simple Higgins boat to the amtrac and eventually to an array of specialized landing craft.

This careful attention to the development of amphibious operations theory and equipment paid dividends when war came. The Allied powers repeatedly proved their ability to seize strongly defended coastal areas in all the major theaters of war. The American strategy of "island hopping" in the Pacific was entirely dependent on such techniques. The selective employment of amphibious assaults against a few strategically significant targets undermined Japan's Pacific empire. "This was the type of strategy we hated most," wrote General Matsuichi Ino. "The Americans attacked and seized, with minimum losses, a relatively weak area, constructed airfields and then proceeded to cut the supply lines to our troops in that area. Our strongpoints were gradually starved out. The Japanese Army preferred direct assault after the German fashion, but the Americans flowed into our weaker points and submerged us, just as water seeks the weakest entry to sink a ship."[1]

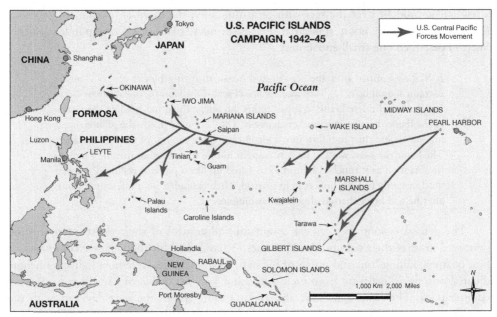

Allied Advances in the Central Pacific

This strategy and early versions of specialized assault craft were tested first at Tarawa atoll in the Gilbert Islands, 2,300 miles southwest of Hawaii. This was not the first American seaborne landing in the Pacific, but it was the first occasion on which strong Japanese forces chose to resist the assault at the water line. The US command selected Tarawa because the enemy had established an airstrip on Betio Island (a two-mile-long, eight-hundred-yard-wide speck that formed part of the atoll), which menaced the approaches to even more desirable targets in the Marshall Islands. Over 4,500 defenders manned fourteen costal defense guns, forty artillery pieces, five hundred pillboxes, and numerous machine-gun nests and rifle pits. The Japanese were determined to repel the enemy.

The Americans brought an armada of seventeen carriers, twelve battleships, and a host of lesser combat vessels to protect the invasion fleet and provide preliminary bombardment and air support for the assault. A continuous "fleet train" of support ships kept the fighting ships well supplied with munitions, fuel, and other necessary provisions. The attack (Operation Galvanic) began early in the morning of November 20, 1943. Heavy fire from two battleships knocked out the four largest costal defense guns and permitted the invasion fleet to sail into the lagoon. Lead elements of the thirty-five-thousand-man attack force boarded Higgins boats and tracked landing craft (LVT "Alligators") headed for the beaches. At this point, an unanticipated and unusual tidal condition (a neap tide) failed to provide enough water for the Higgins boats to clear the island's barrier reef. That left the marines in these boats sitting helplessly five hundred yards from shore. Only the tracked Alligators managed to clamber over the reef and bring their troops to the sea wall on the beach. Meanwhile, most Japanese defenders had survived the initial bombardment and were leaving their protective bunkers to man their artillery and machine guns. Increasingly intense enemy fire now raked the marines at the seawall and those unfortunate troops stranded on the reef.

American officers on the beach knew that keeping up the momentum of the assault was critical. If the attack stalled, the invaders might be pushed back into the sea. They therefore urged their troops forward, even in the face of murderous enemy fire. With the support of a few tanks, brought over the reef with great difficulty, the marines overran the Japanese first line of defense by noon, though at the cost of many casualties. Correspondent Robert Sherrod described one small encounter:

> A Marine jumped over the seawall and began throwing blocks of TNT into a coconut-log pillbox. . . . Two more Marines scaled the seawall, one of them carrying a twin-cylindered tank strapped to his shoulders, the other holding the nozzle of the flame thrower. As another charge of TNT boomed inside the pillbox, causing smoke and dust to billow out, a khaki-clad figure ran out of the side entrance. The flame thrower, waiting for him, caught him in its withering stream of intense fire. As soon as it touched him, the Jap flared up like a piece of celluloid. He was dead instantly but the bullets in his cartridge belt exploded for a full sixty seconds after he had been charred almost to nothingness.[2]

The defenders soon lost critical command and control of their efforts after shelling destroyed most of their communications lines. A naval shell hit the Japanese commander's headquarters, killing him and much of his staff. Japanese units were now fighting uncoordinated actions, in isolation from each other, and were incapable of launching a coherent counterattack. The Americans were able to land more troops the next day and, with the close-in support of naval gun fire, to begin reducing pockets of enemy resistance, though again with heavy casualties. The marines eliminated the last surviving enemy forces on the third day of the battle. Desperate defenders contributed to their own doom by launching virtually suicidal *banzai* charges against well-defended American positions. Over six thousand Japanese, Korean workers, and Americans had been killed in just three days on this tiny speck of coral in the Pacific.

The US Navy and Marine Corps learned valuable technical lessons from this grim experience about the need for better knowledge of local conditions and the requirement for more capable landing vehicles. Beyond that, marine colonel turned historian Joseph Alexander suggests that Tarawa helped steel the American people to accept the realities of a long and brutal conflict: "The Pacific War would become a war of virtual extermination. Tarawa revealed that the road to Tokyo would take time and blood and treasure. Tarawa also provided confidence that Americans could prevail."[3] In the United States, press censorship relaxed enough to allow photographs of American casualties littering the beach and floating in the water.

The American armed forces had now demonstrated that they could bring overwhelming force to bear on a target and accept the high cost of eliminating its determined defenders. This would be the template for the rest of the Pacific war. Historian H. P. Willmott has gone so far as to argue that, "in terms of decision, the Pacific war ended in November 1943. By this time the United States had come into possession of such margins of superiority in the conduct of amphibious operations that its victory in any single landing operation was assured."[4] Moreover, Tokyo's decision for war with the Western powers in 1941 assumed a general Axis victory in the war. By the fall of 1943, Nazi Germany had suffered disasters at Stalingrad and Kursk as well as the defeat of the Afrika Korps and the collapse of Mussolini's regime. The geostrategic calculation upon which Japan gambled its future had collapsed.

Strangling Imperial Japan

While American strength in the Pacific continued to grow at an extraordinary rate through the remainder of the war, Japanese power waned. Part of the explanation is that the island kingdom could never match the industrial capacity of the United States. Another element of the story concerns the extensive interdiction campaign conducted by Allied submarines, bombers, and minelayers that choked the supply of raw materials and fuels to Japanese industry. Securing unchallenged control of the resources of Southeast Asia and the East Indies had been Tokyo's major objective in attacking Britain, Holland, and the United States. The Japanese had conquered those resources (oil, coal, iron ore, minerals, wood, rice, etc.) with relative ease, but they had to ship these commodities by sea to the home islands. There lay Japan's vulnerability. From the beginning of the conflict, the US Navy and its allies declared unrestricted submarine warfare on enemy shipping. Initially, however, the American effort was hampered by inadequate numbers and quality of boats and by defective torpedoes. Seeing the potential to cripple Japan's war economy, the US Navy expanded the campaign, dedicating ever more resources, until it achieved the decisive effect in Asia that Hitler's U-boat campaign had failed to accomplish in the Atlantic. Cryptologists broke the Japanese merchant marine code so that American submarine commanders knew where to find their targets. The navy also introduced a more effective torpedo.

Amazingly, the Imperial Navy never made convoy organization and enemy submarine suppression a priority! When they did launch convoys, American submarines responded by attacking them in wolf packs, with devastating effect. The Japanese did not establish the Grand Escort Command headquarters to coordinate convoy operations until November 1943, and that command had no escort carrier at its disposal until July 1944. It also failed to give its units special training in antisubmarine warfare. US losses in this campaign totaled 50 submarines and 1,300 sailors killed. American submarines sank 2,117 Japanese merchantmen, while British and Dutch subs added another 73 kills.

Equally astounding, the Japanese submarine force made no systematic attempts to interdict the even longer American supply lines from the continental United States to the constantly expanding Pacific perimeter! As American forces captured bases ever closer to Japan and destroyed the capabilities of the once powerful Imperial Navy, bombing and mine laying made the interdiction effort even more successful. By 1945, over 60 percent of Japanese merchantmen, oil tankers, and troopships had been sunk. Tokyo increased its ship construction program, but every year it produced fewer new vessels than the number lost. Production of steel, rubber, manufactured goods, and other vital supplies soon dropped to a tiny fraction of previous totals. In 1943, Japan imported 14.5 million barrels of oil from Sumatra, Java, and Borneo. By the next year, the total was less than half that figure, and in the last year of war it dropped to virtually nothing. Thus by 1945 Japan's strangled economy could no longer support its nation's war effort.

The island fighting in the Pacific, particularly on the larger islands, exposed the weaknesses of the Imperial Army. Relying on "spirit" and "cold steel" to offset deficiencies in heavy weapons and logistics, Japanese forces had been powerful enough to defeat large but even more poorly equipped and poorly led Chinese armies, as well as irresolute British and Dutch colonial defenders in the opening months of the war. Now, however, they came up against well-equipped and determined American and Australian troops. In the judgment of historian Alvin Coox, Japanese "air-ground coordination was rudimentary. . . . Artillery support of ground actions was generally poor. . . . Armored forces were feeble in tank versus tank combat. . . . The foot soldiers still fought with his obsolescent Type 38 (*Sanpachi*) rifle, machine guns, and grenades—without significant air or artillery support and without trucks."[5] He continues, "Reaffirmation of faith in moral attributes and psychological drives amounted to a callous evasion (but not total ignorance) of the realities of modern firepower, mechanization, and aviation."[6]

American forces next moved against the Marshall Islands. The Japanese anticipated the direction of the Americans' drive, but the size of the island group (twenty-nine atolls spread over 750,000 square miles) compelled them to disperse their forces. Two divisions of Major General Holland Smith's 5th Amphibious Corps began their assault on Kwajalein atoll and on the Roi-Namur Islands on January 31, 1944, by capturing small offshore islands for use as artillery firing bases to support the main attacks. The Japanese planned to repel the invaders on the beaches, but, learning from their Tarawa experience, the Americans subjected the target islands to a much heavier bombing and bombardment that destroyed all enemy aircraft and pulverized many of the defenders' entrenchments. Imperial troops fought fiercely, suffering over 95 percent casualties, but their resistance lasted only four days.

US forces next assaulted Eniwetok Island in the Marshall group (350 miles northwest of Kwajalein) on February 17 to gain invaluable airfield and harbor facilities for subsequent attacks against the Mariana Islands. In support of these operations, the US Navy launched a massive strike with carrier-based aircraft, surface ships, and submarines on the only major Japanese naval and air base in the region, Truk in the Caroline Islands group. Employing five large fleet carriers and four light carriers, the American attack destroyed 39 enemy ships and over 250 planes. Like Rabaul, Truk was now effectively neutralized and bypassed. For the first time, American forces had penetrated the "outer ring" of Japan's defenses for its home islands.

The way was now open to strike at enemy bases in the Marianas group of islands, from which, in turn, bombing raids and potentially a full-scale invasion could reach Japan itself. The distance from the island of Saipan to Japan is only 1,400 miles, easily within the reach of the new long-range B-29 bombers. Moreover, the strength and plans of the two rival navies had reversed since the opening of hostilities. The Imperial Navy began the war anticipating an early, decisive encounter with the weaker US Pacific Fleet. By 1944, Admiral King hoped that American attacks in the Marianas would force the much diminished and fuel-depleted Japanese navy to confront his transformed Pacific Fleet, with its numerous new carrier task forces and fast battleships.

The Marianas

The Marianas campaign began with an attack on Saipan (code-named Operation Forager) on June 15, 1944, only ten days after Allied troops stormed the beaches of Normandy in France. Preparatory American air strikes had hit widespread targets around New Guinea, the Palau Island group, and elsewhere, as well as objectives in the Marianas, so as not to reveal where the next landing would occur. The Japanese guessed wrong and transferred aircraft to combat anticipated enemy attacks in New Guinea and the Palaus. They also sailed much of the Combined Fleet 1,600 miles away to the southwestern Philippines to avoid the increasingly heavy US air strikes. Troop strength on Saipan, however, grew from barely a thousand to thirty thousand. American intelligence underestimated enemy strength on the island by half.

However, contrary to some accounts of the battle for Saipan, Japanese commanders had failed to learn the key lesson from their bitter experiences on Tarawa and Kwajalein. Attempts to halt the invaders on the beaches only exposed the defenders to murderous naval gunfire and bombing. Yet the Japanese commander on the island, Lieutenant General Saito Yoshitsugu, ordered his troops to "demolish the enemy landing units at the water's edge."[7] Unlike those tiny atolls, Saipan, an island of seventy-five square miles, was large enough to defend in depth, employing the island's mountains, ravines, caves, coral outcroppings, swamps, and cane fields as natural strongpoints. An entirely defensive, attritional strategy might have slaughtered a great many US troops, but the "*banzai*" mentality of most Japanese officers could not tolerate such a passive tactic. Instead, their plans called for halting the invaders on or near the beaches and then counterattacking with tanks and mass bayonet charges. However, the speed of the American advance caught the Japanese by surprise. When the invasion force struck in mid-June, the preparation of defensive works and the integration of diverse Japanese units were incomplete.

Beginning on June 11, frequent air strikes destroyed 147 enemy planes on Saipan, and starting on the 13th, fire from fifteen battleships battered the island for two days, though most well-dug-in and camouflaged Japanese gun emplacements survived. Much better landing craft, coordination, communications, and logistics enabled the Americans to land eight thousand marines on the 15th. Even these improvements, though, could not take the danger and difficulty out of an amphibious assault. Some amtracs emerged from their carriers at just the wrong time, fell into deep troughs between big waves, and sank with all hands. Getting over the reef was still a problem even for these tracked vehicles. A crewman of an amphibious tank recalled:

> As we approached the reef, our Driver, Allen, had the good sense to down shift all the way to first gear and sure enough we hit that reef at the ebb of the wave. We had to climb that reef before the big wave coming behind us broke down on us and swamped us. An engine stall here would be disastrous. . . . Our Driver had our lives in his hands trying to make it safely across the edge of that barrier reef.[8]

The assault troops encountered heavy enemy artillery and machine-gun fire but managed to establish a beachhead and repulse a Japanese counterattack that night.

The Americans employed one army and two marine divisions under the command of marine general Holland "Howlin' Mad" Smith. On the 16th, elements of the Army's 27th Infantry Division landed and advanced on the airstrip, taking it after a day and night of tough fighting. Mount Tapotchan dominated the island, allowing the Japanese to observe and direct fire at every American unit. The marines attacked up the mountain but were stopped by intense fire. Finally, after three days of bloody combat, they took the objective by flanking attacks, using flamethrowers and explosive charges to overcome enemy resistance in numerous caves.

While the marines pressed up the coast and across the island to cut the enemy's defenses in two, General Holland Smith ordered the army forces to attack up the island's central valley. Already angry that his troops had not completely conquered the island in just three days as originally anticipated, the hot-tempered marine general now made two serious errors that cost many soldiers their lives. He badly underestimated the strength of Japanese resistance, and he ignored the topography of the battlefield—a valley flanked by hills on one side and cliffs on the other, both with many caves that provided strong defensive positions for the Japanese. The initial American attacks were repelled with high casualties, but Holland Smith insisted on more frontal assaults, preferring to believe that the problem was army incompetence rather than his own misjudgment. He dismissed the commander of the 27th Division, army general Ralph C. Smith. That unfortunate commander conceived a better strategy—weaker frontal attacks that would hold the Japanese in their current positions, with powerful flanking assaults to destroy them—which succeeded under the commanders who replaced him.

Many accounts of this battle and the Pacific theater in general have stressed the dysfunctional nature of interservice rivalries and personality clashes among headstrong commanders. There is certainly an element of truth in these contentions, but on balance what stands out is the high degree of cooperation among the Army, Marine Corps, Navy, and Army Air Corps. The complex, combined-arms operations required for the Americans' advance across the Pacific would not have been possible without this collaboration.[9]

As usual, life was miserable for the marines and soldiers on the island. Beyond the rigors of combat and the dangers of Japanese snipers and booby traps, troops had to deal with sweltering heat and humidity, hordes of flies, not showering and wearing the same filthy uniform day after day, sleeping on the hard ground every night, and eating the same tasteless C rations (Spam, dehydrated eggs, dehydrated potatoes, etc.) meal after meal. They suffered the torments of dysentery and various mosquito-borne fevers. They smelled, walked in, and sometimes dove for cover into the "night soil" (human feces) used all over the island for fertilizer. Worst of all, they endured the dreadful, sickly sweet smell of thousands of maggot-infested, unburied corpses.

On June 20, General Saito radioed to Tokyo, "Please apologize deeply to the Emperor that we cannot do better than we are doing. . . . The army will defend its positions to the very end, though that be death. . . . There is no hope for victory. . . . Praying for the good health of the Emperor, we all cry Banzai."[10] Battered and retreating in every sector, on July 7 the Japanese launched a desperate *banzai* charge with the bulk of their remaining forces—the largest *banzai* charge of the war. Their furious assault punched through the American lines, overrunning two army battalions, but the desperate fifteen-hour-long battle proved suicidal for the Japanese, leaving 4,300 of them dead. Before the attack began, Saito had told his troops, "Whether we attack or whether we stay where we are, there is only death. However, in death there is life. We must utilize this opportunity to exult true Japanese manhood."[11] The remaining enemy troops and civilian refugees were soon compressed at the northern end of the island on Marpi Point.

Most surviving Japanese soldiers elected to kill themselves, though for the first time some surrendered. Many civilians also chose suicide, throwing themselves over the cliffs onto the rocks below or into the ocean. Their own troops murdered some who were reluctant to take their own lives. The Japanese had told the local population (the Chamorros) as well as their own civilians on the island that the barbarous Americans would torture, rape, and kill them if they were captured. Twenty-four thousand Japanese troops died in combat, while another five thousand took their own lives rather than surrender. Only 921 were taken prisoner. In addition, twenty-two thousand civilians died during the operation, most as the unintended victims of combat, but some by suicide.[12]

The Americans suffered 3,426 men killed and 10,364 wounded. An operation that was supposed to take no more than three days had required three weeks of bloody struggle. In the view of historian Harold Goldberg, "Japan would continue to fight for another fourteen months after Saipan, but the failure to stop the Americans, on the sea near the Marianas and on the land at Saipan, settled Japan's fate. It was not a surprise that Japan lost the war; it was more amazing that the Japanese were able to resist as tenaciously as they did for another year."[13] The Americans had now broken into Japan's inner ring of defenses. There was one more casualty of the Saipan defeat after the shooting stopped. On July 18, Prime Minister Tojo Hideki resigned.

The Great Marianas Turkey Shoot

While the battle raged on land, the Imperial Navy attempted to disrupt the American invasion—Operation *A-Go*, the First Battle of the Philippine Sea on June 19 and 20. Admiral Toyoda Soemu (now commanding the Combined Fleet) ordered all the ships available in the region to attack the US naval force supporting the Saipan landings. That Japanese battle group included six carriers, five battleships, and a host of lesser war craft of the 1st Mobile Fleet.

The qualitative and quantitative advantage in ships and aircraft, so favorable to the Japanese in the initial stages of the war, had shifted decisively in favor of the Americans. The US Navy now possessed large numbers of faster, better-armed and better-armored ships. Similarly, the quality of its planes and pilots was now markedly superior to those of the enemy. The once-dominant Zero fighter now found itself outclassed by American F6F Hellcats, Thunderbolts, and Corsairs. Toyoda could hope only that the longer range of his carrier-based planes and support from land-based aircraft in the region would offset the American advantage. However, numerous American air strikes on Japanese air bases in the area had already destroyed most of those land-based warplanes. Toyoda was misinformed about the land-based air power available to him because Japanese commanders consistently underestimated and underreported their losses.

US submarines detected the approach of the Japanese fleet, whereupon Admiral Raymond Spruance committed the five carrier task forces of the 5th Fleet, supported by seven modern fast battleships, to a major attack. In the ensuing battle, American planes and submarines sank three Japanese fleet carriers, damaged three other carriers, and destroyed approximately six hundred enemy planes, while suffering damage to only one of their battleships and the loss of 123 aircraft. The encounter was so one-sided that American pilots referred to it as the Great Marianas Turkey Shoot. The Imperial Navy never recovered from this disaster—especially its naval air arm. Replacing the planes was difficult; replacing the skilled veteran pilots was impossible.

Within a few days of the fall of Saipan, American forces struck at the nearby island of Tinian and at Guam. Marines began landing on Guam on July 21. Though enemy artillery sank several of the invaders' landing craft, the Japanese could not prevent American troops and tanks from establishing deep beachheads on both sides of the Orote Peninsula. Once again, Imperial forces contributed to their own slaughter by launching desperate *banzai* charges at the Americans. Running low on both food and ammunition, the Japanese withdrew to the mountainous northern end of the island to make their final stand. After more bitter fighting, the last organized Japanese resistance collapsed by the middle of July.

Meanwhile, American artillery began shelling Tinian from southern Saipan even before the conquest of that latter island was complete. Then, on July 24, lead elements of two marine regiments assaulted Tinian, deliberately avoiding the best landing sites, which the Japanese had prepared to defend stoutly. Once more, fierce counterattacks by the Japanese only served to deplete their forces. Enemy resistance ceased by August 1. Of over eight thousand defenders, only 252 survived the battle. Possession of Saipan, Tinian, and Guam allowed the US Army Air Forces to bomb targets in the Philippines, the Ryukyu Islands, and the Japanese home islands with the long-range B-29 Superfortress bomber. With its four powerful Pratt & Whitney engines and pressurized cabin, the B-29 could fly faster, higher, and farther than any other bomber. On Tinian alone, the United States constructed six 8,500-foot runways for the giant bombers.

The bloodiest, most difficult fight was yet to come—on Peleliu, on the western side of the Carolines group. The Americans wanted the island to protect the flank of MacArthur's advance into the Philippines, though some officers thought it a needless operation. This battle was especially costly in American lives because the Japanese had changed their tactics. Instead of attempting to stop the invasion on the beach, the eleven thousand Japanese defenders were deployed in a defense in depth, using the island's terrain features and a series of bunkers—pillboxes with overlapping fields of fire. For three days before the landing, five battleships and eight cruisers laid down a heavy bombardment on the small island, supplemented by bombing, but the well-fortified defenders remained virtually unscathed. Marines of the 1st Division assaulted the island on September 15, 1944, braving heavy enemy artillery fire that knocked out sixty of their landing craft. They managed to establish a two-mile-long beachhead by the end of the day, at a cost of a thousand casualties. On the next day, American forces captured the airfield, though again with heavy losses. Thereafter, the marines continued the tough job of reducing the enemy pillboxes and bunkers one by one, aided by a new weapon, napalm dropped by dive bombs.

The combat was often hand-to-hand. One marine remembered the Japanese night infiltrations with particular vividness:

> When night came it was like another world. Then the enemy came out of their caves, infiltrating or creeping up on our lines to raid all night, every night. . . . Typically, one or more raiders slipped up close to Marine positions by moving during dark periods between mortar flares or star shells. . . . Suddenly they rushed in jabbering or babbling incoherent sounds, sometimes throwing a grenade, but always swinging a saber, bayonet, or knife.[14]

Heat exhaustion in 115-degree weather also felled many Americans. The toughest fighting took place as the marines assaulted the successive ridgelines of Umurbrogol Mountain, an area they called Bloody Nose Ridge. These outcroppings provided virtually perfect defensive positions for the Japanese. Some marine units suffered 70 percent casualties and had to be relieved by the army's 81st Division. The island was not fully secured until November 27, at a cost of almost ten thousand American casualties.

MacArthur Returns to the Philippines

In the spring of 1944, the Joint Chiefs finally authorized MacArthur to begin planning his return to the Philippines. They had delayed this step because they strongly favored Nimitz's drive through the central Pacific as the most effective way to defeat Japan. At this point, however, several factors coincided to modify their thinking: The projected invasion of Taiwan and areas on the China coast fell apart when the enemy's Operation *Ichigo* overran American air bases in China. New intelligence suggested that while the southernmost Philippine island, Mindanao, was strongly defended, the central island of Leyte was lightly held and therefore an inviting target. The Japanese, in fact, were reinforcing *all* the major Philippine islands, and radio intercepts betrayed this movement; but that knowledge did not change the plans of MacArthur or Admiral Halsey. As the New Guinea campaign wound to a close, MacArthur's troops were available and were much easier to move to the Philippines than forces from the central Pacific. Finally, the American high command realized the mutually supporting nature of the southwest and central Pacific offensives. An attack by MacArthur in the Philippines would dilute Japanese resistance to Nimitz's thrust.

Reconquest of the Philippines required the largest campaign of the Pacific war, employing ten US divisions and five independent regiments, as well as the 5th Army Air Force and a massive fleet of warships. Lead elements of the American 6th Army began landing on the eastern side of Leyte Island on October 20, 1944. Filipino guerrillas joined them to provide invaluable scouting and intelligence assistance. Once a beachhead was secured, MacArthur jumped off his landing craft and waded ashore in a dramatic photo op to proclaim to waiting reporters, "I have returned!" Defeating the Japanese in the Philippines, however, proved a much more difficult and bloody task than the general had predicted. Tokyo rushed reinforcements to the western side of the island but could not build up forces faster than its opponent. American troops made a second landing at Ormoc Bay on December 7 and, after heavy fighting, blocked the access route for any further Imperial Army reinforcements. Fighting would continue for six months, but, cut off from resupply, the defenders were already doomed.

While the battle raged on the island, an even bigger fight broke out at sea, the Battle of Leyte Gulf. Admiral Halsey's powerful 3rd Fleet (deploying fifteen carriers and seven modern fast battleships) and Admiral Thomas Kinkaid's 7th Fleet (with sixteen escort carriers and six older battleships) protected the invasion force. Admiral Toyoda moved to attack the Americans, even though the risk of loss to his own vessels was high. He reasoned that if the enemy took the Philippines, the blockade of Japan would be complete, and his fleet would be immobilized by lack of fuel. The Japanese also took seriously their own pilots' vastly inflated reports of damage inflicted on US warships in previous combat.

An opportunity to destroy a weakened American fleet seemed to be at hand. Toyoda divided his strike force into three groups. Admiral Ozawa Jisaburo's Northern Fleet (including one fleet carrier and three light carriers, but very short of planes and trained pilots) acted as bait, approaching from the north to lure the American warships away from Leyte. Admiral Kurita Takeo's Center Fleet of five battleships (including the super battleships *Yamato* and *Musashi*) and ten cruisers meant to destroy whatever US ships remained to protect Leyte Gulf. A Southern Force under Admirals Nishimura Shoji and Shima Kiyohide (with two battleships and one cruiser) steamed straight for the enemy invasion supply ships. The Japanese fleets made relatively few radio transmissions (having thoroughly war-gamed their operation previously), so radio intercepts did not give the Americans warning of enemy intent.

Two US submarines detected Kurita's approaching fleet on the night of October 22–23. They sank two cruisers and damaged a third. Planes from Ozawa's carrier force attacked Halsey's ships on the morning of the 24th but were driven off. However, Luzon-based bombers managed to sink the light carrier *Princeton*. Halsey's planes struck back against Kurita's ships, registering several bomb and torpedo hits on the *Musashi*, which soon sank, and badly damaged a heavy cruiser. Kurita disengaged to avoid further destruction, giving the Americans the false impression that his fleet had fled the battle.

Halsey then sped north to attack Ozawa's carriers, ultimately sinking all four of them on the 25th. Halsey's departure left only Kinkaid's much weaker force of escort carriers and destroyers protecting the invasion beaches when Kurita's ships suddenly reappeared. His forces sank an American escort carrier and three destroyers but lost three cruisers themselves. The situation was precarious for the Americans. Kurita still had sufficient firepower to devastate the invasion flotilla, but he took two hours to regroup his fleet and then turned away to chase a falsely reported enemy battleship in the area. A potential disaster was averted. In the south, units of the 7th Fleet sank two of Nishimura's battleships and drove him off. This engagement was, in the words of historian Thomas Cutler, "the biggest and most multifaceted naval battle in all of history."[15] The Battle of Leyte Gulf effectively ended the role of the Imperial Navy in the Second World War. It had lost three battleships, four carriers, ten cruisers, and nine destroyers. The US Navy had lost one light carrier and two escort carriers (out of a total of one hundred carriers operating in the Pacific at that time!).

The Battle of Leyte Gulf also included the first large-scale use of deliberate, airborne suicide missions in which Japanese pilots attempted to crash their planes into Allied ships—the *kamikaze* (the term, meaning "divine wind," comes from two typhoons that wrecked attempted Mongol invasions of Japan in the thirteenth century). It was a tactic of desperation. At this point, the Japanese had neither the well-trained pilots, nor the quantities of first-line combat aircraft, nor the supplies of aviation fuel to mount a seriously punishing conventional air assault on Allied invasion forces. Suicide missions, however, could employ freshly recruited, minimally trained pilots and obsolescent warplanes or even trainer aircraft. The ethic of self-sacrifice pervaded Japanese military culture. Suicide attacks in late October sank the carrier *St. Lo* and damaged six other carriers. An additional forty ships (mostly smaller vessels) were hit, five of which sank. Yet overall the suicide bomber technique was ineffective. Most *kamikazes* were shot down or missed their targets, though sailors on the targeted ships found these human bombs especially unnerving.

While the Imperial Navy's attack fizzled, American forces moved quickly to seize the lightly defended island of Mindoro near Manila, where they constructed airstrips to support the subsequent invasion of Luzon. US pilots now flew the new P-51 Mustang fighter that completely outclassed every enemy plane. Then, on January 9, 1945, the first units of a 175,000-man force landed at Lingayen Gulf. By the end of the month, they had retaken Clark Field and soon all but surrounded Manila. General Yamashita, the overall Japanese commander, decided to abandon the capital city and withdraw his over two hundred thousand troops into the mountains, from which to fight a war of attrition. However, a subordinate, Rear Admiral Iwabuchi Sanji, disobeyed orders and kept the twenty thousand naval infantry and soldiers under his control in the city. He enjoined his troops to defend the city to the end, to kill as many of the invaders, and of the local population, as possible. There followed, in the words of historian Lawrence Taylor, "an orgy of burning, shooting, raping, and torture" that, together with American artillery shelling, killed one hundred thousand Filipinos and destroyed much of the city.[16]

American troops finally took the devastated city on March 3 after a month of desperate, house-to-house fighting. MacArthur then ordered the 8th Army to crush the large Japanese garrison on the southern island of Mindanao, though that troop concentration could have been isolated and bypassed. He was determined that US forces should liberate all of the Philippines as soon as possible because of the potentially dangerous divisions among the Filipino resistance movements. Fighting continued against isolated pockets of enemy resistance until the end of the war. The cost of liberating the Philippines was high—almost fourteen thousand American dead and more than forty-eight thousand wounded. Over 336,000 Japanese troops died defending the islands, and more than 12,000 were captured. Some historians have argued that MacArthur's campaign to liberate the Philippines was "strategically irrelevant." The Americans' central Pacific campaign would have defeated Japan without fighting in the Philippines.[17] Of course, that argument can be turned on its head: a massive thrust from the Philippines could have made the central Pacific campaign unnecessary.[18]

Final Steps in the Central Pacific

While MacArthur's troops fought their way through the Philippines, Nimitz's forces in the central Pacific pressed ever closer to the Japanese home islands in 1945, taking Iwo Jima and Okinawa after the bitterest of struggles. Iwo Jima, a small, sulfurous, and vegetationless island with three airstrips, lay halfway between the Marianas and Japan. Both the high command in Tokyo and the local commander, General Kuribayashi Tadamichi, knew that they could not defeat a determined American attack on the island. Yet they resolved to defend it tenaciously to buy time for the preparation of home island defenses and to inflict such heavy casualties on the Americans that Washington might consider a negotiated peace settlement. Just as on Peleliu, the twenty-two thousand Japanese defenders abandoned any idea of stopping the invaders on the beach in favor of constructing a dense network of mutually supporting bunkers and disguised artillery positions, interconnected with eleven miles of tunnels. The Allies' heavy preinvasion bombardment did relatively little damage to these structures.

Three marine divisions began landing on Iwo Jima on February 19, 1945. They met no resistance on the beaches. Only when they moved inland and reached the first enemy line of bunkers did the Japanese open murderous machine-gun and artillery fire. Nonetheless, at a cost of heavy casualties, the marines soon cut the island in two and isolated (on the surface, at least) its high point, Mount Suribachi. The tunnels, however, allowed the enemy to reoccupy previously overrun positions and ambush unsuspecting marines. The most effective weapons against this dug-in enemy were explosive charges and flamethrowers (including Sherman tanks equipped with flamethrowers, which the marines dubbed "Ronsons" or "Zippos").

By the 23rd, the Americans had reached the top of Mount Suribachi, where five marines and a navy corpsman raised an American flag. Joe Rosenthal's photograph of that scene became the most famous image of the Pacific theater. After a month of bitter fighting, Japanese forces were running out of food, water, and ammunition. Only at that point did they begin to engage in desperate frontal attacks. By March 28, US forces controlled the island. Iwo Jima was the only battle in the Pacific in which the Americans experienced higher casualties (twenty-six thousand) than their opponent (nineteen thousand during the struggle, with another three thousand survivors later killed or captured). Debate continues over whether the limited military value of the island was worth this high price.

The next and, as it turned out, last amphibious operation of the war was the invasion of Okinawa, a large island in the Ryukyu chain (485 square miles) only 375 miles from Japan. Over sixty-seven thousand Japanese soldiers and nine thousand naval infantry defended the island, under the command of General Ushijima Mitsuru. The Japanese also drafted thirty-nine thousand of the island's men to serve as militia and laborers, though those formations had little military value. Following the pattern established on Peleliu and Iwo Jima, Ushijima decided not to defend the invasion beaches. Instead, his forces withdrew to inland areas where the topography gave the defenders a natural advantage. The anticipated bombardment—seven days of the most intensive shelling and bombing— killed a great many civilians but scarcely affected the well-dug-in defenders. The landings began on April 1 and were virtually unopposed. American amphibious assault capabilities had developed mightily since that first improvised landing on Guadalcanal. The invaders put ashore sixteen thousand troops in the first hour alone, followed by waves of tanks, heavy weapons, and supplies. By the end of the day, fifty thousand troops were ashore, and two nearby airstrips had been captured.

US Marines raise the flag atop Mount Suribachi on the island of Iwo Jima, February 22, 1945.
Source: Library of Congress

American forces rolled across south-central Okinawa with relative ease for a week. Then the 6th Marine Division pivoted northward, soon compressing enemy defenders into the mountainous and wooded Motobu Peninsula. The marines secured the area by April 18, though only after heavy fighting. Meanwhile, two army divisions turned southward, encountering stronger resistance as they approached the enemy's Shuri defensive line. Attempts to take its first obstacle, Kakazu Ridge, were stopped by defenders fighting from caves, many of which had been reinforced with concrete and steel blast doors. Such fortifications were all but impervious even to the heaviest bombardment. Repeated American assaults were thrown back with alarming losses. Reduction of these cave defenses required small US infantry teams, braving cross-fire from other caves, to creep up to their openings and use grenades, satchel charges, and flamethrowers—a long and bloody process.

The Americans sometimes used gases to clear these caves. When the United States entered the war, President Roosevelt announced that the United States would not use poison gas except in retaliation against an Axis first use of chemical weapons. Because of the appalling casualty rates among American forces in the island-hopping campaigns of 1943–1944, the Joint Chiefs approved the use of poison gas to subdue fiercely resisting Japanese garrisons. President Roosevelt (and subsequently President Truman) vetoed this proposal. However, Miyagi Kikuko, a student nurse on Okinawa, told interviewers that "gas bombs" killed two teachers and ten of her fellow students in a cave where they were hiding.[19] It seems likely that, in their extremely weakened condition, even "nonlethal" chemical agents (tear gases, etc.) could have caused these deaths by asphyxiation.

Ushijima employed the best strategy available to him given his resources and the power of his enemy, but because of the large American losses on Kakazu Ridge, he allowed an impetuous subordinate to launch a nighttime counterattack on April 12. Heavy American fire repelled this assault and more attacks on the next two nights, with serious losses for the Japanese. Futile back-and-forth bloodletting continued. US commanders brought up fresh troops, launched a truly massive bombardment, and attacked the enemy's defense line again. The defenders, however, were securely dug in on the reverse side of the slopes. They survived the intense shelling, emerging to pour heavy fire on advancing American troops. Okinawa marine veteran Eugene Sledge later described his horror at the carnage: "I existed from moment to moment, sometimes thinking that death would have been preferable. We were in the depths of the abyss, the ultimate horror of war. . . . But in the mud and driving rain before Shuri, we were surrounded by maggots and decay. Men struggled and fought and bled in an environment so degrading I believed we had been flung into hell's own cesspool."[20]

At the beginning of May, the Japanese attempted another counteroffensive, trying to sneak past the seaward end of the US line using small boats. Murderous American fire destroyed the operation. Finally, in mid-May, army and marine forces broke through on both flanks of the enemy defensive line, forcing the Japanese to retreat. They were soon trapped on two peninsulas and decimated. General Ushijima, Admiral Ota Minoru, and their staffs committed suicide. The Japanese lost 77,166 troops, while US forces endured 14,009 deaths and over 41,000 additional casualties. The American field commander, General Simon Buckner, was killed by artillery fire in the last week of fighting. A sniper's bullet killed the famous war correspondent Ernie Pyle. These figures do not include the number of men withdrawn from combat because of "combat fatigue" (over twenty-five thousand), also known as "shell shock" and now diagnosed as PTSD—posttraumatic stress disorder. Prolonged exposure to heavy shelling or to close combat fractured the mental stability of many men. Estimates for Okinawan civilian deaths run as high as one hundred thousand people. That total was so large because civilians were often intermixed with Japanese troops and thus subjected to US fire.

While ground troops battled each other on the island, supporting US and British sailors faced a desperate series of attacks by *kamikazes*. From late March through June, suicide air attacks sank 20 ships and damaged 157 more (though the Japanese estimated that they had destroyed as many as 360 ships). Those lost were mostly smaller vessels—destroyers, destroyer escorts, radar picket boats, and landing craft. Flights of suicide planes encountered these smaller ships on picket duty at the outer fringes of the operational area and attacked them first, often mistaking them for bigger vessels. The larger carriers, battleships, and cruisers could put up much heavier antiaircraft fire and were protected by patrolling fighter aircraft.

It was not uncommon for these combat air patrols, flying superior planes and manned by more experienced pilots, to shoot down as many as three-quarters of a *kamikaze* attack wave before it reached Allied ships. Other attackers missed their targets and crashed into the sea. Fewer than 20 percent of *kamikaze* flights managed to hit a ship. There were some hits on carriers and battleships—the carriers *Wasp*, *Franklin*, and *Bunker Hill* were put out of action.[21] The *kamikaze* campaign completely failed in its mission to stop or even slow the American conquest of Okinawa. Nevertheless, for the sailors watching enemy aircraft diving toward them, it was a harrowing and potentially fatal experience.

Japanese commanders, desperate for any hint of good news, seized on inaccurate after-action reports to imagine that their suicide planes were devastating the US fleet. Admiral Ugaki Matome wrote in his diary that on April 15 "two battleships or cruisers seem to have been almost surely sunk."[22] Minimally trained pilots had poor ship recognition skills. They often reported that a comrade had sunk a carrier or battleship when in fact only a destroyer had suffered some damage. With his stock of pilots and planes dwindling rapidly, even Ugaki began to lose confidence in the ability of suicide missions to stave off defeat.

On April 7, the super battleship *Yamato* joined the *kamikaze* campaign, hoping to devastate the American invasion force with its mammoth eighteen-inch guns. It and nine smaller warships sailed from Japan with only enough diesel fuel for a one-way trip. Before going into action, the sailors on *Yamato* gathered for a special ceremony and sang:

> Across the sea, corpses in the water,
> Across the mountain, corpses in the field.
> I shall die for the Emperor.
> I shall never look back.[23]

American scouts detected this small flotilla almost as soon as it left Japanese home waters. US submarines and wave after wave of bombers attacked the giant battleship, scoring numerous bomb and torpedo hits. After hours of torment, the behemoth sank, along with a cruiser and four destroyers.

British leaders reassessed their priorities as the Allies closed in on Japan. Churchill, as always prioritizing recovery of the empire, wanted to focus British strength on liberating Malaya and Burma. His service chiefs and the Commonwealth leaders persuaded him that Great Britain must participate in the battles for Okinawa and Japan itself. They feared that unless Britain and its Dominions bore their share of effort, Anglo-American relations might deteriorate after the war just as they had after World War I. Maintaining an alliance with Washington was a paramount concern. They also believed that their participation in the end game would give London (as well as Ottawa, Canberra, and Wellington) a greater voice in postwar Pacific affairs. British participation was not militarily necessary to ensure the defeat of Japan, but it was a political necessity. Roosevelt and the US service chiefs agreed to joint operations with British and Commonwealth forces for equally political reasons. They wanted the American people to see that their allies were sharing the sacrifices entailed by this bloody conflict.

The Strategic Bombing of Japan

Strategic bombing of Japan's war industries and economic infrastructure had always been a part of the Allies' plans, but until late in the war they did not have adequate bases from which to launch such an offensive. Initially they intended to bomb Manchuria and parts of the home islands, as well as launch tactical attacks on the Japanese army, from bases in the Nationalist-controlled provinces of China. It proved impossible, however, to transport enough supplies from India over the Hump to mount an effective campaign. This strategy fell apart completely in 1944 when the enemy *Ichigo* offensive overran all but one of those bases. The American capture of islands in the Marianas group changed this situation dramatically. US engineers constructed a large air base on the small island of Tinian, only 1,500 miles from Tokyo. Beginning in November 1944, B-29 Superfortress bombers struck frequently against economic targets in Japan—especially urban-industrial complexes, shipping, and the aircraft industry. The results of this daytime, high-altitude, "precision" bombing were as poor in the Far East as they had been in Europe.

At the urging of General Curtis LeMay, the US Army Air Forces switched to nighttime, low-altitude, area bombing. LeMay was unconcerned about damage to the civil population. He once remarked, "There are no innocent civilians."[24] Low-level attacks were now possible because Japanese air defenses had been so degraded by the blockade, which crippled the aircraft industry, and by combat attrition that had eliminated so much of Imperial air power. It was hard to hit a factory from thirty thousand feet, but easy to hit a big city from seven thousand feet or lower. The ordnance used changed as well, from high explosives to incendiary bombs. Fire-bombing was particularly effective given the pervasive use of wood and paper construction in Japanese residential neighborhoods.

This was war against the civilian population, aimed at disrupting its economic activity and breaking its resolve to continue the fight. Japan's biggest cities—Tokyo, Nagoya, Osaka, and Kobe—were pounded relentlessly. Incendiary bombing often created firestorms, like those in Dresden. Over thirty square miles of Tokyo were burned out, and more than one hundred thousand residents were killed. After just three months of this campaign, more than 40 percent of the area of the six largest Japanese cities was destroyed. Smaller cities were attacked, too. The bombing killed about 425,000 people and injured a similar number.[25] The devastation would have been worse, but a significant part of the US bomber fleet was diverted from March to May for tactical strikes on air bases on Kyushu during the battle for Okinawa. Nevertheless, the damage was so extensive that by July, American planners were running out of targets. General LeMay believed that this strategic bombing campaign *by itself* would force Japan to surrender soon. The combined effects of blockade and bombing all but destroyed the Japanese economy. By July 1945, industrial production fell to 40 percent of the previous year's output.

The Downfall of Japan

As the Battle of Okinawa wound to its bloody conclusion, virtually all of Japan's civilian and military leaders realized that defeat was imminent. Their most powerful ally, Germany, had been conquered, and their enemies now enjoyed large margins of superiority in numbers of troops and in quantity and quality of weaponry. The fall of Okinawa meant that the bombing run and invasion route to the Japanese home islands was now under five hundred miles. With the Imperial Navy largely destroyed, Allied warplanes, surface ships, and submarines were strangling Japan by blockading and mining Japanese ports. Food, fuel, and many other vital commodities were running out. Even though Japanese troops still occupied large parts of their overseas empire, the oil, rice, and other riches of those territories could no longer reach the homeland. Factories were grinding to a halt, while hunger spread across the land. Fleets of American heavy bombers now ravaged Japanese cities at will. Under the weight of defeat and privation, morale began to crack—both among the civil population and even among some of the troops. Intelligence analysts perceived the enemy's weakness by April 1944, but Allied commanders ignored their findings, preferring to cling to the stereotype of the Japanese soldier as a fanatical automaton.

Most of the Japanese leadership, however, recoiled from the unbearable prospect of surrender. Many pinned their hopes on one final, climactic battle. If the imminent invasion of Japan could be repulsed with enormous Allied casualties, then the enemy might agree to a less draconian peace. Once again, they deluded themselves that "spirit" mattered more than numbers and equipment, that peasants wielding bamboo spears could somehow overcome tanks. There was also some hope that frictions between the Western Allies and the USSR might make it possible to use Soviet mediation to secure less onerous peace terms.

More realistic men in the Foreign Ministry and at the imperial court focused on preserving the imperial institution. They favored a quick end to the war because they accepted the inevitability of defeat and feared either a military coup or a popular revolution. Diehards in the army, however, held out for much more. They hoped to avoid Allied military occupation of Japan, carry out only partial demilitarization, conduct any war crimes trials themselves, and even preserve some of their overseas empire. Beyond saving the emperor, they expected to maintain Japan's undemocratic political system and the leading role of the armed forces in that system.

Narrow self-interest clouded the judgment of top military and political leaders. Emperor Hirohito was concerned above all with the preservation of his dynasty and the imperial institution.[26] Lord Keeper of the Privy Seal Kido Koichi, the most influential figure at court and a key member of the pro-peace camp, urged a speedy end to the war because he feared a military coup or, even worse, a radical revolution. Navy Minister Yonai Mitsumasa shared that concern, commenting, "The main reason [for seeking an end to the war] is my anxiety over the domestic situation."[27] Behind the patriotic rhetoric of the army officers lay their conviction that the nation could not exist without the predominance of the military. To these men, national suicide seemed preferable to a democratized and demilitarized Japan. By the end of 1944, some leaders and journalists had begun to discuss publicly the heroic extinction of the population. Each element within the decision-making elite seemed unable to envision the Japanese nation apart from its own privileged position within that nation.

While Japanese leaders agonized over some sort of negotiated peace or a fight to the death, American planners projected an invasion of the enemy home islands, Operation Downfall. Navy and army air forces commanders believed that a blockade and continuous bombing would bring Japan to its knees, but the army was sure that a full-scale invasion would be required. Downfall was to be a two-stage assault, first storming the southern island of Kyushu (Operation Olympic) in early November 1945 and then, supported by air bases established on Kyushu, assaulting the Kanto Plain near Tokyo in the spring of 1946 (Operation Coronet). Olympic would deploy thirteen US divisions, commanded by General Walter Krueger, supported by a prolonged naval and air bombardment. The American planners initially expected resistance from six Japanese divisions, three at the southern end of the island where the invasion was to take place and three at the northern end. They also thought that the defenders would have 2,000–2,500 aircraft available to them. Early projections envisioned twenty-six thousand Allied casualties in the first month of the campaign.

Although they had no specific intelligence about American intentions, the Japanese high command accurately anticipated enemy landings in southern Kyushu and on the Kanto Plain. Only those two areas could accommodate a large amphibious invasion force. The Imperial Army adopted a strategy of all-out resistance to the initial assault (code-named *Ketsu-Go*, "Decisive Operation") in hopes that devastating American casualties would cause the United States to reconsider its unconditional surrender demand and lead to an acceptable negotiated settlement. Under this plan, airborne and seaborne suicide strikes were to destroy up to a third of the invader's vessels, especially targeting troop and supply transports. Then units entrenched near the beaches would fight the assault force to a standstill, moving in for close combat to negate the Americans' advantage in firepower. Finally, mobile units would counterattack and destroy the invaders.

Apparently Japanese officers had not learned the bitter lessons from Guadalcanal to Okinawa; they still thought of Americans as a soft, pleasure-loving people who could not endure the grim sacrifices of protracted war. Moreover, the high command in Tokyo readily accepted the self-justifying reports of field commanders who claimed that, although they had lost virtually every battle, they had nonetheless inflicted such suffering on the enemy that he was losing his will to fight. On this illusory hope, Tokyo redeployed troops from Manchuria, Taiwan, Korea, and elsewhere in Japan. They formed new units as well, though most of them were trained only briefly and were poorly equipped. In addition, thousands of Japanese civilians were drafted to build fortifications, bunkers, and tunnels. Most serviceable aircraft, including many obsolete planes and trainers, were transferred to Kyushu to fly *kamikaze* missions. This was the only available strategy because the Allied blockade and bombing campaigns had rendered new combat planes, spare parts, and aviation fuel scarce. The Imperial Navy no longer possessed its mighty fleets, but it would employ suicide speedboats packed with explosives, midget submarines, human-guided torpedoes, and even explosive-carrying swimmers to attack the invading ships.

Ultimately, the Imperial Army believed that the entire able-bodied portion of the civilian population should join in defending their homeland, using shotguns, grenades, knives, and even bamboo spears. Some radical officers envisioned the whole nation resisting the invader to the death. Fatalism displaced professional judgment in the minds of many officers. While they may have boasted of success in public, most of them knew that they had little chance of defeating the coming invasion.[28]

The American high command watched this buildup on Kyushu with growing alarm. By late summer there were as many as nine hundred thousand Japanese defenders there, supported by over 8,500 aircraft (most equipped only for suicide missions). American leaders were already concerned about casualties in an invasion of Japan given the appalling nature of the fighting on Leyte and Okinawa. The initial projections had assumed that the assault force would outnumber the defenders by three to one in the landing zones. Now it seemed that the invaders might be outnumbered—a sure recipe for a bloodbath.

President Truman, Admiral Nimitz, and some other commanders began to have second thoughts about Operation Olympic. The naval and air chiefs again pressed their argument that blockade and conventional bombing would soon compel the enemy to surrender without the need for an invasion. General MacArthur, however, dismissed the evidence of a dangerously large Japanese military buildup on Kyushu. He could not bear the thought of losing command of the largest amphibious assault in history, even bigger than the D-Day landings. General Marshall was so concerned about mass casualties that he explored the possibility of using atomic bombs on the invasion sites. (The effects of radiation poisoning were not well understood at that time.)

Additional concerns supported the strategy of blockade and bombing rather than invasion. After the defeat of Germany, many service members and their families were clamoring for demobilization. The American people were growing war weary. Beyond that, many economists and congressmen raised alarms about the need for a rapid reconversion to a peacetime economy to ensure that prosperity rather than renewed depression followed victory. Historian Lizzie Collingham makes an important point about blockade. Waiting to starve the Japanese into surrender would have taken at least until November. In that time, Allied POWs as well as the peoples of the Far East and the Pacific whom their conquerors had enslaved would have been starving too.[29] For some leaders, the use of atomic weapons seemed to offer a solution to the difficult choice between the high casualties of an invasion and the likely delays before blockade and bombing produced decisive results.

Two other factors came into play at this point. As agreed at the Tehran and Yalta Conferences, the Soviet Union would soon enter the war against Japan by invading Manchuria. It seemed possible that the shock of the Red Army assault might finally bring the Japanese to surrender. Moreover, it was on July 16, while at the Potsdam Conference, that President Truman received the news of the first successful test of an atomic bomb. The Japanese were soon rocked by these twin shocks of American atomic bombs and Soviet invasion. After much debate, the US leadership dismissed the options of an announcement to the enemy about their possession of atomic weapons or a demonstration of the bomb's power against an uninhabited area or a purely military target.

On August 6, a B-29 called the *Enola Gay* released an atomic bomb named Little Boy over Hiroshima. The bomb detonated 1,900 feet above its target, creating a blinding flash of light and a temperature of 5,400 degrees Fahrenheit at the epicenter of the blast. The explosion equaled the force of sixteen kilotons of TNT. Almost five square miles of the city were destroyed. Between seventy and eighty thousand inhabitants died in the blast or in the resulting firestorm, while another seventy thousand were injured. More deaths would follow from radiation poisoning. One dazed survivor recalled this ghastly scene during his escape from the ruins:

> I paused to rest. Gradually things around me came into focus. There were the shadowy forms of people, some of whom looked like walking ghosts. Others moved as though in pain, like scarecrows, their arms held out from their bodies with forearms and hands dangling. . . . They had been burned and were holding their arms out to prevent the painful friction of raw surfaces rubbing together. . . . An old woman lay near me with an expression of suffering on her face but she made no sound. Indeed, one thing was common to everyone I saw—complete silence.[30]

After the bombing, President Truman issued a public warning to the Japanese: "If they do not now accept our terms, they may expect a rain of ruin from the air, the like of which has never been seen on this earth."[31]

Aware of frictions within the Grand Alliance, Japanese diplomats and officers hoped that the Soviet Union, still a neutral in the East Asian theater of war, could mediate to secure more generous peace terms for Japan. Some of them even imagined a new, anti-Western alliance uniting the Soviet Union with Japan and Germany.[32] Their approaches were rebuffed by Stalin, who was now anxious to join the fighting in the Far East to reclaim territories lost by Tsar Nicholas II in 1905 and to secure a Soviet role in the occupation of Japan.

Stalin now saw himself in a race to overrun Manchuria, parts of north China, and perhaps even the northernmost Japanese island of Hokkaido before America's atomic bombs (which he knew about) or its invasion forces compelled Japan to surrender. He had reason to worry. After the successful Alamogordo A-bomb test, the American position had switched from pressing for a Soviet invasion of Manchuria to an ardent desire to secure a Japanese surrender *before* the Russians joined the fight. On August 9 (the day before a second atomic bomb was dropped on Nagasaki), the Soviet army launched a massive invasion of Manchuria and quickly shattered the defenses of Japan's Kwantung Army. Historian Tohmatsu Haruo argues that "it was the Soviet Union's participation in the war that made the Japanese government and military authorities give up trying to negotiate an end to the war and to make up their minds to announce unconditional surrender."[33] Japanese leaders feared not only the battlefield prowess of the Red Army but also the revolutionary implications of a Soviet occupation of their homeland—making surrender to the Americans seem the lesser evil.[34]

Finally, on August 9, a second atomic bomb, dubbed Fat Man, fell on Nagasaki. The results were less dramatic than the Hiroshima bomb (though still appalling) because the Nagasaki bomb fell farther off target than its predecessor and because the hilly topography of Nagasaki shielded parts of the city from the blast. Between thirty-nine and forty-five thousand residents were killed. Using the second atomic bomb only three days after the first did not give the Japanese government much time to ascertain the nature of this new weapon and reformulate its policy on continuing the war. This was deliberate. The Americans hoped to give the false impression that they had a large supply of these devastating weapons, which they would soon employ to incinerate Japan entirely if Tokyo did not surrender immediately. In fact, they had used both bombs then in existence; it would require some time to produce more.

The US decision to drop atomic bombs on Japan has been the subject of sustained controversy among historians. In August 1945, there was little discussion at the highest levels of the American government about whether to use atomic weapons. It seemed simply axiomatic that when the new superbomb was ready, it would be used against any remaining Axis opponents. The president and other members of the administration insisted that use of "the bomb" was necessary to end the war as quickly as possible, to obviate the need for an invasion of Japan, and thereby to save American (and even Japanese) lives. Estimates of Allied casualties for Olympic-Coronet continued to escalate in the postwar period to over a million.

A generation of patriotic historians labored mightily to support this position.[35] Subsequently, however, some American leaders, including General Eisenhower and Admiral William Leahy, expressed regret over using the atomic bomb. Then, beginning in the 1960s, a new generation of revisionist historians attacked the orthodox defense of atomic warfare. They insisted that Japan was already at the point of surrender in August 1945 and that US leaders knew this, but they used the bomb anyway, engaging in "atomic diplomacy" to intimidate their Russian allies.[36] Soviet leaders saw it that way. Iuli Khariton, a key member of the Soviet A-bomb project, later recalled, "The Soviet government interpreted [Hiroshima] as atomic blackmail against the USSR, as a threat to unleash a new, even more terrible and devastating war."[37]

More recently, a "middle ground" position has begun to emerge among historians. The revisionists were wrong in claiming that the Japanese were ready to surrender at the beginning of August on terms that were acceptable to the Allies. However, the traditionalist interpretation is inadequate as well in projecting the decision as an either-or choice between dropping the A-bomb or launching an invasion with hundreds of thousands of casualties. The traditional view is also problematic in ignoring the degree to which President Truman and Secretary of State James Byrnes saw the American monopoly in atomic weapons as an important lever in dealing with their difficult Soviet ally. Byrnes told atomic scientist Leo Szilard that he expected that the atomic bomb would make the Soviets "more manageable" in its dealings with Washington.[38] Truman and Byrnes did practice atomic diplomacy. In the judgment of historian Samuel Walker:

> Was the bomb necessary? In view of the evidence now available, the answer is yes
> . . . and no. Yes, the bomb was necessary, in combination with the Soviet attack on
> Manchuria, to end the war at the earliest possible moment. And yes, the bomb was
> necessary to save the lives of American troops, perhaps numbering in the several

thousands. But no, the bomb was probably not necessary to end the war within a fairly brief time without an invasion of Japan. And no, the bomb was not necessary to save the lives of *hundreds* of thousands of American troops.[39]

Moreover, beyond any geopolitical considerations, vengeance required using atomic weapons against Japan. Pearl Harbor, the Bataan Death March, and other well-publicized Japanese atrocities had aroused the bloodlust of President Truman and most Americans. The use of atomic weapons may not have been militarily necessary to end the war, but probably a political necessity.[40] In a *Fortune* magazine poll taken after the end of the war, the majority of Americans supported dropping two atomic bombs on the enemy, while a large minority thought that the air force should have dropped many more A-bombs before the Japanese had a chance to surrender.[41]

Even before these three dramatic blows of Hiroshima, Nagasaki, and Soviet entry into the Pacific war, a "peace party" had emerged among segments of the Japanese elite. The Foreign Ministry in Tokyo had come to realize that defeat was inevitable and that it was necessary to accept the Potsdam Declaration, with only slight modification to protect the emperor, if Japan were to avoid the complete destruction and abrogation of sovereignty that befell Germany. Lord Privy Seal Kido, the emperor's closest advisor, and other influential figures at court supported this position. Even Admiral Yonai, minister of the navy, gradually accepted the necessity of peace. There were also numerous officers in the army and navy (though certainly not a majority) who understood that the war was unwinnable and that resistance to the end would only result in the destruction of Japan.

Opposed to them stood the "war party," whose adherents hoped that Allied resolve might crack if their casualty count grew high enough. For them, even national extinction was preferable to abject surrender. Members of the peace party had to work in careful secrecy for fear of either assassination by radical officers or a military coup. The head of the government, Prime Minister Suzuki Kantaro (a retired admiral), vacillated between the two camps. Deadlock ensued. Army minister Anami Korechika and army chief of staff Umezu Yoshijiro adamantly opposed anything but a negotiated peace that left Japan fully independent and armed.[42] Under the existing political system, they could block the government from accepting even a modified version of the Potsdam Declaration.

This stalemate in the highest councils of the Japanese regime made the role of the emperor critical. Hirohito had not exerted himself previously to prevent or curtail the tragic series of mistakes—the Manchurian Incident, the Marco Polo Bridge Incident, and the Pearl Harbor attack—that had led Japan to this desperate situation. He was not a strong leader, and he shared many of his compatriots' grievances against the Western powers. As late as May, he too hoped that one last big battle could rescue Japan from defeat. However, his will to fight eroded gradually in the summer of 1945. The desperate supply situation and the horrendous bombing of Japanese cities affected him deeply. After a careful study of the army's plans for one last decisive homeland battle, he concluded that his nation no longer possessed the resources to fend off the enemy. After listening to his ministers and senior commanders rehearse the pro- and anti-peace arguments at an Imperial Conference on the night of August 9–10, Hirohito finally asserted his authority, making a "sacred decision" to accept a slightly modified version of the Potsdam terms and surrender.

Generals Anami and Umezu, although they still wanted to go on fighting, bowed to his majesty's will and ordered the army to comply with the emperor's decree. Hirohito recorded an announcement of surrender to be broadcast throughout Japan and its empire. He told his people that they must "endure the unendurable." One Japanese woman recorded her reaction in her diary: "Although most people think that defeat is extremely unfortunate, in their hearts they generally seem relieved."[43] Historian Samuel Walker has suggested that the atomic bomb gave the military leadership an opportunity to rationalize defeat: "Even the diehards went along, partly out of respect for the emperor and partly because the atomic bomb, ironically, enabled them to save face. They could claim that the war was lost and surrender made necessary because of the enemy's scientific prowess in developing nuclear weapons rather than because of their own mistakes or miscalculations."[44] Navy Minister Yonai referred to both the American atomic bombs and the Soviet invasion of Manchuria as "gifts from the gods" that enabled the Japanese leadership to break the stalemate and accept defeat.

Not everyone in the military was willing to obey the emperor's command, however. On the night of August 14, a group of mid-level officers attempted a coup. When they failed to persuade the commander of the Imperial Guards Division, General Mori Takeshi, to join them, they murdered the general and forged an order in his name for the division to occupy and seal the Imperial Palace and its grounds. They planned to destroy the emperor's recorded public announcement of the surrender and then force the government to reverse its policy. The inept conspirators found neither the record nor the emperor. By the next morning, troops loyal to the emperor had regained control of the palace. The plotters committed suicide. After putting down the coup attempt and ordering Japanese units everywhere to obey the emperor's command, a heartbroken Anami also committed suicide.

But would the Allies agree to Japan's conditional offer to surrender? Secretary of War Henry Stimson and Undersecretary of State Joseph Grew (America's former ambassador in Tokyo) urged acceptance of the Japanese condition that the imperial institution be preserved. Byrnes and his predecessor, Cordell Hull, both opposed the concession, as did the more liberal members of the administration and the Congress. They believed that the emperor system was an integral part of the old militarist, aggressive Japan that had started the war and, as such, should be swept away. Most Americans agreed. President Truman finally conceded that the emperor could remain but that his authority would be "subject to the Supreme Commander of the Allied Powers." He realized that maintaining the emperor's authority would make the surrender of Japanese troops in the homeland and throughout the empire a much smoother process. Truman also pressured Stalin and Chiang Kai-shek to accept this compromise. On September 2, aboard the battleship *Missouri* at anchor in Tokyo Bay, representatives of the Japanese government signed the instrument of surrender, and the bloodiest conflict in world history finally ended.

Notes

1. Quoted in Desmond Flower and James Reeves, eds., *The Taste of Courage: The War, 1939–1945* (New York: Harper & Row, 1960), 726.

2. Robert Sherrod, *Tarawa: The Story of a Battle* (New York: Duell, Sloan & Pearce, 1954), 154–55.

3. Joseph A. Alexander, *Utmost Savagery: The Three Days of Tarawa* (Novato, CA: Presidio Press, 1996), 263.

4. H. P. Willlmott, *War with Japan: The Period of Balance, May 1941–October 1943* (Wilmington, DE: Scholarly Resources, 2002), 158.

5. Alvin D. Coox, "The Effectiveness of the Japanese Military Establishment in the Second World War," in *Military Effectiveness*, vol. 3, *The Second World War*, ed. Allan R. Millett and Williamson Murray (Cambridge: Cambridge University Press, 2010), 34.

6. Coox, "Effectiveness of the Japanese," 39.

7. Harold J. Goldberg, *D-Day in the Pacific: The Battle of Saipan* (Bloomington: Indiana University Press, 2007), 88.

8. Goldberg, *D-Day in the* Pacific, 64–65.

9. Sharon Tosi Lacey, *Pacific Blitzkrieg: World War II in the Central Pacific* (Denton: University of North Texas Press, 2015), 211.

10. Goldberg, *D-Day in the Pacific*, 117.

11. Goldberg, *D-Day in the Pacific*, 172,

12. Alexander Astroth, *Saipan and Tinian, 1944: The Civilian Deaths in Historical Context* (Jefferson, NC: McFarland, 2019).

13. Goldberg, *D-Day in the Pacific*, 102.

14. E. B. Sledge, *With the Old Breed at Peleliu and Okinawa* (Novato, CA: Presidio, 1990), 130.

15. Thomas J. Cutler, *The Battle of Leyte Gulf, 23–26 October 1944* (New York: HarperCollins, 1994), xiii.

16. Lawrence Taylor, *A Trial of Generals: Homma, Yamashita, MacArthur* (South Bend, IN: Icarus Press, 1981), 124–26.

17. Stanley L. Falk, "The Army in the Southwest Pacific," in *MacArthur and the American Century*, ed. William M. Leary (Lincoln: University of Nebraska Press, 2001), 151.

18. David Horner, "General MacArthur's War: The South and Southwest Pacific Campaigns, 1942–45," in *The Pacific War Companion*, ed. Daniel Marston (Oxford: Osprey, 2005), 141.

19. Haruko Taya Cook and Theodore F. Cook, *Japan at War: An Oral History* (New York: New Press, 1992), 356–57.

20. Sledge, *With the Old Breed*, 253.

21. The carrier *Wasp* (CV-18) damaged in this action was named after the carrier (CV-9) sunk in 1942.

22. Donald M. Goldstein and Katherine V. Dillon, eds., *Fading Victory: The Diary of Admiral Matome Ugaki, 1941–1945* (Annapolis, MD: Naval Institute Press, 2008), 588–89.

23. Robert Leckie, *Okinawa: The Last Battle of World War II* (New York: Penguin, 1995), 93.

24. Quoted in Michael S. Sherry, *The Rise of American Air Power: The Creation of Armageddon* (New Haven, CT: Yale University Press, 1987), 287.

25. Richard B. Frank, "The Bomb's Long Aftermath," *Wartime* 61 (2013), 21.

26. Noriko Kawamura, *Emperor Hirohito and the Pacific War* (Seattle: University of Washington Press, 2007), 183–84.

27. Herbert P. Bix, *Hirohito and the Making of Modern Japan* (New York: HarperCollins, 2000), 509–10.

28. Coox, "The Effectiveness of the Japanese," 33.

29. Lizzie Collingham, *The Taste of War: World War II and the Battle for Food* (New York: Penguin, 2011), 314.

30. Michihiko Hachiya, *Hiroshima Diary* (Chapel Hill: University of North Carolina Press, 1955), 4.

31. "Statement by the President of the United States," in *Documentary History of the Truman Presidency*, vol. 1, *The Decision to Drop the Atomic Bomb*, ed. Dennis Merrill (Bethesda, MD: University Publications of America, 1995), 198.

32. Akira Iriye, *Power and Culture: The Japanese-American War, 1941–1945* (Cambridge, MA: Harvard University Press, 1981), 220–23.

33. Tohmatsu Haruo, "The Strategic Correlation between the Sino-Japanese and Pacific Wars," in *The Battle for China: Essays on the Military History of the Sino-Japanese War of 1937–1945*, ed. Mark Peattie, Edward Drea, and Hans van de Ven (Stanford, CA: Stanford University Press, 2011), 440.

34. Tsuyoshi Hasegawa, "The Atomic Bombs and the Soviet Invasion: Which Was More Important in Japan's Decision to Surrender?," *The End of the Pacific War: Reappraisals*, ed. Hasegawa (Stanford, CA: Stanford University Press, 2007), 144.

35. The classic statement of the traditionalist or orthodox position is Henry L. Stimson, "The Decision to Use the Atomic Bomb," *Harper's*, February 1947, 97–107. Herbert Feis, *Japan Subdued: The Atomic Bomb and the End of the War in the Pacific* (Princeton, NJ: Princeton University Press, 1961), is a more

nuanced and widely influential version of the argument. For an updated defense of that position, see Wilson D. Miscamble, *The Most Controversial Decision: Truman, the Atomic Bombs, and the Defeat of Japan* (Cambridge: Cambridge University Press, 2011).

36. Gar Alperovitz, *The Decision to Use the Atomic Bomb* (New York: Vintage, 1996).

37. Vladislav Zubok and Constantine Pleshakov, *Inside the Kremlin's Cold War: From Stalin to Khrushchev* (Cambridge, MA: Harvard University Press, 1996), 42.

38. William Lanouette with Bela Szilard, *Genius in the Shadows: A Biography of Leo Szilard, the Man behind the Bomb* (New York: Scribner, 1992), 265.

39. J. Samuel Walker, *Prompt and Utter Destruction: Truman and the Use of Atomic Bombs against Japan* (Chapel Hill: University of North Carolina Press, 2004), 97.

40. Michael C. C. Adams, *The Best War Ever: America and World War II* (Baltimore, MD: Johns Hopkins University Press, 1994), 44.

41. *Fortune*, December 1945, 305.

42. Noriko Kawamura implies that Anami and Umezu may not have been implacably opposed to peace but maintained a hard line publicly until the emperor's "sacred decision" in order to ensure discipline in the army. *Hirohito and the Pacific War*, 180–81.

43. Thomas R. H. Havens, *Valley of Darkness: The Japanese People in World War Two* (New York: Norton, 1978), 193.

44. Walker, *Prompt and Utter Destruction*, 84.

Part V

A WORLD MADE BY WAR

CHAPTER 21

The Postwar World

Grief and apprehension tempered the joy that greeted the arrival of peace in 1945. As many as eighty million people had died during the war—including twenty-seven million in the USSR and twenty to thirty million in China. Millions more suffered crippling physical or psychological trauma. A hundred million had become refugees in their own lands. The cities of Germany and Japan as well as the western region of the Soviet Union lay in ruins. Reconstruction would be long and difficult given the massive damage to property and the disruption of economic systems. While there were great celebrations in New York and London, in many places hordes of displaced persons roamed the streets or inhabited squalid refugee camps. Gangs of homeless youths, who had never known anything but violence, infested many cities. Moreover, the coming of peace did not mean the end of violence. Some of those who suffered under Axis occupation now sought revenge against their oppressors and those who had collaborated with them. In much of Asia, the war quickly transformed into revolutionary or national liberation struggles. Europeans and many Asians continued to suffer from cold and hunger through 1947. Runaway inflation lasted even longer.

The Second World War shaped life around the globe for decades to come. The war eliminated (at least temporarily) Germany, Italy, and Japan as great powers, while it gravely weakened both Great Britain and France. The United States emerged as a world power, followed by the Soviet Union. Historian Paul Kennedy describes these changes as "a seismic shift in the world order."[1] The wartime alliance between Washington and Moscow quickly disintegrated into a dangerous, nuclear-armed Cold War. The nuclear "balance of terror" between the USSR and USA prevented a new world war but also led to frightening confrontations around the globe as well as proxy wars in Korea, Vietnam, and Afghanistan. That menacing division affected the reconstruction of war-ravaged Europe and the reorganization of Asia.

Overcoming the severe challenges of the Great Depression and fascism, liberal-democratic capitalism emerged reinvigorated from the war—championed by the almost unscathed United States. The Depression and the war suggested to many Europeans that the anarchy of unchecked nation-states and uncontrolled free markets were dangerous modes of organizing human life. Ideas of European union as well as economic and social planning began to take hold. Communism, too, grew in strength and, in some places, established its independence from Moscow's control. Finally, those European empires that had survived the First World War, principally the British and the French, collapsed in the three decades following 1945.

The Cold War

The breakdown of the Grand Alliance and the advent of the Cold War profoundly affected the course of reconstruction in Europe and Asia. Neither the Soviet dictator nor the American presidents intended or even foresaw the rapid disintegration of their alliance and the outbreak of the Cold War. President Roosevelt hoped to construct a just and stable postwar world that would prevent future wars and the reemergence of militarism in Germany and Japan. Woodrow Wilson had attempted this task in 1919 but failed. FDR was determined to learn from that failure. The key to a peaceful future, the American leader believed, was the creation of an international organization more robust and effective than the defunct League of Nations—a new United Nations Organization. Roosevelt was no utopian idealist. An ongoing, cooperative arrangement among the four great powers (Britain, the USA, the USSR, and China—the "four policemen" as he termed them) was to undergird the UN. In his vision, they would use their combined strength to ensure the peaceful resolution of conflicts. That continuing collaboration was particularly important to Roosevelt because he did not envision stationing American troops abroad for long. His plan did not anticipate the rapid breakdown of relations between the Western Allies and the Soviet Union.

Prime Minister Churchill also hoped to maintain some level of cooperation among the Allies, though he was wary of the growing power of the Soviet Union in Europe. He firmly intended to preserve the British Empire, too. His successor as prime minister, Clement Attlee of the Labour Party, understood better than Churchill that Britain, in its weakened state, could no longer hold sway over its far-flung colonies. Stalin also wanted to continue cooperating with his capitalist allies, especially to keep receiving American aid for his war-ravaged country. Roosevelt understood that the USSR would be militarily predominant in postwar eastern Europe and therefore responsible for the region's security under his "four policemen" formula, but he expected Stalin to exercise that responsibility in harmony with the right of self-determination for those nations.

The onset of the Cold War should not have been so surprising. The Western powers and Soviet Russia had been hostile to each other since the October Revolution in 1917. In this sense, it was the Grand Alliance, not the Cold War, that was atypical of the East-West relationship. Moreover, with the defeat of the Axis, the East-West alliance lost its most important rationale. Numerous disputes between the Western powers and Russia during their alliance fueled the reemergence of their mutual hostility.[2] The tardiness of the Western powers in opening a "second front" in western Europe was particularly infuriating to Stalin.

The status of Soviet gains under the Nazi-Soviet Pact raised another vexing problem for the alliance. Stalin insisted that the incorporation of Latvia, Lithuania, and Estonia as well as parts of prewar Poland, Romania, and Finland were irrevocable additions to the Soviet Union. Desperately trying to keep the USSR in the war in the fall of 1941, London recognized these Soviet gains, but Washington declined to concede those seizures publicly, even though Roosevelt knew they could not be pried from Stalin's grip. The Americans' disinclination to recognize the Percentages Agreement over influence in the Balkans, negotiated by Churchill and Stalin, further heightened distrust in both Moscow and Washington.

FDR was sensitive to Soviet security concerns, especially in eastern Europe, where all the states during the interwar period, except Czechoslovakia, had abandoned democracy for authoritarian rule and had consistently pursued policies hostile to the USSR. Moreover, the populations of most of these states were not only overwhelmingly anticommunist but also

The new "Big Three" Allied leaders, British prime minister Clement Attlee, US president Harry Truman, and Soviet premier Joseph Stalin, at the Potsdam summit conference in 1945.
Source: National Archives

deeply anti-Russian. It was a tragic dilemma; security for the Soviet Union and freedom for the peoples of eastern Europe were mutually incompatible.

Stalin initially thought that "friendly" governments along his border would suffice, be he soon concluded that only the imposition of communist regimes throughout eastern Europe could ensure Soviet security. He told Yugoslav communist leader Milovan Djilas, "This war is not as in the past; whoever occupies a territory also imposes on it his own social system."[3] The British and Americans had done as much when they liberated Italy, while the United States insisted on its exclusive control of Japan. At the Yalta Conference, Stalin had promised free and fair elections throughout eastern Europe, but he then bluntly told the Americans, "A freely elected government in any of these East European countries would be anti-Soviet, and that we cannot allow."[4] Roosevelt hoped that his diplomatic skills would enable him to maintain a working relationship with Stalin after the war. After Roosevelt's death, Truman took a much tougher line in dealing with Stalin.[5]

The Anglo-American monopoly of and secretiveness about atomic weapons posed yet another source of discord within the alliance. The president and Churchill agreed not to share information about the atomic program with their Soviet ally. By concluding this agreement, Washington and London created a postwar atomic alliance that inevitably threatened Moscow. Spies provided Stalin with information on the Manhattan Project that his allies were withholding from him. The Soviet leader also knew that the Western powers had cracked German codes but were withholding that information as well.

With the coming of peace, the interests of the Allies diverged in many ways, nowhere more so than in Germany. They divided Germany into occupation zones for Russia, Britain, America, and France, with an Allied Control Commission coordinating matters for the country as a whole. Similarly, the four Allies split control of Berlin, deep within the Soviet zone. The French and (for a time) the British envisioned partitioning Germany into a series of small states, but the Americans and Russians anticipated no partition beyond independence for Austria (also under four-power occupation). Alsace-Lorraine reverted to France while Germany lost about 25 percent of its prewar territory in the east to Poland. The Sudetenland returned to Czechoslovakia. The Allies agreed to dismantle Germany's military-industrial complex so that it could not wage war again and to compel the defeated Reich to pay substantial reparations—mostly to Russia (mainly in industrial equipment) for the extensive damage done on Soviet territory. American planners even flirted briefly with the idea of completely deindustrializing Germany (the Morgenthau Plan).

Stalin expected that Germany, reduced in size and deprived of its military-industrial potential, would remain a united, neutral state. The Cold War made that impossible. Britain and the United States amalgamated their occupation zones (Bizonia) and stopped sending reparations from their zones to the Soviet Union. Ultimately, the growing East-West rift forced the division of Germany along the ideological fault line. The Federal Republic of Germany (West Germany)—liberal, democratic, capitalist, and tied to the Western powers—was established on May 23, 1949. Stalin followed suit, creating the Communist-dominated German Democratic Republic (East Germany) on October 7, 1949. The Western Allies soon reversed their position and allowed the creation of a West German army. Berlin, still under four-power occupation, remained a thorny issue for the former allies. Stalin tried to push the Western powers out of the city in 1948 by blockading the land routes into Berlin. The Americans countered with a massive airlift lasting almost a year, which brought food and fuel to the West Berliners. Both sides carefully calibrated their measures to avoid provoking a major war.

The fate of Poland also caused considerable friction between the USSR and its Western allies. The latter supported the London-based Polish government-in-exile. Stalin distrusted that group of "bourgeois" politicians and broke relations with them after the Katyn massacre became public knowledge. He sponsored an alternative Polish government, based in Lublin and led by Polish communists. He agreed to include two of the "London Poles" in a coalition government and promised to hold free and fair elections, but Polish communists soon pushed the noncommunists out of all positions of authority. Poland became a one-party dictatorship. The new regime nationalized industry and finance and broke up large rural estates. Soviet marshal Rokossovskii took command of the revived Polish armed forces. The key issues for Stalin were territory and security. He had always intended to keep the large part of prewar eastern Poland (populated largely by Ukrainians and Belorussians) that he had already incorporated into the USSR, and he feared that any Polish government not under his control would revert to its traditional Russophobia.

A similar evolution toward one-party dictatorship under Russian tutelage occurred in Hungary, Romania, and Bulgaria. Monarchies were abolished in all three states. "National Front" coalitions inevitably gave way to Communist regimes supported by the two hundred Soviet army divisions stationed throughout eastern Europe. Genuine coalition government lasted longest in Czechoslovakia. Prewar leaders, President Edvard Beneš and Foreign

Minister Jan Masaryk, returned to their homeland after its liberation by the Red Army to head a multiparty administration in a restored democratic republic. Yet even though Beneš had signed a treaty of alliance and cooperation with Moscow in 1943, a Communist coup toppled his government in 1948—another victim of the intensifying Cold War.[6]

Four East European states deviated from this pattern. Communist-led resistance movements liberated Yugoslavia and Albania, which then established communist regimes without substantial Russian assistance. In addition to instituting a socialist economy, Marshal Tito set up a federal system in Yugoslavia, which he hoped would reduce the sharp antagonisms in his multiethnic country. Though allied with the USSR, Tito intended to preside over a fully independent state. That independence angered Stalin, who attempted to depose the maverick marshal. Russia and its satellite states renounced their treaties with Belgrade. They expelled Yugoslavia from the Cominform and denied it membership in the Comecon economic bloc. War seemed imminent. Tito and his regime survived the onslaught, provoking a Soviet-Yugoslav split in 1948. The Belgrade government accepted US aid in order to preserve its independence.

Great power interests also determined the fate of Greece, but in this case it was British, not Soviet, power that intervened. After the Germans withdrew from Greece, the communist-led National Liberation Front (EAM/ELAS) controlled about two-thirds of the country, though not the capital, Athens. The British considered Greece (unlike Yugoslavia) vital to their imperial interests, so they rapidly increased their occupation force from four thousand to fifty thousand troops. They also pressured the EAM to enter a coalition with the returning government-in-exile, though they agreed to delay the return of King George II until a plebiscite on the monarchy could be held.

This fragile truce broke apart over the issue of disarming the various resistance groups and restoring law and order. The plan advanced by Premier George Papandreou and the British envisioned disarming communist-led ELAS units while transforming some of the noncommunist forces into a new national army. Communist ministers resigned from the government in protest and called for massive demonstrations in the capital. On December 3, 1944 (afterward known as Bloody Sunday), the police opened fire on the demonstrators, killing 28 and wounding 140. Civil war flared in Athens. Churchill told his commander on the scene, General Ronald Scobie, *"Do not however hesitate to act as if you were in a conquered city where a local rebellion is in progress."*[7] American planes rushed in two additional British divisions. After fierce battles, ELAS fighters were driven out of Athens. Under British pressure and lacking support from Moscow, the EAM signed a peace agreement in February 1945 and laid down most of its arms. The EAM and the Communist Party were recognized as legal political entities.

Civil war flared again in 1946 and lasted into 1949. The newly founded communist regimes in Yugoslavia, Bulgaria, and Albania supported the Greek communist insurgents, but Stalin, faithful in this instance to the Percentages Agreement, did not. The Soviet leader told Yugoslav communist Milovan Djilas, "The uprising in Greece must be stopped, and as quickly as possible."[8] He did not want to challenge the Western Allies in an area they considered vital to their interests. Washington failed to understand that. The Truman administration believed that Soviet probes in Iran and Turkey, combined with this communist-led insurgency in Greece, exposed a Kremlin strategy to dominate the Middle East and the eastern Mediterranean. The US president cast challenges to US policy in Greece and Turkey as a vital battle in the struggle between "freedom" and "totalitarianism." While Stalin hesitated, American money and arms poured in to sustain the Greek government. This disparity of outside support combined with the Soviet-Yugoslav split to doom the Greek communist insurrection. Greece became a parliamentary democracy (at least for a while) and joined NATO in 1952. More than 108,000 Greeks died during the civil war, over 700,000 became refugees, and much of the country was devastated.

Finland signed an armistice with the USSR on September 19, 1944. That did not end the fighting, however. During the "Lapland War" (September–November 1944), Finns fought to drive the remaining German troops out of their country, expelling the last of them by April 1945. The formal peace treaty with Russia, signed in 1947, deprived Finland of about 10 percent of the territory along its southern and eastern borders, required reparations payments to the Soviet Union, and mandated legalization of the Finnish Communist Party and the banning of all fascist organizations. Unlike most of the countries of eastern Europe, however, Finland did not experience a communist revolution or have a communist regime imposed on it by Soviet forces. Instead of "Sovietization," Moscow settled for "Finlandization"—domestic autonomy but close coordination with the Kremlin in international affairs. The Soviet leader feared that imposing a communist regime on Finland might provoke guerrilla resistance at a time when the Red Army was still battling such movements in Ukraine and the Baltic states.[9] He also worried that a communist Finland might cause neutral Sweden to ally with the West.

The Allies tried to maintain their wartime cooperation after the conclusion of hostilities, at least on some issues. Under American pressure, Stalin withdrew his troops from northern Iran and stopped supporting separatist forces there. He also abandoned his demands on Turkey for naval bases in the Straits. The Soviet Union also withdrew its bid to assume a trusteeship over the former Italian colony of Libya. Britain and the United States tacitly accepted increasing Soviet control of Bulgaria and Romania. The Potsdam Conference proved to be the last summit meeting for ten years. Thereafter, the powers negotiated with each other through conferences of their foreign ministers, but these meetings soon became more acrimonious and less productive.

America responded to the perceived threat of revolutions and Soviet expansionism with money and weaponry. While the USSR consolidated its grip on eastern Europe, the United States used economic power to support the reestablishment of liberal, capitalist democracies in western Europe. The Marshall Plan distributed $12 billion ($150.3 billion in today's money) in recovery aid to nations from Britain to Turkey between 1947 and 1954. The program had an undeniably humanitarian element, but it was also a powerful political tool to blunt the appeals of communism in a traumatized Europe and restore those nations as allies of the United States and eager customers of American exports. Washington sponsored the Bretton Woods Agreement in July 1944 to promote international free trade and freely convertible currencies, the latter objective supported by the creation of the International Monetary Fund (IMF). The US dollar reigned supreme everywhere outside the Soviet sphere, and American goods flooded global markets. The Soviet Union declined to participate in the Bretton Woods system, and it pressured its East European satellites to spurn Marshall Plan assistance. That was one of Stalin's great mistakes, because a Soviet application for Marshall Plan funds might well have derailed the program.

In addition to Marshall Plan aid, the US fought the spread of communism and Soviet influence with widespread military assistance programs. President Truman told Congress on March 12, 1947, "I believe that it must be the policy of the United States to support free peoples who are resisting attempted subjugation by armed minorities or by outside pressures."[10] The Truman Doctrine evolved into a policy of global counterrevolution and

The Cold War divided Europe into mutually hostile Western and Eastern blocs.

containment of any Soviet advance. Both the US and the USSR had begun demobilizing their huge armed forces after the war. By 1949, both powers reversed that trend and entered into a new arms race.

Each side blamed the other for the breakdown of the Grand Alliance, and each accused the other of aggression. In a famous speech in Fulton, Missouri, on March 5, 1946, Winston Churchill declared:

> From Stettin in the Baltic to Trieste in the Adriatic an "iron curtain" has descended across the Continent. Behind that line lie all the capitals of the ancient states of Central and Eastern Europe. Warsaw, Berlin, Prague, Vienna, Budapest, Belgrade, Bucharest and Sofia; all these famous cities and the populations around them lie in what I must call the Soviet sphere, and all are subject, in one form or another, not only to Soviet influence but to a very high and in some cases increasing measure of control from Moscow.[11]

George Kennan, a veteran American diplomat, warned the US government and the public that Marxism drove the Soviet Union to expansionism. However, unlike Hitler, who was a reckless gambler, the Soviet leaders were much more cautious, convinced that their ultimate victory was a certainty. They would probe for weaknesses and flow into vacuums.

The proper American response, Kennan argued, was "containment"—the steady, measured application of counterpressure against Soviet advances.[12] His views were widely accepted because Truman and most senior members of his administration already shared Kennan's underlying assumptions. He advocated the use of political and economic tools to thwart Soviet probes, but the containment doctrine soon produced a series of global military alliances. "The East-West clash also became *systemic*," historian Carole Fink notes, "rooted in almost every institution—economic, military, political, diplomatic, religious, and even cultural."[13] The theory of totalitarianism enjoyed great popularity during the Cold War, not only among academics but among journalists and politicians as well because it transformed the public image of the USSR from valiant ally to menacing foe by claiming to demonstrate that the new enemy—Communist Russia—was identical to the old enemy—Nazi Germany.[14]

NSC-68, a 1950 National Security Council policy statement, replaced mere containment with the goal of "rollback" of communist gains. This document painted a stark picture of East-West relations: "Thus unwillingly our free society finds itself mortally challenged by the Soviet system. No other value system is so wholly irreconcilable with ours, so implacable in its purpose to destroy ours."[15] This policy led to a rapidly increasing military budget, the development of the hydrogen bomb, and expanding commitments to anticommunist allies around the world.

Stalin expected "contradictions" between the US and Britain to sharpen in the postwar years, but he was badly mistaken. His crackdown in eastern Europe had the unanticipated consequence of binding the states of western Europe more closely to America. Two events in 1949, Soviet acquisition of atomic weapons and Mao Zedong's victory in China, shook Western leaders and spurred rearmament programs. The United States and its European allies created the North Atlantic Treaty Organization (NATO) in 1949. Other regional military pacts aimed at containing Russia and "Red China" soon followed. The Soviets countered belatedly with the Warsaw Pact in 1955, linking the USSR and its East European satellites, as a counterweight to NATO.

Moscow joined the East-West war of words with the "Two Camps" thesis, proclaimed by ideology chieftain Andrei Zhdanov in September 1947. Stalin and Zhdanov blamed aggressive American imperialism for dividing the world between the Soviet camp of democracy and peace and the American camp of oppression and war. The Soviets launched the Communist Information Bureau (or Cominform) in 1947 as a replacement of sorts for the Comintern, which had been dissolved in 1943. This body worked to root out any heretical tendencies within East European communism and to present a united front against the West.

Washington and Moscow badly misunderstood each other. Each of them grossly overestimated the threat to their interests posed by the other. American politicians and commentators exaggerated the ability of the war-ravaged Soviet Union to project military force in distant and sustained campaigns. Westerners also inflated the commitment of Stalin's regime to revolution abroad. Communization was a tool for enforcing the loyalty of otherwise hostile East European peoples. The crusading spirit and willingness to take risks for the cause of world revolution, which had been strong in the first years of Soviet power, had atrophied long since. Stalin couched his public pronouncements on international affairs in Marxist jargon, but his foreign policy was, for the most part, geopolitical.[16] He ignored the significance of US war weariness and rapid demobilization in 1946. He also failed to anticipate Washington's responses to his initiatives, which soon led to the remilitarization of America's international posture.

Stalin's xenophobic, paranoid personality also contributed to the breakdown of East-West relations. He had never fully trusted Roosevelt or Churchill, but he had established a tolerable working relationship with them. Both men were gone before the end of 1945. The new British prime minister was a despised "social democrat," while the new American president was an insecure, sometimes abrasive, unknown quantity. America's possession of atomic weapons shook the Soviet leader badly, though he was determined not to submit to US nuclear blackmail. Stalin's own dark fears caused him to anticipate the worst from the Western powers and to cherry-pick the evidence to reinforce those suspicions. Stalin "still did not want a confrontation with his former allies, but he did not know how to avoid it."[17]

Moreover, both Washington and Moscow exaggerated the enemy threat for domestic political effect. For the Kremlin, raising the fear of a new imperialist war justified both the continuing sacrifices required of the Soviet people and the repression of their aspirations for a less authoritarian regime. In America, the Cold War and the arms race it entailed greatly benefited the Republican Party (out of power since 1932) and what President Eisenhower would subsequently call "the military-industrial complex." Many Democrats, too, jumped on the Cold War bandwagon to avoid being crushed by the rightward shift in public opinion.

Life in the Postwar World—Western Europe

Some Europeans hoped that their prewar way of life could be restored, though the more sober minded realized that was an illusion. Others, particularly in the resistance movements, believed that a radically transformed "new Europe" of peace and social justice would emerge from their years of suffering and sacrifice. For many Europeans, the Great Depression and the horrors of the war had discredited the ideal of a self-regulating free market and the international anarchy of uncontrolled competition among sovereign states. The dream of creating a new Europe of social justice, free from war, appealed to many across the political spectrum, from communists to conservative Catholics. Unlike World War I, however, no wave of violent social revolution followed the Second World War in Europe. Europe was also awash with displaced persons (DPs)—concentration camp survivors, millions of foreigners forced to work in Germany, and still more millions fleeing violence in eastern Europe. Despite this devastation and chaos, the countries of Europe (outside the Soviet sphere) reestablished liberal-democratic governments, rebuilt their shattered economies, and constructed a social welfare net for their citizens. By the middle of the 1950s, the countries of Western Europe experienced extraordinary economic growth.

GREAT BRITAIN

Britain emerged from the Second World War severely weakened, deeply in debt, and incapable of maintaining its empire. The United States canceled Britain's $6 billion Lend-Lease debt and provided an additional $3.75 billion loan, though that was a much smaller sum than London's negotiators had sought. In return, the country was required to sign the Bretton Woods Agreement and open its markets to American exports. Wartime food allocations were cut in May 1945; rationing did not end in Britain until 1954. While there had been great celebrations on VE Day, foreign observers soon noticed a pervasive depressed mood.

The cost of two world wars had drained Britain's overseas investments, and now the United States had captured many of Britain's export markets. The nation would endure a much-diminished diplomatic, military, and economic role in the world. Austerity—getting by on less—was the new watchword. Record-breaking cold in the winter of 1946–1947, continuing military expenses in the unsuccessful attempt to keep even part of the empire, and the proliferation of strikes by discontented workers hindered recovery.

In Britain, as on the Continent, most people had come to believe that a completely free market economy could guarantee neither stability nor fairness and that government should play some role in ensuring that citizens had health care, housing, education, and a livable wage. The Labour Party, which won an outright majority in 1945, launched programs to promote full employment, even if that meant an unbalanced budget. Coal, steel, transportation, and some of the service industries were nationalized—though 80 percent of industry remained privately owned. A new National Health Service provided free medical care for all citizens. Education reforms made secondary education available to all students. Progressive income and inheritance levies taxed the affluent to pay for these services. When the Conservative Party came back into power in 1951, its leaders privatized steel and transportation but otherwise left the welfare state intact.

FRANCE

France had suffered many fewer casualties and much less physical destruction than Germany, Poland, or the USSR (and many fewer deaths than it had endured in the First World War). Even so, the Germans had looted the country. Economic recovery was slow, hampered by continuing inflation. Moreover, the humiliation of rapid defeat in 1940 followed by four years of German occupation and widespread collaboration with the enemy would haunt the French conscience for decades. Resistance fighters conducted a "wild purge" in the wake of liberation, in which some seven thousand people were executed as traitors. Twelve thousand women, accused of "horizontal collaboration," were subjected to humiliating rituals—often stripped naked, their heads shaven, swastikas painted on their bodies, and paraded through towns. Many were beaten; some were killed.

Many in the resistance expected the defeat of the Axis to inaugurate an era of sweeping transformation of the social and economic systems. A Paris newspaper's headline screamed, "From resistance to revolution!" Civil war seemed a real possibility. General Charles de Gaulle, backed by the British and the Americans, moved quickly to defang the radical resistance by disarming it. The French Communist Party (PCF), lacking the support of a majority of the working class or of the Kremlin for an armed uprising, gave up its weapons and agreed to participate in electoral politics. Restoring order and reuniting a divided nation were de Gaulle's priorities. Some of the most egregious collaborators were put on trial. Marshal Pétain, head of the Vichy regime, was exiled to an island in the Atlantic, while Pierre Laval, Pétain's odious vice premier, was executed. Amnesty laws in the early 1950s allowed most bureaucrats and business leaders to escape any punishment for their role in the Nazi war effort.

Initially de Gaulle ruled as provisional president of France with the apparent consent of a majority of Frenchmen and the grudging acquiescence of the PCF. Within sixteen months, however, the temperamental general resigned in a huff as the honeymoon of liberation evaporated and political rivalries and the fundamental cleavages in French society reemerged. Voters (with women casting ballots for the first time) established the Fourth

Republic in October 1946. The new democratic, parliamentary system resembled the former Third Republic and, not surprisingly, the political fragmentation and ineffectiveness that had characterized that government soon reappeared.

Most Frenchmen wanted change, but they disagreed sharply over what those changes should be. The Communists shared power in a coalition government but were ejected in 1947, in part because of hardening Cold War battle lines. Cabinets seldom lasted longer than six months. Large-scale industrial strikes swept the county in 1947. Nonetheless, in the postwar years France initiated national economic planning, created a social welfare safety net for its people, reversed its long population decline, played a leading role in bringing Germany back into Europe, and championed European integration. The government nationalized the Renault automobile company and the Bank of France as well as gas, electricity, coal, steel, and insurance companies. A Commissariat du Plan initiated a vigorous program to modernize industry. By 1951, moderates and conservatives replaced the *tripartisme* coalition of communists, socialists, and liberals ruling France, but central planning and social welfare institutions remained in place.

GERMANY

Over six million Germans—soldiers and civilians—died during or soon after the war. Most of Germany's cities lay in ruins, and its industrial production had collapsed. Its distribution system for food and consumer goods had broken down. Agricultural output declined severely due to shortages of labor and fertilizer. Homeless and hungry, six million Germans were refugees in their own land—a number swelled by ten to twelve million more fleeing westward from the Red Army or expelled by the re-created Polish and Czech states. Poland annexed East Prussia and Silesia as compensation for the loss of its prewar eastern provinces to Russia. Germans in those provinces fled westward. No one wanted German-speaking people in their country anymore. Roosevelt, Churchill, and Stalin had sanctioned mass population transfers in eastern Europe at the Yalta Conference. It seemed the only way to establish stable nation-states and minimize interethnic violence. In 1919, Allied statesmen had tried to redraw borders to match populations; now their successors moved people to match borders.

At least half a million Germans died in this exodus from eastern Europe. Those refugees who survived the initial burst of violence by their neighbors and the depredations of robbers along the way to reach Germany safely still lost their homes and lands as well as most of their personal possessions. At the same time, some eight million non-German slaves, contract workers, and refugees were trapped in the defunct Reich, awaiting repatriation. Some of them (French and Dutch workers, for example) were eager to go home, while others (Russian POWs or Croat refugees) were not as anxious to return to the tender mercies of Stalin or Marshal Tito. Ultimately, the Western powers honored their Yalta promise and forcibly returned all Soviet POWs to the USSR, thereby guaranteeing the return of British and American prisoners liberated by the Red Army. Cold, hunger, and loneliness drove many German women into liaisons with Allied soldiers. American GIs could provide food, luxury goods, and a pleasurable evening for women whose existence was otherwise bleak. "But those Lucky Strikes, chocolates, and silk stockings, along with the swing music and the easygoing GI manners," historian Ian Buruma explains, "also represented a culture to women, and many young men, which was all the more desirable for having been forbidden in the oppressive Third Reich."[18]

The Allies mandated a "denazification" process for the defeated German and Austrian population, but its implementation proved difficult. It included the removal of Nazis from positions of authority at every level, the reeducation of Germans in democratic and humanitarian values, and the destruction of Nazi symbols all over the country. Top-ranking Nazis who had not committed suicide or escaped to remote climes, including Göring, Hess, Ribbentrop, Streicher, and Speer, were put on trial for war crimes and crimes against humanity before an international panel of judges in Nuremberg. Twelve of the defendants (including Wehrmacht commanders Jodl and Keitel) received death sentences, while others got long prison terms. Alfred Krupp, the major arms manufacturer, received a twelve-year prison sentence but served only three. Baron Georg von Schnitzler of the IG Farben chemicals complex got a five-year term. Both had used slave labor extensively.

In the US occupation zone, all adults were supposed to fill out a 131-question survey detailing their relationship to Hitler's criminal regime. Many people failed to complete it, while still more lied brazenly. The Nazi system had been so pervasive that most Germans had been members of the party or of the Hitler Youth or the German Labor Front. Many Germans created false biographies for themselves. For example, Dr. Hans Asperger, famed for originating the diagnosis that bears his name, claimed to have saved many children from the regime's euthanasia program. This heroic narrative was widely believed until recently when it was discovered that Asperger willingly sent numerous children to the Nazi death machine.[19]

The denazification process simply overwhelmed occupation authorities, who soon passed it on to German committees that pursued it even less vigorously. The monumental task of reconstructing Germany seemed to require the cooperation of industrialists, financiers, bureaucrats, and others who had been Nazis or who had colluded closely with them. Soviet authorities carried out denazification with only slightly more vigor than their Western counterparts. The whole process virtually ended with the regidification of the Cold War, as each side sought to build up its part of Germany with whatever human resources were available. Moreover, Washington and Moscow welcomed certain categories of Germans who were deemed extremely valuable (like rocket scientists and intelligence experts), regardless of their complicity with Nazi crimes.

Two political parties dominated the revival of democracy in the Western occupation zones. Leaders of the Social Democratic Party returned from the concentration camps and from exile. Under Kurt Schumacher's leadership, they rebuilt the party with broader appeal and less dependence on the trade unions. The Weimar-era Catholic Center Party remerged as the Christian Democratic Union, a conservative party, now including both Catholics and Protestants, under the leadership of Cologne mayor Konrad Adenauer. Neither the right-wing nationalist parties nor the Communist Party enjoyed much support—the former disgraced by their collaboration with the Nazis and the latter discredited by their subservience to Moscow. Both new German states outlawed the Nazi Party, though small underground groups of neo-Nazis persisted. West Germany established friendly diplomatic relations with the new state of Israel and agreed to pay substantial reparations to that nation and to individual Holocaust survivors.

ITALY

As a former Axis member (even though the king and the army had belatedly abandoned their alliance with Hitler), war-ravaged Italy was occupied by the Allies and stripped of its colonies.

In the last stages of the war, the pre-Fascist political parties reemerged in Allied-controlled southern Italy. They expected to re-create the pre-Mussolini parliamentary monarchist regime. In the north, much more radical resistance groups, often led by communists, seized power from the retreating Germans. They sought a sweeping transformation of Italy. However, Stalin sent Palmiro Togliatti, the long-exiled leader of the Italian Communist Party, back from Moscow with orders to tamp down the flames of revolution and participate in electoral politics. Elections for a constituent assembly to draft a new constitution gave the Christian Democrats half the vote, with the Communists and Socialists sharing the other half. Women cast ballots for the first time. The king lost his throne. Italy became a liberal, democratic republic. Marshall Plan dollars, covert help from the CIA, and support from the Catholic Church enabled the conservative Christian Democrats under Alcide Gasperi to dominate Italian politics by 1948. The economy recovered only slowly, at first beset by disastrous inflation and dependence on the black market. Land reform distributed 1.75 acres to each farmer in southern Italy.

TOWARD EUROPEAN UNION

The horrors of the Second World War discredited militarism and, at least temporarily, ultranationalism as well. Visionary leaders saw the need to transcend the anarchy of rival nation-states, working only for themselves, in order to preserve peace and achieve prosperity. Overcoming parochialism was a slow but ultimately successful process. Six West European countries formed the European Coal and Steel Community in 1951. Six years later, France, West Germany, Italy, Belgium, and Luxembourg signed the Treaty of Rome, creating the European Economic Community (or Common Market). More nations joined in the following years, including the United Kingdom.

The Soviet Union

The USSR emerged victorious in the Second World War, having built the most powerful army in the world. Returning servicemen, however, came home to a devastated land. The country suffered twenty-seven million military and civilian deaths. More than 1,700 towns and 70,000 villages were destroyed. Several of the country's most important cities—Leningrad, Stalingrad, Kiev—were shattered. The Germans had wrecked factories, power-generating stations, and mines in the most developed western region of the country. Agricultural output had plummeted. Famine once again ravaged the country. The social dislocation caused by the war was worse than in any other country except China.

Refugees, orphans, and fatherless families were everywhere. Twenty-five million people were homeless. Among Soviet citizens in their twenties and thirties, there were only six men for every ten women. The population was exhausted by the extraordinary sacrifices exacted from them during the war. Historian Nina Tumarkin suggests that the Soviet people may have been suffering collectively from posttraumatic stress disorder.[20] Many in the West feared that a Soviet juggernaut was poised to sweep all the way to the Atlantic Ocean, but the Red Army was demobilizing even faster than American forces. At the same time, anti-Soviet partisan groups continued to fight against the regime in the western borderlands. The largest such group, the Organization of Ukrainian Nationalists (OUN), waged a campaign of terror against any fellow citizens who cooperated in the restoration of Soviet rule.

Soviet citizens hoped that their sacrifices would be rewarded by serious reforms—particularly a less oppressive regime dedicated to enhancing the material well-being of its people. Collective farmers even dreamed of postwar emancipation from their neo-serfdom. These aspirations raised two problems for Stalin. Rather than slackening discipline and devoting resources to raising living standards, the Kremlin leaders needed to mobilize the nation and husband its resources to rebuild their shattered land and, once the Cold War began, to reverse the demobilization of the armed forces. They were even more determined to maintain their power in the face of these liberalizing aspirations. Stalin dashed the hopes of his people. He enforced strict political discipline and economic stringency. The Fourth Five Year Plan (1946–1950) disproportionately favored heavy industry, as had its predecessors, leaving little for agriculture, housing, and consumer goods. Industry rebounded quickly, but agriculture continued to lag. Urban living standards recovered their modest prewar levels only slowly while conditions in the countryside remained abysmal.

The Soviet dictator also moved to combat any liberalizing trends and to counteract the positive view of the Western democracies that had become popular during the Grand Alliance. Stalin and Andrei Zhdanov launched a propaganda campaign, known as the *Zhdanovshchina*, to accomplish these goals. Xenophobic in the extreme, it identified the Great Russian ethnic group (as opposed to the Soviet peoples) as the leading element in the USSR and the "senior brother" of the Slavic nations of eastern Europe. It condemned foreign influences and "rootless cosmopolitanism," while it warned of nefarious foreign plots to undermine the Soviet system. Anti-Semitism resurfaced as well. The Jewish Anti-Fascist Committee was disbanded, and Jewish intellectuals were persecuted. The population of the gulag, which had shrunk during the war, expanded once again. The NKVD subjected the five million liberated POWs and forced laborers returning from Germany to "filtration." Most were allowed to go home, but some of them were sent to prison camps. Soviet citizens living in the areas formerly occupied by the Germans were also subjected to "filtration," with similar results.

America

America's wartime experience finally broke the hold of isolationism on the national psyche and led Washington to establish global political, economic, and military commitments. That same experience profoundly transformed the nature of life in the United States. America was the only major belligerent to emerge from the war both stronger and more prosperous than when the conflict began. The gross national product of the United States more than doubled during the war years. Many economists worried that the cancellation of huge defense contracts after the war would lead to widespread unemployment and the reemergence of the Great Depression. During the first three peacetime years, there was unemployment, inflation, and a wave of strikes. Soon, however, the American economy boomed. Pent-up consumer demand and government policies that fostered economic expansion encouraged a shopping frenzy. After years of rationing, Americans wanted new homes, automobiles, refrigerators, washing machines, and all the luxuries that magazine ads told them they needed. The consumer society was born. Stimulated by GI Bill funding, college attendance soared. College had been the preserve of upper- and upper-middle-class Americans before the war. Now a wave of middle- and working-class veterans washed over campuses.

Not everyone shared in postwar prosperity. Women, African Americans, and Hispanics often lost their well-paying factory jobs to returning white servicemen. Many were forced to return to lower-paying service industry employment. Nevertheless, the freedoms and op-portunities they had enjoyed during the war emboldened many of them to fight for their rights and for a better life in the coming decades. Hitler's murderous regime had given rac-ism, previously perfectly acceptable in most circles, a bad name. That helped to propel the partially successful Civil Rights Movement in the 1950s and 1960s.

The war had changed the human geography of the United States, too. Millions of Americans had moved from rural areas to the defense plants on the Atlantic, Pacific, and Gulf coasts, as well as to midwestern industrial cities. Most of them never returned to their former homes. America became much more urban and its cities even more diverse. Hun-dreds of thousands of veterans' families abandoned the cities and the countryside for newly built subdivisions in the suburbs—funded by the GI Bill. The return of millions of soldiers, reuniting or creating couples, led to a postwar baby boom. The US population jumped from 132 million in 1940 to 179 million in 1960. These spiraling numbers helped to sustain the postwar economic expansion.

For all its wealth and power, the country was troubled by anxieties—particularly the fear of communist subversion and espionage. A new "red scare," much more pervasive than the one following World War I, metastasized across the country. The rapid social changes that had occurred during the war caused many people to feel ill at ease and be more susceptible to conspiracy theories. Revelations by a Soviet diplomatic defector (Igor Gouzenko, a cipher clerk in the Soviet embassy in Ottawa, Canada) of extensive Soviet espionage in America set off a frenzy of spy hunting. Soviet spying was a real, if overblown, threat. Stalin's acquisition of the atomic bomb and Mao's victory in China only heightened the paranoia. However, political opportunism motivated much of the red scare. Republicans (and anti–New Deal Democrats) attacked the Truman administration for allegedly being soft on communism and even harboring communist traitors in its midst. Senator Joseph McCarthy (R-Wiscon-sin) and Congressman Richard Nixon (R-California) used congressional investigative powers to mount public show trials. The State Department and the entertainment industry were purged. Labor unions came under sustained attack as well. No one was shot, as in Stalin's purges, but careers and lives were ruined.

A Troubled Peace Comes to Asia

JAPAN: DEFEAT, DISILLUSIONMENT, AND TRANSFORMATION

Japan surrendered almost unconditionally. The Allies agreed to let Emperor Hirohito re-main on his throne, but under the authority of the Allied supreme commander, General Douglas MacArthur. The emperor was required to renounce his claim to divinity. An Ameri-can military government led by MacArthur ruled the defeated country until 1952. There was an Allied Control Commission, including a Soviet representative, but the Americans completely dominated the defeated nation. The US government chose to retain the emperor as the powerless, symbolic head of state, believing that Hirohito's continued presence on the throne would make the occupation easier for the Japanese people to accept.

That policy entailed ignoring the emperor's complicity in the war and attendant war crimes. An Allied military tribunal tried twenty-eight military and political leaders on various counts of unleashing aggressive warfare, war crimes, and crimes against humanity. All but three were found guilty, with sentences ranging from seven years' imprisonment to death.

Tojo Hideki, prime minister and minister of war for much of the conflict, was executed. Almost six thousand lower-ranking officers and officials were tried in the Soviet Union, the Philippines, the Dutch East Indies, and elsewhere. Still, a great many war criminals went unpunished. The existing bureaucracy, which had made the war possible, remained in office because the US authorities needed it to carry out occupation policies. Some commentators criticized the tribunals for unfair procedures and, more recently, for their overly narrow scope. "One of the most pernicious aspects of the occupation," historian John Dower argues, "was that the Asian peoples who had suffered most from imperial Japan's depredations—the Chinese, Koreans, Indonesians, and Filipinos—had no serious role, no influential presence at all in the defeated land."[21]

Given the ideological fervor displayed by most Japanese troops and many civilians as well, Americans expected occupation to be difficult. The Japanese, however, acquiesced to US control more readily than anyone anticipated. As historian Carole Gluck explains, "the rapid disappearance of *tennosei* orthodoxy in 1945 and 1946 suggests that the relation between experience and ideology had become so strained that the official ideology was relatively easy to abandon once the institutional apparatus that sustained it was dismantled."[22]

Almost three million Japanese soldiers and civilians died in the war. An even larger number endured grave wounds or debilitating disease. A few hundred of the most fanatical officers and bureaucrats committed suicide when the surrender was announced, but most of their colleagues reacted by destroying incriminating evidence and plundering military supply depots. All major cities were extensively damaged by bombing, and 30 percent of the urban population was homeless. The economy was severely disrupted. Hunger swept the land. Cities teemed with the unemployed and war orphans living by their wits—often by theft, prostitution, or working in the black market. Gangs of feral children roamed the streets in search of food, while platoons of *panpan* girls offered their sexual services to GIs for small amounts of money or packs of cigarettes (the main currency of the black market).

There was little sympathy among the American public for Japan's plight, but the United States had to provide relief supplies to maintain an orderly occupation and allay the specter of communism. Even with US and UN aid, many people depended on the black market to sustain themselves. About six and a half million Japanese soldiers and civilians were stranded throughout Asia and the Pacific. It would be many months, in some cases years, before most of them returned to their homeland. Hundreds of thousands of them died in the process. Over a million Koreans and large numbers of Chinese, Okinawan, and Taiwanese conscripted laborers and prisoners of war remained in Japan. Almost all of them (except the collaborators) were desperate to return to their native lands.

Political forces that the militarists had suppressed—trade unionists, socialists, and communists—now reemerged to champion social and political reform. Land reforms transformed a mass of tenant farmers into small farm owners. As the Cold War intensified, however, American occupation authorities took steps to curb the power of the left. The conservative Liberal Democratic Party ruled the country from 1955 to 1993. Japan signed a peace treaty with the Allies in 1951 and emerged as a self-governing parliamentary democracy the following year. The new constitution renounced war as a means of settling international disputes. Continuing antimilitarist sentiment allowed nothing more than a small Self-Defense Force. With the United States shouldering Japan's defense burden, national leaders were free to devote more of their resources to economic reconstruction. Japan gradually emerged as an economic superpower, with annual GDP growth rates averaging 9.2 percent between 1957 and 1973.

KOREA

Korea had not e
grievously nonetl
and tens of thous
women. The Japa
guage. After Tokyc
while US troops ga
hardened the suppo
separate, mutually he
Il-sung and an antico
to reunite the peninsu
clashes between the two
in 1950 and the Korean

CIVIL WAR IN CHINA

The Allied leaders agreed a
territories lost to the Japane
the Kurile Islands. The status
golia. Russia could lease a nav
of Dalian, and control the Ch
each a recovery of previously lo
Chinese. Moreover, the Russian
churia worth an estimated US\$3 billion.

...ls at the port
...ria. These latter measures,
... decided without the participation of the
... industrial equipment and raw materials from Man-

Both the Nationalists and the Communists began preparing for a showdown as soon as Japan was defeated, while at the same time talking about peace and cooperation. Soviet forces in Manchuria allowed the Chinese Communists to acquire the weapons left behind by the defeated enemy. The Communists intended to occupy all of Manchuria's large cities immediately, but the United States and the Soviet Union blocked that effort. The USSR had signed a Treaty of Friendship and Alliance with the Nationalist government in 1945. Securing GMD acquiescence in Soviet territorial gains was more important to Stalin than bolstering the CCP's position in Manchuria. Nonetheless, when the Soviet army began to withdraw from Manchuria in the spring of 1946, it facilitated the occupation of Mukden, Harbin, and other cities by Chinese Communist forces. After the Japanese surrender, the Americans used their airlift and naval capacity to rush Nationalist troops to Nanjing and Shanghai and later to Beijing and even some ports in Manchuria. To facilitate these transfers, American forces occupied five key ports. The United States also sent marines to Beijing and Tianjin. Japanese units were ordered not to surrender to Communist troops but to wait for GMD officials to arrive.

Under heavy pressure from both Washington and Moscow, the Guomindang and the Communists consented to negotiate an agreement for cooperation in rebuilding China. Stalin told the Chinese Communists bluntly that the outbreak of civil war would be a disaster. Both sides entered the talks cynically. Each hated and was determined to destroy the other. However, after long negotiations, the GMD and CCP agreed on paper to establish a democratic state, unify all troops under the command of Chiang Kai-shek, and organize a

Chiang Kai-shek and Mao Zedong at doomed peace negotiations in August 1945. Civil war was inevitable since each leader intended to impose his own rule and system on China. Source: Wikimedia Commons

political consultative conference to work out the details of their collaboration. Both parties were playing a duplicitous political game to appease domestic and foreign opinion. Each side anticipated blaming the other when this truce ultimately broke down. Mao privately told Soviet representatives that civil war was "virtually inevitable."[23]

President Truman wanted a strong, united, noncommunist China. Lend-Lease aid for China continued, along with a US military advisory group to support Nationalist forces. When the People's Consultative Conference opened in January 1946, Chiang Kai-shek promised full civil rights for each citizen, the freeing of all political prisoners, and legal equality for every political party. In January 1946, Chiang and Mao publicly ordered their respective forces to stop fighting each other, but both were pouring troops into Manchuria, and clashes soon erupted. The first major battle occurred in March when Nationalist troops drove Mao's troops from Mukden. The following month, Communist units ousted Chiang's soldiers from Changchun.

In 1946, everything seemed to be going Chiang Kai-shek's way. The generalissimo's troops won most of their battles in both Manchuria and north China, while he convened a National Assembly that the Communists boycotted. However, several factors combined to diminish Chiang's popularity with the Chinese people. Corruption riddled the Guomindang regime at every level. Chiang was aware of the problem but thought it necessary to defeat the Communists first before addressing the issue. Out-of-control inflation wrecked the urban economy and undermined the government's reform projects. Spiraling military expenses thwarted all attempts to bring down the inflation rate. In 1945 it took 1,500 *fabi* to buy a US dollar. By the beginning of 1948, the exchange rate was 180,000 to 1! The authoritarianism of the regime in practice belied its proclamations of democratic intent. The GMD security services frequently employed intimidation, violence, and even assassination. Anti-Guomindang protests on the island of Taiwan, for example, were savagely suppressed, resulting in more than twenty thousand deaths. Despite his rhetoric about representative government, Chiang had always believed that the Chinese people were not ready for democracy.

Lack of prior planning for the reoccupation of Japanese-held areas led to appalling conditions and mass suffering. The Guomindang mismanaged that process badly. The people of postwar China yearned for a better standard of living, social justice, and more freedoms. Chiang's regime failed to meet these expectations. The mass migrations of the war years further weakened the Guomindang by breaking down the traditional social order based on family, clan, and regional allegiances. The old elites lost their economic bases of power and were unable to defend the country or their social legitimacy. The previous hierarchy was replaced by a process of social leveling—in the words of historian Diana Lary, a "the grim equality of suffering."[24] In the process, Chiang Kai-shek's government lost the proverbial Mandate of Heaven.

The Guomindang regime squandered whatever legitimacy it previously enjoyed not only because it lost almost every battle in the first eighteen months of the Sino-Japanese War but also because, through callousness and panic, its defense strategies often harmed the Chinese people far more than they hurt the Japanese aggressors. In the view of historian Keith Schoppa, the Nationalist regime was not able to engage in state building or even state maintenance during the war but suffered from "state erosion."[25] Conversely, Communist soldiers were under strict orders as they took Nationalist cities not to harm civilians, destroy property, or interrupt business, insofar as possible. The Communists defeated the Guomindang in the most important battle—the struggle for the hearts and minds of many Chinese.

Chiang Kai-shek believed that his forces were not strong enough to oust the Communists from Manchuria, but a series of Nationalist victories in 1946 and encouragement from General George Marshall changed his mind. Some historians believe that the decision to hold the land north of the Great Wall at all costs was the fatal mistake that doomed Nationalist China.[26] Manchuria became a sinkhole for the Nationalist army. Chiang repeatedly rushed troops there, only to see them surrounded and decimated. The Communists had partially abandoned their guerrilla strategy to form large armies and confront GMD forces frontally. By November 1948, Manchuria had been lost.

At this point Communist forces outnumbered Chiang's army and were almost as well equipped (with Japanese and captured American weapons). Now northern and central China came under siege. As the People's Liberation Army overwhelmed one Nationalist army after another, it often absorbed the survivors into its ranks. The Soviets, who had been careful earlier to avoid the appearance of intervention in the Chinese civil war, now sent trainloads of military equipment to the PLA. With GMD cities and armies in central China falling to the enemy, the generalissimo dispatched his navy, air force, many of his remaining troops, and China's gold reserves to the island of Taiwan. The majority of GMD civil officials and troops were left to their fate on the mainland. When the Nationalist navy mutinied in April 1949, Communist forces were able to cross the Yangzi River. Nationalist-held south China was doomed. Chiang Kai-shek fled China and reestablished his Republic of China on Taiwan.

On October 1, 1949, Mao Zedong proclaimed the founding of the People's Republic of China. He quickly discarded the liberal rhetoric of the "New Democracy." Instead, Mao established a one-party dictatorship and initiated radical measures for the confiscation of private property. He negotiated an alliance with the Soviet Union and, within a year, was at (an undeclared) war with the United States in Korea. The United States refused to recognize the People's Republic until 1979, though Great Britain established diplomatic relations with Mao's regime in 1950.

Decolonization

The Second World War greatly accelerated the already existing process of decolonization. Since the days of Woodrow Wilson, if not before, US policy had anticipated the demise of Europe's colonial empires. Americans wanted a world of free trade and global interdependence, guaranteed by democratic, antimilitarist governments—a world in which their industrial prowess would allow them not just to profit but to dominate. Roosevelt clashed sharply with British and French leaders over this issue. Churchill famously proclaimed, "I have not become the King's First Minister in order to preside over the liquidation of the British Empire." He also supported the postwar reconstitution of the French, Dutch, and Belgian Empires. A conference of French colonial governors convened in January 1944 by Charles de Gaulle in Brazzaville, Congo, insisted, "The goals of the work of civilization undertaken by France in the colonies exclude all ideas of autonomy, all possibilities of development outside the French block of the Empire; the possible constitutional self-government in the colonies is to be dismissed."[27]

However, Washington saw most of the colonial peoples of Asia and Africa as immature and unready for immediate self-government. Therefore, the United States sanctioned the temporary return of the European imperial powers to their former colonies—France in Indochina and Algeria; Britain in Malaya, Burma, and Hong Kong; etc. Colonies belonging to the defeated Axis states were to be administered by "trusteeships" awarded to the great powers. Under either arrangement, the authorities were obligated to prepare their subjects for independence. All this assumed that the powers would continue to cooperate with each other in peacetime at least as well as they had during the war. It also assumed that native people, long chafing under colonial rule, would wait patiently until their former masters pronounced them "ready" for freedom.

The imperial powers intended to retain some of their colonies because they seemed too valuable to lose or because others were deemed "unready" for independence. Even in those colonies that they were prepared to grant self-rule, the powers anticipated the process to be long and peaceful, resulting in newly established states that remained in the political and economic orbit of their former masters. Those expectations proved illusory. Decolonization after the Second World War was rapid, disorderly, and often violent. National liberation

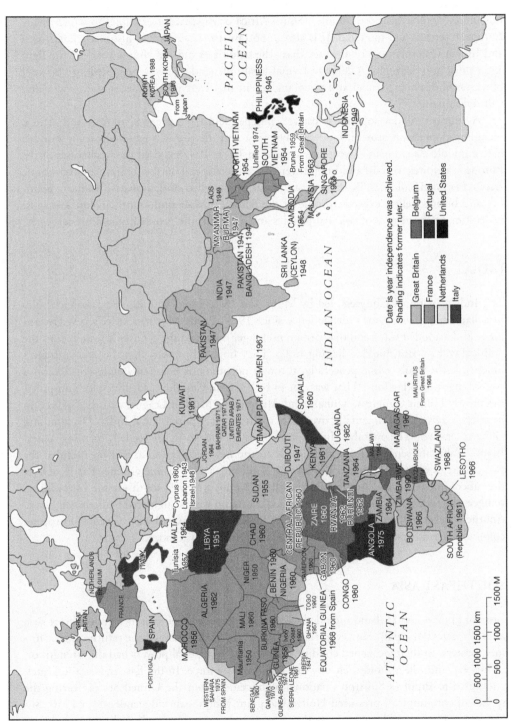

Postwar Decolonization

wars flared in many places. Sometimes the withdrawal of European control sparked revolutions or civil wars—battles between rival elites or savage ethnic conflicts. The situation was more complex in those colonies (South Africa or Algeria, for example) to which many European settlers had migrated. It is also important to remember, as historians Jan Jansen and Jürgen Osterhammel remind us, that "the colonizers did not simply turn off the light and vanish into the night. A colony's formal-legal independence was integrated into broader processes of disentanglement and re-entanglement that were political, economic, social and cultural in nature."[28]

A number of developments fostered independence movements in Asia and Africa, including population growth, food supply crises, and the rise of a nationalistically minded native middle class. Japan's sweeping victories in 1941–1942 exposed the weaknesses of the European empires. Britain and France were forced to depend on the military and economic resources of their colonies. By the end of the war, large, self-confident, native military, political, and business elites existed in some of the colonies. Most importantly, colonialism lost its legitimacy in the eyes of colonial peoples and at least some people in the imperial states.

INDIA

The Indian National Congress, led by Mohandas "Mahatma" Gandhi and Jawaharlal Nehru, had been pressing for independence since 1929. Prime Minister Attlee's new government understood at war's end that Britain no longer possessed the economic resources or the political will to continue dominating India. They hoped, however, that the subcontinent's independence would come peacefully, through negotiations between London and various competing Indian factions. That was not to be. Despite Gandhi's calls for peace and unity, the mostly Hindu Congress, Muhammad Ali Jinnah's Muslim League, and the Sikh community disagreed fundamentally over how to structure a postcolonial India. Division and violence ensued. The mainly Muslim provinces in the north succeeded, forming a new Islamic Pakistan, separate from and hostile to the new secular India. Within months, the two countries were at war over the region of Kashmir. Savage ethnic violence flared all over the subcontinent as well. Muslims fled north as Hindus streamed south—some 14.5 million refugees. In addition, as many as five hundred thousand were slaughtered by their neighbors. Another twelve million became homeless. A Hindu fanatic assassinated Gandhi. European colonialism had begun to crumble, but the process was messy indeed.

SOUTHEAST ASIA

Britain, France, and Holland intended to resume control of their colonies in Southeast Asia after the defeat of Japan. However, the peoples of the region resisted the return of their former masters. In their weakened condition, none of the imperial powers had the strength or, ultimately, the will to hold their unwilling colonies by force. In the East Indies, the Dutch attempted to suppress Sukarno's nationalist movement, but the United States, fearing the spread of communism, pressured Holland to grant Indonesian independence in 1950. Sukarno struggled to weld a cohesive nation out of the new country's ethnically and religiously diverse population. On the Malay Peninsula, British plans to continue dominance, ruling through traditional regional leaders, sparked resistance from the (mostly ethnically Chinese) communists. Malaya (modern-day Malaysia) became an independent member of the British Commonwealth in 1957, though counterinsurgency warfare dragged on until 1960. Under the leadership of Aung San, Burma (now Myanmar), too, gained its independence from the British Empire in 1947 and, unlike India and Malaya, declined membership in the Commonwealth. It was a troubled independence marred by ethnic violence. The United States had promised independence to the Philippines before the war. It honored that pledge in 1946. Communist Hukbalahap rebels resisted the new government and waged class warfare in some areas until the last of their cadres were destroyed in 1955.

After the surrender of Japan, the Chinese Nationalist army occupied northern Vietnam while British forces took control in the south. The British helped France reestablish its power in the south, but Ho Chi Minh's communist and nationalist Viet Minh movement took over the north. A bitter guerrilla war ensued against the French and their Francophile, Catholic Vietnamese supporters. The United States backed the French because communists led the insurgents. American aid was not enough, however. The Viet Minh inflicted a decisive defeat on the French at Dien Bien Phu in 1954. Enthusiasm for this colonial conflict waned in France. Vietnam became independent after the Geneva Conference of 1956—the north under communist rule and the south under an anticommunist regime.

The Middle East

The Second World War transformed the Middle East once again. Britain and France, which had largely dominated the region, were no longer able to maintain their hegemony. Lebanon, Syria, Jordan, Iraq, and Egypt gained independence during or soon after the conflict. Hitler's "Final Solution" swelled Jewish migration to Palestine, where Zionism and Arab nationalism inevitably clashed. The UN proposed a division of Palestine into separate Jewish and Arab states, but Arab leaders rejected the plan. Zionist authorities established the new state of Israel in May 1948, leading to the First Arab-Israeli War. Approximately eight hundred thousand Jews were expelled or fled to Israel from other Arab lands, while a similar number of Palestinian Arabs fled from Israel to become refugees in bordering Arab countries.

Africa

Believing them unready for full independence, British authorities attempted to retain their African colonies by granting them limited self-rule. Jomo Kenyatta, Kwame Nkrumah, and other African nationalist leaders rejected this snail's-pace emancipation. Their movements were mainly nonviolent, but some groups like the Mau Mau in Kenya used terror, demanding immediate *uhuru* (Swahili for "freedom"). British resolve crumbled. All those colonies populated mainly by black Africans received their independence in the late 1950s or the 1960s. Conversely, in colonies with significant white settler populations—South Africa and Southern Rhodesia—white successor regimes continued to dominate and oppress their black populations for decades. The white elite in South Africa had enjoyed self-government since 1910 and gained full independence in 1961. It oppressed and segregated the much larger black population. Black South Africans did not receive full political rights and an end to apartheid until the early 1990s. Similarly, the majority black population of Southern Rhodesia (now Zimbabwe) did not gain freedom until 1980.

The French, too, lost their African colonies. Rebellion broke out in Algeria in 1954. Paris prevented its spread to Tunisia and Morocco only by granting them quasi-independent status. That was not an option for Algeria because more than a million European colonists (*colons*) lived there. The government sent half a million troops to Algeria in a futile attempt to suppress the insurrection. Another long and bloody war ensued. When it seemed that the government was tiring of the struggle, a rebellion broke out among the *colons* and French troops that soon brought down the Fourth Republic and propelled de Gaulle back into power. A thoroughly traumatized France, having barely averted civil war, finally relinquished control of Algeria in 1962, whereupon nine hundred thousand *colons* fled to France. French determination to keep its black African colonies collapsed after the disasters in Indochina and Algeria. Those colonies received independence in 1960. French troops suppressed an uprising on the island of Madagascar in 1947 but finally permitted the establishment of the Malagasy Republic in 1958. Portuguese Angola and Mozambique also became independent in 1975 after protracted anticolonial rebellions.

The Ecological Impact of War

The impact of the war on the Earth's ecosystems was dramatic and extensive. Natural habitats were blasted on Pacific islands, in the Balkan Mountains, and elsewhere. Thousands of ships sank during the war. All of them leaked diesel fuel into fragile ocean ecosystems. Heightened wartime demand for wood led to significant deforestation. Beyond obliterated cities, cratered battlefields, and radioactive fallout, the war burned forests, inundated low-lying areas, and introduced alien species of flora and fauna in many places. It left millions of land mines and much unexploded ordnance across combat zones. Ramped-up production in factories and oil fields left toxic waste with little concern for environmental hazards. The pressing need to increase food production led to extensive use of chemical fertilizers and pesticides, creating a much more toxic world. These effects were not limited to the belligerents but also affected neutral countries.

In some cases, nature soon repaired the environmental destruction done on battlefields, but ecological damage caused by massive wartime industrial mobilization has been an enduring plague. Because of the wartime emergency, those few environmental regulations in place at the time were ignored with impunity. In the view of three pioneering researchers, "the Second World War became one of the main forces that rewrote the environmental history of the latter part of the twentieth century." They argue that "World War II also meant the birth of global environmental catastrophism."[29]

Three environmental disasters stand out. In 1938, Nationalist Chinese forces detonated the Huayuankow dike across the Yellow River, flooding millions of hectares of agricultural land. In 1944, the Germans intentionally opened the dikes of Holland, flooding some two hundred thousand hectares of farmland with salt water. In that same year, as the Germans retreated westward across the Soviet Union, they devastated human and animal populations and destroyed economic, transportation, and communications systems.

Fighting extensively damaged the ecosystems of many Pacific islands. Even where no combat occurred, the building of air bases and garrisoning of troops for sustained periods covered the best gardening land with compacted coral. Such construction decimated bird populations on Midway Island. US troops also accidentally introduced rats onto the island in 1943. On Betio Island near Tarawa in the Gilberts, heavy shelling ruined inshore fisheries. Whales were slaughtered because they looked like submarines on radar screens or because they swam into minefields. Although Allied forces did not use poison gases against the Japanese army, they did stockpile them. Decades later, mustard gas canisters were found on Guam and on Banika in the Solomons. Americans deliberately introduced *Mikania micrantha* ("American rope") into the western Pacific as a rapidly growing vine for camouflage. It is still a problem today, since it quickly overwhelms other plant life. The Japanese brought giant African snails to the islands as a food source. These voracious breeders and eaters decimated native plants and spread fungi that further damaged flora. Brown tree snakes (*Boiga irregularis*) were inadvertently brought to Guam—probably in equipment shipped from Australia or New Guinea. Lacking natural predators, these snakes have decimated bird and forest vertebrate populations.

Since most battles in the Pacific were fast moving and not prolonged, nature was able to repair even extensive damage, sometimes in a few years. At one site of major combat between Australian and Japanese forces on New Guinea, a veteran who returned to the place seven years later commented, "The entire ridge was blasted bare of vegetation, but today the foliage and kunai [grass] have covered much of the scene, and the mass-grave of the Japs killed there are not to be found. Nor could I distinguish the once important features."[30]

Scientists and military leaders expected the atomic blasts unleashed on Hiroshima and Nagasaki to kill many people and destroy much of these cities. They did not understand the effects of radiation that would kill many more and increase rates of cancer and birth defects, nor did they foresee how fallout would remain in the soil and enter the food chain. Atomic warfare affected the environment in America as well. The United States produced the fuel for its atomic bombs at Oak Ridge, Tennessee, and Hanford, Washington. Both plants created large amounts of radioactive waste without the technology for safely neutralizing it. At Hanford, workers dumped contaminated water into the Columbia River and released radioactive isotopes into the air. Scientists believed (mistakenly) that such wastes would bond with the soil and dissipate.[31] The United States also conducted atomic bomb tests in the atmosphere at Alamogordo, New Mexico, in 1945. Subsequent tests were conducted in Nevada and on Bikini Atoll in the western Pacific. Residents of the atoll were relocated beforehand and were promised that they could return when the testing ended. That proved impossible because of radioactive pollution of the soil and water.

Environmental historian Judith Bennett points to a global environmental problem completely unrecognized at the time: "Among the intangible or at least invisible at the time was the unnoted and uncalculated but huge burden of carbon dioxide thrown up into the atmosphere by the factories producing processed food, clothing, and war materiel, and by machines burning fossil fuels—ships, tanks, jeeps, bulldozers, and airplanes—from the lands of the protagonists. . . . World War II was a major building block in the process of global warming."[32] Mobilization and production for war inflicted more environmental damage than the fighting itself. In many places—European battlefields or roads cut through Asian jungles—nature soon began to reassert its dominance over the work of men. Flora covered the scars of combat, and plants grew through disintegrating airstrips and roadways. However, the deleterious effects of excessive mining, overcutting timber, and the toxic waste products released by tens of thousands of war factories remained for decades.

The War in Memory

Memory has become a hot topic among historians—how individuals and groups chose to remember or forget or reimagine the past. Memories of the Second World War often focus on one's national experience—so much so that historian Carol Gluck suggests that the result is "a memory of a *world* war with the *world* left out."[33] These national myths emphasized heroism and/or victimization. Inconvenient truths are simply ignored.

UNITED STATES

After the conflict, most GIs wanted to forget their traumatic ordeal and get on with their civilian lives. Only later, in middle age and beyond, would many of them begin to reminisce publicly about their experiences. It is telling that a great national memorial in Washington for the men and women who fought in the Second World War opened only in 2004. Total victory at a price much less dear in human lives (419,000) than that paid by any other major belligerent combined with a booming postwar economy and Washington's new status as leader of the "free world" to encourage American triumphalism.

After the divisive and disappointing Vietnam War, however, Americans reimagined World War II as a selfless crusade in which everyone came together as one in the fight for freedom and democracy. It was, in the sarcastic phrase of a later historian, "the greatest war ever."[34] Journalist Tom Brokaw's best-selling 1998 book, *The Greatest Generation*, epitomizes this trend. America and Americans fought the war not for personal gain or simply because they were drafted but because it was "the right thing to do." Brokaw is not wrong in emphasizing the accomplishments of veterans Daniel Inouye, Mark Hatfield, Robert Dole, and others during and after the war, but his characterization of the war and those who fought it is greatly oversimplified. This heroic narrative had little room for strikes, race riots, Japanese Americans in concentration camps, war profiteering, and Jewish refugees turned way at the ports. Professional historians have been quick to challenge such myths, pointing out how disruptive the war was to the lives of soldiers and those on the home front (including a flourishing black market, increasing juvenile delinquency, and rampant marital infidelity).[35] Academic correctives have been slow, however, to percolate into public consciousness.

GERMANY

German historians and the public needed to come to terms with their traumatic wartime experience and the terrible defeat suffered by their nation. In East Germany, the press and scholars were forced to follow the Soviet interpretation of recent history: The capitalist system imposed Nazism on unwilling German workers, a tragedy from which the people had been saved by the Soviet Union. In West Germany, a different narrative of national victimhood emerged. This account emphasized the massive destruction caused by the Anglo-American bombing campaign, the many rapes of German women by Soviet soldiers, and the mass expulsion of Germans from postwar eastern Europe, while ignoring the imperialist and exterminationist character of the war Germany unleashed. Blame for the war itself and for the Holocaust was limited to Hitler, the Nazi Party, and the SS. In this view, the German people had been seduced and coerced by the Nazis into the most destructive war in world history. Popular memory emphasized resistance to Nazi policies by such religious leaders as Archbishop August von Galen, Dietrich Bonhoeffer, and Martin Niemöller.

Debate over German guilt erupted in the 1986–1987 *Historikerstreit* (historians' dispute). Conservative nationalist historian Ernst Nolte asserted that Germans should not bear any special measure of guilt because Hitler's regime and his war were an understandable reaction to the assault on "civilization" embodied in Soviet communism. Nolte's language was convoluted, but his message was clear—it was the Russians' fault. Similarly, Andreas Hill-gruber relativized German guilt by arguing that Allied bombing of German cities, Stalin's crimes, and the Holocaust were moral equivalents. Liberal and leftist historians were quick to challenge these views. Some of them argued that Germany had not followed the normal course of modern, industrializing societies but had evolved along its own unique path (*Sonderweg*). In this view, Hitler, world war, and mass murder emerged almost inevitably from the deformations of the German past (widespread anti-Semitism, Prussian militarism, etc.). Unlike most scholarly debates, this one jumped the bounds of academic discourse and splashed across the mass media.

The "myth of the unblemished Wehrmacht" prevailed for several decades. Numerous memoirs by German officers depicted a "clean" war fought by "decent" soldiers, entirely separate from the crimes of the SS. Those same self-serving memoirs blamed Hitler for the German army's defeats, exonerating senior commanders of responsibility. The title of Field Marshal Erich von Manstein's memoir—*Lost Victories*—epitomized that approach. The onset of the Cold War and the creation of a West German army required the rehabilitation of German military tradition and the remembrance of soldiers who had fought not for conquest and ethnic cleansing but to halt the spread of communism in Europe (without acknowledging Hitler's authorship of that idea). Some historians began to challenge that sanitized picture of Germany's war in the 1960s. Gerald Reitlinger characterized the SS as the "alibi of a nation," and by the 1980s, several German historians had demonstrated the Wehrmacht's extensive complicity in war crimes. Not until the major, controversial photo exhibit *Crimes of the Wehrmacht* in 1995, however, did the public in Germany fully confront the complicity of the German army in the horrors perpetrated on the eastern front and elsewhere.[36]

BRITAIN

The British also remember the Second World War as a time of national unity and heroic resistance to evil. It was "the People's War," and in Churchill's famous phrase, it was Britain's "finest hour." The British people were proud of having stood "alone" against Hitler after the fall of France and before the entry of the United States into the war. Churchill's views were particularly influential, especially his six-volume *The Second World War*. Having won the war without suffering enemy occupation, the British did not have to face the terrible moral dilemma that beset their Continental neighbors. Upbeat, heroic books and films about the war remained popular. During the first decades after the war, historians and social scientists argued that the conflict sparked a "revolution" in attitudes that made possible the postwar welfare state. More recently, historians have backed away from claims of a national revolution—some changes were in process before the outbreak of hostilities, and others were less sweeping than originally characterized.[37]

FRANCE

Anxious to unify his country, Charles de Gaulle propagated the myth of France as "a nation of resisters," a country that fought valiantly and helped win the Second World War. In his imagination, the collaborationist Vichy regime was a mere footnote, unrepresentative of the great French nation, in no way tainting the postwar Fourth Republic. That was a popular view, for it veiled the moral ambiguities of the French defeat in 1940 and the subsequent German occupation. The Gaullist myth also ignored the communist prominence in the resistance. The communists created their own mythology, which disregarded their passivity during the period of the Nazi-Soviet Pact. Yet the stunning collapse of France in 1940 could not be ignored. Explanations divided along the political fault line. Conservatives blamed the weakness and alleged corruption of the Third Republic, while those on the left accused proto-fascists of betraying the republic.

Although Gaullists labored to suppress memory of the Vichy years, that era continued to trouble many Frenchmen. American historian Robert Paxton's 1972 book, *Vichy France: Old Guard and New Order*, reopened the unhealed wound. He documented the popularity of Pétain's regime and its willing cooperation with the Nazis. French cinema ignited debate as well. Louis Malle's gripping *Lacombe Lucien* (1974) depicted the experiences of a young French Gestapo auxiliary, while Marcel Ophuls's documentary *The Sorrow and the Pity* (1971) explored the multiple reasons Frenchmen collaborated. French historian Henry Rousso suggested that a "Vichy Syndrome" tormented the French people, or at least their political and intellectual elite.[38]

Only in 1995, however, did a prominent Gaullist, President Jacques Chirac, acknowledge, for the first time, France's responsibility for the crimes of the Vichy regime. A series of trials in the 1990s publicized the role of Vichy officials in the Holocaust. Maurice Papon, for example, had organized the transport of 1,600 Jews from Bordeaux to death camps. Papon had gone on to senior civil service posts in the Fourth Republic. On the radical right, Jean-Marie Le Pen's National Front continued to praise the values of the Vichy regime and minimize the Holocaust.

ITALY

The long period of Fascist rule and Italy's alliance with Nazi Germany are a troubling heritage for modern Italians. Early postwar accounts focused on the anti-Fascist resistance of 1943–1945, with heroic freedom fighters redeeming the national stain of fascism. They largely ignored the broad support that Fascism had enjoyed for most of its reign. Mussolini continued to be a controversial figure. Renzo De Felice's influential, massive biography of Mussolini sought to rehabilitate the dictator as a revolutionary modernizer at home and a pragmatic statesman abroad. Comparing the Duce favorably with Hitler, De Felice minimized atrocities committed by Italian troops in their empire as well as Italy's role in the Holocaust. In stark contrast, Federico Fellini's 1973 film *Amarcord* lampooned the ridiculous posturing and intellectual vacuity of Mussolini and Fascism. Since then, Italian historians have explored more fully the repressive nature of the Fascist regime, the brutalities of Italian forces in Ethiopia and the Balkans, and the role of the Salò Republic in the Holocaust. Nonetheless, "Mussolini's legacy," historian Martin Clark suggests, "*is* a real challenge to contemporary Italian and European society, because his values in general have become so politically incorrect but are still in fact widely shared."[39]

RUSSIA

The myth of the Great Patriotic War (the Soviet designation for the battles on the eastern front) was the most important component in defining the identity of the Soviet peoples after 1945. It was yet another triumphalist narrative. The Russian people, under the wise leadership of Stalin and with the organizing skill of the Communist Party, had defeated the mighty German war machine (almost single-handedly). The Red Army had saved Europe from the scourge of fascism. In the minds of Soviet leaders—and in their propaganda—the victory demonstrated the superiority of the Soviet system and validated all the sacrifices of the revolution, civil war, forced-pace industrialization, collectivization of agriculture, and even the Great Purges. The war was, in a sense, "the Armageddon of the Revolution"—the long-expected, climactic confrontation with the capitalist world. The victory gave the Soviet leadership an enormous boost in confidence.

Stalin would not share credit for the victory, however. He prohibited senior officers from publishing memoirs. Marshal Zhukov lost his post as commander of the Red Army and was sent off to head a minor military district. Other prominent commanders were similarly exiled, demoted, or even imprisoned. The regime also tried to minimize the terrible cost of the war to Russia. It published ridiculously low figures for Soviet dead and wounded. It swept war cripples off the streets of Moscow. Orders 270 (equating POW status with treason) and 227 (not one step back) disappeared from the war narrative.

After Stalin's death, in the "de-Stalinization" process under Nikita Khrushchev, some wartime mistakes were admitted, but they were blamed solely on the generalissimo and a few of his evil henchmen. The heroic war myth continued to justify the party's reign and even reached new heights under Leonid Brezhnev. Memoirs, novels, and movies poured out—as long as they followed the official line on the nature and meaning of the struggle.

Most scholars have seen this cult of World War II as a device cynically manufactured by the Communist regime to justify its power and policies.[40] Other researchers, however, maintain that the war was a transformative experience for the Russian people and that the memory of that ordeal remains central to their national self-conception. Amir Weiner argues that the phenomenon had deep roots: "The hegemonic status of the myth of the war cannot be traced solely to the Soviet state and its propaganda machine, but at least as much to the identity of the articulators of the myth in the localities, the peasant soldiers, for whom the war turned into an autobiographical point of reference and point of departure."[41]

During the administration of Mikhail Gorbachev and even more so under his post-Soviet successor, Boris Yeltsin, the archives opened, at least partially, and a vigorous debate erupted over the origins and course of the war. Revisionist Russian historians explored the Nazi-Soviet Pact, Stalin's many military mistakes, the regime's dysfunctional repression of its own people, the Katyn massacre, and even atrocities committed by Soviet troops. Against them stood a national-patriotic school of Russian historiography that recapitulated much of the previous party-line analysis of Russia's role in World War II, though not with the motive of showing the Communist Party as inerrant. Members of this school seemed to be reacting to the drastic fall in the international position and prestige of Russia. They sought to reestablish a heroic and usable past out of which a resurgent, proud, nationalist Russia might be reborn. More recently, Vladimir Putin clearly favors the creation of a national history that is both noble and uncomplicated—particularly regarding the virtually sacred myth of the Great Patriotic War. Much of the Russian public seems to agree with him.

JAPAN

In Japan, popular memory focuses on a narrative of victimization that absolves ordinary people of responsibility because a ruthless military cabal seized control of the nation and forced it into an unwinnable war. The 1930s and early 1940s were, in this view, a "dark valley" in which the Japanese people were forced to submit to the dictates of a military police state. There is also a tendency in Japan to ignore or minimize Japanese atrocities committed against other Asian peoples. Some Japanese writers and filmmakers have examined the rape of Nanjing, comfort women, and the use of biological weapons, but their work remains controversial. In contrast to popular opinion, a few Japanese researchers have focused on the widespread popular support for aggressive foreign and military policies.

Since 2012, the government of the late Shinzo Abe and various conservative private organizations have promoted a sanitized, revisionist account of Tokyo's war effort that downplays Japanese atrocities and defends the militarists' imperial ambitions. These efforts are aimed at both domestic and foreign audiences. Internationally, this campaign dovetailed with Abe's more assertive stance against China. Japanese liberals and much of the academic community reject this revisionism.[42] This sanitized version of Japan's war effort has also complicated relations with Korea and China.

CHINA

During Mao Zedong's lifetime, Beijing focused on the Communist victory in 1949, rather than the "War of Resistance against Japan," as the key event in modern Chinese history. Its narrative of the war years emphasized the heroic role of Communist guerrillas, to the exclusion of Nationalist and Allied war efforts. Official memory highlighted the wartime betrayals and atrocities carried out by its Nationalist predecessor rather than the war crimes committed by the Japanese foe. That view began to change after Mao's death in 1976.

The evolution of the People's Republic toward a Communist Party–dominated mixed economy produced an economic boom but left an ideological vacuum. Deng Xiaoping and his successors replaced revolutionary Maoism with nationalism as the core of Chinese identity. A reconstructed memory of the Second World War facilitated this transition to an emphasis on nationalism. According to Rana Mitter, "the trauma of events such as the Great Leap Forward and the Cultural Revolution . . . gave way to China's own 'good war' in which noble Chinese patriots, Communist and Nationalist, fought against Japanese devils."[43] Although there is still a tendency to attribute a "leading role" to Communist-led resistance, the suffering of the Chinese people and heroic fighting by Guomindang units are memorialized in historical markers, displays, and museums all over China. A recent Chinese film, *The 800*, directed by Hu Guan, portrays the virtually suicidal resistance of a Nationalist regiment to the Japanese attack on Shanghai in 1937. This new emphasis on World War II also supports Beijing's foreign policy by ascribing a much larger role in the war to China and thereby justifying its claim to greater influence in East Asia and the world.[44]

Notes

1. Paul Kennedy, *Victory at Sea: Naval Power and the Transformation of the Global Order in World War II* (New Haven, CT: Yale University Press, 2022), xv.

2. Gabriel Gorodetsky, "The Origins of the Cold War: Stalin, Churchill and the Formation of the Grand Alliance," *Russian Review* 47, no. 2 (April 1988): 145–70.

3. Milovan Djilas, *Conversations with Stalin* (New York: Harcourt, Brace & World, 1962), 90.

4. Norman A. Graebner, *Cold War Diplomacy, 1945–1960* (Princeton, NJ: D. Van Nostrand, 1962), 24.

5. Before becoming vice president, Senator Truman opined, "If we see that Germany is winning we ought to help Russia, and if Russia is winning we ought to help Germany, and that way let them kill as many as possible." David McCullough, *Truman* (New York: Simon & Schuster, 1992), 262.

6. Whether or not Stalin had a master plan to dominate East Europe (and beyond) remains a subject of controversy among historians. Russian émigré historians Vladislav Zubok and Constantine Pleshakov argue that Stalin was willing to tolerate "popular front" coalition governments in eastern Europe before the challenge of the Marshall Plan, after which he insisted on Communist Party dictatorships. *Inside the Kremlin's Cold War: From Stalin to Khrushchev* (Cambridge, MA: Harvard University Press, 1996), 131. Cf. Gerhard Wettig, who contends that Stalin always intended to dominate the region by imposing communist regimes there, but the process had to be delayed and concealed while the groundwork was laid. *Stalin and the Cold War in Europe: The Emergence and Development of East-West Conflict, 1939–1945* (Lanham, MD: Rowman & Littlefield, 2008).

7. Winston S. Churchill, *The Second World War*, vol. 6, *Triumph and Tragedy* (New York: Houghton Mifflin, 1953), 289, italics in original.

8. Djilas, *Conversations with Stalin*, 182.

9. Zubok and Pleshakov, *Inside the Kremlin's Cold War*, 118.

10. *Documents on International Affairs, 1947–1948* (London: Oxford University Press, 1952), 2–7.

11. https://www.cia.gov/library/readingroom/1946-03-05.pdf.

12. Kenneth M. Jensen, ed., *Origins of the Cold War: The Novikov, Kennan, and Roberts "Long Telegrams" of 1946*, rev. ed. (Washington, DC: United States Institute of Peace Press, 1993), 17–31, and the anonymously published "X" [Kennan], "The Sources of Soviet Conduct," *Foreign Affairs* 25, no. 4 (1947), 566–82.

13. Carole K. Fink, *Cold War: An International History* (Boulder, CO: Westview, 2017), 56.

14. Abbott Gleason, *Totalitarianism: The Inner History of the Cold War* (Oxford: Oxford University Press, 1995), ch. 2.

15. NSC-68, 8, https://www.trumanlibrary.org/whistlestop/study_collections/coldwar/documents/pdf/10-1.pdf.

16. Gabriel Gorodetsky argues that Stalin's "statesmanship was to a large extent entrenched in Tsarist Russia's legacy, and responded to challenges which had deep historical roots." "Geopolitical Factors in Stalin's Strategy and Politics," in *Russia in the Age of Wars, 1914–1945*, ed. Silvio Pons and Andrea Romano (Milan: Feltrinelli, 2000), 236. Cf. Zubok and Pleshakov, who argue for a "revolutionary-imperial paradigm" in Soviet foreign policy, meaning that Moscow's goal was a communist world, but it would rely increasingly on measures of traditional statecraft to achieve its objectives. *Inside the Kremlin's Cold War*, 4–5, 18.

17. Zubok and Pleshakov, *Inside the Kremlin's Cold War*, 39.

18. Ian Buruma, *Year Zero: A History of 1945* (New York: Penguin, 2013), 43.

19. Edith Sheffer, *Asperger's Children: The Origins of Autism in Nazi Vienna* (New York: Norton, 2018).

20. Nina Tumarkin, *The Living and the Dead: The Rise and Fall of the Cult of World War II in Russia* (New York: Basic Books, 1994), 242.

21. John W. Dower, *Embracing Defeat: Japan in the Wake of World War II* (New York: Norton, 1999), 27.

22. Carol Gluck, *Japan's Modern Myths: Ideology in the Late Meiji Period* (Princeton, NJ: Princeton University Press, 1985), 284–85.

23. Sergei N. Goncharov, John W. Lewis, and Xue Litai, *Uncertain Partners: Mao, Stalin and the Korean War* (Stanford, CA: Stanford University Press, 1993), 11.

24. Diana Lary, *The Chinese People at War: Human Suffering and Social Transformation, 1937–1945* (Cambridge: Cambridge University Press, 2010), 32.

25. R. Keith Schoppa, *In a Sea of Bitterness: Refugees during the Sino-Japanese War* (Cambridge, MA: Harvard University Press, 2011), 308.

26. E.g., Jay Taylor, *The Generalissimo: Chiang Kai-shek and the Struggle for Modern China* (Cambridge, MA: Harvard University Press, 2011), 378.

27. Robert Gildea, *France since 1945* (New York: Oxford University Press, 1996), 16.

28. Jan C. Jansen and Jürgen Osterhammel, *Decolonization: A Short History* (Princeton, NJ: Princeton University Press, 2017), 15.

29. Simo Laakkonen, Richard P. Tucker, and Timo Vuorisalo, "Conclusion: World War II and Its Shadows," in *The Long Shadows: A Global Environmental History of the Second World War*, ed. Laakkonen, Tucker, and Vuorisalo (Corvallis: Oregon State University Press, 2017), 317, 325.

30. Judith A. Bennett, *Natives and Exotics: World War II and Environment in the South Pacific* (Honolulu: University of Hawaii Press, 2009), 201.

31. Jacob Darwin Hamblin, "Environmental Dimensions of World War II," in *A Companion to World War II*, ed. Thomas W. Zeiler and Daniel M. DuBois (Oxford: Blackwell, 2013), 704.

32. Bennett, *Natives and Exotics*, 304.

33. Carol Gluck, "Operations of Memory: 'Comfort Women' and the World," in *Ruptured Histories: War, Memory, and the Post-Cold War in Asia*, ed. Sheila Miyoshi Jager and Rana Mitter (Cambridge, MA: Harvard University Press, 2007), 48.

34. Michael C. C. Adams, *The Best War Ever: America and World War II* (Baltimore, MD: Johns Hopkins University Press, 1994).

35. Kenneth D. Rose, *Myth and the Greatest Generation: A Social History of Americans in World War II* (New York: Routledge, 2012). Rose suggests, "The best way to honor this [wartime] generation is not to falsify it but to humanize it. The only way that can be done is to follow the truth where it leads, and to include the blemished as well as the valorous" (p. 3).

36. Gerald Reitlinger, *The SS: Alibi of a Nation* (New York: Viking, 1968); Klaus Naumann, "The 'Unblemished' Wehrmacht: The Social History of a Myth," 417–29, and Omer Bartov, "Whose History Is It, Anyway? The Wehrmacht and German Historiography," 400–416, in *War of Extermination: The German Military Experience in World War II, 1941–1944*, ed. Hannes Heer and Klaus Naumann (New York: Berghahn Books, 2004).

37. Richard J. Overy, "Great Britain: Cyclops," in *Allies at War: The Soviet, American, and British Experience, 1939–1945*, ed. David Reynolds, Warren F. Kimball, and A. O. Chubarian (New York: St. Martin's, 1994), ch. 5.

38. Henry Rousso, *The Vichy Syndrome: History and Memory in France since 1944*, trans. Arthur Goldhammer (Cambridge, MA: Harvard University Press, 1991). Cf. Gertram M. Gordon, "The 'Vichy Syndrome' Problem in History," *French Historical Studies* 19, no. 2 (1995): 489–518.

39. Martin Clark, *Mussolini* (Harlow: Pearson, 2005), 332.

40. E.g., Tumarkin, *The Living and the Dead*, 101.

41. Amir Weiner, *Making Sense of War: The Second World War and the Fate of the Bolshevik Revolution* (Princeton, NJ: Princeton University Press, 2001), 20–21.

42. Jeff Kingston, "Japanese Revisionists' Meddling Backfires," *Critical Asian Studies* 51, no. 3 (2019): 437–50.

43. Rana Mitter, "China's 'Good War': Voices, Locations, and Generations in the Interpretation of the War of Resistance to Japan," in Jager and Mitter, *Ruptured Histories*, 174.

44. Rana Mitter, *China's Good War: How World War II Is Shaping a New Nationalism* (Cambridge, MA: Harvard University Press, 2020), 217.

Selected Readings

Read More about It

This is not a comprehensive bibliography of World War II studies, nor is it a list of works cited in the endnotes. Rather, it is a highly selective list of some of the better English-language works for readers who wish to study the topics discussed in this book in more depth.

Adams, Michael C. C. *The Best War Ever: America and World War II.* Baltimore, MD: Johns Hopkins University Press, 1994.

Alexander, Joseph H. *Storm Landings: Epic Amphibious Battles in the Central Pacific.* Annapolis, MD: Naval Institute Press, 1997.

Alexievich, Svetlana. *The Unwomanly Face of War: An Oral History of Women in World War II.* New York: Random House, 2017.

Atkinson, Rick. *An Army at Dawn: The War in North Africa, 1942–1943.* New York: Henry Holt, 2003.

Baime, A. J. *The Arsenal of Democracy: FDR, Detroit, and an Epic Quest to Arm an America at War.* Boston: Houghton Mifflin, 2014.

Barber, John, and Mark Harrison, *The Soviet Home Front, 1941–1945: A Social and Economic History of the USSR in World War II.* London: Longman, 1991.

Barnhart, Michael A., and Larry N. Shyu, eds. *Chinese Collaboration with Japan, 1932–1945: The Limits of Accommodation.* Stanford, CA: Stanford University Press, 2002.

———. *Japan Prepares for Total War: The Search for Economic Security, 1919–1941.* Ithaca, NY: Cornell University Press, 1987.

Bartov, Omer. *The Eastern Front, 1941–45: German Troops and the Barbarisation of Warfare.* 2nd ed. New York: Palgrave, 2001.

———. *Hitler's Army: Soldiers, Nazis, and War in the Third Reich.* New York: Oxford University Press, 1991.

Bergen, Doris L. *War & Genocide: A Concise History of the Holocaust.* Lanham, MD: Rowman & Littlefield, 2009.

Bergerud, Eric M. *Fire in the Sky: The Air War in the Pacific.* Boulder, CO: Westview, 2001.

———. *Touched with Fire: The Land War in the South Pacific.* New York: Penguin, 1997.

Bess, Michael. *Choices under Fire: Moral Dimensions of World War II.* New York: Knopf, 2006.

Black, Jeremy. *Rethinking World War Two: The Conflict and Its Legacy.* London: Bloomsbury Academic, 2015.

Blatt, Joel, ed. *The French Defeat of 1940: Reassessments.* Providence, RI: Berghahn Books, 1998.

Borg, Dorothy, and Shumpei Okamoto, eds. *Pearl Harbor as History: Japanese-American Relations, 1931–1941.* New York: Columbia University Press, 1973.

Browning, Christopher R. *Nazi Policy, Jewish Workers, German Killers.* Cambridge: Cambridge University Press, 2000.

———. *Ordinary Men: Reserve Police Battalion 101 and the Final Solution in Poland.* New York: Harper Perennial, 1998.

Buckley, John. *Monty's Men: The British Army and the Liberation of Europe, 1944–5*. New Haven, CT: Yale University Press, 2013.

Budiansky, Stephen. *Blackett's War: The Men Who Defeated the Nazi U-Boats and Brought Science to the Art of Warfare*. New York: Knopf, 2013.

Carley, Michael Jabara. *1939: The Alliance That Never Was and the Coming of World War II*. Chicago: Ivan R. Dee, 1999.

Citino, Robert M. *Death of the Wehrmacht: The German Campaigns of 1942*. Lawrence: University Press of Kansas, 2007.

———. *The Wehrmacht Retreats: Fighting a Losing War, 1943*. Lawrence: University Press of Kansas, 2012.

Clark, Martin. *Mussolini*. Harlow: Pearson Longman, 2005.

Collingham, E. M. *The Taste of War: World War II and the Battle for Food*. New York: Penguin, 2012.

Cutler, Thomas J. *The Battle of Leyte Gulf: 23–26 October 1944*. New York: HarperCollins, 1994.

Dallek, Robert. *Franklin D. Roosevelt and American Foreign Policy, 1932–1945*. New York: Oxford University Press, 1979.

———. *The Lost Peace: Leadership in a Time of Horror and Hope, 1945–1953*. New York: HarperCollins, 2010.

Deák, István. *Europe on Trial: Collaboration, Resistance and Retribution during World War II*. Boulder, CO: Westview, 2015.

Doubler, Michael D. *Closing with the Enemy: How GIs Fought the War in Europe, 1944–1945*. Lawrence: University Press of Kansas, 1994.

Dower, John W. *Embracing Defeat: Japan in the Wake of World War II*. New York: Norton, 1999.

———. *War without Mercy: Race & Power in the Pacific War*. New York: Pantheon, 1986.

Drea, Edward J. *In the Service of the Emperor: Essays on the Imperial Japanese Army*. Lincoln: University of Nebraska Press, 1998.

———. *Japan's Imperial Army: Its Rise and Fall, 1853–1945*. Lawrence: University Press of Kansas, 2009.

———. *MacArthur's Ultra: Codebreaking and the War against Japan, 1943–1945*. Lawrence: University Press of Kansas, 1992.

Edele, Mark. *Stalinism at War: The Soviet Union in World War II*. London: Bloomsbury Academic, 2021.

Edgerton, David. *Britain's War Machine: Weapons, Resources, and Experts in the Second World War*. Oxford: Oxford University Press, 2011.

Ellis, John. *Brute Force: Allied Strategy and Tactics in the Second World War*. New York: Viking, 1990.

Evans, Richard J. *The Third Reich at War*. New York: Penguin, 2008.

Fennell, Jonathan. *Fighting the People's War: The British and Commonwealth Armies and the Second World War*. Cambridge: Cambridge University Press, 2019.

Frank, Richard B. *Downfall: The End of the Imperial Japanese Empire*. New York: Random House, 1999.

———. *Guadalcanal*. New York: Random House, 1990.

Friedländer, Saul. *Nazi Germany and the Jews*. Vol. 1, *The Years of Persecution, 1933–1939*. Vol. 2, *1939–1945, The Years of Extermination*. New York: Harper Perennial, 1998 and 2008.

Fritz, Stephen G. *The First Soldier: Hitler as Military Leader*. New Haven, CT: Yale University Press, 2018.

———. *Frontsoldaten: The German Soldier in World War II*. Lexington: University Press of Kentucky, 1995.

Fritzsche, Peter. *Germans into Nazis*. Cambridge, MA: Harvard University Press, 1998.

Fussell, Paul. *Wartime*. New York: Oxford University Press, 1989.

Gatu, Dagfinn. *Village China at War: The Impact of Resistance to Japan, 1937–1945*. Vancouver: UBC Press, 2008.

Glantz, David M. *Barbarossa: Hitler's Invasion of Russia, 1941*. Stroud: Tempus, 2001.

———. *Colossus Reborn: The Red Army at War, 1941–1943*. Lawrence: University Press of Kansas, 2005.

———. *Stumbling Colossus: The Red Army on the Eve of World War*. Lawrence: University Press of Kansas, 1998.

———. *Zhukov's Greatest Defeat: The Red Army's Epic Disaster in Operation Mars, 1942*. Lawrence: University Press of Kansas, 1999.

Goldberg, Harold J. *Daily Life in Nazi-Occupied Europe*. Santa Barbara, CA: Greenwood, 2019.

———. *D-Day in the Pacific: The Battle of Saipan*. Bloomington: Indiana University Press, 2007.

Goldhagen, Daniel Jonah. *Hitler's Willing Executioners: Ordinary Germans and the Holocaust*. New York: Knopf, 1996.

Goldman, Wendy Z., and Donald Filtzer. *Fortress Dark and Stern: The Soviet Home Front during World War II*. New York: Oxford University Press, 2021.

Gooch, John. *Mussolini and His Generals: The Armed Forces and Fascist Foreign Policy, 1922–1940*. Cambridge: Cambridge University Press, 2007.

Gorodetsky, Gabriel. *Grand Delusion: Stalin and the German Invasion of Russia*. New Haven, CT: Yale University Press, 1999.

Gripentrog, John. *Prelude to Pearl Harbor: Ideology and Culture in US-Japanese Relations, 1919–1941*. Lanham, MD: Rowman & Littlefield, 2021.

Gross, Jan T. *Neighbors: The Destruction of the Jewish Community in Jedwabne, Poland*. Princeton, NJ: Princeton University Press, 2001.

———. *Revolution from Abroad: The Soviet Conquest of Poland's Western Ukraine and Western Belorussia*. Princeton, NJ: Princeton University Press, 2001.

Habeck, Mary R. *Storm of Steel: The Development of Armor Doctrine in Germany and the Soviet Union, 1919–1939*. Ithaca, NY: Cornell University Press, 2003.

Harmsen, Peter. *Shanghai, 1937: Stalingrad on the Yangtze*. Philadelphia: Casement, 2013.

Harrison, Mark, ed. *The Economics of World War II: Six Great Powers in International Comparison*. Cambridge: Cambridge University Press, 2000.

Hartcup, Guy. *The Effect of Science on the Second World War*. New York: Palgrave Macmillan, 2003.

Hasegawa, Tsuyoshi, ed. *The End of the Pacific War: Reappraisals*. Stanford, CA: Stanford University Press, 2007.

———. *Racing the Enemy: Stalin, Truman, and the Surrender of Japan*. Cambridge, MA: Harvard University Press, 2005.

Havens, Thomas R. H. *Valley of Darkness: The Japanese People and World War II*. New York: Norton, 1978.

Heer, Hannes, and Klaus Nauman, eds. *War of Extermination: The German Military in World War II*. New York: Berghahn Books, 2004.

Hendricks, Waldo, and Marc Gallicchio. *Implacable Foes: War in the Pacific, 1944–1945*. New York: Oxford University Press, 2017.

Hill, Alexander. *The Red Army and the Second World War*. Cambridge: Cambridge University Press, 2017.

———. *The War behind the Eastern Front: The Soviet Partisan Movement in North-West Russia, 1941–1945*. New York: Frank Cass, 2005.

Hinsley, F. H., and Alan Stripp. *Codebreakers: The Inside Story of Bletchley Park*. Oxford: Oxford University Press, 1993.

Hotta, Eri. *Pan-Asianism and Japan's War, 1931–1945*. New York: Palgrave Macmillan, 2013.

Iriye, Akira. *The Origins of the Second World War in Asia and the Pacific*. London: Longman, 1987.

———. *Power and Culture: The Japanese-American War, 1941–1945*. Cambridge, MA: Harvard University Press, 1981.

Jackson, Ashley. *The British Empire and the Second World War*. Hambledon: Continuum, 2006.

Jackson, Julian. *The Fall of France: The Nazi Invasion of 1940*. Oxford: Oxford University Press, 2003.

———. *France: The Dark Years, 1940–1944*. Oxford: Oxford University Press, 2001.

Kagan, Robert. *The Ghost at the Feast: America and the Collapse of the World Order, 1900–1941*. New York: Knopf, 2023.

Kaiser, David. *No End Save Victory: How FDR Led the Nation to War*. New York: Basic Books, 2014.

Kawamura, Noriko. *Emperor Hirohito and the Pacific War*. Seattle: University of Washington Press, 2015.

Kay, Alex J. *Exploitation, Resettlement, Mass Murder: Political and Economic Planning for German Occupation Policy in the Soviet Union, 1940–1941*. New York: Berghahn Books, 2006.

Keegan, John. *Six Armies in Normandy: From D-Day to the Liberation of Paris, June 6th–August 25th, 1944*. New York: Viking, 1982.

Kennedy, Paul. *Engineers of Victory: The Problem Solvers Who Turned the Tide in the Second World War*. New York: Random House, 2013.

———. *Victory at Sea: Naval Power and the Transformation of the Global Order in World War II*. New Haven, CT: Yale University Press, 2022.

Kershaw, Ian. *Fateful Choices: Ten Decisions That Changed the World, 1940–1941*. New York: Penguin, 2007.

———. *Hitler, 1889–1936: Hubris*. New York: Norton, 1999.

———. *Hitler, 1936–1945: Nemesis*. New York: Norton, 2000.

Khan, Yasmin. *India at War: The Subcontinent and the Second World War*. Oxford: Oxford University Press, 2015.

———. *The Raj at War: A People's History of India's Second World War*. London: Bodley Head, 2015.

Knox, MacGregor. *Hitler's Italian Allies: Royal Armed Forces, Fascist Regime, and the War of 1940–1943*. Cambridge: Cambridge University Press, 2000.

Koshiro, Yukiko. *Imperial Eclipse: Japan's Strategic Thinking about Continental Asia before August 1945*. Ithaca, NY: Cornell University Press, 2013.

Lary, Diana. *The Chinese People at War: Human Suffering and Social Transformation, 1937–1945*. New York: Cambridge University Press, 2010.

Linderman, Gerald F. *The World within War: America's Combat Experience in World War II*. Cambridge, MA: Harvard University Press, 1997.

Lower, Wendy, *Hitler's Furies: German Women in the Nazi Killing Fields*. Boston: Houghton Mifflin Harcourt, 2013.

MacKinnon, Stephen R. *Wuhan, 1938: War, Refugees, and the Making of Modern China*. Berkeley: University of California Press, 2008.

MacKinnon, Stephen R., Diana Lary, and Ezra F. Vogel, eds. *China at War: Regions of China, 1937–45*. Stanford, CA: Stanford University Press, 2007.

MacMillan, Margaret. *Paris 1919: Six Months That Changed the World*. New York: Random House, 2003.

Manzower, Mark. *Dark Continent: Europe's Twentieth Century*. New York: Vintage, 2000.

———. *Hitler's Empire: How the Nazis Ruled Europe*. New York: Penguin, 2008.

Marks, Sally. *The Illusion of Peace: International Relations in Europe, 1918–1933*. New York: Palgrave, 2003.

Marrus, Michael R., and Robert O. Paxton. *Vichy France and the Jews*. New York: Schocken, 1983.

Marston, Daniel, ed. *The Pacific War Companion: From Pearl Harbor to Hiroshima*. Oxford: Osprey, 2005.

Martel, Gordon, ed. *The Origins of the Second World War Reconsidered: A. J. P. Taylor and the Historians*. 2nd ed. New York: Routledge, 1999.

Marwick, Roger D., and Euridice Charon Cardona. *Soviet Women in the Second World War*. New York: Palgrave, 2012.

Mawdsley, Evan, ed. *The Cambridge History of the Second World War*. Vol. 1, John Ferris and Evan Mawdsley, eds., *Fighting the War*. Vol. 2, Richard J. B. Bosworth and Joseph A. Maiolo, eds., *Politics and Ideology*. Vol. 3, Michael Geyer and Adam Tooze, eds., *Total War: Economy, Society and Culture*. Cambridge: Cambridge University Press, 2015.

———. *Thunder in the East: The Nazi-Soviet War, 1941–1945*. London: Hodder Arnold, 2005.

———. *The War for the Seas: A Maritime History of World War II*. New Haven, CT: Yale University Press, 2019.

May, Ernest R. *Strange Victory: Hitler's Conquest of France*. New York: Hill & Wang, 2001.

Megaree, Geoffrey. *War of Annihilation: Combat and Genocide on the Eastern Front, 1941*. Lanham, MD: Rowman & Littlefield, 2007.

Merridale, Catherine. *Ivan's War: Life and Death in the Red Army, 1939–1945*. New York: Metropolitan Books, 2006.

Militärgeschichtliches Forschungsamt. *Germany and the Second World War*. 9 vols. Oxford: Oxford University Press, 2014–2015.

Millett, Allan R. *Military Innovation in the Interwar Period*. New York: Cambridge University Press, 1996.

Millett, Allan R., and Williamson Murray, eds. *Military Effectiveness*. Vol. 3, *The Second World War*. Cambridge: Cambridge University Press, 2010.

Mitter, Rana. *Forgotten Ally: China's World War II, 1937–1945*. Boston: Houghton Mifflin Harcourt, 2013.

———. *The Manchurian Myth: Nationalism, Resistance, and Collaboration in Modern China*. Berkeley: University of California Press, 2000.

Morley, James William, ed. *Deterrent Diplomacy: Japan, Germany, and the USSR, 1935–1940*. New York: Columbia University Press, 1976.

Moskoff, William. *The Bread of Affliction: The Food Supply in the USSR during World War II*. Cambridge: Cambridge University Press, 1990.

Mueller, Rolf-Dieter, and Gerd Uebershaer. *Hitler's War in the East: A Critical Assessment*. 3rd ed. New York: Berghahn Books, 2009.

Muscolino, Micah S. *The Ecology of War in China: Henan Province, the Yellow River, and Beyond, 1936–1950*. Cambridge: Cambridge University Press, 2014.

Naimark, Norman. *The Russians in Germany: A History of the Soviet Zone of Occupation, 1945–1949*. Cambridge, MA: Harvard University Press, 1995.

———. *Stalin and the Fate of Europe: The Postwar Struggle for Sovereignty*. Cambridge, MA: Belknap Press, 2019.

Nish, Ian. *Japanese Foreign Policy in the Interwar Period*. Westport, CT: Praeger, 2002.

Noakes, Jeremy, ed. *The Civilian in War: The Home Front in Europe, Japan and the USA in World War II*. Exeter: University of Exeter Press, 1992.

Nord, Philip. *France 1940: Defending the Republic*. New Haven, CT: Yale University Press, 2015.

O'Hara, Vincent. *Torch: North Africa and the Allied Path to Victory*. Annapolis, MD: Naval Institute Press, 2015.

O'Neill, William L. *A Democracy at War: America's Fight at Home and Abroad in World War II*. Cambridge, MA: Harvard University Press, 1993.

Overy, Richard. *The Bombers and the Bombed: Allied Air War over Europe, 1940–1945*. New York: Viking, 2013.

———. *Russia's War: A History of the Soviet War Effort: 1941–1945*. New York: Penguin, 1997.

———. *War and the Economy in the Third Reich*. Oxford: Clarendon Press, 1995.

Paine, S. C. M. *The Wars for Asia, 1911–1949*. Cambridge: Cambridge University Press, 2014.

Pavone, Claudio. *A Civil War: A History of the Italian Resistance*. London: Verso, 2013.

Paxton, Robert O. *Vichy France: Old Guard and New Order, 1940–1944*. New York: Norton, 1972.

Peattie, Mark. *The Japanese Wartime Empire, 1931–1945*. Princeton, NJ: Princeton University Press, 1996.

Peattie, Mark, Edward Drea, and Hans van de Ven, eds. *The Battle for China: Essays on the Military History of the Sino-Japanese War of 1937–1945*. Stanford, CA: Stanford University Press, 2011.

Prange, Gordon W. *At Dawn We Slept: The Untold Story of Pearl Harbor*. New York: Penguin, 1981.

Prange, Gordon W., with Donald M. Goldstein and Katherine V. Dillon. *Miracle at Midway*. New York: Penguin, 1982.

Ragsdale, Hugh. *The Soviets, the Munich Crisis, and the Coming of World War II*. Cambridge: Cambridge University Press, 2004.

Reese, Roger R. *Why Stalin's Soldiers Fought: The Red Army's Military Effectiveness in World War II*. Lawrence: University Press of Kansas, 2011.

Reynolds, David, Warren F. Kimball, and A. O. Chubarian, eds. *Allies at War: The Soviet, American and British Experience, 1939–1945*. New York: St. Martin's, 1994.

Rieber, Alfred J. *Stalin and the Struggle for Supremacy in Eurasia*. Cambridge: Cambridge University Press, 2015.

———. *Stalin as Warlord*. New Haven, CT: Yale University Press, 2022.

Roberts, Geoffrey. *Stalin's Wars: From World War to Cold War, 1939–1953*. New Haven, CT: Yale University Press, 2006.

———. *Victory at Stalingrad: The Battle That Changed History*. Harlow: Longman, 2002.

Roberts, Mary Louise. *What Soldiers Do: Sex and the American GI in World War II France*. Chicago: University of Chicago Press, 2013.

———. *Sheer Misery: Soldiers in Battle in World War II*. Chicago: University of Chicago Press, 2021.

Rossino, Alexander B. *Hitler Strikes Poland: Blitzkrieg, Ideology, and Atrocity*. Lawrence: University Press of Kansas, 2003.

Sarantakes, Nicholas E. *Allies against the Rising Sun: The United States, the British Nations, and the Defeat of Imperial Japan*. Lawrence: University Press of Kansas, 2009.

Schoppa, R. Keith. *In a Sea of Bitterness: Refugees during the Sino-Japanese War*. Cambridge, MA: Harvard University Press, 2011.

Shaller, Michael. *Douglas MacArthur: The Far Eastern General*. New York: Oxford University Press, 1989.

Shepherd, Ben H. *Hitler's Soldiers: The German Army in the Third Reich.* New Haven, CT: Yale University Press, 2016.

Sherwin, Martin J. *A World Destroyed: Hiroshima and Its Legacies.* Stanford, CA: Stanford University Press, 2003.

Shin Gi-Wook and Daniel Sneider. *Divergent Memories: Opinion Leaders and the Asia-Pacific War.* Stanford, CA: Stanford University Press, 2016.

Showalter, Dennis. *Armor and Blood: The Battle of Kursk; The Turning Point in World War II.* New York: Random House, 2013.

Sledge, E. B. *With the Old Breed at Peleliu and Okinawa.* Novato, CA: Presidio Press, 1990.

Slepyan, Kenneth. *Stalin's Guerrillas: Soviet Partisans in World War II.* Lawrence: University Press of Kansas, 2006.

Smethurst, Richard J. *A Social Basis for Prewar Japanese Militarism: The Army and the Rural Community.* Berkeley: University of California Press, 1974.

Snyder, Timothy. *Black Earth: The Holocaust as History and Warning.* New York: Tim Duggan Books, 2015.

———. *Bloodlands: Europe between Hitler and Stalin.* New York: Basic Books, 2010.

Spector, Ronald H. *Eagle against the Sun: The American War with Japan.* New York: Free Press, 1985.

Stahel, David. *Operation Barbarossa and Germany's Defeat in the East.* Cambridge: Cambridge University Press, 2009.

Stargardt, Nicholas. *The German War: A Nation under Arms, 1939–1945; Citizens and Soldiers.* New York: Basic Books, 2015.

Steiner, Zara. *The Lights That Failed: European International History, 1919–1933.* New York: Oxford University Press, 2005.

———. *The Triumph of the Dark: European International History, 1933–1939.* New York: Oxford University Press, 2011.

Stoler, Mark A. *Allies in War: Britain and America against the Axis Powers, 1940–1945.* London: Hodder Arnold, 2005.

Stone, David R., ed. *The Soviet Union at War, 1941–1945.* Barnsley: Pen & Sword, 2010.

Symonds, Craig L. *The Battle of Midway.* New York: Oxford University Press, 2011.

Taaffe, Stephen R. *MacArthur's Jungle War: The 1944 New Guinea Campaign.* Lawrence: University Press of Kansas, 1998.

Takaki, Ronald. *Double Victory: A Multicultural History of America in World War II.* Boston: Little, Brown, 2000.

Taylor, Jay. *The Generalissimo: Chiang Kai-shek and the Struggle for Modern China.* Cambridge, MA: Harvard University Press, 2011.

Terkel, Studs. *"The Good War": An Oral History of World War Two.* New York: Ballantine, 1984.

Thorne, Christopher. *Allies of a Kind: The United States, Britain, and the War against Japan, 1941–1945.* London: Hamish Hamilton, 1978.

———. *The Issue of War: States, Societies, and the Far Eastern Conflict of 1941–1945.* New York: Oxford University Press, 1985.

Thurston, Robert W., and Bernd Bonwetsch, eds. *The People's War: Responses to World War II in the Soviet Union.* Champaign: University of Illinois Press, 2000.

Toll, Ian. *Pacific Crucible: War at Sea in the Pacific, 1941–1942.* New York: Norton, 2012.

———. *The Conquering Tide: War in the Pacific Islands, 1942–1944.* New York: Norton, 2015.

———. *The Twilight of the Gods: War in the Western Pacific, 1944–1945.* New York: Norton, 2020.

Tooze, Adam. *The Deluge: The Great War, America and the Remaking of the Global Order, 1916–1931.* New York: Viking, 2014.

———. *The Wages of Destruction: The Making and Breaking of the Nazi Economy.* New York: Penguin, 2006.

Trachtenberg, Marc. *A Constructed Peace: The Making of the European Settlement, 1945–1963.* Princeton, NJ: Princeton University Press, 1999.

van de Ven, Hans. *China at War: Triumph and Tragedy in the Emergence of the New China.* Cambridge, MA: Harvard University Press, 2018.

————. *War and Nationalism in China, 1925–1945.* London: RoutledgeCurzon, 2003.

van de Ven, Hans, Diana Lary, and Stephen MacKinnon, eds. *Negotiating China's Destiny in World War II.* Palo Alto, CA: Stanford University Press, 2014.

Vinen, Richard. *The Unfree French: Life under Occupation.* New Haven, CT: Yale University Press, 2006.

Wakabayashi, Bob Tadashi, ed. *The Nanking Atrocity, 1937–1938: Complicating the Picture.* Brooklyn, NY: Berghahn, 2017.

Walker, J. Samuel. *Prompt and Utter Destruction: Truman and the Use of Atomic Bombs against Japan.* Chapel Hill: University of North Carolina Press, 2004.

Weinberg, Gerhard L. *Germany, Hitler and World War II.* Cambridge: Cambridge University Press, 1995.

————. *Visions of Victory: The Hopes of Eight World War II Leaders.* Cambridge: Cambridge University Press, 2005.

————. *World in the Balance: Behind the Scenes of World War II.* Hanover: University Press of New England, 1981.

Willmott, H. P. *The War with Japan: The Period of Balance, May 1942–October 1943.* Wilmington, DE: Scholarly Resources, 2002.

Willmott, H. P., with Tohmatsu Haruo and W. Spencer Johnson. *Pearl Harbor.* London: Cassell, 2001.

Yamashita, Samuel Hideo. *Daily Life in Wartime Japan, 1940–1945.* Lawrence: University Press of Kansas, 2016.

Young, Louise. *Japan's Total Empire: Manchuria and the Culture of Wartime Imperialism.* Berkeley: University of California Press, 1998.

Zuccotti, Susan. *The Italians and the Holocaust: Persecution, Rescue, Survival.* New York: Basic Books, 1987.

Index

Page references for figures are italicized.

About the Author

Teddy J. Uldricks, PhD, has taught college-level courses on the Second World War for over forty years. He is an emeritus professor of history, University of North Carolina, Asheville, and now teaches a variety of courses on World War II at the University of Nevada, Las Vegas. Dr. Uldricks has written extensively on Russia and the origins of the Second World War, including an earlier book, *Diplomacy and Ideology: The Origins of Soviet Foreign Relations*. He is widely regarded as a leading authority on Soviet foreign affairs in the interwar years. His current research projects focus on the appeasement of aggressors in the 1930s as a global phenomenon and on the political and military uses of rape in World War II.

Made in the USA
Las Vegas, NV
11 January 2024

84193235R00313